The
Progress
of Redemption

The
Progress
of Redemption

*The Story of Salvation from
Creation to the New Jerusalem*

Willem VanGemeren

Baker Books

A Division of Baker Book House Co
Grand Rapids, Michigan 49516

©1988 by Willem A. VanGemeren

Published by Baker Books
a division of Baker Book House Company
P.O. Box 6287, Grand Rapids, MI 49516-6287

Paperback edition published 1995 by Baker Book House
First printing, October 1995
Cloth edition published 1988 by Academie Books, Zondervan Publishing House

Printed in the United States of America

ISBN 0-8010-2081-6

To
Evona, my wife,
and to
Nurit
Tamara
Shoshanna
my children

You make Psalms 127—128 come alive

Contents

Figures

Tables

Preface

It is my pleasure to present a study of God's work of redemption as it began in creation and as it progresses toward the full and final development in his New Jerusalem. In telling the story of redemption, the Bible reveals the progression of God's plan for his people; both Old and New Testaments witness to the glory prepared for the new people of God in Jesus Christ. We will look at the Bible as the book of God and as the book of man and, for each phase in its unfolding of redemption history, will consider in particular the respective *literary forms,* the *canonical function,* or meaning of the passage as a divine message for the community to which it was given, and the *redemptive-historical significance,* or relevance of each period in light of God's purposes in all the other stages in redemption. This book thus introduces the reader to the Old Testament, the intertestamental period, the New Testament, church history, and the prophetic future. The flow of redemptive history witnesses both to the diversity in God's revelation and also to the unity of his plan. According to George Ladd,

> The entire Bible finds its unity in what can best be called holy history—*Heilsgeschichte.* It is a record and interpretation of the events in which God visits men in history to redeem them as persons and also to redeem them in society—in history. This means finally the redemption of history itself.
>
> Diversity occurs because of different stages along the redemption line and the differing ways in which the redemptive event may be interpreted. The prophets see this event from the perspective of promise, with a strong emphasis on the earthly and historical meaning of this divine visitation.[1]

I address a wide range of topics in this book and sense keenly my own limitations in dealing with each one adequately. A vacuum exists, however, in current evangelical literature, as few writings trace the progressive development of redemptive history. I am greatly indebted to the writings of Geerhardus Vos, whose epochal work *Biblical Theology: Old and New Testaments* was printed some forty years ago, and to Edmund P. Clowney and Richard B. Gaffin, Jr., for introducing me to the redemptive historical approach, while studying at Westminster

15

Theological Seminary. In spite of this book's shortcomings and errors, I trust that it will help Christians to ground themselves in the history of the people of God, serve the Christ better, and become filled with the Spirit of restoration as we look toward the glorious redemption prepared for God's people in his New Jerusalem.

I am grateful to my students for their encouragement—at Geneva College (1974–78); Reformed Theological Seminary, Jackson (1978–92); and Trinity Evangelical Divinity School, both the Deerfield campus and the many extension campuses (1992 to the present). I am also grateful to Jim Weaver of Baker Book House for his support in having this book published under the Baker banner. I am deeply grateful to God for my family, to whom I dedicate this work. Their sacrifice, constant love, and the spiritual ties that bind us together have given me a sense of God's blessing that renews and refreshes. I praise the Lord for the love of my wife, Evona, over these nearly thirty years and for her interest in our international community at the seminary; for the spiritual growth and sensitivity of our seminarian daughter, Nurit; for the social development of our college daughter, Tamara, who is engaged to Bryan Betts; and for the "flowering" of our high school daughter, Shoshanna. Praise be to God!

I pray now that the reader may catch glimpses of the Eternal One in these pages and may find shelter under the wings of the Almighty, who has revealed himself in the Son and who, through the Holy Spirit, assures us of the certainty of the future.

Introduction

The Bible is the book of God and man. God speaks through the mouths of men, and men and women hear the voice of God. Though the men God spoke through lived millennia ago, the church still listens. Its way of listening, however, depends on its own historical situation. Since the nineteenth century, serious challenges to the inspiration, canonicity, and inerrancy of the Bible have arisen. Scholars look at the rise of the critical approach to Scripture as a watershed and refer to the literature before and after this development as pre- and postcritical. The critical approach has deeply affected the way the Bible is studied in universities and seminaries as well as how it is expounded in churches. Biblical critics have been accused of leading the church into a Babylonian exile—the scholarly practitioners of exegesis debate subtle points of interpretation while God's people thirst for the Word.

Evangelicals have gradually responded to the challenges. Though they have been accused of elevating the Scriptures to the lofty status of oracles of God and of showing little regard for the historical, literary, and cultural manner in which the Bible has come to us, Evangelicals do care about these matters. Out of concern for interpreting the Bible in a way that is both realistic and relevant, I present in this book the *redemptive-historical approach*. This approach to the Bible shows an appreciation of God's Word as it has come to us in space and time, by paying attention to the historical and grammatical analysis as well as to the literary and canonical functions. This method of interpreting the Bible begins with the presupposition that the Bible is both the Word of God and the word of man. As the Word of God the Bible reveals the triune God and his plan of salvation and life for human beings in relation to his grand design for the renewal of heaven and earth.

As the word of man the Bible is the collection of the literary works written by men of God and inspired by the Spirit of God. These literary treasures were written in human languages over many centuries, reflecting different literary conventions and cultures. As such the Scriptures are related to specific cultures. God spoke to the writers in the language of accommodation, and he still speaks to us in a way that we can understand. The recognition of a theological commitment to the

Bible as Scripture is not a hindrance to understanding but aids in understanding, as does the focus on the literary forms, the canonical function of Scripture, and the sequence of continuity and discontinuity throughout the history of redemption. The concern with both the divine and the human aspects creates tensions that relate to the most basic question of interpretation: "Do we really understand what we read?" To answer this question leads to seven additional questions:

1. How can an event described in the Bible be relevant for a twentieth-century Christian?

2. What is the relationship between a theological tradition or confessional statement and the continuing need for a fresh reading and study of the Bible?

3. What is the place of "faith" in the reading and study of Scripture, including the Old Testament?

4. How are the Old and New Testaments related to each other?

5. What is the theological center, or the dominant theme, of the Bible?

6. What elements in an interpretation vitally involve the interpreter?

7. How does biblical exegesis apply to practical life? How does the Bible lead to continual transformation?

ANCIENT EVENTS AND THE FAITH OF THE MODERN CHRISTIAN

How does the biblical text, set in its ancient context, touch us today? The issue of relevance is as old as the Bible but was raised most pointedly by Hegel, a nineteenth-century German philosopher of history. Hegel posited the concept of spirit in history as the link that connects present to past. For Hegel, the event itself is insignificant; only its connection with other events is important. Process alone is revelatory. The relevance of the past depends on its bearing on the present. In Hegel's view, then, Biblical events and history are relevant only insofar as they relate to the present.

The separation of faith from history resulted in a negative attitude toward Old Testament history and a subsequent erosion of the authority of the Old Testament.[1] New Testament scholars extracted the historical Jesus from the theological interpretation of Jesus in the early church. The quest for the historical Jesus led Bultmann to introduce the concept of demythologization, in an effort to separate Jesus of Nazareth, or the historical kernel, from the Jesus of faith. The critical method dissected the individual biblical books into literary fragments produced by a multiplicity of traditions. Klug well states the reaction of Evangelicals to the critical dilemma: "The historical-critical practitioners had themselves become morticians at the funeral and burial of the Word of God."[2]

The process of interpretation should never create a separation between the interpreter and the text, between the ancient event and the twentieth century. Hegelianism creates such a separation. Higher criticism also accentuates the difference. Certainly differences exist, but the process of interpretation involves the modern reader of the Bible. The authentic interpretation reverberates the ancient message to each reader of the Bible in a similar but not identical manner. God has spoken and still speaks to men and women by the operation of the Holy Spirit. The revelation of God through Moses, the prophets, our Lord, and the apostles still witnesses in the modern context to individuals who open their ears to the voice of God. Jesus said that his sheep hear his voice (John 10:1–5), and that voice comes to us in the Holy Scriptures. Those who believe on the Christ of God are grafted into the history of God's acts, so they can exclaim with the psalmist,

> Great is the LORD and most worthy of praise;
>   his greatness no one can fathom.
> One generation will commend your works to another;
>   they will tell of your mighty acts.
> They will speak of the glorious splendor of your majesty,
>   and I will meditate on your wonderful works.
> They will tell of the power of your awesome works,
>   and I will proclaim your great deeds.
> They will celebrate your abundant goodness
>   and joyfully sing of your righteousness.
>
> (Ps. 145:3–7)

BIBLICAL EXEGESIS AND THEOLOGICAL TRADITIONS

Throughout the history of the church the Bible has been firmly connected to its life and teaching. The actual practice and teaching may have deviated at one point or another, but at no time was the Bible completely replaced. The place of the Bible, however, is in continual tension with the traditions of the church or denomination. This tension was augmented during the Reformation, and since then its resolution has given birth to many denominations.[3] Tradition has a place in church life because each generation cannot relive the tensions, theological issues, and practical problems of the previous generations. We are heirs of the church fathers who hammered out the doctrinal formulas of the Trinity. We are heirs of the Reformation, with its emphases on Christ (vs. the church), justification by faith, salvation by grace, the priesthood of all believers, and the primacy of Scripture (vs. the traditions of the church). Moreover, many evangelical churches have a creed, confession,

19

covenant, or statement of belief by which the members are bound together. Tradition gives a sense of historic continuity and of identity and solidarity. Moreover, the admission of a preunderstanding (i.e., a culturally conditioned approach) in biblical interpretation helps the reader of the Bible to guard against misunderstanding.[4]

On the other hand, tradition is dangerous when it is independent from the reformational principle of the primacy of Scripture (*sola Scriptura*). The reformational *sola*s (Christ alone, faith alone, grace alone, and Scripture alone) were set in contrast to theological and ecclesiastical traditions. The Reformers embraced wholeheartedly the primacy of Scripture. From the Scripture they supported their position—the sufficiency of Christ for salvation and the immediate appropriation of his benefits through faith and through grace—against ecclesiastical authorities. Undaunted by the force of tradition and the power of Rome, they returned to the Word of God as the chief source of their faith. The danger continually exists of living at ease with our theological formulations and not knowing the excitement of fresh interpretation. Barr thus encourages a return to biblical interpretation as a way of appropriating one's heritage. "For a great deal of interpretative work, freshness will not mean departure from tradition . . . but the reappropriation of the tradition with greater depth of understanding."[5]

Our position today is not greatly different from the period before the Reformation. The Middle Ages were united by the acceptance of the "rules of faith," as taught and transmitted by the church. Scripture was secondary in importance to tradition. The modes of interpretation were inconsequential to the teaching of the church. The danger to modern evangelical Christianity is the extraction of values from the Bible, without a due concern for listening to it carefully. Emil Brunner laments the fact that many do not hear the biblical text nor apply the text appropriately, and some seek a hidden "spiritual meaning." He rightly objects that the chaos resulting from a mishandling of the Bible is not reformational but is reminiscent of the pre-Reformation period: "We can only warn people most urgently against this confusion of thought, which inevitably leads us back to a religious position which the Reformers had overcome; indeed, this victory constituted the Reformation."[6]

THE PLACE OF FAITH
IN THE INTERPRETATION OF SCRIPTURE

Over against traditionalism is the world of biblical scholarship. Modern biblical scholarship is only about one hundred years old, but its impact on the approach, depth, and breadth of biblical studies is undeniable. One of the fascinating results of Old Testament scholarship in the last century was the proliferation of articles, monographs, and commentaries integrating the results of the broader studies of the ancient Near East and the Old Testament text. The comparison of a commentary of the early nineteenth century on any book of the Old Testament with its mid-twentieth-century counterpart will reveal the differences. Early Christian, medieval, and reformational commentaries were set aside in favor of the insights from philosophy, philology, comparative religion, archaeology, and history. Coupled with the rejection of the past was the incessant search for newness.

The scholarly community did not necessarily intend to take the Bible out of the church. Critical scholarship aimed at reconstructing the original contexts in which the biblical books arose and assumed that more information would make the message only clearer. The results were different, however, as Childs observes: "It is simply not the case that the more historical and literary knowledge acquired, the better one is able to understand the biblical text."[7]

The study of the Bible is unlike the study of any literary or religious text. It presupposes a personal faith and calls for a commitment of one's whole being. Out of concern for the authoritative (canonical) claim of the Bible and in light of Judeo-Christian traditions through the centuries, the student of the Bible can and must appropriate the Bible with a faith commitment.

This assumption has two implications. First, one does not arbitrarily dismiss the testimony of the Fathers, Reformers, Puritans, or any other conscientious readers of the biblical text. We are part of a historical continuum. Knowledge has not begun with us, nor will it cease with us. As Childs has observed, "The term 'pre-critical' is both naïve and arrogant."[8]

Second, Christian students of the Old Testament *must pass by the cross of Jesus Christ on their return to the Old Testament,* and as such they can never lose their identity as a Christian. Childs's call to return to a theological apprehension of the Old Testament has awakened the scholarly community. In his article "Interpretation in Faith," he showed that the fundamental error of critical scholarship was found in its common assumption that the goal of exegesis was objectivity. Instead, he argued in a plausible way in favor of a return to the reformational model:

> The Reformers read the Old Testament in order to hear the Word of God. They began with the presupposition of the Christian faith that both the Old and New Testaments witness to the one purpose of God with his people. . . . They read Scripture with faith that this witness was directed to Someone who had done something.

21

Childs thus proposes a return to exegesis within a theological context. He claims that one can attain a theological understanding only if one "enters into the hermeneutical circle of genuine exegesis."[9]

Childs's method provides for a way of proclaiming the biblical message in the modern church. The hermeneutic affirms that:

1. the context of the single text is the whole Old Testament, and the whole Old Testament must be understood in the light of the single text;

2. the Old is interpreted in the light of the New and the New in the light of the Old, in accordance with the "one divine purpose";

3. the exegete moves from the Old and New Testaments to the theological reality itself (and vice versa); "The Biblical text is not a dead vestige from the past age but a living vehicle for a divine action which lays claim upon its reader."[10]

THE RELATIONSHIP BETWEEN THE TWO TESTAMENTS

Essential to interpretation in faith is the issue of how the two Testaments relate to each other.[11] The problem arose when the New Testament took its place along with the Old as part of the canon. Marcion, a second-century theologian, argued against the place of the Old Testament in the church on philosophical and theological grounds. For him the Old Testament was Jewish, earthly, full of the wrath of God, and unspiritual. Marcion's position has had its advocates throughout the history of the church. Adolph von Harnack's defense of Marcionism represented the anti-Semitic mind-set that ultimately led to the Holocaust. Friedrich Delitzsch likewise argued,

> The Old Testament is full of deceptions of all kinds: a veritable hodge-podge of erroneous, incredible, undependable figures, . . . in short, a book full of intentional and unintentional deceptions . . . a very dangerous book, in the use of which the greatest care is necessary.[12]

This problem was highlighted in the Reformation. The different approaches of Calvin and Luther to the Old Testament stem from different conceptions of the relationship between the two Testaments. Luther approached the sacred Scriptures with the yardstick of *was Christum treibt* ("what deals with Christ") and subjected the Old Testament to this perspective. "Gospel," as defined in the New Testament, became a yardstick for analyzing the relevance of the Old Testament.[13] On the one hand, Luther found sections of the Old Testament that clearly anticipate the proclamation of the Christian gospel. On the other hand, parts of the Old Testament he found legalistic and Jewish. Luther distinguished "law" over against "gospel" and concluded that much of the Old Testament has little relevance:

"Leave Moses and his people together. They are a thing of the past and none of my business. I hear the word that concerns me. We have the gospel. . . . I pay no attention to [Moses], he does not concern me."[14]

Calvin's position on the Old Testament, which is reflected in the Reformed confessions, arose out of the confrontation with Rome and the Anabaptists. Rome used the Old Testament to argue in favor of the mass, the liturgy, the place of good works, the priesthood, and various and sundry laws, whereas all the Reformed confessions emphasize the aspect of completion or fulfillment introduced by the coming of Jesus Christ. The church was not a mere continuation of Israel with its cultic and civil requirements. The church is a spiritual community, composed of all the people of God who profess faith in Jesus Christ. The biblical teachings emphasizing the newness of the new age (the better covenant, the fulfillment and completion of Jesus' work) thus provided solid reasons for rejecting Rome's claim of continuity between the Old and the New Testaments. The Reformers rightly appreciated the distinct differences between the communities of the Old Covenant and those of the New Covenant. Christians were encouraged to throw off the bondage of Rome and enjoy "the freedom of the Christian man."

Over against the Anabaptists, however, who rejected the Old Testament completely and looked on it as inferior to the New Testament revelation, Calvin maintained to a certain extent the abiding relevance of the Old Testament law. He gave careful attention to the place of Israel and the Old Testament in his exegesis. In Calvin's understanding, God made a covenant with Abraham and his seed, a relation that has a special, redemptive nature. The Old Testament and the New Testament are two forms of one divine administration of grace, which includes all specific covenants.[15] The covenants and both Testaments are most significantly based on the one foundation: Christ, the Mediator of the covenant (1 Tim. 2:5), who fulfills the Old Testament promises while ensuring greater fulfillment at his glorious coming. Calvin attempted to hold in tension both the unchangeable nature of God and the description that Scripture gives of various redemptive stages as being "new." In this way he sought to balance the static (i.e., the eternal aspect of redemption) with the dynamic (i.e., the historic aspects) in his understanding of revelation.

The relatively fluid position of Calvin became more fixed in the distinctive approaches of two seventeenth-century theologians, Cocceius and Voetius.[16] The followers of Cocceius emphasized Calvin's love of biblical and exegetical theology. The followers of Voetius emphasized Calvin's ability to systematize. Calvin's points of tension have thus become polarized up to the present day. The tensions may best be represented by the pairing of law and gospel, promise and fulfillment, token and reality.

Law and Gospel

In Calvin's theology, the difference between the two Testaments lies in the distinction between law and gospel, which reflects the historical period of each: the law was given in the Old Testament, and the gospel in the New Testament. By "law" he understands more than the legal aspects and demands given in the law of God—it is the Old Testament *administration* of the covenant. The Old Testament is not merely preparatory for the coming of Christ. It is a revelation of redemption whose subject is the promised Messiah, the center of the covenant. The period of law, as an expression of the covenant of grace, extended forgiveness, adoption, and covenantal privileges on the basis of the finished work of Christ. In other words, "The gospel points out with the finger what the Law foreshadowed under types."[17]

Law contrasts with gospel in that the former is at best a guide to Christ. The law, with its requirements and penal code, preaches condemnation as opposed to the gospel, which makes alive by the Spirit. The law prepares for the coming of Christ, who is the goal of the law. The law, then, with Christ as its object, has a proper place as an administration of the covenant of grace. The demands of the law change into the experience of liberty, according to which believers willingly obey their heavenly Father.

Promise and Fulfillment

Another way to distinguish between the two Testaments in Calvin's thought is that of promise and fulfillment. In both cases, salvation is the point of contact. Hence, the New Testament revelation is not simply the "fulfillment" and the Old Testament the "promise"; the two Testaments are complementary. The Old Testament saints already experienced salvation, even though they expected a fuller salvation to come. Calvin soberly reminds us that our position is similar to that of the Old Testament saints:

> Although, therefore, Christ offers us in the gospel a present fullness of spiritual benefits, the enjoyment thereof ever lies hidden under the guardianship of hope, until, having put off corruptible flesh, we can be transfigured in the glory of him who goes before us.[18]

The whole nature of biblical revelation is (1) the proclamation and experience of *promised redemption* in the present and (2) the anticipation of a *greater fulfillment* in the future. This truth is reflected in the imagery of "token" in the Old Testament and "reality" in the New Testament. This latter reality, however, is in turn dwarfed by the promise of the greater fulfillment of redemption awaiting the children of God at their final glorification.

24

Token and Reality

Thus far we have noticed that Calvin saw no radical distinction between the Old and New Testaments; rather, they display different emphases. Calvin posited the experience of Israel as the childhood of the church:

> The same church existed among them, but as yet in its childhood. Therefore, keeping them under this tutelage, the Lord gave, not spiritual promises unadorned and open, but ones foreshadowed, in a measure, by earthly promises. When, therefore, he adopted Abraham, Isaac, Jacob, and their descendants into the hope of immortality, he promised them the Land of Canaan as an inheritance. It was not to be the final goal of their hopes, but was to exercise and confirm them, as they contemplated it, in hope of their true inheritance, an inheritance not yet manifested to them.

There is, then, a spiritual nature attached to the earthly blessings. The Old Testament believer received God's benefits as a token of his *shalom*, or peace, with God: "Then he adds the promise of the land, solely as a symbol of his benevolence and a type of the heavenly inheritance." This insight explains the prophetic language, with its pictures and representation, of the earthly blessedness in the state of completion:

> Yet the prophets more often represent the blessedness of the age to come through the type that they had received from the Lord. . . . We see that all these things cannot properly apply to the Land of our pilgrimage, or to the earthly Jerusalem, but to the true homeland of believers, that heavenly city wherein "the Lord has ordained blessing and life forevermore" (Ps. 133:3).[19]

THE THEOLOGICAL CENTER OF SCRIPTURE

Is there any unity in the literary and historical traditions of Israel and the church? The emphases and themes of the Bible are so intertwined, showing significant variation from epoch to epoch and book to book, especially from Old Testament to New Testament, that it is difficult to see any unity. God's love for variety shows up in creation and in his revelation. But we like to distinguish harmony, integration, and direction both in the world of nature (science) and also in the study of his Word. Hence, the quest for a unifying theme or center.

The history of biblical theology gives little hope that students will agree on a single center.[20] Eichrodt asserted that the unifying concept was the covenant. Sellin proposed the holiness of God as the center of the Old Testament. Kohler proposed the lordship of the God of Israel. Others have suggested equally intriguing possibilities, such as the kingdom of God, the people of Yahweh, or the relation of Yahweh to his people. Von Rad rejected offhand any simplistic constructions of Old Testament theology in favor of a variety of emphases that come to expression in the history of Israel.

Definition and agreement upon a center concern evangelical scholars as well.[21] Kaiser's concern with a center arises from a conviction that Scripture reveals the plan of God. Out of this concern he developed an Old Testament theology around the "promise" motif:

> The divine promise pointed to a seed, a race, a family, a man, a land, and a blessing of universal proportions—all guaranteed, according to Genesis 17, as being everlasting and eternal. In that purpose resides the single plan of God. In that single plan lies a capability of embracing as much variety and variegation as the progress of revelation and history can engender. In that unity of goal and method unfolded a march of events which the writers described, and in a series of interconnected interpretations they likewise boldly announced God's normative views on those events for that generation and those to come.[22]

Theological centers such as promise (Kaiser), covenant (Robertson; McComiskey), and kingdom (Van Ruler) have the advantage of serving as organizing principles from which the biblical revelation may be approached. The recognition of a theological center highlights one aspect of God's plan in distinction from others. God is a God of order. He has a purpose for everything. Out of that conviction I propose to focus on Jesus Christ as the center. *Jesus is the revelation of the salvation of God.*

The history of redemption unfolds a progression in the outworking of God's plan of redemption that will unfold completely in the restoration of all things. All blessings, promises, covenants, and kingdom expressions are reflections or shadows of the great salvation in Jesus Christ that is to come at the end of the age. In other words, the Old and New Testaments together witness to the great salvation as restoration. Old Testament saints and Christians share the common experience of receiving the grace of God in Christ Jesus. The enjoyment of the experience of salvation increases as God's revelation clarifies the nature of the Messiah and the messianic age.

Christian interpreters of the Old Testament cannot limit their focus to one of the many themes.[23] They cannot isolate the Old from the New. In their approach to the Old Testament, they must remember that they stand in a tradition that goes back to the midpoint of redemptive history, namely, the incarnation, death, and resurrection of Jesus, the Messiah.

> The Christian church confesses to find a witness to Jesus Christ in both the Old Testament and the New. . . . The form of the Christian Bible

> . . . lays claim upon the whole Scripture as the authoritative witness to God's purpose in Jesus Christ for the church and the world. . . . The Old Testament is interpreted by the New, and the New is understood through the Old, but the unity of its witness is grounded in One Lord.[24]

The heartbeat of the Scriptures has increased rapidly since the coming of Jesus. The New Testament authors show an excitement and intensity in their preaching and writing about the new era that has been introduced since the resurrection of Jesus. Consider Peter, for example (Acts 2:22–24; 4:11–12; 10:42–43; 1 Peter 1:12), or Stephen (Acts 7:52) or Paul (Acts 13:32–33; 17:30–31; 26:22–24; 28:28; 2 Cor. 1:19–20; Phil. 1:18). *The center of the Bible is the incarnate and glorified Christ, by whom all things will be renewed.* All the acts of God, all the revelation of his promises and covenants, all the progression of his kingdom, and all the benefits of salvation are *in Christ.*[25]

All the acts and blessings of God in any age are thus based on the death of the Christ in anticipation of the new age. We do not know the exact nature of that new age, because the prophets and apostles speak in metaphors and parables. We do know that the age of salvation will establish complete freedom from the death, anxiety, and judgment that characterize the present world. Since that world is so foreign (and so glorious!) to believers before and after Christ's first coming, all believers share in common hope, or faith (Heb. 11). By having hope in the coming world of righteousness (Gal. 5:5; 2 Peter 3:13), faith focuses on the Christ, the King of Glory, in whom shadow, token, and promise will become light, reality, and fulfillment. In view of the shadowlike existence of all God's saints—from Adam to the present—it would be presumptuous for us to reduce God's gracious acts, revelations, covenants, and promises to "mere shadows." We, too, are still living in the shadow of the great age to come!

THE INTERPRETATION OF THE BIBLE

Exegesis is the art and science of biblical interpretation in accordance with the rules of hermeneutics. Hermeneutics refers to the manner in which we listen to the text, relate it to other texts, and apply it. Hermeneutics calls for a discipline of mind and heart, by which the student of Scripture may patiently study the biblical text in its various contexts, including historical, grammatical, literary, and cultural. This approach is best known as *historical-grammatical analysis.*[26]

Such analysis, however, cannot be separated from interpretation "in faith." The Bible requires continual submission of our understanding to what the Spirit of God has inspired (1 Cor. 2:12–15) and requires a personal transformation, application, and alteration of our presuppositions. Each interpreter of the biblical text approaches the meaning of the text theologically, existentially, psychologically, or as a literary phenomenon.[27] One's prior understanding, however, must continually come under the transforming power of the Spirit of God, witnessing through the Word of God. Interpretation of the Bible requires submission of one's spirit to the Holy Spirit, a walk with God, a diligent study of the Word, and an openness to the insights of other believers. God speaks and we must listen.

The Art of Bible Study

Bible study in many ways resembles the study of a work of art. The Bible, too, is actually a work of art—a literary masterpiece, or, better, a collection of literary masterpieces. Art may be inspiring, but the Bible is inspired. Art may be uplifting, but the Bible is transforming. Its power to transform by the Spirit is not independent of discipline and diligent study, as the study of the Bible requires *more*, not less, than the study of any piece of art. Art, we could say, captures the spirit of the artist, but the Bible is the work of the Holy Spirit. Students of the Bible may surround themselves with Bible reference books and may diligently study the history of redemption and biblical theology. They may master ancient Near East history and Semitic languages and literature. But if they do not have the Spirit of God, the Bible is a mere collection of books that may or may not be inspiring. The Holy Spirit is the author of Scripture and teaches the deep things of God to those who search (1 Cor. 2:10–16; 2 Peter 1:21). When the student of the Bible approaches the Bible with openness to the Spirit, the Holy Spirit witnesses to the authority of the Word, illumines and transforms the life, and permits increasingly deeper understanding of relations between the biblical books as well as of thematic and historical developments.

The Spirit's presence, however, is no excuse for failure to study the Bible diligently. Far too often, the student of the Bible opens God's Word only in order to find the answer to an immediate problem. Contexts and relationships are disregarded. Many students of the Word are like people who know little about art and who walk through a museum reacting only with likes and dislikes. Comparable with the proper study of art, in studying the Bible one must penetrate the structure of biblical thought. If one can feel the heartbeat of the books by understanding their cultural, historical, and literary background, as well as how one portion relates to other parts of Scripture, one can better understand and appreciate the book. If understanding structural relations is important in the study of arts and sciences, how much more must the student of the Bible learn to appreciate the structure of biblical thought and expression. Otherwise, the Western reader of the Bible may come to conclusions significantly different from those of a third-world reader. Because the Bible is studied in different cultures and subcultures, we must bring harmony into our study of the Bible by searching for those structures of biblical thought that are inherent in the Bible itself. According to Torrance,

> There are structures of biblical thought and speech found in the Old Testament which have permanent value, both for the New Testament and for the Christian Church. That is why the Church is built upon the foundation not only of the apostles but of the prophets, and in that order, for the Old Testament Scriptures are now assumed within the orbit of the New Testament, for they provide the New Testament revelation with the basic structures which it used in the articulation of the Gospel, although the structures it derived from Israel were taken up and transformed in Christ.[28]

Analysis and Synthesis: A Trifocal Approach to the Biblical Text

If we are to come closer to the structure of biblical thought, we must learn to study patiently the interrelationships between Old Testament and New Testament, as well as individual books of the Bible, authors, people, land, history, and geography. Through a study of the various components of the text (analysis) and their interrelationships (synthesis), the structures of biblical thought can present themselves powerfully to us today. (See figure 1, page 43.)

Analysis is that part of the interpretation of the text in which the student of Scripture pays attention to meaning (words, phrases, grammar, and syntax), relationships (verses and paragraphs), and text-critical issues. In addition to the analysis of words, phrases, and verses, the analyst also examines the use of the text in parallel passages or in quotations elsewhere in the Old or New Testament. As part of a careful analysis the student of Scripture should study the cultural, socioeconomic, geographic, and historic background of the text.

Armed with a thesaurus of background material and with linguistic, semantic, and textual information, the student of the Bible is at least more aware of the constituent parts of the text. The problem with the historical-grammatical method, however, is that students of the Word may be tempted to think that they have control over the text when all they have done is examine its constituent parts—but what grasp do they really have of its message? Only after seeing how the parts fit together and how they relate to the rest of the book and to the rest of Scripture can the student master the clear message of the text. Proper exegetical theology, therefore, requires synthesis.

Synthesis is that part of the interpretation of a text that considers its meaning within the context of the book and within the whole of the

Scriptures. The process of synthesis is the most important ingredient in truly understanding the biblical text. Exegetes, however, after duly recognizing the subjectivity involved in bringing the components of the text together in a holistic fashion, often content themselves with being mere observers of the text. The text is there, however, not only to be analyzed but also to have an impact on modern men and women. The connection between Old Testament text, as a historically conditioned event, and the twentieth-century Christian is complicated by the subsequent events in redemptive history, especially the coming of Jesus Christ. It is further complicated by the various theological assumptions we bring to the text that form an interpretive framework. We must therefore make a conscious effort to listen to the text in an honest and methodologically sound manner. We must resist the temptation to disregard the author's intended meaning in order to use the passage as a proof text. Finally, we must avoid reading too much New Testament into the Old, whether by christological, typological, or existential application of the text.

The three aspects of synthetic exegesis provide linkages between a text and the surrounding corpus of texts. The trifocal elements all assume the importance of the historical-grammatical method and show a sensitivity to the fact that biblical revelation, while divinely inspired, is historically conditioned. The Bible is not an oracle of God but the Word of God mediated in time and communicated in human language. The Word of God is infallible in everything it affirms, but we are limited in our perception. The study of the Bible, therefore, aims at thinking God's thoughts after him by being willing to ascertain the *literary forms* (i.e., the human forms of written communication), the *canonical context* (i.e., the function of the literary forms within the community that received the inscripturated Word of God as indeed God's Word), and the progress of *redemptive history* (i.e., the orderly flow of God's acts and revelation).

Literary Form

Each book of the Bible has a purpose, and every text must be read in the light of the purposes of the book. In order to discover how the text under consideration contributes to the argument of the whole book, the former must be read as a distinct literary expression within the book as a whole. It has a literary form, or genre, that requires special attention, since the form is always related to content. The reader must compare one passage with passages that have a similar literary form. By permitting passages of the same genre to interpret the text under consideration, one allows Scripture to interpret Scripture.[29]

Canonical Place

Sensitivity to the canonical function begins with the simple recognition that the Bible as we now have it developed over a long period of time. The "canon" was at one time a dynamic concept, as the various parts came together under the inspiration and providence of the Holy Spirit.

First, one must be sensitive to *canonical relations*. In other words, one must consider a book within its respective place in the canon, whether *Pentateuch, Prophets* (divided into the so-called Former Prophets [Joshua through 2 Kings] and Latter Prophets [the major prophets Isaiah, Jeremiah, and Ezekiel and the twelve minor prophets]), *Writings* (Psalms, Job, Proverbs, the five "Scrolls" [Ruth, Song of Songs, Ecclesiastes, Lamentations, and Esther], Daniel, Ezra-Nehemiah, and 1-2 Chronicles), *Gospels, Acts, Epistles,* or *Revelation.* Sensitivity to canonical relationships also concerns the time in which the people of God received the particular writing. By relating a text to the entire book, one may come to a fuller synthetic understanding of the message as a whole.

Second, sensitivity to the *canonical function* of the text appreciates the historical context in which God's people originally received the individual books. The needs of his people varied from era to era, and we may look at the biblical canon as a collection of canons, that is, individual books given to a particular people who received each one as the Word of God. Brevard S. Childs has made an invaluable contribution by raising scholarly sensitivity to the importance of the canonical function of a book. According to Childs, "To speak of canonical function is to view the book from the perspective of a community whose religious needs and theological confessions are being addressed by the divine word." The interpreter of the Bible must sensitively note those signs within the biblical book that reveal the book's function within the community of faith. "It is our thesis . . . that the diversity of function has been carefully structured within the book in order to establish guidelines for its authoritative role within the community."[30]

Redemptive-Historical Significance

Biblical revelation interprets God's activities in human history and reveals God's gracious response to the needs of human beings. The history of God's self-involvement through his mighty acts of redemption and revelation forms the subject of so-called redemptive history. The redemptive-historical approach assumes that the Bible was primarily given not to convey history or morals but to record God's fidelity to the nations, the patriarchs, Israel, and the church of Jesus Christ. Through a study of redemptive history, the purpose of God in Christ becomes

31

more evident. This method provides a framework for connecting the parts of Scripture into a coherent whole, but it also displays the many themes as a mosaic. The variety and harmony of Scripture are held in tension by the assumption that now we know in part and by the confidence that God knows the end from the beginning.

The redemptive-historical approach pays careful attention to the text, to the particular redemptive-historical period, and to the relationship of that period to the coming of Jesus as the Savior and Restorer of heaven and earth. Those who take a redemptive-historical approach to exegesis recognize that they have not fully achieved a holistic understanding of Scripture, but they strive together as a community of exegetes toward the goal.[31]

The interpreter asks what the text has to do with the coming of Jesus and our hope in the restoration of all things at his return. The redemptive-historical approach respects the channels of human communication and civilization by paying careful attention to the text given in its original context of history, culture, literature, and community of faith. This message is considered to be christological in the sense that the whole of the Bible (both Old and New Testament) focuses on Jesus the Messiah, who will restore all things to the Godhead. Since this restoration has not yet taken place, however, the redemptive-historical perspective contemplates the process in light of the revelation of the end, or consummation, of redemptive history. The progression of redemption did not culminate in Jesus' first coming but anticipates the coming of Christ in glory, when he will inaugurate the era of consummation, the new heavens and the new earth. Interpretation, therefore, is both christological and eschatological. If it limits the fulfillment to Jesus' first coming, it tends to contrast the Old Testament with the New. If, however, it focuses on the restoration of all things as the goal of the history of redemption, then the Old Testament and New Testament are brought more closely together as witnesses to the hope that this Jesus has been appointed to make everything subject to the Father (Acts 2:34–36; 1 Cor. 15:25; Heb. 1:13; 2:8; 10:13; Rev. 2:27; 12:5; 19:15).

With this concern in mind, I describe in this book twelve periods of redemptive history. Each period is distinct and relates organically to the previous and succeeding epochs. Each period reveals elements of continuity and discontinuity and contributes to a greater appreciation of the overall plan of God. (See table 1.)

The twelve periods serve as convenient dividers along the long road of redemptive history. Rather than looking at the acts of God in a general way, the reader of the Bible may discover certain markers— high points, or watersheds—in the progression of God's salvation. The number 12 is arbitrary, but the concern for continuity and discontinuity

TABLE 1. TWELVE PERIODS OF REDEMPTIVE HISTORY

Approx. Beginning	Period	Scripture	Themes
—	Creation in Harmony	Gen. 1–2	Yahweh is Creator King; humans are viceregents of the great King; covenant with creation
—	Creation in Alienation	Gen. 3–11	Rebellion against God's kingship; state of alienation, two kingdoms: kingdom of God and of man; Noahic covenant
2000 B.C.	Election and Promise	Gen. 12–50	Promise, Abrahamic covenant, and faith
1400 B.C.	A Holy Nation	Exod.–Josh.	Consecration of Israel, Mosaic covenant, presence of Yahweh, kingdom of God in Israel
1200 B.C.	A Nation Like the Other Nations	Judg. 1–1 Sam. 15	Israel's rebelliousness and Yahweh's sovereignty; necessity of human kingship in Israel
1000 B.C.	A Royal Nation	1 Sam. 16–1 Kings 11 1 Chron. 1–2 Chron. 9	Davidic covenant, the glory of the theocratic community, and Yahweh's presence in the temple
931 B.C.	A Divided Nation	1 Kings 12–2 Kings 25 2 Chron. 10–36	Israel's rebelliousness and Judah's vacillation; the failure of the Davidic dynasty; prophetic message: remnant, day of the Lord, exile, and restoration
538 B.C.	A Restored Nation	Ezra, Neh., Prophets	Restoration: renewal of the covenants
4 B.C.	Jesus and the Kingdom	Gospels	Jesus' proclamation, miracles, death, and resurrection: the presence of the glorious kingdom in the Son, renewal of the covenants, the new people of God, preparation for the glorious coming of Jesus
A.D. 29	The Apostolic Era	Acts, Epistles	Rule of Jesus, his presence in the Spirit, advance of the church, apostolic transmission of the tradition: New Testament writings
A.D. 100	The Kingdom and the Church	—	Progression of the church: challenge of being a holy and royal people in the world
—	The New Jerusalem	Gen. 3:1–Rev. 22:21	Transformation and restoration: a new heaven and earth; redemption of creation; a holy people; the beneficent presence and rule of God and of his Messiah

is relevant for understanding how to read the Bible and how to relate a particular text to the whole movement of God's acts. It is easy to focus on one theme or center, such as covenant or promise, but the twelve periods together provide many avenues of relationships, all of which converge in Jesus Christ.

From creation to new creation, the Lord is working out his purpose of creating a renewed humanity to enjoy his restored creation. The integration of redemption with creation reveals God's royal concern as the Creator-Redeemer-King. Each stage of redemptive history reveals the gracious acts of God in spite of human disinterest, waywardness, and rebellion. The council of the great King stands, and his love cannot be thwarted by individuals. The struggle between the kingdom of God and the kingdom of man has already lasted thousands of years, but the outcome is secure. The patience and love of God is evident in his care and blessing of all of his creation. God's love, however, is balanced with his wrath. The God who redeems also avenges and vindicates. Throughout redemptive history the Lord intervenes with blessing and judgment and thus reminds all persons of the great day when he will finally and climactically establish his kingdom.

BIBLICAL INTERPRETATION AND TRANSFORMATION

Interpretation "in Community"

Critical and conservative biblical scholars alike have seen the need to let the ancient biblical witnesses speak to us today. The first question is not how the Scriptures can be made relevant but how we can develop a methodology that permits us to hear the voice of God and to respond to it. Evangelicals have challenged their own community to take the Bible seriously in preaching.[32] Interpreters of the Bible are involved in the process of interpretation as a member of the community of God's people. They cannot be satisfied with feeding their own soul, but as a Christian they value the unity of Scripture, the guidance by the internal testimony of the Holy Spirit, and the words of God in their heart and life.

Non-Evangelicals, too, challenge their community to listen to the text. Stuhlmacher opts for a "hermeneutics of consent" in which the exegete affirms the tie with the textual and spiritual tradition. The question is not primarily "how we relate to the texts and how the texts . . . can be ranked in an ancient context of events" but also "what claim or truth about man, his world, and transcendence we hear from these texts." By hearing the historical text, exegetes may involve themselves with what Stuhlmacher calls "a critical dialogue with the tradition." The conclusions must always be verifiable. The methodology must not contradict the attitude of consent but must permit modern readers "to rediscover and recapture dimensions of existence which have been forgotten and believed to be lost." In this way exegesis remains communicable and does not "become an intuitive vision, limited to an individual or group."[33]

In spite of the theological differences, both evangelicals (Kaiser and Maier) and Stuhlmacher approach exegesis with the desire to interpret the biblical text in community. Both advance a hermeneutics of consent, of hearing the Word of God. Both oppose individualistic exegesis. Both desire to be faithful to the Apostles' Creed ("I believe in Jesus Christ"). The main difference lies in the relative value placed on history, historical research, and the relationship between the past and the present.

The isolation of the Bible from the life of the church has produced, in Stuhlmacher's words, a vacuum that often is filled with unwarranted interpretation.

> Among the older and younger theologians at work in the church this distancing effect is accompanied by an enormous and at times even alarming uncertainty in their use of scripture. . . . For them biblical criticism has produced a vacuum which causes them to despair of the possibilities of a useful, historical-critical interpretation of scripture, and in part to seize at hair-raising theological substitutes.[34]

The concept of vacuum describes the compulsion to satisfy one's spiritual thirst *regardless of the means*. Subjectivism and pragmatism have left us with a bankruptcy of biblical scholarship. Distrusting the guidance from scholarship, students of the Bible have rediscovered the need for the Holy Spirit, the priesthood of all believers, and the perspicuity of Scripture in order to understand God's Word. Spirituality in biblical interpretation is most important, but the urge for immediacy and pragmatic results have had as detrimental an impact on Evangelicalism as the results of criticism have had on liberalism.

The Jews in exile from Jerusalem and the temple were alienated from God, but Christians today may feel equally abandoned when the Bible remains a closed book for them or when its value is reduced to being a treasury of proof texts or inspirational thoughts. The vacuum has been filled by an emphasis on personal experience, devotional practice, and personal Bible study. The community worships, but individuals feed their own soul. The polarization of community and the individual is regrettable and can lead only to an impoverishment of the Christian community. Real dialogue takes place when the church as a whole and the individual Christian relate at the same level to the biblical text.

Interpretation "in Dialogue"

Richard L. Rohrbaugh presents an example of how a pastor can be involved exegetically. He defines parish hermeneutics as "a ministry that attempts to take the biblical literature as a serious partner in the ongoing dialogue of God's people." Hermeneutics is not a process in which the biblical scholar takes a text and gives the single correct interpretation of the text, after which the pastor transforms the exposition into proclamation. Rohrbaugh wants to break the chain that links exegesis with scholars alone.

> ... it is the pastor, as the one who most regularly and most often interprets Scripture in the life of the church, who becomes a link in the hermeneutical chain that stretches from the biblical literature itself, through the varied scholarly processes that raise the questions cited above, and finally to the particular person who is doing the interpreting in the church. ... The context and person of the one doing the interpreting is a key link in the process of re-creating the meaning of the Scriptures in the church.[35]

Gerhard Ebeling, as a representative of the new hermeneutic, adds a valuable insight regarding how to begin the process of dialogue. For him the sermon is not just an exposition of the experience of God in the past; the event must be re-created so that the minister helps his people to experience God in the present as God's people did in the past. Such a sermon is proclamation![36] Through the sermon the minister aims at helping God's people experience the transforming power of the Word of God. The interpreter is involved with the context of the text but must show an equal concern for God's people in a different context. Interpretation has been likened to two horizons—the past and the present—but interpretation also fuses these two horizons.[37] This fusion must capture accurately the clear meaning of Scripture.[38]

Evangelical study of the Bible can be lively and relevant, reflecting careful interpretation (analysis and synthesis). The resulting transformation by the Spirit of God exalts God. Interpretation not based on the Spirit's intent but motivated by an ingenious search for redeeming values may lead God's people to say,

> "We cannot explain the Bible like our Minister, he ... is so clever, and so ingenious—he can 'find Christ' in every part of the Bible!" This means that such people will probably do one thing or the other: *either* they will give up their own private Bible reading altogether: *or* they will try to imitate their Minister; then they will indeed fall into a pit, and indulge in flights of the wildest allegory![39]

To be relevant the student of the Bible must stand with one foot in the world of the Bible and one foot in today's society. Bible study is work and requires personal involvement. Its insights may throw new light on one's thoughts and beliefs.[40] But in the end, the individual and the community of God's people benefit greatly by permitting the Spirit of the living Christ to speak through the ancient Scriptures in our modern context.

CONCLUSION

For the believer in Jesus Christ the Bible is the book of God and man. The Lord accommodated himself to human beings in different cultures and in distant historical epochs, but in each case the same God spoke (Heb. 1:1–3). In both Old and New Testaments the Bible unfolds God's plan, as his acts in creation and in redemption witness to his love and determination. This inspired record of God's fidelity challenges modern people and the church to look to the God and Father of Jesus Christ as the Redeemer of the world. He will complete what he planned from the foundation of the world.

How this plan unfolds is the object of biblical interpretation—that is, the process of studying the Bible, of relating the various parts of Scripture, and of applying the ancient text to a modern situation. Interpretation is both an art and a discipline. The interpreter of Scripture studies the biblical text in the presence of the living Christ, who operates in the believer by the power of the Spirit of God. Interpretation is dynamic, as the Bible calls for continual transformation. The vision of God has an impact on our vision of the world and of God's creation. Bible study requires a faith commitment to the triune God. Rather than approach any book of the Bible solely from within the historical situation of that book, readers must admit unashamedly that they come to the reading of that book with colored glasses. They live between the times of Christ's resurrection and his glorious appearing, and they also live between the horizon of their time and that of the ancient books. But God speaks to them within their own cultural milieu, including their own confessional framework. The Bible speaks because God speaks!

The vantage point from which the student of the Bible comes to Scripture determines what the text may or may not say. Biblical history and the study of past events seem unrelated to twentieth-century men and women, but for the Christian they form a part of the story of God's special acts in unfolding his plan of redemption. Living in the twentieth century, individuals may not be able to free themselves from nearly two thousand years of church history, from pressing modern issues, or from their own theological framework; but they can renew their Christian commitment, self-understanding, and theological convictions by a fresh study (exegesis) of the Word of God. Insofar as Bible study includes the

37

acquisition of facts and analysis, the historical-grammatical method is helpful in recovering the meaning of the ancient words and the life-situation of the text.

Interpretation not only involves the analysis of the text but also includes a synthesis, or integration of the text within its literary setting, the canonical situation (i.e., the Word of God as addressed to God's people in a particular historical context and received as canon), and redemptive-historical developments. The interpretation of a text is like a snapshot, whereas the hermeneutic of redemptive-history may be likened to a movie. The latter relates the individual pictures to each other and continues to alter the perceived relationships so as to permit the Bible to tell its own story of God's redemptive involvement in the history of Israel and the church. Furthermore, the Spirit of God requires transformation, by which the horizons of the past culture and that of the present cultural situation are fused. As Ramm wrote, "Exegesis without application is academic."[41]

Interpretation also involves equal concern for the Old and New Testaments. When the two parts of the Bible are held in careful balance, the continual tension between law and gospel, token and reality, promise and fulfillment, present age and future restoration, Israel and the church, and earthly and spiritual only enhances a christological and eschatological focus. God's revelation in Jesus is the watershed—the midpoint of redemptive history.[42] Jesus is the focus of Scripture. We cannot say, however, that the Old Testament is fulfilled in the New. Nor did Jesus completely fulfill the Old. In a real sense the Scriptures have an eschatological focus, as Old and New together point forward to the era of consummation, when all things will be made new. Jesus the Messiah is thus the hope of saints, both before and after his first coming.

Part 1

Creation in Harmony

Introduction to Part 1

The Bible begins with the account of creation (Gen. 1–2) and ends with a description of a more glorious creation (Rev. 21–22). Between these accounts lies the story of redemption.[1] The movement from creation to restoration is one organic development whereby God works out his plan for the redemption of a new humanity from all the nations (Rev. 5:9; 7:9). Creation, in a real sense, is the preamble to the history of redemption. In this part I consider the biblical account of creation as a proclamation, specifically, that:

1. God, the Redeemer, is the Creator;
2. God rules over his creation in accordance with his royal nature (glory, power, wisdom, and fidelity);
3. his creation itself reflects these royal attributes;
4. human beings are uniquely endowed to mirror the royal attributes of the great King;
5. God, who created by his Word, maintains his relationship with individuals by the Word;
6. although the original creation was good, it had to be consecrated and perfected; therefore,
7. Jesus Christ had to come to consecrate all things to God (Eph. 1:9–10).

In order to understand rightly the biblical account of creation, we must learn to adjust ourselves to the structures of biblical revelation. The teaching about creation is God's message to Israel, a proclamation that had an authoritative function in shaping Israel's faith. When God revealed the creation story, he revealed it first to Israel. The Israelites were concerned not with twentieth-century scientific presuppositions and models but with who Yahweh is.[2] He had made a covenant with Abraham and had led them out of Egypt. They were concerned with their survival, sustenance, and God's protection. They faced pagan cultures that had a different view of gods, nature, human beings, and life in general. God's Word on creation came to his people in their historical context as authoritative; that is, it came as *canonical*.

The creation account also came to them as a majestic, *literary*

40

masterpiece. The movement of the narrative unfolds in simple strokes as the activities of the Creator. By analyzing the biblical account of creation, taking into consideration the *redemptive-historical* purposes of God, the canonical context of ancient Israel, and the literary conventions of another era and culture, we can apprehend the structures of biblical thought. The dynamic message of God's Word, having been heard, can then be proclaimed and applied to a new generation.

CHAPTER 1

A Theocentric Focus on Creation

The biblical description of creation comprises two accounts (Gen. 1:1–2:3; 2:4–25).[1] The first consists of ten commands set within a series of stereotyped expressions and is more poetic. The second represents the narrative form. The two accounts present creation from perspectives that are different yet harmonious and complementary. The first has been called the fiat creation; the second, the action creation.[2] Both portray God in human terms, and both focus on the creation of man. The theocentric perspective gives harmony to the anthropocentric focus. Only in view of the revelation of God can one appreciate humankind's unique position! Genesis 1 portrays God as a *ruler*, by whose command the world comes into being. The second account portrays God as a *potter* who shapes the man from the dust of the ground (2:7), as a *gardener* who plants a garden (v. 8), and as a *builder* who made the woman out of the rib (v. 22). As anthropocentric accounts, both place the emphasis on the human beings as the special creatures of God, endowed with unique gifts and having a special relationship with their Creator that he has graciously initiated and confirmed. We consider further in this chapter the literary contribution of each account. (See figure 1.)

GOD MAKES A HOME FOR MAN (GEN. 1:1–2:3)

The prosaic style of the first chapter of Genesis is characterized by schematization and symmetry. It is a literary masterpiece, intended to give readers a sense of wholeness and harmony and to fill them with awe for the wonderful Creator, by whom the heaven and earth came into being. (See, e.g., Ps. 139:14: "I praise you because I am fearfully and wonderfully made; your works are wonderful, I know that full well.") The symmetry, or balance and harmony, of the first chapter is linguistic and schematic.

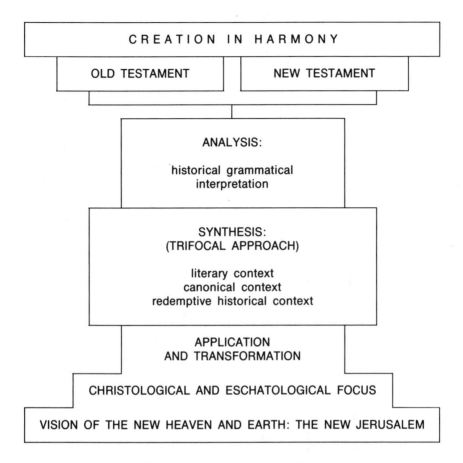

Figure 1. Total Interpretation

Linguistic Symmetry

In linguistic, or verbal, symmetry repetition of words and phrases creates balance and an aesthetic sense of harmony. The Israelites no doubt readily saw such symmetry, because it reflected the literary conventions of their time.[3] The major symmetry of the first chapter is the repetitive use of seven stereotyped phrases. (See table 2.)

The intensification of repetitive phrases pertaining to days three and six, each with two separate creative acts, represents a closing off of days 1–3 and days 4–6 as subsections of the account. Moreover, each transition is marked by changes in vocabulary and repetition of significant words.[4] The dissonance thus created is like a signpost marking a change in direction.[5] By means of crescendo and dissonance

TABLE 2. LINGUISTIC SYMMETRY IN GENESIS 1:1–2:3

Phrases	Days[a]						
	1 (1:3–5)	2 (1:6–8)	3 (1:9–13)	4 (1:14–19)	5 (1:20–23)	6 (1:24–31)	7 (2:1–3)
1. and God said	1	1	2	1	1	4	—
2. let (there be)	1	2	2	1	2	2	—
3. and it was so	1	1	2	1	—	2	—
4. [descriptive phrase telling what God did]	1	1	2	1	—	2	—
5. [word of naming or blessing]	1	1	1	—	1	1	1
6. (very) good	1	—	2	1	1	1	—
7. and there was evening, and there was morning—the—day	1	1	1	1	1	1	—

[a]The numbers under each day indicate the number of occurrences of each phrase type.

the reader is invited to pay more attention to the fourth, sixth, and seventh days. (See figure 2.)

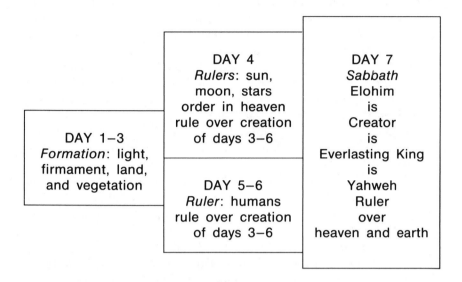

**Figure 2. Literary Movement in Genesis 1:1–2:3
(Emphasis on Days 4, 6, and 7)**

The Fourth Day

The account moves in a crescendo from the first day to the fourth. (See table 2.) The fourth day marks the end of the sequence of the first three days by repeating the vocabulary of the first three days. It marks a crowning point in creation, as the formative process described in days 1–3 comes to completion (see "Schematic Symmetry" p. 47). Dissonance results from the use of infinitives ("to separate" [used twice], "to give light" [twice], and "to govern") and from the introduction of a new root word—*mšl*, "to govern"—used three times in Genesis 1:16 and 18. The dissonance functions to emphasize a new element: *governance.* God has appointed light-bearers for governance in the expanse of heaven (v. 17). On the one hand, the fourth day belongs to the formative aspect of God's creation (days 1–3) and, on the other hand, it is part of the filling of the created world (days 4–6), as God fills space with the sun, moon, constellations, and stars. The fourth day, therefore, forms a bridge between the first three days and the last three days.

The Sixth Day

The rhythm reaches another climax on the sixth day. God had blessed the creation of fish and fowl on the fifth day (Gen. 1:22). He also blessed man on the sixth day. The significance of the sixth day, however, lies in the fourfold repetition of the phrase "and God said" (which appears only twice in the description of the third day), the twofold repetition of the verb "created" (v. 27), and the threefold repetition of the noun "image" (vv. 26–27). Dissonance is conveyed by the phrase "let us" and by the words "image" and "likeness." Whereas *mîn*, "kind," in verses 11–12, 21 (2x), 24, and 25 signifies the botanical and zoological reproductive powers, the human beings differ by their being like God. They are not of the nature *(mîn)* of God, nor do they belong to the world of vegetation and animal life. The rapid repetition of the words "image" and "likeness" builds momentum and emphasis: "in our image, in our likeness . . . in his own image, in the image of God" (vv. 26–27).

Another element of dissonance is created by the verbs translated "rule" *(rdh; kbš)*. Man's rule differs from that of the light-bearers (for which the verb *mšl* is used in vv. 16–18). The introduction of different verbs *rdh* and *kbš* calls the reader's attention to the importance of the humans' rule over creation on earth. The fourth day marked a high point in that the "rulers" of heaven were ordained by God. The sixth day is another high point, as God ordains men and women to rule over all creation (v. 28). Finally, dissonance is also created by changing the stereotyped phrase "it was good" to "it was very good," thus concluding the creation story.

The Seventh Day

The repetition of the seven formulas comes to an abrupt end in Genesis 2:1. The change in rhythm calls special attention to the distinctiveness of the seventh day—the day that completes creation and the only day that God consecrates. The author focuses on the completion of the activities by repeating "completed" (2x), "his work" (3x), and a form of the verb *'śh*, "do" (3x in MT; 2x in NIV).

The author also highlights the significance of the seventh day by repeating "the seventh day" (3x) and by using the verb *šbt*, "rested" (2x). He further creates dissonance by shifting from the familiar phrase "and he blessed" (1:22, 28) to a new phrase, "and he sanctified" (2:3). The God *Elohim* (his name appears three times in vv. 2–3), who had made everything, is the God who rested from his creation. The consecration of the seventh day was unique, however. The God who had *blessed* the first human beings *consecrated* the seventh day. The God who had observed that everything was "good," even "very good," called only the seventh day "holy." Creation itself is not marked by perfection or holiness; only the seventh day is so distinguished.

Schematic Symmetry

Symmetry is evident in the order of the days of creation. The schema of the seven days is a literary figure that frames the totality of the created order within a sequential development.[6] These days are usually understood as depicting merely the sequence of events or as the basis for providing information on the length of the days. A symmetric reading may avoid such issues altogether. The impression of sequence may at first give a sense of progression, but questions of how all the created world coheres, including the issues posed by modern science, become secondary when the meaning of creation in the Genesis account is considered. The sequence of the days reveals the *orderliness* of creation, rather than the *order* of creative events.

The first set of three days depicts the *formation* of man's home, while the second set of three days presents the *filling* of the world of creation—in heaven above, the earth, and the sea. The sequence of the days brings out the internal harmony in the created world. God first prepares the stage, we might say, for the humans' habitation (light and darkness, heaven and earth, waters and dry ground with vegetation) and then fills that stage with light-bearers, birds, fish, animals, and human-kind. The sequence is climactic, moving from formlessness (days 1–3) to fullness (days 4–6) and from inanimate creation to animal life and finally to human life, the climax of his creative acts. The days also show parallelism in each day having a counterpart. The six days of creation may be placed in synthetic parallelism, each day finding its complement in another day.[7] The first day and the fourth day are thus a pair, as are the second and fifth, and the third and sixth. (See table 3.) Only the seventh day stands alone and has significance of its own.

TABLE 3. SYNTHETIC PARALLELISM IN GENESIS 1

Formation of the World Item Created		*Filling of the World* Item Created	
Day		Day	
1	darkness, light	4	heavenly light-bearers
2	heavens, water	5	birds of the air; water animals
3	seas, land, vegetation	6	land animals; man; provision of food

The creativity of the author brings us from concern with the physical world, as we know it, to a reflection on man, created in God's image, vested with the rule over God's creation, and blessed by the Creator-King. The significance of human beings in God's creation is suggested by their creation (1) at the climax of the creation week; (2) by divine decree ("let us"), over against the usual form of command ("let"); (3) in the image of God (Gen. 1:26–27); and (4) with a divinely established purpose (vv. 26–27). Finally, the creation of humankind is distinctive because to them alone God speaks (vv. 28–30).

If we look only at the balance of forming and filling in days one through six, we miss the significance of the seventh day. The importance of the seventh day is first made clear by the threefold repetition of "the seventh day." As we have seen, the repetition of words and phrases is significant in the development of the first creation narrative. Furthermore, it is remarkable that God "blessed" and "sanctified" the seventh day. The verb "call" is associated with the first three days, and the verb "bless" is associated with the last two days of creation. It seems that the author progressively moves us from calling to blessing and then to the consecration of the seventh day. He introduces the new concept of holiness, as God consecrated a day by declaring it holy (i.e., set apart)— because he rested on it. The sanctity of the day lies in God's declaration and opens up eschatological dimensions. The male and female were blessed but not consecrated. If human beings are to enter into the sanctity of the day, they too must be holy. To be holy requires divine approval, which individuals did not have merely because they were created in God's image. A probation was required in which the humans had to demonstrate their absolute loyalty to their Creator-King. Only then would they receive their consecration. The symbol of this probation, or test, is introduced in the second creation narrative, and the probation itself is told in chapter 3. The seventh day concludes God's creative activities and opens up the question regarding how individuals might enter into the rest from their activities (see Heb. 4:4–11).

GOD MAKES MAN AT HOME IN THE WORLD
(GEN. 2:4–25)

Whereas God stands apart from his creation by speeches and commands in the first chapter, he is involved with his creation through actions in the second chapter. This difference in theological focus should not obscure the fact that the second chapter, like the first, contains evidence of symmetry in its literary form. Chapter 2 may be divided into three narrative comments (vv. 4b–6, 10–14, 24–25), three narratives (vv. 7–9, 15, 19–22), and three dialogues (vv. 16–17, 18, 23). The symmetry in Genesis 2 brings the various elements together in a masterful development of the whole narrative.[8] Moreover, several motifs are distinct to this chapter and are not found in chapter 1. In introducing these different ideas, the author nevertheless demonstrates

48

the complementary relationship of the two creation accounts. (See figure 3.)

Genesis 1—God (Elohim) at work	Genesis 2—Yahweh God at work
Focus: orderliness; man is the acme of creation	Focus: God loves man, male and female
Creates heaven, firmament, sea and land, including vegetation, animal life, and man	Serves man by making him a home and by making the family structure; loves human beings and cultivates their loyalty

Figure 3. The Two Creation Accounts

First, the covenant name Yahweh (ten times in the narrative and once in 2:4, the superscription) takes precedence over the title Elohim ("God") in chapter 1. The former name reveals God's concern with establishing a world in which human beings experience God's presence in blessing (12:2–3) and holiness (Exod. 19:6). He is the God of promise, whom Israel knew by his mighty acts and revelation. He is Yahweh ("LORD" in English translations), the covenant Redeemer-God. Genesis 2 thus teaches an astounding fact: Yahweh, the Redeemer of Israel, is the Creator! Yahweh is Elohim! This exciting revelation is unfortunately obscured by the translation of *Yahweh Elohim* as "LORD God." If instead we translate the phrase as "Yahweh God," we can sense the excitement of this chapter. Yahweh, the Creator, formed a man from the dust, planted a garden, made the animals, fashioned a woman, and brought man and wife together. Yahweh did it all!

Second, the emphasis in chapter 2 is on the garden instead of the earth. The garden was a beatific place with vegetation and rivers, where God provided for the irrigation of the soil and for the first humans' food and work. It is the setting of Adam and Eve's temptation and expulsion (chap. 3). As such, the twofold repetition that God placed the man in the garden (2:8, 15) is symmetrical with the two verbs reporting the expulsion of the pair from the garden (3:23–24). But the hope in a return to that garden has been alive and is encouraged by the prophets, our Lord, and the apostles. Paradise regained will be infinitely more beautiful than Paradise lost (Rev. 22:1–5).

Third, through his Word God gives man permission to eat (2:16), a prohibition not to eat from the fruit of the tree of the knowledge of good and evil (v. 17), and a promise to make a suitable helper (v. 18).

Like the animals the man is permitted to eat of the vegetation (1:29–30; 2:16), but this very broad permission excludes two trees, namely, the tree of the knowledge of good and evil and the tree of life (2:17). The former tree is the focus of the testing. The tree of life becomes the main concern only toward the end of the narrative (3:22). The prohibition has thus introduced us to the tree of the knowledge of good and evil as the symbol of temptation, as well as to the tree of life, which is a symbol of human hope; namely, that people will later obtain life from the world of death, which is associated with God's judgment on nature since the Fall.

Fourth, the emphasis in Genesis 2 is on the family unit. The author has already introduced man and woman in the first chapter as the objects of God's blessing and as the ones who will fulfill the cultural mandate (1:26, 28).[9] The second chapter begins with the man and develops his relationship to the garden and to the animals. Only after the naming of the animals is the woman formed, in anticipation of the relationship of man and woman before and after the Fall. The purpose of the woman is to complement the man. The woman is to help the man in remaining faithful to God's commandments, which include the prohibition not to eat from the tree of the knowledge of good and evil. Man and woman together must be submissive to the Lord and be accountable to him. They are uniquely designed by God and are uniquely brought together and therefore must live in harmony with each other within the institution of marriage. The purpose of marriage, as such, is to develop their different gifts in such a way that they will be accountable to God and also to each other. From the beginning, the family unit was God's means of extending his blessed presence and fellowship to the ends of the earth. He dealt with husband and wife as a family. Creation was not complete until this unit had been established. The family is thus prominent throughout the Bible. The covenant with the patriarchs and Israel, including the blessings and the sign, was given within the family structure.

The central thrust of Genesis 2 is to show God's special interest in humankind by (1) the unique formation of the first man and God's breathing into the man's nostrils the breath of life (v. 7); (2) his placing the man in the garden that he formed for man's delight and cultivation (vv. 8–15); (3) the commandment to eat, the prohibition not to eat from the forbidden fruit, and the promise to make a helper for man (vv. 16–18); (4) the special act of forming the woman as a unique creature with a distinct, but complementary, nature to the man (vv. 20b–23); and (5) the repeated use of the covenant name Yahweh in the narrative.

CONCLUSION

The literary thrust of Genesis 1 and 2 has a theocentric, rather than a scientific, focus. God is the Creator, who is interested in humankind.

The theocentric interest correlates with the anthropocentric concern. The correlation of God and man is the very ground for the history of redemption. God does not need men and women, but in his purpose he created them, made a home for them in his world, and placed them in charge of his creation. Furthermore, he made the world an enjoyable place to live by creating a variety in his works, by providing for human needs, and by endowing humankind with his image, which male and female each reflect in a complementary manner.

The two versions of the creation account instill an overwhelming sense of the majesty of the Creator. He is a God of order and concern. All things exist by him and cohere in him. He established order in space, ordaining the solar system to regulate life on earth; he also established order on earth, ordaining humankind to interact culturally with his creation. The order of space and earth exists in microcosm in the human family, which the Lord ordained and blessed as part of his creation order.

The Creator found pleasure in his creation. He saw that it was good, even very good. The sign of his approval and of his love for creation is the Sabbath day. He is holy, he declared the Sabbath holy, and he purposed to share this special day with a holy people. He gave this day as a sign of his love as they await the glorious renewal of the creation.

CHAPTER 2

The Canonical Perspective—
God's Word to Israel

As we have seen, the function of the creation narrative is to show the Israelites that Yahweh is the Creator. The Israelites had been marvelously rescued out of Egypt by God's mighty hand and had received his revelation at Mount Sinai. He showed himself in the midst of smoke, fire, and earthquake with the words "I am the LORD [Yahweh] your God, who brought you out of Egypt, out of the land of slavery" (Exod. 20:2). Through the delivery out of Egypt, through the provisions of water, manna, and quails, and through the theophany at Mount Sinai, Yahweh had revealed himself as their Redeemer-King. He is the God who made a covenant with the patriarchs Abraham, Isaac, and Jacob; confirmed his covenant with Israel at Mount Sinai; and swore fidelity to his Word. In the context of Yahweh's revelation at Sinai he made known to Israel that he is the Creator. The creation narrative is a proclamation that Yahweh alone is God, that he alone created everything, and that he had granted men and women, whom he created in his image, a high position in his kingdom.

This story provided Israel with a credo, or statement of faith. As a credo Genesis 1 and 2 upholds Yahweh to Israel as the great King over all creation who has elected humankind to rule under him. To this purpose, he graciously endowed human beings with "the image of God." The creation narrative as a statement of faith is supported by the literary analysis of these chapters.

The biblical account of creation also has a polemical function, as it dismisses in a literary way the pagan accounts of the origin of the world. Among the nations of the ancient Near East, the Babylonians and the Egyptians also had creation accounts, or cosmogonies.[1] These stories reflect a belief in a pantheon of gods in which one of the gods rose to supremacy. These cosmogonies were, in fact, a validation of the leadership of one god over the other gods. The pagan accounts were in reality theogonies, explanations of how the *gods* came into being! Furthermore, these accounts of creation were independent from the history of these nations. As a literary contribution, however, the biblical account has a vastly different nature. It assumes the existence of God and relates creation to the history of Israel. It does not attempt to *demonstrate* that the Creator-God is Yahweh. Rather, it *presents* Yahweh as the Creator.

The creation narrative also forms a prologue to the history of redemption. This narrative was revealed to a people who had come to know Yahweh as the God of the mighty acts of redemption and of Mount Sinai. This God is the Creator and the Ruler over all the world. The emphasis of the two chapters can be best appreciated by gleaning from the Psalms and Prophets a sense of the faith of Israel in the Creator-God. Genesis 1 and 2 introduce us to the Ruler of the universe, whose kingdom encompasses all of his creation and whose attributes of glory, wisdom, and power are visible in his creation. His creative work comes about by his Word, by which also he sustains a covenantal relationship with his people. In order to understand better how ancient Israelites felt the impact of these themes in their reading of Genesis 1 and 2, we shall briefly consider the canonical significance of (1) God who creates, (2) God who speaks, and (3) God who rules.

GOD WHO CREATES

The opening words of the Apostles' Creed, "I believe in God the Father Almighty, maker of heaven and earth," seem to our secular contemporaries a relic from the distant past. People in this post-Christian age think that they know, understand, and make personal plans with little reference to God. For the Israelites, however, belief in God the Creator was the most significant difference between them and the pagan cultures around them. They believed that Yahweh is Elohim ("God"). To the Hebrew mind, the phrase "in the beginning God" had a confessional ring.

In using the phrase "in the beginning God," the Bible begins with a statement of God's supremacy over all pagan conceptions. When the people of Israel came out of Egypt, they were not ignorant of idolatry, pagan rites, magic, priestcraft, or myths explaining the origins of the universe and the hierarchy of the gods in the Egyptian pantheon. The names of the deities and the systems of beliefs differed from nation to nation, but in essence all the ancient peoples were pagans. Their gods had "job descriptions" associated with sun, moon, earth, sky, sea, vegetation, mountains, and other forces of nature. In Egypt, Horus/Re was the sun-god who ruled supreme; in Canaan, Shemesh was the sun-god, while El was the supreme deity; and in Babylon, Shamash was the sun-god, and Marduk the chief god. Because the ancients divided their world into areas ruled by different forces, the pagan religions could not explain how everything holds together.

Paganism in essence was a commitment to unpredictable forces that may cooperate with each other or that may work against each other with destructive results for life on earth. In the context of paganism Yahweh revealed himself as "Elohim." This plural form of *El* ("God"), or the name of the chief god of the Canaanites, sums up the revelation: the God of Israel is gods. As strange as it may sound, *the God of Israel is in himself everything the pagans allocated to their many gods.* The phrase "in the beginning Elohim" carries polemical force, as God's revelation counters the world of paganism. Yahweh, the God of Israel, alone holds all the forces of nature together: sun, moon, stars, sea, vegetation, fertility, life, and death. The confession of the Creator demands that every created thing be related to him. This same theme is carried through into the New Testament, where we are commanded to submit ourselves to Jesus, "the image of the invisible God, the firstborn over all creation," in whom "all things hold together" (Col. 1:15, 17). Submission to this God gives rise to worship and praise. To Israel coming out of Exodus the Lord says, "Why be afraid of cosmic forces or fate?" God is the Creator of heaven and earth! Psalm 148 expresses the excitement of God's people as they praise the Creator:

> Praise Yahweh.
> Praise Yahweh from the heavens,
> praise him in the heights above. . . .
> Praise Yahweh from the earth,
> you great sea creatures and all ocean depths, . . .
> Let them praise the name of Yahweh,
> for his name alone is exalted;
> his splendor is above the earth and the heavens.
>
> (vv. 1, 7, 13)

GOD WHO SPEAKS

Belief in the Creator requires attention to his Word. The Word of God is powerful and effective. Creation and revelation are two aspects of God's Word. Creation resulted from God's Word, and God's revelation to humankind is the Word by which individuals must be re-created, or formed, into the likeness of God.

At Mount Sinai Israel received the word of revelation. There Yahweh impressed upon Israel the importance of living in accordance with his Word, which consists of the commandments and statutes of the great King. His words were life-giving (Deut. 30:15–16; Ps. 119). He required of Israel faith, love, and obedience (Deut. 6:4–5; 30:20), even as he did of Adam and Eve in the garden. Israel as a nation faced the same life-or-death choice that Adam did; like Adam, Israel was challenged to hear and obey the Word of God. Against the background of this revelation, Israel learned about the creative Word of Yahweh.

At creation, the Word of God was effective; nothing frustrated it. Psalm 33 reflects this understanding of creation by the Word. Facing the strength of the enemies of God's people (vv. 10, 13–17), the psalmist encourages the godly to put their trust in the Lord (vv. 18–22). His plans and purposes will be fulfilled, regardless of the opposition. He had shown to Israel that his Word is faithful, and he promised to remain faithful (vv. 4, 22). The reason for the psalmist's confidence and even jubilance lies in his commitment to the Lord, by whose Word everything came into being, by whom everything is upheld, and who will fully execute his purposes.

> By the word of the LORD were the heavens made,
>   their starry host by the breath of his mouth.
> He gathers the waters of the sea into jars;
>   he puts the deep into storehouses.
> Let all the earth fear the LORD;
>   let all the people of the world revere him.
> For he spoke, and it came to be;
>   he commanded, and it stood firm.
> The LORD foils the plans of the nations;
>   he thwarts the purposes of the peoples.
> But the plans of the LORD stand firm forever,
>   the purposes of his heart through all generations.
>   (vv. 6–11)

In the myths of Israel's neighbors, fate was unavoidable. They posited many gods to explain the various forces, but they could not provide a coherent explanation for all the phenomena. The world of creation, however, is not controlled by fate or by random happenings. The God of creation gives coherence to everything. He plans, speaks, executes, gives his Word of promise, and completes his plans from beginning to end. "He engages in conscious volition (in contrast to the 'strivings' of the cosmogonic powers in the religions)." His words are not magical incantations common to the nations.[2]

The purpose of the revelatory Word of God is to prepare individuals to respond to that Word when it is addressed to them (Gen. 2:16–17). Throughout the Old Testament, God speaks to his people and creates his own people by his Word. The revelation to Abraham, Moses, and Israel was a Word revelation. The prophets spoke the Word of God. The Word became incarnate in Jesus Christ. He was full of grace and faithful love as he spoke and called on people to respond to the Father (John 1:1–14). The Bible witnesses that the God who spoke at creation continued to speak through Moses and the Prophets and, in a climactic way, through the Son (Heb. 1:1–4; 3:1–6).

GOD WHO RULES

Belief in the Creator presupposes the revelation that he alone is King. The designation of God as Elohim is not intended to obscure his kingship. Rather, it signifies that all the metaphors of kingship attributed to the gods of the nations (royal glory, power, and wisdom) have reality in the God of Israel, who alone is King. This revelation was made to Israel at the Exodus and, before that, to Abraham.

Abraham encountered Melchizedek, a priest-king of Salem (Jerusalem) who professed faith in the Creator-God, El-Elyon (".God Most High"). Melchizedek blessed Abraham in the name of the Creator-Ruler: "Blessed be Abram by God Most High, Creator of heaven and earth" (Gen. 14:19). Abraham, in turn, took an oath by the same Creator-Ruler (v. 22). The designation of God as El-Elyon signifies that he alone is supreme. He is King over all.

When the Israelites had crossed the Red Sea, Moses led them in a song that praised God for his rule over the gods and nations of this world:

> Who among the gods is like you, O LORD?
> Who is like you—
> majestic in holiness,
> awesome in glory,
> working wonders?
> You stretched out your right hand
> and the earth swallowed them. . . .
> The LORD will reign
> for ever and ever.
>
> (Exod. 15:11–12, 18)

Phenomena, powers, forces, and deities do not control. God rules!

The Glory of the Great King

The great King has shared his glory with his creation. There is visible beauty in the heavenly bodies and on the earth. A glorious beauty is in nature, derived from a glorious King. Nature, therefore, is not to be worshiped for its beauty; rather, we worship the God who has vested it with his own glory. The angels in heaven ascribe glory to him as the majestic ruler over all the earth (Ps. 29:1). The seraphim proclaim God's universal glory in the presence of Isaiah, "Holy, holy, holy is the LORD Almighty; the whole earth is full of his glory" (Isa. 6:3). Heaven and earth continuously show forth his glory as a witness to his kingship and sovereignty (cf. Rom. 1:20). Psalm 8 celebrates his glory as revealed in the heavens, on earth, and particularly in human beings ("What is man that you are mindful of him?" [v. 4]). Psalm 19 associates the revelation of his glory in the world of creation with the glory of his Word. The great King is exalted above his creation, and therefore all creatures must praise his name.

> Let the name of the LORD be praised,
>> both now and forevermore.
> From the rising of the sun to the place where it sets
>> the name of the LORD is to be praised.
> The LORD is exalted over all the nations,
>> his glory above the heavens.
> Who is like the LORD our God,
>> the One who sits enthroned on high,
> who stoops down to look
>> on the heavens and the earth?
>
> (Ps. 113:2–6)

The Power of the Great King

Creation is the result of God's power and is upheld by his power. He spoke, and it came to be. The awesome power to bring things into existence demonstrates his sovereign ability to rule effectively. The special abilities ascribed to the many gods by the pagans are united in Elohim, the one God of Israel. Psalm 29 encourages the godly with the portrayal of God's continuous power over nature: over water, thunder, lightning, earthquakes, and the entire earth. To this God belongs glory and strength:

> Ascribe to the LORD, O mighty ones,
>> ascribe to the LORD glory and strength. . . .
> The LORD sits enthroned over the flood,
>> the LORD is enthroned as King forever.
> The LORD gives strength to his people;
>> the LORD blesses his people with peace.
>
> (vv. 1, 10–11)

The Wisdom of the Great King

The scriptural witness to the wisdom of the King highlights the orderliness, coherence, and completion of his creative activities. The characteristic of wisdom in the Old Testament is to plan and execute one's plans successfully. It was usual for kings to meet with their counselors in a planning session (2 Sam. 16:20; 17:5; 1 Kings 22:6; Prov. 8:14–16), and the wise were characterized by their openness to counsel (Prov. 1:5; 9:9). Even the pagans portrayed their gods as meeting in joint council. But God did not need a council.[3] He planned, spoke, executed, and brought everything to a successful completion by the seventh day (Gen. 2:1). Proverbs 3:19 declares, "By wisdom the LORD laid the earth's foundations, by understanding he set the heavens in place." His wisdom receives particular emphasis in the Wisdom

Hymn (Prov. 8:22–31). There wisdom, personified as a lady, is exalted because she was with God in all his works: "The LORD possessed me at the beginning of his work, before his deeds of old" (cf. v. 22). When Genesis 1 and 2 are read from the perspective of Israel's poetry and wisdom literature, it becomes clear that the author intended to stress God's wisdom in creation. In both accounts the manifold wisdom of God is focused on the human beings he created (1:26–28; 2:22). Their creation marks the completion of God's designs.

Recognition of God's wisdom should lead to the humble recognition of our inability to comprehend God's creation. The finite cannot grasp the infinite. This view flies in the face of the assumption that people can and must come to the defense of God in debates between science and the Bible.[4] Rightly does Houston speak of the mystery of creation.

> No infinite amount of time—even the twenty billion years now being postulated for the "big bang hypothesis" for the origin of the universe,—nor any infinite amount of space, can help us to conceive the ineffable mystery of the creator and his eternity of being. When we talk of God as creator and of "knowing him," we are thus introducing a qualitative difference that no amount of scientific data can either prove or disprove. It is an altogether different way of knowing. Yet with simple majesty the writer of Genesis 1 outlines this mystery of creation.[5]

Genesis, with its magnificent opening, calls forth a sense of awe in the presence of the great King. Awe leads to humility, praise, and dependence on God.

CONCLUSION

The credo "I believe in the Creator" signified for Israel the confessional position that the whole world was the handiwork of the great King. By his Word the world of creation came into being. A belief in the Creator-God challenges any power attributed to gods or any mythological conception. Such a belief renounces absolute loyalty to any being or institution other than the great King and evokes a response of love, adoration, and worship. The great King endowed the world and especially humankind with his glory, power, wisdom, and love. This great King has made everything, but he has chosen men and women to respond to his love!

CHAPTER 3

Creation as a Preamble
to the History of Redemption

The literary forms unveil the richness of the creation story and help us to appreciate the story's canonical function in ancient Israel. On the one hand, the literary devices of symmetry and dissonance enhance the aesthetic sense of balance, order, and movement under the majestic administration of the great King. Readers look beyond themselves and their world to the Creator-God, who has made everything so magnificently. They ask the questions, Who is man that you have endowed him with your glory, wisdom, power, and love? and Who is man that you have made everything so enjoyable?

On the other hand, God's message to Israel in its canonical situation evokes a response from men and women. The sense of awe at the creation leads to worship of the Creator. The order inherent in creation is derived from God and is possible only because the Lord sustains everything by his orderly rule. This view of the world was radically opposed to the pagan and humanistic conception of the world as an uncertain place. Moreover, God loves this world. His concern with the world and especially with human beings calls forth devotion, gratitude, and loyalty to the one Creator of heaven and earth. To him be the glory! The redemptive-historical approach builds on canonical conclusions by emphasizing the rule of God on earth and the interrelation of man and his Creator.

THE RULE OF GOD ON EARTH

Although not explicitly taught in Genesis 1–2, the idea of the rule of God provides a conceptual approach to the story of creation. The essence of God's rule as it relates to his creation is poignantly displayed in his free and gracious involvement with the created universe. God is King over creation because, as the Genesis narratives show, the heavens and the earth depend on God for their existence, not vice versa. Creation does not exist out of necessity—rather, God creates freely and continues to be involved with his creation, ruling in faithfulness, orderliness, and wisdom.[1]

The Covenant of Rule

The continuous relationship between God and nature could be called a covenant of creation, although the word "covenant" is rarely used in Scripture with this meaning. When Jeremiah refers to God's "covenant with day and night and the fixed laws of heaven and earth" (Jer. 33:25), the term "covenant" *(berît)* is parallel to "fixed laws" *(huqqôt,* Job 38:33; Jer. 31:35; and *huqqîm,* Jer. 31:36). For Jeremiah, God's gracious and free relationship with heaven, earth, sun, moon, stars, and the sea is evident by the regularity of day and night, the seasons, and the ebb and flow of the sea. It is a picture of his special covenant relationship with his people. Jeremiah argues that, since God keeps covenant with creation, he will even more surely take care of his covenant children (vv. 35–36; 33:25–26) and the descendants of David, to whom he also covenanted his fidelity (v. 26; cf. 2 Sam. 7:15).

Instead of using "covenant" to designate God's relationship to creation, I choose the word "rule," one that has deep roots in Israel's theology. Psalm 148 employs diverse conceptual imagery as it reflects on God's kingly rule. It calls on all creation to praise him: the creation in heaven (angels, heavenly hosts, sun, moon, and stars), the living creation on earth and in the sea (sea creatures, fruit trees, cedars, wild animals, cattle, small creatures, flying birds, kings, nations, princes, rulers, young men, maidens, old men, and children), and the inanimate elements on earth (lightning, hail, snow, clouds, stormy winds, mountains, and hills). In this context, too, the psalmist speaks of "decree," or "fixed law" *(hōq;* v. 6), as an expression of his rule. The Ruler is cautiously and anthropomorphically portrayed as having an exalted name and as the one whose "splendor is above the earth and the heavens" (v. 13). Then the psalmist makes a quick transition to show God's concern for his people, similar to that of Jeremiah: "He has raised up for his people a horn, the praise of all his saints, of Israel, the people close to his heart" (v. 14). Both Jeremiah and the psalmist begin with the general and established concern of God for his creation and then extend it to the particular concern he has for his own people.

The Nature of the Rule

The rule of God is characterized by *order.* At creation he established the order and has maintained it even after the Fall (Gen. 8:22). The created world is not unpredictable or filled with brute facts that randomly interact with each other. Scientific inquiry is not only possible but expected by the Creator, who rules over his creation in an orderly manner.[2]

The rule of God demonstrates his absolute *power.* The prophet Isaiah shows us creation as an expression of God's continuous power over his realm. He introduces God, the Redeemer of his people, as the Creator of heaven and earth (44:24). God overthrows the magic incantations and spells and the mantic oracles of the nations (v. 25) but confirms his own Word as spoken by the prophets (v. 26). His purpose will be fulfilled, even if it requires the miraculous drying up of streams (v. 27) or the raising up of Cyrus the Persian (v. 28). Isaiah proclaimed Yahweh as the only God, who, by his fiat creation, has shown his absolute claim over everything (45:5–6) and who will demonstrate to every generation that he is "the LORD, and there is no other" (v. 6). Then he challenges the critics and cynics and compares the Creator to a potter who has full authority over his clay:

> Woe to him who quarrels with his Maker,
>   to him who is but a potsherd among the
>   potsherds on the ground.
> Does the clay say to the potter,
> "What are you making?"
>
> (v. 9)

The absolute power of the Creator is manifested in his continued working out in an orderly, contingent, and gracious way his plan for the world and particularly for his children (vv. 11–25).

The rule of God is characterized by *faithfulness*. It guarantees that God's absolute power is not that of a dictator but that of a good, beneficent ruler. Since the universe not only is created out of nothing but is maintained in its creaturely being through God's constant interaction with it, who will not let it slip away from him into nothing but grounds its existence on his eternal faithfulness, the universe is given a stability beyond anything of which it is capable in its own contingent state.

The Christological Focus of God's Rule on Earth

The rule of God over creation has a christological focus. The creation was not consecrated. In Hebrew categories things are either common or holy, clean or unclean. The repeated statement that creation was "good" or "very good" expresses God's pleasure with his universe. However, he consecrated only the Sabbath day! The created world was still to be consecrated. With the acts of individual rebellion (Gen. 3–11; see Part 2), consecration was no longer a possibility but a necessity. Israel, living in that world of evil, had been called out to be God's holy people and to live in a holy manner in his presence. For them the creation narrative had an eschatological significance. They had received a foretaste of the promises of God in their special status as a covenant people and were guaranteed a greater restoration in the Promised Land. To this end the prophets spoke under divine inspiration of the coming restoration of all things in the messianic age. Only Jesus, the Second Adam, can and will inaugurate that great era of redemption, for which all creation is still groaning (Rom. 8:19–21).

The plan of God the Father involves Jesus the Son as the cosmic Redeemer (Col. 1), by whom all things will be restored to himself. The christological focus provides a sharp contrast to concepts of order, power, faithfulness, and goodness because God did not spare his Son for the sake of the redemption of humanity and creation. Torrance writes, "It was from the great movement of God's love to the world in Jesus Christ that [the Gentiles] learned that the world is not only the creation of God but the object of his love and unceasing care." Though the world may be filled with revolutions and natural disasters and may show the evidence of fragility, belief in Christ undergirds one's faith in "the constancy of God's wisdom and love."[3]

The biblical teaching of God's rule established in creation correlates with God's involvement in redemption. Creation anticipates a *telos*, or end. The God who freely, graciously, and powerfully rules creation has a goal: the new creation in his Son Jesus Christ (Gal. 6:15). Even though we await the full revelation of the new creation, God assures us of his constant care for all creation in general and for his own children in particular. He is father of all his creation, but in a special way to his children. Our Lord Jesus expressed God's fatherly care when he taught that the Father causes the sun to rise and the rain to fall on the evil and good (Matt. 5:45) and that the one who cares for the birds of the air and the lilies of the field knows also the needs of his children (6:25–32).

THE CREATOR AND MAN

The Image of God

The focus on men and women as creatures is on their likeness to God, not on their physical existence. They are flesh and spirit (Gen. 2:7; Mal. 2:15). The image of God in humankind lies in the gifts endowed by the King to the creature, graciously chosen to rule over the earth and to enjoy his fellowship. The image involves accountability to the Creator (as implied by the commandments, as in Gen. 1:28; 2:16–17), personal dignity (derived from God's kingship and majesty), and the ability to rule under the watchful eye of the Creator. The dignity of men and women is expressed in their relationship to the Creator and to the created world. The royal dignity of man consists in his rule over creation and in his abilities to civilize the earth and is cause for marvel:

> You made him a little lower than the heavenly beings
>   and crowned him with glory and honor.
> You made him ruler over the works of your hands;

62

> you put everything under his feet:
> all flocks and herds,
>   and the beasts of the field,
> the birds of the air,
>   and the fish of the sea,
>   all that swim the paths of the seas.
> O LORD, our Lord,
>   how majestic is your name in all the earth!
>
>   (Ps. 8:5–9)

Men and women are also like God in their derived ability to communicate, to affect things, to show power, and to care—in this way they reflect the glory of the Creator. Human beings, in the totality of their body and spirit, reflect the image of God in their whole creative existence, including their body. Mankind, however, is two: male and female.[4] In this distinction lies the need for fellowship, companionship, and human relations. In the union of male and female, wholeness may be experienced:

> The man said,
> "This is now bone of my bones
>   and flesh of my flesh;
> she shall be called 'woman,'
>   for she was taken out of man."
>
>   (Gen. 2:23)

Man's likeness to God has far-reaching consequences for the history of redemption. Fellowship with God requires likeness to him and a living in harmony with the kingdom of God. An individual's life in the presence of God is an expression of covenant (the technical term defining the relationship between two or more parties).[5] Since God has defined the terms and the nature of that relationship, an individual's happiness and meaning are in the covenantal relationship. Isaiah's language of God's covenantal commitment is a most important commentary on Genesis 1 and 2. He uses words for creation ("form," "make," "create") not only to refer to God's creative activities in forming the world but also to signify God's election, grace, love, and loyalty to Israel.[6] The words for creation are, therefore, also covenantal terms.

The Hope of Humanity

The lack of perfection of the created world and particularly of man opens up the story of creation to the question, What now? The story of creation is not finished with the formation of the man and his wife, or even with God's Sabbath rest. Elements in Genesis 1 and 2 point to a future unfolding. In the dynamic tension between the event of creation and its purpose lies the human factor of possibility. Openness is marked by the remarkable absence of God's consecration of his creation. "The statement that the world was created good . . . even very good . . . was wrongly taken as evidence of perfection; [good] however is not 'perfect,' but 'suitable for its purpose,' namely communion between God and man."[7]

The Garden of Eden is a prototype of the world planned by God— the world of restoration. The history of redemption, therefore, does not begin with a high point only to end up with the new earth as an equally high point. The new creation is better than the first because it will be perfect, holy, and characterized by the presence of God the Father and the Lord Jesus Christ (Rev. 21:22). It is a world without pain, sin, or the possibility of sin, a world of the redeemed, whose bodies have been transformed gloriously. For that reason we must look upon Christ as the very purpose of God's creation. He is what Berkhof calls "the pattern of existence for which creation is intended."[8] His redemptive work from the Incarnation to the Resurrection was no accident, nor was it suddenly necessary in order to correct the course of an unforeseeably fallen creation, but it was fully in view when God created the world. Creation is, therefore, the beginning, or the preamble, of the history of redemption.

God required faith and obedience from Adam and Eve. Complacency with the status quo was wrong. He required that they be loyal to him and that they trust their Creator to endow them with life and knowledge *in his time*. The tree of the knowledge of good and evil and the tree of life were eschatological symbols of hope. Hope is an expression of faith that says, "As a promise, the creation is intended to be elevated and to become a world that is centered upon and that serves a radically new form of humanity, in conformity to the image of the glorified Christ."[9]

The history of redemption is a process in which God purifies the world and prepares it through his Son to share in his glory, wisdom, and rule:

And they sang a new song:
You are worthy to take the scroll
   and to open its seals,
because you were slain,
   and with your blood you purchased men for God
   from every tribe and language and people and nation.
You have made them to be a kingdom and priests to serve our God
   and they will reign on the earth.

(Rev. 5:9–10)

The created world is therefore not a hostile environment, and man is not a cosmic orphan. The perfection of men and women is achieved not by self-fulfillment or denial of the world but by living in harmony with the Creator *and* the creation. Meaning for an individual is found, therefore, in living before God in harmony with his revelation.[10]

The creation story is thus incomplete. It is characterized by openness to the future (i.e., it implies an eschatology) and by hope in the perfection and consecration of the creation, including human beings. Will they be declared holy? Will they enter God's rest? How will they respond to the prohibition? Will they taste of the fruit of the tree of life? Truly, "The message of the beginning anticipates a message about the end."[11]

Conclusion to Part 1

God's interest extends to all of his creation by virtue of his involvement with his work. The great King is not an absentee landlord. His rule distinguishes itself by his generosity, wisdom, love, and fidelity. He has created and prepared the world for his people. From a redemptive-historical perspective, God has made creation for his people who will enjoy the benefits of his presence on the new earth. The creation chapters thus shed light on the glorious hope in the restoration, in the Messiah, and in the fidelity of God. He will continue until everything is holy and perfect. Between the act of creation and the glorious conclusion of God's work of redemption, the children of God have enjoyed the benefits of his continual love, of being endowed with his image, and of receiving the promises—life is not in vain—God is the Creator and the Redeemer. The flow of redemptive history rushes on till the full revelation of God's presence and the perfection of creation.

This first period, "Creation in Harmony," thus witnesses to:

1. the glory, wisdom, power, and fidelity of the Creator;
2. the magnificence and variety of God's creation, as it reflects the divine perfections;
3. the splendor of man (male and female), being in the image of God in glory, wisdom, power, and fidelity;
4. the orderliness and harmony of creation in heaven under the rule of the solar system and in earth under the rule of men and women, God's appointed vice-regents;
5. the goodness and the enjoyment of God's creation, which exists for God's purpose and for the sake of human beings;
6. the place of the Word of God in ordering the world and the expectation that human beings too will live orderly in obedience to God's Word; and
7. the hope that individuals will enjoy the consecration of creation, for the Lord who consecrated the Sabbath has planned to consecrate men and women and to share his rest with a renewed and holy mankind. This hope is rooted in God's plan of redemption in Jesus Christ.

Part 2

Creation in Alienation

Introduction to Part 2

The revelation of creation was a watershed in the development of Israel's faith. It provided a radical new way of looking at the world, and as such was revolutionary in a pagan world. It also provided Israel with a defense of the faith that ultimately transformed Western culture. The Redeemer-God is the Creator-God! Of what value is redemption, if the world is separated from a beneficent creator who upholds all things?

The credo "I believe in God the Father Almighty, Maker of heaven and earth" forms one connection between the Old and New Testaments. Faith in the Creator opens up a wholly new way of looking at God, the created world, man, history, the Word of God, and the death of our Lord Jesus on the cross. Thus far we have seen that faith in the Creator-God requires (1) a complete submission to God the Father, the Son, and the Holy Spirit; (2) a commitment to the sovereignty (or rule) of God; (3) a transformation of one's life by the sanctifying power of the Word of God; (4) praise of the great King and a joyful living in the presence of God; (5) a working out of one's God-given potential in accordance with the cultural mandate; (6) a regard for the family unit as a creation ordinance; and (7) a growing anticipation of the glorification and consecration of the whole world of creation.

Faith in the Creator-Redeemer also confesses that the world of our experience is continuous with the world of creation, and yet radically different. The world of our experience is filled with alienation, sickness, death, meaninglessness, oppression, chaos, and destructive forces. The creation story raises these questions: What has happened to the goodness and order of creation? Why do men and women suffer from guilt? Why do we experience broken relations, sickness, and death? How did sin enter the world? What is the source of evil? Why did God permit the entrance of Satan and of sin? The Bible does not attempt to answer these pressing questions individually. It affirms, instead, the folly of man's revolution against the Creator, which is the essence of sin. The world we know is the "shadow" side of creation. "It is incomplete, unfinished, defective."[1] This world was "subjected to frustration . . . by the will of the one who subjected it," that is, God himself (Rom. 8:20). Here we stand before a mystery: God in some sense willed the present.

The movement backward from redemption to creation, from the Redeemer to the Creator, from Yahweh to Elohim, brings us to the inevitable fact of human rebellion. Between the creation and the international situation known to ancient Israel, a tragic moment in human history occurred. Human beings were deceived. They rebelled willingly against the Creator and continued in their state of rebellion. This rebellion took on an increasingly hostile attitude, culminating in the great revolution at Babel. The accounts of Genesis 2:4–11:26 vividly portray the rebellious human nature at all levels: individual, familial, societal, and national.

Genesis 2:4–11:26 perpetually witnesses to human hostility against the Creator and to God's response in judgment and in grace. This period highlights the progression of man's alienation from God and the continuity of God's rule in grace, forbearance, and resolve. In our approach to this passage we shall bring together the literary, canonical, and redemptive-historical dimensions of the text. The trifocal approach allows us to explain (1) the change in the creation order from harmony to alienation; (2) the reality of evil, anguish, and alienation; and (3) the actuality of God's gracious rule. The fidelity of God in the face of the reality of evil is the ground for hope that this world will be changed into a more glorious world.

CHAPTER 4

The Generations From Adam to Terah

In this chapter we will look at the literary structure of Genesis 2:4–11:26, the literary variations of narrative and genealogy bridging the span of time between creation and Abraham, and the relation of this passage to the epics of Israel's neighbors.

THE *TOLEDOT* FORMULA

The Book of Genesis is structurally held together by ten occurrences of the phrase "this is the account of" (*'ēlleh tôl∙dôt*, lit., "these are the generations of").[1] The tenfold use of the formula is not incidental, as Genesis reveals structured repetition. This formula bridges the story of creation (1:1–2:3) with that of Israel in Egypt (Exod. 1). Each occurrence of the phrase forms a link in the history of redemption up to God's revelation to Israel in Egypt. The linkages indicate that Genesis is more than simply a collection of ancient traditions that were copied down without any editorial reworking.[2] The *toledot* formula provides a redemptive-historical way of looking at the past as a series of interrelated events. (See table 4.)

The phrase "this is the account of" occurs symmetrically five times in the development from Adam to Abraham and five times in the development from Abraham to Israel in Egypt. The bridge from Adam to Israel thus consists of two spans, each consisting of five links. (See figure 4.) The literary linkage device connects the narratives and genealogies of Genesis 11:27–50:26 with the narratives and genealogies of the primeval history (2:4–11:26). Through the revelation in these chapters Israel could trace its origins back to Abraham, Terah, Shem, Noah, Seth, and finally to Adam. It demonstrates that in Adam, Israel has a common ancestry with the nations. Israel, too, shares with the nations in the history of grace, rebellion, and revolution, long before God's election of Abraham.

A closer examination of the structure of Genesis 2:4–11:26 shows an interesting alternation of narratives and genealogies. The narrative of the formation of Adam and Eve, the Garden of Eden, the expulsion from the garden, Cain's sin, and the building of the city (2:4–4:26) concludes with Cain's genealogy (4:17–24). The genealogy of Adam in chapter 5 reveals a symmetry with the genealogy of Shem in 11:10–26. Both contain ten generations, and both end on three sons, one of whom is chosen to be the link. (See table 5.)

TABLE 4. TOLEDOT STRUCTURE OF GENESIS

Toledot Phrase	Passage	Contents
(In the beginning God)	(1:1–2:3)	(Creation)
1. This is the account of the heavens and the earth	2:4–4:26	Creation and man's disobedience
2. This is the written account of Adam's line	5:1–6:8	Genealogy, Seth–Noah
3. This is the account of Noah	6:9–9:29	Man's corruption; Flood; covenant
4. This is the account of Shem, Ham, and Japheth	10:1–11:9	Table of Nations; man's rebellion at Babel
5. This is the account of Shem	11:10–26	Genealogy, Shem–Abraham
6. This is the account of Terah	11:27–25:11	Story of Abraham
7. This is the account of Abraham's son Ishmael	25:12–18	Genealogy of Ishmael
8. This is the account of Abraham's son Isaac	25:19–35:29	Transition of blessing from Isaac to Jacob
9. This is the account of Esau	36:1–37:1	Genealogy of Esau
10. This is the account of Jacob	37:2–50:26	Joseph; Israel in Egypt

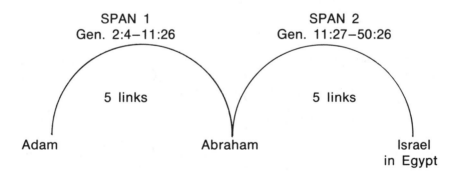

Figure 4. Literary Bridge From Adam to Israel in Egypt

The center of Genesis 2:4–11:26 is the lengthy narrative of the

Flood and the covenant with creation, which contains God's affirmation that, regardless of humankind's wickedness before and after the Flood, the Creator remains faithful to his creation. The five sections fit together in a schematic way.[3] The narratives give a select and symmetrical presentation of (1) *human sinfulness* before the Flood (Cain and mankind) and after the Flood (Canaan and mankind); (2) the continuity of God's *rule in judgment* before the Flood (curse of Cain and the destruction of human beings) and after the Flood (curse of Canaan and the scattering of people at Babel) and his *rule in grace* before the Flood (for Adam and Eve [3:21]) and after the Flood (Noahic covenant and existence of the nations, languages, and territories in accordance with his will), and of (3) *God's purpose* in establishing relations with individuals and their families before the Flood (Enoch and Noah) and after the Flood (Noah, Shem, and Abraham).

TABLE 5. THE TEN-GENERATION GENEALOGIES IN GENESIS

No.	From Adam	From Shem
1.	Seth	Arpachshad
2.	Enosh	Cainan*
3.	Kenan	Shelah
4.	Mahalel	Eber
5.	Jared	Peleg
6.	Enoch	Reu
7.	Methuselah	Serug
8.	Lamech	Nahor
9.	Noah	Terah
10.	*Shem*	*Abraham*
	Ham	Nahor
	Japheth	Haran

*See LXX and Luke 3:36; this name is missing in the MT.

The reader gains an insight into redemptive history by understanding why the author emphasized the two genealogies (Gen. 5; 11), each containing ten generations and each ending with three sons. First, the genealogies form a link between (1) Adam and Abraham, (2) the Garden of Eden and Canaan, and (3) the old humanity and the new humanity (Israel). Second, the genealogies demonstrate godliness at an individual level: Enoch and Noah walked with God (5:22, 24; 6:9) and Lamech expressed his hope in the grace of God's comfort in a world affected by judgment (5:29). Third, the genealogies develop the renewal of blessing: Adam received the original blessing (1:28); Noah was chosen to be the new father of mankind after the corruption of God's creation by the descendants of Adam; and Shem was the recipient of a special blessing (9:26–27) which the Lord confirmed to Abraham, son of Terah (12:2). The Lord thus sustains mankind graciously and renews with Abraham the promises given to Adam and Noah. By combining narratives and genealogies in Genesis 2:4–11:26, the *toledot* sections lay a foundation for God's promises to Abraham. God's saving grace is all the more necessary because of the sinful and rebellious nature of human beings.

The central section (6:9–9:29) bears out these concerns. The author there describes the sinfulness of mankind (6:11–12; 8:21), the grace of God (in preserving Noah and his family), the patience of God with human beings (9:8–17, the Noahic covenant, or covenant of forbearance), God's grace to humankind (vv. 1–3, 7–17), and a promise that God's blessed presence will return through Shem (v. 27).[4]

A BRIDGE BETWEEN CREATION AND ABRAHAM

As we have seen, the *toledot* formulas form a bridge between creation and the story of Israel in Egypt, using ten separate structural components. The first five components span the primeval history (2:4–11:26), whereas the last five components span the story of Abraham till Israel arrives in Egypt (11:27–50:26).

A comparison of Genesis 1:1–2:3, which presents an ordered world in which God attests to the goodness of his creation and implies how he expects men and women to respond positively to its beneficial Creator, with Genesis 11:1–9, a world of chaos and rebellion, brings out how the world has undergone radical change prior to the world of Abraham. Genesis 1–11 forms a unit, and as a unit it sets the stage for Abraham's appearance as the agent of God's special grace. The story of Adam and Eve's fall (chap. 3) begins the movement leading to the dispersion of the nations (11:1–9). Genesis 3 is set within the literary unity of Genesis 2:4–4:26 (the first *toledot* section), and as such it is best read in the context of the literary unit as a whole. The narratives and genealogies of Genesis 2:4–11:26 move climactically from the story of God's involvement with man at creation (2:4–25) to the narrative of man's revolution at Babel (11:1–9) and the genealogy of Shem, by whom the potential of blessing is transferred to Abraham (vv. 10–26). The world of human beings (11:1–26) is set in contrast to the world of creation (1:1–26) as a world of revolution, but it is still a world in God's control.

A World of Revolution

The contrast of the beginning (creation) and the end (the Tower of Babel) indicates that something radically wrong has happened to creation. The words of God, "Let us make man" (Gen. 1:26), are in sharp contrast to the words of man, "Let us make . . . bake . . . build . . .

make a name for ourselves" (11:3–4). The unity and consolidation of the people at Babel (11:1, 4) are contrary to God's command to fill the earth (1:28; 9:1, 7). The human city with its "tower that reaches to the heavens" (11:4) in the valley of Shinar forms a stark contrast to the kingdom of God that was lowered to this earth in the Garden of Eden. The city and tower symbolize the human desire for virility and perpetuity, which cannot be compared with the harmony of the garden, in whose center stood the tree of life, symbolic of eternal blessedness and life (2:9; 3:22). Moreover, the portrayal of a human community—a family unit—in fellowship with God (2:20b–23) has become a community characterized by rebellion against the Creator. The creative, sustaining, and complementary union between husband and wife (the "one flesh") has turned into the external solidarity of mankind, as symbolized by the repetition of the word "one" in 11:1 (translated "one language" and "common speech"). The world of order and harmony has become a world of confusion (v. 9). The story of Babel dramatizes climactically humankind's revolution against the rule of God. Although God came to establish his rule on earth and to crown it with his presence, he is practically cast out by those he created.

The contrast between the beginning (Gen. 1–2) and end (11:1–9) underscores the contrast between the rule of God and the rule of man, unity and diversity, order and confusion, blessing and judgment![5] Instead of enjoying freedom, royal power, and glory, men and women are filled with tension, anxiety, and alienation. Instead of experiencing communion with God, they run from God and seek an autonomous establishment of their own kingdom on earth. Genesis 1–11 is a sober reminder that sin has come into the world and that the pervasiveness of sin cannot be rationalized; its effects on individuals cannot be explained away. The originally good creation has not become perfect. Human beings are not consecrated to God but have been alienated from him. The theme of Genesis 1–11 is "the radical seriousness of the sin that, from the beginning of the rebellion of mankind, has marred and stained God's good work."[6]

A World in God's Control

The control, or rule, of God comes to clearest expression in the development of the blessing from Adam to Abraham. This blessing is gradually particularized in Genesis 2:4–11:26. First, God blessed Adam and Eve and, in them, all humankind (1:28; cf. 9:1, 7). This blessing pertains to the orderly process of propagation and is not essentially different from the blessing of other creatures (1:22). Man's blessing is greater than that of the animals because he is endowed with the image of God and rules over the animals. Human beings, though, share in created existence; after the introduction of sin in the world, God's blessing still rests on his creation.

> The blessing as a power of fertility belongs to all organic life; these they have in common, however differently man and beast may develop. The power of the blessing as the power of fertility means not only the capacity to beget, conceive, and bear, but the whole process of propagation through conception and birth, from the choice of partner right up to the care and education of the child. It is this that binds man and beast together; as long as man exists, and just because this shared possession is included in the very act of man's creation, it is considered as something thoroughly positive . . . something promoting man's progress as man. This is what blessing means.[7]

The development of Genesis 2:4–11:26 traces the continuity of God's blessing on human beings (even in their rebellion!) and the particularization of God's blessing on individuals and their families. The Fall introduced judgment and curse, but still man was not abandoned by his heavenly Father. Through the narratives and genealogies a line of promise connects God's special blessing of Adam to Abraham (12:3). (See figure 5.)

CREATION

Blessing—on the elect	*Judgment*—on humankind generally
Adam and Eve	Adam and Eve
Seth	Cain
Noah	Flood
Shem	Canaan
Terah	Babel and the nations
Abraham	

Figure 5. Blessing and Judgment in Genesis

The renewal of the blessing of God is important because it marks the continuity of his working in the history of redemption. The drama of Eden intensifies outside of the garden from the story of Cain and Abel to the corruption of mankind, leading into the Flood narrative. After the Flood, the drama builds up to a climax in the Babel narrative. In each case, God renews his blessing and focuses it more particularly on one of the descendants of Adam. First, he renews his blessing with Seth, then with Noah and Shem, and finally with Terah and Abraham.

In conclusion, the five *toledot* units of Genesis 2:4–11:26 link creation with the story of Abraham's election. As a linking formula, their significance is:

1. to trace the development of humankind from Adam to Abraham;

2. to present the degeneracy and rebellion of the human race;

3. to reveal God's concern with mankind, as his grace extends to all creation (chap. 9);

4. to demonstrate that God's special blessing is renewed and given sharper focus in the development of God's dealings with men and women; but

5. not to give a complete history or sufficient data for reconstructing the antiquity of mankind or for getting lost in the names and numbers of the genealogies.[8]

PARALLELS WITH MESOPOTAMIAN MYTHS

For Israel the *toledot* sections transform historical data, names, narratives, genealogies, and human developments into a coherent framework for understanding the world. The Sumerians and Babylonians had explained their world in a mythological fashion in literary material that has many parallels in the ancient Near East. As we have already observed, the biblical creation account had a polemical purpose to counter common notions about the gods, nature, and the formation and purpose of human beings. The ancient peoples had transmitted stories about a paradise, heroes, and the Flood. The contribution of Genesis 2:4–11:26 lies both in its polemic against paganism and in giving a coherent account of events from creation to the call of Abraham.

The Biblical narrative of the garden, the tree of life, the tree of knowledge, and the serpent stands apart from pagan magic and symbolism. The Genesis account uses symbols (the two named trees and the serpent), but it naturalizes them so as to shift the focus from magic and unpredictable forces to the humans' responsibility and their response to God.[9]

The most familiar ancient Near Eastern myth is the Babylonian flood story. There are many parallels between the biblical and Babylonian narratives: the divine decree, a heroic character, details on building, a boat, animals, the sending out of birds, the boat's resting on a mountain, and the sacrifice.[10] Again the biblical account is a polemic against the mythological elements. Instead of many gods, there is one God who decrees the Flood. He does not need food, unlike the Babylonian gods, who "crowded like flies" when Gilgamesh offered a sacrifice.[11] More important, God's decree to flood the earth with water and to destroy all living creatures is related to the creation story. It is in a sense a return to the creative beginnings, as if man and animals do not exist: originally "darkness was over the surface of the deep, and the Spirit of God was hovering over the waters" (Gen. 1:2). After the Flood, God graciously renews his blessing (9:1, 7) and covenants to sustain creation by nourishment (8:22) and promises not to destroy all life in the waters of another flood (8:21; 9:8–17). The biblical flood story is set against the background of human corruption and brings out vividly God's royal nature, justice, and grace. Men and women are left without excuse because they are sustained every day by the grace of their Creator-King.

CONCLUSION

Through the *toledot* structure, the Lord revealed to Israel the unity of the human race, the rebellious nature of humankind, and the existence of nations and languages. He also revealed how he had selected Noah and Abraham as instruments of his faithfulness to mankind. The literary materials (genealogies and narratives) thus connect Israel with human prehistory. The genealogies link Israel with Adam. The narratives collectively portray human beings in rebellion against God as well as his sovereign control over mankind, revealing a linkage between Israel's prehistory and the canonical concerns of Israel as one nation among the nations. To this latter concern we now turn our attention.

CHAPTER 5

Israel and the Nations

From Genesis 2:4–11:26, Israel learned that the world as they knew it did not result from Yahweh's inability to rule or lack of wisdom. He is not like the gods of the nations, who, according to mythological accounts, sin and become angry so that the earth languishes because of their infighting, magical incantations, and sicknesses. Yahweh did not fail man; man failed Yahweh. The effects of human failure explain the present condition of the world.

To Israel also belonged the revelation that Yahweh is sovereign over the nations (Exod. 15:13–18). The Israelites had witnessed his sovereign rule over the Egyptian Pharaoh in the ten plagues and particularly in the passage through the Red Sea (7:14–14:31). They wondered how these great nations, such as Egypt, came into being; why the nations opposed the will of Yahweh; why the Ruler-God did not destroy the nations that revolted against his will; why Canaan had been chosen as their patrimony; what Israel's relation to the nations was; and how nationalism, with its political, geographical, and linguistic overtones, had arisen. Genesis 2:4–11:26 answers these questions.

At no point did Yahweh abandon his creation. His judgments are not expressions of abandonment but forms of discipline. Moreover, the discipline of God has a purpose for the world and for mankind as a whole. A canonical reading of Genesis 2:4–11:26 therefore teaches us concerning (1) Israel's election out of the nations, (2) the beginning of restoration, (3) the place of revelation over against religion, and (4) the contrast between earthly and heavenly wisdom.

THE ELECTION OF ISRAEL

The Word of God came to Israel in the wilderness. The Israelites first received the revelation of Yahweh's name and of his promises to the patriarchs in the context of their redemption from Egypt. In the wilderness God revealed to them that he is the Creator and that his kingship is universal. He rules over all nations, but the Lord graciously and freely elected Israel out of all the nations of the world to be his people.

> You yourselves have seen what I did to Egypt, and how I carried you on eagles' wings and brought you to myself. Now if you obey me fully and keep my covenant, then out of all nations you will be my treasured possession. Although the whole earth is mine, you will be for me a kingdom of priests and a holy nation. (Exod. 19:4–6)

God had not rejected the other nations, but he planned to do his work of redemption through the nation of Israel. A new beginning had become necessary because of the rebellious nature of humankind so evident in Genesis 2:4–11:26. The election of Israel as "the people of God" was not based on any vast population or any righteousness but was an expression of the grace, love, and fidelity of God.

> The LORD did not set his affection on you and choose you because you were more numerous than other peoples, for you were the fewest of all peoples. But it was because the LORD loved you and kept the oath he swore to your forefathers that he brought you out with a mighty hand and redeemed you from the land of slavery, from the power of Pharaoh king of Egypt. (Deut. 7:7–8; see also 9:5–6)

The promises, covenants, blessings, the Exodus, the giving of his Word, and the conquest of Canaan are acts of God foreshadowing the restoration of heaven and earth. What God does in Israel is, on a small scale, what he plans for all the nations. The land of Canaan is a microcosm of the earth. Israel and Canaan form the bridge between God's concern for the nations before Abraham and God's love demonstrated through Jesus the Messiah in the redemption of the elect from all the nations after Pentecost.

It is apparent that God's blessing rests on the nations. God graciously preserved Noah and his sons from the destructive waters of judgment. The account of the Flood includes six separate indications of God's preservation of Noah's family in anticipation of the genealogy of the nations.[1] The nations, too, could trace their genealogy back to Noah and to God's grace and blessing extended to Noah's sons. Moreover, God pronounced his blessing on Noah and his sons. The process of procreation and genealogical development, as well as the population of the earth, was within God's will and received his blessing (Gen. 9:1, 18–19).

The purpose of the Table of the Nations (Gen. 10) is not to give a complete listing of all the nations or to give historical information pertaining to the period in which a nation arose or even to set certain nations off as more prominent. Rather, it presents a brief picture of the unity and diversity of the nations. The rapid increase of mankind came as an expression of God's blessing in accordance with his will. God willed the nations! The relevant passages (vv. 5, 20, 31) lead to only one conclusion: geographical, political, and linguistic diversity is not sinful. God willed it from the beginning (1:28). Multiplication, migration, population of the earth, and the rise of civilizations are natural expressions of the blessing of God. The Table of the Nations contains no comment or allusion to the natural superiority of any region, race, or political entity. The more extensive attention given to the genealogy of Shem is for the canonical purpose of showing in greater detail the relationship of Israel to Shem. For this reason his genealogy is covered last (vv. 21–31) and repeated in a different form in 11:10–26.

A comparison of Genesis 10 with 1 Chronicles 1:1–27 supports the contention that the Table of the Nations has a canonical significance for Israel. Only Israel has been chosen out of all the nations. Israel's election and blessing, however, is not to be misunderstood as God's complete disregard of the other nations. Cassuto, a Jewish exegete, argues that the table contains seventy nations. The number 70 (7 x 10) is not accidental, because the author shows a fondness for numbers and significant repetitions. From this fact Cassuto concludes that the seventy nations evidence the abundance of children as a result of God's blessing of the nations.[2] This number matches the seventy persons of Jacob's family that entered Egypt (Exod. 1:5). The blessing on the nations finds its parallel in God's special blessing on Israel. Deuteronomy confirms this perspective and further brings out the truth that the election of Israel is a status of privilege.

> Remember the days of old;
>> consider the generations long past.
> Ask your father and he will tell you,
>> your elders, and they will explain to you.
> When the Most High gave the nations their inheritance,
>> when he divided all mankind,
> he set up boundaries for the peoples
>> according to the number of the sons of Israel.
> For the LORD's portion is his people,
>> Jacob his allotted inheritance.
>
> (Deut. 32:7–9)

The election and privilege of Israel also have a positive significance for the nations. God willed to increase his blessing to the nations through Israel (Gen. 12:3). God's involvement in Israel is thus for the purpose of redeeming mankind to himself. The Table of Nations teaches that (1) God has created and blessed the nations; (2) Israel's election is by grace; (3) Israel's mission is not apart from, but in relation to, the nations; and (4) God rules over the nations as well as over Israel.

THE BEGINNING OF RESTORATION

Israel's expulsion from Egypt is a return to God's favor, presence, and blessings! The Exodus event forms a contrast to Adam's expulsion from the Garden of Eden, which signified removal from God's presence and hence from the immediacy and abundance of God's favor and blessings. Adam and Eve were condemned to live in a state of alienation. The Exodus is God's concrete act of reconciliation.

The early chapters of Genesis contain the good news to Israel that, in spite of Adam and Eve's rebellion in the garden and their subsequent expulsion from Eden, God has renewed a people to himself and has prepared Canaan, a new "garden," for them. Genesis 1–11 provides the background for redemption. Israel could not appreciate what God was doing in and through them unless they understood their roots.

Israel shared a common heritage with the nations as descendants of Adam and Noah. In Adam they shared created existence and God's special endowment of his image to man. In Noah they shared in God's common grace toward all life. In Shem they had participated in humankind's rebellion at Babel. In spite of Israel's identity with the nations and participation in a world under God's judgment, they were heirs of the promises in Abraham. The Lord had reconciled them graciously to himself. He freely loved them and promised to restore to them his blessings in the Land of Promise, Canaan! God had placed Adam in the garden (2:8) and expelled him (3:24). But he was free in placing Israel in the land of Canaan, whose fertility, productiveness, and richness in natural resources was a reminder of the Garden of Eden.

> For the LORD your God is bringing you into a good land—a land with streams and pools of water, with springs flowing in the valleys and hills; a land with wheat and barley, vines and fig trees, pomegranates, olive oil and honey; a land where bread will not be scarce and you will lack nothing; a land where the rocks are iron and you can dig copper out of the hills. When you have eaten and are satisfied, praise the LORD your God for the good land he has given you. (Deut. 8:7–10)

The Israelites were also heirs of Noah's blessing of Shem. Noah had predicted that Yahweh would dwell in the tents of Shem.

> Blessed be the LORD, the God of Shem!
> May Canaan be the slave of Shem.
> May God extend the territory of Japheth;
> may he [MT] live in the tents of Shem,
> and may Canaan be his slave.
> (Gen. 9:26–27)[3]

To Israel God revealed his glorious presence. He had kept people away from his presence after Adam's expulsion from Eden and dramatically symbolized the impossibility of reentrance by stationing the cherubim at the entrance of Eden (Gen. 3:24). When Yahweh came to dwell in Israel, however, he had Israel make gold cherubim and place them over the ark of the covenant in order to symbolize his presence "in the tents of Shem" and the possibility of access to his glory through the ministry of the high priest.

The presence of God was more fully manifest in the incarnate Christ, who now dwells in each believer with his Spirit of glory. The Holy Spirit witnesses in our hearts to the great glory awaiting all the children of God in the new heaven and earth; the New Jerusalem. Then the triune God will dwell among the renewed humanity (Rev. 21:3).

THE REVELATION OF GOD

Yahweh had given his Word to Israel, by which he might rule Israel and the world. The creative word brought the world into existence, endowed with his glory and design. By the redemptive word, the Lord chose Israel from the scattered peoples of the earth. His Word is not the word of judgment or curse (Gen. 3–11) but of warning, encouragement, and promise. His Word is clearly a renewal of the commandment first given to Adam: "You are free . . . but . . ." (2:16–17). The freedom to enjoy life, family, food, drink, and all good expressions of creaturely existence is inseparable from the exceptions ("but"), that is, his commandments and prohibitions.

Because of disobedience to God's commandment, Adam lost the full enjoyment of freedom and life. He and his descendants were bound to a course of rebellion against the Creator because they had become slaves to autonomy and self-gratification. God's Word to the serpent, Adam, Eve, Cain, and mankind generally therefore pertained to judgment and curse. The change in language was from "do this and live" to "because you have done this, I will bring judgment (curse) on you."

In the context of the judgment, however, God gave a word of grace to all life, set forth in the covenant of forbearance, traditionally called the Noahic covenant. Israel thus is taught that, though God's Word has come to Israel as a word of redemptive grace, the whole world is sustained by his word of forbearing grace and is not consumed by his wrath.

Israel believed that they had received the Word of God that gives regularity and order to creation and that is destined to give order and renewal to God's people:

> Your word, O Lord, is eternal;
> it stands firm in the heavens.
> Your faithfulness continues through all generations;

you established the earth, and it endures.
Your laws endure to this day,
    for all things serve you.
If your law had not been my delight,
    I would have perished in my affliction.
I will never forget your precepts,
    for by them you have preserved my life.
                                        (Ps. 119:89–93)

EARTHLY AND HEAVENLY WISDOM

The wisdom of God was not a theoretical concept for Israel. They knew that Adam and Eve disobeyed God by eating from the tree of the knowledge of good and evil. They knew that human beings had a moral consciousness and an accountability to the great King. They also knew by revelation that God's wisdom is different from the wisdom of the Egyptians. They were familiar with nontheistic ways of finding meaning in life. The Lord revealed to them how to order their activities to achieve balance, harmony, and success in life. Biblical wisdom, unlike Egyptian wisdom, is related to godliness. It is a way of life, involving an individual's relations with God, other people, and the world of creation, giving personal guidelines for religious, cultural, and social behavior.

From Genesis 1–11, Israel learns that God's wisdom is different from that of the nations, who seek comprehensive knowledge so as to obtain a sense of their own divinity. The nations also seek life apart from God in their mythological conceptions that the divine and human come together in the world and experience of human beings. The allusion to the tragic encounter between the sons of God and the daughters of men (6:1–4; see chapter 6) is a perennial reminder that God has set boundaries between his heavenly image-bearers and his earthly image-bearers. Man is not divine. Kings are not divine. There are no supermen, and there will never be a super race! Moreover, human wisdom reflects the spirit of secularism and humanism. The story of the Tower of Babel with its repetitive "let us," with its creative expressions, and with its intended goal ("a name for ourselves") reminds Israel that the nations live apart from the true Creator-Ruler. The nations still reflect the divine image, but they seek by civilization, independence, and false religion to obtain their own goals.

God does not want the spirit of autonomy in his own people. He expects Israel to be wise. With whom does he delight? Who is wise? The people who call on his name (Gen. 4:26), who walk with him as Enoch and Noah did (5:22, 24; 6:9), and who are blameless (righteous) in his sight (6:9). In such people he delights. They are wise! They also receive their reward, which no one can take away. Enoch was taken up by the

Lord (5:24). God found favor with Noah and chose to renew mankind through him. The human way brings judgment, but godly wisdom is encouraged because it is borne out of a responsive heart to the Creator. Israel had to learn this distinction between good and evil, between the way of man and the way of God, between the ways of the nations and the way of Yahweh!

> He brought out his people with rejoicing,
> > his chosen ones with shouts of joy;
> he gave them the lands of the nations,
> > and they fell heir to what others had toiled for—
> that they might keep his precepts
> > and observe his laws.
> Praise the LORD.
>
> > > (Ps. 105:43–45)

CONCLUSION

The canonical function of Genesis 2:4–11:26 is to present Israel with the background necessary for understanding God's rule over the nations in their great variety of languages, territories, and cultures. Humankind collectively shares the guilt, condemnation, and anguish of human existence. The Lord restrained the potential evil of men and women by expelling them from the Garden of Eden, by keeping them from his presence by the cherubim, by reducing their longevity, and by splitting their collective potential for evil through the phenomena of different languages, nations, and geographical limits.

Despite man's sin, rebellion, and revolution against the Creator-King, the Lord remained faithful, blessing his creatures with food, procreative abilities, and protection. Moreover, the story of redemption anticipates the special privileges enjoyed by Israel: the presence of God, the protection of the cherubim, a renewal of God's fellowship, and access to the revelation of God. Furthermore, for Israel the prospect of Canaan was a reminder of the Garden of Eden, of their privileges under God's special blessings, and of their distinct responsibility to the Redeemer-God. As the new people of God, Israel represents a new era in the progression of redemption!

CHAPTER 6

Man's Revolution and God's Rule over the Earth

The narratives and genealogies of Genesis 2:4–11:26 trace the pervasiveness of human rebellion against the Creator. The Lord responds in judgment and grace to the growing intensity of the revolt. He judges Adam and Eve, Cain, and the generation of the Flood and later scatters humankind over the earth. He is also gracious in removing Adam and Eve from the tree of life, in reducing the human life span, in breaking up the solidarity of man's evil power, and in blessing human beings in their depravity. In this chapter we shall consider (1) the Father's care in the face of man's revolution, (2) human life in alienation from God, and (3) the community and individual responsibility.

THE FATHER'S CARE AND HIS CHILDREN'S REVOLUTION

A dominant theme in these early chapters of Genesis is the pervasiveness of sin: it exists at all levels, both in the Garden of Eden and outside of it (Gen. 3:1–4:24), both before and after the Flood (3:1–11:9). The Bible does not explain the origin of evil, but it clearly describes the entrance of sin into the world of man. Sin *(ḥaṭṭā't)* is often defined negatively as "missing the mark," but in biblical language, sin involves "rebellion" *(peša')*, an act of opposition to God's rule. From the first days in the Garden of Eden to the dispersion over God's earth, the history of mankind shows a persistent tendency toward revolution against God's rule.

What was conceived in lust (3:6), then developed into sin and guilt (vv. 6–8), grew up as corruption (6:5, 11–12), and matured into a full-scale revolution against the Creator-Ruler (11:1–9). God's response to sin does not fit the usual caricature of a God of wrath. In the garden he responds with wonder, asking, "Where are you?" (3:9); "Who told you that you were naked? Have you eaten from the tree that I commanded you not to eat from?" (v. 11); "What is this you have done?" (v. 13). Even his reaction to Cain's sin seems to be an expression of astonishment: "Where is your brother Abel?" and "What have you done?" (4:9–

10). These expressions are demonstrations of his concern for his creatures. In the Flood narrative too, God's concern for his creatures becomes sorrow: he grieves over the corruption of man, as a father grieves over the loss of a son. Men and women have gone away from the Creator-Father, who pains deep in his heart (6:6)! God is deeply affected by their alienation from him, and he deals with this crisis in a personal way.[1] Finally, the story of the Tower of Babel presents us with a compassionate God who determines what is best for human beings. God deals with the situation with kindness and determination, not like a father who is enraged by the affront of his little child.

God's fatherly concern and love for his creation is also evidenced by his restraining the power of sin in the world. In chapters 3, 6, and 11, he (1) put "enmity" between man and evil (3:15); (2) caused human beings to become occupied with their creaturely existence (vv. 16–19); (3) decreed a natural end to human physical existence (v. 19b); (4) expelled Adam and Eve from the garden so as to keep them from another offense; (5) reduced the human life span to 120 years (6:3); (6) instituted responsibility, justice, and the law of retaliation (vv. 5–6); and (7) broke up the solidarity of humankind by the introduction of languages (11:1–9).

In spite of the pervasiveness of sin, God cares for mankind and his world. He has reserved a place for people in this world as the object of his affection. These motifs are brought out in Genesis 3–11 in three specific areas: (1) human desire, sin, and guilt; (2) human corruption; and (3) human revolution.[2]

Human Desire, Sin, and Guilt (Gen. 3)

Man has been endowed with a glory far above the rest of creation. Because men and women are created in God's image, they reflect God's glory in the world. They have been given a headship, the ability to rule over the world, but this headship is derived from God. In ruling the earth, individuals thus realize not only that they must act in conformity to the Creator but also that they have a real dominion over the creation.

A crisis developed because man and woman are created in the image of God (1:27) and yet are free, desiring to be like God. Their desire to obtain this knowledge and "be like God, knowing good and evil" (3:5), led them to believe that they could become wise without learning to do God's will. By eating from the tree (vv. 6–7), the man and woman thought they were obtaining comprehensive knowledge, with wisdom and power to execute their plans.

Upon eating the fruit, Adam and Eve immediately became aware of their nakedness and frantically searched for leaves to cover themselves. This action, as well as their hiding from the sound of the Lord, reveals their dread of God and alienation from him. A new stage of history is ushered in by alienation, whereby the Lord allows his children to experience fear, anguish, anxiety, and uncertainty of God's blessings and of life itself. Alienation affects every aspect of existence: God, work, family life, and society.

The alienation is not complete, for humankind is not completely controlled by evil. God has graciously and sovereignly imposed an enmity between man and evil, Satan, and demonic powers. This relation of hostility places on individuals a full responsibility to continue to seek God and do his will. God has thus not abandoned his rule over the earth but will reassert it in accordance with his plan.

God is determined to keep men and women from falling into a state of alienation and anguish. Their autonomy, alienation from God, and sense of anguish may drive them to eat from the fruit of the tree of life (3:22). If people were to live forever in their state of anguish, the alienation would be complete and everlasting. By removing them from the garden, God keeps Adam and Eve from exercising an unlimited freedom from God. It is an act of grace, because only God blesses individuals with the blessings of life, family, children, culture, work, and recreation.[3]

Human Corruption (Gen. 4:1–16; 6:1–9:17)

Adam and Eve shared in sin and judgment. Cain was alone in his sin and alone when he received the judgment of God. Sin had passed from parents to child. Cain's sin lies in jealousy, hatred, and murder (Gen. 4:3–8; cf. Heb. 11:4; 1 John 3:12–15). His story is not told in order to warn us of the dangers of jealousy and hatred. Rather, it shows the solidarity of the human race in Adam's sin (cf. Rom. 5:12–21); sin has been passed on to the next generation. Moreover, it demonstrates the alienation between an individual, his brother, and his God. Brueggemann observes, "It is the brother and God together that create conflict for Cain."[4] Cain resolves that conflict by disobeying God (4:6–7) in order to pursue his own interests. The spirit of secularism is thus born. Cain's departure from the presence of God (v. 16) is a statement of life without God. Though his descendants were involved with high cultural pursuits (vv. 20–22), the story of Cain concludes with the expression of hatred, bitterness, and vengeance, as expressed in the song of Lamech,

> Adah and Zillah, listen to me;
> wives of Lamech, hear my words.
> I have killed a man for wounding me,
> a young man for injuring me.
> If Cain is avenged seven times,
> then Lamech seventy-seven times.
> (4:23–24)

The spirit of humanism and secularism inevitably leads to corruption (Rom. 1:18–32). Nevertheless, the secular spirit is not devoid of myths, images of spirituality, or a sense of accountability. Its religion, however, is simply a human effort to achieve greater realization of self under the guise of serving God or the gods.

Further background for human corruption is given in the brief allusion to the interaction between "the sons of God" and "the daughters of men" (Gen. 6:1–4). This intersection of the divine and human takes place outside the will of God. The sons of God are not the pious descendants of Seth nor the dynastic kings but the lowest order of angelic beings. They are "heavenly," that is, nonterrestrial beings.[5] The daughters of men ('*ādām*) are human, of this earth ('*dāmâ*). The wrong alluded to is the attempt at divinity. Human beings again grasped at becoming "like God," as a plan to develop a super race. God's judgment in the form of the Flood wipes out the possibility of a super race. The fallen angels are reserved for judgment (2 Peter 2:4; Jude 6), and the human life span is reduced to 120 years. God's judgment is that mankind is and remains flesh, or mortal (Gen. 6:3). His life-giving spirit will therefore not remain forever in men and women. Man is man; not the author of life. His life span is subject to the decree of God.

Another summary of human corruption is given in 6:5–7: "Every inclination of the thoughts of his heart was only evil all the time" (v. 5). The hardness of the human heart contrasts sharply with the grief and pain of God's heart—the LORD was grieved that he had made man on the earth, and his heart was filled with pain" (v. 6). The author thus contrasts the way of men and women with the love of the grieved heavenly Father. After all, man is God's creature, whom he still loves. In pain, the Father determines to remove life in order to save life (vv. 7–8).

God's love for mankind is demonstrated in the escape provided for Noah and his family in the ark. The ark becomes symbolic of God's continuing plan for his creation. He even renewed his blessing to Noah and his sons (Gen. 9:1, 7). As a final act of loyalty to all of life, God made a covenant with life (vv. 8–17) in which he guaranteed the continuity of his blessings. The account of the Flood (6:9–9:17), therefore, contains these balanced aspects: the judgment of God and the love of God; the execration of life and the blessing of life; the end of an era as well as the beginning of a new era.[6] This new era is characterized by God's remembrance of human frailty, of his commitment to life, and of his covenant.

> But God remembered Noah and all the wild animals and the livestock that were with him in the ark. (8:1a)

> I will remember my covenant between me and you and all living
> creatures of every kind. Never again will the waters become a flood to
> destroy all life. Whenever the rainbow appears in the clouds, I will see
> it and remember the everlasting covenant between God and all living
> creatures of every kind on the earth. (9:15–16)

God gave the rainbow as a sign of his covenant. It is a sign by which
God "remembers" his creation, a sign of assurance for his creatures. It is
a token that he will not abandon his purpose for creation.[7] The bow
extends his grace from creation to the new creation, when he will have
purified mankind and renewed the earth (see 2 Peter 3:10–13; Rev.
21:1–3). The symbolism of the rainbow is appropriately developed by
Isaiah as a token of God's redemption. Since God has been loyal to the
Noahic covenant, how much more will he be faithful to the redeemed
humanity!

> "To me this is like the days of Noah,
>   when I swore that the waters of Noah would never again
>   cover the earth.
> So now I have sworn not to be angry with you,
>   never to rebuke you again.
> Though the mountains be shaken
>   and the hills be removed,
> yet my unfailing love for you will not be shaken
>   nor my covenant of peace be removed,"
>   says the LORD, who has compassion on you.
>
> (Isa. 54:9–10)

Human Revolution (Gen. 11:1–9)

God's grace in renewing his blessing on the human family is no
license to sin—but men and women went on sinning. Just as it was
before the Flood, man's heart is corrupt, "every inclination of his heart
is evil from childhood" (Gen. 8:21). God has already restrained sin and
human sinful inclinations by imposing an enmity between Satan and
mankind (3:15), by mixing his blessings with the anguish of human
existence (vv. 16–19), by expelling the humans from the Garden of
Eden (vv. 23–24), by reducing the human life span to 120 years (6:3),
and by instituting law, justice, and governance (9:5–6).

In spite of these restraints and God's blessing on human society (9:1,
7), people developed a civilization without God. The Tower of Babel is
a symbol of man's revolutionary spirit against God, who is Creator,
Ruler, and Sustainer. The repetition of "let us," the intent to reach "the
heavens," the goal to make a name, and the motivation not to be
"scattered over the face of the earth" bring out dramatically the careful
planning of humanity not only to interfere with God's plan but also to
usurp God's authority on earth and in heaven. The city and the tower

are part of a grand scheme to draw God into battle with man. Humankind brazenly challenges God to a duel and is confident of victory and recognition.

God's judgment comes in the form of another limitation: the diversity of languages. The variety of languages is not in itself a curse, but it is a divinely instituted means of controlling the human desire for absolute control of one's destiny apart from God.[8] God disrupts man's unified revolutionary spirit. That spirit remains, and it recurs in the form of various political and economic programs, but it is restrained.

Babel/Babylon becomes in the Bible a symbol of a self-reliant, imperialistic secularism: control without accountability to the Creator. The spirit of secularism can coexist with religions and deities, but not with the absolutism of the Creator-God. Humanism and secularism are bound to run counter to theism. Isaiah saw this spirit in the imperial ambitions of Assyria and Babylon (10:7–11; 14:4–6; 47:5–7, 10). John the apostle symbolically speaks of the Roman Empire and all kingdoms to follow as Babylon the Great. Babylon, the seducer of nations, kings, and merchants will fall (Rev. 18)!

HUMAN LIFE IN ALIENATION FROM GOD

The blessing of God in Genesis 1:28–29 extends to every area of human life on earth and presupposes a continuing relationship between Creator and creature. Blessing is always associated with the presence and pleasure of God with his creatures. Whoever pleases the Lord is called "blessed" (Ps. 1:1).

A disruption in the relationship removes man from the presence of God. When Adam and Eve rebelled against him, they went into hiding, guilty and terrified before the presence of the great King (Gen. 3:8–10). The relationship had been broken. God expelled the humans from his presence in the Garden of Eden in order to dramatize the fact that he cannot trust his creature and consequently that man is not worthy of fellowship with the Creator. Since the alienation of men and women from God, their lives have been characterized by anguish and by hope.

Anguish

Death entered into the world with sin (Rom. 5:12). God's condemnation and judgment was quick and affected each element of his blessing. His judgment, however, should be distinguished from his curse. The judgment of God lies over this world like an invisible shield that keeps it from developing its full potential. This judgment limits both the human family and nature, so that all of creation is now characterized by groaning (Rom. 8:22). A curse, however (Gen. 3:14), is a final verdict that permits no redemption. The one cursed, namely Satan, is to be forever separated from the presence of God in this life and the world to come.[9]

The power of sin and the sting of death are now associated with created existence. The story of the temptation and God's judgment explains in literary form that the world was originally good: it distinguishes between creation and the Fall. With the introduction of sin at the human level, God judged man and cursed Satan and the ground. How did the judgment on human beings affect the blessing of God?

First, God cursed the serpent, who is identified with Satan (see Rom. 16:20). It is his plan ultimately to remove Satan completely from the creation (see Rev. 20:10). The curse on Satan is good news, for it means that he is still responsible to the Creator. He has to "bite the dust," a metaphor of his submission to God.[10] Another aspect of the good news is the declaration of enmity between Satan and man. Human beings are guilty, but they are also victims.[11] Though they have been seduced by the Evil One, they are not to be overpowered by evil.

Second, the judgment on men and women directly affects their enjoyment of blessing, but not the blessing itself. Their guilt changes the family structure and their means of physical sustenance and rule over the earth.

In the first place, the relationship between husband and wife is altered. The complementary expression of God's image in male-female relations still exists, but it is changed. The family bond is now preserved by the woman's "desire" for her husband and by the husband's role as the one responsible for the well-being of the family. His "rule" (Gen. 3:16) is to be marked neither by dictatorship nor by dominion, otherwise God would have taken from the woman the rule that he graciously had bestowed on both male and female (1:28).[12]

In the second place, the family is a divine institution in which children are raised. The offspring, likewise, share in bearing the image of God (Gen. 5:2–3). Hope lies in the children (3:15), but hope is a blessing mixed with fear, anguish, and shame. Fear results from the uncertainty associated with birth, childbearing, and the raising of children. Anguish grows out of the inability to predict the outcome, because no one has control over the genetic processes, the environment, or the individual traits of the offspring. Shame comes from the inability to have children. The women in Genesis were all too familiar with the "pain" of being women. Eve lost Abel ("vanity," "vapor") by the hand of Cain. Sarah, Rebekah, and Rachel suffered from barrenness. Rebekah's frustration with her children (27:46) is a powerful commentary on 3:16.

In the third place, pain is experienced in providing for the family needs (3:17–19). By the verdict of the just Judge, work becomes toil. The thorns and thistles symbolize the harshness of human existence and of human frailty in responding to the challenges of nature. Dominion over the earth does not come easily. It is associated with sweat; the returns are generally not as great as the expected yield. Moreover, human existence is continually overshadowed by the specter of death and failure, making life all the more uncertain. Human beings desired certainty and absolute control over life when they ate from the fruit of the tree of knowledge but instead ended up with their world crumbling beneath them.

God's blessing is not removed, however, even in view of life's uncertainties and man's corruptible nature. Family, provisions, and cultural expressions are still within the sphere of God's rule. As a good ruler, he takes care of his creation. It is most significant, therefore, that after the Fall God renews his pledge to provide people with food by the regularity of the seasons (8:22), to bless the human family (9:1, 7), and to help man in his relation to animal life (v. 2). Our very existence today is an expression of his blessing on the human race.

Hope

In spite of the anguish of life, God's blessing finds special expression in hope. He gives to man the hope of an end to the seemingly meaningless cycle of human existence, promising that he will be patient with mankind.

In the first place, God gives men and women hope in regard to their struggle with Satan. The first promise of the seed (Gen. 3:15) has at times been called the *protoevangelium*, or first mention of the gospel. This interpretation, however, is highly unlikely. Satan and man are locked in a battle, over which God is like a referee, establishing perpetual enmity between the powers of evil and humankind. Each party must guard against the moves of the opponent. Man in his erect position has the ability to stamp on the serpent's head but at the same time must guard his heel. The deadly serpent can strike the man at any time and inject deadly venom into his heel.

The translation of Genesis 3:15 in its context should not be read too optimistically as if the victory of the Messiah (Jesus) is revealed from the beginning of the history of redemption. Rather, it should reflect the fact that the seed is collective and that the personal pronoun in "he will crush" refers back to the seed.[13] I propose the following translation:

> And I will put enmity
> > between you and the woman,
> > between your seed and her seed;
> > they may crush your head,
> > and you may strike at their heel.

Human beings must recognize the fight on two fronts: the struggle of existence in their involvement with nature and the struggle with the realm of spiritual powers. The command to subdue the earth has thus been enlarged to include the subjugation of evil. In spite of their deteriorating condition, the responsibility of humans is extended. This text contains both a warning and hope: warning that, if salvation depends on man, he will suffer defeat, and hope that a descendant of Adam and Eve may one day be victorious.

These two elements of hope and responsibility come together in Cain, of whose name Eve says, "With the help of the LORD I have brought forth a man" (4:1). Eve has fixed her hope on Cain. Because of his jealousy, however, the Lord warned Cain to master sin, which is like an animal "crouching at your door" (v. 7). After Cain's sin, judgment, and expulsion by the Lord, Eve focused her hope on Seth, saying this time, "God has granted me another child in place of Abel, since Cain killed him" (v. 25). The genealogy of Seth shows evidence of hope in Enoch and especially in Lamech. What a contrast between this Lamech's words and the vindictive words of Lamech, a descendant of Cain (vv. 23–24)! The former Lamech called his son Noah and expressed the hope, "He will comfort us in the labor and painful toil of our hands caused by the ground the LORD has cursed" (5:29). Final victory did not come through Noah, but God did begin a new work in him. In the covenant of forbearance the Lord guaranteed to sustain life on earth and to renew his blessing as an expression of his commitment to humankind (9:1, 7).

Hope becomes more focused in Shem. In Noah's blessing of Shem, he expresses hope that the Lord will dwell in the tents of Shem! The redemptive historical development of hope and blessing in Genesis 2–11 is thus slowly taking place. It begins with Adam and Eve and follows the genealogy of Seth to Noah, ending with the blessing on Shem, whose genealogy concludes these chapters and leads to Abraham, the heir of the promises (11:26).

According to Genesis 3:15, hope had to come from a descendant of Adam. Jesus is fully human, being a descendant of Adam, Noah, Shem, and Abraham (see Luke 3:33–37)—he is also fully God! He is the God-Man, the divine Warrior, who revealed his royal splendor while on earth (John 1:14). When he was on earth, he struggled with Satan and overcame (Col. 2:15; Heb. 2:14; 1 John 3:8). The hope of humankind thus lies in Jesus Christ, who alone has authority to shatter the kingdom of evil and to restore creation and to share his victory and glory with redeemed humanity. We need not fear Satan, because his rule on earth, together with all human kingdoms, will fall (see Matt. 16:18; Rev. 12:10–12).

In the second place, human beings gain hope from the forbearance of God as revealed in the unfolding of his plan for redeeming mankind. God is committed by the act of creation to people. He knows our frailty

(Gen. 8:21), yet he pledges himself by covenant to remember his commitment to all of creation (9:16). The sign of that covenant is the rainbow, a magnificent symbol of all the blessings and gifts God bestows on creation. Through the very combination of clouds, rain, and sunshine, the rainbow suggests his commitment to nourish his creation. As Vos wrote, "But [the rainbow] is produced upon these [clouds] by the rays of the sun which in the symbolism of Scripture represent the divine grace."[14] Peter's comment on the seeming delay of judgment reminds us that God desires to give all mankind an opportunity to repent before he fulfills the promise of the complete renewal of heaven and earth (2 Peter 3:9).

THE COMMUNITY AND THE INDIVIDUAL

A change occurs with the introduction of sin and guilt. Mankind's accountability before the Creator continues to be in line with his expectations of Adam and Eve. All people will render an account and are judged on the basis of their works (Acts 17:31; Rev. 20:13). God judged mankind as a whole in the garden, in the Flood, and at Babel. His blessing on humankind, whether righteous or ungodly (Matt. 5:45), is an expression of "corporate solidarity," or of how God treats the human family as a whole. Corporate solidarity, however, also means corporate guilt and punishment. This idea forms the basis of Paul's doctrine of the universal condemnation of humankind before God:

> Consequently, just as the result of one trespass was condemnation for all men, so also the result of one act of righteousness was justification that brings life for all men. For just as through the disobedience of the one man the many were made sinners, so also through the obedience of the one man the many will be made righteous. (Rom. 5:18–19)

On the other hand, individuals are not necessarily doomed to sin, condemnation, and death. Although solidarity of the human race is clearly taught in Genesis 2–11, individual responsibility is also emphasized. The story of Cain's murder of Abel dramatizes individual responsibility. The Lord graciously warns Cain not to be overtaken by his emotions but to take seriously his personal responsibility. He must learn to master sinful inclinations and do what is right. "If you do what is right, will you not be accepted? But if you do not do what is right, sin is crouching at your door; it desires to have you, but you must master it" (4:7). Cain could not excuse himself by justifying the murder or by blaming his parents. He knew he had personally sinned against God and submitted himself to the judgment of God. The course of action he had chosen also affected his descendants, among whom is Lamech, the self-avenger (vv. 23–24).

The genealogy from Adam to Noah contains encouraging developments. In stark contrast to the genealogy of Cain, marked by autonomy and self-vindication, is the brief observation, "At that time men began to call on the name of the LORD" (4:26). Enoch walked with the Lord, and so did Noah—that is, their heart was responsive to God and was characterized by integrity and righteousness (see 17:1).

From the cases of Adam, Cain, and Noah, it should be apparent that, while God singles out the individual, he deals with individuals in the context of their family. God does not disregard the institution of the family when he bestows grace on an individual. In Noah's family God's grace extended to Noah's wife, children, and even in-laws. The incident of Noah's drunkenness and the curse on Canaan further illustrates how curse and blessing are connected with the manner of response. In this case, however, the redemptive-historical significance goes a step further. The curse of Canaan finds corporate expression on his descendants (9:25), whereas the blessing of Shem anticipates the special role of his genealogy in the unfolding of salvation. The author traces Abraham back to Shem and thereby to the promise.

Tension is therefore maintained both between the solidarity of the human community and the individual and also between the solidarity of the family and the responsibility of the individual member. Special privileges may come to the children through the parents, but special grace is given only to those who walk with the God of their fathers!

The revelation of God in Genesis 2:4–11:26 requires men and women to uphold his ordinances, such as worship of the Creator, support of marriage and the family, involvement in labor and culture, personal integrity, absence of malice or murder, and avoidance of meat with blood or of strangled animals (Gen. 9 as a whole; cf. Acts 15:29).[15] In essence, God expects people to respond with integrity to the Creator, to the family, to their fellow human beings, and to life in general by virtue of their position of responsible rule over the earth. Life is truly a sacred trust. The responsibility of individuals before God is the basis for calling people back to commitment to their Creator. They cannot excuse themselves by blaming God for their identification with Adam and the imputation of Adam's sin, because individuals are responsible for their own acts.[16] But when a person repents and lives in the presence of God, God graciously deals with that one and with that one's seed (i.e., family)! In his choice of Abraham and his seed, God is not forgetting his commitment to mankind, on whom his blessing still rests. For that very reason, the Lord purposefully links Abraham and the nations in his promise that "all peoples on earth will be blessed through you" (Gen. 12:3).

Conclusion to Part 2

The period I have called Creation in Alienation is a transition from Adam to Abraham; more important, it explains the world of human beings between the first and last periods (Creation in Harmony and The New Jerusalem). This world is characterized by anguish, alienation, and rebellion against the Creator. Far from being vexed, however, the Creator is grieved by human sin. He maintains control over his creation and, like a father, continues to care for his creatures. Though the sinfulness of men and women increases and affects the family structure, cultural developments, and the world at large, the Lord is constant in his fidelity. He restrains the potential of human evil at each stage of rebellion by imposing enmity between Satan and the human, by expelling the first people from the garden, by reducing human life span, and by breaking up the solidarity of mankind. The anguish of human existence in birth, raising children, interpersonal relations, sickness, making a living, and death affect all members of the human race, regardless of ethnic, political, religious, or linguistic background. The hope of the human race, however, lies in the God with whom Enoch and Noah walked. In the Noahic covenant he has promised to deal kindly with his creation and to dwell again on earth ("in the tents of Shem"), to bless and protect the people among whom he dwells in a special manner. To this end he expects individuals to be loyal to him, living like Noah, who was "righteous in his generation."

The literary, canonical, and redemptive-historical foci give us a window into Israel's world as well as our own by these seven perspectives:

1. Human beings sinned, rebelled, and revolted against God's rule.

2. Individuals live continually between anguish and hope.

3. The nations live in a state of revolution against the Creator, but the Creator has limited the power of evil.

4. God rules over all the nations in grace and judgment.

5. God's concern with mankind is that of a grieved father, who works with his children to bring them to repentance. Responsibility lies with individuals.

96

6. The special blessing on humankind finds its focus in Shem, an ancestor of Abraham.

7. Israel's special position as an elect nation is an expression of God's free grace, whereby Israel is invited to the experience of restoration in Canaan by the glorious presence and blessing of God, conditioned on its responsiveness to the Creator-Redeemer.

Part 3

Election and Promise

Introduction to Part 3

The failure of men and women to respond to God's grace is the theme of the primeval prologue (Gen. 1–11), which portrays humankind as thoroughly corrupt. The plan of God to sanctify and glorify his creation has been momentarily frustrated by the rebellion of human beings against their Creator-King (11:1–9). But God's grace shines through in his division of mankind into nations by means of another creative act: the multiplication of languages! Individuals are still corrupt, but their revolutionary nature has been curbed because they no longer can confront God as an expression of solidarity. Even in their state of rebellion, men and women are still human, made in God's image, the object of his free grace, and under his watchful eye.

The third epoch in redemptive history begins with the account of Terah (11:27) and continues with the subsequent story of the patriarchs. This story explains why Israel was first chosen out of the nations to be the people of God. God's election of Abraham and Israel and their becoming God's new people represent an important development in the history of redemption. This period, like all others, is only a stage in a series of developments, each of which separately and together reveals a magnificent design.

The developments of this period are fundamental to each subsequent period in the history of redemption. The chief contribution lies in the revelation of God's special, redemptive (or restorative) grace. His special grace is not new, as all his acts of redemption from Adam to Abraham were expressions of his grace. What is new is the *covenantal* aspect. Through Abraham and his descendants as heirs of the covenant, the Lord himself promises to be their God and to accept them as his people. This period witnesses to the first clear development of the biblical motif of *the people of God*. In this part we shall consider the following important developments in the history of redemption:

1. God makes a commitment to renew humankind through Abraham and his descendants.

2. God graciously and freely initiates the promises to Abraham concerning descendants, the blessing of God, land, and other nations.

100

3. God's plan includes other nations, kings, and lands, because they too will be blessed by the God of Abraham.

4. God's school of faith involves testing and requires endurance amid trials.

5. God's promises and covenants are transmitted through the institution of the family—from Abraham, Isaac, and Jacob (Israel) to the tribes of Israel.

6. God's school of hope includes alumni such as Abraham (the father of the faithful) and Jacob (the father of Israel), who excelled because they looked patiently to the Lord for the fulfillment of the promises.

7. God's promises and covenant converge in Jesus Christ, "the hope of the nations."

In my approach to Genesis 12–50, I shall seek to bring together the various literary, canonical, and redemptive—historical dimensions of the biblical text. Once again we shall see how the use of this threefold approach keeps us closer to the intentions of the biblical author and also helps us to understand the purpose of the patriarchal history for the nation of Israel and for the church of Jesus Christ.

CHAPTER 7

Promise in an Alienated World

The patriarchal narratives and genealogies understandably receive a more elaborate treatment than mankind's primeval history from Adam to Abraham. God revealed to Israel who they were in relation to the nations by the *toledot* structure of Genesis and also who they were as defined by the promises given to the patriarchs.

THE *TOLEDOT* FORMULA

The *toledot* formula ("this is the account of . . .") functions as a signal to show the movement from creation to Israel in Egypt (2:4–50:26). The story is divided into ten structural divisions: five sections from creation to Terah (2:4–11:26) and five sections from Terah to Israel (11:27–50:26). There are five such headings in the patriarchal narratives: the accounts of Terah (including the story of Abraham, 11:27–25:11), Ishmael (25:12–18), Isaac (25:19–35:29), Esau (36:1–37:1; cf. 36:1 and 9), and Jacob (37:2–50:26).

Length

The difference in the comparative length of the accounts is the most striking feature. The first (Terah) and last (Jacob) accounts each have fourteen chapters, and the middle portion (Isaac's account) is about ten chapters long. But the accounts of Ishmael and Esau are really no more than genealogies, occupying only seven verses and one chapter respectively. The bulk of the narrative material is given to the lives of Abraham, Isaac, Jacob, and Joseph. Ishmael and Esau are set aside as not being heirs to the covenant and promises. (See figure 6.)

Symmetry

In very general terms, the accounts of Terah and Jacob are longer than that of Isaac because they function as the beginning and end of the patriarchal history. The story of Abraham, the first patriarch, thus balances the story of Jacob, the father of the twelve tribes of Israel. Isaac's account has no counterpart; yet, as the central story, it must receive adequate attention. In it we learn of the transmission of God's blessing from Abraham through Isaac to Jacob. What takes place in the center of the patriarchal history, therefore, functions as a pivot or a hinge for the progress of God's redemptive plan.

Terah/Abraham	(11:27–25:11)
Ishmael	(25:12–18)
Isaac	(25:19–35:29)
Esau	(36:1–37:1)
Jacob	(37:2–50:26)

Figure 6. Patriarchal Accounts in Genesis

The *toledot* formulas and the literary structure that they create further highlight the movement of redemption in terms of the theme of election. In each successive generation of patriarchs there is the question of which son will receive the blessing and be heir to the promises. The whole literary movement of Genesis 12–50, therefore, takes the reader from God's election of Abraham to his election of Jacob, the father of all Israel. When we consider the amount of material given to the patriarchs themselves, the literary feature of symmetry becomes important.

Abraham and Jacob

The structural development concentrates on Abraham and Jacob, whereas Isaac is a transition figure between them. The emphasis in the Abraham story is on his migration from Ur and Haran to Canaan, God's call, the divine promises, the testings in his life of faith, the covenant, the rivalry between Sarah and Hagar, the birth of Isaac, and his struggles in the land of promise. The focus is on Abraham, the father of the faithful, as he represents all the faithful in the reception of the promises, the covenant, and the testings.

The story of Jacob also shows an internal symmetry in that he returned to his ancestral homeland, returned to Canaan, received God's promises at Bethel, and was severely tested in the development of his faith, in the rivalry of his wives and the birth of his sons, and in the personal anguish over his sons (Simeon and Levi at Shechem; Joseph and his brothers). The focus here lies on Jacob's place as the "father of the tribes." He represents all of Israel in his reception of the promises, covenant, and patriarchal blessing.

Crises

The stories of the patriarchs unfold a series of crises associated with the promises of God. Interaction between the Word of God and the challenge of faith is the focus of the structural development of Genesis. In the response to the crises, the promises are confirmed and undergo slight modifications, and the patriarchs are transformed into "heroes of faith." The structural development thus highlights the promises and the personal struggles, anguish, and the testing of the patriarchs.

THE PATRIARCHAL PROMISES

If we described the *toledot* formulas as the skeletal structure of Genesis, then we would certainly have to designate God's promises to the forefathers as the circulatory system: "the scarlet thread . . . [that] runs through the subsequent history of the patriarchs."[1] To say that the promises to the patriarchs are the theme (or at least a primary motif) of Genesis or even the Pentateuch as a whole is to say nothing new. Conservative and critical scholars alike have pointed to the centrality of the patriarchal promises in the study of Genesis.[2]

What, then, are the promises, and where are they found in the patriarchal narratives? The four basic areas of promise are (1) a seed, or offspring; (2) a land, namely, the land of Canaan; (3) a blessing to the patriarchs, specifically, the presence of God in protection and guidance; and (4) a blessing to the nations through the patriarchs. (See table 6.)

A vital aspect of the promises is their location within the text of Genesis. The occurrences of God's promises to the patriarchs fully support my earlier contentions about the significance of the *toledot* structure. Isaac and Jacob, to the exclusion of Ishmael and Esau, share in these promises.[3]

Another aspect of the promises that is evident from table 6 is that in only four passages do all promises occur together: Genesis 12:1–3, 7; 22:17–18; 26:3–4; 28:13–15. Each patriarch received the fourfold promise of God. The promises are reaffirmed most frequently to Abraham and to Jacob.

Another general feature of the promises is the repetition they show in language and vocabulary. Many statements of the promises may better be called reaffirmations precisely because they repeat words and phrases found in preceding passages containing the promises. A brief study of the language of the four promises will reveal both the similarities and differences in vocabulary.

TABLE 6. THE PATRIARCHAL PROMISES IN GENESIS

Promise	PATRIARCHS				
	Abraham		*Isaac*	*Jacob*	
Seed	12:2a; 13:16 15:5	17:5–6 18:18 22:17	26:4 (24)	(28:3) 28:14 35:11 (48:4)	
Land	12:7 13:15, 17 15:18–21	17:8 22:17	26:3	(28:4) 28:13	35:12 (48:4)
Personal Blessing	12:2b (15:1) 17:7ff	22:17	26:3	(28:3) 28:15 35:11	(48:3)
Blessing to Nations	12:3 18:18	22:18	26:4	28:14	

The Promise of Seed

The most frequent of the four promises is that of a seed. It is the first promise given by God to Abraham: "I will make you into a great nation" (12:2). Every promise of a seed describes either what the offspring will be like (e.g, "like the dust of the earth" [13:16; 28:14]) or what it will become (e.g., "a community of peoples" [28:3]). Sometimes the Lord focuses on the patriarchs themselves, and other times on the offspring itself. In each case God's use of language makes the promise of seed a powerful vehicle for communicating the grand nature of his unconditional election of the patriarchs.

We note that the Lord uses the language of simile ("like the dust," "like the stars," "like the sand of the sea") with each of the patriarchs to stress the magnificence of the promise. Second, the interchange between "I will make" (e.g., 48:4) and "be fruitful and increase" (e.g., 35:11) shows us that the original command given to Adam (1:28) and Noah (9:1, 7) is still relevant in the covenant community and that the success is guaranteed by divine promise. Third, the goal of the promise goes beyond Abraham's receiving a son, even beyond the nation of Israel, to the inclusion of the nations and kingdoms. Through Abraham and his descendants, the Lord plans to redeem to himself "a community of peoples" (28:3; 48:4).

The Promise of Land

The promise of the land is the second most frequent promise, with at least twelve occurrences in Genesis. Although there is great variation in the language of the land promise, the form is relatively constant. It consists of two parts: the recipients of the land and a specification of the land (e.g., "The whole land of Canaan . . . I will give as an everlasting possession to you and your descendants after you" [17:8]).

The focus of the land promise is the land to the west of the Jordan River, extending from the Negeb to the Euphrates, that is, the land area occupied by the descendants of Canaan (see Gen. 10:15–19). As the descendants increase, they are expected to extend the borders in all directions. As an expression of God's curse on those who do not bless Abraham and his descendants, the Canaanites' lands and cities will be taken away (22:17; cf. 24:60).

The land promise, while incorporated into the covenantal structure, is not specific. Its relevance was far removed from the situation of the patriarchs. The Lord had forewarned Abraham that his descendants would first have to suffer oppression before the land would vomit out its native inhabitants and be given to Israel (15:13–16). The patriarchs themselves are portrayed as seminomadic wanderers between the region of the Euphrates and Egypt, with a concentration on Shechem, Hebron, Beersheba, and the Negeb.

The final words of Genesis close the story of the patriarchs with a brief mention of Joseph's death in Egypt. The reader is left wondering how the promise of the land will be fulfilled. Whereas the promise of the seed showed signs of development, the promise of the land seems far from realization.

The Promise of Blessing to the Patriarchs

This promise may seem to be a catchall for various expressions of God's relationship with the patriarchs, but within the diversity of language pertaining to blessing there is most certainly a unifying theme. The Lord has promised to be with the patriarchs, and this constant relationship may be expressed in terms of blessing (12:2b; 22:17; 26:3; 28:3), presence (26:3; 28:15; 31:3; 46:4; 48:21), protection (15:1; 26:24; 28:15), or covenant (15:18; 17:7).

Once again the unconditional character of the promises is clearly revealed. The covenant that the Lord made with Abraham (chap. 15) depended solely on God's sovereign Word for its fulfillment. When the covenant is confirmed with the sign of circumcision (17:10–14), Abraham must respond with faith and obedience. The Lord's sovereign protection and presence also calls for a faith response.[4]

The themes of presence and protection are closely tied together. If this great covenant God is with the patriarchs, then his presence should be evident in their lives. Perhaps the most eloquent witness to God's presence with the patriarchs is given by Abimelech of Gerar and by Phicol, the commander of his army. They told Abraham, "God is with you in everything you do" (21:22). Later they told Isaac, under similar circumstances, "We saw clearly that the LORD was with you" (26:28). When those who threaten God's chosen people recognize his presence with them, there can be no denying the reality of his power and the veracity of his promise!

The Promise of Blessing to the Nations

The patriarchs and their seed are to be the channel for God's blessing to the nations. This mediatory status comes as a result of the blessings God has given to them. The language in the initial promise to Abraham indicates this movement from the patriarch(s) to the peoples of the earth (Gen. 12:2–3); the NIV obscures the purpose clause of the original Hebrew: "I will bless those who bless you, and whoever curses you I will curse; *so that* all peoples on earth will be blessed through you."[5]

The Table of Nations (Gen. 10) and the story of Babel (11:1–9) indeed depict the many nations in need of salvation. But we should be cautious lest we underemphasize the blessing to the patriarchs. God's blessing is first to Abraham and his family and secondarily to the nations. In spite of the close relationship between the two types of promises of blessing (to the patriarchs and to the nations), the blessing to the nations occurs the least frequently of all the four major areas of promise (12:3; 18:18; 22:18; 26:4; 28:14).

The blessing to the nations occurs in those passages containing all four promises as well as in Genesis 18:18, where God mentions it as a reason for informing Abraham of the coming destruction of Sodom and Gomorrah. Even though this promise is an integral part of God's election of the patriarchs, the Book of Genesis does not articulate a fully developed doctrine of salvation for the Gentiles. Indeed, nowhere in the patriarchal narratives is the exact nature of the blessing to the nations defined.

Summary

Thus far we have seen that both the *toledot* formulas and the internal movement of the election and promise of God build upon the history of redemption set forth in Genesis 1–11. The *toledot* structure highlights the narrowing of God's focus begun in the primeval history, moving from Adam to Seth, Noah, Shem, Terah, Abraham, Isaac, and Jacob. The promises express God's continuing concern for his creation, particularly fallen humanity. Just as the Lord provided new beginnings with Seth, Noah, and Shem, so he works out his plan of redemption for the scattered nations through the chosen family of Abraham. God still purposes to have a people for himself, and his call of the patriarchs opens a new phase in the history of redemption.

THE INDIVIDUAL PATRIARCHS

The literary approach to the patriarchal history makes the great purposes of God very clear. The literary features that arise in the narratives concerning the individual patriarchs reflect the themes of election and promise in several ways. We may examine the lives of Abraham, Isaac, Jacob, and his sons as set forth in Genesis 12–50 by focusing on the respective themes and plots that the author develops.[6]

Themes: Continuities and Discontinuities

Continuities

One common feature of the patriarchal narratives is the *promises* that God gave. At least once in their lives, Abraham, Isaac, and Jacob each heard the Lord speak the gracious promises of a seed, a land, a personal blessing, and the blessing to the nations (see 22:17–18; 26:3–4; 28:13–15). They also received the covenant (17:7, 19).

Second, Abraham, Isaac, and Jacob all lived as *aliens* in the land of Canaan, wandering among the peoples who had settled there before them. This nonsedentary life was reflected in their relationship with the Lord. Genesis mentions no organized patriarchal religion; instead, the narratives tell us only that the patriarchs built altars to the Lord where they pitched their tents (12:8; 13:4, 18; 26:25; 33:20) or where they heard the Word of God (12:7; 22:9; 35:1, 3, 7; see also 28:18–22).

A third area of continuity is that each of the patriarchs faced similar problems with respect to their *family lives*. Their wives all experienced barrenness before they gave birth to the promised sons—Sarah (11:30; 15:2–3; 16:1), Rebekah (25:21), and Rachel and Leah (29:31; 30:9, 17, 22). Abraham and Isaac had to wait twenty-five and twenty years, respectively, for the birth of their sons. Moreover, Abraham and Isaac faced similar experiences in dealing with foreign kings who wanted to take away their wives: Sarah with Pharaoh (12:10–20) and Abimelech (chap. 20), and Rebekah with Abimelech (26:1–11). Isaac and Jacob, on the other hand, both married non-Canaanite women from within the patriarchal family (24:3–4; 28:2). Finally, all three patriarchs witnessed intense rivalry between their sons. Abraham ultimately sent Ishmael away from his son Isaac according to the wishes of Sarah, who knew that Ishmael could never share in Isaac's inheritance (21:8–21). The conflict between Jacob and Esau, both before and after their birth, is well documented in the biblical narratives (25:22–26, 29–34; 27:1–45).

And it was the jealousy of Jacob's older sons toward Joseph that triggered the events that led to the chosen family's move to Egypt (37:4, 11, 18).

Finally, as the patriarchs lived in the hostile environment of the ancient Near East, they each faced *other crises* that reflected the negative effects of creation in alienation. In addition to the difficulties surrounding the birth of their children, they faced natural catastrophes, acts of hostility, and jealousy. Abraham, Isaac, and Jacob dealt with severe drought and famine (12:10; 26:1; 41:56–42:2). Abraham and Isaac were troubled with the issue of ownership of wells (21:25–30; 26:18–25, 32). Abraham fought against the kings who had kidnapped Lot (14:13–17) and made a treaty with Abimelech of Gerar (21:22–34), as did Isaac (chap. 26). So great was the jealousy of the Philistines toward Isaac over God's lavish blessings that he had to move away from them. The patriarchs lived continually in the tension of blessing and alienation. It is clear that the covenant people cannot live together with the nations. The history of the Old Testament bears out how the people of God evoke hatred, jealousy, bitterness, war, and other acts of hostility. Jacob's experience with the Shechemites resulted in the death of the native population rather than in treaty (34:25–26). Instead of being a blessing to the nations, Jacob became a "stench to the Canaanites and Perizzites" (v. 30).

Discontinuities

Although we have seen several similarities in the life experiences of the three patriarchs, the differences in the way God dealt with them are just as striking. We have already noted how little space is given to the life of Isaac (chaps. 24–26) in comparison with the space given to the lives of Abraham (chaps. 12–23) and Jacob (chaps. 27–35). The lack of biographical information about Isaac is coupled with the fact that he received the promises only once (Gen. 26:3–4). Moreover, we clearly see the overall scarcity of God's appearances or revelations to Isaac (only in 26:2–5) in comparison with those to Abraham (12:1–3, 7; 13:14–17; chap. 15; 17:1–22; chap. 18; 22:1–18) and Jacob (28:13–15; 31:11–13; 32:1, 24–29; 35:1–13; 46:2–4). All three patriarchs encountered difficulties concerning the objects of the promises (they waited for sons to be born; they sojourned in the land of Canaan; they fought the peoples around them), but the way in which they faced these problems was different.

Abraham's faith struggle was primarily directed toward God: why would not the Lord fulfill his promise of a son? Isaac's waiting for a son, on the other hand, is recorded in only one verse (25:21), even though he had to wait almost as long as Abraham (whose twenty-five-year wait covers ten chapters)! Jacob and Abraham are depicted as active characters, but Isaac is everywhere shown to be passive: in Ishmael's ridiculing (21:8–10); in his nearly being sacrificed (chap. 22); in the choice of a wife (chap. 24); in the struggle between his sons (25:22–34; here God speaks to Rebekah, not Isaac!); and in his blessing of Jacob and Esau (chap. 27). Except for his dealings with Abimelech (chap. 26), most of the important events in Isaac's life simply happen to him. In definite contrast to Isaac is his son Jacob, who knows what he wants from life and struggles to obtain it: the birthright and blessing (25:29–34; 27:1–29); his wives, especially, Rachel (29:16–30); Laban's flocks (30:25–43); and the blessing from the "man" with whom he wrestled (32:22–32).

Purpose

The writer of Genesis did not accent these similarities and differences in his narration for the sole purpose of maintaining the reader's interest in the story. His reason for including some facts about the patriarchs while excluding others is fully in keeping with the overall *toledot* structure of the entire book. The writer intended for his audience to see the relative importance of Abraham and Jacob (and their struggles with faith and obedience), compared with Isaac. Again, the literary features prove to be significant in demonstrating the history of the promise from Abraham ("the father of the faithful") to Jacob ("the father of the tribes of Israel"), with Isaac playing a transitional role. Both Abraham and Jacob experienced the world in alienation, anguish, pain, evil, and death. The fathers of the promise were tested in their faith and persevered! In the tension between alienation and the promises, they developed in faith, love, and hope. The patriarchs modeled to Israel the way of faith: tension between this world and the world to come, the kingdom of God and the kingdom of evil.

Plot: Symmetry and Movement

The overall balance and symmetry in the patriarchal narratives (between Abraham and Jacob, with Isaac as the middle component) also finds expression in the individual biographies of the patriarchs. In other words, the writer develops the plot to its overall conclusion by relating only certain events. In the narratives concerning Abraham and Jacob, in particular, the device of symmetry helps the reader to identify the central themes and to focus on the movement in God's plan of redemption.

Abraham

The major portion of the story of Abraham deals with his life as he waits for God to give him a son by Sarah. The ten chapters devoted to this theme cover twenty-five years, recording events relating to each of the promises: the seed, the land, and the covenant. (See figure 7.) Through his selectivity of events, the writer builds suspense for the reader. Will Sarah be the mother of the promised son or become the wife of Pharaoh (chap. 12)? Will Lot inherit some of the Promised Land (chap. 13)? Will Abraham always live in an antagonistic relationship with the nations (chap. 14)? When will the covenant blessings come into existence (chap. 15)? The events before and after chapter 16 are symmetrical to each other, although the eleven years covered in chapters 12–16 (cf. 12:4 and 16:16) are balanced by only one year in chapters 17–21!

A. Promises stated (Gen. 12:1–9)
    B. In Egypt with Sarah (Seed) (12:10–20)
        C. Lot and the land (to Sodom) (chap. 13)
            D. Abraham and the nations (14)
                E. The covenant—initiation (15)
                    F. Hagar, Ishmael, and Abraham (16)
                E'. The covenant—confirmation (17)
            D'. Abraham and the nations (18)
        C'. Lot and Sodom and Gomorrah (19)
    B'. In Gerar with Sarah (Seed) (20)
A'. Promise of son fulfilled (21)

Figure 7. Structure of the Abraham Narrative

This structure brings out that in chapter 16 Abraham hits the low point of his faith, attempting to bring about fulfillment of the promise of a son by his own efforts. A thirteen-year period of waiting follows the birth of Ishmael. (Note how the writer condenses this long wait in between two verses, 16:16 and 17:1.) With the renewal of the covenant and the sign of circumcision (chap. 17), however, Abraham's waiting is over. In chapters 17–20 he faces the same basic issues and problems of chapters 12–15, until the birth of Isaac (chap. 21). Chapters 21–22 give further proof that the writer of Genesis carefully selected his materials. The only episodes from Isaac's youth that he recounts are the ridiculing by Ishmael and the sacrifice story, in between which must surely be a jump of several years. Both the writer's arrangement of the events and the movement within the plot, therefore, serve to present Abraham as the patriarch who in faith struggled with the Lord.

Jacob

Two other sections within the patriarchal narratives exemplify symmetry and movement in the development of plot: the story of Jacob's journey (28:10–35:15; within the *toledot* of Isaac) and the story of Joseph and his brothers (chaps. 37–50; within the *toledot* of Jacob). The story of Jacob's journey to Haran is symmetrical, being framed between the accounts of God's two appearances to him at Bethel (28:10–22; 35:1–15). On both occasions, God reaffirmed the patriarchal promises to Jacob, showing that the Lord has been with Jacob throughout his journey, from beginning to end. God is "the God of Bethel" (31:13). (See figure 8.)

Bethel: first appearance (Gen. 28:10–22)

1. Away from Bethel: dealing with Laban (chaps. 29–31)
Arriving in Paddan Aram (29:1–14)
Laban's deception: marriage (29:15–30)
Children: *promise of seed* (29:31–30:24)
Laban's deception: flocks (30:25–43)
Leaving Paddan Aram (chap. 31)

2. Returning to Bethel: dealing with Esau (chaps. 32–33)
Preparation (32:1–21)
Wrestling with God: *promise of blessing* (32:22–32)
Meeting (chap. 33)

3. Approaching Bethel: dealing with Shechem (chap. 34)
Dinah violated (34:1–5)
Agreement: *land and nations* (34:6–24)
Shechemites murdered (34:25–31)

Bethel: second appearance (35:1–15)

Figure 8. Structure of the Jacob Narrative

In between the two appearances are three stories of Jacob's struggles, each dealing with an aspect of the promises. In the central section Jacob's character is most severely tested as he wrestles with God. His concern for self, preeminence, riches, and trickery fades in his confrontation with God. Abandoned to his God, he asks for nothing less than to know God (32:29). Jacob, blessed by God, knew that God had been there at Peniel (or "Face of God"; v. 31). Jacob was a changed man.

Jacob's stay at Shechem disrupts what would have been a well-balanced movement away from Bethel and back again. Jacob had been commanded to return to the land of his fathers (31:3; cf. 28:15), and in settling at Shechem, Jacob walks in the footsteps of Abraham (12:6–7).

Like Abraham, his grandfather, he came to Shechem, but God did not confirm the promise at Shechem as he had done to Abraham. Like Abraham, Jacob departs from Shechem, but unlike him, Jacob receives the confirmation at Bethel (35:1–15). Jacob's return to the original site of promise marks the end of his pilgrimage of faith. He has been tested and has persevered. He, too, is a hero of faith, a son of the covenant!

Joseph

The literary movement in the story of Joseph and his brothers reflects their geographical movement from Canaan to Egypt.[7] (See figure 9.) The author unfolds this movement in an orderly fashion, allowing time after each development to establish the necessary conditions for the subsequent stage. For example, chapters 39–41 see Joseph slowly come to power through two episodes of dream interpretation. By the time his brothers arrive (chap. 42), Joseph is in a position of authority, controlling the affairs of state that have control over his kin. The journey of the brothers actually involves two round trips, creating intrigue and suspense: When will Joseph, who is several times overcome with emotion (42:24; 43:30–31; 45:1–2), reveal himself? What will become of Simeon (42:24) and Benjamin, who is supposedly caught with stolen property (44:12)? Will Jacob accept the fact that Benjamin must go with his brothers for the second journey (42:20, 38)?

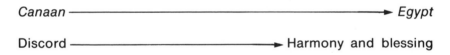

Canaan ——————————————————→ Egypt

Discord ——————————————————→ Harmony and blessing

    A. Jacob's family (Gen. 37–38)
        B. Joseph (39–41)
        B'. Joseph's brothers (42–45)
    A'. Jacob's family (46–50)

Figure 9. The Narrative of Joseph and His Brothers

The opening and closing chapters of this story (37–38; 46–50) balance each other in a problem-solution motif. The lack of family harmony manifested by the brothers' hatred and jealousy finds its counterpart in the reconciliation of the brothers at the end of the story (45:15; 50:18–20). The individual sons of Jacob, who seem to blend together in their personal faith and character (except Reuben and Judah, 37:21–29), are set in their proper light at the end of the story when they receive appropriate blessings (49:28). The whole narrative is dominated by the unmistakable theme of God's providence, which enabled the family to survive the famine and arrive in Egypt. As Joseph would say on two occasions: "You intended to harm me, but God intended it for good to accomplish what is now being done, the saving of many lives" (50:20; see also 45:5–7).

CONCLUSION

The selective biographies of the individual patriarchs clearly demonstrate the importance of literary analysis in biblical interpretation. These stories not only confirm the centrality of election and promise but also probe deeply into the nature of living faith in the midst of struggles and temptations. The patriarchal narratives help the reader to see two distinct but interrelated levels of God's plan of redemption. There is, of course, the general picture of God's narrowing focus upon the patriarchal line; all the while God assures his people that they will survive difficult experiences on their way to Egypt. But within this more general movement of redemptive history, however, the reader is swept into the drama of God's ways with individuals whom he calls and to whom he promises descendants, land, blessing, and a place in his purposes for the nations of the earth.

The *toledot* structure unfolds by symmetry and crisis situation the development of promise from Abraham to Israel in Egypt. The literary materials give a cross section of the joys and pains of the patriarchs. On the one hand, they received the promise and covenants, and the Lord assured the continuity of the transmission by his speaking directly with Abraham, Isaac, and Jacob. Of these three, Abraham gained his prominence as the father of the faithful and Jacob as the father of the tribes. Isaac remains a transition figure. On the other hand, the patriarchs experienced the anguish of this world in alienation: childlessness, quarrels, war, selfish plotting, corruption, and famine. Not only were they real residents of a world in alienation, they also were sojourners. As such, they had limited rights, which often put additional strains on them. The Lord committed to them his word of promise and assured them by covenant that they and their family were heirs of the promises regarding descendants, land, and blessing. They were God's objects of blessing as well as his instrument of restoring his blessing to the nations. But they were also God's subjects on the stage of redemptive history. Their faith, love, and hope in face of crises and testings brings the promise down to the world of reality in which blessing and alienation coexist.

CHAPTER 8

The God of the Fathers
Is the God of Promise

We have previously seen how Genesis 1–11 taught the people of Israel during their early history to recognize Yahweh, their Redeemer, as the Creator-God of the universe and as King of the nations, which he dispersed by his sovereign will. Israel had to know that it had a long history in common with the nations and that its privileges were because of God's sovereign grace to the patriarchs (Gen. 12–50).

As a people, the Israelites would surely want to know about their origins: How did they come to be a populous nation from the humble beginnings of Terah's clan? What kind of men and women were their ancestors, and what struggles did they endure? What were the promises attached to the Abrahamic covenant? How is Yahweh the God of the fathers—the God of Abraham, of Isaac, and of Jacob? Did they come to Egypt by accident or by divine purpose? Literary analysis of Genesis 12–50 has shown that these patriarchal narratives helped Israel to see that Yahweh was the God who had elected their forefathers, Abraham, Isaac, and Jacob. Structures within the larger narrative in chapters 12–50 as well as the symmetry and movement in the individual accounts focus on the providence of God in choosing Isaac and Jacob instead of Ishmael and Esau. And the story of Joseph and his brothers in chapters 37–50 would be understood by Israel as part of their prehistory, showing them how their ancestors came to be in Egypt.

The startling, miraculous promises given to the patriarchs would inspire the nation of Israel with great hope: God would lead them to a land of their own. The patriarchal narratives relate to the infant nation how they have a place within Yahweh's magnificent plan to renew earth and its peoples and to effect a glorious re-creation and fulfillment of his original intentions. The patriarchal history taught Israel that (1) Yahweh was the God of the fathers, (2) they had a unique relationship to the nations, and (3) the revelation of God demanded an appropriate response from his people.

YAHWEH IS THE GOD OF THE FATHERS

The final forty years of Israel's slavery in Egypt was a significant period in at least two respects. First, Yahweh had sovereignly and providentially provided for the survival and preparation of a deliverer for his people, namely Moses (see Exod. 2). Second, and perhaps more important for the entire flow of redemptive history, the Lord God inaugurated a new stage in his self-revelation to his people. In the context of the great deliverance brought about at the Exodus, the descendants of Jacob began to realize that the God of their salvation was the God of their fathers.[1]

In the early chapters of Exodus the identification of Yahweh as the God of the patriarchs is clearly revealed in two separate statements to Moses (chaps. 3–4, 6). No less than six times does Yahweh identify himself as the God of the fathers—the God of Abraham, the God of Isaac, and the God of Jacob (Exod. 3:6, 15–16; 4:5; 6:3, 8). During the momentous era of the Exodus and the giving of the law at Mount Sinai, God not only provided the fresh revelation of his name (Exod. 3:13–15; 6:2–4) but also, by his very identification as the God of the patriarchs, placed Israel's traditions about their forefathers in a new context. (See table 7.) God's previous covenant with the patriarchs is directly related to the name Yahweh in the following:

> God also said to Moses, "I am the LORD. I appeared to Abraham, to Isaac and to Jacob as God Almighty, but by my name the LORD I did not make myself known to them. I also established my covenant with them to give them the land of Canaan, where they lived as aliens. Moreover, I have heard the groaning of the Israelites, whom the Egyptians are enslaving, and I have remembered my covenant." (Exod. 6:2–5)

TABLE 7. THE NAMES OF THE LORD

Name	Emphasis	Activities
Elohim	Creator-Ruler	Rules over the nations; rules in Israel
El Shaddai	God of the Fathers	Gives covenant promises
Yahweh	Covenant-Redeemer	Reveals his name and law; consecrates Israel as his own

This passage communicates at least three important facts about Yahweh's revelation. First, although the patriarchs perhaps knew and used the name *Yahweh*, their relationship with God is better understood through the designation *El Shaddai* ("God Almighty").[2] In a balanced study of the problem, B. S. Childs says that the emphasis in Exodus 6:3 is clearly on the revelation of God's character; that is, the name "Yahweh" affirms the patriarchal promises.[3] At the same time, by the use of the divine name, God is obviously trying to say that a new era is beginning. He is now to be known as the Savior-God of Israel. Second, with the raising up of Moses as Israel's leader during the Exodus, God will reveal himself in a new way, demonstrating that he is both the Creator-God and the Savior-God of Israel who is with his people. Finally, on the basis of these two truths, the imminent salvation of Israel from Egypt (see 6:6–8) is seen to be a logical—indeed necessary—result of the patriarchal covenant!

Genesis 12–50 thus taught Israel that Yahweh, their God and the God of their fathers, had long ago promised to keep covenant with them as his people. The close relationship between the four patriarchal promises and the Abrahamic covenant is brought out in Genesis 15 and 17. In the former chapter the covenant is instituted by Yahweh, whereas in the latter it is confirmed (fourteen years later) by the sign of circumcision. In both chapters, however, *the promises are made an integral part of the covenant* (see Gen. 15:5–6, 18–21; 17:2, 6–8). If we understand the word "covenant" as "sovereign administration of grace and promise," then the promises of a seed, a land, a blessing, and the nations' blessing are the very core of what the covenant-making God will do for his people as he oversees the development of his plan of redemption.[4] And because this covenant includes the descendants of the patriarchs (specifically those who will suffer as slaves [Gen. 15:13–14]), we are able to see much more clearly the message of Exodus 6:3–8. The covenant-making God of the fathers is now revealed to be the covenant-keeping God of Israel through the punishment of Egypt, the Exodus, the revelation at Sinai, and the conquest of Canaan!

According to this perspective, therefore, the patriarchal promises take on a whole new significance. Until we have seen Genesis 12–50 in the larger canonical context, the exact nature of the fulfillment of the promises remains unclear. But in the Book of Genesis, "The divine words of assurance have been set within an eschatological pattern of prophecy and fulfillment which now stretches from Abraham to Joshua. The promises function only as a prelude to the coming exodus, and extend into the distant future."[5]

This so-called eschatological pattern is felt by the reader as a tension between promise and fulfillment. The promise of a land is an excellent example of apparent nonfulfillment of the promise. Due to the patriarchs' constant mobility, "the patriarchal narratives take place outside the Promised Land almost as much as inside it." And "at the end of the book [the heirs of the promise] are firmly outside the land and settled in Egypt." The narratives also create tension through what Clines calls "partial fulfillment and partial nonfulfillment."[6] The promise of a seed held forth great hopes for Jacob's descendants. There was certainly an inkling of hope at the close of Genesis, where the family of Jacob numbered at least seventy descendants (46:26–27). But not until the opening chapter of Exodus do we see the promise of a seed being fulfilled in greater measure: "But the Israelites were fruitful and multiplied greatly and became exceedingly numerous, so that the land was filled with them" (v. 7; note the extensive use of promise vocabulary).

When Genesis 12–50 is taken as a part of the greater whole of the Pentateuch, we see how the Lord was fulfilling his promises to the patriarchs. As the Israelites sat in the plains of Moab, awaiting the conquest of Canaan, they would no doubt recognize the validity of the promises and the veracity of Yahweh, the God of their fathers. For this reason Moses calls the people to renew the covenant before entering the Promised Land.

> You are standing here in order to enter into a covenant with the LORD your God, a covenant the LORD is making with you this day and sealing with an oath, to confirm you this day as his people, that he may be your God as he promised you and as he swore to your fathers, Abraham, Isaac and Jacob. (Deut. 29:12–13)

ISRAEL AND THE NATIONS

The people of Israel, under the leadership and teaching of Moses, would have looked to Genesis 12–50 not only to understand their self-identity but also to know what sort of relationship they were to have with the nations around them. Israel knew that they had a unique standing among the nations. The Lord had told them, "Now if you obey me fully and keep my covenant, then *out of all nations* you will be my treasured possession. Although the whole earth is mine, you will be for me a kingdom of priests and a holy nation" (Exod. 19:5–6; italics mine). Even a cursory reading of the patriarchal narratives would have shown Israel that God's plan of redemption found its central focus in the descendants of Abraham. Whatever God intends for the nations (in light of the story of Babel, Gen. 11:1–9) will not come about apart from his relationship with Israel. *Redemptive history hinges on Yahweh's salvation of Israel.*

Crises and Isolation

The nations, however, are not totally removed from the scene of patriarchal history. Abraham, Isaac, and Jacob live and move *among* the nations. The Canaanites are in the land (Gen. 12:6); the lands of other nations are promised to Abraham's seed (15:19–21; 22:17); Abraham must fight against the nations (chap. 14); he has dealings with Egypt 13:10–20); both he and Isaac arouse jealousy in the Philistines (chap.

20; 26:1–31); Abraham pleads for Sodom and Gomorrah (18:16–33); and Jacob experiences strife with the Shechemites (chap. 34). Indeed, more than one-fourth of Genesis (chaps. 37–50) is set against the background of Egypt.

These facts about the ancient Near Eastern background of the patriarchs' lives would have come as no surprise to Israel during the era of Moses and Joshua. They knew what it was like to be slaves of Egypt; to seek passage through Edom, a brother nation (Num. 20:14–21); to fight against the nations, such as the Amalekites (Exod. 17:8–16) and the Amorites and Bashan (Num. 21:21–35); and to be led astray by the Moabites (Num. 25). Israel's tenuous relationship with other peoples was partly a result of God's blessings, which caused the nations to be jealous of the Israelites (see esp. the story of Isaac and Abimelech of Gerar in Gen. 26). Israel cannot coexist with the nations of this world of alienation. The primeval prologue of Genesis had taught Israel that the nations were under the judgment of God. God is also patient with the nations, as Israel had to wait out the promise in Egypt for hundreds of years. Their suffering was fully in line with God's purpose, as revealed to Abraham, that his descendants would possess the land of Canaan only when "the sin of the Amorites" had "reached its full measure" (Gen. 15:16).

The sinfulness of the Amorites and Canaanites was the primary reason why Israel was warned to avoid friendly relations with the inhabitants of the Promised Land. If the Israelites made a treaty with them, they would become a "snare" to Israel (Exod. 34:12). The very next verse explains that idolatry was the ultimate danger. For these reasons, the nations had to be driven out of the land, assuring that Israel would dwell peacefully in the Promised Land. Jacob's blessing on Judah is consistent with the attitude of Israel's future dominance of the nations. He told Judah, "Your hand will be on the neck of your enemies," and stated, "The obedience of the nations is his" (Gen. 49:8, 10).

Blessing

All that we have considered about Israel's isolation from (and animosity toward) the nations is, of course, only one side of the larger picture of God's plan for all peoples. The many hints regarding God's gracious intentions for the nations and peoples of the earth find renewed focus in the patriarchal promises, specifically, in the blessing on the nations through the seed of Abraham. From the outset of the patriarchal era, the Lord made it clear that Israel would have a mission to the nations: "All peoples on earth will be blessed through you" (Gen. 12:3). Abraham and his descendants are promised to be the means whereby the nations will receive God's blessing.

Although much of the Pentateuch conveys a thoroughly negative attitude toward the nations, there are some indications that Israel, once established in the land, was to be open to foreign peoples. The alien living among the Israelites was not to be mistreated but to be loved as an Israelite, because the Israelites themselves were once aliens in Egypt (Lev. 19:33–34). Moreover, if an alien was circumcised, he would be able to partake of the Passover meal as if he were an Israelite (Exod. 12:48–49). By joining oneself to the community of faith in Israel, the blessings of Yahweh would surely be extended to any person (see the story of Ruth). Behind this attitude of acceptance was the compassion of Abraham, who, when faced with the judgment of God on Sodom and Gomorrah, interceded for an utterly sinful, foreign people (Gen. 18:16–33). The restoration of the earth and its peoples would begin with and through the nation of Israel, itself called out of slavery and sin.

REVELATION AND RESPONSIVENESS

Another important aspect of Yahweh's relationship with his people is the freedom and graciousness of God's actions. The Lord's calling of Israel out of slavery in Egypt, as well as his call of Abraham, was not dependent on any particular characteristic within the ones called. As Moses was to tell the Israelites,

> The LORD did not set his affection on you and choose you because you were more numerous than other peoples, for you were the fewest of all peoples. But it was because the LORD loved you and kept the oath he swore to your forefathers that he brought you out with a mighty hand and redeemed you from the land of slavery. (Deut. 7:7–8)

Jacob was but a "wandering Aramean" who "went down into Egypt with a few people and lived there" (Deut. 26:5). The patriarchal narratives would help Israel to see clearly that their forefathers were called out of their homeland to a land that God would show them (Gen. 12:1). This free choice of God expressed his gracious intent to have a holy people for himself. In initiating his relationship with the patriarchs, the Lord revealed himself through the spoken word (e.g., Gen. 12:1), a theophany (e.g., 18:1), the angel of the Lord (22:11–18), or a vision (15:1).

Family

The Israelites of Moses' day would have recognized that, as surely as Yahweh dealt with the patriarchal family, he had revealed himself to the nation at the time of the Exodus. From the earliest expression of the promises to the confirmation of the covenant (Gen. 17), the Lord intended to work in and through the family line of Abraham. That the sign of the covenant, circumcision, was administered to infant males is proof that the Lord desired families as whole units to follow after him. And although the faith and life experiences of Abraham and Jacob were emphasized above those of Isaac, there is no doubt that Isaac fully shared in the covenant.

Individual Responsiveness

Nevertheless, within the larger structures of family and nation, there was the vital necessity of individual responsiveness to Yahweh. As a father, Abraham was responsible for directing "his children and his household after him to keep the way of the LORD by doing what is right and just, so that the LORD will bring about for Abraham what he has promised him" (Gen. 18:19). Individual family members are not exempt from faith and obedience simply because the family as a whole, or even the nation of which they are a part, has been called by God out of one place into another!

CONCLUSION

The Book of Genesis functions as the "roots" of Israel. They learn from the various genealogies, promises, narratives, and blessings that the Lord is King over the nations, that they belong to the nations, and that they are set apart from the nations by divine election. Their privilege is on account of God's promises to the patriarchs. The chief promise was his commitment to bless and protect the family of Abraham and all the clans, nations, and kingdoms that would seek shelter with the God of Abraham. Enjoyment of the privileges was by birth, but the continued enjoyment of the covenantal blessings came only by a heartfelt response to the God of Abraham. As such, the development in the school of faith as well as the victory of faith served to model for Israel the proper response to Yahweh's goodness.

CHAPTER 9

Promise, Grace, and Fidelity

The growing and struggling nation of Israel would have derived a sense of both hope and challenge from the patriarchal narratives as they fought to possess the Promised Land. But the canonical approach is not the only perspective by which we may understand Genesis 12–50. The patriarchal narratives occupy a significant place in the entire history of redemption. The dual themes of (1) God's election and promise and (2) the patriarch's faith and obedience highlight a redemptive-historical interpretation of Genesis 12–50.

GOD'S ELECTION AND PROMISE

Yahweh's call of Abraham and the patriarchs was based upon his free grace. The family of Terah, and that of his son, Abraham, after him, was set apart by God for his purposes. The transitional genealogy of Genesis 11:10–26 (from Shem to Terah) demonstrates the narrowing focus of God: from Abraham on into the remainder of the Old Testament, God works with the seed of Abraham. This nation of Israel becomes the focus of the plan of redemption; they are the means whereby the nations and peoples of the earth will be blessed.

But this general overview of God's election of the patriarchs fails to do justice to the precise function of Genesis 12–50 in the whole history of redemption. If the patriarchal narratives and the promises contained in them were excised from the Scriptures, would the plan of redemption read any differently than it does now? Are any elements that arise later in Scripture inexplicable apart from the events, revelation, and message of the patriarchal history?

One statement in particular summarizes the role of Genesis 12–50 in redemptive history: *Yahweh's gracious promises to Abraham, Isaac, and Jacob are the very platform of the history of redemption.* In other words, having set forth the four areas of promise in Genesis 12–50, Yahweh is committed to fulfilling his Word. He will not be content until the fullness of the promise is realized. We might also say that the covenant promises are, in a real sense, the plan of redemption itself. While we should not exclude later amplification of the promises, those found in Genesis do contain the center of the plan of redemption. They tell us the direction and purpose of God; they point to where salvation history is heading.

Seed

Each of the four areas of promise illustrates this movement, from the statement of the promise, through its gradual fulfillment, to its fullness. The promise of a seed does not appear in Genesis 12:2 as something totally new and unseen. In Genesis 3:15, God had held forth hope for the community of human beings in their perpetual battle with evil. Within the larger context of the plan of redemption, the promise of a seed to Abraham first functioned as a renewing of God's purpose for mankind in general. The Lord would seek to bring about his program for humanity by beginning with one family.[1] In order for this family to achieve the goals of redemption, however, they would have to expand and become a great nation.

Land

The promise of land, which was delayed in its fulfillment until the Conquest, is referred to repeatedly by Moses in his sermon in Deuteronomy (e.g., 1:8, 21, 25, 35–36; 2:31; 3:18, 20). The later history of Israel, however, revealed an even greater fulfillment during the reigns of David and Solomon, who extended the borders of Israel to those mentioned in Genesis 15:18–21: "Solomon ruled over all the kingdoms from the River to the land of the Philistines, as far as the border of Egypt" (1 Kings 4:21).

Blessing and God's Presence

The promise of blessing and God's presence finds a new expression as the Lord commands Israel to build a tabernacle for his glorious presence (Exod. 25–27). When the tabernacle is completed, the Lord comes to be with his people in a way in which he had not been with human beings since the Garden of Eden: "Then the cloud covered the Tent of Meeting, and the glory of the LORD filled the tabernacle. Moses could not enter the Tent of Meeting because the cloud had settled upon it, and the glory of the LORD filled the tabernacle" (Exod. 40:34–35).

Much the same thing occurred when Solomon's temple was completed (1 Kings 8:10–11). The Lord was now with his people, just as he had promised to be when he confirmed the covenants with Abraham and Moses (Gen. 17:7–8; Exod. 34:10).

123

Nations

The promise of blessing to the nations may have been the most uncertain of the promises as far as the visible evidence of its fulfillment is concerned. Nevertheless, the tenuous relationship between Israel and the nations eventually included Rahab, Ruth, David's friendship with Hiram of Tyre (1 Kings 5:1), and Solomon's international ties (4:34; 10:1–13).

Promises and Progressive Fulfillment

The Exodus, the Conquest (period 4, the holy nation), and the era of David and Solomon (period 6, the royal nation) marked the most significant progress toward fulfillment of the original promises. By and large, however, Israel failed, missing out most basically because of unbelief. Finally, the people went into exile. The downfall of Israel and Judah due to sin—the destruction of Jerusalem and the temple and the Assyrian and Babylonian exiles, in 722 B.C. and 586 B.C. respectively— placed all four promises in an uncertain status. Had the Lord broken his unconditional and eternal covenant promises?

When this question is raised some answer that, because the people of Israel were disobedient, Yahweh was no longer obliged to keep "his side of the covenant." Such a view contains a misunderstanding of the significance of individual response. Those who sinfully reject Yahweh's grace will forfeit their participation in the covenant; but Yahweh's Word stands forever (note Isa. 40:8 and its context). Even before the Babylonian exile, Yahweh promised through Jeremiah the coming of a new era with a covenant renewal (Jer. 31:31–34). The return from exile would mark a new era in the history of the promises. Judah was no longer a great nation: their land was a waste; the temple, the symbol of God's presence, lay in ruins; and they were under the rule of other nations and in danger of attack from neighboring peoples (see the Books of Ezra and Nehemiah). Yet the Lord had long ago promised through Moses that the promises would be renewed after exile:

> Even if you have been banished to the most distant land under the heavens, from there the LORD your God will gather you and bring you back. He will bring you to the land that belonged to your fathers, and you will take possession of it. He will make you more prosperous and numerous than your fathers. The LORD your God will circumcise your hearts and the hearts of your descendants, so that you may love him with all your heart and with all your soul, and live. (Deut. 30:4–6)

All of the promises would begin to be fulfilled, but only in the Lord's time. The temple that was built after the Exile appeared small in comparison with the former temple, but the Lord assured them, "The glory of this present house will be greater than the glory of the former house" (Hag. 2:9).

The four hundred years of prophetic silence between the Testaments caused many Israelites to believe that Yahweh had forgotten them, but the New Testament declares that the coming of the Messiah was in the fullness of time, or "when the time had fully come" (Gal. 4:4). For all of those who have lived after Jesus' first advent and who look toward his second coming, the apostle Peter states, "The Lord is not slow in keeping his promise, as some understand slowness" (2 Peter 3:9). To give perspective, Peter comments that "with the Lord a day is like a thousand years, and a thousand years are like a day" (v. 8). Just as the Lord gave Abraham a son, "at the very time God had promised him" (Gen. 21:2), so will the Lord fulfill all of his covenant promises according to his wisdom and in his perfect time.

With the coming of Jesus Christ and his ministry, death, and resurrection, the patriarchal promises reach their most significant focus. Not only are all of the promises to be fulfilled in and through Jesus Christ, but also in him all true believers become recipients of the promises. In other words, Jesus' life and ministry is like a lens at the center of redemptive history.

As the apostle Paul later said, "For no matter how many promises God has made, they are 'Yes' in Christ" (2 Cor. 1:20). It is no longer just the Jews who are heirs of the promises. That wall of partition that divided Jew and Gentile has been broken down by Christ (Eph. 2:14). Indeed, "If you belong to Christ, then you are Abraham's seed, and heirs according to the promise" (Gal. 3:29). Ever since the coming of Christ we rightly shift our language from singular to plural, from "a great nation" and "the land of Canaan" to those "from every tribe and language and people and nation" (Rev. 5:9). Obedience to the Great Commission of Christ (Matt. 28:18–19) will be the means whereby "all peoples of the earth will be blessed."

Furthermore, through Christ men and women may know the presence of God as never before. Not only did he live for a while among us (John 1:14), he also is with us always (Matt. 28:20). He maintains his continual presence through the Holy Spirit, who has descended upon the church (Acts 2) and now dwells within the hearts of believers in Christ (John 14:17). But even this magnificent fulfillment of "God with us" is not the final one, for one day all of God's people will dwell with him and he with them, for all eternity:

> And I heard a loud voice from the throne saying, "Now the dwelling of
> God is with men, and he will live with them. They will be his people,
> and God himself will be with them and be their God. He will wipe
> every tear from their eyes. There will be no more death or mourning

125

or crying or pain, for the old order of things has passed away." (Rev. 21:3−4)

THE PATRIARCHS' FAITH AND OBEDIENCE

Although Genesis 12−50 places a premium on the election and promise of God, it does not do so apart from a continual emphasis on the faith and obedience of Abraham, Isaac, and Jacob. The concepts "faith" and "obedience" should not be too sharply contrasted; rather, they are to be distinguished from one another as two aspects of a holistic approach to life that is lived out in the presence of God. Perhaps a more appropriate term for this kind of responsiveness is *living faith*. Such faith pleases the Lord. All three of the patriarchs manifested living faith during their lives, but, as we have seen from our literary analysis, the active figures of Abraham and Jacob stand out over against the more passive Isaac.[2]

A literary study of Abraham and Jacob revealed that the biblical writer sought to organize the important events of their lives so as to give the reader an impression of the dynamism of faith. The bulk of the narrative follows their struggles to supply their material needs. Both men experienced three distinct stages in their lives of faith: an early encounter with the Lord involving mystery and awe, an event or struggle that called for the exercise of living faith, and a long period of waiting. In addition, at the outset of their respective pilgrimages, each man heard Yahweh state all four promises (Gen. 12:2−3, 7; 28:13−15), and after they have found something of what they sought, Yahweh reaffirmed the promises to them (22:17−18; 35:11−12).

Each man seemed to have been concerned with just one of the promises: for Abraham it was the seed, or more precisely, a son; for Jacob, it was the blessing of Yahweh's presence and protection. At face value it may appear that these men were selfish and worldly in their lack of concern for the other promises. Was Abraham's complaint against the Lord (Gen. 15:2−3) merely because he did not want his wealth to go to his servant, Eliezer of Damascus? Was Jacob's vow simply a means of trapping the God of Bethel into keeping him alive in unknown territory? On the contrary, these two promises were rightly identified by the patriarchs as the most important for them in their respective situations. Abraham was very old, with a wife past childbearing age (18:11); all of the promises depended upon having a son by Sarah. Jacob faced a similar situation. None of the other promises would have any significance for him if Yahweh did not protect him and bring him safely back to his homeland. At the early stage of their walk with the Lord, they were thus only beginning to express a living faith in Yahweh.

A broader redemptive-historical perspective shows that the New

Testament placed Abraham's faith in a category by itself. It is the prime example of living faith, without which "it is impossible to please God" (Heb. 11:6). Jesus told the Jews of his day that they "would do the things Abraham did" if they were truly Abraham's children (John 8:39; note the emphasis on faith in action implied in the word "did"). Paul's entire fourth chapter of Romans is an exposition of Genesis 15:6, "Abram believed the LORD, and he credited it to him as righteousness." Whereas Paul seems to focus more on the *relationship* between God and sinful people that justifying faith makes possible, James emphasizes the ongoing, *dynamic nature* of living faith, which brings forth works of righteousness as evidence of justification (James 2:21–24).[3] Living faith enabled Abraham to hope for the eternal home that Yahweh had prepared for him (Heb. 11:13–16). And the several struggles he endured (vv. 8–12; see Gen. 12–20) so strengthened his faith that he was willing to offer up Isaac, because "Abraham reasoned that God could raise the dead" (Heb. 11:19). The initial faith he placed in Yahweh (Gen. 15:6) was "made complete by what he did" (James 2:22).

Because Abraham is the ancestor of Jesus Christ, those who believe on Christ are heirs of the promises (Gal. 3:29), the covenant (Acts 3:25), and the blessings (Gal. 3:14). The kind of living faith exemplified by Abraham is now the means whereby all men and women receive new life from God. Indeed, it is through their faith in Jesus that God is preparing a new humanity for himself. As the apostle Paul recognized,

> Those who believe are children of Abraham. The Scripture foresaw that God would justify the Gentiles by faith, and announced the gospel in advance to Abraham: "All nations will be blessed through you." So those who have faith are blessed along with Abraham, the man of faith. (Gal. 3:7–9)

Paul points further to the great purpose of God when he addresses the nations:

> You are no longer foreigners and aliens, but fellow citizens with God's people and members of God's household, built on the foundation of the apostles and prophets, with Christ Jesus himself as the chief cornerstone. In him the whole building is joined together and rises to become a holy temple in the Lord. And in him you too are being built together to become a dwelling in which God lives by his Spirit. (Eph. 2:19–22)

The patriarchal hope in God's promises continues to be the hope of the church. At Babel mankind sought to build a temple, rising to the heavens, to unite all people. Instead, God scattered the peoples. In the midst of this hopeless confusion, however, he was at work singling out the family that would bring redemption to the earth. Now the descendants of Abraham are being built up together in fulfillment of

God's promises and purposes. A holy people is no longer a dream but an ever-developing reality! The goal of God's promises and of redemptive history is the establishment of God's kingdom on earth. With Dumbrell, we may view Genesis 12:1–3 as being God's response to Genesis 3–11.[4]

Conclusion to Part 3

The period "Election and Promise" inaugurates the special grace of God in at least seven respects:

First, in the *election* of Abraham and his descendants. The Lord initiates the restoration of heaven and earth by renewing the relation between human beings and himself.

Second, in the Abrahamic covenant as *the sovereign administration of grace and promise*, by which the Lord secures a people for himself.

Third, in the fourfold *promise*: multiplication of his people, the gift of the land, the Lord's presence in blessing and in protection, and the instrumentality of Israel to the nations.

Fourth, in the *progression of redemption* in time and space. From this period onward the Lord works out the promises in accordance with his purpose and time. The progression of the fulfillment of the promises constitutes the history of redemption, but the perception of fulfillment is restricted by human inability to know the beginning and the end. More important than our knowledge of God's plan of salvation is the enjoyment of that salvation in this life and the anticipation of the grand realization of all of his promises.

Fifth, in the sequence of developments that lead us to the inauguration of the messianic era and the new heavens and new earth. The Abrahamic covenant is the basis for all of *God's covenantal dealings*: the Mosaic, Davidic, and the New Covenant in Christ. The biblical revelation bears out four eschatological goals: (1) a people of God, consisting of all nations, tongues, tribes, and regions; (2) the renewal of the heaven and earth; (3) the presence of the Lord on earth, evident in his blessing and protecting his people; and (4) the inclusion of the nations in the Abrahamic covenant for blessing and the exclusion of all who do not submit to and love the God of Abraham.

Sixth, in the *continuity* of God's covenantal and promissory relationship. The promises of the Abrahamic covenant reveal a continuity and growth in the progression of the history of redemption. It becomes apparent that the God of Abraham is the Creator-King who planned to renew his grace to the nations in and through Abraham. To this end he begins with the family as the smallest unit and plans through the believing family to prepare a new and loyal humanity for himself. In the coming of his Son, he confirms this commitment to blessing (a new earth, a holy people composed of Jews and Gentiles) and to judgment.

Finally, in the life of *faith*. The way of blessing requires radical discipleship and a forswearing of the ways and systems of this world. Individuals of faith are free, because of God who sets them free from the restrictions of creation in anguish and who promises to set his children completely free by the promise of his presence!

Part 4

A Holy Nation

Introduction to Part 4

The Old Testament devotes great attention to the fulfillment of God's promises in the history of Israel. The five great books, Exodus through Joshua, interpret the redemptive-historical developments in the various stages of the Exodus and the Conquest: Israel's formative period. To understand the nature of the Old Testament revelation, the law, the fulfillment of God's promises, the covenantal status, and especially the ministry of our Lord and the apostles, we must pay careful attention to Exodus, Leviticus, Numbers, Deuteronomy, and Joshua. These biblical books portray God faithfully fulfilling the patriarchal promises and confirming the Abrahamic covenant to Israel as a nation.

Central to these books are Moses and Joshua. Moses received the original commission to lead the people out of the land of Egypt into the Promised Land, and Joshua, the mantle bearer of Moses, received the privilege of fulfilling this mission. Through these giants in the history of redemption, the Lord began to fulfill his promises as he brought the nation of Israel as his people into Canaan.

Moses is uniquely the "servant" of God, by whom he constituted Israel as his people. Abraham, to be sure, is the "father" of the faithful, but through Moses the Lord mediated his covenant and his law. God's revelation through Moses was not inferior to that given to the patriarchs; in fact, it was deeper, more extensive, and more frequent. Through Moses, God revealed more clearly his divine nature as a caring Father for his people, as the King over Israel, and as the Ruler over the nations. Through Moses he revealed his glorious and holy presence.

This period also witnesses the establishment of the Mosaic covenant. *The Mosaic covenant is the administration of grace and promise by which the Lord consecrates a people to himself by the sanctions of law.* During this stage God deals with his people as children, binding them together by the sanctions of his law and leading them into the maturity of faith.

Characteristic of the Mosaic era is the mediatorial nature of God's communion with his people. He was present with them in the tabernacle, in their encampment, and in the theocratic offices. But he mediated his grace through Moses, the priests, and leaders of his people. Through his laws and regulations, the Lord taught Israel the seriousness of sin and the appropriate response to his holy presence in their midst. The sacrificial system, the regulations of holiness and purity, and the tabernacle served as tokens of his presence and of Israel's consecration as the people of God. Israel knew herself to be saved by grace and in need of God's mercy and forgiveness through his appointed institutions and ministers. In order to assure that Israel would live in accordance with his expectations, the Lord established covenant (or theocratic) officers—priests, Levites, prophets, kings, judges, and elders.

Though the Mosaic administration is an era characterized by law, institutions, and symbolism, we must emphasize the reality of God's presence and his gospel (grace) during this period. Surely this era marks a significant stage in the fulfillment of his promises! The period of Israel the as holy nation under Moses and Joshua presents us with:

1. a fuller revelation of God as Yahweh, King, and Divine Warrior;

2. the place of Moses as the servant of God and as the mediator of the Mosaic covenant;

3. the consecration of Israel as the royal priesthood and the holy nation;

4. the establishment of God's kingship in Israel;

5. the grace and patience of God in response to Israel's unbelief;

6. the gracious fulfillment of the promises and confirmation of the covenant with Israel; and

7. the eschatological hope of greater blessings.

This period in redemptive history is continuous with the past. The Lord continued to require that individual Israelites come to him in faith. He expected maturity from them, even as Abraham had demonstrated a walk of integrity (Gen. 17:1; 26:5). He freely and sovereignly loved them. During this period in particular, he showed the depth of his love in great signs and wonders, in the Exodus, in his care for Israel in the wilderness, and in their marvelous entry into the Promised Land.

Israel's response, however, was immature. When they were about to enter into Canaan, God expressed his disappointment with them: "Oh, that their hearts would be inclined to fear me and keep all my commands always, so that it might go well with them and their children forever!" (Deut. 5:29). Moses also pleaded with the people in his final speeches, contained in the Book of Deuteronomy, to have heart, both to listen to God and to love him: "Love the LORD your God with all your heart and with all your soul and with all your strength" (6:5).

If we are to understand Paul's positive summary of the Mosaic covenant, the glory, and God's fatherhood (see Rom. 9:4), we must reevaluate the books of Exodus through Joshua. If we are to understand the nature and necessity of the Atonement, the attributes of the Father (which Jesus confirms in his teaching), and the nature and privileges of the people of God, we must begin here. In other words, it is impossible to understand the gospel unless we understand the law.

CHAPTER 10

The Literary Record
of Promise and Fulfillment

EXODUS

The literary structure of Exodus is not as transparent as that of Genesis. The book lacks a literary key, overarching motifs, and clear transitions between the narrative and legal materials. Most critical scholars look on Exodus as a work that grew out of various traditions, reflections, and elaborations over long periods of time, culminating in a mass of contradictions and problems.

The interweaving of different motifs contributes to a complex, but grand, design. The narrative sections are set in a chronological framework, but the relationship between them is not always clear. Moreover, the narratives are interrupted by blocks of legal material (Exod. 21–23; 25–31; 35:1–3). The book gives the impression of movement, but the narratives collectively have little structural unity, and the book has no comprehensive literary framework. The individual sections, however, contribute to the literary development of Exodus. Even with its literary variety, the book presents a sense of harmony that creates a total impact "far more than the sum of its parts."[1] In spite of this variety in literary units and material, the book evidences symmetry. At its center (C, C') is Israel's consecration as a covenant people (19:1–24:18) and the revelation of God's glorious and holy presence in the midst of Israel (chaps. 25–31). (See figure 10.)

A. Royal power (chaps. 1–13)
   B. Royal provisions and Israel's complacency (14–18)
      C. Covenant; consecration of Israel as God's own (19–24)
      C'. Plans for tabernacle (25–31)
   B'. Israel's idolatry, forgiveness, covenant renewal, and royal presence (32–34)
A'. Royal glory (35–40)

Figure 10. The Presence of God in Exodus

At Mount Sinai (C, C'), Israel reacted with terror to God's revelation

135

and demanded that Moses be their mediator (Exod. 20:18–20; Deut. 5:4–5). Moses served in this capacity by giving Israel the law of God (Exod. 20:22–23:19); the promises of God's presence, protection, and fidelity (23:20–33); the confirmation of the Sinaitic covenant (chap. 24); the revelation concerning the tabernacle worship (chaps. 25–27; 31:1–11); the Aaronic priesthood (chaps. 28–30); the Sabbath as the sign of the Mosaic covenant (31:12–17); and the tablets of the Testimony (31:18). Moses' mediatory ministry was publicly recognized: the Lord, who had previously shown his glory in the wilderness (16:10), now revealed his glory as Moses ascended the mountain (24:15–18), and especially after Israel's apostasy with the golden calf. The narrative of the calf brings out most pointedly the importance of a mediator, who intercedes three times (32:11–14, 30–35; 34:8–10) on behalf of the people, who by now have shown their true character (see 34:9).

The acceptance of Moses in his mediatorial office is confirmed by God's response to Moses' request to see his glory (33:17–18). Moses not only sees the glory of God but also receives on behalf of Israel the magnificent revelation of Yahweh's covenant fidelity (34:6–7) and a second set of tablets (vv. 27–28). All Israel now knows that they have a true mediator who is not only the giver of the laws but also an intercessor for the people. His divine appointment radiated in his face (vv. 29–35; see also 2 Cor. 3:13–16)!

The first and last blocks of material (A, A') display the fidelity of God and the infidelity of Israel. In the first section (chaps. 1–13), the Lord is faithful to his people in multiplying them (1:7, 12, 20), in raising up Moses (chap. 2), in hearing their groans (2:23–25; cf. 1:8–22), in promising to be with them (3:7–17; 6:1–8), in showing his glorious power in the ten plagues in Egypt, in protecting his people in Egypt (chaps. 8–12), in redeeming them from Egypt (12:31–13:16), and in giving a visible token of his presence in the glory-cloud (13:20–22).

The last block (chaps. 35–40) reveals that God is faithful in spite of Israel's repeated acts of rebellion, evidenced so soon after the covenant agreement (chap. 24) in the idolatry of the golden calf (chap. 32). The Lord demonstrates that his holy and glorious presence will dwell among a sinful people. Moses prays that the Lord's presence will not depart from Israel, even though it is "a stiff-necked people" (34:9). The Lord answers that prayer in a wonderful demonstration of his presence when the tabernacle is completed. He fills it with his glory (40:35) and remains with Israel in its journeys (vv. 36–38; see also Num. 9:15–23; 10:34–36). In contrast with the beginning of Exodus (chaps. 1–13), the Lord is more vividly present: in his great grace, love, and loyalty, he actually dwells among his people!

The literary structure of Exodus also impresses on the reader the necessity of divine revelation. Israel's nature was not different from that of the nations. If Pharaoh, representative of the nations at large, is hard-hearted, so is Israel. The central section of Exodus (B, B') places at Mount Sinai the theophany of the Lord's holiness (19:23) and glory (24:17), the revelation of the Decalogue (20:1–17) and the moral, civil, and ceremonial laws (21:1–23:19; 25:1–31:17), and the promises of his presence (23:20–33) in between the narratives of Israel's murmuring and hardness. By itself Israel could not and would not have developed into a God-fearing nation.[2] The literary structure also brings out the grace and patience of Yahweh. He desired to have a holy nation, a royal priesthood, by which to establish his kingdom on earth (19:4–6). Instead, he condescends to Israel's request to glorify Moses as his servant, by whom he mediated his royal law. In the present literary ordering, the instructions pertaining to the construction of the tabernacle of his presence and the priesthood are before the narrative of Israel's sin of the golden calf. After having forgiven his people, Yahweh does not alter his plans. The detailed description of the construction of the tabernacle (chaps. 35–40), which follows Israel's apostasy, is clear evidence of the grace and the patience of the Lord. He knows the frailty of his people and still plans to dwell in their midst.

In conclusion, the present structure assures Israel of God's continued presence before and after the rebellion at Mount Sinai (23:20–23; 33:12–16). The glory-cloud filling the tabernacle was proof positive that the covenant with Israel was confirmed, even though the people were known to be sinful and rebellious by nature. Yahweh's love, forgiveness, and patience triumphed over their sin and need of restoration.

LEVITICUS

The laws of Leviticus are framed by an introductory and concluding reference to Moses, the mediator of the covenant (1:1; 27:34). The literary framework and the formulas connecting the priestly laws and regulations establish Moses' authority as mediator of the priestly, cultic, and sacrificial systems. The various literary divisions of Leviticus are all related to Moses.

But why should Israel listen to Moses? First, Moses is the divinely appointed servant of God by whom he revealed his will for his covenant people. Second, through Moses God gave the regulations pertaining to holiness, not only to remind Israel of Yahweh's holiness, but to sensitize Israel to become a holy community. The offerings and sacrifices (chaps. 1–7), the institution of the priesthood and the inauguration of the sanctuary (chaps. 8–10), the laws of impurities (chaps. 11–16), and the laws of holiness (chaps. 17–26) advanced the awareness of God's holiness and called for Israel's appropriate response. "I am the LORD who brought you up out of Egypt to be your God; therefore be holy, because I am holy" (11:45).

Particularly in the laws of holiness, God reminds them of their redemption from Egypt (22:32–33), their election out of the nations (20:26), and their consecration by covenant (20:7–8, esp. the priests [21:8, 15, 23; 22:9, 16]). In fact, the phrase "I am the LORD," repeated in the laws of holiness (e.g., 18:5–6, 21), is an abbreviation of his covenantal relationship ("I am Yahweh your God"; e.g., 19:2–4, 10) and of his holy presence among them ("I, Yahweh, am holy"; e.g., 19:2; 20:26). The commandment to be a holy people is rooted in the covenant relationship, in which Israel was consecrated by grace to the Lord: "Consecrate yourselves and be holy, because I am the LORD your God. Keep my decrees and follow them. I am the LORD, who makes you holy" (20:7–8).

The effect of the literary structuring is to show that the holiness of God extends beyond the cult to the community and even to the individual. The combination of the sacrificial laws, the laws of impurities, and the laws of private, public, and priestly holiness have the overall effect of integrating holiness and purity. Though God dwells in his holy tabernacle, he requires his people in their cultic acts and rituals, in their communal life, and in their private lives to be a holy and pure people. The laws of impurities and of holiness remind the people constantly of the divinely established distinctions. Israel had to learn to respond to their covenant God in all areas of life: cultic, dietary, personal relations, and work.[3] The regulations are God's laws, mediated by Moses, to be obeyed! The Lord treats Israel as his holy nation, who, like the priests of Aaron's descent, must learn to live in accordance with the divine will. Therefore, any attempt to find an ethical, cultural, sociological, or medical justification for these laws is contrary to their primary purpose.

NUMBERS

The Book of Numbers represents a multifaceted collage witnessing God's concern for a clean and holy people. It includes descriptions of the encampment (chaps. 1–4); the offerings and sacrifices (chaps. 7, 15, 28); feasts and festivals (9:1–14; chaps. 28–29); priestly portions (chap. 18); relations of priests, Levites, and people (9:1–14; chaps. 17–18); and regulations of purity (chaps. 5–6, 19). God's concern for holiness is evidenced by his judgment and expressions of wrath on the person who does not celebrate the Passover (9:13); on the complaining community (11:1–3, 33–34; 21:4–9); on Miriam (12:10–15); on Israel's rebellion (chap. 14); on the Sabbath breaker (15:32–36); on the rebellion of Korah, Dathan, and Abiram (chap. 16); and the idolatry at Baal Peor (chap. 25). God must be treated as *holy* in the midst of his holy nation. Whoever desecrates or offends his holiness will not escape his wrath. Even Moses and Aaron were judged for not regarding his holiness: "The LORD said to Moses and Aaron, 'Because you did not trust in me enough to honor me as holy in the sight of the Israelites, you will not bring this community into the land I give them'" (20:12).

The framework of the first and second census (chaps. 1 and 26) confirms Yahweh's goodness.[4] In spite of Israel's history of rebellion at all levels, Yahweh is constant in his promise. At Sinai Israel counted 603,550 men who were at least twenty years old (1:46). Though the adult generation that had left Egypt had died in the wilderness, Israel still numbered 601,730 at the end of the forty years (26:51). By means of interweaving the narratives of Israel's rebelliousness with records of the Lord's cultic regulations (holiness and purity, Levites and priests, offerings and sacrifices, holy days, and vows; see 3:1–9; chaps. 15; 18–19; 28–30), with the framework of Israel's encampment around the tabernacle (chap. 2) and her tribal allotment in the land (chaps. 27; 32; 33:50–56; chaps. 34–36), and with Israel's movement from Mount Sinai to the plains of Moab (10:11–14:45; 20:14–21:35; 33:1–49), the author demonstrates the grace, forbearance, and fidelity of God. Though the people rebel, their God remains faithful. The book has a significant theological function as it lifts up Yahweh's grace and constancy in keeping covenant. This quality is most evident in his sovereignty over Balaam, the Aramean soothsayer. The Lord changed Balaam's curse into a blessing, and thereby he confirmed each of the promises made to Abraham (chaps. 23–24).

By the institution of the tabernacle, by his own presence, and by the offerings and sacrifices, regulations about holiness, purity, feasts, and festivals, the Lord assured Israel that restoration was always close at hand.[5] Even the borders of the land, the Levitical cities and the cities of refuge, and the regulations of inheritance (chaps. 34–36) express God's concern for holiness and purity in the land. As the encampment of the tribes around the tabernacle was determined by God's decree (chaps. 2–3), so also does the Lord determine specifically the inheritance of the tribes. The cities of refuge protect those who shed blood innocently. They preserve justice on the grounds that God requires Israel to keep the land clean and that he will continue to dwell in their midst, even as he did in the wilderness encampment.

> Do not pollute the land where you are. Bloodshed pollutes the land, and atonement cannot be made for the land on which blood has been shed, except by the blood of the one who shed it. Do not defile the land where you live and where I dwell, for I, the LORD, dwell among the Israelites. (35:33–34)

139

DEUTERONOMY

The fifth book of the Pentateuch also has a narrative framework that is of secondary significance to the single focus of the book.[6] In its present form Deuteronomy is not primarily a programmatic interpretation of the history of Israel, a code of law, an ideal projection, or even a covenant affirmation. A holistic reading of Deuteronomy presents us with a series of speeches in which Moses presents Israel about to enter the Promised Land with *the continuity of covenant and promises*, graciously extended by the Lord to the new generation, and urges them to respond to Yahweh in faith and obedience for the sake of the future generations.[7] The five major divisions of Deuteronomy support this perspective.

In chapters 1–4, Israel's past is reviewed in order to *motivate the new generation to hold fast to the Lord* so that they may enter the land and enjoy the promised blessings (4:4–8). The generation that came out of Egypt perished because of rebellion and disobedience (1:34–35; 2:14–15). As the new generation is about to enter the land, Moses expounds to them what it means to be a covenant people (1:5ff.). The Sinai revelation and covenant were unaffected by Israel's disobedience. The Lord has been faithful, so he expects loyalty from his people, lest they perish from the land (4:25–28). Yet, even in Israel's apostasy and judgment, there is hope, if Israel returns to him with all of their heart and soul (v. 29), because the God of the covenant is forgiving in nature: "The LORD your God is a merciful God; he will not abandon or destroy you or forget the covenant with your forefathers, which he confirmed to them by oath" (v. 31).

Chapters 5–11 *extend the covenant obligations to the new generation* by repeating the Decalogue (5:6–21), strongly requiring loyalty (6:4–5), and pleading for the internalization of the law (v. 6). They also exhort Israel to teach its children (vv. 6–9). Each generation must receive for itself the revelation of God, given at Mount Sinai, incorporated in the covenant, and mediated by Moses (5:22–33). The continuity of the covenant involves God's ongoing expectation of a heart commitment in those who keep his commandments: "Oh, that their hearts would be inclined to fear me and keep all my commands always, so that it might go well with them and their children forever!" (v. 29).

Chapters 12–26 give a complex, though unsystematic, *presentation of the laws to a new generation* that is about to enter the land. Any variation here from the laws of Exodus, Leviticus, and Numbers must be interpreted as an updating. Moses applies the law of God to the new situation, as Israel moves out of its encampment structure (cf. Num. 2–3) and into its tribal territories in the land. This land is God's gift (Deut. 11:11–12) and trust for an obedient, loving people (vv. 13–15), the recipients of God's blessings (vv. 22–32). The new situation envisions a centralized place of worship, in continuity with the central position of the tabernacle (chap. 12), the institution of kingship (17:14–20), and the continuity of a prophetic ministry like that of Moses (18:14–22). This section concludes with an affirmation of Israel's covenant position in continuity with the past generation:

> The LORD your God commands you this day to follow these decrees and laws; carefully observe them with all your heart and with all your soul. You have declared this day that the LORD is your God and that you will walk in his ways, that you will keep his decrees, commands and laws, and that you will obey him. And the LORD has declared this day that you are his people, his treasured possession as he promised, and that you are to keep all his commands. He has declared that he will set you in praise, fame and honor high above all the nations he has made and that you will be a people holy to the LORD your God, as he promised. (26:16–19)

The next section, chapters 27–30, *calls for a response to the lessons from history, to the covenant, and to the revelation of God*, as given in chapters 1–26. The new generation must now respond to God's covenant expectations and to the evidences of his grace. Moses envisions the renewal of the covenant at Mount Ebal (27:1–8), when Israel will be reminded of the curses and the blessings of covenant disobedience and loyalty (27:9–28:68). Then he calls for an immediate response, on the basis of their sharing in the fulfillment of the Abrahamic covenant (29:13) as well as in God's mighty acts of redemption from Egypt, in the wilderness, and in the first stage of the conquest of Transjordan (vv. 2–8). The penalty for following in the footsteps of their fathers will be to experience God's "furious anger" and "great wrath" (v. 28). In the covenant relationship the Lord offers life to those who are obedient and "death," or expulsion from the covenant fellowship, to those who reject it (30:11–20). Each generation is responsible for the generations to come:

> This day I call heaven and earth as witnesses against you that I have set before you life and death, blessings and curses. Now choose life, so that you and your children may live and that you may love the LORD your God, listen to his voice, and hold fast to him. For the LORD is your life, and he will give you many years in the land he swore to give to your fathers, Abraham, Isaac and Jacob. (30:19–20; see also 29:19–20)

Finally, chapters 31–34 *project the new situation of Israel.* Moses' successor, Joshua, is publicly recognized as God's servant, by whom Moses' ministry will be continued (31:1–8, 23). Moses instructs the Levites to read the law in the form of Deuteronomy regularly every

141

seven years during the Feast of Tabernacles (vv. 9–13) and to keep it by the ark (v. 26). The Book of Deuteronomy is the record of covenant renewal with the new generation (v. 9; cf. 29:1). Moses further solemnly instructs each successive generation to renew its covenant loyalty and to separate itself from the "rebellious and stiff-necked" spirit of human autonomy (31:27). The Song of Moses functions as a perpetual warning against covenant disloyalty and as an encouragement to be loyal to the God who is always faithful to his covenant (chap. 32). God's purpose for Israel will be accomplished, when the nations rejoice with his people (v. 43). Through Moses' blessing on the tribes, God assures all Israel that he loves them, rules over them, blesses them, and has constituted them as his special people:

> Blessed are you, O Israel!
> Who is like you,
> a people saved by the Lord?
> He is your shield and helper
> and your glorious sword.
> Your enemies will cower before you,
> and you will trample down their high places.
>
> (33:29)

Just as the Lord has been faithful to his people through his servant Moses (34:10–12), he will continue to be with them in Joshua (v. 9).

JOSHUA

Joshua is intimately connected with Deuteronomy by what is called the deuteronomistic perspective.[8] The literary connection between Deuteronomy and Joshua is clear with regard to the continuity of leadership, covenant, God's presence, the covenant community, the covenantal sanctions (obedience and disobedience; blessings and curses), and the fulfillment of the promises. The Book of Joshua pulls together the various motifs of Deuteronomy and brings into reality the promises and hope of the Pentateuch. The stage of the Conquest under Joshua functions as a closure of the Mosaic era and the generation after Joshua. The interweaving of motifs, narratives, and details on the division of the tribal territories illustrates the literary connection between Deuteronomy and Joshua. The discontinuities arising from the new situation (Joshua's leadership, presence in the land, no new revelation added to the law of Moses) are overshadowed by the continuities (God's presence, fulfillment of his Word, the law of Moses, covenant blessing, and loyalty). The book contains five major divisions, framed between the era of Moses and that after Joshua. (See figure 11.)

The Book of Joshua describes a *continuity of leadership*. Toward the end of Deuteronomy Moses prepares Israel for the new situation, including the transfer of leadership from himself to Joshua. Joshua is charged with the military leadership as the instrument of fulfilling the promise pertaining to the land (Deut. 31:7–8). Joshua receives the assurance of the Lord's presence (v. 23) on the condition of Israel's obedience to the written law (vv. 19–22, 24–29; 32:46–47). Joshua also receives the spirit of Moses, which was "the spirit of wisdom," by the laying on of hands in the presence of all Israel (34:9; cf. Num. 27:18–23). The Book of Joshua projects Joshua as the leader appointed by the Lord who continues to lead Israel in the spirit of Moses and with the presence of the Lord (see Josh. 1:1–9). Like Moses, he leads Israel through a body of water (chaps. 3–4; cf. Exod. 14–15), leads Israel in a celebration of the Passover (Josh. 5:10–12; cf. Exod. 12:1–28), calls on Israel to renew the covenant at Mount Ebal (Josh. 8:30–35; cf. Deut. 27–28), shows authority over the priests and Levites (Josh. 4:10, 17; cf. Deut. 31:9–13, 25–29), makes intercession on behalf of Israel (Josh. 7:6–9; cf. Deut. 9:25–29), consecrates them (Josh. 3:5; 7:13; cf. Exod. 19:10), calls Israel to covenantal loyalty (Josh. 23:1–24:27; cf. Deut. 29–30), and leaves "witnesses" as reminders of God's mighty acts and of Israel's external commitment (Josh. 4:19–24; 24:26–27; cf. Deut. 31:19–32:47). He too was exalted in the eyes of Israel: "That day the LORD exalted Joshua in the sight of all Israel; and they revered him all the days of his life, just as they had revered Moses" (Josh. 4:14; cf. Deut. 34:9).

Mosaic era (1:1)
    Joshua's commission (Josh. 1:2–9)
        Joshua's leadership (1:10–5:12)
        The conquest (5:13–12:24)
        Division of the land (chaps. 13–22)
    Joshua's last words to Israel (23:1–24:28)
New era (24:29–33)

Figure 11. The Literary Structure of Joshua

Blessings and curses, associated with obedience and disobedience, are operative in the period of the Conquest. The Lord leads Israel into victory and promises to continue his victorious presence and protection if Israel proves itself loyal (Josh. 10:14; 23:10–11; cf. Deut. 3:22; 12:29). On the other hand, their defeat at Ai, because of Achan's sin, demonstrates how the sin of an individual may bring God's curses on Israel as a whole (Josh. 7; cf. Deut. 28:25). Joshua challenges Israel to remain loyal so that they may continue to enjoy God's blessings (Josh.

23:6–7; 24:14). This appeal is based not only on God's mighty acts shown to the previous generation (e.g., in the Exodus) but also on the faithfulness of God to Joshua's generation. He has fulfilled his promise of the land, given to Abraham and renewed through Moses to Israel (23:14). But God is sovereign in his gifts, and he may sever the relation of the land and people, when they sin against him:

> But just as every good promise of the LORD your God has come true, so the LORD will bring on you all the evil he has threatened, until he has destroyed you from this good land he has given you. If you violate the covenant of the LORD your God . . . the LORD's anger will burn against you, and you will quickly perish from the good land he has given you. (23:15–16)

The fulfillment of the land promise, like the evidences of love in the Exodus and the wilderness, *is not conditioned on Israel's response* (Josh. 21:43–45; cf. Deut. 7:7–9; 32:1–14). On the other hand, the fulfillment of the land promise *is conditioned on covenant loyalty*. The tension of grace and reward goes back to Deuteronomy and is best reflected in the literary structuring of Joshua. The first twelve chapters portray a quick mobilization of Israel's forces against the Canaanites and a full Israelite victory, as we read in this summary statement: "So Joshua took the entire land, just as the LORD had directed Moses, and he gave it as an inheritance to Israel according to their tribal divisions. Then the land had rest from war" (Josh. 11:23).

The next section (chaps. 13–24) generally assumes that there is still land to be conquered (13:2–7; 18:2; 23:4), although some passages assume a total conquest (21:43–45). Apparently the emphasis is on continuity between Moses and Joshua and the miraculous nature of the Conquest. In its excitement over the fulfillment of God's promises, the account is reminiscent of God's goodness in Egypt and the wilderness. The land is divided in accordance with the ideal lines, without considering how the ideal was generally not yet reality. The realization is dependent on a continuation of the Conquest (17:18) and on loyalty to the Lord, the giver of the land (23:4).

The Book of Joshua thus moves us beyond an idealized reality to the hope of a full and final fulfillment. The realization of the promises is one of a progressive fulfillment of God's Word. As long as the leaders of the Conquest were still alive, Israel remained faithful (24:31). With the burial of Joshua and Eleazar, the high priest, a new era dawned on Israel.

CONCLUSION

The books Exodus through Joshua give perspectives on God's determination in fulfilling the covenant with the patriarchs, on the acts and perfections of Yahweh, on the important moments in Israel's early history (Exodus, the law given at Sinai, Conquest), on Israel's failure to respond to Yahweh's grace in faith, and on the glory granted to Israel as the people of God. The Lord dealt patiently with Israel as he educated them in the school of faith, obedience, holiness, and purity. If the people responded in faith and absolute loyalty, his blessings, to which both Moses and Joshua witnessed, would be unleashed on them. If instead they rebelled, his curse and judgment would overtake them.

CHAPTER 11

The Revelation of Yahweh
and the Consecration of Israel

The story of Israel's redemption from Egypt, of God's revelation, of his guidance, and of the conquest of Canaan shaped Israel's corporate solidarity as the people of God. Individual Israelites were to ground themselves through the canonical writings in the roots of the people as a whole; namely, God's grace, promises, revelation, covenant, and expectations. Biblical revelation in the books of Exodus through Joshua was recorded to teach, exhort, and proclaim. In this chapter I follow the canonical approach as a road into the diverse materials in these books. On this road of investigation we shall consider the emphases on the nature of Israel, the nature of God and the revelation to Moses, the presence of God and the Mosaic covenant, and the matter of personal commitment.

THE NATURE OF ISRAEL

The canonical books of Exodus through Joshua functioned as God's witness to each generation in ancient Israel that they received gratuitously the privileges of being heirs of the covenants, the promises, and the blessed presence of God. These blessings were not obtained by birthright, nor were they denied because of Israel's rebellious ancestors (Deut. 7:7–9; 9:5–6). The promises were theirs because of the covenant Yahweh had made with Abraham, because of his loving patience, and because of his readiness to be reconciled with them. But even when they enjoyed prosperity, the promises and covenant blessings were not automatically theirs by virtue of their descent from Abraham. The Lord required faith, repentance, reconciliation, and devotion to himself. Israel was both privileged and accountable; it was undeserving and received grace upon grace. The canonical portrayal of Israel is filled with tensions.

Israel as God's Son

The canonical portrayal of God's love for Israel is that of a father's care for his son.[1] He exalts them before the Egyptians as his "firstborn

146

son" (Exod. 4:22). He carries them out of Egypt "on eagles' wings" and brings them to himself (19:4). Like a caring parent, he meets their needs (Deut. 32:10–14) yet teaches them by his fatherly discipline (8:1–5). To this end, he tested them by sending adversities in the wilderness, which was to lead Israel to a mature relationship with him. But Israel could relate to him only as a young child (cf. Gal. 4:1–3). This fact explains why Israel, delivered out of Egypt with a demonstration of God's royal, glorious power and adopted as sons (see Deut. 26:18; Rom. 9:4), often expresses preference for the material cultural advantages of Egypt over the lessons in God's school of spiritual maturity.

Israel as the People of God

In fulfillment of God's Word to the patriarchs, Israel became the people of God (Gen. 17:7; Exod. 6:7–8; Deut. 26:18). God called Israel to serve him (Exod. 4:22–23), but the people preferred to serve the Egyptians (14:12). They had seen how the Lord judged the hardened heart of Pharaoh, but they did not seek to have a heart that loved God and kept his commandments or that understood what he had been doing in their midst (Deut. 5:29; 29:3–4).

As the people of God, they were to reflect their separation as God's nation from among the other nations (Deut. 26:18–19) by observing his regulations pertaining to holy living, by reflecting their knowledge of God, and by establishing his rule on earth. The new generation that entered into the Promised Land knew that their position as the people of God was not due to the loyalty of the generation that perished in the wilderness. Rather, the benefits of God's revelation, the covenant, and his love were theirs on account of God's fidelity to the patriarchs (7:7–9). The promises of God will always be applicable to all who renew their allegiance to their God: "The LORD your God will circumcise your hearts and the hearts of your descendants, so that you may love him with all your heart and with all your soul, and live" (30:6).

Israel as a Holy and Glorious Nation

The Lord promised Israel that they would be his people in fulfillment of his word of promise to the patriarchs. As the people of God, they were to be set apart to the Lord. The act of setting Israel apart (i.e., of consecration) was singularly important. It meant that the holy God of Israel had separated this nation apart for himself from all the nations of the world (Exod. 19:5). The consecrated nation has no king other than the Lord, and the Lord has no people other than Israel (see Deut. 26:17–18). Israel has become the "treasured possession" (*segullâ*; Exod. 19:5) of the great King. The Hebrew word *segullâ* is derived from the Akkadian *sikiltū*, a word that signifies a personal possession, one set apart for one's personal use. From the use of *segullâ* in the Old

Testament, we see that Israel is the object of God's love and devotion, his election, his expectation of covenant fidelity (obedience), and the promise of great rewards and honor associated with their privileged position (Exod. 19:5; Deut. 7:6; 14:2; 26:18; Ps. 135:4; Mal. 3:17). The significance of *sᵉgullâ* is further described in two parallel phrases: "a kingdom of priests" and "a holy nation" (Exod. 19:6). The words "kingdom" and "nation" are parallel, as are "priests" and "holy." The Lord thus promises to take Israel as his consecrated nation, set apart to himself and privileged to serve the great King as a visible manifestation of God's kingdom on earth.[2]

Israel, the Praise of the Nations

The adoption of Israel as his son, his people, his holy nation, and his royal dominion was for the purpose of exalting God's name among the nations. He desired to establish one faithful, responsive, and loving people on earth to do his will, as the angels obey his wishes in heaven. The Lord promised them blessings, conditioned on their observance of his law, but they could never claim to be heirs of the promises as a reward for their righteousness (Deut. 9:5).

The close identification of Yahweh with his people struck terror into the nations (Exod. 15:13–16) and made them jealous (Deut. 4:6–8). The covenant nation was destined to be God's "praise, fame and honor high above all the nations" (26:19). As his people they were to rule over the nations: "The LORD will make you the head, not the tail. If you pay attention to the commands of the LORD your God that I give you this day and carefully follow them, you will always be at the top, never at the bottom"(28:13).

THE NATURE OF GOD AND THE REVELATION TO MOSES

During the patriarchal period the Lord revealed himself directly to the patriarchs. He made and confirmed covenant promises to Abraham. While the personal relationship between the Lord and the patriarchs was very close, he was known to them chiefly as El or El Shaddai. "I appeared to Abraham, to Isaac and to Jacob as God Almighty [*El Shaddai*], but by my name the LORD [*Yahweh*] I did not make myself known to them" (Exod. 6:3). To the patriarchs God was known as the Creator-God (Gen. 14:22), the Protector (15:1), the God of Bethel (31:13), the Fear of Isaac (31:53), and the Mighty One of Jacob (49:24). He is *El* ("God"), the source of promise. In the period of Moses and Joshua, God reveals himself more fully in his name, mighty acts, and personal attributes.

The Covenant Name Yahweh

God revealed his name to Moses. The significance of the name Yahweh is found in the context of Israel's redemption from Egypt.[3] When the Lord called Moses to be his prophet to Israel (Exod. 3:10–12), he assured him of his divine *presence*, with the sign of the burning bush, and of his *purpose* of using Moses to bring Israel out of Egypt to meet with God at Mount Sinai before leading them into the Promised Land.

I Am Who I Am: Yahweh

When Moses asked God to confirm his mission to Israel by giving his name, the Lord answered, "I AM WHO I AM" (*'ehyeh 'ašer 'ehyeh* [Exod. 3:13–14]). We may make several observations about this name. Note first that this phrase should not be understood primarily in an abstract, philosophical sense (meaning something like "being" or "self-existent one"). Second, the Hebrew phrase "I am who I am" contains a repetition of two verbs *(hyh)*, to which the divine name Yahweh *(hyh hwh)* is cognate. Third, there is a certain ambiguity in God's answer. His name is clearly given, but the meaning of his name is ambiguous. Fourth, some meaning may be deduced from the context. Yahweh is a God who is (*'ehyeh)* with his people, as he promised to be with Moses (Exod. 3:12).[4] Furthermore, the play on the verb *hyh* identifies Yahweh with the God who is the God of the fathers (v. 15). The use of the imperfect rather than the perfect presents God as the God of past, present, and future, signifying, "I shall be who I shall be." He is the God of the patriarchs, of Israel—the God on whom they may rely forevermore. He loves the descendants of Jacob, caring for them and protecting them in order to fulfill his promises to the patriarchs (Exod. 6:6–8; cf. 2:24–25).[5] The Lord's name is the concrete confirmation, the ironclad proof, that God will fulfill his promises. In his self-revelation he declares to Moses, "I am who I am" as a strong affirmation that he is wholly involved in the redemption of his people. He exists *for* his people!

The self-revelation "I am who I am" also guarantees God's *freedom* in his involvement. The seeming tautology "I am who I am" may also be translated, "I shall be *whoever* I shall be."[6] Yahweh conceals the manner of how and when he will fulfill his promises to his people. In other words, Yahweh declares that he is free in the progression of fulfillment of his promises. Time and space cannot bind him! His people cannot restrict him. Further, no one can predict how or when he will work out the full redemption of his people (cf. Acts 1:7).

I Am Yahweh

Another way in which God identifies himself is by the phrase "I am the LORD" (Exod. 6:2). In the Hebrew text, this phrase consists of only two words, "I Yahweh" (*'anî Yahweh*). The identification "I am Yahweh" is extremely important in the Old Testament: it signifies God's characteristic faithfulness, by which he binds himself to his covenant and to the fulfillment of its promises. The threefold repetition confirms God's promises of (1) the deliverance from Egypt (Exod. 6:6), (2) the consecration as the covenant people (v. 7), and (3) the inheritance of the land (v. 8). The phrase "I am Yahweh" serves as God's signature, certifying that the great King has the power and the fidelity to work out all of his promises. The separate acts of Yahweh in fulfillment of his promises are intended to instill in his people the confidence that he is faithful and able to deliver them.[7] Sacred history—that is, the history of redemption—tells a story so that God's people in all ages may know that he is Yahweh.[8]

"Yahweh" in English

The name Yahweh is usually translated in English versions as LORD and spelled with capital letters, in accordance with the practice of the Septuagint, the translation of the Old Testament into Greek. (In contrast, the word *Adonai*, meaning "master," is spelled "the Lord" in translation.) In the Old Testament, "the LORD" is not a title but a designation of a relationship between God and his people, a name that the covenant people may take on their lips in their prayers, praise, speech, and holy vows. The God of the Old Testament has a name, and his name is Yahweh!

Yahweh is the God of Israel, not only the God of the fathers. He has promised to be with Israel to the thousandth generation. He is their Father by adoption. Each God-fearing Israelite enjoyed the privileges of a father-child relationship. A reader of the English Bible can enter more deeply into the spirit of closeness and personal fellowship that existed between God's ancient covenant people and Yahweh if he or she substitutes the name Yahweh for "the LORD" (when it is capitalized in this way).

God's Mighty Acts

Kingship was demonstrated to Israel in Yahweh's mighty acts and in the revelation of his attributes. The mighty acts themselves are not devoid of revelation. In the light of his self-identification, they also reveal his nature, as may be seen in Psalm 111:

> Great are the works of the LORD;
> they are pondered by all who delight in them.

150

> Glorious and majestic are his deeds,
>   and his righteousness endures forever.
> He has caused his wonders to be remembered;
>   the LORD is gracious and compassionate.
>
> (vv. 2–4)

In a summary of Moses' ministry an anonymous author writes about Moses as God's instrument: he "did all those miraculous signs and wonders. . . . For no one has ever shown the mighty power or performed the awesome deeds that Moses did in the sight of all Israel" (Deut. 34:11–12). The Lord had authorized Moses to perform these wonders (Exod. 4:21), signs (7:3), and judgments (v. 4) that through them the Egyptians would come to know that Yahweh, the God of Israel, is sovereign in his judgments over the Egyptians and gracious in delivering his own people (v. 5). In and through the process of hardening Pharaoh's heart against these demonstrations of Yahweh's royal power (3:19; 4:21; 6:1, 6; 7:3–5), Yahweh planned to demonstrate an even greater power. Not only would he send the ten plagues as wonders and judgments on Egypt, but he delivered Israel with "a mighty hand" (e.g., Exod. 3:19; 6:1) and "an outstretched arm" (e.g., Exod. 6:6; Deut. 5:15).

His mighty acts carried a powerful message to the nations. They too should fear the God of Israel and cooperate with him by giving aid and support to Israel. In a powerful, poetic expression Moses sang the praise of Yahweh's glorious acts as evidences of his love for the redeemed people (Exod. 15:11–13), but inspiring the nations with terror:

> The nations will hear and tremble;
>   anguish will grip the people of Philistia.
> The chiefs of Edom will be terrified,
>   the leaders of Moab will be seized with trembling,
> the people of Canaan will melt away;
>   terror and dread will fall upon them.
> By the power of your arm
>   they will be as still as a stone—
> until your people pass by, O LORD,
>   until the people you bought pass by.
>
> (vv. 14–16)

The acts of God further reveal Yahweh as the *warrior-God*, who is determined to establish his kingdom on earth in Israel. The revelation of the Lord to Israel and the demonstration of his mighty works can best be understood under the comprehensive framework of God's kingdom in Israel. Yahweh took upon himself the responsibility for his people by providing them with his protection and in securing their well-being. His role conformed to that of an ancient Near Eastern king, as Mendenhall concludes,

> Yahweh was the one who exclusively exercised the classic functions of the king, as described in the prologue to the Code of Hammurabi. . . . The administration of law internally, the waging of war, and the economic well-being of the diverse population are here already the three prime functions of the king.[9]

The great King fights for, protects, and defeats the enemies of his people. He established his kingship at the parting of the Red Sea (Exod. 15:18), when he vindicated Israel and avenged them against the Egyptians. Moses recognized this event as nothing less than God's warring on behalf of his people:

> The LORD is a warrior;
>   the LORD is his name.
>   (Exod. 15:3; cf. Rev. 15:3, 4)

Yahweh is the *Divine Warrior* who rules with righteousness and equity, delivering his people from their enemies and avenging the enemies in his wrath.[10] Clearly, the Exodus and Conquest demonstrate the rule of the Creator-Redeemer (Ps. 136). He brought them victoriously out of Egypt, protected them in the wilderness, and assured Israel of his victorious conquest of the Promised Land. He further promised Israel that he would continue to fight for them in the land (Josh. 23:5). Yahweh is committed to reestablish his rule over the earth through Israel and to be their Divine Warrior, their Savior, King, and Vindicator. It is noteworthy that the New Testament affirms the continuity of Jesus' ministry with this Old Testament concept. He is the Divine Warrior who will establish his sovereignty over all creation in his kingdom rule, in the deliverance of the saints, and in vengeance on the enemies of the saints (cf. 2 Thess. 1:7–10; Rev. 19:11–20:6).[11]

God's Attributes

God revealed his attributes to Moses. In the revelation of his glory, the Lord revealed more clearly his nature as a covenant God. In the context of Israel's act of rebellion with the golden calf, the Lord proclaimed the depth of his commitment, love, and forgiveness. He explained the dynamic and lasting significance of his name:

> [Yahweh] passed in front of Moses, proclaiming, "The LORD, the LORD, the compassionate and gracious God, slow to anger, abounding in love and faithfulness, maintaining love to thousands, and forgiving wickedness, rebellion and sin. Yet he does not leave the guilty unpunished; he punishes the children and their children for the sin of the fathers to the third and fourth generation." (Exod. 34:6–7)

God thus revealed not only his law to Moses but also his royal grace and glory!

Along with his name and the mighty acts, God revealed seven attributes of his kingship. We should remember that these attributes cannot be isolated from each other; rather, together they reveal a balanced view of the nature of God. An emphasis on his holiness must be balanced by an awareness of his readiness to forgive sin. It is easy to be overcome by awe of his glory, but one must see that he is also full of compassion and grace. He is jealous, but also full of love and faithfulness. He hates sin, but he is also patient.[12] Israel received the revelation of the attributes in the context of their covenant rebellion. Such is the compassion, grace, love, faithfulness, patience, and forgiveness of God!

Holiness

Yahweh is "holy," that is, "set apart." God's holiness separates him from everything he has created: he is *different from* his creation. But God's holiness also reaches out to his creation, as the Creator will not rest until his creation and especially his people are consecrated (i.e., made holy). At creation he sanctified only the Sabbath day, but at Sinai he sanctified Israel as a holy nation (Exod. 19:6).

"Holiness" is a positive concept: separation *unto* the Lord. The holy and jealous God *chose* to establish his "sanctuary" (*miqdāš,* lit. "holy place") among people. Even though they had sinned against him both before and after the revelation at Mount Sinai, Israel became "God's sanctuary" (Exod. 15:17; Ps. 114:2)! So the Lord begins the restoration of a holy and renewed creation in Israel. He extends to them the invitation to approach his holy presence, to enjoy the holy Sabbath day, and to be his alone (i.e., holy to him). However, the covenant invitation is in the form of a sovereign administration. Israel can never take for granted God's holiness and their consecration. In his holiness Yahweh is free in his love, forgiveness, and judgment (cf. Hos. 11:9). He is God and not human!

Glory

The God of Israel shows his glory by his acts. He displayed his glory by defeating the Egyptians in the Red Sea (Exod 15:1, 11). His glorious presence appeared in a cloud to the Israelites in the wilderness (13:21–22) and was evident when God graciously provided quails and manna for the people (Exod. 16:13), when Moses went up Mount Sinai (Exod. 24:16–18), and when Moses reflected God's radiant glory upon his return (Exod. 34:30–35). Everything associated with the great King reflects his glory.

The wonder lies in Yahweh's condescension to *dwell* in the midst of

Israel, a people who had experienced abandonment in Egypt (Exod. 1) and witnessed the descent of the glory cloud and Yahweh's glorious and royal presence in the Tent of Meeting (Exod. 40:34–35). What a contrast between the beginning and the end of Exodus! More than that. Every *act*—the ten plagues, the Exodus, the passing through the Red Sea, manna, water, victory, the making of the covenant—reveals his glory. Yahweh is Israel's glorious king.[13]

The glory of God is nothing less than the revelation of his hiddenness. This revelation consists of acts, word revelation, and his perfections (cf. Exod. 33:18; 34:6, 7). The godly respond with awe and praise to the revelation of the *hiddenness* of God, thankful for seeing something of his glory and struck with awe by the splendor of his majesty. But the complacent people reduce the mystery of God's glory to common human forms of expression and imagination. They deprive the Lord of the honor due to him (Mal. 1:6; cf. vv. 11, 14).

Compassion

God is filled with *compassion* and *grace*. Although he is full of glory and exalted above his people, he stoops down and shows compassion to the oppressed, poor, and brokenhearted. In his compassion he *freely* redeems them, feeds them, heals them, and exalts them so that they no longer feel shame and deprivation (Ps. 113:5–8). Israel's needs in the wilderness were both physical and spiritual, and the Lord met all of them. He extended grace upon grace, even when they were unresponsive.

Long-suffering

The Lord is also *long-suffering*, infinitely patient with his people. He is like a "father" who understands the weaknesses of his children. He is patient with the spiritual development of his children, and when they wander he is like a father beckoning his wandering children to return home (cf. Luke 15:20; 2 Peter 3:8–9). His patience extends to the godly (cf. Ps. 103:8, 13–16), to future generations (103:8–18), and to all his creation (Ps. 145:8–9; Jonah 4:2, 11).

Love and Faithfulness

The dual qualities of "love" (*ḥesed*) and "faithfulness" (*ʾemet*, Exod. 34:6) affirm his continual care for his people. The Lord expresses his love for Israel by his goodness to them in order that they may confess with the psalmist, "Surely goodness and love will follow me all the days of my life" (Ps. 23:6). The rendering "truth" (KJV, NKJV), instead of "faithfulness," fails to do justice to the unity of the qualities. "Truth" and "love" are two aspects of a *single* attribute. The love (*ḥesed*) of God is faithful (*'emet*, "truth"), i.e., enduring. His fidelity is the ground of the dynamic covenant relationship (cf. Ps. 25:10; 61:7; 86:15; 89:1).

Forgiving

The Lord is not like other rulers in the ancient Near East. They *do not* forgive the rebellious acts of their subjects. Yahweh does forgive a breach in the covenant relationship, even though he is the great King and dwells among his people. Israel experienced real forgiveness as individuals and as a nation (cf. Num. 14:20; Ps. 32; 103). God forgave in anticipation of the death of his Son, typified by the institutions of priesthood and sacrifice. Sin breaches the relationship, but God graciously restores that relationship by initiating the process of reconciliation and forgiveness (Ps. 103:3, 10–12; Mic. 7:18–19). All he requires is a "truly" penitent spirit (Ps. 32:5).

Jealousy

The manifestation of God's jealousy is far removed from any connotation of petty human rivalry. It signifies that Yahweh alone is God, "For the LORD, whose name is Jealous, is a jealous God" (Exod. 34:14). He tolerates no infringement on his royal authority, infraction of the covenant stipulations, detraction from his glory, and dilution of loyalty from his people. God is jealous for his own people, as they are the partakers of a special relationship with him. But if any individual detracts from his being God, he is free to discipline, judge, and remove the offender, because he is "a consuming fire" (Heb. 12:29).

THE PRESENCE OF GOD AND THE MOSAIC COVENANT

The revelation of God on Mount Sinai, as embodied in the Mosaic covenant, is the revelation of *Yahweh*. Even though Moses' name is associated with this covenant, the canonical witness stresses God's involvement, initiation, and condescension to dwell with Israel. Although the people respond out of fear and rebel against the Lord, he persists in revealing his glory and perfections to Israel. He, the great King, is not quickly deterred from his royal plans! The Pentateuchal witness sets forth the greatness of God's patience and love for his covenant people in his dwelling with them, revealing his law, and consecrating all areas of covenant life with his presence—including the feasts and festivals, the offerings and sacrifices, the Sabbath, and also their family life, work, pleasure, covenant villages and cities—both when near the sanctuary and when far away. He richly bestowed grace on Israel and revealed his glory: the presence of his kingship in Israel; the assurance of his nearness in blessing, protection, promise, forgiveness, and adoption; and consecration of the people to himself (see Rom. 9:4–5).

The Presence of God

The glorious truth of God's presence was revealed to Israel, even after they had shown their true nature as a rebellious and sinful people. Israel was like any other nation. Their only distinction was that the Lord had graciously called their ancestor Abraham and had freely promised himself to the descendants of Abraham, Isaac, and Jacob. In the canonical shaping of Exodus, Leviticus, Numbers, Deuteronomy, and Joshua, each generation of Israel is confronted by their unworthiness for having God's presence in their midst. The promise made to Shem of God's presence among the descendants of Shem (Gen. 9:26–27) was fulfilled to Israel, but they did not deserve his presence any more than any other nation.

The Lord first guided Israel "in a pillar of cloud" and "a pillar of fire" (Exod. 13:21) to Mount Sinai. There he revealed his awe-inspiring presence, with the intention of impressing them with his holiness (19:18–19) as he gave them the Ten Commandments. Not until they had ratified the covenant did they receive a glimpse of his glorious presence on top of the mountain (24:17).

The canonical shaping of these books served to remind each generation of Israel that Yahweh was determined to dwell in their midst as an expression of his free grace, even though he well knew their stubborn hearts. To this end the revelation of all the laws in Exodus, Leviticus, and Numbers were recorded in the context of Israel's redemption from Egypt and its migration to the Promised Land. If Israel is to enjoy the continued presence of God, with all its blessings and benefits, they must listen to the words recorded in the covenant and laws of God. (See table 8.)

Covenant, law, and tabernacle worship have significance only when they are related to the central motif of Yahweh's presence in the midst of his people. It is therefore important to see that, in the literary structuring of Exodus, the revelation of covenant, divine presence, and Sabbath are placed in the context of Israel's rebelliousness. The people with whom the Lord makes a covenant, among whom he dwells, and to whom he gives the Sabbath are sinners. By grace the Lord dwelt in the midst of Israel and by grace he sustained Israel with his fellowship. The gospel in Exodus is the affirmation that Yahweh desires to meet and fellowship with his people (Exod. 25:8–9; 29:42–46). The revelation of how to construct the tabernacle and of the Sabbath (chaps. 25–31; 35–40) brackets the revelation of God's forgiveness and renewal of the covenant, necessitated by Israel's idolatry (chaps. 32–34).

The tabernacle, as the central symbol of God's presence, of his revelation, communion, and holiness, witnesses to something of much greater significance. Yahweh, the great King, has established *his kingdom on earth*. The tabernacle could be called the footstool of his kingship on earth, for it reflects the glory and holiness of the Divine Warrior (Num. 10:35–36; Ps. 132:8). More particularly, the ark of the covenant (Num. 10:33) is the unique symbol of his presence, of the covenant, and of his kingship. The cherubim on the ark represent the ministering angels who guard the entrance into the presence of the great King. The Divine Warrior is in the midst of his people to keep them, graciously to provide for them, and to grant them his peace (6:24–26). All who love him need not be afraid, because he intends to bless them and to answer their prayers (see 1 Kings 8:6–11, 23–30). The atonement made on the mercy seat, or "the atonement cover" (Lev. 16:14; Heb. 9:5), on the annual Day of Atonement (Lev. 16) assured the people of God that God the Divine Warrior had forgiven their sins and was ruling over them in deliverance, blessing, and protection. The sign of the covenant benefits was the ark (Exod. 25:22).

TABLE 8. GOD'S FIDELITY TO THE PATRIARCHAL PROMISES

Book	God's Action
Exodus	God redeems Israel from Egypt; he gives the Mosaic covenant and consecrates Israel.
Leviticus	The Lord teaches the people to be holy, separate from the nations.
Numbers	God shows his holiness in his judgment and grace.
Deuteronomy	Despite Israel's record of infidelity, disobedience, and rebellion, God gives a new opportunity for a new generation.
Joshua	God continues his presence with Joshua and brings the people into the Promised Land.

The very presence of God also necessitates regulations. As an earthly king enjoys a protocol, so the Lord revealed the decorum expected of his people in worship and in private and social life. All areas of life, close to the sanctuary or far away from it, are under the scrutiny of his holy eye. This understanding of God explains the extensive regulations of holiness and purity, the rituals of offerings and sacrifices, the regulated life of the priestly and Levitical functionaries, and the ordinances pertaining to Israel's distinctive way of life at every level.

The Mosaic Covenant and Law

God revealed himself, his divine will, and his wonders to Moses in a direct way (Deut. 34:10–12). Moses was greater than any prophet, priest, king, or leader in Israel's history. When Aaron "the priest" and Miriam "the prophetess" challenged Moses' special status, the Lord spoke approvingly of "my servant Moses; he is faithful in all my house. With him I speak face to face" (Num. 12:6–8). The attributes of God were all mediated through the man Moses, whose ministry was continued in Joshua. He closely adhered to Moses' law, mission, and prophetic leadership. The mantle of Moses was clearly evident upon Joshua. Continuity of leadership also meant continuity of the mediatorial office in Israel. Israel fared well under Joshua's leadership, as it had under Moses.

The promises of the covenant are associated with Abraham, and the promise of kingship has its fountainhead in David. Moses is to be remembered as the mediator of the covenant God made with Israel, known as the Sinaitic, or Mosaic, covenant. The Mosaic covenant *applies the divine administration of grace and promise to a particular people, namely Israel*. Regrettably, the negative view of law in society and even in Christian circles diminishes Moses' importance. From a canonical perspective, Moses is "the servant" of God who instructed God's people in the nature of God. The revelation of God through Moses was not made irrelevant by the coming of Jesus, the Son of God (see Heb. 3:5–6).

The presence of God is intimately connected with the revelation of the Mosaic covenant.[14] Under this covenant *the Lord consecrates his people to himself under the sanctions of his royal law*. Negatively, the covenant administration signified a bondage, as the Lord binds his children together by the sanctions of law.[15] He treated them as little children or servants (see Gal. 4:1–7, 21–31) because of their hardness of heart and slowness to respond to his grace (Deut. 5:29). For the unbelieving Israelites the law was a burden and served to condemn them. Positively, the law was a means of grace for the godly in Israel, as it led them to look to the Lord's salvation, provided for in Jesus the Mediator. They delighted in every expression of God's will (Ps. 1:2). The law in all its many details served as the Father's way of bringing his children to understand what it means to walk humbly in his presence, to love righteousness and justice, and to pursue love and fidelity (Mic. 6:8). By the administration of law the Lord bound individuals and tribes together into one nation with the intention of fulfilling his promises and of securing his grace to those who live in fellowship with him.

The Mosaic covenant is therefore not inferior to the Abrahamic covenant. The main differences lie in the national character of the

158

Mosaic covenant over against the individual or clan nature of the promises in the Abrahamic covenant and in the manner whereby the promises are guaranteed. McComiskey's recent contribution to this issue finds a delicate balance between the greater benefits of the New Covenant and the proper appreciation of the Mosaic covenant.

> The law is not the promise; it is a covenant distinct from the promise covenant. It establishes the conditions under which the terms of the promise could be maintained. The promise is the eternal expression of God's will. The law is the temporary framework that prescribed the terms of obedience for the people of God in the Mosaic era.[16]

Though the people were expected to respond in faith, they were bound together as one nation by the consecration of law. The law of the Old Testament is not to be viewed over against the gospel; rather, the gospel is the good news that God loves his people, cares for them, and expects an appropriate response from them.[17] The Lord proclaimed the good news of his presence, protection, blessing, forgiveness, and grace to Israel. Because of the spiritual immaturity of the people, the Lord regulated their communion with him and their private and societal life by giving his laws, statutes, and ordinances. The laws dealt with the individual, the family, and the nation as a whole. The Lord guaranteed and preserved the promises by the law. Through the revelation of his law the godly come to know that God expects from those who walk with him nothing less than he expected from Enoch, Noah, and Abraham; namely, perfection. The meaning of *tāmîm*, "perfect" (e.g., Gen. 17:1), signifies "integrity," as further defined in Psalm 15:2; 24:4; Isaiah 33:15; Micah 6:8. This attitude toward God and other people is identical to what Jesus expects from his followers (Matt. 5:3–10): the pursuit of holiness, justice, righteousness, love, and peace for the sake of God.

Law and Moses

God revealed his *law* to Moses. All parts of the law came to Israel through Moses, *the* mediator of the Mosaic covenant by divine appointment (Exod. 19:3, 9), by the will of the people (Exod. 20:19), by his special relationship as intercessor for Israel (Exod. 32–34), and by the glory God bestowed on him (Exod. 34:29–35). The Torah associates all the laws with Moses.[18] The authority of the law lies in Moses' position as *the* lawgiver, *the* spokesman for God, and *the* mediator between God and Israel. He received, wrote down, taught, applied, and expounded God's law. He repeatedly, lovingly, and patiently called God's people to faith, commitment to the Lord, and to an internalization of the law (cf. Deuteronomy). He was fully aware of the dangers of legalism, hypocrisy, and fideism. His concern was that Israel might come to know the grace and love of God by the circumcision of the heart (Deut. 30:6) and that out of response to his grace they would readily keep his commands (30:10). The "law" was not the *end* but a means of binding God's people together as a holy people. Through the external law they could get a sense of the unique responsibility of being a holy people privileged to enjoy God's holy presence among them, of understanding what sin is, and of returning to the Lord for forgiveness. The law was a gift of God (Rom. 9:4) and a positive means of instructing his children to walk in his presence (Lev. 26:11–13; cf. 2 Tim. 3:16–17). Yes, there was grace, because God consecrated his people, even under the tutelage of law.[19]

Law as Law

Old Testament "law" is a complex phenomenon. The traditional division of the law into three categories (moral, ceremonial, and civil) does not do justice to the intricate relationship of the laws, because the laws function on many different levels.[20] The distinction between *apodictic* laws and *casuistic* (or "case") laws has the advantage of categorizing the biblical laws in accordance with their literary form. The apodictic—that is, necessarily true—laws provide absolute principles of right and wrong. They have the form of positive commands and negative commands ("you shall not") as in the Decalogue.[21] They also occur in the form of a generalized statement ("anyone who"), curse formula ("cursed") or in an asseveration of the death penalty ("he will most surely die"). A study of the Book of the Covenant (Exod. 20:22–23:33) and the Holiness Code (Lev. 18–20) reveals that the apodictic laws cut across all segments of Israelite life: (personal, familial, communal, cultic), whether at home, at work, at war, asleep, or on vacation.[22] God's concern pertains to the imitation of himself: holiness, purity, righteousness, justice, peace, and love in all areas of life.

The casuistic laws reinforce the conclusion that the Lord is concerned with all of life, as the case laws flow out of the apodictic laws and reinforce the application of the law of God. The case laws are in the form of "if . . . then" or "when . . . then." They pertain to moral, ceremonial, and civic areas of personal and community life. Israel's life was ordered by the law of God as a means of grace to help the godly in living their lives to the glory of God.

The Lord provided Israel with a basic groundwork for personal and societal ethics (the apodictic laws), with a practical application of these laws to life's circumstances (casuistic laws), and with a framework of adapting to new circumstances. This framework encouraged the judges and priests to interpret and apply the law of God to a variety of situations. The development of a case system of legal opinions assured the continual relevance of God's law. But over time the traditions of humans could become oppressive. This was certainly the context of

Jesus' teaching. The traditions of the rabbis (oral law), legalism, and keeping the law for its own sake, rather than for the sake of God (cf. Matt. 5:19, 20), hindered the Jews from seeing God's spiritual and pedagogical purposes in the law. It became an external burden rather than an internal joy (Deut. 30:11–14; cf. Matt. 11:28–29).

Covenantal Reminders

God's people had visible markers to remind themselves continually of their covenantal status.[23] They marked the doorframe of their houses (Deut. 6:9). They wore fringes around their garments in order to signify that they were the covenant people (22:12). They were to remind each other, both in their daily walk and in their times of relaxation, that they were God's people (6:6–7).

Feasts and Festivals

Israel was to be like and also unlike the nations. They could resemble the nations in enjoying special seasons of rejoicing and feasting. The festivals of Israel, however, were always enjoyed in the presence of the Lord. The Lord himself therefore instructed his people to be different from the other nations by shunning the magic and immorality of their pagan counterparts.[24]

The Lord specified an annual calendar of events by which all the tribes had an opportunity to celebrate in their own locale or in the community around the tabernacle (Exod. 23:14–17; 34:18–23; Lev. 23; Deut. 16:1–17). The "festivals" *(mō'ēd)* of Israel consisted of the weekly Sabbath, the monthly new moon, the annual festivals (the Festival of Acclamation and the Day of Atonement), and the three pilgrimage "feasts" *(ḥāg*; Passover or the Feast of Unleavened Bread, the Feast of Weeks or Firstfruits, and the Feast of Tabernacles).

Through the framework of feasts and festivals, the Israelites transmitted their redemptive history. They passed on from generation to generation the stories of the exodus from Egypt, the miraculous happenings in the wilderness, the revelation of the law and covenant, and the conquest of Canaan. Through these celebrations they developed a consciousness of being God's people and of having been specially blessed:

> Three times a year all your men must appear before the LORD your God at the place he will choose: at the Feast of Unleavened Bread, the Feast of Weeks and the Feast of Tabernacles. No man should appear before the LORD empty-handed: Each of you must bring a gift in proportion to the way the LORD your God has blessed you. (Deut. 16:16–17)

The people also developed a greater awareness that their history and election were only by grace, as they confessed, regardless of tribal descent, their connection with the wanderings of Abraham, Isaac, and Jacob (see Deut. 26:5–10).

Sacrifices and Offerings

The ritual of sacrifices and offerings (Exod. 20:24–26; Lev. 1:1–7:21; chap. 17; 19:5–8; Num. 15:22–29; Deut. 12) guaranteed Israel's continued status as a holy people. The people could never forget that God's presence was a token of his grace, not a reward for might or righteousness (Deut. 8:17–18; 9:4–6). Through the sacrificial system the Lord taught his people that privileges were freely given to all who looked to him for meaning, that he expects holiness and righteousness from them, and that any infraction is punishable by death. Through this system the Lord taught his people that their sins may be atoned for (expiated) and forgiven.[25] By the shedding of blood—anticipating the blood of our Lord Jesus Christ—there is forgiveness for sin (Heb. 9:22), because the Lord is a gracious and forgiving God. Ultimately, the people had to look to God for forgiveness and could not expect pardon by mechanically fulfilling the external requirements (Isa. 1:11–17; Mic. 7:18–20). Through the sacrificial system the Lord taught his people to express their devotion to him in gratitude for his redemption, protection, and provisions. He taught them that they are one covenant people, in whose communal celebrations and expressions the covenant God delights. To express these various purposes, we distinguish between three kinds of offerings and sacrifices.[26] (See table 9.)

TABLE 9. OFFERINGS AND SACRIFICES

Category	Offering Types	Function
Propitiatory	Sin, guilt	Foreshadows the atonement of our Lord
Dedicatory	Burnt, grain, drink	Expresses loyalty, gratitude, and a spirit of devotion
Communal	Fellowship, freewill, votive, thanksgiving	Indicates communal joy, celebration, thanksgiving, and love

Paul exhorts us to present ourselves as a dedicatory offering (Rom. 12:1–2), and the Book of Hebrews calls on the Christian community to "offer to God a sacrifice of praise—the fruit of lips that confess his name" and "to do good and to share with others, for with such sacrifices God is pleased" (13:15–16). The communal offerings find expression in the Lord's Supper and in Christian love feasts (fellowship suppers). The three divisions of sacrifices and offerings remained in force till the atonement made by our Lord Jesus. His is the final propitiatory offering (Heb. 10:1–14; Rom. 3:25). Though the system of prescribed offerings has been set aside, the modern equivalent of dedicatory and communal offerings are still applicable.

Holy and Clean

Other regulations specified the categories of holiness and cleanness. In their daily walk the godly Israelites had to think constantly of their relationship with God by evaluating whether an object was holy or common, clean or polluted. The Lord had revealed to them the laws of impurities (Lev. 11–16) and the laws of holiness (chaps. 17–27) to consecrate them to himself and to separate them from the practices of the Canaanites. The customs of Israel in eating, marriage, dealing with sickness and death, and so forth were based on divine revelation. These laws of holiness and cleanness, while being observed by pious Jews, gradually increased in number and intensity, because of human traditions. Our Lord upheld the spirit of the law, while rejecting the burdensome nature of the traditions. He taught that people defile themselves by their thoughts, speech, and actions, rather than by what they eat or by the manner in which they eat (Matt. 15:1–20). Similarly, Paul upheld the principles of holiness and purity, while rejecting human customs (1 Cor. 10:27–31; Galatians; Col. 2:8–23).

The principles of holiness and cleanness served before the incarnation of our Lord to teach Israel to consecrate themselves when they had polluted what was clean. They divided the whole world into "common" and "holy." A person (e.g., Levite, priest, Nazarite) or object (e.g., sacrifice, vessels) was holy only after it had been consecrated to the Lord. The holy could become profane by using it again in a "common" way, or it could be polluted by coming into contact with an unclean object or person. On the other hand, what was unclean could become clean through a ritual of purification, thus becoming clean and common. (See figure 12.)

In the regulations of holiness and purity, the Lord taught Israel to watch constantly how they lived in his presence. He is holy and expects nothing less than conformity to his will. Though certain regulations may seem odd at first sight, the Lord taught his people thereby to distinguish themselves from the nations, to listen to his Word without questioning the reasons, and to examine their hearts. At issue was not how much God required or how little but whether they had a heart to listen to him (Deut. 5:29).[27] A responsive heart began with the fear of the Lord (Prov. 1:7) and exhibited itself in humility (Mic. 6:8). God was not pleased with external conformity but delighted in those children who

163

had a heart fully devoted to him (Deut. 6:5; Ps. 51:17). Such inner motivation is also known as "circumcision of the heart" (Deut. 30:6).

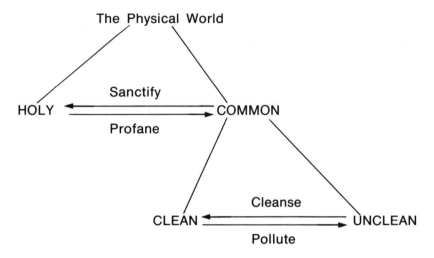

Figure 12. The Distinction Between Holy and Clean

The Sabbath as the Sign of the Covenant

The sign of the Abrahamic covenant was circumcision, and that rite was carried on into the new administration (Lev. 12:3; see Exod. 4:24–26; Josh. 5:1–9). The newness of the Mosaic era called for another covenantal sign, namely, the Sabbath. In the Decalogue, Israelites were commanded to observe the Sabbath day (Exod. 20:8–11; Deut. 5:12–15). The Sabbath commandment also embodies or encompasses the covenant as a whole. The Sabbath was an everlasting sign of God's covenant, "a sign between me and you for the generations to come, so you may know that I am the LORD, who makes you holy" (Exod. 31:13).

While the other commandments in the Decalogue pertain to our worship of God and our dealing with other people, the Sabbath commandment focuses on the relationship between Yahweh and his people. By resting on the Sabbath, Israel was invited to rest with God (Exod. 31:17; Gen. 2:1–3). They would thus be conformed to his holy image. God, who had sanctified the Sabbath to himself at creation, consecrated Israel so that they might share in the holy day. The Sabbath is a day holy to the Lord, which the holy God shares with his holy people (Exod. 31:13). Childs concludes from the canonical correlation of the covenant, the tabernacle, and the Sabbath (Exod. 20–31) that the Sabbath is the sign of the covenant relationship and of God's presence, symbolized by the tabernacle.[28] The Israelites might be far away from the tabernacle or temple, but in the celebration of the Sabbath they had a sign of God's kingship, of his relationship with them, and of his presence in blessing and protection.[29]

The Sabbath also has a sacramental value as a sign of covenantal relationship: it assures us of the restoration of all things.[30] Those who observe the Sabbath enjoy the rest to which the promises of the restoration point. The Sabbath rest is beautifully illustrated in the double provision of manna on the sixth day so that the people would not have to gather any manna on the seventh day and could enjoy the Lord's provision (Exod. 16:22–26). One may easily see, therefore, how the Sabbath commandment required God's people to have faith in him. One who attended to one's own affairs doubted God's faithfulness to provide. The prophet Isaiah challenged this unbelieving attitude and practice and urged Israel to "call the Sabbath a delight" (58:13; see also vv. 3–5).

The Tabernacle

The tabernacle was the central symbol of the presence of the great King, the Divine Warrior. He was present in blessing and protection. He had established his rule in Israel, and the tabernacle was a symbol of his earthly "palace," a miniature model of his heavenly palace (cf. Heb. 9:24). The encampment of the tribes of Israel around the tabernacle in the wilderness symbolically represented the extension of God's kingdom to Israel (Exod. 19:6; 25:8; 29:45–46; Lev. 26:11–13; cf. Ps. 114:2).

The tabernacle represented God's holy and glorious kingdom in Israel.[31] The various parts of the tabernacle, too, symbolize his royal presence, covenant relationship, and his care in maintaining this relationship. The Most Holy Place (Exod. 26:31–33; cf. Heb. 9:3–5) was an area of fifteen by fifteen feet, separated by a veil (Exod. 26:31–33) from the Holy Place. In it stood the ark of the covenant, *the* symbol of God's rule over Israel. It was the "footstool" of his throne in heaven. The imagery of throne and footstool metaphorically express God's universal dominion and his special rule over his people (1 Chron. 28:2; Ps. 99:5; 132:7–8; cf. 66:1; Matt. 5:35). The cherubim above the ark represent the ministering angels around God's royal throne in heaven, guarding God's holiness (Ezek. 10:15–19; cf. Gen. 3:24). They serve him willingly and protect his royal splendor from those who transgress against him. Yet their being positioned above the mercy seat (*kappōret*, NIV "atonement cover," Exod. 25:17–22; Heb. 9:5) assures Israel that the great King readily forgives his people. The objects in or associated with the ark symbolize God's commitment to his people: the two tablets of the law (Exod. 25:16, 21; 40:20; Deut. 10:1–5), the pot of manna (Exod. 16:33, 34; Heb. 9:4), and Aaron's rod (Num. 17:10; Heb. 9:4).

The significance of the Most Holy Place lies in the ark as a token of Yahweh's present kingship among his people, of the meeting place of God and man (Exod. 25:22; 30:36), of divine atonement (Lev. 16), and of the covenant relationship between Yahweh and Israel. To accentuate the privilege of his dwelling among Israel, once a year on the Day of Atonement, the Lord permitted the legitimate heir of Aaron to enter into the Most Holy Place to make atonement for Israel (Lev. 16; cf. Heb. 9:7–10).

Entrance to the Holy Place was limited to the priests. They were God's servants in his earthly sanctuary, even as the angels are his heavenly servants. The priests sacrificed sacred incense (Exod. 30:34–38) at the incense altar (Exod. 30:1–10; 37:25–28); placed the bread of the presence (shewbread; Exod. 25:23–30; 37:10–16) on the table, symbolic of Israel's fellowship before the Lord and of his readiness to bless each of the tribes of Israel; and kept the lampstand burning (Exod. 25:31–40; 37:17–24; 40:24) with sacred oil (Exod. 27:20, 21), symbolic of Yahweh's continual vigilance over his people.

In the court outside the tabernacle, priests and Levites served the Lord on behalf of Israel. The altar of burnt offering (Exod. 38:1–8), on which the priests offered the sacrifices and offerings for the purposes of atonement, dedication, and communion, was prominent. By the entrance of the Holy Place was the laver, or basin, (Exod. 30:17–21; 38:8; 40:29–32), whose water the priests used for ritual washing when entering the tabernacle.

PERSONAL COMMITMENT

Israel, the natural descendants of the patriarchs, received the promises and the covenants by which the twelve tribes were transformed into a nation with a special relationship to Yahweh: he became their God, and they were to be his people. This relationship is often called the covenantal relationship. In this relationship Israel was known as his *segullâ*, or "special possession"; his "people" (*'am*), and his "inheritance" (*naḥᵃlâ*; cf. Deut. 9:26, 29; 1 Kings 8:51; Ps. 94:5).

Each of the tribes, regardless of its location in the land of Canaan or its prominence in the further developments in Israel's history, enjoyed a common tradition with the other tribes. Though the physical geography of Canaan and of Transjordan encouraged separationism, and in spite of tribal differences, they were all God's people. Although the people were encouraged always to remember to what tribe they belonged, there was a commonness in their history, traditions, and divinely revealed law, which bound them together, as it were, by a divine constitution.

To this end also the biblical books were given. They portray the common experience of all the tribes in the land of Egypt (Exod. 1–12).

All the tribes celebrated the passover in Egypt and were commanded henceforth to maintain its celebration (12:1–30, 43–50). All the tribes passed through the Red Sea and were fed by God in the wilderness. They all received the covenant and God's law at Mount Sinai, joined together in rebellion against the Lord and Moses, shared in the experience of the wilderness wanderings, and participated in the conquest of the land. Psalm 105 celebrates the commonness of God's people as they received God's grace in their journey from Egypt to the Promised Land:

> Remember the wonders he has done,
>> his miracles, and the judgments he pronounced,
> O descendants of Abraham his servant,
>> O sons of Jacob, his chosen ones.
>
> (vv. 5–6)

In Psalm 106, the psalmist remembers the love of God in the Exodus and Conquest. He confesses on behalf of all the tribes that they are sinners by nature and share in a history of rebellion against the Lord:

> We have sinned, even as our fathers did;
>> we have done wrong and acted wickedly.
> When our fathers were in Egypt,
>> they gave no thought to your miracles;
> they did not remember your many kindnesses,
>> and they rebelled by the sea, the Red Sea.
> Yet he saved them for his name's sake,
>> to make his mighty power known.
>
> (vv. 6–8)

The expressions of God's judgment, the threats of the judgments of the covenant, and the teaching about the holy anger of the Lord remind Israel in every generation that the Lord holds each person and each generation responsible. Each Israelite is one with the people of God. Achan's sin brought disgrace, defeat, and death on Israel (Josh. 22:20). If Israel persists in its rebellion, the united biblical witness is that the whole people will be exiled and scattered among the nations. Yet, out of their sordid history, the tribes, clans, families, and individuals in Israel were called upon to devote themselves completely to the Lord their Redeemer, to consecrate themselves to him, and to be the light to the nations. To this end, the law of Moses called on individual Israelites to respond to a gracious offer. Forgiveness, covenant relationship, and blessing were not automatic but required loyalty to the Lord. God expected nothing less from his Old Testament people than he does today. The saints were those who were circumcised of heart, or "regenerate."[32] The Lord sustained them with his grace and favor in a special way, as a father provides for the needs of his children. The

Mosaic covenant is an expression of solidarity, but in the renewal of the covenant after the idolatry by Mount Sinai, the Lord made it clear that only those who respond to him live in grace, whereas sinners—even Israelites—will perish (Exod. 33:19; 34:5–6). Moses and Joshua appeal to individuals and their families to take upon themselves the yoke of God's kingdom (Deut. 26:16–19; 30:11–20; Josh. 23–24).

The basis for ethics in Israel is threefold. First, the presence of the great King in their midst calls forth a response of faith and loyalty. He has chosen Israel to be his treasured possession and has demonstrated his love in acts of deliverance, protection, vindication, and blessing. Second, the call for separation unto the Lord distinguishes the ethics from Sinai. Ethics is not merely for the good of a community, but it delimits Israel from the nations as his royal priesthood. They have been called to serve the great King. Third, the eschatological perspective intrudes in the area of ethics. Godly living is not only theocentric and incarnational, but it is also future-oriented. In a manner of speaking, ethical living brings in more clearly the rule of God on earth. Furthermore, those who live for God will receive their reward in this life and in the world to come. They are heirs of the promise, and as heirs they willingly sacrifice themselves and their personal rights and natural ambitions for the sake of the kingdom of God.

CONCLUSION

The canonical function of the five books from Exodus to Joshua is manifold. The place of the Torah (Genesis–Deuteronomy) became established in Judaism from the Exile onward, but even before that time the godly derived their identity as the people of God from these sacred writings. For them the Torah was the Word of God, spoken through his servant Moses, as the Lord confirmed their election as his people, their consecration as a holy priesthood, and their unique position as exalted above the nations. To Israel he revealed the significance of his name Yahweh, the acts of redemption, and his perfections (holy, glorious, compassionate, long-suffering, loving, faithful, forgiving, and jealous). The Lord chose to dwell in their midst, consecrating his people by the sanctions of law, committing himself by covenant, and securing the continuity of the blessed covenantal relationship by the feasts and festivals, laws of offerings and sacrifices, and the regulations on holiness and purity. The tabernacle was the physical token of his presence, and the Sabbath was the spiritual token (or sacrament) of their holiness, calling, and privilege of enjoying fellowship with their God. Over against these many benefits, the Lord expected nothing less than wholehearted devotion.

CHAPTER 12

God's Kingdom and His Promise

The biblical revelation of Exodus through Joshua was God's Word to each new generation in Israel so that they may know the good news of

1. the Lord's love for Israel;

2. his determination to dwell in the midst of Israel;

3. the revelation and significance of his name, his attributes, and his mighty acts, revealing that Yahweh is King, Judge, and Deliverer;

4. the privileges and obligations of the terms of the Mosaic covenant;

5. God's "servant" Moses and the need to pay careful attention to God's revelation through him (see Mal. 4:4);

6. the establishment of his kingdom in Israel; and

7. his blessings, conditioned on the depth of Israel's devotion and love.

The literary structure and canonical context illustrate the importance of the grace of God, Israel's covenantal status, the presence of God, the place of Moses, and the centralization of Israel's worship. The redemptive-historical significance of this epoch lies in (1) the establishment of God's kingship in Israel, (2) the institution of the theocratic officers as a means of continuing and protecting his kingship, and (3) the fulfillment of the promises.

GOD'S KINGSHIP IN ISRAEL

From the beginning the Lord's purpose was to take Israel to be his own people (Exod. 6:7).[1] The word "people" gradually acquired the significance of an elect nation, to whom the Lord gave the privilege of being his own kingdom, characterized by royalty and holiness (Exod. 19:5–6). The Lord adopted the people of Israel as his nation ('am). Out of all the nations of the world, he elected Israel to be his *theocratic kingdom,* granted Israel the adoption of sonship, revealed his glory to Israel, and bestowed on it the covenants, the temple worship, and the promises (Rom. 9:4).

The fulfillment of the promise of Israel's nationhood and unique relationship to God was not conditioned on its responsiveness to the Lord. Both before the revelation of God at Mount Sinai and after the ratification of the covenant, Israel had proven itself to be a thoroughly stubborn and rebellious people who did not have the heart to love the Lord. The revelation of God, the redemption from Egypt, the revelation at Mount Sinai, the ratification of the covenant, and the glorious presence of God in the tabernacle witness to the love and grace of God that was showered on an undeserving people. It was clearly God's plan to establish his kingdom on earth through Israel, regardless of their responsiveness. In the covenantal contract, however, the Lord expected his people to respond in love (Deut. 6:5) that was not an emotional response but that was an expression of devotion or loyalty.[2]

THEOCRATIC OFFICERS

The purpose of the covenant was to inaugurate the kingship of Yahweh over Israel and to consecrate Israel as his people. From its beginnings, Israel had been divided into twelve tribes. Each tribe maintained a clan leadership of elders and leaders of hundreds and thousands.[3] The clan leadership was an ancient institution that developed in Israel while they were in Egypt. Because they were to be constituted the people of God, however, the need arose for a divinely appointed leadership.

In the first place, the necessity for theocratic leadership became clear soon after the evidences of Israel's rebelliousness (Exod. 14–18). Moses was God's agent, appointed with a particular mission of bringing Israel out of Egypt and leading them into the Promised Land. Jethro, Moses' father-in-law, observed that the burdens of leadership were too great for Moses. Not only was he the national leader of the people, but he was also the court at all levels. He himself heard the cases and rendered judgment. Jethro's advice to appoint judges as helpers of Moses was a common-grace insight. Moses listened to Jethro's counsel and thus received significant help (Exod. 18:24).

Second, leadership became essential because of the people's history of complaining and grumbling. After the Israelites left Mount Sinai (Num. 10:11–13), Moses felt it was too difficult to lead the people and asked for his own death as a form of resignation. The Lord responded to Moses by having him appoint seventy elders (11:16). The elders received a part of Moses' spirit (v. 25) so that they might properly assist him. When two of the elders who were not at the tent of meeting prophesied, Moses expressed the hope that *all* of Israel would be prophets (v. 29). He realized that the very goal of the theocracy is the presence of God's Spirit in all of God's people. With this Spirit there is no room for grumbling.

Finally, the deaths of Moses and Joshua created a vacuum of godly leadership. After Moses a gradual breakup of theocratic leadership took place. Moses had served Israel as judge, military leader, cultic official, mediator of the covenant, and prophet. As we have seen, however, even during his ministry he had to share his leadership with others. His work as covenant mediator was taken over by the priests and elders who shared in judging the people. Joshua took over the military leadership while Moses was alive and received his ordination directly from Moses to be the charismatic leader over Israel (Num. 27:15–23; Deut. 31:1–8, 14, 23; 34:9; see also Josh. 4:14). God spoke to Israel through Joshua (see Josh. 1), but after his death the Word of the Lord became "rare" (Judg. 2:7; 6:13; 1 Sam. 3:1).[4]

The goal of the theocratic offices was that God's people may learn to live in harmony with the Lord, their Creator-Redeemer, and with their fellow Israelites. As long as they were living in harmony with their God and his covenant people, they expressed the covenant ideal: *the people of God.*

Priests and Levites

Only the descendants of Aaron served as priests (Lev. 9), but the entire tribe of Levi was devoted to the service of the Lord.[5] They assisted the Aaronic priests in the tabernacle. It seems that the Aaronic priesthood was God's appointed institution by which he administered his blessings and forgiveness to his people. Korah, Dathan, Abiram, and 250 leaders of Israel challenged the Aaronic priesthood, arguing that all Israel was holy and that the priesthood need not be limited to Aaron and his descendants (Num. 16). In the episode of the budding rod, God confirmed his will to limit the priesthood to Aaron and his descendants (chap. 17).

The family of Levi was God's gift to the priests to facilitate their work (Num. 8:19; 18:6). Likewise Moses' work was shared by Aaron, the high priest. The Lord clearly intended the descendants of Aaron to continue to serve, because he confirmed this office also by covenant. The grandson of Aaron, Phinehas, showed his loyalty to the Lord at the time when Israel gave itself to immorality and idolatry. As a reward the Lord confirmed the priestly function by covenant (Num. 25:11–13). Malachi is also familiar with the covenant of peace that the Lord made with the priesthood, and he challenges the priests after the Exile to be faithful to the original covenant the Lord made with them (Mal. 2:4–8).

Prophets

The Pentateuch also foresees a class of people by whom Yahweh will reveal his will to the new generation. The prophets stand in the footsteps of Moses as they, too, receive God's revelation. While Moses received the Word of the Lord as a direct revelation, the prophets received the Word of the Lord indirectly, by means of visions and dreams (Num. 12:6–8). The standards of the prophetic institution substantiate the authenticity of God's revelation to Moses: prophets are judged by their faithfulness to the Word revealed to Moses (Deut. 13:1–3).

A prophet was also to be a fellow Israelite (Deut. 18:15). A good prophet did not receive his revelation by means of witchcraft or sorcery (vv. 9–12) but rather from the Lord. His word may be authenticated by determining whether it comes to pass (vv. 15–22). When the prophet has spoken, it is as if God himself has spoken. The function of Moses as the mediator of the covenant is thus continued. In Israel's history, the prophetic role shifted from covenant mediator to covenant prosecutor from the time of Elijah onward.

Kings

The institution of Israelite kingship is intimated in the Pentateuch in only one passage. In Deuteronomy 17, Moses details the nature of theocratic kingship. The king is to be raised up from the Israelites by the Lord and is not to be like any pagan king. He must be sensitive to the law of the Lord and delight in it (vv. 19–20). He is not to multiply material possessions or power to himself (vv. 16–17). The king's heart must be right with the Lord; otherwise, he cannot lead his people into the covenant blessings, as Moses had done. If he is the servant of God, he is the servant of God's people. Kingship in Israel was to be different from the tyrannical, despotic, absolute rulers of the nations.[6] The concept of theocracy assumes that all leaders, including kings, minister in a servant role for the benefit and welfare of the people.

PROMISE AND FULFILLMENT

Yahweh's revelation to Israel as the God of Abraham, Isaac, and Jacob (Exod. 3:15–16) implied his fidelity to the fourfold promise made originally to Abraham.

Seed

By the time of the Exodus, Israel had become very numerous. On the eve of their entry into the Promised Land, Moses observed that they had become like the stars in number (e.g., Deut. 1:10; 10:22), and he blessed them, praying that the Lord might increase them "a thousand times" (1:11). From among the tribes, Levi, Judah, and Ephraim/Manasseh had risen to prominent positions.

The prominence of *Levi* is due both to God's choice of his descendants to serve as Levites and to the ordination of the descendants of Aaron (a Levitical family) as priests. The priestly-Levitical work pertains to the maintenance of the tabernacle, the offerings and sacrifices, and the reading and observance of the law of God. The Levites were living reminders of God's holiness, glory, grace, and forgiveness and also of his holy requirements as embodied in the law of Moses.

The important role of *Judah* was enhanced by Caleb's report that the land of Canaan was a good land and could be taken with the Lord's help (Num. 13:30; 14:5–9, 24). In the listing of the division of the land, Judah's position is most prominent, because it is connected with Caleb's possession of Hebron (Josh. 14:6–15:63).

The importance of *Ephraim/Manasseh* is also because of the faithfulness of a spy, namely, Joshua (Num. 14:6-9, 38). Joshua, an Ephraimite, had remained faithful to the Lord and to Moses from the beginning (Exod. 17:9–13). His tribe, together with Manasseh, received a major portion of the land. The tribal territories of Judah, Ephraim, and Manasseh (Josh. 15–17) make up about half of the available land in Canaan!

The significance in these early happenings lies in the later division of the nation into two rival kingdoms: Judah and Israel, centered in the Ephraim-Manasseh region. The Bible thus gives us some explanation for the rivalry and enmity among the tribes. The charismatic leadership of Moses and Joshua is barely able to keep the tribes united. The tribes are easily provoked (see, e.g., Josh. 22) and show too much concern for their own standard of living. This attitude led Reuben, Gad, and some of the clans of Manasseh to request the extension of the inheritance to include Transjordan (Num. 32), and the tribe of Joseph (which includes Ephraim and Manasseh) urged Joshua to give them more land (Josh. 17:14–18).

Overall, the spiritual condition of the people of God was weak. Greed, selfishness, bitterness, immorality, impurity, idolatry, hatred, discord, fits of rage, dissension, factions, orgies, and complaints all characterized God's people! They were a stubborn, stiff-necked, and hardened nation. Though they had become numerous, as is clear from the first census, taken at Mount Sinai (Num. 1), and from the census shortly before entering the land (chap. 26), yet the promise of the increase had not guaranteed that the spiritual condition of the descendants of Abraham would be like "the father of the faithful." This period clearly demonstrates the truth that physical birth and the sign of circumcision (see Josh. 5:1–9) do not guarantee a sensitivity to God, the evidence of a spiritual circumcision of the heart.

The promises were, nevertheless, restated and fulfilled to the descendants of Abraham. The grace of God is clearly evident in his patient dealings with the people under Moses and Joshua's leadership.

The promises, including that of the seed, are still given "to you and to your seed." For this reason, communal and family instruction is important. The prophets make it abundantly clear, however, that only those who truly respond to Yahweh in faith, love, and loyalty belong to his "treasured possession" (see Isa. 65:13–16; Mal. 3:16–18). Moses laid the groundwork for the concept of the seed within the seed, the people within the people, and the circumcised of heart among the circumcised of the flesh.

The Land

The promise of the land was given to the patriarchs (see Deut. 1:7–8).[7] When the people of Israel finally moved toward the land, after spending thirty-eight years in the wilderness, they were denied the southern entry into the land. They had to travel into Transjordan south of the Dead Sea and make their approach into Canaan from the east, across the Jordan. As a consequence of this detour, they faced the opposition of Sihon, king of Heshbon, and Og, king of Bashan (Num. 21:21–35; see also Deut. 3:1; 29:7; Ps. 135:11; 136:19–20). They also avenged themselves on the Midianites (Num. 31). This activity resulted in an extension of the Promised Land to include the Transjordan territory, where Reuben, Gad, and some clans of Manasseh were permitted to settle (chap. 32). This additional land was a mixed blessing, because the Transjordanian tribes were somewhat cut off from the rest of Israel. Israel's history demonstrates that, except for the great prophet Elijah, who hailed from the Gilead region, those tribes failed to contribute to the spiritual welfare of Israel.

The land of Canaan was taken under Joshua's leadership. The indigenous population was opposed to Israel and was in great fear of Yahweh (Josh. 2:11, 24; 6:27; 10:1–2). They came out against Israel (see 11:20), and the Lord gave the land into the hands of his people, because he fought for them (10:42). Joshua dealt with the native population and occupied the land, "just as the LORD had directed Moses" (11:23). Again following Yahweh's command through Moses, he divided the land into tribal territories by lot (14:2). By the end of Joshua's ministry it could be said that God's promise of the land was fulfilled in such a way that Israel enjoyed rest from the enemies and that they had reaped the benefits of the Land of Promise, the new Garden of Eden.[8]

> So the LORD gave Israel all the land he had sworn to give their forefathers, and they took possession of it and settled there. The LORD gave them rest on every side, just as he had sworn to their forefathers. Not one of their enemies withstood them; the LORD handed all their enemies over to them. Not one of all the LORD's good promises to the house of Israel failed; every one was fulfilled. (21:43–45)

The promise, however, was still promise. There was still much land to be occupied.[9] Moreover, the promise of perpetual rest was conditioned on covenantal loyalty. If Israel failed to respond, the Lord forewarned them of troubles, exile, and dispersion (Deut. 4:25–28; 28:64–68; Josh. 23:12–16; 24:20). The enjoyment of the land was thus a token of an even greater fulfillment that Israel never experienced in any enduring way. "So I declared on oath in my anger, 'They shall never enter my rest'" (Ps. 95:11; cf. Heb. 4:3–11).

The Presence and Protection of God

The blessed presence of God was with his people in Egypt, in the wilderness, and in the Promised Land. The ark of the covenant in the Most Holy Place of the tabernacle was the symbol of his presence. During the wilderness journey, the Lord's presence was clearly visible in the cloud and the pillar of fire. With the construction of the tabernacle, the ark became the symbol of God's rule over his people as well as of his covenant.[10] During the Conquest the ark had been placed at Gilgal, and from there it was moved to Shiloh. With all the evidences of the Lord's presence, the people still awaited fulfillment of God's promise that he would choose one place as the resting place for his ark. That place would signify the unique place of God's rule and the center of his worship.[11]

Yahweh blessed Israel with his presence in numerous ways: by sparing them during the ten plagues; in the Exodus and the crossing through the Red Sea; in the glory-cloud; in providing Israel with food, drink, and victory over the Amalekites; in the theophany at Mount Sinai; in the covenant and in the sanctuary of his presence; in the institutions of tabernacle, priesthood, offerings and sacrifices, and feasts and festivals, by which Israel was regularly reminded of his presence and assured of his forgiveness; in the giving of the law as a detailed expression of his will; in the giving of the land; and in making Israel victorious over its enemies. Truly, God's Word of blessing, presence, and protection was fulfilled during this epoch.

God's presence has yet another side: curse and judgment. He expressed his judgment on the Egyptians (in the plagues and in their defeat at the Red Sea), on the Amalekites, on the kingdoms of Sihon and Og, and on the Canaanite kings. But he also demonstrated his wrath to Israel. After the revelation at Mount Sinai he made it clear that he punishes the guilty. He is a consuming fire (Exod. 24:17; Deut. 4:24; Heb. 12:29). He "consumed" rebellious Israelites by plagues (Exod. 32:34–35; Num. 11:33; 14:37; 16:46–50; 25:9), by fire (11:1–3; 16:35), by earthquake (vv. 31–34), and by snakes (21:4–6). He is a jealous God who is in the midst of his people but who does not tolerate any infringement on his holiness and glory.

Only Yahweh's covenant loyalty prevented him from consuming all

Israel. He continued to be present, to dwell in their midst, and to guide, protect, and bless them *for his sake*, on account of the promises made to the patriarchs (Exod. 32:13; cf. Josh. 7:9). He is jealous of his name, but he is also patient, loving, and forgiving (Exod. 34:6–7; Num. 14:17–19).

The law was God's appointed instrument to teach Israel as a nation how to live in his presence. Through it he taught Israel to be like him in character, as the law advanced in a practical way the concepts of holiness, purity, justice, righteousness, love, and peace. His blessing, however, did not rest on mere legalism. He expected inward loyalty, not formality. Loyalty to God, though, includes loyalty to his revelation. Devotion to God is never separated from obedience and sanctification. He promised blessings in abundance to those who lived in harmony with him and his will (Lev. 26:1–13; Deut. 28:1–14) but also punishment for disobedience (Lev. 26:14–39; Deut. 27:15–26; 28:15–68). Yet, he always held out forgiveness and full restoration, conditioned on repentance (Lev. 26:40–45; Deut. 4:30–31).

The Blessing to the Nations

The historical context of this period helps us to understand why so little is said about the inclusion of the nations in the covenant blessings. First, the concern of this period is with Israel's national existence, namely, its redemption from Egypt, consecration as a nation, and theocratic status. Second, Israel is seen as apathetic, disobedient, and outright rebellious. Israel cannot yet serve as a light to the nations. The nation receives the light of God's self-revelation and of his oracles (Rom. 3:2), but it is as yet a poor steward of the privileged position. Third, Moses and Joshua challenge Israel to conform to the grace given. If it conforms, the nations will observe its wisdom granted by God (Deut. 4:6), the presence of God (v. 7), and God's glory bestowed on Israel (26:19). It is indeed God's plan to make his people to be "a kingdom of priests" (Exod. 19:6). Fourth, the historical context of the Exodus and the Conquest also explains why the focus is on Israel. Israel was taught the lesson of separatism: it was neither to perpetuate the ways of Egypt nor to adopt the Canaanite customs. The negative emphasis on the lewd practices of the nations reinforced the importance of Israel's holiness and purity. God expected his people to cleanse their hearts so that he might extend his kingdom to the nations. One clear example of covenant inclusion in this era is Rahab, the prostitute! She put her trust in Israel's God (Josh. 2:8–13) and was spared with her family. She was fully incorporated into the covenant: she married into the tribe of Judah, through which she became the mother of Boaz and the ancestor of David and of our Lord (Ruth 4:21; Matt. 1:5).

Moses anticipates that the nations will have cause to rejoice with

Israel (Deut. 32:43; see **LXX** and Dead Sea Scrolls). The apostle Paul explains that this promise has been fulfilled in the Gentile inclusion into the church by the mercies of God (Rom. 15:9–10). This promise, too, is one of those that was fulfilled in Jesus Christ, although first given to Moses and Israel. Though Balaam declared both the rule over and subjugation of the nations by the "star" and "scepter" that would arise out of Israel (Num. 24:17), Moses openly predicted also the enjoyment of the covenant privileges by Gentiles!

Conclusion to Part 4

The significance of Israel's calling to be "the holy nation" underlies the history of redemption from Moses till Jesus' coming in glory. Even as the present world reflects the continuity of creation in alienation, so Christians are rooted in the story of God's acts of redemption and revelation. They are heirs of the history of redemption: God's commitment to Abraham. The kingship of God confirmed in Jesus Christ was first granted to Israel. The New Testament emphasis on the presence of the kingdom thus goes back to God's acts in the Exodus, the revelation at Mount Sinai, and the Conquest. Both Moses and Joshua, God's servants, and Jesus as the Son speak of the kingdom of God as entering into the world of man. Moreover, the use of the designations "people of God," "congregation" (qāhāl, ekklēsia), and similar terms in both Testaments witnesses to the continuity of the church of Jesus Christ as the people of God. The officers of the church likewise go back in function to the Old Testament theocratic officers, as the Lord is pleased to use men ordained by him to keep his children pure and holy as well as to minister to their needs by upholding his kingdom principles of righteousness, justice, peace, and love. Though the Lord's dealing with Israel was on the basis of their being under the guardianship of law, his goal of establishing his kingship since Jesus' coming and the ministry of the Spirit remains the same. He desires nothing but a holy and undefiled people who respond willingly to their privileged position of being children of the living God!

Throughout the unfolding of the history of redemption, the Lord proves his fidelity by fulfilling his promises. He expects his children to look with great anticipation to him as they live in the tension of this world and the world to come. He is faithful—yesterday, today, and forever! Israel's experiences under Moses and Joshua were a foretaste of the glory of the new age, confirmed in Jesus Christ. We too enjoy a foretaste of the benefits of our great Lord as we look forward to the realization of the rest, the renewal of the earth, and the blessedness of God's people in which both Jews and Gentiles have a share.

In several respects the period of Israel as "the holy nation" has an important bearing on the subsequent flow in redemptive history:

1. The Lord revealed himself in the name *Yahweh*, in his acts of deliverance and judgment (acting as the Divine Warrior), and in his perfections (Exod. 34:5–6).

2. The Lord established his kingship on earth in Israel, revealed his royal glory to Israel, and established his royal dwelling among Israel in the tabernacle.

3. The Lord consecrated Israel as his people. On that basis he openly accepted them as his people, sanctified them, and defined the future of redemptive history in connection with Israel.

4. The Lord sealed the relationship by covenant—a sovereign administration of grace and promise by which the Lord consecrates a people to himself by law—and mediated the covenant blessings and the stipulations through Moses.

5. The Lord revealed his forbearance with Israel in his responding graciously and with forgiveness to Israel's history of rebellion (see Ps. 78).

6. The Lord sovereignly and freely acted in the Exodus and Conquest in fulfillment of the promises made to the patriarchs.

7. The Lord witnessed repeatedly through Moses to a greater fulfillment, to blessings, and to rest (see Heb. 3:5). He expects a response of fidelity and devotion to his kingdom purposes, but the outworking of his purposes is independent of individual human response. He will establish his kingdom—the new heaven and the new earth—at his time and for his saints!

Part 5

A Nation Like the Other Nations

Introduction to Part 5

With the death of Joshua and the other leaders of his generation, Israel was left without a direct voice from God. The voice of warning sounded by Moses and Joshua continued to echo, but it no longer affected the heart of the nation. A period of growing indifference set in, resulting in intermarriage with the Canaanites and worship of their gods. The "holy nation" became endangered by acculturation and syncretism. In the providence of God, they could not enjoy long periods of peace and prosperity in their identification with the nations, because the Lord troubled them with wars and adversities. When the surrounding nations whose friendship they sought became their enemies, the tribes found that they could not defend themselves. They were particularly vulnerable to the incursions of the newly settled Philistines. The Israelites were also embroiled in intertribal disputes. The religious, social, political, and moral distinctions of Israel as a holy nation were being obliterated by its refusal to live up to God's expectations.

This period is also marked by expressions of God's discipline. Israel was not consumed by his wrath, though they deserved to be. Though he had every right to do so, the Lord did not break the covenant. When he was provoked by Israel's flirtations with paganism, he afflicted them with hostile raids and incursions by the surrounding nations: the Moabites, Ammonites, Midianites, Amalekites, Canaanites, and Philistines. He thus brought adversity on his people, but not to destroy them. Out of his fatherly concern he made Israel feel uncomfortable with the nations so as to bring them back to himself. When they cried out to him, he listened to them as a father who hears the cry of his hurting child.

This fifth period is therefore characterized by Yahweh's undeserved favor to Israel. Instead of provoking Israel to the breaking point, he sent them deliverer after deliverer in the office of judge. The judges were often regional, charismatic leaders, whose first duty was to deal with the threatening situation and only secondarily to lead or rule.

But the judges only dimly reflected the charismatic leadership of Moses and Joshua. Under them there was almost no progress in Israel's history. Israel went from crisis to crisis. Out of these crises developed the monarchy, which was associated with Samuel, Israel's last and greatest judge. He perceived the situation as it truly was. The people did not ask to be ruled by a theocratic king, whose rule would be characterized by an adherence to God's law and by a concern for the unique, covenantal status of Israel, as set forth in Moses' law (Deut. 17:14–20). Rather, Israel conformed to the practices of the surrounding nations in their conception of kingship. They wanted a king like the kings of the nations. In the presence of Samuel, one of the greatest leaders in the Old Testament, the tribes of Israel again showed a recalcitrant spirit. The Israel of Samuel's day was as stiff-necked as the Israel of Moses' day.

The first king of Israel was Saul. Though he was anointed by Samuel, he was a king after the heart of the people. He was tall, handsome, and a capable warrior. He unified the tribes, but as he consolidated his power, he spurned the law of God and had little regard for the aging Samuel. Through Saul the Lord taught Israel again what paganism is like. It is ruthless, power-hungry, and despotic. It neither reflects God's kingship on earth nor regards the covenantal relationship. Yet, the grace of God was again evident through the ministry of Samuel, because through him David was anointed. Though it seemed that Israel's history showed no movement, going from one crisis to another, yet the Lord was still in control of the affairs of his people. Saul's rule was overshadowed by David, the man after God's own heart.

The significance of this period lies in the following elements:

1. Israel's inability to live up to the theocratic ideal;
2. the lack of significant advance in redemptive history;
3. restrictions on the fulfillment of God's promises because of Israel's lack of responsiveness;
4. the patience and grace of God over hundreds of years in sustaining his people by judges/deliverers;
5. the prophetic ministry of Samuel, through whom God again ministered to his people, revealing his presence as he had in the days of Moses and Joshua;
6. the sovereignty of God in Israel's history; and
7. the eschatological hope that was focused on David, the anointed of the Lord.

A brief survey of the literary, canonical, and redemptive-historical aspects of this period supports the contention that Yahweh's patience and grace kept alive the hope of the rule of God over his people. The flickering flame of the theocratic ideal flared up in Samuel's rule, was nearly put out in Saul's despotic regime, but was kept alive as long as David escaped from Saul's hands.

CHAPTER 13

A Story with Little Movement

Judges, Ruth, and 1 Samuel provide us with the scriptural perspective on this period. Though these books are historically reliable, they do not convey the data for the sake of historical interests alone. They are literary creations with a theological message. Our interest here is with the literary structure of these books as each one reflects a particular theological concern.[1]

JUDGES

The Book of Judges is a literary work composed of a prologue with two introductions (1:1–3:6), the story of the judges (3:7–16:31), and an epilogue with two stories (chaps. 17–21).

Prologue

The first introduction in the prologue functions to connect the Book of Judges with the story of the Conquest, while the second relates more to the situation at the time of Samuel. The two introductions seem to be related to the two final speeches in Joshua (chaps. 23–24), and the last verse of the epilogue anticipates the introduction of kingship in the days of Samuel.[2]

The long period of time covered by the book underlines the message that, in spite of the many judges raised up by the Lord, little of real significance happened. The *political introduction* (1:1–2:5) harkens back to the great era of Joshua and thereafter, when the tribes set out to establish themselves in the tribal territories allocated to them by Joshua. They enjoyed the fulfillment of God's promise, but not completely. The tribes were not able to subjugate the Canaanite enclaves successfully. At best, they could only put them to forced labor (1:28, 30, 33, 35; see also Josh. 17:13). Israel's political weakness had great social, and therefore religious, implications: Israelites began to treat the Canaanites on an equal footing socially. They adopted Canaanite ways of life, including their idolatry (Judg. 2:1–3).

In the *theological introduction* (2:6–3:6), the narrator approaches the problem posed in the first introduction from a different vantage point. He shows that Israel repeatedly departed from the Lord by intermarriage and by the adoption of pagan cultic practices. Though they sinned greatly, the Lord expressed his patience and mercy by sending deliverers in the form of the judges (2:18). But Israel did not listen long to the Lord, nor did they pay great attention to the judges. Rather, "they quickly turned from the way in which their fathers had walked" (v. 17). Because they refused to return to covenantal loyalty (v. 19), the Lord restricted their enjoyment of the covenantal promises. Rather than destroying them, desolating the land, or dispersing them among the nations, however, the Lord chose the merciful course. He permitted the remaining indigenous people (the Canaanites) to dwell in the land and trained Israel in the midst of conflict (vv. 21–23). This tension provides the setting for the Book of Judges.

Epilogue

The conclusion, or epilogue (chaps. 17–21), demonstrates how deeply Israel had fallen. The stories of Micah, the cultic site, and the migration of the Danites (chaps. 17–18) illustrate the political problems in Israel and the people's religious depravity. The story of the Levite and his concubine, who was repeatedly raped in Gibeah of Benjamin, brings out the moral corruption, the intertribal tensions, and the concern for the welfare of all the tribes (chaps. 19–21).

The epilogue holds together in the refrain, which states that there was no king in Israel (17:6; 18:1; 19:1; 21:25). The fourfold repetition is symmetrical, with each story repeating this observation twice. The intent is to demonstrate the inferiority of the judges. Great as they were, they were unable to make a lasting contribution to Israel's spiritual, social, moral, and political dilemmas. The narrator thus gives his commentary on the period and at the same time establishes a divinely inspired rationale for a divinely appointed monarchy.

The prologue and the epilogue together present a period in Israel's history characterized by little movement. The Danite migration northward epitomizes the tribes' inability to rid the land of the Canaanites.[3] The social, moral, and religious problems are dramatically portrayed in the stories about Micah's cult and the Levite with his concubine. A clear political shift, however, is also noticeable. The unity of Israel as the people of God was now shaky. Where were the other tribes when Dan could not keep its appointed patrimony? Why did the tribe of Benjamin foolishly risk war with the other tribes of Israel? The last two verses of Judges provide a commentary on this period, as they witness to the tribal independence and to the need for a permanent leadership to solidify the tribes and to advance the kingdom of God: "At that time the Israelites left that place and went home to their tribes and clans, each to his own inheritance. In those days Israel had no king; everyone did as he saw fit" (21:24–25).

Cycles of the Judges

The second introduction (2:6–3:6) prepares us for a cyclical pattern in the stories: Israel's disobedience, the Lord's provocation in the form of the raids of the enemies, Israel's cry to the Lord for deliverance, the appointment of a judge, deliverance, and a period of rest, followed anew by Israel's disobedience. The pattern reinforces the meaninglessness in this period of Israel's history. There is no movement or purpose as Israel goes from one crisis to another.[4]

In the middle of crisis situations, the Lord raises up a judge. The literary clue to this phenomenon is given by the phrase "the Spirit of the LORD came upon him" (3:10; see also 6:34; 11:29; 13:25; 14:6, 19; 15:14). The Spirit of God, who had rested on Moses and Joshua, also fell on the judges as a manifestation of God's continued care for his people. But there was no continuity in the judges from one generation to another. Moreover, the judges ruled over regions or tribes but never consolidated power over all of the tribes. In essence they were tribal leaders. The word "judge" occurs only in the prologue (2:16–19), whereas the usual designation of the leaders is "deliverer" (e.g., 3:9, 15).

The representative and selective nature of the stories of the judges appears in the alternation between the brief notices and the longer accounts. There are six *minor judges*, who receive only a small notice, and six *major judges*, of whom some details are given up to a full story of one or more of their exploits. The accounts of the minor and major judges are woven together to create a fabric out of the separate stories. The decreasing frequency of major judges corresponds to the increase in the number of minor judges, until the story of Samson.[5] (See figure 13.)

The judges were tribal leaders who could never rally the support of the whole nation. The greatest judges mobilized the forces of only four to six tribes. Gideon, for example, came from Manasseh, which was trampled by the seminomadic incursions of the Midianites and Amalekites.[6] His troops came from Asher, Manasseh, Zebulun, and Naphtali (6:35). When Ephraim heard about the battle, they criticized Gideon sharply for not having called them to the battle. Gideon adroitly averted a civil war. Intertribal relations, obviously, were quite tense. Involvement, or lack of it, depended on who was the judge and which tribe was occupied by foreign invaders.

In addition to the prologue and epilogue and the narratives and brief notices pertaining directly to the judges, the book contains several intriguing literary masterpieces: Deborah's hymn (chap. 5), Jotham's fable (9:7–15), and the story of Samson (chaps. 13–16).[7]

186

Major	Minor
1. Othniel	
2. Ehud	
3.	Shamgar
4. Deborah	
5. Gideon	
6.	Tola
7.	Jair
8. Jephthah	
9.	Ibzan
10.	Elon
11. Abdon	
12. Samson	

Figure 13. The Twelve Judges

RUTH

The Book of Ruth is cast in the middle of the period of the judges (1:1). The departure of Elimelech, Naomi, and their sons Mahlon and Kilion is necessitated by the famine in the region of Bethlehem. Evidently, the curses of the covenant (including famine) were unleashed on the inhabitants, in addition to enemy raids. The family migrated from Bethlehem to the Moabite plains, where Mahlon and Kilion married Moabite women, Ruth and Orpah.[8] The story quickly focuses on Ruth and her loyalty both to Naomi and to the God of Israel. The literary artistry of the book is self-evident. The author softly paints the beautiful character of this Moabite woman, full of loyalty, love, and concern. Boaz observes that, in her own unique way, Ruth is "a woman of noble character" (3:11), or wise (see Prov. 31:10). What a contrast to the portrayal of Israel's apostasy during this period! The Lord used a Gentile woman to silence the Israelites! She was committed to him and to the covenant people.

The story of Ruth, however, is more than a literary masterpiece about Ruth's marriage to Boaz. While there was lack of movement in the narratives of the judges, here there is evident movement—although it was not planned by Elimelech, Naomi, or Ruth. Even Boaz is subject to the workings of God. The Lord works in the ordinary circumstances of ordinary Israelites and a sojourner in Israel.[9] Through Ruth and Boaz he planned to renew theocratic leadership in Israel. Through the dynasty of

187

David God's glorious plans and promises would be fulfilled. The genealogy at the end of the book bears out the significance of the literary creation. The genealogy spans the time from Perez, a son of Judah by Tamar (Gen. 38:29), to King David (Ruth 4:18–21; cf. Matt. 1:2–16).

THE BOOKS OF SAMUEL

The first book of Samuel bears this same theological perspective. Though it forms part of a collection known as the Book of Samuel in the Hebrew Bible, in the LXX and in the English Bible it is divided into two books. The literary structure, however, shows the unity of the Books of Samuel as one whole.[10] For our purposes we shall treat the books as a unit, fully realizing that our present treatment already anticipates the more glorious era of the Davidic monarchy.

In contrast to the anarchy and lack of movement in the period of the judges, the Books of Samuel show real development in Israel's history. Their focus is on the Lord, who acts in ordinary human situations to work out his plan of redemption. The literary structuring develops the basic theme contained in Hannah's song, in which she gives praise to the Lord, the Holy One and the Rock of Israel (1 Sam. 2:2). He is sovereign in all his activities. He breaks the bows of warriors, humbles and exalts, and "will give strength to his king and exalt the horn of his anointed" (vv. 4, 7, 10). The editor of the whole work developed the activities of God in a most sensitive way. The Lord made war to cease, destroyed the temple at Shiloh and raised Samuel as his priest, and then brought down the mighty Saul and raised up David. The critical contention that the structure of the book is hardly discernible has failed to appreciate the theological interpretation of redemptive history.[11]

Together with Hannah's song, chapters 21–24 of the second book of Samuel form an inclusion. The inclusionary motifs are that human history unfolds the purposes of God and that God plans to use his anointed king (his messiah) in establishing his kingdom on earth. Two psalms of David (2 Sam. 22 [Ps. 18] and 23:1–7) echo the words of Hannah's song. She praised the power and strength of the Lord, who is holy, just, and loving to his own and who will raise up his messiah. David also praises God's power and strength. He is "the Rock" (2 Sam. 22:2, 47), who gives victory to his messiah, namely "to David and his descendants forever" (v. 51). In 2 Sam. 23:1–7, David thanks the Lord for having made an everlasting covenant, which guarantees the culmination of redemptive history:

Has he not made with me an everlasting covenant,
arranged and secured in every part?

(v. 5b)

Within the broader structural motif, the editor has set the outworking
of redemptive history in the hands of three characters: Samuel
(Hannah's son), Saul (Israel's first king), and David (Ruth's great-
grandson). There is an evident overlap in the stories of each of these
characters until the kingship of David. Though attempts were made to
snatch David's kingship from him (by Absalom and then Sheba), they
utterly failed. (See figure 14.)

Introduction (1 Sam. 1–2)

   Eli and Samuel (1 Sam. 3–8)

      Samuel and Saul (1 Sam. 9:1–16:13)

         Saul and David (1 Sam. 16:14–31:13)

           David (2 Sam. 1–20)

Conclusion (2 Sam. 21–24)

Figure 14. The Literary Structure of the Books of Samuel

Samuel

Like John the Baptist, Samuel stands on the threshold of a new era.
He witnessed the beginning of the downfall of Saul's kingship and
anointed David king. However, his eyes did not see the working out of
God's salvation and kingdom. He was God's tragic instrument, rejected
by his contemporaries and hated by Saul for having taken away his
kingship by divine decree.

The first book of Samuel develops the sovereign working of God in
the birth of Samuel (1:1–2:11), the downfall of the house of Eli, the
high priest at Shiloh (2:12–4:22), and the capture and return of the ark
(chaps. 5–6). Through Samuel, the judge-priest-prophet, the Lord gave
Israel victory over the Philistines and peace with the Amorites (7:13–
14).

Samuel and Saul

The next section (1 Sam. 9–16) treats the rise of the monarchy.
Within the complex of developments, two separate strands appear.
According to one perspective, the monarchy was against the will of God.
Samuel represents this sentiment in his negative portrayal of the power
of the king (8:11–18). On the other hand, the editor describes kingship
as God's instrument of bringing peace, victory, and prosperity to God's

189

people (9:1–10:16; chap. 11). These two strands are further worked out in the stories surrounding the incompatibility of Saul and David. After Samuel has given his farewell speech as a final exhortation to covenantal loyalty (chap. 12), in the spirit of Moses (Deut. 29–32) and Joshua (Josh. 23–24), Samuel openly confronts Saul, until he has demonstrated that Saul is not sensitive to the will of God. The prophet Samuel declares that he will not be present with Saul any more. His presence signified the presence of God with Saul. The separation of Samuel from Saul thus sealed the removal of Saul's dynasty from perpetual rule over Israel (1 Sam. 15:26, 28).

Saul and David

With the anointing of David, the working of God comes into clearer focus (1 Sam. 16). As long as Saul was alive, these two men symbolized the struggle of the kingdom. In and through the struggles, however, the kingship desired by God as his instrument of bringing blessing to his people came into focus.[12] David was God's choice as king (16:12); Saul was the people's choice. David represented the divine kingdom; Saul typified the human kingdom.

David

After Saul was dead and the civil war between supporters of Saul's dynasty and David's men had come to an end (1 Sam. 31–2 Sam. 4), David was crowned king over all Israel. He captured Jerusalem and brought the ark there (2 Sam. 6). This rapid sequence of events illustrates David's concern for the welfare of all the tribes and for the worship of God in Jerusalem.

The Lord richly rewarded David by giving him victory over his enemies (2 Sam. 8–10), but even more so by promising him a lasting dynasty (7:5–16). The successes of David, however, are balanced by his personal failures. Because of his involvement with Bathsheba and the murder of her husband, Uriah, the Lord also brought a curse to David (chap. 11). David is a man under both blessing and curse. The curse brings death and alienation to his family, and ultimately a civil war (chaps. 12–20). In and through the portrayals of David as a real man of flesh and blood, the literary movement leads the reader to hope. Unlike the kingship of Saul, characterized by lack of movement, there is progress in David's regime. The last section (chaps. 21–24) keeps alive the hope that, through the descendants of David, with whom God has made a covenant, the kingship with all its glories as a greater expression of God's presence may be established.

CONCLUSION

The literary materials give a condensed presentation of Israel's unresponsiveness and acculturation. The lack of movement during this period was not because of God's inability to deliver. He remained faithful, as he tolerated only so much suffering among his people before he raised up another deliverer-judge. His people had chosen the path of least resistance, and the Lord withheld his blessings and fulfilled the curses that were part of the covenant.

In the Book of Judges, the narrator has chosen incidents out of the life of Israel representing the dark days of the judges in order to illustrate the variety of incursions and troubles as well as the involvement of most of the tribes. No tribe was spared the trouble of wars, oppression, and incursions. Moreover, no tribe could claim supremacy, because the judges represented many tribes. All of these developments demonstrate clearly Israel's lack of unity, which stemmed from the inability of any one leader to effect a return to the theocratic ideal.

The cycles, the judges, the tribal squabbles, the enemies, and Israel's continual apostasy from the Lord make the lack of movement in Israel's history evident. The tribes of Israel did not gain perpetual victories, nor did they enjoy the fullness of the inheritance of the land. God was always there, but his working was behind the scenes. At times he reminded Israel of its rebelliousness by sending an angel (2:1–5), a prophet (6:7–10), or a divine judgment speech (10:6–16). Such messages affected minor reforms, but by and large Israel was unresponsive and hence became like one of the nations. Israel was not the envy of the nations, nor was it much of a theocracy. In spite of Israel's shortcomings, however, the author portrays the constancy of the Lord, who sovereignly disciplined and led his people out of the cycles toward a new era.

This new era is marked by the inauguration of the prophetic office (Samuel) and of the royal office (Saul and David). During this period these offices were defined in a way that would set the stage for further developments. However, the new era came into being only amid crisis.[13] Saul's callousness to Samuel's ministry and to the theocratic ideal created a deep rift between God's prophet-priest and the king. Moreover, Saul's pursuit of David posed a threat to the future of redemptive history. Saul is a lonely and transitory figure between two great men, Samuel and David. They reminded Israel of the leaders of a past era (Moses and Joshua) but also gave a foretaste of a greater reality of the kingdom of God on earth. Unlike the kingdom of Saul, God's kingdom is established not by human power but by the Spirit of God.

CHAPTER 14

Lessons from Israel's History

The Books of Judges, Ruth, and Samuel were probably composed during the period of the early monarchy. They served a parenetic function, teaching Israel lessons against syncretism, paganism, and despotism. The canonical approach of the books also aided Israel in viewing its own history from God's perspective, thus providing a kerygmatic function. These books contain preachable material for the people of God in all ages. The literary beauty has a quality that enables the godly to experience weeping, joy, laughter, confidence in God, and, above all, a deep sense of mystery at the working of God in history. Finally, the canonical books served a didactic function. They taught Israel what had happened, why the promises had not been fulfilled, and why the monarchy became necessary.

DIDACTIC FUNCTION

The people of God who first heard the words of the Book of Judges already lived in the new era. They had heard about the Conquest and the great promise of full claim to the land. They had heard about the great wonders of God in the days of Moses and Joshua. But they had not witnessed the theophany at Mount Sinai or the deliverance from Egypt or the sovereign working of God in the conquest of the land. They could identify with Gideon, who said to the angel of the Lord,

> If the LORD is with us, why has all this happened to us? Where are all his wonders that our fathers told us about when they said, "Did not the LORD bring us up out of Egypt?" But now the LORD has abandoned us and put us into the hand of Midian. (Judg. 6:13)

They were all members of a new Israel that felt the disadvantage of receiving traditions. To a large extent, they "knew neither the LORD nor what he had done for Israel" (Judg. 2:10). At this time also "the word of the LORD was rare; there were not many visions" (1 Sam. 3:1). Instead they knew a new kind of world, characterized by limitations. The Canaanite enclaves were a reality. Israel had suffered from enemy raids and oppressions. Since the battle of Deborah and Barak, the Canaanites were no longer a great force to be reckoned with (Judg. 4–5), but the threat of the Philistines was growing. The Philistines had migrated to the coast of Canaan about the same time as or shortly after the Conquest. Israel was hedged in between the Moabites and Ammonites on the east and the Philistines to the west, with the reality of Canaanite towns and villages within their tribal territories.

They also knew the effects of the Canaanites in their midst. By means of intermarriage and cultural and religious assimilation, the purity of Israel's worship and theocratic expression had been lost.[1] Several hundred years of decline and apostasy had left a deep scar on Israel's faith and practice. The traditions of the fathers had been altered by generations of improper instruction. The Levites, the priests, and the people had not escaped the destructive forces of assimilation.

Finally, the new generation needed further instruction as to who they were and what had happened to God's plan from the writing of the Book of the Law and the Conquest. To this end the Book of Judges particularly fills the gap by explaining the world of Israel's past as it related to their present context.

The Presence of Foreign Enclaves in Canaan

Canaan did not meet the expectations associated with the phrase "promised land." Joshua had left much land that had to be taken (Josh. 13:1–5; cf. Judg. 1). Jerusalem was a Jebusite city until the reign of David. In addition to the Canaanite presence, Israel encountered opposition from a new people who had settled in the southern coastal plains: the Philistines. The plains, valleys, international roads, and many fortified cities were in the hands of non-Israelites; whereas the covenant people occupied the hill country, being unsuccessful in taking or holding on to the richer valleys and plains. The foreign enclaves caused serious difficulty for Israel. The Philistines destroyed Shiloh, where the tabernacle stood in the days of Eli (1 Sam. 1:3; cf. Jer. 7:12–15; 26:6, 7). They enjoyed a monopoly on iron and, consequently, controlled the development of Israel's military weaponry and even of its agricultural implements (cf. 1 Sam. 13:19–21). Their power was so great that the tribe of Dan was forced to migrate to a new territory (cf. Judg. 18).

The natural questions posed by any pious Israelite were, "What has happened to the promises of God to the patriarchs?" and "Why did the mission of Moses and Joshua fail?" Underlying these questions was a more basic issue: "Is Yahweh faithful to his promises?" The Book of Judges explains that the presence of non-Israelites in the land was not due to God's lack of faithfulness or to his inability. Instead, Israel was fully to blame for their own situation. Because of their continued apostasy, the Lord decreed that they would not enjoy rest from their enemies (Judg. 2:20–3:4; Ps. 95:11; cf. Heb. 4:3–11). Through the continued existence of the nations, in and among Israel, the Lord tested the fidelity of his people (Judg. 2:22, 23; cf. Josh. 23:13).

The Breakup of Israel's Solidarity

After the death of Joshua the solidarity of Israel's tribes became a phantom. With the gradual deterioration of relations, tensions arose between the northern and the southern tribes and between the tribes settled on either side of the Jordan. For example, Deborah rebuked the Transjordan tribes and the outlying districts of Dan and Asher for failing to respond to her call for help (Judg. 5:15–17). Gideon barely avoided a civil war when the Ephraimites criticized him for not including them in his war against the Midianites (8:1). Jephthah was drawn into civil war with the Ephraimites (Judg. 12:1–6).

The story of Samson, a Danite, portrays the single-handed operation of a lonely frontier man against the Philistines (13:1–16:31).[2] The victories were not crowned with great success, because the Danites were forced to leave their homestead for another region (chap. 18). Childs correctly observes that Samson "personifies the tension between promise and fulfillment, ideal and actuality, freedom and servitude which also constitutes the tragedy of the nation under the judges."[3]

The tragic story of the Levite and his concubine bears out moral and political corruption. The men of Gibeah were guilty of multiple rape, but the tribe of Benjamin protected the guilty and faced the ire of the sister tribes, which resulted in civil war (Judg. 20). So severe was the bloodshed in Benjamin that the tribe approached extinction (21:17). Clearly, the unity of God's people had suffered from geographical isolation as well as regional and political strife. The contrast between the unity of the tribes in the period of the conquest and settlement and the disunity in the period of the judges is evident by comparing the beginning and end of the Book of Judges. In the beginning the tribes fought against the *Canaanites* under the leadership of Judah (1:1, 2). At the conclusion of the book they fought against Benjamin, *one of their own,* also under the direction of Judah (20:18).

Proliferation of Cultic Sites

Acculturation by intermarriage and syncretism as well as intertribal jealousies affected Israel's way of life more than the law of Moses ever had. Cultic sites grew in number until each city could boast of its own "high place," or *bamah,* where offerings and sacrifices were presented to Yahweh or to some pagan deity, often resulting in an admixture of Yahwism and paganism (syncretism). Special cultic significance was attached to Shechem and Bethel because of the importance of these sites in the lives of the patriarchs. Other sites gained significance by association with a great personage (Gideon's ephod at Ophrah, Judg. 8:22–27) or by reputation (Micah's ephod and idols, Judg. 17–18).

The story of Micah's idols, their seizure by the Danites, and the Levite's promotion to the priesthood, first by Micah and then by the Danites, is a sad commentary on the religious values of the Israelites. Idolatry and an illegitimate priesthood developed separately from the cultic center at Shiloh (cf. Judg. 18:30–31).

Samuel stepped into this world of Israel's lost religious heritage.[4] Not only had the pure worship of God suffered because of the wanton behavior of Eli's sons, but also the ark had been taken by the Philistines, and Shiloh was in ruins (1 Sam. 4–6, Ps. 78:60–61; Jer. 7:12–15; 12:6–7; 26:6).[5] During the time Samuel judged Israel, he had an altar constructed at Ramah, his hometown, where the people assembled at the high place (*bamah*) for sacrifice (1 Sam. 7:17; 9:12). Samuel led the people in local sacrifices and offerings at Gilgal (10:8; 11:14–15) and at Bethlehem (16:4). But even after David had the ark of the covenant transported to Jerusalem, the people continued to worship the Lord at local shrines.

The Need for a King

The Book of Judges provides a rationale for kingship. The conditions of anarchy, deterioration of tribal relationships, proliferation of cultic sites, and immorality called for a centralized leadership. The judges had been important instruments of God. By sending "judges," Yahweh had kept the tribes from complete destruction by foreign invaders. However, the judges were not national leaders. At best they rallied support from only a few tribes. Only Samuel came close to being a national leader, for he judged all of the tribes "from Dan to Beersheba" (1 Sam. 7:15; cf. 3:20).

The Book of Judges explains the danger inherent in kingship as well as its necessity. On the one hand, Israel was prone to selfcenteredness and autonomy, "In those days Israel had no king; everyone did as he saw fit" (21:25; cf. 17:6; 18:1; 19:1).[6] On the other hand, Israel needed a king in order to bring cohesion and to reduce the potential of absolute anarchy. Within this tension of independence and need for unity, the Book of Judges offers both a rationale for kingship and a warning regarding the dangers inherent in human kingship. What Israel needed was a centralized, self-perpetuating government that would be sensitive to the law of God, support the worship of God, bring unity to the tribes, and give Israel rest from her enemies. Samuel had provided this form of leadership but could not continue forever. The ideal would be a dynastic kingship, but the story of Gideon and his son Abimelech was a painful reminder of the danger of giving the rule to one family.[7] Gideon had refused kingship,[8] but his son Abimelech encouraged the leadership of

Shechem to crown him as king. In order to rid himself of would-be contenders, he had his seventy siblings executed, except for Jotham, who escaped. In his fable Jotham forewarned the people of the dangers inherent in despotic kingship (Judg. 9:7–15). The attempt at monarchy quickly soured when Abimelech killed a thousand men and women in the tower (vv. 22–49). Finally he was killed when he attempted to set the tower of Thebez on fire (vv. 50–55). Thus the tragic experiment in "dynastic" kingship ended.

The story of Abimelech taught Israel that kingship was not a guaranteed blessing. On the one hand, they needed a king as a symbol of tribal unity. On the other hand, a king could become oppressive and scorn the law of God. The subsequent history of Israel demonstrated to each generation how unpredictable the institution of kingship could be.

PARENETIC FUNCTION

God's Word also has a parenetic, or hortatory, function. The Books of Judges and Samuel contain important lessons for Israel and all of God's people. The pious Israelites who heard these books read would have been horrified at the apostasy and immorality of their predecessors. Even though they may have preferred the direct experience of God's rule without the institution of kingship, they had to learn from Israel's history that kingship ordained by God is good for the sake of the nation. Support of the institution, regardless of who was ruling, expressed trust in a sovereign God who had ordained that particular king for that particular hour (see 1 Sam. 24:6). Anarchy, oppression from enemy forces, and religious and moral deterioration would be much worse.

The books also warned the godly not to overemphasize tribal allegiance. The judges came from all tribes and regions. Though some were more important in the canonical accounts, the criterion of selection for more extensive coverage is seldom the tribal affiliation. Deborah, Barak, and Gideon represent Israel's difficulties from incursions from the north and the east. Jephthah hails from Transjordan and is engaged with the Ammonites, who had even crossed into the hill country of Judah, Benjamin, and Ephraim (Judg. 10:9). Samson, a Danite, dramatizes the difficulty of his little tribe against the Philistines, their southwestern neighbors. God's people had to learn to put aside tribal pride and isolationism.

The concern for tribal and regional divisions is also related to a deeper concern. The accounts of the angel of the LORD at Bokim (Judg. 2:1–5), the prologue (2:6–3:6), the repetitive descriptions of Israel's idolatry, the words of the prophet (6:7–10), the Word of the Lord against an apostate people (10:11–16), and the occasional expressions of repentance (2:4–5; 10:16) spoke to the people of God. In the expressions of the patience and mercy of God, they learned that God is concerned with loyalty. All of Israel's troubles in warfare and famine came from the curse of God against his people's disobedience.

A theocratic king had to be more sensitive to the law of God. The welfare of God's people depended on his leadership. He had to be sensitive to the Word of God through the prophets and to establish and foster the central cult, which was vital to the unity of God's people. The story of Saul dramatizes the importance of loyalty to Yahweh. Despite the fact that he was able to rally the support of the tribes, Saul was repeatedly disobedient to the Lord. Tribal unity without loyalty to Yahweh did not constitute a theocratic kingdom. Therefore, the kingdom was removed from his family.

> Does the LORD delight in burnt offerings and sacrifices
> as much as in obeying the voice of the LORD?
> To obey is better than sacrifice,
> and to heed is better than the fat of rams.
> For rebellion is like the sin of divination,
> and arrogance like the evil of idolatry.
> Because you have rejected the word of the LORD,
> he has rejected you as king.
>
> (1 Sam. 15:22–23)

In his last address to Israel, Samuel sums up the situation very well (1 Sam. 12). As a godly leader (vv. 1–5), he reminded them of their past. In spite of their sins, Israel was not consumed but repeatedly experienced the evidences of God's love. The period of the judges is full of "the righteous acts performed by the LORD for you and your fathers" (v. 7). The patience of God, however, is not an excuse to continue in evil. Samuel forewarned that such stubbornness would cause both people and king to perish: "Yet if you persist in doing evil, both you and your king will be swept away" (v. 25).

THE KERYGMATIC FUNCTION

The good news of this period is God! In spite of the changes in the judges and the expressions of Israel's rebellious spirit, the Lord graciously meets the needs of his people, exhorts them to covenantal loyalty, gives Israel the institution of kingship, and amplifies his Word through the prophetic ministry of Samuel. God raised up judges who were adequate to meet the military challenges of their time. He sent his Spirit, who had previously guided the ministry of Moses and Joshua, upon these theocratic leaders (see Judg. 3:10; 11:29; 13:25; 14:6, 19; 15:14).

At the same time, the Lord was preparing Israel for a new era. The ministry of Samuel signified the transition from an era of individual theocratic leadership to an era of full-fledged monarchy with clearly prescribed expectations of the theocratic leaders: king, prophet, priest, and Levite. The offices are related to, but also independent from, the controlling interests of any one party. Each officer has a place within the operation of the kingdom of God and is responsible to God for his actions. The history of redemption traces the development of each office under the old and new administration of the covenant.

Of overarching significance is the institution of kingship. The Book of Judges prepared Israel to see the benefits of a king over against the anarchy and meaninglessness of the intervening period between Moses/Joshua (the period of Israel as "a holy nation") and David/Solomon (Israel as "a royal nation"). During the cycles of the judges the Lord prepared the way for David and his dynasty. The little Book of Ruth testifies to his grace. The tragic circumstances of the famine, migration, and death of loved ones experienced by Naomi was transformed into joy by the romance that developed between Ruth and Boaz. But the romance was not an end in itself. Out of the marriage of a Judean and a Moabite, a new family was created from which David was born. The ordinary circumstances of life in the period of the judges were sovereignly and graciously transformed into a new era: the Davidic dynasty.[9]

GREAT EXPECTATIONS

Finally, the people of God had reason to look at the new era with great expectations. As they lived in the early days of the Davidic dynasty, they greeted the change with a welcome sigh of relief. The days of the judges were over, and new hope was focused on the anointed servant of God who was to bring unity to the tribes, lead Israel into perpetual victory over the enemies, establish a centralized rule, foster the worship of the Lord, and promote the fear of God. The Israelites of Samuel's era had experienced a token of the new era in Samuel's ministry. Would David now be God's instrument for establishing the just rule of God to the ends of the earth, of which Hannah had spoken in her prayer (1 Sam. 2:1–10)? Would the era of David bring into reality the Word of the Lord that was spoken by the man of God: "I will raise up for myself a faithful priest, who will do according to what is in my heart and mind. I will firmly establish his house, and he will minister before my anointed one always" (v. 35)? The many ways in which David, the anointed of the Lord, was spared were a silent testimony to an affirmative answer. The eyes of faith were directed to look to God for the establishment of his kingdom.

CONCLUSION

The stories of the judges and Saul serve as sober reminders of how blessing is related to responsiveness to the Lord. God places his people in concrete situations in which they must respond, either to the favorable conditions and structures of this world or else to him. The self-serving interests of Israel undermined the blessedness they could have experienced, if only they had put their confidence in the Lord. Samson serves as a model of apostate Israel. He was powerful in the Lord's Spirit, but powerless in his own.

Israel destroyed itself, as tribe rose against tribe, immorality prevailed, and cultic sites proliferated. The end of Judges serves as a tragic reminder of the immorality, bloodshed, and hostility. Nevertheless, the Lord was present in providing deliverance, raising up judges, giving his Word to Samuel, and choosing David to be his servant. The end of the period is set off by Saul's death. The fall of Saul and his family at Gilboa opens up the realization of a new era that the Lord had been preparing for generations: David, son of Jesse, grandson of Obed, and great-grandson of Ruth, the Moabite! Kingship is of the Lord!

CHAPTER 15

God's Faithfulness
and Israel's Unresponsiveness

The significance of this period in redemptive history lies in the *acts of God*. These acts were different from those in the previous period. In the past he worked wonders in the eyes of Israel, but Israel had failed to respond to the revelation of his glory. In this period, he tests Israel's responsiveness to him. The canonical Books of Judges, Ruth, and Samuel blame Israel's troubles during the period of the judges on their failure to respond. The adversities (wars, foreign occupation, famine) were due to Israel's infatuation with paganism. God's acts are expressions of fatherly discipline and concern. He sends adversities and then deliverers. First he closes his ears to an unresponsive people, and then he listens to their cries. He abandons them to the despotic rule of King Saul, preparing Israel for the gracious reign of King David. God's acts are disciplinary and lead Israel gradually to him.

Behind the scenes the Lord is preparing his people for a new era. The present era is characterized by independence, apostasy, and meaninglessness. Even the great Samuel was unable to effect significant changes. He was, however, God's forerunner of the new era: the kingship of David. Actually, Samuel knew little of the working out of God's plan. By the time he passed away, he had been put aside by Saul and knew only of David's troubles at the hands of Saul. The future of the theocracy and particularly of kingship in Israel was questionable from a human perspective.[1] Yet, God was working over a period of hundreds of years to lead Israel to the fuller revelation of his plan to install the Davidic dynasty in preparation for the kingship of Jesus the Messiah. The redemptive-historical themes of this period focus on the sovereign working of God, the needs of the people, and the hope for the coming of God's kingdom.

THE SOVEREIGN WORKING OF GOD

The prophetic author of the second prologue in Judges (2:6–3:6) saw the finger of God in Israel's history. God sent enemies to oppress Israel as a consequence of their disobedience. The pattern established in

Deuteronomy became incorporated in Israel's history. Prosperity and adversity do not just happen. They evidence the respective reward and judgment of God. They are forms of encouragement and discipline from the Lord to draw his children to himself. To this end he uses two basic means of communication: his Word and his acts.

God's Word

God sent his Word to Israel through the angel at Bokim (Judg. 2:1–5), the prophet (6:7–10), an unidentified messenger (10:11–14), and particularly through the great prophet Samuel (1 Sam. 3:19–4:1a; chap. 12). Samuel uses a legal-prophetic form known as the *rîb* ("charge") pattern to charge the people with infidelity. The statement consisted essentially of (1) a reminder of God's acts of loyalty toward Israel, (2) a statement of his charges against them, and (3) a solemn warning of judgment, if his Word remains unheeded. Samuel's farewell speech (1 Sam. 12:6–25) brings together the period of the judges from God's perspective. The past has been a dismal failure, and now is the time to repent: "But be sure to fear the LORD and serve him faithfully with all your heart; consider what great things he has done for you. Yet if you persist in doing evil, both you and your king will be swept away" (vv. 24–25).

The Word of God was rare in the period of the judges (1 Sam. 3:1); Israel had to learn to respond to Moses' revelation. The infrequency of new revelation confirmed the finality of his Torah ("instruction") through Moses (see Judg. 3:4). Only when Israel had consistently failed to respond did he send Samuel as a living witness to himself. The renewal of revelation should have shaken Israel's national conscience, but Samuel's ministry seemed to have little impact (see 1 Sam. 12:24–25).

God's Acts

The work of God is most evident in the *cycle* characteristic of the period of the judges. The enemies that troubled Israel were his instruments of justice, teaching Israel to look up to him.

Though Israel was slow to learn, God was patient and compassionate. The nations he permitted to remain were left to refine Israel. Joshua had forewarned the people that the nations would become "snares and traps . . . , whips on your backs and thorns in your eyes" (Josh. 23:13; cf. Judg. 2:3). When Israel succumbed to the military and cultural pressures of the nations, especially the Philistines, God gave them over to famine, wars, and foreign occupation. Yet, he also delivered them by the judges, especially his servant Samuel, a theocratic leader like Moses and Joshua. Samuel simultaneously held the three offices of judge, priest, and prophet. Through Samuel's ministry God encouraged Israel, exhorted them, and gave them victory over the Philistines (1 Sam. 7:14).

In response to the growing pressure for a dynastic kingship, the Lord provided Israel with another hard lesson: Saul's despotic rule. As long as Saul was in the shadow of Samuel, he led Israel to victory. But he failed miserably when he was in the shadow of David. He was occupied with an all-consuming passion to rid himself of David, whom "all Israel and Judah" loved (1 Sam. 18:16).

The anointing of David was crucial in redemptive history. It anticipates the glorious rule of David, the founder of the Davidic dynasty by the grace of God. But the event of the anointing cannot be related to the righteousness of David. That David's heart was right with God is not at issue (see 1 Sam. 13:14; 16:7). The issue, rather, is the mysterious working of God for generations. David was the son of Jesse, the grandson of Obed, and the great-grandson of Ruth and Boaz. One of the purposes of the Book of Ruth is to give us a glimpse into the sovereign working of God in raising up a family through whom David and ultimately the Messiah would come. The Lord had sovereignly rejected Ephraim as leader in favor of Judah (Ps. 78:67–72).

David was from the tribe of Judah, the city of Bethlehem, and a great-grandson of a Moabite woman, who had shown more faith and loyalty to the Lord and his covenant people than many an Israelite. Israel found the ideal shepherd-king in David, the great-grandson of a Gentile proselyte, in whom was God's Spirit.

Israel's Responsiveness

Rare and precious were the moments when repentance was expressed on a national level. At Bokim they wept aloud and offered sacrifices to the Lord (Judg. 2:4–5). In response to the Ammonite pressure and to occupation of Gilead and parts of Judah, Benjamin, and Ephraim, Israel realized that they had sinned against the Lord, removed their idols, and served the Lord (10:15–16). Samuel led Israel in a short-lived national revival, when they confessed their sin to the Lord. Finally, in response to Samuel's farewell address and the sign of the thunder and rain, they asked Samuel to intercede on their behalf (1 Sam. 12:19).

We are able to affirm that God's purposes are being achieved even in those portions of biblical history when Yahweh's people fall into sin and experience great difficulties. At the level of Israel's historical awareness, however, it seemed that there was little movement or direction. The seeming meaninglessness was due to retrogression and progression. (See figure 15.)

Israel experienced *retrogression* in her covenantal privileges: the absence of Yahweh's blessing and protection. Instead of enjoying the glorious liberty of being God's children, the Israelites experienced tribal factions, oppression, and want, interspersed with moments of relief under God's appointed judges. The people may have thought that Yahweh owed them his blessing and protection, even when they flaunted their immoral and idolatrous behavior. In this context the Lord demonstrated that he is free in giving and in withholding his blessing and protection.

PROGRESS

—because of Yahweh's Word and acts
—hope in David's kingship as God's means of restoring and fulfilling the promises

DECLINE

—because of Israel's sin
—despair over the loss of the tabernacle and the ark, as well as over foreign invasion and rule

Figure 15. Progress and Decline Before David's Rule

The symbol of God's freedom was the ark of the covenant, the token of God's beneficent kingship. For a while it seemed as if Shiloh was the central place of worship of which Moses had spoken (Deut. 12:5). The tabernacle was set up at Shiloh, and the ark was in the tabernacle in the days of Eli the priest. But Eli and his sons showed contempt for the holy and glorious presence of the Lord and thus brought about God's judgment upon the priestly family (1 Sam. 2:12–27, 29–34; 3:11–12). The people, too, treated God's presence with contempt when they used the ark of the covenant as a magical symbol in their war against the Philistines. Yahweh demonstrated his freedom in permitting the ark to be captured by the Philistines (1 Sam. 4:11, 17, 22). The name Ichabod ("the glory is departed") reinforces the significance of the capture of the ark, for with its departure the symbolic glory of Yahweh departed (4:19–22). After the destruction of Shiloh, the capture of the ark, and the desolation of the tabernacle (cf. Ps. 78:60; Jer. 7:12, 14), Israel did not have a centralized place for the worship of Yahweh. Even when the ark was returned to Israel, it remained at Kiriath Jearim (1 Sam. 7:2) until David brought it to Jerusalem (2 Sam. 6:3–17).

In her continual wars against the Philistines Israel thought that the solution was in military power, symbolized by a centralized government under a powerful king. The victory achieved under Samuel's leadership at Mizpah (1 Sam. 7:11) and the subsequent weakening of the Philistines during the rest of his life (7:13) served as a reminder that Yahweh grants his blessing and protection through a godly leader. Israel desired a continuation of dominance by electing kingship and military power (*Realpolitik*) in favor of *theocracy*. Though Israel's first king, Saul, defeated the Ammonites at Jabesh Gilead (chap. 11) and his son, Jonathan, brought temporary respite from the Philistines (chap. 14), the writer of Samuel summarizes the military situation under Saul's kingship in this way: "All the days of Saul there was bitter war with the Philistines" (1 Sam. 14:52).

Israel experienced *progression* under Samuel and Saul as they paved the way for a new era. They were catalysts in bringing unity among the tribes. The renewed sense of solidarity comes to expression in phrases such as "all Israel" (1 Sam. 3:20; 4:1; 7:3, 5, 6) or "all the elders of Israel" (8:4). The confederate tribes had finally come to the realization that they could not live independently of each other. They believed that a king would enhance the tribal federation in its political struggle against enemy forces. They wanted a king like the nations (1 Sam. 8:20). They received what they asked for: Saul. He symbolized *Realpolitik*: military power, administrative skills, and political skills. But his reign ended in a fiasco.

In contrast David became a symbol of *theocracy*. The Books of Samuel develop in a masterful way the fact that the symbol of a theocratic kingdom lies in a godly king. David was dependent on the Lord, jealous for Yahweh's holiness and glory, zealous for the presence and kingdom of the Lord, and recognized by all the tribes, "all Israel and Judah loved David" (1 Sam. 18:16a). In spite of all of Saul's plotting against David, David relentlessly trusted in the Lord to give him the kingdom (1 Sam. 16–31). Israel's future was in David, the king after God's heart, under whose kingship Israel might find rest from her enemies. Only with the appearance of the Davidic kingship does Israel have hope for a restoration to covenantal privilege.

THE PROMISES OF GOD AND THE
NEEDS OF THE PEOPLE

The period of the judges was a low point in redemptive history. Israel was living dangerously close to the edge of God's judgment. The previous period was characterized by fulfillment under the ministry of Moses and Joshua, but Israel had since lost direction and was drifting from one experience to another. God had promised to make Israel chief of the nations (Deut. 26:19; 28:13), but instead it was often overrun by the nations (v. 45).

The Land and Israel

Apostasy affected every area of life. Most prominent was the way in which the promises were curtailed. Israel's borders changed continually, depending on its strength. At the beginning of the period of the judges, there was a latent hope that they could drive out the indigenous population with the help of the Lord (Judg. 1). By God's decree to permit the nations to remain (2:3, 21–3:4), Israel had to accept coexistence with the Canaanite enclaves and respond appropriately to the challenge of either being like the nations or showing loyalty to the Lord by keeping his Torah. From this period on, Israel would, by divine decree, seldom enjoy rest in the Promised Land (Ps. 95:11). Early on, Samuel warned Israel that failure to respond to the Lord would lead to exile from the land (1 Sam. 12:24–25).

God's Blessings

Israel's troubles foreshadowed greater difficulties, but God's acts of compassion demonstrated his great love for them. War, famine, and adversities were concrete expressions that the people were not blessed by the Lord. Yet, he graciously sustained them so that they would not be wiped out. He remained faithful to them so that no one could charge him with lack of love and mercy for his own people. As Samuel said, "For the sake of his great name the LORD will not reject his people, because the LORD was pleased to make you his own" (1 Sam. 12:22).

The inspired poetic interpretation of Israel in the wilderness and their occupation of the land gives an insight into their unresponsiveness to God's mighty acts (Ps. 78). The more he did for them, the more they rebelled. Ephraim had been greatly blessed in population and land (Josh. 16–17), in accordance with the blessings of Jacob and Moses (Gen. 48:15–20; 49:22–26; Deut. 33:13–17). Its independent and bellicose attitude provoked God's anger, however, so its prominence was given to Judah (Ps. 78:67–68). Each person, each clan, and each tribe had to be loyal to the Lord if they were to experience his blessings, which could be limited or given to another tribe!

Blessing to the Nations

Israel was too occupied with its own problems to be a light to the nations. In spite of Israel's obstinacy, the Lord sovereignly worked out the conditions that led Elimelech to take his family to Moab. The story of Ruth is an illustration of the magnificence of God's grace to the nations. He brought Ruth into the covenant community as he had done earlier with Rahab. These women are examples of the many who joined the covenant and thus became sons and daughters of Abraham. The story of Ruth is also a perpetual warning to the covenant people that God is free to extend his blessing to the Gentiles. He fulfills his purposes in spite of his own people.

SAMUEL AND THE HOPE FOR THE FUTURE

The canonical books also give hope to the godly: hope focused on the care of God shown in his patience and mercy. After all, he sent them judges, even though he had not promised this means of deliverance to Moses or Joshua. He also sent them his Word, especially in the ministry of Samuel. In Samuel, God further developed the kind of leadership associated with the period of the Exodus and the Conquest. Samuel was a prophet of the Lord, who ministered to the king. He was the fountainhead of the prophetic office in the Old Testament. Through Old Testament prophets God revealed his presence with his people, spoke his Word in visions and dreams, demonstrated his power by signs, exhorted Israel to return to the Mosaic revelation, charged his people with their offenses, decreed punishment, and corrected the king when he led the people astray. The prophet was God's spokesman, and Samuel was the first to occupy this office (Acts 3:24).

Samuel is also directly associated with the institution of the kingship. Even though he remained opposed to it, he was God's messenger. He looked forward to the righteous rule of God in David and to the extension of God's blessing first to Israel and then also to the nations. His place in redemptive history is like that of John the Baptist. Both men were important as messengers proclaiming a new era in this history of redemption, but each was overshadowed. Samuel was overshadowed by David, and John was dwarfed by Jesus.

THE NEW ERA

Brief glimpses of the new era are found in Hannah's song, the word of the anonymous prophet, and the Word of God to the young boy Samuel.

Hannah's Song

Hannah's song (1 Sam. 2:1–10) provides the interpretive framework for the two books of Samuel. The books begin with the ministry of Samuel and climax with King David's expectations of God's fidelity to the covenant with him and his descendants. Hannah's song expresses (1) confidence in God, the Rock of Israel; (2) hope in the Lord's victory over Israel's enemies; (3) hope in the restoration of the fortunes of his people; (4) hope in the establishment of his kingdom on earth; and (5) an allusion to the anointed (messiah) of the Lord. These expressions of hope have united the children of God in both the Old Testament and New Testament periods. The focus of hope in the coming redemption gradually changes over the course of redemptive history from David to Solomon and from Solomon in turn to Hezekiah, Josiah, Zerubbabel, and ultimately Jesus Christ in his exaltation and glorification. Mary's Magnificat confirms that Jesus is the focus of hope as God's ultimate expression of his mercy, by whom God keeps covenant with the fathers (Luke 1:46–55).

The Anonymous Prophet

An anonymous prophet predicted the end of Eli's dynastic priesthood (1 Sam. 2:30–36). The deaths of Eli, Hophni, and Phinehas set the course for the fulfillment of this word, ultimately fulfilled by Solomon in the removal of Abiathar, a descendant of Eli, from the priesthood (1 Kings 2:27). The prophet also spoke of a new era in which God would raise up for himself "a faithful priest, who will do according to what is in my heart and mind," who would serve perpetually before his anointed (1 Sam. 2:35).

The combination of a faithful priest and a faithful messianic king has its initial focus on the era of David and Solomon and the institution of the Zadokite priesthood. Eli was a descendant of Aaron and had received the Aaronic priesthood by heredity. He served at the Shiloh tabernacle. However, the Lord abandoned the tabernacle at Shiloh (Ps. 78:60; Jer. 7:12, 14) in favor of establishing a central sanctuary in Jerusalem. The abandonment of Shiloh in the hill country of Ephraim signified his rejection of the importance of the tribes of Joseph in favor of the tribe of Judah:

> Then he rejected the tents of Joseph,
>   he did not choose the tribe of Ephraim;
> but he chose the tribe of Judah,
>   Mount Zion, which he loved.
> He built his sanctuary like the heights,
>   like the earth that he established forever.
> He chose David his servant
>   and took him from the sheep pens.
>   (Ps. 78:67–70)

The prophetic word anticipates fulfillment in the Solomonic era. Through David, God established Jerusalem as the religious center of the kingdom. The ark of the covenant had been taken by the Philistines, but it had afflicted them as it was taken from one Philistine city to another (1 Sam. 5). Finally it was returned to Israel (6:1–7:1). During David's early years as king over the twelve tribes, it was brought to Jerusalem (2 Sam. 6) to await the building of the Solomonic temple (see 2 Sam. 7:11–13; 1 Chron. 22:2–26:32; 28:1–29:20).

Through Solomon, the Lord fulfilled his Word given by the anonymous prophet. Solomon deposed Abiathar, a descendant of Eli, thus making room for the Zadokite priesthood (1 Kings 2:26–27, 35;

1 Chron. 29:22; Ezek. 40:46; 44:15; 48:11). The Solomonic era was to be a climactic fulfillment, as the temple was erected in Jerusalem, the priesthood of Zadok was established, and the anointed kingship of David's dynasty ruled over all the tribes of Israel.

Clearly, the prophecy of the anonymous prophet points to the Davidic era and beyond the Solomonic era to our Lord Jesus. It is possible to appreciate more deeply the combination of these theocratic offices in his ministry in fulfillment of the prophecy of Zechariah, who predicted the close cooperation between the royal and priestly offices (Zech. 4).

God's Word to Samuel

Finally, the Lord forewarned the prophet Samuel of these changes in a vision of the night (1 Sam. 3). Samuel did not clearly understand the implications of the death of Eli and his family. After these events, he knew that he had been uniquely chosen to serve Israel as judge, prophet, and priest. Even though he had not come from a priestly family, he was chosen by the Lord to serve Israel in the absence of an ordained leadership. Through this servant of the Lord, God focused the hope of the faithful beyond the era of the judges and the monarchy to a new era, to a new kind of kingship, and to a greater expression of his presence and blessing on his people. As the apostle Peter said to the crowd in Jerusalem,

> Indeed, all the prophets from Samuel on, as many as have spoken, have foretold these days. And you are heirs of the prophets and of the covenant God made with your fathers. He said to Abraham, "Through your offspring all peoples on earth will be blessed." When God raised up his servant, he sent him first to you to bless you by turning each of you from your wicked ways. (Acts 3:24–26)

Conclusion to Part 5

The fidelity of God expressed itself in a variety of ways, despite Israel's lack of responsiveness. He multiplied his acts of deliverance, sent his Word through Samuel, and worked quietly to establish his kingship in David. God's sovereign and gracious work was one aspect that Israel learned to appreciate years after the event. The people of God in any age may learn from this period of seemingly meaningless movement that God is still sovereign. In the process of refining, God was preparing his people for the new era, when the messianic king would lead the people into an experience of solidarity and blessing. By itself, however, the period is marked by lack of movement. Israel went through the treadmill.

Even in the most adverse circumstances, the Lord expects his own to be zealous for him and to remove any form of idolatry. Israel remained idolatrous because idol worship was culturally acceptable, and hence it seemed to solidify success in life. Samuel defined the essence of covenantal loyalty: "If you fear the LORD and serve and obey him and do not rebel against his commands, and if both you and the king who reigns over you follow the LORD your God—good!" (1 Sam. 12:14).

Samuel remains significant as the forerunner of the prophetic office. He is a transition figure between Moses, with whom the Lord spoke face to face, and Elijah, who inaugurated the covenant-prosecutor role in its usual sense. Samuel warned the people of the impending dangers of the course that they had taken.

The Lord's purposes remained constant. Regardless of Israel's response, he planned to fulfill the promises of raising a people to himself, including Gentiles. Ruth serves as an encouragement to all Gentiles and as a reminder of the universal purposes of God. Hope in God is sustained by the conviction that the Lord will be victorious over all his enemies and that he will vindicate his children and permanently establish his kingdom.

The period of Israel as "a nation like the other nations" brings out how short-lived Israel's enjoyments of the covenantal benefits were and how the Lord disciplines his people like a father. The negative and positive features of this period may be summarized as follows:

1. Israel failed terribly in maintaining the theocratic ideal.

2. Israel's leadership was incapable of looking beyond the regional and temporary interests. The tribes were constantly embroiled in intertribal squabbles and warfare.

3. The people of Israel suffered greatly on account of their infidelity, regretted the consequences of their acts, but did not repent.

4. Israel's history took a meandering course, as major and minor judges led the tribes out of the oppression and harassment occasioned by the invading and occupying forces.

5. The Lord, nevertheless, was present in raising up judges, in not permitting the nations to rule over his people, in preparing his people for kingship, in disciplining his people, and in laying his hand on David as the anointed of the Lord.

6. The Lord raised up Samuel as the first of the prophets, by whom he kept his people and refined them in preparation for the greater revelation of his kingdom on earth.

7. The Lord is the object of hope because he has planned to give his people rest through his king, through the ordained priesthood, and through the prophetic word. The theocracy was threatened, but the Lord is faithful!

Part 6

A Royal Nation

Introduction to Part 6

The period of Israel as "a royal nation" marks a most important development in the history of redemption. In previous periods God had been faithful to his promise to Abraham. Nations and kings had risen out of him. Through him the Lord had begun to renew the earth and a people for himself. This renewal had developed during the stage of Moses and Joshua in God's promise to Israel that it would be his holy nation out of all the nations. Israel was consecrated as Yahweh's people, and they became holy by God's dwelling among them. Moreover, he had given them the Land of Promise, as his holy land (Exod. 15:17).

Yet, there were great limitations. The land was only partially taken; the people were by nature rebellious and unresponsive. They had become like the other nations. The period of the judges, in which the Lord raised up these nations as oppressors, is a low point in the history of redemption. Despite the great leaders, none until Samuel was able to unite the nation under theocratic leadership. Even when Samuel united the people and led them as priest, prophet, and judge, the damage of the preceding centuries under the judges was too great for him to correct. When his sons proved unable to succeed him, the people looked for a greater and more enduring kind of leadership, craving a king like that of the other nations. Under these circumstances, the institution of national kingship arose.

The Lord knew the hearts of his people and gave them the kind of king they desired—one who turned out to be a despotic, selfish tyrant. King Saul had ably unified the tribes by administrative reforms, but he was concerned primarily with his own position and that of his sons. His kingship was taken away and given to David, God's chosen servant, through whom the Lord restored the benefits of theocratic kingship to Israel.

David was a man after God's own heart, a picture of the Messiah. David's character is presented to us in the Books of Samuel in such a way that we may understand the kind of Messiah God would send to earth. The era of David and Solomon was one of *great fulfillment*. Not only did God promise that there would be kings to sit on the throne of David forevermore, but he fulfilled elements of both the Mosaic and

212

Abrahamic covenants. The Mosaic covenant spoke only of "a place" where God was to be worshiped. That place was specified in David's choice of Jerusalem. The era of David and Solomon was one of peace, justice, righteousness, and the presence of God. Israel became the head and not the tail, as they had been in the previous era (Deut. 28:13, 44). In the Abrahamic covenant the Lord promised to bless his people, to prosper them and their families in the land, to make Abraham's name great, and to bless the nations through the descendants of Abraham. The promises became a reality during this era. In addition, the Lord further committed himself to perpetuate the promises of both covenants by making a covenant with David. The Davidic covenant assures the perpetuity of God's covenants and the promises inherent in them through an enduring kingship of David's dynasty.

A study of this period further helps us to appreciate the background of the prophetic metaphors used later in portraying the messianic age. After this period, the writers of Scripture would look back to the era of David and Solomon as a model describing the glories of the messianic age. From our perspective after the coming of our Lord Jesus Christ, David may seem to be only a faint reflection of the true Messiah. If we are surprised that the prophets looked back on the past in projecting the glorious messianic age, we must remember that they had not yet seen the glory of the Son of God. Since the fullness of the messianic age still lies in the future, we too must use the historicized language of the Old Testament to portray the glory of the messianic age. A reflection on the era of David and Solomon helps us to understand such language. The image of the royal nation under David and Solomon points to a greater, more lasting fulfillment. Maranatha!

In this period we shall witness several important developments:

1. a greater fulfillment of the promises guaranteed in the Abrahamic covenant;

2. the fulfillment of God's dwelling among his people in the place that he would choose, namely Jerusalem, chosen as the religious and administrative center;

3. a renewal of theocratic leadership (reminiscent of Moses and Joshua) in David's true heart-commitment to God, to the Mosaic covenant, and to theocratic leadership as a shepherd over all the tribes of Israel;

4. the establishment of the Davidic covenant as the expression of God's kingdom on earth;

5. the enthronement of wisdom evident in the lives and works of David and Solomon;

6. the closeness of God's relationship to David and Solomon, the glories of the royal era, the upholding of justice and righteousness,

the enjoyment of the covenant blessings of peace and prosperity, the shepherd-like leadership, and the fulfillment of the theocratic ideals (which later formed the basis of the prophetic projection of the messianic kingdom marked by God's presence, wisdom, peace, and prosperity); and

the expectation of another era, not marred by the personal failures of David and Solomon, which would be characterized by an even greater and more permanent fulfillment.

CHAPTER 16

Yahweh Is the Rock of Israel

The records of the period of Israel as "the royal nation" separately and collectively witness to the grandeur of David and Solomon. These literary materials come from various historical contexts and address different needs of the community, but regardless of their diversity and canonical function, one unifying theme is clear: Yahweh is the Rock of Israel. Because of him Israel tasted a greater sense of fulfillment of the Abrahamic and Mosaic covenants. Because of his promise to David in the Davidic covenant, the people remained hopeful that he would be faithful in restoring the benefits of this period on a grander scale.

A study of the Books of Samuel, Kings, and Chronicles simultaneously with the royal psalms (Pss. 2; 18; 20; 21; 45; 72; 89; 101; 110; 132) and the prophetic portrayals of the Davidic Messiah contributes to a holistic reading. Such a large picture is necessary to appreciate the canonical function, the theocentric perspective, and the eschatological dimension. It is clear that the canonical writings are selective. They do not purport to give us a complete history of this period. The historian may lament what Gottwald calls the "narrow historiographic base," but the Spirit of God witnesses in the diversity of the literary sources to the God who is faithful in working out his purpose in the history of humankind.[1]

THE BOOKS OF SAMUEL: DAVID THE MAN OF GOD

The Books of Samuel were already introduced in the previous chapter. Its literary structure unfolds a concern with the workings of God, "the Rock of Israel," in three major characters: Samuel, Saul, and David.

Hannah's Song and David's Psalms

The book is held together by motifs developed in Hannah's prayer (1 Sam. 2:1–10) at the beginning and David's psalms toward the end (2 Sam. 22:1–23:7; see chap. 13 above). The materials included in the book show the editor's concern to develop the themes of Hannah's prayer: (1) the Lord's deliverance of Israel from its enemies (v. 1), (2) the instrumentality of the Lord's anointed king (v. 10), and (3) the resultant prosperity, honor, and protection of his people (vv. 1, 4–5, 8–9).

In the concluding chapters of the second book of Samuel, the editor uses psalms of David to point out that Hannah's prayer finds fulfillment in David. In the first psalm (2 Sam. 22:2–51 [Ps. 18]), David expresses his trust in the Lord as "my rock" (2 Sam. 22:2–3). He confesses that, in the name of the Lord, he was victorious over his enemies (vv. 35–46). He is the anointed (messiah) with special qualities: faithfulness, integrity, purity of heart, and humility (vv. 26–28). Yahweh graciously granted him victory and continuity in his dynasty:

> He [Yahweh] gives his king great victories;
> he shows unfailing kindness to his anointed,
> to David and his descendants forever.
>
> (v. 51)

In another psalm (2 Sam. 23:1–7), the editor affirms the qualities of David's regime: the presence of God's spirit (v. 2), fear of God (v. 3), righteousness (v. 3), blessedness (v. 4), perpetuity (v. 5), and absence of malice (vv. 6–7). David's rule was like "the light of morning" and like "the brightness after rain" (v. 4) in comparison with the dark period of the judges and Saul. The impact of both psalms is to move the reader to make the literary connection between beginning and end. The long-awaited messiah is David, the man of God and the shepherd of Israel!

The portrait of David as a godly man, patient, wise, righteous, humble, whose heart was right with the Lord is developed throughout the Books of Samuel.[2] The books present three characters, two major (Samuel and David) and one minor (Saul). Each character is studied in terms of his contribution to the expectations raised in Hannah's song, namely, the Lord's sovereignty in beginning an era of deliverance, peace, and prosperity.

Samuel and Nathan

Samuel made a great contribution (1 Sam. 7:13–15) but was limited due to his age (8:1). Samuel's farewell speech (chap. 12) gives a summary of Israel's past and its problems and ends on a severe warning of exile. Saul's disobedience as king meant his rejection by God (13:13–14). Israel, however, was not rejected, as is evident in Samuel's anointing of David (chap. 16). The kingship and Israel, however, were in danger (see 12:25). By the grace of God, however, Samuel's warning in his farewell speech finds its complement in God's promises to David through Nathan, in which the Lord graciously promised not to end Israel or the institution of kingship.

216

The Davidic covenant provides a messianic hope for the dawning of a new age. The Lord favored David with the covenant in which he guaranteed David and his descendants (1) continuous rule over Israel as the shepherds of his flock, (2) his presence with them, symbolized by the temple, (3) the blessedness and rest of his people, (4) his covenant loyalty and love to David's descendants; and (5) a father-son relationship, expressed by discipline of David's descendants who prove not to be loyal to him (2 Sam. 7:5–16).

Narratives

The narratives in the books are structured around prayers (songs), speeches, and laments. This literary structuring accentuates Samuel as the great prophet, priest, and judge and David as a man of godliness, trust, fidelity, and wisdom (see Ps. 78:72)—but dwarfs Saul.[3] Though Saul was jealous of David and pursued him all over Judah, David never gave in to the temptation to avenge himself on evil Saul. He patiently waited for the Lord. Moreover, the lament on the occasion of the death of Saul and Jonathan (2 Sam. 1:19–27) reveals that David truly loved Saul. This lament functions as a pivot in the structure of the Books of Samuel.

When a civil war broke out between David and the new leadership of Ish-Bosheth and his military commander, Abner, David was anxious to pursue a course of reconciliation and did nothing to provoke the ruthless murders of Abner and Ish-Bosheth (2 Sam. 3:6–4:12). The kingdom fell into his hands by the Lord's will when the people requested him to be king over all the tribes, because they knew that it was of the Lord (5:2).

The selection of the narratives from chapters 8 to 20 presents us with two diverse pictures of David: David under blessing and David under judgment.[4] (See figure 16.) Under blessing, he led Israel into victory and rest. David, however, also experienced God's judgment through discipline: death in his family, unrest, and civil war.

The last four chapters summarize the period of David by a selection of episodes and psalms. The four major themes are (1) David's acts toward Saul's family, (2) David's victory over the enemies, (3) David's godly qualities and godly leadership, and (4) David's sin, reaction to judgment, and concern for reconciliation.

The Books of Samuel close with David's offering on the threshing floor of Araunah. The literary structure has pushed David forward as the anointed of the Lord, by whom Israel received rest, and Jerusalem as the chosen capital. However, there was no temple and no central altar. David had accomplished much, but the fullness of the promises had not been realized under David. At the close of the book, therefore, the editor invites us to look beyond David to a new age of altar, temple, and a greater sense of the presence of God through the messianic king.

Blessing	Curse
Concern for Ark and Temple (2 Sam. 6–7)	Adultery and murder (11:1–12:23)
Loyalty to Jonathan's family (chap. 9)	Family troubles (chaps. 13–14)
Military victories (8:1–4; chap. 10; 12:26–31)	Rebellion of Absalom (chaps. 15–19) and Sheba (20:1–22)
Rule over the twelve tribes (8:15–18)	
Solomon's birth (12:24–25)	

Figure 16. David Under Blessing and Curse (2 Samuel)

THE BOOKS OF CHRONICLES: THE PRESENCE OF GOD

The Books of Chronicles were composed some time after the Exile. The exact date is debated, as is the question of whether it belongs to a trilogy with Ezra-Nehemiah or whether it is an independent contribution.[5] In its present literary structure it uses genealogy to connect the Israelites with the nations via Adam and Noah (1 Chron. 1:1–27), with Abraham (vv. 28–54), and with each other as descendants of Jacob, or Israel (2:1–9:1). Prominence is given to the genealogies of Judah and David (chaps. 2–4) and the genealogy of Levi (chap. 6), including the temple musicians.

The perspective of Chronicles is postexilic. The author presents a coming together of the remnant of the twelve tribes out of exile ("those from Judah, from Benjamin, and from Ephraim and Manasseh") to resettle the land, particularly Jerusalem (1 Chron. 9:1–3). He structures the records of Israel and Judah with particular emphasis on Judah and the Davidic dynasty as guardians of the theocracy, on the kingdom of God, and on the temple. To this end he by-passes Saul's kingship with a record of his genealogy (chap. 8) and a brief report of his death (chap. 10), whereas the accomplishments of David and Solomon cover twenty-eight chapters (1 Chron. 11–2 Chron. 9)![6]

The period of David and Solomon provided a paradigm for the Chronicler. He looked back to the "temple-structured society of David and Solomon and the kingdom of God leadership that it represented" in order to inflame the hope of his contemporaries that, through their commitment to the temple and to the theocratic ideals, they might witness the establishment of God's kingdom.[7] The literary structure of Chronicles relates the past events to the existential needs of the postexilic community. For example, the brevity of the genealogies of the Transjordan tribes may be due to their no longer occupying a place in the restored community, because they had come under prophetic condemnation of their apostasy, were exiled by Tiglath-Pileser (Pul), and did not share in the restored community (1 Chron. 5:26). On the other hand, the genealogies of the tribes that formed the reconstituted kingdom of Israel are more extensive and conclude on a more positive note—the remnant of Israel lived together with the remnant of Judah and the Levites in Jerusalem after the Exile (9:1–34). The final twenty-seven chapters trace the development of the Davidic dynasty, the temple, Jerusalem until its fall, the destruction of the temple, and the carrying away of the holy temple vessels into Babylon.

THE BOOKS OF KINGS:
THE FULFILLMENT OF PROMISE

In between the final redaction of the Books of Samuel and Chronicles lies the great work of Kings, composed during the exile of Judah. It too employed many sources and selected from a vast body of material those portions that contributed to the major literary intent and development. These materials documented the period from the last days of David (c. 975 B.C.) to the release of Jehoiachin from prison in exile (c. 561 B.C.). The material is structured in three major blocks: Solomon's succession to the throne and his kingdom (1 Kings 1–11), the kingdoms of Judah and Israel till the exile of Israel (1 Kings 12–2 Kings 17), and the kingdom of Judah till its exile (2 Kings 18–25).[8]

The Books of Kings unfold the messianic motif of the Davidic kingship. This kingship is based on the promises of God and is not contingent on the response to theocratic kingship by the descendants of David and the tribes. On one hand, the books portray God's justice, by whose word Israel and Judah are blessed and judged. On the other hand, they have an underlying kerygmatic message, or proclamation of good news, that Yahweh is loving, merciful, and forgiving. He does not want his people to perish completely but uses judgment as a form of discipline to call his people back to himself. In judgment, as opposed to curse, there is still the possibility of reconciliation and forgiveness. To this end the editor appended the last section of Jehoiachin's release. The Lord raised up King Jehoiachin from prison and permitted him to enjoy a measure of royal dignity even in exile (2 Kings 25:27–30).

Solomon

The Solomonic era consolidated David's aspirations for peace, international recognition, and, above all, the presence of God in the Jerusalem temple (1 Kings 1–2). Once Solomon had consolidated his power, he continued in the pattern of kingship laid out for him by his father. The editor presents the reader with a king whose concern was for the well-being of his people. Solomon preferred a wise rule (chap. 3) and a judicious administration (chap. 4). He prepared for the building of the temple and his own palace and carefully executed the plans (5:1–8:9). He led Israel in prayer for God's presence and blessing (8:23–53), calling upon Israel to be loyal to the Lord (v. 61), and presenting offerings to the Lord (v. 63). It was evident to all people that the Lord was present, because his glory filled the temple (v. 10).

The pattern of David and Solomon's kingship, evidenced in their concern with integrity, fear of God, wisdom, justice, righteousness, and a caring attitude for the people of God, was thus crowned by the Lord's presence. The Lord warned Solomon and all his descendants that he expected nothing less:

> As for you, if you walk before me in integrity of heart and uprightness, as David your father did, and do all I command and observe my decrees and laws, I will establish your royal throne over Israel forever, as I promised David your father when I said, "You shall never fail to have a man on the throne of Israel." (1 Kings 9:4–5)

Division and Unity

The shaky beginning of the united monarchy under Saul ended up in the same sorry state under Solomon. Solomon became syncretistic because of the idolatry introduced by his wives (1 Kings 11). The Lord raised up adversaries (vv. 14–40), but Solomon did not repent as David his father had done. He persisted even to the point of trying to kill Jeroboam, whom Ahijah had anointed to rule over the northern tribes (vv. 26–40). Because Solomon's heart was divided before God, at his death God split the monarchy into the northern and southern kingdoms. From this time onward there was little movement in the kingdom. Apart from several great kings and the prophetic ministry of Elijah and Elisha in the north and Isaiah in the south, the period of the divided kingdom was another dark time in the history of God's people.

The literary structuring of the Books of Kings attempts to hold together the unity of the people of God, though divided into north and south, by giving a synchronic analysis of selected events in the two kingdoms. The fragmentation, however, did adversely affect the unity of worship and loyalty to Jerusalem and to David's dynasty.

CONCLUSION

The Lord demonstrated that he is Israel's king by establishing his kingship in David's dynasty. The rule of God was gloriously manifest in this period of "the royal nation." Hannah had prayed that the Rock of Israel would remember his lowly people by raising up a leader through whom the people of God would again receive the fulfillment of the covenantal blessings. This prayer was being answered in the appointment of David and his descendants. The Lord delighted in appointing him as his messiah, or anointed one, in preparation for his Son, the Messiah. For David, the Lord was none other than "the Rock of Israel," as he relied on his Father in heaven to give him victory and to establish God's kingdom on earth.

Nevertheless, David and Solomon were men, each with their own shortcomings. Depending on the loyalty of the Davidic king to the great King, God's people prospered or suffered. As in the period of the judges, Israel's suffering was not on account of the Lord's inability to deliver. Suffering ensued from the weakness of the Davidic king, by whose sins Israel came under God's curse. David experienced division within his own family and held the kingdom of the twelve tribes together only because he was sustained by God's grace. Solomon's position was strengthened because of the consolidation of the kingdom under David. He too, however, had to put up with threats to the harmony of his kingdom. It becomes apparent that, great as David and Solomon were, the kingdom of God, the fulfillment of his promises, and the joy of Israel were dependent on the Lord. He is the Rock of Israel. Even in the division of the kingdom and in the fragmentation and exile of his people, the Lord strengthened them with the hope that his Word is true. He had covenanted himself with the patriarchs, with Israel at Mount Sinai, and with David. Regardless of the political vicissitudes, the weaknesses of the Davidic king, and Israel's unresponsiveness, the Lord is still faithful!

CHAPTER 17

God's Presence in the Kingship
of David and Solomon

DAVID: A MAN AFTER GOD'S HEART

David was clearly a man appointed by the Lord. When Samuel went to anoint David, he was looking for a warrior type, someone not unlike Saul in appearance. But God forewarned Samuel not to look at the outward appearance, because the Lord looks at the heart (1 Sam. 16:7). David is known as having a heart that loved God (13:14). After years of being pursued by Saul, God raised David up as the king over Judah and ultimately over all of Israel: "And David knew that the LORD had established him as king over Israel and had exalted his kingdom for the sake of his people Israel" (2 Sam. 5:12).

David also had the support of the leaders and the people. They also recognized that David was the man that God had sent as king (1 Chron. 12:18, 38). Moreover, the Lord made David's name famous among the nations. Through Nathan, the Lord told David, "I have been with you wherever you have gone, and I have cut off all your enemies from before you. Now I will make your name like the names of the greatest men of the earth" (17:8).

Although his God-given greatness could have made him proud, David remained submissive to the Lord. In battles, civil war (2 Sam. 15:26), when cursed by enemies (16:10–12), or when rebuked by the Lord (24:14), David willingly received whatever the Lord had appointed for him. Except in the case of Uriah the Hittite, he did not further rationalize his way out of a problem. He did not scheme or plot but believed that the Lord's will would be done in his life. In his old age he could truly say, "As surely as the LORD lives, who has delivered me out of every trouble" (1 Kings 1:29). David indeed was a man after God's heart, walking humbly before the Lord.

Because he was a man of God, David accomplished much during his forty-year reign. He typified *theocratic* kingship.[1] He was a shepherd to the people of Israel (2 Sam. 5:2; 1 Chron. 11:2). The theocratic king led his people into a period of peace and prosperity. He protected them and saw that they followed Yahweh's statutes (see Deut. 17:18–20). As an undershepherd of the Lord (Ps. 23:1), David's leadership was neither individualistic nor despotic. By delegating authority and depending on his fellow officers, David's theocratic kingship flourished to the benefit of all Israel.

David's qualities of kingship are those that the prophets celebrate and anticipate in the messianic king, namely, love, justice, righteousness, wisdom, and the presence of God's Spirit. David is particularly known for his love, and Solomon is renowned for his wisdom. Both men were clearly filled with the Spirit of God and sought justice and righteousness. Too often their shortcomings come to our minds and overshadow the great character of these men. If we can learn to be like God in forgiving David and Solomon, we may more readily assess the strength of their character.

The Love of God and Man

David was preeminently a man given to the love of God and of other people. The Hebrew word for love *(ḥesed)* is better translated "loyalty," as love is always associated with loyalty. Love is constant. When David established a relationship with a person or a family, he remained loyal, regardless of the treatment he received.

David's loyalty to Saul and his family was evidenced by his sincere grief at the death of Saul and Jonathan. He grieved because Saul was the anointed of the Lord and because Jonathan was his covenant friend (2 Sam. 1:19–27; see 1 Sam. 20). He showed his concern when Ish-Bosheth was ruthlessly murdered (2 Sam. 4:8–12) and when Abner was killed by Joab (3:22–30). He concretely demonstrated his loyalty to Jonathan by giving the possessions of Saul's family and the privilege of the royal table to Mephibosheth, Jonathan's son (chap. 9). He later sealed his friendship with Saul's house by having the bodies of Saul and Jonathan properly buried (21:13–14).

Justice and Righteousness

David was also a man of great justice and righteousness. He repeatedly honored Saul, even when the latter pursued and persecuted him (1 Sam. 24:6, 10; 26:9, 11, 23). This respect for God's anointed led to his just sentencing of the man who reported Saul's death (2 Sam. 1:16). He also avenged the death of Ish-Bosheth, who had been killed while asleep (4:12).

The desire for justice was particularly evident when he charged Solomon to repay all those who had done wrong during David's reign. He made it clear that Joab needed to die for shedding the innocent blood of Abner and Amasa (1 Kings 2:5–6). Shimei also, to whom David had shown mercy, was to die (vv. 8–9). Both of these men represented a threat to the establishment and security of Solomon's rule. David thus had rightly gained a reputation for justice in his days:

"David reigned over all Israel, doing what was just and right for all his people" (1 Chron. 18:14).

Wisdom

David displayed God-given wisdom in the manner in which he dealt with people and ruled over his extensive kingdom. He inspired people with his leadership (1 Sam. 22:2; 2 Sam. 5:1–3). The Bible does not speak explicitly about David's wisdom, mainly because it was so apparent. As a demonstration of his own respect for wisdom, he prayed that Solomon, who was still a youth, might have wisdom to rule the people of God: "May the LORD give you discretion and understanding when he puts you in command over Israel, so that you may keep the law of the LORD your God" (1 Chron. 22:12).

The Presence of God

David's rule was particularly characterized by God's presence. The Lord was with David in all his accomplishments. Israel's defeat at Mount Gilboa just prior to David's reign would be transformed into victory and ultimately peace and joy by the time of David's departure. His forty years were good ones for Israel, and the people remembered the blessings of his rule. From Psalm 78 it is apparent that the Lord had favored Judah by choosing David's dynasty and that he had favored his people by his willingness to dwell in Jerusalem (vv. 66–72). The God of David would condescend to dwell among his people even after David's death. God was with David even as he had been with Moses, Joshua, and Samuel: "And David became more and more powerful, because the LORD Almighty was with him" (1 Chron. 11:9). When David had Solomon crowned, Benaiah, Solomon's new military commander, expressed a similar desire for David's son: "As the LORD was with my lord the king, so may he be with Solomon to make his throne even greater than the throne of my lord King David!" (1 Kings 1:37).

Theocratic Concern

The final characteristic of every great theocratic leader is his charge to God's people. Like-Moses (in Deuteronomy), Joshua (Josh. 24), and Samuel (1 Sam. 12) before him, David exhorted Israel and Solomon to be loyal to Yahweh. After he had sung the praises of Yahweh (1 Chron. 29:10–13), he called on the people to join with him in blessing the Lord (v. 20). And to Solomon he said,

> And you, my son Solomon, acknowledge the God of your father, and serve him with wholehearted devotion and with a willing mind, for the LORD searches every heart and understands every motive behind the

thoughts. If you seek him, he will be found by you; but if you forsake him, he will reject you forever. (28:9)

He encouraged Solomon with words similar to Moses' charge to Joshua: "Be strong and courageous, and do the work. Do not be afraid or discouraged, for the LORD God, my God, is with you. He will not fail you or forsake you until all the work for the service of the temple of the LORD is finished" (v. 20).

The Chronicler reminds us that with David there is a return to—as well as a development beyond—the Mosaic era. The era of David recapitulates that of Moses and Joshua. Through these servants God's people inherited the land; through David they enjoyed peace and prosperity in the Land of Promise. However, it was also an era marred by imperfections and sin. The Davidic-Solomonic era was not the fulfillment of all of God's promises. Each Davidic king failed in one way or another to conform completely to the theocratic ideal.

SOLOMON: THE RISE AND FALL OF GLORY

Solomon, David's son by Bathsheba, is also known as Jedidiah (2 Sam. 12:24–25), meaning "beloved of Yahweh" and signifying that the Lord truly loved Solomon. God called on Solomon to accomplish what David had desired to do: build the temple. By the end of Solomon's life, God's people had enjoyed peace and prosperity for nearly eighty years.[2] It seemed as if the Mosaic covenant was completely fulfilled and all of God's promises to the patriarchs and Israel had been realized. Except for Solomon's failure to remain faithful to the Lord, such an estimate may well have been true. The kingdom was divided under Solomon's son, and a new era began, leading to the exile of both Israel and Judah. Only after the Exile would God's covenant with Abraham, Isaac, Jacob, and the people of Israel be renewed. As we consider Solomon's important reign, we shall study his relationship with the Lord, his accomplishments, his wisdom, and some important issues during his reign.

The Presence of God

According to the succession stories (2 Sam. 15–1 Kings 2), the Lord who loved Solomon raised him up against impossible odds. Absalom made his claim to kingship, and thereafter Sheba tried to divide the kingdom. When David was old, Adonijah led an insurrection, supported by Abiathar and Joab as well as many leaders of the people. In a providential turn of affairs, Solomon succeeded David as king (1 Kings 1). During David's last days, he knew that the leaders and the people had recognized Solomon as king (v. 47; 1 Chron. 29:23). God had blessed the transition from David to Solomon! Solomon's kingship was established. He did not suffer from political problems until the end of his reign. Most of his rule was characterized by God's blessing,

> The LORD highly exalted Solomon in the sight of all Israel and bestowed on him royal splendor such as no king over Israel ever had before. (1 Chron. 29:25)

> Solomon son of David established himself firmly over his kingdom, for the LORD his God was with him and made him exceedingly great. (2 Chron. 1:1).

By means of Solomon's kingship the Lord's own name was magnified and the praise of Israel was made known to the nations.

One clear demonstration of Solomon's deep understanding of Yahweh and his ways is his prayer at the dedication of the temple (1 Kings 8:22–53). This beautiful prayer focuses on the Lord's relationship with Israel, highlighting Solomon's concern that God hear the prayers of his people. Solomon knew how great Yahweh was (vv. 23, 27) and all that he had promised to David (vv. 24–25). The king's special hope was for God to hear Israel's prayers during times of need, whether involving national sins, conflict with enemies, draught and famine, or exile (vv. 30–52). Solomon even asked Yahweh to listen to the prayers of foreigners who might come to the temple. Surely Solomon believed that Yahweh was with his people and was concerned with their needs, because he had called them to himself (v. 53).

Solomon, however, did not manifest the same love for God that his father, David, had shown. Although Solomon "showed his love for the LORD," he also "offered sacrifices and burned incense on the high places" (1 Kings 3:3) and later was involved in idolatry (11:1–8). Solomon's love for the Lord was indeed marred by the absence of complete loyalty to the Lord. Unlike David, Solomon's heart was divided. He served the Lord, but he loved his wives: "As Solomon grew old, his wives turned his heart after other gods, and his heart was not fully devoted to the LORD his God, as the heart of David his father had been" (v. 4). God assured him of a special place in redemptive history by means of his great wisdom (3:5–13) and by virtue of his being the son of David (9:1–9). God explicitly warned Solomon not to follow after other gods, lest Israel be cut off from the land (9:6–7). But Solomon disobeyed, and "the LORD became angry with Solomon because his heart had turned away from the LORD, the God of Israel, who had appeared to him twice" (11:9).

Solomon's Fame

In spite of this sad ending to his reign, the early stability of his kingdom permitted Solomon to accomplish much for God and the people, as well as for himself. All of the potential difficulties he inherited from David were dealt with in such a way that his kingship was secure from the very beginning (1 Kings 2:12; cf. v. 46). Solomon divided the kingdom into twelve administrative districts in order to make possible a centralized rule, and he appointed district governors with the authority to raise taxes in support of the royal household (4:1–19, 27–28). He established fortifications throughout Israel, such as the wall of Jerusalem, the royal cities of Hazor, Megiddo, and Gezer, as well as Lower Beth Horon, Baalath, and Tadmor in the wilderness (9:15–19).

In addition to these internal policies, Solomon developed good relations with distant countries. He enhanced Israel's economy by building a fleet manned by mariners from Phoenicia (1 Kings 9:26–28; 10:11, 22). The fleet brought the Solomonic kingdom great wealth in gold, silver, wood, ivory, and even rare animals. Solomon also advanced commercial relations by caravans (10:15). He made Jerusalem an important commercial center in the ancient Near East. It was admired and respected by the kings of other nations who came to Jerusalem for an audience with Solomon (4:34; 10:24).

The pinnacle of Solomon's accomplishments was the building of "a temple for the Name of the LORD" (1 Kings 5:3). The writer of Kings revels in the glory of God's house, giving every detail of the planning and building (chaps. 5–6; 7:13–51).[3] Although different from the tabernacle in its specific dimensions and layout, the temple, like the tabernacle, was intended to be symbolic of Yahweh's presence with, and his kingship over, his people. There the ark of the covenant with the cherubim would rest and sacrifices would be made. Even the names of the two bronze pillars point to God's covenant faithfulness: *Jakin* ("he will establish") and *Boaz* ("in him is strength"; 7:21).[4] The great expense is never questioned or criticized by the biblical writer. For him the temple reveals a theology of God's beauty and glory.

Solomon's Wisdom

The extensive internal developments and the foreign alliances and trade relations showed the depth of Solomon's wisdom. When the Lord would grant Solomon anything he chose, Solomon asked for the wisdom to be able to rule God's people properly (1 Kings 3:5–9). Often we think of Solomon's wisdom as something he used only once in the case of two harlots (vv. 16–28). But the purpose of that event was to demonstrate and confirm Solomon's wisdom to rule: "When all Israel heard the verdict the king had given, they held the king in awe, because they saw that he had wisdom from God to administer justice" (v. 28).

Other expressions of his wisdom were his 3,000 proverbs and 1,005 songs (1 Kings 4:32). He contributed to the biblical books of Psalms (e.g., Ps. 72) and Proverbs (chaps. 1–29) and very likely authored the Song of Songs. He also clearly inspired the writer of Ecclesiastes.[5] He was able to speak intelligently about all of nature (including vegetation, birds, and animals). His knowledge of the world of his day was greater than that of any person on earth (1 Kings 4:30–31). His wisdom was also recognized by those outside of Israel (5:7; 10:8).

Solomon and the Promise

Solomon's rule started off well. He built the magnificent temple. In the course of time, however, glory, riches, and wisdom corrupted him. Solomon's rule was marred by self-glorification and love of foreign cultures, including idolatry. He did not share David's absolute commitment to Yahweh. He had been forewarned by David to maintain loyalty for the sake of Israel and the future generations:

> Observe what the LORD your God requires: Walk in his ways, and keep his decrees and commands, his laws and requirements, as written in the Law of Moses, so that you may prosper in all you do and wherever you go, and that the LORD may keep his promise to me: "If your descendants watch how they live, and if they walk faithfully before me with all their heart and soul, you will never fail to have a man on the throne of Israel." (1 Kings 2:3–4)

The Lord also reminded Solomon that the king, as the theocratic leader, was the means by which the covenant community was either blessed or cursed:

> As for this temple you are building, if you follow my decrees, carry out my regulations and keep all my commands and obey them, I will fulfill through you the promise I gave to David your father. And I will live among the Israelites and will not abandon my people Israel. (6:12–13; see also 3:14; 9:6–9)

While Solomon tasted many of the benefits of the covenant, he was not able to bring in the fullness of the covenantal relationship because of his marriage to women from nations into which God had forbidden Israel to marry (Deut. 7; 1 Kings 11:1–2). Solomon consequently fell into idolatry and did not fully follow the Lord (vv. 4–8). Because of these inconsistencies, the Lord brought troubles on Solomon toward the end of his reign. He raised up adversaries such as Hadad the Edomite, Rezon the Syrian, and Jeroboam the Ephraimite. In addition to these troubles, the Lord told Solomon that he would tear most of the kingdom away from the house of David and give it to someone else (vv. 11–13). Only because of Jerusalem and David would the Lord remain loyal to Solomon's sons (v. 13). God's purpose, however, was to reunite all of the tribes of Israel and Judah and bring them together under one descendant of David (v. 39).

CONCLUSION

David and Solomon were chosen by the Lord to establish his kingship on earth. David received the kingdom from Saul, not without Saul's struggle to maintain the rule of Israel or the opposition of Ish-Bosheth, his son. David was God's man, who at God's time was crowned by popular acclamation over all the tribes of Israel. Solomon similarly had to overcome major obstacles. First, he was not the first-born of David and had to contend with rivalry to the throne. Second, he was the son of Bathsheba, who had been married to a foreigner (Uriah the Hittite) and who had become David's wife through adultery and murder. In spite of these limitations, the canonical perspective presents Solomon as God's man. Both David and Solomon responded with loyalty to their suzerain, Yahweh. The kingdom was established in peace, justice, righteousness, and wisdom. The nature of their rule and the beneficence of Israel as the royal people gave God's people hope that in future generations the Lord would again establish the Davidic dynasty as in the former times (see Mic. 4:8), when the twelve tribes of Israel were united under one king and enjoyed the reality of God's presence, blessing, and protection.

This period, however, is marred by the sins of David and Solomon. These great men were consumed with a theocratic concern for building God's kingdom, for establishing Jerusalem as the city of God ("Zion"), and for guiding God's people in safety and prosperity as the shepherd of God. But they sinned grievously. The canonical function of the biblical account is such that, in the worst of times, the faithful were sustained with hope that the Lord would reestablish his kingdom or would more evidently inaugurate his kingdom on earth. Since Yahweh was gracious and forgiving to David and Solomon, the reality and glory of his kingdom depends not on the frailty of even the greatest men but on himself. He is the Rock of Israel!

CHAPTER 18

The Covenant with David

GOD'S SURE MERCIES TO DAVID

During the era of David and Solomon, the Sinaitic covenant underwent significant developments.[1] One of the most prominent of these was Yahweh's choice of David's dynasty as the theocratic expression of God's rule on earth. Whereas Moses, Joshua, and Samuel had no heirs to succeed them, David was assured by divine oath that he would have. Another distinctive feature of the Davidic covenant is its promissory nature, over against the obligatory emphasis of the Mosaic covenant. The continuity of Israel and God's rule on earth is guaranteed by promise and is not dependent solely on Israel's loyalty to the Lord.

Though the word "covenant" is noticeably absent in 2 Samuel 7, God's word of promise is guaranteed by his commitment, or *hesed* ("loyalty"), to David.[2] The expressions of his love and loyalty to David, his descendants, and the people are thus expressions of a covenant he made with David. David clearly understood God's promise as a covenant:

> Is not my house right with God?
>> Has he not made with me an everlasting covenant,
>> arranged and secured in every part?
> Will he not bring to fruition my salvation
>> and grant me my every desire?
>
> (2 Sam. 23:5)

The structure of the covenant resembles the Near Eastern "royal grant," in which a king gave rights to a loyal servant.[3] Centuries later a psalmist calls on God to continue his love (*hesed*) to David by bringing in the messianic era:

> O Lord, where is your former great love,
>> which in your faithfulness you swore to David?
>
> (Ps. 89:49)

Isaiah also foresees the renewal of God's love to Israel as an expression of his covenantal loyalty to David:

> Give ear and come to me;
>> hear me, that your soul may live.
> I will make an everlasting covenant with you,
>> my faithful love promised to David.
>
> (Isa. 55:3)

We consider here four aspects of the Davidic covenant: (1) God's promises, (2) God's purposes, (3) the fulfillment, and (4) the eschatological dimensions.

God's Promises

God's promises to David were fivefold. First, the Lord promised to *raise up David's heirs* and thus establish his throne forevermore. This dynastic expression of theocracy was the most important development in the history of redemption after Moses. The period of the judges demonstrated the need for continuity of leadership. Because there was no leader to unify the people, they went their own ways, and the tribes tended to separate from each other (Judg. 21:25). The purpose of the theocratic king, as the shepherd over all the tribes, would be to unify the people (2 Sam. 7:8).

Second, God promises to *be a father to David's descendants*. The close relationship of father and son is to characterize the relationship of the Lord and his anointed ruler (2 Sam. 7:14). God's presence would be so clear during the messianic rule that the people would know God was with their king. Because of his presence, the Lord's blessings would also rest upon the people at large. The greatness of the king was a manifestation of the presence of God with him (see 1 Chron. 11:9).

Third, like Moses, the Davidic king would *emphasize the worship of God*. Under Moses' service as priest, the tabernacle was erected, the priesthood and the Levitical system were instituted, and sacrifices were begun. Likewise, David and Solomon were concerned about the worship of the Lord. Although David was not permitted to build a temple (because God's plan was for him to establish peace), God assured David that his son Solomon would accomplish this project (2 Sam. 7:12–13).

Fourth, the Lord promised to *be loyal to David and his heirs forevermore*. As we have seen, the Hebrew term for "loyalty" is *ḥesed* or faithfulness in action (translated in 2 Sam. 7:15 in the NKJV as "mercy"). God's promise not to remove his lovingkindness, or loyalty, was his assurance that the throne of David would be established forever (v. 16). David himself made the connection between loyalty (vv. 15–16) and goodness (v. 28) in the shepherd's psalm:

> Surely goodness and love will follow me
>> all the days of my life,
> and I will dwell in the house of the LORD
>> forever.
>
> (Ps. 23:6)

The Lord's goodness and loyalty represented his covenantal faithfulness to David and his descendants.

Fifth, God *chose Jerusalem* as the place where he would put his name (2 Sam. 7:13).[4] David captured Jerusalem, made it his capital city, and brought the ark of the covenant there. He wanted the Lord to dwell in Jerusalem (see 1 Chron. 23:25). Although an earthly temple cannot contain a God who is greater than heaven (2 Chron. 6:18), the Lord is willing to dwell among his people in order to bless them. Furthermore, though not clearly stated, the promise of universal rule is implied (see Pss. 2; 132). An interpretation of the various passages pertaining to the promise affirms that God has appointed the house of David to be his instrument for establishing his kingdom on earth.[5]

God's Purposes

By means of his loyalty to David's dynasty, God planned to accomplish the purposes he originally set forth in the Sinaitic covenant. The purposes of God are threefold: (1) to plant his people, (2) to establish his kingship, and (3) to exalt his people.

God desired to plant his people in the Land of Promise. Even though the people of Israel had come into the land, they had been continually harassed by the indigenous population and by other nations. God permitted those nations to remain in order to test his people and to encourage them to cast themselves upon the Lord's mercy (Judg. 2:20–23). Under David, however, the Lord renewed his covenantal loyalty by reducing the power of the indigenous population and by subduing the surrounding nations (1 Kings 4:21; 9:20–21).

God also wanted to establish the presence of his kingship through the agency of the theocratic king. He had been with Abraham, Moses, Samuel, Joshua, and David. God also promised to dwell with his people if Solomon and his descendants would obey his Word (1 Kings 6:12–13). On the basis of God's promise, Solomon prayed that the Lord would readily forgive the sins of his people, prosper them by sending rain, and renew his covenant love when they depart from him (chap. 8). God's kingship would also mean the existence of peace, justice, and righteousness and the manifestation of God's wisdom.

God's third purpose was to exalt his people as he exalted their ruler. God's exaltation of David and Solomon among the rulers of the nations had a direct effect upon the whole people of God (1 Chron. 14:2). The fear of the Lord fell on the nations: "So David's fame spread throughout every land, and the LORD made all the nations fear him" (v. 17). The nations brought their gifts to Jerusalem (2 Chron. 9:9–11) and readily made alliances in order to cooperate with the king.

Fulfillment

The Solomonic era indeed fulfills much of God's promise to David and his purposes for his people. God further established the throne of David by raising up Solomon and establishing him (1 Kings 1:48; 2:12, 46). Solomon built the temple of the Lord, the glory of which was legendary among the nations.[6] When the temple was dedicated, God was pleased to send his glory as a visible token of his presence: "And the priests could not perform their service because of the cloud, for the glory of the LORD filled his temple" (8:11). When the Lord had made the temple his footstool, Solomon was assured that the Lord had fulfilled his promise to David: "You have kept your promise to your servant David my father; with your mouth you have promised and with your hand you have fulfilled it—as it is today" (v. 24; see also v. 20 and 2 Chron. 6:10).

Solomon's kingship brought the people rest and joy. They rejoiced when the temple was dedicated, because God's covenantal loyalty was apparent to them (1 Kings 8:66). Solomon called upon the people to respond to the Lord's blessing by being loyal to the covenant. In so doing, the Lord would continue to be with his people:

> Praise be to the LORD, who has given rest to his people Israel just as he promised. Not one word has failed of all the good promises he gave through his servant Moses. May the LORD our God be with us as he was with our fathers; may he never leave us nor forsake us. May he turn our hearts to him, to walk in all his ways and to keep the commands, decrees and regulations he gave our fathers. (vv. 56–58)

The people of Israel saw themselves not simply as heirs of God's promises to *Moses*. Under Solomon, there was also a further realization of the *patriarchal* promises. (See figure 17.)

> The people of Judah and Israel were as numerous as the sand on the seashore; they ate, they drank and they were happy. . . . During Solomon's lifetime Judah and Israel, from Dan to Beersheba, lived in safety, each man under his own vine and fig tree. (1 Kings 4:20, 25; cf. Gen. 22:17; 32:12)

Moreover, the borders of the land were exactly where God had promised Abraham they would be (1 Kings 4:21; cf. Gen. 15:18). Finally, the nations recognized the greatness of God's kingdom as established in Solomon (1 Kings 10:6–10, 23–24; cf. Gen. 12:2).[7]

Eschatological Dimensions

As we look beyond the era of David and Solomon, we must consider the eschatological dimension of the Davidic covenant. In the narratives about Solomon the writers of Kings and Chronicles emphasize both the fulfillment of the promises and the challenge to covenantal loyalty. God challenged Solomon to be faithful (1 Kings 6:12; 9:4), but Solomon was disobedient and thereby brought God's judgment upon the people. After his death, the kingdom was divided into the nations of Israel and Judah, both of which were eventually exiled (in 722 B.C. and 586 B.C., respectively). Solomon's death thus ended the era of God's messianic blessing for his people.

Messianic kingship of Jesus Christ: Jesus is Lord over all creation and his church, the community of the redeemed. He administers all the benefits of the covenants to his people: grace, promise, forgiveness, presence in protection and blessing. He has received the full authority of rule in deliverance and in vengeance.

Davidic covenant: Sovereign administration of grace and promise by which Yahweh consecrates a people to himself through his messianic king. Rule of God through his vassal for blessing and protecting his people.

Mosaic covenant: Sovereign administration of grace and promise by which Yahweh consecrates Israel to himself by the sanctions of divine law. Rule of God through his law for blessing and keeping his people consecrated to himself as his kingdom on earth; royal and glorious presence of Yahweh among his people; forgiveness of sin; and fellowship with the Lord of glory.

Abrahamic covenant: Sovereign administration of grace and promise. Fourfold promise pertaining to creation and redemption; Yahweh is the Father of the covenant community.

Covenant with creation: Sovereign administration. Yahweh is the Creator-King-Father. He rules over his creation in patience, blessing, and judgment.

Figure 17. The Progression of Yahweh's Covenants

From this point onward the faithful remnant looked for a messiah of David with whom God would be present and by whom he would extend his peace, justice, righteousness, and wisdom to his people. Only a few kings that followed David and Solomon responded positively to God's challenge. Such kings helped to bring in the kingdom of God among the people. Unfortunately, those periods were like oases in the desert of

234

Judah's history. After the Exile, the faithful continued to look for the fulfillment of the promises based on God's oath to David.

In Jesus, the people of God saw the focus of the Old Testament Scriptures. Jesus is *the* Messiah! He is the gospel of the messianic kingdom (Mark 1:1). In his teachings, life, miracles, suffering, and resurrection, the Spirit of God testifies that Jesus is the long-awaited Messiah. Yet, the complete fulfillment of all the expectations and promises has to this point been further delayed. While the promises are focused in him as the appointed means of ushering in the era of restoration, hope looks forward to the time when Jesus will rule over the earth. His rule will be characterized by the presence of God, justice, righteousness, loyalty, and wisdom. He will also bring peace, healing, joy, rest, and prosperity to his people. His rule, however, differs from that of David and Solomon in that it will not be marred by sin or lack of loyalty to the Father. Moreover, his rule will last forever and ever! Come, Lord Jesus, come!

THE DAVIDIC COVENANT AND THE MOSAIC COVENANT

There are certain elements of continuity and of discontinuity between the Davidic and Mosaic covenants. Continuity is most evident in the blessedness of the covenant people, the institution of a theocratic king, the establishment of temple worship, and the centrality of Jerusalem.

When God redeemed Israel out of Egypt, he sought one nation for himself, a blessed, covenant people. David recognized this goal when he prayed,

> And who is like your people Israel—the one nation on earth whose God went out to redeem a people for himself, and to make a name for yourself, and to perform great and awesome wonders by driving out nations from before your people, whom you redeemed from Egypt? (1 Chron. 17:21)

Indeed, the people of God were united by their experience of the Exodus and their reception of the covenant at Mount Sinai. They were also united by the promises God had given to Abraham. Israelites under David's dynasty were thus the heirs of both the Abrahamic and Mosaic covenants. We saw above how the patriarchal promises of descendants, land, blessing, and blessing to the nations were all being fulfilled during the Davidic and Solomonic eras. Israel under the united kingdom had a sense of inheritance from the past, a continuity with the fathers.

A further example of continuity between the covenant administrations is the ideal of theocratic leadership. Under Moses, God had instituted theocratic officers. Although Moses was the chief mediator between God and the people, the Lord also chose priests, Levites, and prophets to continue theocratic leadership. Especially important here, however, is the fact that Moses foresaw the time when the people would be ruled by a king of God's choosing (Deut. 17:15). This king was to be responsive to the law, unlike Saul, who disobeyed the word of the Lord. With David, the Lord set up a dynasty that met the requirements of Deuteronomy 17:16–20. After the death of Moses and Joshua, there was a lack of firm theocratic leadership among God's people. As great as Joshua and Samuel were, they could not fill the vacuum left by Moses (34:10). But David and Solomon were able to continue in Moses' tradition of great leadership.

Their contributions may be seen as building on the foundation laid by Moses. Whereas Moses led Israel to the borders of Canaan, David and Solomon brought peace and rest from the enemies. This rest was seen as a fulfillment of the earlier covenant: "Praise be to the LORD, who has given rest to his people Israel just as he promised. Not one word has failed of all the good promises he gave through his servant Moses" (1 Kings 8:56; cf. Deut. 12:10). Under David and Solomon, Israel experienced a golden age of exaltation above all nations. Their glory was the first blessing of obedience stated in the Mosaic covenant: "The LORD your God will set you high above all the nations on earth" (Deut. 28:1).

The developments instituted by David and Solomon in the worship of Yahweh were continuous, at least in their purpose, with much of the tabernacle worship in the Sinaitic covenant. Moses had ordained that the Levites should assist the priests in the maintenance of the tabernacle, and many Levites continued to serve the Lord in this function (1 Chron. 23:2–26:32). But David divided the Levites into other functions not originally taught in the law of Moses. There were musicians, choruses, gatekeepers, and guardians of the threshold (9:17–23; 25:6–7; 26:1–19). In addition, Levites served as judges, temple craftsmen, and supervisors (23:4, 28).

Along with these basically continuous aspects of the covenant administrations (involving people, leadership, and worship), there are some altogether new developments in the Davidic covenant. The most obvious one is the concept of dynasty. Moses may have hinted at the idea when he taught that the king, through obedience, "will reign a long time over his kingdom in Israel" (Deut. 17:20). But apart from such hints, the biblical writers before the Books of Samuel do not anticipate a kingly dynasty that would play an essential role in God's redemptive plan. Nevertheless, Yahweh's purpose in establishing a line of good kings was to provide a means of bringing in his kingdom on earth. The Davidic covenant has nothing less in view than a glorious and universal rule of the Davidic king.

A second form of discontinuity occurred in Solomon's appointment of Zadok as high priest. During David's lifetime the priestly house of Eli continued, but God's judgment upon that house would have to come according to the prophecy of the man of God (1 Sam. 2:30–36). Soon after Solomon became king, Eli's descendant Abiathar was removed from office, and God's Word was fulfilled (1 Kings 2:27). In the house of Zadok the prophecy came to pass, "I will raise up for myself a faithful priest, who will do according to what is in my heart and mind. I will firmly establish his house, and he will minister before my anointed one always" (1 Sam. 2:35).

Any changes made by David and Solomon, such as the expanded role of the Levites, were necessary in light of the new glory of temple worship. Because these provisions were not inconsistent with the spirit of the Sinaitic covenant, the Lord blessed such changes. The discontinuity also appears in the choice of David's dynasty through which he promised to lead his people to paradisaical bliss. In and through these various changes, God progressively moved his people along toward his goal. In David and Solomon, Yahweh further focuses his plan, bringing greater fulfillment to past promises but also calling for hope in a future that will be even more glorious than the present golden age.

Conclusion to Part 6

This period stands in a direct relation to the eras of promise and election (Abrahamic covenant) and the constitution of Israel as the people of God under Moses (Mosaic covenant). The affirmation of the perpetuity of rule to David (Davidic covenant) guaranteed the establishment of God's kingdom on earth, the realization of the promises made to Israel, and the enjoyment of God's blessings.

It becomes apparent that the promises of God are not wholly dependent on human response. Yahweh works out his plan of salvation in history, but he chooses human institutions and leaders. If his plan of restoring a people to himself under the fullness of blessing were dependent on men such as Moses, Samuel, and David, his people would never live in the security of the hope of the kingdom to come.

The Davidic covenant guarantees to the Lord's people that Yahweh has pledged himself to be responsible for establishing his presence and blessing to Israel and to the nations that find shelter under its wings. It is also clear, however, that there is no salvation outside of the Lord or outside of the messiah whom he has chosen. Rejection of the divinely appointed king signifies a rejection of the Lord, who has accepted the Davidic king as his son. The Lord thus prepared Israel for the coming of the Messiah, his Son. Acceptance of the Son-Messiah signifies loyalty to Yahweh, whereas rejection of the Messiah is a mark of apostasy.

In the Old Testament economy the Lord had further established his kingdom in Zion. David had conquered the city, the Lord had blessed it, and Solomon had been granted permission to build a temple to the Lord in it. Jerusalem became a symbol for the city of God. Rejection of Jerusalem was tantamount to repudiating the Lord. A devotion to Jerusalem was an expression of devotion to the Lord who dwelt in Zion (Ps. 122:6–9). With the corruption of Jerusalem (see, e.g., Isa. 1), the godly looked beyond the immorality of the leadership and the idolatrous practices in the temple to the Lord himself. He was their hope. For them the physical Jerusalem was a token, even though weak, of Zion, "the City of God" (Ps. 46). The prophets clearly understood this message. Isaiah, for example, called on God's people to recognize that God's kingship is not limited to Jerusalem (Isa. 66:1–2) but extends over all his creation. With the coming of Jesus the Messiah of God, Jesus further clarified that the heavenly Father looks for people who worship him "in spirit and in truth" (John 4:24) and that the place of worship is of secondary importance.

The period of Israel as a royal nation served as a golden era to which God's people looked back with appreciation at how the Lord fulfilled the Abrahamic and Mosaic (Sinaitic) covenants in the Davidic covenant. The Davidic covenant is *a sovereign administration of grace and promise by which the Lord consecrates a people to himself through his messianic king, under whose leadership he endows them with royal splendor.* A synopsis of this period includes the following highlights:

1. the fulfillment of the Abrahamic covenant: in population explosion, enjoyment of land, experience of God's blessing and protection, presence of God in the midst of Israel, and the blessing of the nations through Israel;

2. the fulfillment of the Mosaic covenant in the righteous and wise leadership of David and Solomon, by which God's people prospered and achieved a name among the nations;

3. the development of the Abrahamic and Mosaic covenants into the Davidic covenant, by which the Lord decrees that the benefits of the two covenants will be realized in and through his messianic king;

4. the establishment of the kingdom of God in Israel in a more permanent manner, namely, the Solomonic temple; the Lord hereby guaranteed the fulfillment of the Davidic covenant (see Ps. 132);

5. the modeling of the shepherd role of the theocratic king in David and Solomon, which secured rest, peace, provisions, glory, and enjoyment of the covenant benefits and which required exemplification of wisdom, justice, righteousness, love, and fidelity from the messianic ruler (see Isa. 11:1–9);

6. the failure of Israel's model kings in securing the permanence of God's blessings, because of their personal infraction of the covenant; David was plagued by problems in his household and within his kingdom, threatening the break-up of Israel's solidarity as a nation; upon Solomon's death the northern tribes formally seceded from Judah;

7. the impermanence of the "glory of Israel"; since it depended on descendants of David, Israel was subject to plagues, judgments, and internal and external disturbances. The golden era thus provided a conceptual model for the prophets who predicted the messianic kingdom, one that would be even more glorious than the era of David and Solomon!

Part 7

A Divided Nation

Introduction to Part 7

The glorious kingdom of David and Solomon was followed by a low point in Israel's history, the division of the kingdom in 931 B.C. The "glory years" had begun with great expectations of seeing all the promises to the patriarchs fulfilled. Not only had Israel become "a great nation" (Gen. 12:2), they had also begun to possess "the cities of their enemies" (22:17). Under Solomon, Israel truly began to stand out among the nations. The magnificent glory of that era drew people from every nation (1 Kings 4:34), including the queen of Sheba (1 Kings 10). Evidently, the nations were being blessed through Abraham's seed (Gen. 12:3).

But this era was by no means the ultimate fulfillment of God's promises. It soon came to an end. The ensuing age began when the kingdom split in two between Judah and Israel and ended on the lowest point in the entire flow of salvation history since the days of the patriarchs: the Exile. The Exile marks Yahweh's judgment upon the great wickedness of both Israel and Judah, against which he had repeatedly warned them through his servants the prophets.

The era of the divided nation presents a blending of themes, developments, and perspectives. A sensitivity to diversity is thus required to appreciate the overall picture. Understanding this epoch involves three levels of approach. First, it demands attention to the interrelationship of temple, Torah, Davidic dynasty, and the prophetic ministry. Second, the epoch from the secession of Israel to the fall of Jerusalem (i.e., from 931 B.C. to 586 B.C.) unfolds the tensions between the obedience and disobedience of Israel and the patience and judgment of Yahweh. Third, the prophetic perspective on the developments in Israel and Judah holds out both a condemnation and consequent judgment on Israel and Judah as expressions of the Day of the Lord as well as the hope of (1) a remnant from all twelve tribes, (2) restoration of the people to the land, (3) restoration of the Davidic dynasty (messianic kingdom), (4) restoration of the covenant, (5) restoration of the theocratic kingdom, and (6) the inclusion of the Gentiles as recipients of his blessings.

The Books of Kings, Chronicles, and the preexilic prophets witness to the importance of this period. Though both Israel and Judah ended up in exile and experienced alienation from God, the history of the kingdoms is not simply a history of failure. It presents the working of God in purifying a people for himself—"the remnant." Yet, while doing so, the Lord shows concern for all of his people, including those in the northern kingdom. They too are his. This era anticipates a renewal of God's people and of his favor. On the one hand, the era of the divided kingdom brings to a climax the history of Israel's rebelliousness in the final judgment of God: the Exile. On the other hand, this period raises a new hope, focused on God's promises to the prophets. In an era of restoration he will reestablish his kingdom in a new people, ruled permanently by a Davidic King and richly blessed and restored by the Spirit of God.

CHAPTER 19

Literary Perspectives

THE BOOKS OF KINGS

The two separate Books of Kings in the English Bible were originally one book. The material is structured around three separate concerns: the Solomonic era (1 Kings 1–11), the story of the divided kingdoms of Israel and Judah from the secession to the exile of Israel in 722 B.C. (1 Kings 12–2 Kings 17), and the story of the kingdom of Judah till its exile and Jehoiachin's release in 561 B.C. (2 Kings 18–25).

The author employed a variety of literary sources in portraying the story of theocracy in Israel and Judah from the death of David to the release of Jehoiachin. The structuring of these literary materials reflects a combination of annalistic documentation, literary traditions, prophetic narratives, and editorial remarks. The annalistic documents of the northern kings follow a semirigid formula: "X, son of Y, became king of Israel, and he reigned over Israel Z years. As for the other events of X's reign, are they not written in the book of the annals of Israel? X rested with his fathers and was buried in L." The annals of the southern kings are somewhat different: "In the Nth year of X, Y became king of Judah, and he reigned in Jerusalem M years. His mother's name was Z. As for the other events of Y's reign, are they not written in the book of the annals of Judah? And Y rested with his fathers and was buried in the City of David. And Y1 his son succeeded him as king."[1] (See table 10.)

The author added some kind of theological statement on the religious and moral climate of the kingdom. For the northern kings, the comment has roughly the form "He did evil in the eyes of the LORD, walking in the ways of his father and in his sin, which he had caused Israel to commit" (1 Kings 15:26, 34; 22:52; 2 Kings 13:2, 11; 14:24; 15:9, 18, 24, 28). In the case of the southern kingdom, a positive or negative comparison with David would be made; for example, "He committed all the sins his father had done before him; his heart was not fully devoted to the LORD his God, as the heart of David, his forefather had been" (1 Kings 15:3).

The appearances of the prophetic narratives are unpredictable. Depending on circumstances, the prophets play either a supportive role or stand critically against the king. They relate God's Word mainly to the kings of Israel. (See table 11.)

TABLE 10. KINGS OF ISRAEL AND JUDAH, 931–715 B.C.

ISRAEL		JUDAH	
Jeroboam I	931–910	Rehoboam	931–913
		Abijah/Abijam	913–911
Nadab	910–909	Asa	911–870
Baasha	909–886		
Elah	886–885		
Zimri	885		
Omri	885–874		
Ahab	874–853	Jehoshaphat	872–848
Ahaziah	853–852		
		Jehoram/Joram	853–841
Joram/Jehoram	852–841	Ahaziah	841
Jehu	841–814	Athaliah	841–835
		Joash/Jehoash	835–796
Jehoahaz/Joahaz	814–798		
Jehoash/Joash	798–782	Amaziah	796–767
Jeroboam II	793–753		
		Azariah/Uzziah	790–740
Zachariah	753		
Shallum	752		
Menahem	752–742		
Pekahiah	752–732	Jotham	750–732
Pekah	742–740		
Hoshea	732–722	Ahaz	735–715

Source: E. R. Thiele, *A Chronology of the Hebrew Kings* (Grand Rapids: Zondervan, 1977) with modifications. For a comparison of other chronological arrangements and a bibliography, see Hayes and Miller, *IJH*, 682–83; Childs, *IOTS*, 284–85.

The variety of literary sources, the absence of consistency, and the seeming patchwork of literary traditions arise from the theological concerns of the book. After the division of the kingdom the author shifts back and forth between Israel and Judah. He includes prophetic traditions, yet at times shows little regard for the accomplishments of kings who made significant political contributions (e.g., Omri, Ahab, and Jeroboam II).

The author of Kings reflects a deuteronomistic perspective, that is, an interest in the theological contribution of Deuteronomy. Such emphases include loyalty to Yahweh (e.g., Deut. 5:32–33; 8:10–11, 18), devotion to a central shrine (12:5, 11, 14, 18), and the relationship of blessings or curses with obedience or disobedience (6:2–3, 18, 24; 7:12–8:9). By employing such a deuteronomistic perspective, the author creates a tension between human guilt and divine mercy in relation to the Davidic covenant.[2] David became a model of all the kings of Judah, and hope remained alive that God would renew his covenant with all of Israel through another king like David.[3] The Books of Kings offer a profound commentary on the theological importance of the Davidic covenant. As long as hope for a better era is focused in a Davidic king, the ups and downs in the history of Judah and Israel permit hope for the fulfillment of God's promises. Though these hopes were dashed when Judah went into exile, the book leaves the possibility open for a new era, by ending with the seemingly insignificant observation that Jehoiachin was released from prison and was royally treated.

TABLE 11. PROPHETS OF ISRAEL AND JUDAH (1–2 KINGS)

Prophet	King of Israel	King of Judah	Text	
Ahijah	Jeroboam I	—	1 Kings	11:26–40
				14:1–18
Shemaiah	—	Rehoboam	1 Kings	12:22–24
Anonymous	Jeroboam I	—	1 Kings	13
Hanani	—	Asa	2 Chron.	16:7
Jehu	Baasha	—	1 Kings	16:1–4
Elijah	Ahab, Ahaziah	—	1 Kings	17:1–
			2 Kings	2:12
Anonymous	Ahab	—	1 Kings	20:13–43
Micaiah	Ahab	—	1 Kings	22:1–36
Elisha	Joram, Jehu,	—	1 Kings	19:19–21
	Jehoahaz, Jehoash		2 Kings	2:1–8:15
				13:14–21
Jonah	Jeroboam II	—	2 Kings	14:25–27
Isaiah	—	Hezekiah	2 Kings	18:17–20:21

The literary structure also explains the editor's concern with Israel's apostasy and its need for repentance and forgiveness. It seems that the inclusion of the prayer and blessing of Solomon and the Lord's response (1 Kings 8:22–9:9) reveal the corporate responsibility of both king and people to the nations. Solomon prays, for example, for blessing on Israel "so that all the peoples of the earth may know that the LORD is God and that there is no other. But your hearts must be fully committed to the LORD our God, to live by his decrees and obey his commands, as at this time" (8:60–61).

Although failure and unresponsiveness later resulted in war, famine, plague, and ultimately exile and destruction of the temple (1 Kings 8:33–40; 9:6–9), the hope of forgiveness and restoration to the land remained alive (8:34, 50–51). The selection of the materials in Kings brings out the manifoldness of God's judgment. Yet with the reality of the Exile, the prayer of Solomon led the godly to hope for a new future:

> If they have a change of heart in the land where they are held captive, and repent and plead with you in the land of their conquerors and say, "We have sinned, we have done wrong, we have acted wickedly"; and if they turn back to you with all their heart and soul in the land of their enemies who took them captive, and pray to you toward the land you gave their fathers, toward the city you have chosen and the temple I have built for your Name; then from heaven, your dwelling place, hear their prayer and their plea, and uphold their cause. And forgive your people, who have sinned against you; forgive all the offenses they have committed against you, and cause their conquerors to show them mercy; for they are your people and your inheritance, whom you brought out of Egypt, out of that iron-smelting furnace. (vv. 47–51)

The inclusion of this prayer gave both hope and a program for expressing true contrition. It functions like a theological marker in Kings, even as Samuel's speech (1 Sam. 12) and Nathan's promissory words (2 Sam. 7:5–16) do in the Books of Samuel. The destruction of the temple thus did not signify the end of the relationship, because the Lord's dwelling place is *in heaven*.[4] Solomon's prayer extends hope for God's gracious dealings beyond Israel and Judah to include Gentiles. The godly in exile and thereafter were thus encouraged not to limit God to themselves but to speak freely about the Lord, who dwells in heaven and who responds to prayer (see 1 Kings 8:41–43). The stories of the queen of Sheba (chap. 10), the widow at Zarephath in Phoenicia (17:7–24), and Naaman the Aramean (2 Kings 5) support the universal applicability of the Books of Kings, as God shows himself to be the God of the Gentiles also.

In conclusion, by incorporating into Kings various literary strands—prophetic traditions, documentary annals, the story of Solomon, and his prayer—the editor has given a powerful prophetic interpretation of the history of Israel and Judah, with an emphasis on covenant loyalty, Israel's sin and guilt, judgment and curse, divine patience and mercy, the rule of God over Israel and Judah and the world at large, the favor of God on his people and on the Gentiles, and a hope of restoration and a messianic era.

THE BOOKS OF CHRONICLES

Chronicles was composed after the Exile.[5] The author used many different sources to trace the roots of postexilic Israel, from Adam to the decree of Cyrus. He shows familiarity with biblical writings such as the Pentateuch, the Former Prophets (Joshua, Samuel, and Kings), and the prophetic writings. He apparently also uses additional sources.

Regardless of one's observations about the materials, it becomes clear that the documentation serves a distinctive literary purpose. By giving a uniquely postexilic perspective, the author does more than copy from the contents of Joshua through 2 Kings. The existential needs of the community of faith, separated from their ancestors by hundreds of years, dictated a retelling of the history of redemption showing how the present relates to the past and through which the postexilic remnant learned positive and negative lessons from their history.[6]

There is little agreement concerning the purpose of the Chronicler's writing, since conclusions here depend on the interpretation of the literary materials and dating of the book. For our purposes we shall consider the literary materials, the way the Chronicler used them, and then look at several aspects of his purpose for writing.

The Literary Materials

As we have already seen, the Chronicler gives an extensive genealogy from Adam to the postexilic community, emphasizing the tribes of Judah and Levi, the remnant of Israel, and the Davidic dynasty. His interest in the early history of the monarchy is not in Samuel and Saul but rather in David and Solomon (1 Chron. 11–2 Chron. 9), a focus evident in his delineation of the developments in the southern kingdom. Twenty-seven chapters (2 Chron. 10–36) are given to the story of Judah's kings from Rehoboam to the decree of Cyrus, with a virtual exclusion of the history of the northern kingdom.[7]

The Chronicler presents a schematic interpretation of Israel's history, different from that presented in Samuel and Kings. He is familiar with these writings; about half of the material in Chronicles finds a parallel there. The other half reflects historical schematization by harmonization, supplementation, typology, and interpretation of Israel's history. To this end, he employs the written materials together with annals available to him, as well as prophetic books and sources. In his theological concern for providing the postexilic community with a framework for interpreting their existence as the people of God, the Chronicler uses several methods of relating past events to present concerns. These methods may be called "sermonic" or "midrashic," but we must not assume that the Chronicler wrote inferior history. His purpose was to give a sense of redemptive history.[8] In using the written materials the Chronicler stays within the broadest limits allowed by the text. After all, he wrote a reflection on Israel's history and not a history for history's sake.

In the employment of the literary materials, he shows great regard for the law of Moses. For example, in Solomon's prayer he substitutes "to walk before me according to my law" (2 Chron. 6:16) for "to walk before me" (1 Kings 8:25). The work and involvement of the priests and the Levites is more clearly brought in line with the law, reducing tensions and resolving possible questions. To this end the Chronicler specifies the roles of the Levites and the priests in the transportation of the ark to Jerusalem, in the service as singers and trumpeters before the ark, and as doorkeepers (1 Chron. 15:1–28). The celebration of the Passover in the days of Hezekiah and Josiah is told in great detail, establishing harmony with the law and continuity with their heritage.

The inclusion of the prophetic speeches reveals a concern for the ministry of the prophets.[9] The inclusion of the royal speeches and prayers also shows a concern with loyalty to the Lord, as evidenced by a strict adherence to the law and a concern for purity of worship (e.g., 1 Chron. 16:7–36; 28:2–10, 20–21).[10] Finally, certain moments in Israel's worship and acts of loyalty are glorified to bring out the continuity with the epochs of great fulfillments, namely, those of Moses, Joshua, and David. Some examples are David's words to Solomon (22:11–13; cf. Josh. 1:9), the glory-cloud in the Solomonic temple (2 Chron. 5:13–14; cf. Exod. 40:34–35), the freewill offerings (2 Chron. 24:8–14; cf. Exod. 35:20–36:7), and the descriptions of the loyal kings.

Authorial Intent

The Chronicler creatively uses existing material (Samuel and Kings, annals, and prophetic writings). His purpose is not to write a history of Israel but to relate the post-Exile community to their past. It is as much an inspired reflection on Israel's past as a commentary on his own times.[11] His primary concern is to demonstrate continuity in Israel's worship in the priority of the Aaronic priesthood, in the service of the Levites as support personnel, and in the Davidic dynasty. To this end he reveals a strong sense of the authority of the Word of God as revealed in the Law and the Prophets. The members of this postexilic community are the heirs of the legal and prophetic heritage and must carefully heed the Word of God, lest they perish like the generation of the Exile (2 Chron. 36:15–20).

The Chronicler further painstakingly points out the connection between human responsibility and God's judgment or blessing. Individuals must seek the Lord (2 Chron. 15:2), walk according to the law of God (6:16), and have faith in the prophetic word (20:20). The victories or defeats of Judah's kings reflect on their loyalty to the Lord (e.g., 13:15–18; 17:10; 20:22–25). This point of view supports the canonical status of the Law, the Former Prophets, and the Prophets. Postexilic Israel must learn to live in accordance with the Word of God (see Mal. 4:4).

CONCLUSION

The Books of Chronicles are as much a commentary on the postexilic concerns as a literary contribution to the epoch of the divided kingdom. Kings, written for the sake of exilic Israel and Judah, reflects a closer use of the documentary materials. Chronicles, while historical, applies the lessons of history for the sake of rebuilding the theocratic community out of the ashes of the exilic era. The concern for continuity with the institutions of kingship, temple, and the priestly and Levitical systems, as well as the parenetic concern with Israel's history, expresses the Chronicler's desire that the "second" Israel may pay careful attention to the revealed Word of God, which holds before them the hope of a greater fulfillment of the prophetic word.[12]

CHAPTER 20

Israel and the Prophetic Ministry

THE DIVISION/SECESSION OF THE KINGDOM

From the canonical perspective the division of the kingdom upon the death of Solomon (931 B.C.) was a historic reality. The Israelites and Judeans during and after the Exile did not need to reflect on all the reasons that may have led to that division. Israel's biblical books and the traditions do not permit an extensive reconstruction of all the political, sociological, economic, or theological factors that may have led to that division. From the perspective of Judah, the division was no more than a secession of the northern tribes from Judah (Isa. 7:17).[1]

The narratives and the prophetic speeches make it clear, however, that division was the will of God, as a judgment on Solomon's idolatrous practices (1 Kings 11:1–13). Solomon had already experienced a challenge to his sovereignty by the rebellions in Aram and Edom and by the threat of a political overthrow inspired by Jeroboam (vv. 14–40). Even so, the Lord spared Solomon the misery of the disintegration of the Davidic empire.

The prophet Ahijah, who announced to Jeroboam I that the secession of Israel was the will of Yahweh, also made it clear that this division was not to be permanent. The people of God had to know that Yahweh would bring an end to the secession and would rejoin the two peoples into one nation: "I will humble David's descendants because of this, but not forever" (1 Kings 11:39). The word "humble" often carries the sense of discipline or humiliation, and it seems that Yahweh purposed to purify his people through shame and humiliation. Even though this purpose is not stated explicitly, the literary context of the stories of Solomon's failures and the division of the kingdom indicates to the postexilic people that there was a connection between Solomon's sin and the division of the kingdom and that the Lord who divided the kingdom by his will has the authority to rejoin the tribes. Soon after Rehoboam was crowned king over Judah, the northern tribes sought an occasion to test the nature of the new leadership. When it became apparent that the new administration was unresponsive to their needs, they repeated an old cry of secession from the days of Sheba and David,

> What share do we have in David,
>   what part in Jesse's son?
> To your tents, O Israel!
> Look after your own house, O David!
>
> (1 Kings 12:16; cf. 2 Sam. 20:1)

The division of the kingdom became a reality in 931 B.C. From this time till the Exile, the two kingdoms remained divided. The political focus in the north shifted from Shechem, Mahanaim, and Tirzah to Samaria, where Omri established the capital city. Samaria became the focal point of cultural and religious innovations. To the prophets, "Samaria" signified a foreign way of life in which the culture of the nations was accepted. Samaria easily adapted its culture to that of the Phoenicians, the Arameans, and other surrounding nations. The leaders of Samaria encouraged political alliances and trade relations. Samaria was not representative of the common people. Rather, it was the political, cultural, and financial center of the aristocracy of the northern tribes.

"Jerusalem," on the other hand, signified the place where the temple of God was located and where the throne of David was established.[2] Jerusalem remained more isolated from international intrigue but was not sufficiently isolated to remain faithful to Yahweh. The policies of Jerusalem were marked by conservatism. (See figure 18.)

Samaria	Jerusalem
10 tribes	2 tribes
9 dynasties, all evil kings	1 dynasty (house of David), good and bad kings
no affiliation with Jerusalem temple	location of Solomonic temple
cultic centers at Bethel and Dan	retention of original cultic center
change in liturgical calendar	original liturgical calendar
widespread acculturation	conservatism

Figure 18. Samaria and Jerusalem Contrasted

Israel's political separation from Jerusalem and the Davidic dynasty entailed a religious commitment away from Yahwism. Yahweh was associated with Jerusalem and the Solomonic temple. The extensive refrain of the religious ills of the northern kingdom may be traced back to their separation from Jerusalem. Jerusalem, the temple, and a Davidic ruler were bound together by the will of Yahweh. Rejection of one or the other of these three signified a rejection of Yahweh himself. The postexilic community learned, however, that the separate status of the northern tribes was not permanent. The remnant of Israel together with the remnant of Judah returned to the worship of Yahweh in the postexilic temple (1 Chron. 9:3).

Religious innovations had brought down the northern kingdom. The canonical traditions put the responsibility for Israel's exile on Jeroboam I, Israel's first king (see, e.g., 1 Kings 15:34). Jeroboam consecrated his own priests out of Israel's laity, instituted two cultic sites at the borders of his kingdom (Dan and Bethel), and changed the liturgical calendar.[3] Jeroboam apparently began his cultic innovations because of fear that, if Israel went up to Jerusalem to bring their offerings and sacrifices, they might desire to end the secession (12:26–27).

The religious changes may have been forced upon the people, thus leading to religious persecution. Many left for Judah. Chronicles reminds the postexilic community that Levites and God-fearing Israelites had joined with Judah long ago:

> Those from every tribe of Israel who set their hearts on seeking the LORD, the God of Israel, followed the Levites to Jerusalem to offer sacrifices to the LORD, the God of their fathers. They strengthened the kingdom of Judah and supported Rehoboam son of Solomon. (2 Chron. 11:16–17)

This crossover is significant for understanding the religious background of the northern kingdom. With so many godly Levites and Israelites leaving for Judah, there would necessarily be a tremendous decrease in the level of moral consciousness and religious concern among the ten tribes. This factor goes far toward explaining why Israel as a whole consistently wallowed in idolatry.

ISRAEL: A KINGDOM AMONG THE NATIONS

Generations after the fall of Israel in 722 B.C., the materials of Israel's history were edited with a selectivity that was determined by the canonical situation, that is, by the needs of the people of God who received these books as the Word of God. In this selectivity, we may observe four important themes: (1) the unrighteousness of Israel's kings and people, (2) the necessary judgment of Yahweh upon the covenant breakers, (3) the power of the prophetic word, and (4) the mercy of God.

The Unrighteousness of Kings and People

The northern kingdom was different from the southern kingdom in many ways. The northern kingdom had nine dynasties in over 210 years of political existence. The nine dynasties were all characterized as evil, following in the sins of Jeroboam, the first king of the first dynasty. The biblical narrator comments on fifteen of the nineteen northern kings that, for example, they walked "in the ways of Jeroboam and in the sin he had committed and had caused Israel to commit" (1 Kings 16:19). Two of these dynasties receive special prominence in Kings, those of Omri and Jehu.

Omri put Israel on the map of the ancient Near East. Omri's relocation of Israel's capital from Tirzah to Samaria symbolized a cultural and political reorientation. He made Israel a power to be reckoned with. His son Ahab likewise strengthened his position as an international figure by adopting Baalism as Israel's official religion.[4]

Jehu's kingship is significant in that God used him to end Omri's dynasty.[5] Whereas the first four dynasties lasted no more than forty-five years each, the house of Jehu (the fifth dynasty) was blessed with ninety years of rule! The length of the dynasty is seen as an expression of God's grace to Jehu for removing Baalism (2 Kings 10:30).

All the kings of Israel fell far short of the Davidic model. They did not seek to bring the people into fellowship with Yahweh or to advance the theocratic ideal. The kings were instead political opportunists who came to the throne by subterfuge and rebellion. They surrounded themselves with aristocratic leaders and thus were able to control the political situation in the country from Samaria.

The most important points in Israel's history of unrighteousness were Jeroboam's introduction of worship apart from the Jerusalem cult and Ahab's establishment of Baal worship. The latter held Israel in its grip for about thirty years, until Jehu killed the ministers of Baal (2 Kings 10:18–28). Syncretism as a mixture of Yahwism and paganism then became more prevalent and destructive than Baalism.[6] Even Jehu, having destroyed Baal worship in Israel, "did not turn away from the sins of Jeroboam son of Nebat, which he had caused Israel to commit— the worship of the golden calves at Bethel and Dan" (v. 29). More telling than this evaluation of Jehu, however, is the writer's summary of the reasons for Israel's downfall. After having described the many ways in which the people went astray, he concludes:

> When [Yahweh] tore Israel away from the house of David, they made Jeroboam son of Nebat their king. Jeroboam enticed Israel away from following the LORD and caused them to commit a great sin. The Israelites persisted in all the sins of Jeroboam and did not turn away from them. (17:21–22)

The Necessary Judgment of Yahweh

It is difficult to separate the unrighteous actions of Israel from both the promised and the actual judgments that came upon them. Just as there were different stages in Israel's sinful practices, so also there were different periods of fulfillment of God's judgment.

The earliest statement was given in the reign of Jeroboam I after he had initiated the worship of the golden calves. So significant was his idolatry that Yahweh responded with a prophetic word of doom upon the altar at Bethel: "O altar, altar! This is what the LORD says: 'A son named Josiah will be born to the house of David. On you he will sacrifice the priests of the high places who now make offerings here, and human bones will be burned on you'" (1 Kings 13:2). This prophecy overshadows the entire history of the northern kingdom till its exile and beyond, until it was fulfilled in the last days of Judah.

Another prophecy that haunted Israel all its days was that of Ahijah. He reminded Jeroboam of Yahweh's promise to establish his kingship, conditional upon obedience (1 Kings 14:7–8). The autocratic rule of Jeroboam brought God's judgment on himself and on Israel: his son would die, Jeroboam's dynasty would be cut off, and Israel would ultimately go into exile beyond the Euphrates (vv. 10–15). As the narrative progresses, the writer observes that each of these prophecies was fulfilled (1 Kings 14:17–18; 15:29–30; 2 Kings 17:21–23). The most far-reaching of these, regarding the Exile, spans a period of two hundred years between its proclamation and its fulfillment.

The prophet Elijah brought four charges against Israel: the people had abandoned the covenant, destroyed the altars, murdered the prophets, and were seeking to end his own life (1 Kings 19:10, 14). The charges provide a lucid commentary on the evil practices of the northern kingdom during Ahab's regime. The Lord responded by assuring the prophet that he would raise up Hazael as the Aramean aggressor, Jehu as the head of a new dynasty, and Elisha as a new prophet (vv. 15–16). Through external pressures, internal changes, and the ministry of the prophets, God would rebuke, judge, and purify the people, thus ensuring a remnant of godly Israelites (vv. 15–18).

During the period of the divided kingdom, prophetism developed in two ways. First, with the ministry of Elijah, the prophet became God's appointed *covenant prosecutor*. Second, in the eighth century, prophetic oracles began to be written down. The writing, editing, collecting, and organizing of the prophetic oracles mark the beginning of *classical prophetism* as a distinct development in Israelite prophetism. Two of these latter prophets, Amos and Hosea, directed their attention to the northern kingdom during the reign of Jeroboam II (c. 790–750), truly the golden age of Israel. Yahweh was gracious in spite of their sin: the economic prosperity in Israel was due, not to the repentance of the people, but solely to God's care for his people, lest they perish (2 Kings 14:26–27).

Hosea charged the people with disobedience and infidelity to Yahweh:

> Hear the word of the LORD, you Israelites,
>> because the LORD has a charge to bring
>> against you who live in the land:
> "There is no faithfulness, no love,
>> no acknowledgment of God in the land.
> There is only cursing, lying and murder,
>> stealing and adultery;
> they break all bounds,
>> and bloodshed follows bloodshed."
>
> (Hos. 4:1–2)

Specifically, Hosea heaps guilt on the priests and the royal leaders (5:1–7). Even as Israel has rejected the prophets (9:7–8), so too,

> My God will reject them
>> because they have not obeyed him;
>> they will be wanderers among the nations.
>
> (v. 17)

Amos identifies the sins of injustice, immorality, and idolatry (Amos 2:6–8) and declares the certainty of judgment upon Israel. According to Yahweh's Word,

> On the day I punish Israel for her sins,
>> I will destroy the altars of Bethel;
> the horns of the altar will be cut off
>> and fall to the ground.
> I will tear down the winter house
>> along with the summer house;
> the houses adorned with ivory will be destroyed
>> and the mansions will be demolished.
>
> (3:14–15; cf. 9:4)

Even so, both Hosea and Amos hold out hope that a remnant will return from the punishment of exile and be renewed by God's grace (Hos. 14:4–5; Amos 9:11–12).

The Prophetic Ministry of Elijah and Elisha

The stories of both Elijah and Elisha are found only in Kings and not in the parallel history of the Chronicler, primarily because the latter has a Judean focus.[7] Chronicles is concerned with the priesthood, whereas the Books of Kings develop the place of the prophetic word in the history of redemption. For this reason the Hebrew canon placed Kings among the "Former Prophets" and put Chronicles as the last book of the

"Writings." The canonical perspective of Kings focuses on the redemptive history of the ministry of the prophets.

Long before Elijah came on the scene (1 Kings 17), prophets both named and anonymous had played a vital role in the history of Israel and Judah. God's Word came through Ahijah and an unnamed "man of God" to Jeroboam I (11:29–39; 13:1–9; 14:2–18), through Shemaiah to Rehoboam (12:22–24), and through Jehu to Baasha (16:1–4). More significant than the naming of the prophets and their prophecies is the editor's care in showing how each of these prophecies was fulfilled exactly according to the Word that God had spoken (1 Kings 14:17–18; 15:29–30; 22:18, 38; 2 Kings 9:36; 10:10, 17; 17:21–23).

Elijah the Tishbite, however, is unique among the prophets. Through Elijah's ministry Yahweh declared his judgment on Baalism, the Omride dynasty, and on Israel, while continuing to establish a righteous remnant for himself. While there were indeed other prophets contemporary with Elijah (see 1 Kings 18:4; 20:13–14, 28; 22:8–28), Elijah became one of the forerunners of classical prophetism as it developed in Israel and Judah. Elisha is closely connected with the ministry of Elijah his master, whom he affectionately called his father (2 Kings 2:12).

Elijah occupies a distinct place in the history of redemption. Though he left no prophetic book, Elijah was one of the greatest Old Testament prophets and has a special place next to Moses and Samuel. The prophetic movement in the Old Testament developed along the lines of the ministry of Elijah. So important is his place in the history of redemption that Malachi predicts that Elijah will come again (Mal. 4:5–6). The angel Gabriel told Zechariah that his son would go before the Lord "in the spirit and power of Elijah" (Luke 1:17). Jesus himself acknowledged that John the Baptist was Elijah (Matt. 11:14; Mark 9:13). Moreover, it was Elijah with Moses, representing the Prophets and the Law, who spoke with Jesus on the Mount of Transfiguration (Matt. 17:3–13).

Even as Elijah led a renewed people of God, so too John the Baptist prepared the way for our Lord Jesus and the beginning of a new humanity during the last days. This remnant, as Jesus pointed out (Luke 4:25–27), consists of Gentiles as well as Jews, for Elijah certainly passed by many needy Israelites in order to minister to the widow of Zarephath. Finally, Elijah stands as a great example of a godly man, by whose faith the Lord accomplished great things. For the Christian, Elijah is a God-given encouragement to pray fervently (James 5:17).

Elisha, the son of Shaphat of Abel Meholah, was an important instrument of God's mercy to Israel. He was anointed by Elijah (1 Kings 19:16, 19–21) and played an essential part in the forthcoming judgment (v. 17). The Scriptures tell us little about the life of Elisha, but his continuity with Elijah is important to the writer of Kings, who recounts the events before and after Elijah's ascension to heaven. Elisha receives the cloak of Elijah, as God's response to Elisha's desire to inherit "a double portion" of the prophetic spirit of Elijah (2 Kings 2:9, 13).

Elisha receives the spirit of Elijah and is given the authority to divide the water in the same manner as Elijah—as a sign of continuity to the sons of the prophets who witnessed both acts. They thus can say, "The spirit of Elijah is resting on Elisha," and their subsequent obeisance confirms the sincerity of their words and their respect for the prophet (2 Kings 2:15).

Elijah and Elisha stand as two great figures in the age of the divided kingdom. This pair of prophets is often likened to Moses and Joshua. Moses and Elijah were at Mount Sinai: the former as a covenant mediator and the latter as a covenant prosecutor. Joshua and Elisha both succeeded great men, both were authenticated by a miraculous crossing of the Jordan, and both maintained a position of authority.

The Mercy of God

Though God pronounced his judgment through the prophetic word of men such as Ahijah, Elijah, Elisha, Amos, and Hosea, he showed great mercy for his people. First, his mercy is shown in his *patience*. From the very beginning of Israel's secession, God's judgment was clearly announced by his prophet Ahijah (1 Kings 14:7–16). The Lord did not eradicate the northern kingdom immediately, though the deterioration of religious and political life in the northern kingdom brought God's judgment upon it as declared by Ahijah. Ahijah announced the fall of the northern kingdom, some two hundred years before it happened. In the meantime the Lord continued to tolerate the northern kingdom until the cup of wickedness was full. Dynasties rose and fell, but evil prevailed. The pious in Israel thanked the Lord for bringing the dynasties of Jeroboam, Baasha, Omri, Jehu, and others to an end. With the end of each dynasty there flickered some hope that the next era might be better. In the end, none of the dynasties was acceptable to the Lord. Finally, he brought upon the ninth dynasty the judgment of exile and destruction.

Second, his mercy is shown in *prosperity and blessing*. During the era of the Omride dynasty, Israel prospered. A century later, Israel enjoyed a golden age under Jeroboam II. As an expression of God's displeasure with Israel, Hazael of Aram had been permitted to harass and oppress Israel (1 Kings 19:15–17). Hazael almost succeeded in bringing Israel to its knees, but the Lord's mercy sustained it. He eased Israel's pain with prosperity, not because it had become more righteous, but out of sheer compassion (2 Kings 14:26–27).

Third, his mercy was also shown in the *prophetic ministry*. The

258

prophets were tokens of hope, encouraging the remnant to persevere. Through prophets such as Elijah and Elisha, the Lord ministered his grace, renewing his people with his marvelous powers of feeding, healing, and raising the dead. They witnessed with visible signs that the Lord is Yahweh, the God of the Exodus, the God of the fathers. The deliverance of the Divine Warrior was granted to Israel in fulfillment of his Word through Elisha (2 Kings 13:18–19) and Jonah (14:25).

Fourth, his mercy *extended through and beyond judgment.* After all these demonstrations of his mercy, his judgment was still upon the people. The weight of it finally fell in 722 B.C., when the armies of Shalmaneser V and Sargon II devastated the land and exiled the people. With the exile of the northern kingdom the covenant was suspended indefinitely. The people were accursed and forced to live among the nations. But Sargon II left a small remnant behind. It was this small remnant that had the potential of being rejoined to Judah, thus creating a remnant of all twelve tribes as one nation under one God. God was still concerned about the remnant in the northern kingdom, even as he had promised the prophet Elijah (1 Kings 19:18).

The canonical account clearly asserts that a remnant of the ten tribes joined in with Judah before the Exile and was thus incorporated into the covenant community. Judah's godly kings Hezekiah and Josiah were shepherds of Israel, concerned with all of the twelve tribes. Chronicles portrays Hezekiah as being greatly interested in the remnant of Israel who lived in the territory of the Land of Promise after the majority of the population had been exiled. His kingship unfolds the Davidic ideal in that, after the purification of the temple (2 Chron. 29), he called on the Israelites to join him in a great Passover celebration (30:1). A proclamation was made from Dan to Beersheba, calling on the people to repent so that the Lord might again be gracious:

> People of Israel, return to the LORD, the God of Abraham, Isaac and Israel, that he may return to you who are left, who have escaped from the hand of the kings of Assyria. Do not be like your fathers and brothers, who were unfaithful to the LORD, the God of their fathers, so that he made them an object of horror, as you see. Do not be stiff-necked, as your fathers were; submit to the LORD. Come to the sanctuary, which he has consecrated forever. Serve the LORD your God, so that his fierce anger will turn away from you. (vv. 6–8)

Hezekiah believed in God's promises, as he spoke of God's compassion on the remnant:

> If you return to the LORD, then your brothers and your children will be shown compassion by their captors and will come back to this land, for the LORD your God is gracious and compassionate. He will not turn his face from you if you return to him. (v. 9)

The response of those Israelites left was not positive. The people of Ephraim and Manasseh scorned the couriers (2 Chron. 30:10). However, some from Asher, Manasseh, and Zebulun came to Jerusalem. The small remnant of Israel joined together with the people of Judah in the great celebration of the Passover for fourteen days. The festival was so great that there had not been anything like it since the days of Solomon (v. 26)! When God's people had assembled in Jerusalem and had been blessed by the priests (v. 27), the Israelites were so inspired that they joined with the Judeans in smashing the idols in Judah, Benjamin, Ephraim, and Manasseh (31:1). At that time they had returned to their own cities in order to continue the occupation of the land by the covenant people.

The reunion of North and South was even greater during the days of Josiah. Like Hezekiah, Josiah invited the people of Israel to join him in celebrating a Passover. It was the highest point in the history of the divided kingdom, when the ritual was closely kept in accordance with the instructions of David and Solomon. Again, representatives of the twelve tribes were in Jerusalem. The union of the people and their submission to King Josiah and to the Lord brought to mind the days of David and Solomon (2 Chron. 35:4–5). The celebration was the greatest Passover since the days of the prophet Samuel (vv. 18–19)!

CONCLUSION

Though the canonical account reflects negatively on the 210 years of the northern kingdom, there was some light both at the beginning and at the end. In Israel's early history (c. 930 B.C.), Levites and a godly remnant of the northern tribes joined with Judah in their loyalty to Yahweh. After the fall of Samaria in 722 B.C., a remnant of the twelve tribes joined together with Judah in the service of Yahweh. With the return of the remnant of Israel to Judah, the twelve tribes joined together in their worship of God in Jerusalem and in their submission to the house of David. Yet, these individuals who believed in Yahweh, held to the Davidic dynasty, and hallowed the temple were not yet constituted as one nation. The remnant of Israel and Judah was yet to undergo the purifying fires of war and exile. The prophetic word assured them, however, that the Lord would restore them from exile to the land as one nation, that he would renew his covenant with the remnant, and that they would enjoy his kingship and protection under the leadership of one shepherd: the Messiah of David's dynasty (see Hos. 3:5).

The assurance of God's judgment, purification, and restoration of his favor to the remnant lies in the ministry of Elijah and Elisha. From Elijah's complaint to the Lord on Mount Sinai onward, the prophets speak of judgment and transformation. They sustain the godly remnant with hope in the kingdom of God, while warning the ungodly of the terrible day of God's judgment. The prophet has become the symbol of the continuity of God's purposes, especially when the light of theocratic kingship shone dimly. Throughout redemptive history the word of the prophets would sustain the godly who were awaiting the righteous establishment of God's kingdom (see Mal. 4:5–6).

CHAPTER 21

Judah and the House of David

THE KINGDOM OF JUDAH

From a redemptive-historical perspective, Judah had much more going for it than did Israel at the secession of the northern tribes. Judah possessed the temple of God in Jerusalem and the promises to the Davidic dynasty. Though Rehoboam may have acted unwisely toward the leadership of the northern tribes, he enjoyed the privilege of being in the Davidic line and therefore was the heir of God's promise (see 1 Kings 11:35–38). Moreover, the hope of the reunion of the twelve tribes under Davidic rule remained alive (v. 39).

In addition to the privileged position of the Davidic dynasty, the southern kingdom offered a special attraction to the godly in Israel and Judah. After all, Jerusalem was the city Yahweh had chosen. The temple symbolized God's presence. With the influx of Levites and godly people from the ten tribes, Judah's position was strengthened.

Another of Judah's advantages was its geographical isolation. From a political and military aspect, Judah was removed from the major highways and was more defensible by royal and fortified cities. These military garrisons guarded the access roads that led into the hill country. Judah's insular position may help to explain its conservatism with regard to linguistic, cultural, political, and economic developments.

In spite of these advantages, Judah was not immune to idolatry, temptations, and rebellion against the covenant. Its history reveals no consistent apostasy akin to that of its northern neighbor, yet the nation moves often meaninglessly from a high point of religious zeal to a low point of idolatry and apostasy, only to return to a greater commitment to Yahweh. Since the king figures prominently in his shepherd role as political, economic, and religious leader, the nature of the leadership of the Davidic king is carefully evaluated in Kings and Chronicles. These books tell us little about ordinary people or about events merely for the sake of history itself. The editors of Kings and Chronicles each have a unique concern in retelling the story of Judah.

The author of Kings is concerned with the relationships of obedience to blessing and of disobedience to curse. Some kings were good shepherds of Judah who loved the Lord and had concern for his temple. The kings who led Judah into defeat and economic strangulation, however, were idolatrous and despotic in their regimes. By God's judgment he delivered his people from evil, entrusting the theocratic rule to another king.

Yet, the author also brings out the extent of God's mercy. Even though Judah was often guilty of covenantal rebellion, Yahweh remained loyal to the nation. Because of this loyalty, Judah was not consumed at the same time as was Israel. The 136 years between Israel's fall and Judah's exile were not because of Judah's righteousness. The Bible makes it clear that the Lord spared Judah for his own purposes. He promised to remain with his people in Judah, though they had gravely sinned (see Isa. 8:6–10).

Moreover, hope remained focused on the Davidic king, who filled the important role of shepherd. Not only was the Davidic king compared with his forefather David, but each generation thought of him as being able to bring in a new era of peace and prosperity, just as David and Solomon had introduced the era of the royal nation. Hope was possible only because of God's grace, by which he was ready to forgive the sins of the father and renew his covenant with the son. God's grace and forgiveness to the Davidic kings reveals that the Lord, rather than any earthly Davidic king, is the object of hope. With him is forgiveness and grace.

The author of Chronicles has different concerns. Over against the often colorless kings of Judah portrayed in Kings, the Davidic kings of the Chronicler are made to live. The Book of Kings is still too close to the ravages of the Exile and explains Judah's fall essentially through the portrayal of Israel's fall. The days of Judah after Israel's fall (2 Kings 18–25) focus on the Assyrian threat to Hezekiah (chaps. 18–19), Hezekiah's illness, and the envoys from Babylon (chap. 20; cf. Isa. 36–39). Manasseh's long reign receives brief treatment (2 Kings 21), compared with the more lengthy consideration of the law and the renewal of the covenant in Josiah's days (chaps. 22–23). The last chapters unfold the last days of Judah before and during the Babylonian invasions and captivity (chaps. 24–25). The relationship between the Davidic king and the Torah is important to the editor of Chronicles. The good kings are those who encourage the popular instruction of the Torah and who show an interest in the welfare of the temple.

These varied concerns may best be illustrated by comparing the canonical accounts of Rehoboam, Judah's first king after the secession. The narrative in Kings is unusually short (1 Kings 14:21–31). The acts of Rehoboam are set in between the annalistic materials (vv. 21, 29–31) pertaining to his age at the coronation, the length of his rule, his mother's name, a reference to "the other events of Rehoboam's reign"

263

as recorded in the annals of the kings of Judah, and his burial in the city of David. Apart from these data the author places the responsibility for a growing idolatry with the people of Judah (vv. 22–24). He mentions the invasion of Pharaoh Shishak, who carried off treasures from the Jerusalem temple (vv. 25–26), without drawing a relationship of cause and effect. He also makes clear that Rehoboam ruled in Jerusalem, "the city the LORD had chosen . . . in which to put his Name" (v. 21). Judah's weakened position is illustrated by the substitution of bronze shields for the gold shields of Solomon, taken by Shishak (vv 26–28; cf. 10:17).

The Chronicler's interest in Rehoboam is quite different. Not only is the account much more extensive, but the treatment is representative of how he evaluates other kings of Judah. First, when Rehoboam receives a word from the Lord by the prophet Shemaiah, he responds positively (2 Chron. 11:2–4). Second, Rehoboam secures Jerusalem by fortifying Judah's defense towns (vv. 5–12). Third, Rehoboam shows a concern for the Jerusalem temple. He promotes the worship of the Lord by welcoming the Levites and godly remnant from the northern tribes, displaying his continuity with David and Solomon (vv. 13–17). Fourth, Rehoboam enhances the position of the Davidic dynasty by setting up his leaders in Judah (vv. 18–23). Fifth, Chronicles connects Judah's apostasy and military defeat in a cause-and-effect relationship (12:1–5). Sixth, the Chronicler teaches the importance of responding to the law of the Lord and to the prophets. He explains that, when the people and the king repented from their rebelliousness, they were not completely destroyed (vv. 6, 7, 12). God's grace is evident as Yahweh explains through Shemaiah, "Since they have humbled themselves, I will not destroy them but will soon give them deliverance. My wrath will not be poured out on Jerusalem through Shishak" (v. 7).

THE DAVIDIC KING

Though Kings and Chronicles have different emphases, the canonical and redemptive-historical themes of these books are highly complementary and include the following four elements: (1) the importance of the Davidic ideal, (2) the king's responsiveness to the theocratic ideal, (3) the royal support of the temple, and (4) the unity of the twelve tribes.

The Davidic Ideal

The Davidic ideal clearly takes on special significance for Judah because its kings were in David's family line. He was not just the pattern for Judean kings; he was their *father*. David's style of kingship was the goal that the kings ought to attain; he was the standard to which they are compared. The king's heart was to be loyal to Yahweh (e.g., "Asa did what was right in the eyes of the LORD, as his father David had done" [1 Kings 15:11].) The Davidic ideal pertained to covenantal loyalty and to the benefits extended to God's people. The extent to which they fulfilled or failed that purpose determined whether a king was considered good or evil.

The king was to be the shepherd of Yahweh's people and to seek their welfare in both material and spiritual ways. Although the majority of southern kings fell far below this standard, a few kings were considered to have been good. The best examples of the "good" southern kings who led the people in righteousness were Hezekiah and Josiah. Both are likened to David (2 Kings 18:3; 22:2), and both followed kings who were particularly evil (Ahaz and Manasseh).

The kings were "good" when they followed in David's footsteps, that is when they: (1) had a zeal for the defense of Jerusalem and for the fortification of Judah (2 Chron. 26:9–15); (2) upheld the Davidic covenant for the benefit for all of God's people through economic and judicial measures (2 Chron. 19:8–10); (3) had a concern for the spiritual welfare of the people by devotion to the temple in Jerusalem (2 Kings 18:4; 2 Chron. 13:10–12; 24:13; 29:1–31:21) and by fostering the instruction in God's law (cf. 2 Chron. 19:10; 23:18); (4) had a receptivity to God's Word through his prophets (2 Chron. 12:5–8; 20:14–17; 34:23–32; Isa. 36–39) and whenever possible to the reunification of the twelve tribes (2 Chron. 30:5).

Responsiveness to the Theocratic Ideal

The good kings of Judah protected their people and led them in spiritual reformation. They were also judged by their responsiveness to Yahweh. The so-called theocratic ideal revolves around the proper relationship of the king to the Lord and the theocratic officers: the priests, Levites, and prophets. The king is evaluated in terms of his loyalty (or lack of responsiveness), the loyalty of his people, and the loyalty of the other officers of the covenant to the ideal of God's rule (theocracy). A concern for the theocratic ideal focuses more on the relationship of the kingship to the temple and priesthood, all twelve tribes, and the prophetic ministry.

The Place of the Temple, the Priests, and the Levites

The good kings encouraged the development of the priests and the Levites in and outside of the temple cult. David is the paradigm, as he transferred the ark to Jerusalem and made plans for building the temple. Whereas Moses had instructed the Levites to be the porters of the parts and vessels of the tabernacle as well as of the ark of the covenant (Num. 4:1–33), David instituted new duties for the priests and Levites: doorkeepers (1 Chron. 9:22–27; 15:23–24); singers and musicians, in particular, Heman, Asaph, Ethan, and their descendants (6:31–47; 15:16); and caretakers for the holy vessels and the preparation of the bread of the presence, cereal offering, and incense (6:49–53; 9:28–32).

Chronicles traces the continuity and discontinuity between Moses/David and the postexilic situation through the period of the kings of Judah. Care of the temple and the priestly and Levitical system was rewarded by evidences of God's blessedness: victory, prosperity, and peace. Lack of loyalty to the temple became associated with assassination, disease, war, and adversity, which eventually culminated in the Exile. A harmonious relationship between king, temple, and priesthood secured God's blessings on his people (see 2 Chron. 13:12).

The Religious Unity of the Twelve Tribes

With the secession of the northern tribes, the possibility of one people's worshiping at one temple came to an end. Jeroboam I saw to it that the northern tribes had their own cultic system, centralized at Dan and Bethel, their own priesthood, and their own religious calendar. Even the good southern kings could do little to effect changes in the religious system of their northern contemporaries. The fall of Samaria, however, marked a new era. The northern tribes had been exiled, and a remnant had been left in the land under an Assyrian governor.

Hezekiah responded by asserting his royal prerogatives as king over all Israel. Though he could not reclaim the territory of the northern tribes politically, he made a valiant attempt to win the hearts of the northerners by naming his son "Manasseh," after one of the leading northern tribes. Moreover, he invited all the people from Beersheba to Dan to a Passover celebration (2 Chron. 30:5). So great was the joy that the resultant celebration reminded the people of "the days of Solomon son of David king of Israel" (v. 26)! The worshipers, intoxicated with the religious zeal of Hezekiah, smashed idolatrous sites in Judah and Israel (31:1). With the return of the Israelites "to their own towns and to their own property" (v. 1), Hezekiah had achieved the beginnings of the restoration of the twelve tribes submitted to a Davidic ruler and the law of Yahweh.

> Hezekiah's cultic reform was a movement combining religion and nationalism and also a territorial and political project whose aim was to prepare the road for the incorporation of the former area of the kingdom of Israel under the reign of the house of David.[1]

Josiah followed in the footsteps of Hezekiah. When the Assyrian Empire was disintegrating, he extended his borders, possibly even reclaiming much of the territory formerly held by Israel (2 Chron. 34:6–7).[2] He appealed to the remnant of the northern tribes to be loyal to Yahweh and to his king by inviting them to the Passover celebration.

Not since the days of Samuel had such a Passover been observed (35:1–19).

The work of restoration began before the Exile in the renewal of God's favor to the remnant of Israel together with Judah. Josiah's contemporary, the prophet Jeremiah, made it a point to stress that the future glory, restoration, and covenant renewal belonged to the remnant of both Israel and Judah. For him the continuity of Davidic king (Jer. 33:14–18), land (32:1–33:13), priesthood (33:19–22), the twelve tribes (33:23–26), and the renewal of the covenant (31:31–37) belong to all descendants of Abraham (33:25–26). The work begun by Hezekiah and Josiah, in continuity with the national concerns of Samuel, David, and Solomon, would extend beyond the Exile!

CONCLUSION

The hope of the southern kingdom was in the Davidic dynasty. Judah, because its history was replete with examples of idolatry and acts of apostasy, did not owe its long national existence (from 931 to 586 B.C.) to its own righteousness. Instead, God's covenant with David assured Judah of Yahweh's fidelity. In his grace the Lord raised up godly kings who more or less approximated David's loyalty to the Lord and his concern for the people.

The good kings of Judah cared for the people by providing for Jerusalem's defense, by encouraging economic development, and by giving spiritual leadership. The godly kings promoted the worship of the Lord. They related harmoniously with the temple leadership; they provided royally for the needs of the temple, the priests, and the Levites; and they modeled the worship after the practices laid down by Moses and David. Moreover, even though the kingdom had been divided and the northern tribes had been defiled by about two hundred years of idolatrous practices, godly kings such as Hezekiah and Josiah did everything to include the godly from the north and thus to foster unity of worship.

CHAPTER 22

Prophetism

Like the kings in Israel, the Judean kings received direct confrontation and encouragement from the messengers of God. Whereas Kings shows an interest in the relation of prophets and the northern kings, Chronicles concentrates on God's prophets in the southern kingdom. God's Word explained the purposes of God. For example, Shemaiah, "the man of God," explained to Rehoboam that Israel's secession was the Lord's doing (2 Chron. 11:2–4). The challenge of Azariah, son of Oded, to King Asa was God's invitation to each generation of God's people: "Listen to me, Asa and all Judah and Benjamin. The LORD is with you when you are with him. If you seek him, he will be found by you, but if you forsake him, he will forsake you" (15:2; cf. Isa. 55:6; James 4:8).

In order to pay the tribute exacted by Ben-Hadad, Asa emptied out the temple treasury. Hanani, "the seer" (2 Chron. 16:7–9), rebuked Asa for making such a political alliance with Ben-Hadad of Aram against Baasha, rather than relying on the Lord. Similarly, Jehu, "the seer" (19:2), and Eliezer, son of Dodavahu (20:37), condemned the alliance between Jehoshaphat and the house of Omri (Ahab and Ahaziah).

Zechariah, son of Jehoiada, was a prophet-priest who resisted the idolatry of Joash. Joash had him executed by stoning (2 Chron. 24:21), for which he was later assassinated by his own servants (v. 25). King Amaziah received a message from "a man of God" when he had allied himself with Israel against the Edomites. The prophet encouraged him to go in the strength of the Lord without military help from Israel (25:7–9). The Lord was with him, until he set up Edomite idols (v. 14). He ordered a prophet who rebuked him not to speak a word from the Lord (v. 16). But the prophet pronounced God's judgment on him. Jehoash, king of Israel, attacked Judah. Jerusalem was sacked, and vast booty was taken, including the treasuries of the temple and the palaces (vv. 20–24).

The prophets encouraged, promised, warned, and pronounced God's judgment on the kings. By the time King Uzziah resisted the prophet-priest Azariah and was stricken with leprosy, a new development in the prophetic movement was taking place—classical prophetism. The classical prophets spoke God's Word to the king, leaders, or people. They charged them in a *rîb* ("accusation") pattern, condemned the people, pronounced the judgment of a coming "Day of the Lord," and predicted a new era that the godly remnant would enjoy. In the announcement of the new era they proclaimed that the Lord would continue with his people, but the continuity would be qualified by certain elements of discontinuity.

As it did in the north, prophetism in the southern kingdom developed from the prophet's function as a counselor to the king to his calling as God's spokesman to the people at large. The prophets encouraged and warned the kings of their proposed, present, or future actions. The approach to prophetism in Chronicles reveals an increasing hardness toward the prophetic word. King after king insisted on his rights and spurned the prophetic ministry.

Gradually, the prophetic movement changed direction. By the eighth century the prophetic function was enlarged to that of *preacher*, whose inspired message was cast into distinct forms of prophetic speech.[1] The prophet was a *covenant prosecutor*, commissioned by the Lord to indict Judah, declare it guilty, and forewarn it of the coming judgments of the Lord. The prophet was also a *visionary*, speaking of a new age. This message of another day was marked by comfort, hope, and a call for an individual response of love for the Lord, with whom is mercy and forgiveness.

Beginning in the late eighth century, the prophets had their messages written down as a witness to posterity of the judgments and of the restoration to come. Even as Moses and Joshua had left a written witness against the future generations (Deut. 31:24–29; Josh. 24:25–27), the ministry of the prophets of Judah was perpetuated by the collection and preservation of their oracles. The extension of the prophetic office into public proclamation and literary output signifies a new development in Judah.[2]

PROPHETS OF THE EIGHTH CENTURY

Isaiah

Isaiah, whose name means "salvation is the Lord's," began his ministry in the year of King Uzziah's death (Isa. 6:1), approximately 740 B.C. Of the remaining three kings in whose reigns Isaiah prophesied (Jotham, Ahaz, and Hezekiah), only Ahaz is reckoned wicked. This fact is significant because the prophet identifies great sinfulness among the people, despite the goodness of the king. Much of what Isaiah attacked was the oppression, immorality, and injustice that was so rampant in

Judah (3:13–26; 5:8–23; 9:8–21; 22:1–13; 28:1–4; 29:1–16). In essence, Judah and Jerusalem had broken the covenant (24:5). Now Yahweh's righteous anger was directed against them (3:1–12; 5:1–7). The very blessing of a prosperous land would be revoked, and Israel and Judah would be removed from the land by Assyria and Babylon. Isaiah's oracles also address nations that had oppressed, troubled, and seduced Judah (see chaps. 13–23). Yet, in the midst of all of this judgment, Yahweh promised to preserve a remnant that will ultimately be restored to the land (chap. 27).

Isaiah gave hope for the future of the Davidic dynasty. He spoke of God's presence in the great Immanuel prophecy (Isa. 7:10–17) and of the messianic era of righteousness and peace (9:1–7; 11:1–11). Isaiah looks forward to the renewal of God's favor after the Exile. He ministers comfort (40:1) by assuring the people that God's kingdom will come in power, their sins will be forgiven, and a remnant will return to the land. Several passages focus on the majesty of Yahweh, the only true God (40:12–26; 41:1–7; 44:6–8; 45:18–19). This truth is intended to calm the fears of the remnant as they return to the land (40:27–31; 41:8–10; 43:1–7). The so-called Servant Songs distributed among chapters 40–55 speak of Yahweh's sovereign purpose for (49:3) and the coming of a special servant who would bear the sins of his people (52:13–53:12). In his prophecies of the era of restoration, Isaiah telescopes the history of redemption into a grand renewal of heaven and earth (chaps. 65–66) in which God's people share but from which the ungodly are banned. The progression of restoration takes place over centuries, even millennia, but all of the blessings of God enjoyed in time foreshadow the eternal glorious and victorious blessedness of his saints, consisting of both Jews and Gentiles.[3] Isaiah concludes his prophecies with a vision of the final glory of Yahweh's consummated kingdom in the new heavens and the new earth.

Micah

Micah, Isaiah's younger contemporary (see Mic. 1:1), brought a similar message of judgment (vv. 2–16), focusing particularly on the sinful leadership of rulers, prophets, and priests (2:6–11; chap. 3). Much of the responsibility for the coming disaster lies with them:

> Therefore because of you [leaders],
>   Zion will be plowed like a field,
> Jerusalem will become a heap of rubble,
>   the temple hill a mound overgrown with thickets.
>
> (3:12)

As with Isaiah's message, judgment will also come upon Assyria (5:5–6) and all of Israel's enemies (v. 9). For his part, Micah provides a beautiful vision of Yahweh's reign in Zion and Judah's participation in teaching the nations the will of the Lord (4:1–3). He also speaks of the revitalization of the Davidic kingship and the glory of Yahweh's reign (5:2–5). In his magnificent prayer (7:14–20), Micah asks Yahweh to keep his covenant with Abraham and Jacob, to forgive the people's sins, and to restore them to the land with the renewal of his blessing.

PROPHETS OF THE SEVENTH AND SIXTH CENTURIES

A century later Judah was close to its fall. The nation had just come through the darkest period in its history, one dominated by the fifty-five-year reign of Manasseh, the most wicked of Judah's kings. God's judgment was inevitable. Even though the religious reforms of Josiah were favorably accepted by the Lord, he had decreed to bring Judah to its end. The generation between Josiah's reforms and Judah's fall was a creative period, during which major prophets in Jerusalem (Jeremiah) and in the Exile (Ezekiel) called on the faithful to seek the Lord—the only proper response to the impending fall of Jerusalem, burning of the temple, and exile.

Both Jeremiah and Ezekiel spoke the Word of God, even though their contemporaries refused to accept the fact that Jerusalem would fall. Both men spoke of the coming judgment and of the restoration that would follow. Jeremiah and Ezekiel were God's messengers who encouraged the faithful remnant to persevere in hoping for the renewal of the covenant, the outpouring of the Spirit of God, and the restoration of God's people to the Land of Promise.

Jeremiah

The prophet Jeremiah had a ministry that lasted about forty years. He was called in the thirteenth year of King Josiah (627 B.C.) and witnessed the fall of Jerusalem (586 B.C.).[4] Shortly thereafter he was forced by his compatriots to seek refuge in Egypt. He witnessed the reign of Josiah, with its great reforms, as well as the rule of the petty kings Jehoahaz, Jehoiakim, Jehoiachin, and Zedekiah.

His ministry reached beyond Jerusalem and Judah to encompass the nations, and he is known as the prophet to the nations (Jer. 1:5, 9–10). Jeremiah's ministry included an explanation of God's judgment upon Judah and Jerusalem and the kingdoms of the earth (chaps. 42–51), including Babylon, the agent of destruction. At the same time Jeremiah also proclaimed God's outstanding promise of restoration and the inclusion of the Gentiles into the covenantal fellowship. His proclamation consisted of oracles of destruction and of restoration (see 1:9–10).

The message of Jeremiah was not unlike that of other prophets. His historical context, however, set him apart from other prophets. He was

God's messenger to Jerusalem at the hour of the destruction of the city, the burning of the temple and palaces, and the exile of the people. He bore witness both before and after the event that the judgment was in no way an accident of history but was intended by the Lord (Jer. 1:15). Jeremiah knew that God's indictment and judgment of Judah were justly deserved (11:20; 12:1). The people had broken the covenant (chap. 11). They had abandoned Yahweh and had gone their own way (2:13). The covenant curse was now invoked (11:3). God would no longer deal in mercy as he had in the past (15:1).

Nevertheless, the prophet spoke words of comfort. In the new age a "righteous Branch" will come from David. He will be righteous, unlike Zedekiah (whose name means "the Lord is righteous"), and he will rule over all the tribes of Israel.

> "The days are coming," declares the LORD,
> "when I will raise up to David a righteous Branch,
> a King who will reign wisely
> and do what is just and right in the land.
> In his days Judah will be saved
> and Israel will live in safety.
> This is the name by which he will be called:
> The LORD Our Righteousness."
> (Jer. 23:5–6; cf. 33:15–16)

The message of comfort and restoration was the basis of hope in the postexilic community and at the time of our Lord Jesus Christ. The people continued to look for the fullness of the New Covenant. As Jesus was about to be betrayed, he told his disciples that the fullness of the restoration could not come unless he died. With his death, the New Covenant about which Jeremiah prophesied (31:31) has taken on greater significance, because in the New Covenant God reaffirms his intention to restore humankind to himself and to restore the heavens and the earth (Matt. 11:28; 26:28; 1 Cor. 11:25; 2 Cor. 3:6; Heb. 8:8–12). Moreover, the magnificent prophecies of Jeremiah pertaining to the nations will always be the basis of hope for God's inclusion of the Gentiles together with his people Israel, as one covenant people. Jeremiah said comparatively little about the exact nature of the messianic kingdom and its messianic king. He did, however, bear witness in a period of perverse leadership, as he looked ahead to the restoration of God's kingship on earth.

Ezekiel

The ministry of the prophet Ezekiel can also be best understood against the backdrop of his time. If we assume with Origen that the vague reference to "the thirtieth year" (Ezek. 1:1) marks the age of the prophet, he may have been born around 622 B.C., during the rule of King Josiah of Judah (c. 632–609 B.C.). In his youth he witnessed the growing power of Babylon, when Egypt and Assyria were defeated by Nebuchadnezzar at Carchemish (605 B.C.). The Babylonians pushed further south to Jerusalem and made the first deportation of Judah's leading men, including Daniel. Nebuchadnezzar left King Jehoiakim on the throne to rule as his vassal.

After three years, however, Jehoiakim rebelled against his overlord, repeating the mistake of his predecessors by relying on Egypt for support. This policy brought the full wrath of Nebuchadnezzar upon Judah, though by the time the Babylonians arrived, Jehoiakim had died and his son Jehoiachin had succeeded him.

A second deportation followed the destruction of the city. Jehoiachin and thousands of other leading citizens were taken into captivity. Among these deportees was Ezekiel, the son of Buzi (1:3), and a member of a priestly family. He was then approximately twenty-five years old. Although it is not known whether he actually served in the temple as a priest, he was clearly preoccupied with the temple as a symbol of God's presence.

In exile, Ezekiel the prophet-priest spoke God's Word regarding the future of the temple to his fellow exiles who were settled at Tel Abib, a place located by the canal of Chebar. Here the thousands of deportees eked out a meager existence, hoping for a change in the international situation that would allow their speedy return to Judah. Their hope was inflamed by the spirited preaching of the prophets of positive thinking. Ezekiel compares them to jackals among ruins (13:4). They deceived the people with their message of peace, at a time when God's judgment was about to be poured out on Jerusalem (v. 10). Ezekiel spoke clearly of the imminence of God's judgment (e.g., 12:23) in words, visions, and symbolic acts.[5]

Ezekiel: The Prophet-Priest

As a priest, Ezekiel was concerned with the future of the temple. The temple was the sacred symbol of God's presence, covenant, and rule (1 Kings 8:10–11). While in exile Ezekiel had a vision of God's glory. The Lord assured Ezekiel of his call (Ezek. 1:4–2:2) and of God's departure from the temple in Jerusalem (8:1–4; 10:1–22; 11:22–25). The God of glory appointed Ezekiel to be a "watchman" over Israel (3:16–19). His witness to Israel was for the express aim of national repentance, so that sinners might be restored upon repentance from their sins (3:18–19).

Symbolism figures prominently in Ezekiel's writing. Possibly his priestly background had prepared him for communicating God's Word in symbolic acts and representations. More likely, he chose this vehicle as the most effective means of communicating God's Word to those who, hardened in their sin, waited optimistically for their release from exile and return to Judah. He enacts Jerusalem's siege on a clay tablet (4:1–3), Israel's iniquity by lying on his sides (4:4–8), the siege of Jerusalem by partaking of rationed food and drink (4:9–17), and Jerusalem's fateful destruction by fire and sword by cutting off his hair (5:1–4). Further, three parables set forth the apostasy, present uselessness, and judgment of Israel: a piece of charred wood (chap. 15), an adulterous woman (chap. 16), and a vine (chap. 17).

The Restoration

Ezekiel's ministry was not crowned with success. The exiles preferred to listen to the blind optimism of the false prophets (chap. 13; "shepherds" in chap. 34), who fattened themselves at the expense of the flock (34:2–3). God promised to be the faithful shepherd of the remnant by gathering the flock, by feeding them, and by caring for them (vv. 11–15). The promise of God includes restoration to the land and restoration of the Davidic dynasty, "I the LORD will be their God, and my servant David will be prince among them" (v. 24). The renewed relationship between the Lord and Israel under the messianic ruler is sealed with a new covenant, the "covenant of peace." The covenant assures God's blessing in harvest (vv. 26–27) and in protection (vv. 25–29).

Chapter 34 is the key to the message of restoration. It sets the stage for the interpretation of the following chapters. The emphases include the outworking of the frequently repeated verse, "They will be my people, and I will be their God" (11:20; cf. 34:30; 36:28). The most significant aspects of the restoration theme include: (1) the divine and gracious initiation of the renewal of the covenant relationship (36:20–36; 37:23, 26; 39:25); (2) Israel's return to the land (36:1–15, 24; 37:14–23; 39:27); (3) the spiritual transformation of the people (36:25–27; 37:14; 39:29); (4) the covenant blessings (36:8–12, 29–30, 33–35; 37:26), including victory over enemies (35:1–15; 36:36; 37:28; 38:1–39:24); (5) the restoration of a Davidic king, the Messiah (37:24–25); and (6) the restoration of the temple (37:26–27). In brief, the Lord promised to renew all the covenants: the Abrahamic, the Mosaic, and the Davidic. The renewal would mark an even greater fulfillment, because the restoration has in view the final triumph over all evil and the blessedness of God's people.

THE PROPHETIC WITNESS

In addition to the so-called major prophets (Isaiah, Jeremiah, and Ezekiel), the Lord sent other prophets with his oracles—the "minor prophets." The difference between the major and minor prophets lies only in the size of their books, not in the significance of their message. Four minor prophets spoke God's Word concerning Judah and the nations. Nahum and Obadiah spoke of God's judgment on the nations, particularly Assyria and Edom. Zephaniah and Habakkuk spoke of the Day of the Lord that comes on the house of Judah and extends to all the nations. The message of the minor prophets to us today is that the Day of the Lord is certain and is very close at hand. However, those who trust in God need not fear; they will receive the redemption of the Lord.

Nahum

Nahum was a seventh-century prophet who, like the prophet Jonah in the previous century, addressed God's Word to Nineveh. Nahum witnessed the rise and fall of Assyria and the exile of many nations, such as the northern kingdom. He lived during the reign of Manasseh, king of Judah, some time between the fall of Thebes (664–663 B.C.) and of Nineveh (612 B.C.). The emphasis of his message is that the Day of the Lord will come upon Assyria because of the great oppressive wickedness with which the Assyrians ruled. In that day, judgment will extend beyond Assyria, engulfing all the wicked (1:15).

The Day of the Lord is an era of judgment and of restoration. Though the Lord is filled with jealousy and vengeance for his sacred name, to the point of annihilating the wicked, he is tender in his love for his own. Nahum affirms the Lord's goodness to those who trust in the Lord. Ultimately the Lord will take care of his own:

> The LORD is good,
>   a refuge in times of trouble.
> He cares for those who trust in him.
>
> (1:7)

The proclamation of the Lord's vengeance upon the wicked nations therefore demonstrates the concern and the goodness of God to his beloved. The Day of the Lord is a day of peace for the godly and of trouble for the wicked (v. 15).

Zephaniah

Zephaniah prophesied about 630 B.C., after the wicked reign of King Manasseh and at the beginning of Josiah's kingship over Judah. He proclaimed that the Day of the Lord would come upon all flesh: human, animal, bird, and fish. This judgment rests upon all creation and includes both the people of Judah and the nations (chaps. 1–2). Zephaniah waxes poetic when he describes the terrible day of God's ire:

> That day will be a day of wrath,
>   a day of distress and anguish,

> a day of trouble and ruin,
>   a day of darkness and gloom,
>   a day of clouds and blackness.
>
> (1:15; cf. 2:2)

Even though the judgment would come upon all flesh, the prophet also includes a word of encouragement for the godly. Redemption will extend to both Jews and Gentiles. The Gentiles will come to worship the Lord, and their worship will be acceptable to the Lord (2:11; 3:9). He encourages the people of God with the message that the Lord will again be in their presence as the great King (3:15, 17). God's people need not be afraid, regardless of what disasters may come upon them. The people of God are exhorted to rejoice in the Lord. He will reinstate their fortunes so that they will experience the fullness of restoration (vv. 18–20). Zephaniah thus foresaw the great era of restoration that began after the Exile and was accentuated in the ministry of our Lord. This restoration extends to our own day in the proclamation of the gospel and will find its fullness and completion in the return of Jesus Christ.[6]

Habakkuk

The prophet Habakkuk ministered God's Word shortly after the battle of Carchemish (605 B.C.). The people of Judah had witnessed the fall of Assyria and the ascendancy of the Babylonian Empire. Though Habakkuk is fully aware of the great wickedness of his people, he is concerned that the Lord is using a more wicked nation in judging his own wicked people (1:5–17). He presents his case before the Lord and waits for his response (2:1). The Lord assures him that the commencement of Jerusalem's fall is the beginning of the end. He commands Habakkuk to write the vision of the end, which will extend from the fall of Jerusalem to the great judgment of humankind (v. 3). This vision assures the godly that God will judge all evil (vv. 5–20). Though the nations may cause great devastation on earth, the Lord is in his holy temple in heaven; his judgment will silence their swelling rage (v. 20).

Habakkuk also speaks of the great era to come, when

> the earth will be filled with the knowledge of the glory of the LORD,
>   as the waters cover the sea.
>
> (2:14)

In the tension between the wickedness of the present age and the glory of the future age, the Lord exhorts the remnant to remain faithful:

> See, [the proud man] is puffed up;
>   his desires are not upright—
>   but the righteous will live by his faith.
>
> (2:4)

The Lord is looking for those who trust in him. To them he extends his righteousness.

Finally, the prophet is reconciled with the belief that the Lord is the victorious King who has shown his ability to lead and rule the nation he brought out of Egypt (chap. 3). Since God is the great God who is to be feared by all the nations, the prophet expresses in his prayer the conviction that the Lord is the strength of those who believe in him and that God's people therefore need not fear (3:18–19).

Obadiah

With Obadiah we return to the theme of judgment on a particular nation. He condemns Edom for the way it dealt with Israel and Judah throughout its history, particularly at the time of the fall of Jerusalem in 586 B.C. He describes how the Edomites were anxious to help the Babylonians massacre the people of Judah and Jerusalem. Edom will also see the Day of the Lord, when he comes in his great wrath. The prophet extends the language of judgment to include all the nations:

> The day of the LORD is near
>   for all nations.
> As you have done, it will be done to you;
>   your deeds will return upon your own head.
>   (v.15)

He too encourages the godly to trust in the Lord because in him there is deliverance (v. 17). The purpose of God is to establish his kingdom; judgment of his enemies and the restoration of his people will accomplish this goal (v. 21).

Daniel

Daniel's ministry was unique. Nebuchadnezzar deported him to Babylon in 605 B.C. Here he enjoyed an education to prepare him for statecraft. Daniel's natural gifts and unique and divine endowment gave him immediate recognition as the spokesman for the Lord, the God of heaven. Through the interpretation of dreams (chaps. 2; 4), of handwriting on the wall (chap. 5), and of the visions of the four beasts (chap. 7), the ram and the he-goat (chap. 8), the seventy weeks (chap. 9), and troubles on earth and God's ultimate victory (11:2–12:13), the Lord upheld his sovereignty over Babylon and the nations, while comforting his people with the message of hope. Hope lies in the God of heaven, who shall establish his sovereignty over all nations and who will share his dominion with his saints.[7]

Conclusion to Part 7

The epoch of "the divided nation" unfolds the interrelationship between sin and judgment, disobedience and condemnation, unfaithfulness to the covenant and exile from the Promised Land. The warnings, judgments, and curses of the Mosaic covenant, as echoed by the prophets, have come to fulfillment in the desolation of Israel and Judah.

The picture, however, is more complex. Within the historical developments of the two kingdoms, an intricate web of interrelated developments reveals an ebb and flow in the history of redemption. From a redemptive-historical perspective the development of the prophetic institution is of utmost importance in understanding the complexity of social, political, cultural, and religious events. Both in the northern and southern kingdoms, the Lord raised up his servants the prophets.

Through their ministry the Lord revealed in miniature the terrible effects of the Day of the Lord on the nations and kingdoms of the world, through the exile of Israel and Judah. The prophets who had first spoken to, counseled, and exhorted the kings of Judah and Israel had then turned to the people and had their oracles transmitted in written form as a witness to the people. The prophetic witness against the people and their leaders was in the form of a *rîb*, or legal suit, in which the prophets as covenant prosecutors charged them with infidelity and consequently with a breach of the covenant. The Exile, though a harsh and cruel punishment, was a just one. The people had acted treacherously against the presence of the holy and glorious God of Israel.

Through their ministry the Lord also revealed the transformation of the Mosaic covenant, which the Lord would graciously renew for a purified people, composed of representatives ("a remnant") from all tribes, to whom would be given a new heart and the Spirit of God to keep the covenant. All institutions would undergo a transformation: temple, priesthood, and kingship. The new age of which the prophets spoke revealed the continuity and importance of the covenant, the presence of God, the theocracy, the Davidic monarchy, the temple and priesthood, and the promises and blessings of God. The difference is that the Lord promised to involve himself even more in the unfolding of the history of redemption. The secession of the northern tribes would end, and all tribes would again be led by a Davidic king as God's appointed shepherd.

The new age of restoration will consist of a strengthening of the relationship among the Lord, his messianic king, the temple, the priesthood, and the people. The restoration of the covenant, kingdom, and theocracy will have a great impact on the nations, as they too will participate in the benefits of the messianic era. The prophets anticipate a new age, characterized by peace and the worship of the Lord, in which both Jews and Gentiles share. The accomplishments of the good kings of Judah in the strength of the Lord will be greatly magnified in the messianic age. In all these proclamations of hope, the Lord reveals his fatherly concern for his people, who undeservedly receive the promises of God's favor, renewal of the covenants, restoration of the people to the land, and personal spiritual transformation.

> The promise is for you and your children and for all who are far off— for all whom the Lord our God will call. (Acts 2:39)
>
> Indeed, all the prophets from Samuel on, as many as have spoken, have foretold these days. And you are heirs of the prophets and of the covenant God made with your fathers. He said to Abraham, "Through your offspring all peoples on earth will be blessed." When God raised up his servant, he sent him first to you to bless you by turning each of you from your wicked ways. (3:24–26)

Part 8

A Restored Nation

Introduction to Part 8

This era is one of the most fascinating periods in redemptive history. For several reasons, however, it has been greatly neglected: its length (from about 538 B.C. to A.D. 30), the variety of the literary materials (the Bible, Apocrypha, pseudepigrapha, rabbinic literature, Dead Sea Scrolls, Josephus, et al.), the complexity of the historical and cultural developments (Persian, Macedonian, Seleucid/Ptolemaic, Hasmonean, and Roman), and an underlying desire to rush from the last period of the Old Testament to the coming of the Messiah. These factors also have an effect on the dynamic relationship of Old and New testaments as they may give rise to the following questionable assumptions:

1. God was finished with Israel when he sent them into exile.

2. Israel's history ended up being a fiasco, which necessitated the sending of his Son.

3. Jesus' correcting the Pharisaic traditions and the attitudes of the Jews is a criticism of the whole Old Testament.

4. The world into which Jesus stepped was essentially similar to the world of the postexilic era.

5. The silence of God during the intertestamental period signifies his lack of involvement with the Jewish people.

We must not forget, however, that the history of redemption unfolds God's total plan for renewing this earth and that the postexilic restoration was part and parcel of this plan. Moreover, the dynamics of the six-hundred-year period reveal a gradual process, which crystallized in *Judaism*, the way of life and point of view of the Jewish community at the time of Christ.

Only a minority of the exiles responded to the challenges of the prophets. This minority from Israel and Judah, known as "the remnant," reflected on their past, returned to their God, and were renewed in spirit. Some of them returned to the land of Canaan and reestablished temple worship. Others remained in the *Diaspora*, or dispersion. Whether they lived in Judea or in Egypt, Babylon, or Rome, the pious Jews were united in their devotion to the Torah of God and to the

Sabbath, in their sense of solidarity of being God's covenant people, and in the prophetic hope.

The Exile witnessed the beginnings of Judaism. Judaism further developed as the Jews returned to Canaan and were free to worship the Lord and as the Jewish people integrated their view of God and his Torah with cultures that were hostile to monotheism and to divine revelation. Out of the purification of the Exile, Diaspora Judaism developed as a live organism. It continued to respond to the political and cultural shifts of the ancient Near East. As an organic movement, Judaism developed in many forms. The variety of traditions evolved into groups, sects, systems, and theologies during the intertestamental period. Jesus' ministry is, therefore, set against the backdrop of a multifaceted Judaism that had evolved over many centuries from its exilic background.

This era compares to the Exodus in formative importance. In the period of the Exodus, the Lord brought together the diverse elements of the twelve tribes through the experiences of the ten plagues, the Feast of Unleavened Bread, the deliverance from Egypt, and the passing through the Red Sea. He brought one nation into being, and he became their King. The Exile affected every aspect of life, as the tribes were scattered among the nations. It now looked as if they were no longer a nation, no longer had a God, no longer were his people, and no longer had Yahweh as their King. Who ruled? Who was in control over the terrible effects of war? Who cared for the rebellious nation that had provoked the Lord so many times? The story of the Exodus seemed to end in the story of the Exile. Whatever the Exodus had confirmed seemed to be undermined by the Exile.

The era of restoration, however, is both climactic and transitory. It is climactic because it brings upon the twelve tribes the fullness of God's wrath and judgment. He freely dissociates himself from his people, removing his presence, grace, and compassion. The curses of which Moses and the prophets had forewarned fell upon the twelve tribes: sickness, famine, starvation, fire, blood, and war. The covenant people have joined the lot of the rest of the nations that were left in darkness, anguish, and alienation. The period is also transitional, though, because judgment and alienation mark the road that leads from Babylon to Bethlehem.[1] On the one hand, the covenants confirmed to Abraham, Israel, and Moses were broken, and Israel existed as a non-nation. On the other hand, the Lord raised up a new people from the ashes of the conflagration. They were the remnant, the heirs of the promises. In this period I shall stress the correlation of three stages: the Exile, the postexilic restoration, and the intertestamental period.

THE EXILE

God executed his justice in the exile of Israel and Judah. His people were scattered abroad among the nations because of their obstinacy, rebellion, apostasy, and stubbornness.[2] The godly remnant took upon themselves the responsibility for the sins and judgment upon God's people. They too experienced his wrath and alienation but knew that it was deserved, as they came together for prayer, as they remembered the past, as they grieved over Jerusalem's fate, and as they longed for the redemption of Zion.

The exile was a productive and creative stage in Israel's self-awareness of God. Out of the processes of reflection and interpretation of the past in the light of the exilic situation, a new commitment was born. This new devotion to the Lord, to his Torah, to the covenant ideal, and to the Sabbath gave birth to Judaism.

THE POSTEXILIC RESTORATION

The restoration of the people to the land by the decree of Cyrus in 538 B.C. was a sign of the renewal of all the covenants: Noahic (creation), Abrahamic, Mosaic, and Davidic. The renewal is a gracious, sovereign, progressive, and greater realization of the working out of God's plan of redemption and his promises. The prophetic word and ministry (of Haggai, Zechariah, and Malachi) in the era of restoration embraces the ministry of reconciliation, hope, proclamation of the good news, anticipation of God's triumph in history, and also the exhortation regarding how God expects his people to bring in his kingdom.

The postexilic period continued the tension between promises and fulfillment, between fulfillment and greater fulfillment, and between the joy of restoration and the anguish of creation awaiting redemption. Under the leadership of Zerubbabel, Joshua, Ezra, and Nehemiah, the prophetic promises became closer and more tangible. Yet, the prophets held out a greater fulfillment, which would come, not by might or power, but by the Spirit of God. Through the writings, proclamation, and exhortation of the prophets and the encouragement of their contemporaries, the godly respond to the challenges with faith, hope, and love and begin to manifest a new spirit. The godly purify themselves, and the well-wishers fade away.

THE INTERTESTAMENTAL PERIOD

Complex developments took place from the end of the biblical writings to the revelation of God in Jesus Christ. In response to the political, social, cultural, and religious changes, Judaism splintered into many parties, sects, and belief systems. Among the major divisions were Sadducees, Pharisees, Essenes, and Zealots. Judaism had developed traditions from the Old Testament revelation (law, wisdom, and apocalyptic) in response to the world outside, but each system tended to develop one or more strands of biblical revelation in isolation from the others.

This period sets the stage for the ministry of Jesus. Our Lord came to restore the continuity between the work of God in the postexilic era and to inaugurate more fully the restoration to which the prophets bear witness. His teaching is a return to the Old Testament revelation of God, rather than a setting aside of God's witness through Moses and the prophets.

CHAPTER 23

The Literature of the Exilic/Postexilic Era

The Lord left a testimonial to what he had done to his people in the Exile as well as in the restoration from exile. Through his revelation he explained why he brought disgrace on Israel and Judah and why he restored his favor. In the negative and positive acts of God, we find a marvelous manifestation of who Yahweh is. Regrettably, the exilic and postexilic periods are often regarded as a digression from God's redemptive design. It may seem that, in comparison with the highlights of Old Testament redemptive history (Abraham, the Mosaic covenant, the Conquest, the Davidic era), this period flows downward until the coming of Christ.

What accounts for the obvious lack of interest in the acts of God during this period? Many perhaps regard the Exile simply as a prelude to the coming of the Messiah. The flicker of light in the postexilic restoration seems dim indeed in comparison to the presence of God in Christ. Moreover, not enough attention has been paid to the reality of covenantal renewal in the postexilic era. Another reason for the lack of appreciation for the developments in the exilic and postexilic period lies in the obvious scarcity of materials. Gottwald has observed, "For exilic and postexilic history there is nothing to equal the fullness and continuity of the historical and history-like materials of earlier Israel."[1]

The literary sources of the exilic and postexilic periods are composed of those books that primarily detail the fall of Jerusalem, the exilic situation, and the postexilic reconstruction. This corpus of material comprises Daniel, Haggai, Zechariah, Malachi, Esther, Ezra-Nehemiah, Chronicles, Lamentations, several psalms (42, 43, 74, 137), and possibly Joel. They have a canonical function but pose frustrating historical problems in reconstructing the complex developments of this period. The issues and questions are many; for our purpose here, we shall focus on the canonical significance.

In order to develop a greater understanding of this period, biblical scholars have complemented the study of the biblical materials with all available literary sources from Egypt, Mesopotamia, and Palestine, including the apocryphal writings, as well as archaeological artifacts.[2]

Because of the complexity of this period and the variety of literary sources (biblical and nonbiblical, Jewish and non-Jewish), I confine myself here to brief comments on the relevant biblical books.

LAMENTATIONS

Lamentations contemplates the last days of Jerusalem and covers the fall of Jerusalem, the reasons for and effects of the exile of Judah, and the experience of abandonment. The book consists of four acrostic poems of the alphabetical type (chaps. 1–4) and a nonacrostic poem (chap. 5). The first two and last two poems consist of twenty-two verses, whereas the central poem consists of sixty-six (3 x 22) verses. The number 22 is significant as it represents the number of consonants in the Hebrew alphabet.

Though the authorship of Lamentations is often associated with Jeremiah (witness the English ordering of Lamentations after Jeremiah), the author is anonymous.[3] The absence of a clear movement within the chapters heightens the importance of thematic repetition. The repetition of themes, the selection of certain literary forms (acrostics, dirge, complaints, and confession), and the poetic descriptions of Judah's suffering have made the poetic work a lasting form of prayer, confession, and hope for God's people in subsequent centuries.

CHRONICLES, EZRA-NEHEMIAH, AND ESTHER

The contribution of Chronicles lies both in its sense of continuity with the past (law, temple, priests) and in its adaptation of the history of Israel to the new situation of the restored community. It achieves its purposes by means of a selective and interpretive employment of the literary resources, including the books of Samuel and Kings, and by focusing on the contemporary needs of the restored community. Chronicles, together with Ezra-Nehemiah, employs literary materials of the past to establish the roots of the postexilic people. It contributes to a new sense of unity and purpose of the people, whose nationhood was lost in exile. The returnees were few in number but were permitted to reestablish themselves as a small province in the large Persian empire.

The Book of Chronicles was written for the postexilic situation. Together with Ezra-Nehemiah, it forms the background for the transformation from exiles to Jews, from an exiled people to a law-abiding people of God, from individualism to a common concern for law, temple, and Jerusalem. To this end, the personages and roles of Ezra and Nehemiah were important. They shaped Judaism.

The approach to the literary materials of Chronicles and Ezra-Nehemiah is complicated by several literary-critical issues.[4] First, the literary development of Chronicles, Ezra, and Nehemiah may have taken place over the course of a hundred years.[5] Second, theological motivation may explain the chronological difficulties.[6] Childs suggests that the final editor of *Ezra-Nehemiah* presents "the restoration as a theological model for the obedient and holy people."[7] This explains the canonical order: (1) Ezra's concern with the law and with covenantal loyalty to Yahweh (Ezra 7–10), (2) Nehemiah's contribution to rebuilding Jerusalem's walls (Neh. 1–6), and (3) an account of how Ezra and Nehemiah both join in the religious and political "transformation" of the restored community (Neh. 8–12).[8]

The composite work of Chronicles-Ezra-Nehemiah gives the postexilic community a sense of continuity with the past. This work renewed the sense of destiny, as the idealization of the Davidic monarchy is transformed into a community given to the law of Moses, to separatism, and to the temple worship through the dynamic leadership of Ezra and Nehemiah.[9]

The situation with Esther is quite different. The story of Esther takes us far away from Jerusalem to Susa, a foreign court.[10] The Book of Esther is one of the five *megillôt*, or scrolls, the others being Ruth, Song of Songs, Ecclesiastes, and Lamentations. One of the functions of Esther is the theological teaching of God's providence, who protects his people from any attempt at genocide. The account of Haman's hostility against the Jews, which is directed against Mordecai, and the story of King Ahasuerus's love for the Jewess Esther (Hadassah) set the stage for a drama, directed by the Lord God of Israel. Though the name of God does not occur in Esther and though it seems that Mordecai and Esther were integrated into Persian society, the Lord was working through these faithful ones to deliver his own people and to set up an example through Haman's death. Amid powers too great for the Jews and being surrounded by non-Jews, they are cared for by the Lord. The celebration of Purim, the feast of lots, is a continual reminder that God cares even today for his ancient covenant people.[11]

THE PROPHETS

The renewed emphasis on the law and the temple was accompanied by the renewed outpouring of the Holy Spirit on God's servants, the prophets.

Haggai and Zechariah

These two prophets encouraged the small remnant to rebuild the temple in 520 B.C. (Ezra 5:1–2). With their encouragement, the restored community renewed its allegiance to the Lord. They called on their contemporaries to reassess their priorities. If they continued

justifying themselves because of the uncertainty associated with home-
steading on land that had lain fallow for two generations, life would
become more complex and less rewarding. On the other hand, a life
given to seeking God's honor would be richly blessed indeed.

Malachi

Malachi ministered to God's people shortly before the work of
Nehemiah.[12] He prepared the Jews for the reforms instituted by
Nehemiah, as he dealt with social problems, the priesthood, tithes, the
Sabbath, and marriage with heathen wives (cf. Neh. 5:1–13; 13:7–27).
Malachi's disputational style consists of a series of rhetorical questions
and answers, by which the prophet aims at bringing his audience to
respond appropriately, lest they become subject to God's judgment.[13]

Joel

The date of Joel has received great emphasis, ranging from the time
of Joash (835–796 B.C.) down to the postexilic era or as late as the fifth
century B.C.[14] The literary contribution of Joel, however, is more
important than rooting his message in a given socioreligious background, because the theological contribution is unaffected by dating his
message. The significance of the prophetic word lies in its affirmation of
hope, which comes through the experience of catastrophe, fasting, and
repentance, and the promise of the new age of the Spirit. He is the
Spirit of *restoration,* who bears witness to the certainty of blessing
(2:18–26), of the covenant relationship (2:27), protection during the
progression of the Day of the Lord (3:1–16), and of the progression of
restoration of all things: the New Jerusalem (3:17–21).[15] The message
of Joel is always relevant, as Childs observes: "No technique is required
to extract Joel's message from its form. All that is needed is that true
witness is borne: 'Tell your children of it, and let your children tell their
children, and their children another generation' (1:3 RSV)."[16]

CHAPTER 24

Exilic Perspectives

During the Exile the godly drew their hope from the prophetic word, as it told of God's judgment, but at the same time it told of his plans of restoration. The prophetic witness together with the Torah of Moses formed the testimony by which the Lord continued to speak to his people, even when they were physically separated from the land and from the temple. Those who remained loyal to the Lord and those who returned to the God of their forefathers constituted the new people of God: the "remnant" from both Israel and Judah. The remnant underwent a radical transformation throughout the exilic period. Their reflections and aspirations formed the foundation of what was to become *Judaism*. The godly emerged from this period with a new concern for the Lord, his law, and the temple and also a commitment to an ethnoreligious identity. The exilic synthesis flourished, because of the manifold witness of God's servants, the prophets who followed the exiles wherever they went.

During the Exile the godly reflected on the prophetic ministry. The prophets had spoken as God's covenant prosecutors, bringing God's charge and stating God's verdict. Experiencing the reality of the Exile, a small group responded to the prophetic word by repenting and having hope for deliverance. Through the ordeal of exile the Lord purified and shaped the remnant as a new people for himself. Their experience of having been cast out of God's favor, the anguish of their existence, their questions, their search for hope, and the transformation of the diverse elements to a new community cannot be forgotten. It is a part of the canon, and the canonical witness brings this part of the history of redemption to bear on every generation.

In this chapter we shall get a sense of (1) God's contention with his people, (2) the ferocity of God's wrath as felt by the exiles, (3) the creative and reflective import of the Exile, (4) the response of the godly, and (5) the impact of the Exile in the crystallization of Judaism.

GOD'S CONTENTION WITH HIS PEOPLE

Among the various forms of prophetic speech, the prophets utilize the *rîb* pattern.[1] In this legal suit the prophet, as the covenant prosecutor, charges the rebellious people in the name of the Lord with breach of the covenant. The elements of the *rîb* pattern are (1) the charges, (2) the acts of God's love in the past, (3) the witnesses, and (4) the verdict.

The Charges

The charges are best summarized by the word "rebellion"; that is, lack of loyalty to the covenant.[2] In the ancient Near East a suzerain, whether king or lord, expected absolute loyalty from his vassal. If there was a breach of the treaty, the suzerain had every right to reduce the city of the offending vassal to rubble or to replace the vassal with someone more submissive. The prophets charged Israel and Judah with covenantal infidelity, as they had rebelled against their great King (see, e.g., Isa. 3:14).

The Love of God Rejected

Above all, the people have rejected the love of God. God's past acts of love, as enumerated by the prophets, refer especially to the exodus from Egypt. The prophets reminded the people of how the Lord had loved them, had brought them from Egypt, and had led them through the wilderness. During the wilderness journey the Lord demonstrated what might be called honeymoon love. The people had received many evidences of his tender care, including the land of Canaan, but had not responded (see, e.g., Jer. 2–3).

The Witnesses

In ancient Near Eastern treaties the witnesses that the suzerain invokes are the gods of heaven and earth.[3] But because the Lord, as Creator of heaven and earth, alone is God, he can swear only by himself. He is *the* witness against his own people (see Jer. 42:5; Mic. 1:2; Mal. 3:5).

The Verdict

In the verdict the prophets speak about God's judgment on Israel and Judah as an expression of the Day of the Lord. The prophets before and after the Exile declared Yahweh's judgment in terms of the Day of the Lord (Isa. 2:12; Ezek. 13:5; Joel 1:15; 2:1; Amos 5:18; Zeph. 1:7). That day will be great and terrible as the Lord vindicates himself, roots out evil, and, expressing his jealousy, disciplines his people with a holy anger. While no one can escape that judgment, he promises to protect his own. The Day of the Lord denotes the final judgment of God, when all rebellious nations and evil will be put down. God revealed through the prophets, however, that his people were not exempt from the judgment and that they were subject to his wrath in the form of the

291

exile of Israel and Judah.[4] The prophets prayed for relief and mercy, as they, like Moses, served their people as intercessors. On the day of judgment, however, prayers no longer avail (Jer. 15:1).

THE FEROCITY OF GOD'S WRATH

God's enmity toward his people is an expression of his righteous anger that is manifested on the Day of the Lord. On that day the Lord brings terrible destruction. Many in Israel apparently thought of the Day of the Lord as an era of prosperity, but the prophets condemned this popular optimism. Rather than blessing for Israel and curse for the nations, the Lord includes the members of the covenant community in the coming judgment. Amos, for example, exclaims,

> Woe to you who long
> for the day of the LORD!
> Why do you long for the day of the LORD?
> That day will be darkness, not light.
>
> (Amos 5:18)

He asks further,

> Will not the day of the LORD be darkness, not light—
> pitch-dark, without a ray of brightness?
>
> (v. 20)

Zephaniah proclaimed that nothing would deliver the people "on the day of the LORD's wrath":

> In the fire of his jealousy
> the whole world will be consumed,
> for he will make a sudden end
> of all who live in the earth.
>
> (Zeph. 1:18; cf. 2:2)

Lamentations, written shortly after the fall of Jerusalem, describes the effect of the defeat upon God's people. The author recognizes that what has happened to Judah and Jerusalem was an expression of the Lord's anger:

> How the LORD has covered the Daughter of Zion
> with the cloud of his anger!
> He has hurled down the splendor of Israel
> from heaven to earth;
> he has not remembered his footstool
> in the day of his anger.
>
> (Lam. 2:1)

There are several ways of describing the effect of God's enmity toward his people. The prophets taught that the outstretched arm or hand, which formerly signified the lovingkindness of the Lord, would now carry out God's intent to judge his people (Isa. 5:25; 9:12; Jer. 21:5) because the Lord had departed from his people. Ezekiel described this departure of the Lord in a visible way: "The glory of the LORD went up from within the city and stopped above the mountain east of it" (Ezek. 11:23, cf. chap. 10). With the departure of God's glory the people were left without protection, and their enemies were given complete control.

It is difficult for us to imagine life without the mercy of God. We know that God extends his general grace even to the nations by providing them with food and shelter. How much more does he deal kindly with his own! Yet, when he removes his *special* and *general* grace, the question must arise, Who can survive his judgment? (see Amos 7:2, 5; Nah. 1:6). Habakkuk, predicting the fall of Jerusalem to the Babylonians, asks how the Lord can permit a wicked nation like Babylon to destroy Judah and Jerusalem (Hab. 1:13). The Lord promises Habakkuk that, out of his judgments, a new earth will result that will be filled with the knowledge of his glory (2:14). Today, we are able to look at our Lord Jesus Christ, who experienced God's wrath on the cross. God the Father became like an enemy to his Son. He removed himself, covered his Son with darkness, and permitted him to be disgraced and then killed by humans. Our Lord Jesus Christ thus took upon himself the reproaches that belong to us. He carried the enmity of God in order that, through him, we might be reconciled to God. "Therefore, since we have been justified through faith, we have peace with God through our Lord Jesus Christ" (Rom. 5:1).

THE CREATIVE AND REFLECTIVE IMPORT OF THE EXILE

Among those Judeans who went into exile, there were various reactions to the captivity. (See figure 19.) Many lived their lives only on a material level, survived the horrors of war, and ultimately were not affected by the exilic experience. They quickly adapted themselves to their new environment and achieved prosperity. They assimilated themselves by intermarriage and lost their identity as having belonged to the covenant community.

The situation of the faithful remnant was quite different. They took their new lot seriously, reflecting on the spiritual significance of the Exile. They remembered the history of redemption and the many acts of God's love, including the covenants. For them the exilic experience was bittersweet. It was bitter as they remembered what had happened and how much they had lost. Their fellowship with God was broken because of their exile from Jerusalem and the temple. It was sweet as they drew near to the Lord and remembered his promises. Several passages of Scripture reflect on the exilic experience (see Pss. 42–44, 89, 137 and Lamentations). What did they remember?

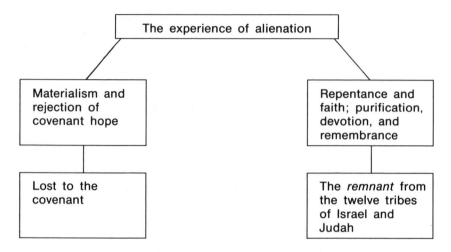

Figure 19. Two Responses to Exile

First, they remembered *their sins*. One of the primary purposes for the Exile was to show that, when God judged his people, he was serious about sin. The God whose glory dwelt in Jerusalem could also destroy his temple and desecrate the altar erected to his glory. Thus Ezekiel speaks of the Exile as a process of purging the rebels (Ezek. 20:38).

Second, the people also remembered *the word that the Lord had spoken to his servants the prophets*. For many years the prophets had predicted the fall of Jerusalem and Judah, but the response of the people had been minimal. Even before the prophets came the Lord had warned his people through Moses that the curses of the covenant could overtake them. Now they knew that Moses and the prophets had been right:

> The LORD has done what he planned;
> he has fulfilled his word
> which he decreed long ago.
> (Lam. 2:17)

Third, the people remembered *how different their lot could have been*, if they had been obedient. Isaiah well expressed what God promised his people when they had listened to him as their teacher. They would have experienced both peace and righteousness, and their descendants would have increased and been blessed (Isa. 48:17–19). All along, God's intention was to lead his people into greatness.

Fourth, and most important, the people remembered *their God*. Their reflections on Mount Zion and Jerusalem were actually their thoughts about God himself and the covenantal loyalty he had shown to his people in the past. Psalm 137 is an example of how the faithful community swore to continue their remembrance of their God:

> If I forget you, O Jerusalem,
>> may my right hand forget its skill.
>>> (Ps. 137:5)

The remembrance of Zion (v. 1) and the exaltation of Jerusalem (v. 6) signify the deep longing God's people had for their restoration to the Land of Promise, where they might worship the Lord again in his holy temple.

THE RESPONSE OF THE GODLY

In the midst of the exilic experience, the remnant did more than remember the past. Indeed, their remembrances led them to respond in appropriate ways to their present situation. The Lord had given them an opportunity of returning to him. They responded in confession, repentance, hope, fasting, and questioning.

The remnant's initial response was *confession*. As they remembered their sins and the sins of their ancestors, they called upon the Lord to forgive them. Although the godly remnant may have been faithful, they took the sins of the people upon themselves because of their solidarity with the people. Lamentations is such a moving book precisely because the author, probably a godly Judean, presents himself as being responsible for the Exile:

> See, O LORD, how distressed I am!
>> I am in torment within,
> and in my heart I am disturbed,
>> for I have been most rebellious.
> Outside, the sword bereaves;
>> inside, there is only death.
>>> (Lam. 1:20; cf. Ezra 9:5–7;
>>> Neh. 9:16–31; Dan. 9:4–14)

Yet, with this attitude, and writing in first person singular, he leads God's people as a whole to think through carefully what has happened to them (see also Lam. 3:40–42).

The second response to the Exile by the remnant is to call themselves to *repentance*, to return to the Lord. Before the Exile, the Lord himself called upon his people to return, even though they had greatly sinned against him (Jer. 3). The ground for hope that God would receive them lay in the fact that God is merciful and expects his people to return to him and receive his fatherly compassion.

Third, the people, knowing that they had no right to God's mercy, still responded with *hope*. They are called upon to wait for God and to seek him. Their sins have separated them from God's mercy. When the Lord is ready to show his loyalty again, his people need to be prepared to accept his grace. The basis for their patience is found in the Lord's loyalty and faithfulness to his people, so beautifully expounded in Lamentations 3:23–25. Another ground for hope in seeking the Lord is that he is the great King. Psalm 44 remembers the mighty acts of God and calls for confidence in the Lord because he is King over his people (v. 4). Though his people are now covered with scorn and derision (v. 13), the psalmist knows that in time the Lord will respond to the needs of his own. The waiting process is not merely passive, being inactive until something happens. It is a time of reflection on the past and especially hope in the future. The ground for hope lies in God's faithfulness, his kingship, and his covenant.

Fourth, as a further expression of their dependence upon the Lord, the people turned to *fasting* during the Exile. The prophet Zechariah alludes to these fasts as they were practiced during and after the Exile. A question came up during the regime of Darius concerning whether the people should continue fasting and mourning after the pattern of the previous years (Zech. 7:3). God's response is that the new era of restoration calls for rejoicing instead of fasting. Joy is more in accordance with the lovingkindness of the Lord (8:19).

Fifth, the people also responded to their situation by *questioning*. Why has God forsaken his people (Ps. 43:2; 44:24)? Even though the people knew that they had sinned and that God had sent his judgment, this question was important because it provided the basis for hope. The very fact that the psalmist could speak of Judah as "God's people" indicates his belief that the remnant would ultimately enjoy their relationship with God.

Why were they disturbed and discouraged (Ps. 42:5–6, 11; 43:5)? Although the people remembered God's former expressions of loving-kindness, they continued to question within themselves what the future would hold. They were in a state of deep spiritual agony, in which the darkness was much greater than any light that might be dawning on the horizon. They could only hope that the Lord might send his light and lead them back to Jerusalem (v. 3).

Why does God hide his face and forget the affliction and oppression of the people (Ps. 44:24)? They knew that God could see their strife, and they also believed that God is King over the whole earth. And yet it seemed that God was distant from and blind to their affliction.

From where might their comfort come? They certainly received no comfort from their enemies (Lam. 1:3, 9), and in their own anguish they could not provide comfort for each other. They would ask, "What can I say for you?" (2:13). Their grief was so intense that it seemed as if God was against his people.

Arising out of these responses, all of which are based ultimately on the character and acts of God, are specific concerns for the future. There were several objects of the remnant's hopes and prayers. In the first place, they longed for a renewal of God's compassion for them (Lam. 3:24–26). The second object of their hope was that their enemies might be avenged. The people remembered the fall of Jerusalem and the shouts of exultation by the Babylonians and the Edomites. They prayed that the Lord's judgment would come upon the enemies of the Lord and his people (Ps. 137:7–9). The people of God also hoped that, with the vengeance on the enemies and the renewed demonstration of God's love, a new era would begin. They prayed that, instead of his anger and rejection, they would experience his love and the newness of life that only he can give (Lam. 5:21–22).

It is no wonder, then, that the reaction to the Exile was mixed. On the one hand, the people felt that God was constant in his love. On the other hand, they experienced alienation and adversity. They could not help but turn to him; and yet, as they turned to him, they did so with anguish and uncertainty.

THE IMPACT OF THE EXILE IN THE CRYSTALLIZATION OF JUDAISM

The Exile greatly influenced the godly remnant and thus had a profound effect on the history of the Jews. But what exactly did the Exile mean for the Jews as a people? To answer this question, we may speak of the historical, cultural, and religious effects of the Babylonian captivity.

From a *historical* perspective, the Jews in exile experienced a real continuity with the past. Even in the early days of the captivity, Jeremiah sent a letter to the exiles, exhorting them to settle there and continue life as normal (Jer. 29). He asked them to make for themselves the best living possible under the circumstances. They were free to get married, build houses, plant gardens, and raise a community of Jews in exile (vv. 5–6). Historical evidence from Babylonian documents indicates that Jews indeed became a part of Babylonian society. They were involved in the agriculture, commerce, crafts, arts, and sciences, as well as administrative functions. The story of Daniel and his friends demonstrates how Jews participated at a high level in the government of Nebuchadnezzar (see Dan. 1). Among themselves, they enjoyed the system of elders that they had inherited from Moses (see Jer. 29:1). The prophet Ezekiel sat with the elders in exile (Ezek. 8:1; 14:1; 20:1). According to the genealogical listings of Ezra and Nehemiah, the families remained organized in order to demonstrate continuity with the past (Ezra 2; Neh. 7).

The Exile provided much time for reflection, during which the people had an opportunity to develop a greater appreciation for the sacred Scriptures that they had received. In fact, the Jewish captives were instrumental in the writing and editing of additional Scriptures. From this period came the final editions of the Books of Kings, Jeremiah, Ezekiel, and Lamentations and also several psalms. Under the inspiration of the Holy Spirit, the writers/editors reflected on the exilic experience and interpreted redemptive history before the Exile in light of their present situation. These books thus both recount the events that led to Israel and Judah's downfall and also include rays of hope that God will again show favor to the Jews.

On a *cultural* level, the influence of Babylonian society would mark Judaism from this time onward. This influence was felt in such small things as Babylonian names (e.g., Sheshbazzar, Zerubbabel, Shadrach, Meshach, Abednego, and Belteshazzar [see Ezra 1; Dan. 1]). Linguistic changes are also evident in the names of the months. After the Exile, the Jewish names of the months were replaced by Babylonian names (e.g., Tammuz, Marchesuan). On a larger scale, Aramaic was the international language of the Babylonian empire, and it became the prominent language among the Jews in exile because of its close relationship to Hebrew and because it was the language of culture, commerce, and diplomacy. Aramaic is found in the Bible in several passages (Ezra 4:8–6:18; 7:12–26: Dan. 2:4b–7:28) as well as isolated Aramaisms. (Aramaisms are words that are wholly or partly derived from Aramaic and are especially found in the Hebrew portions of the Old Testament that come from the exilic and postexilic periods.)

The *religious* developments during the exilic era may be summed up by the term "Judaism." What has come to be known as Judaism has its roots in the Babylonian exile. A transformation took place among those who had repented from their sins and had returned to their God. The small community of the faithful became more concerned about doing the will of God as it had been revealed in the law. Hence, the study of the law of God became less a study for academic purposes and more a task that called for obedience, for God's glory (see Neh. 8:8, 13–18; 9:3; 10:28–29). In Dumbrell's phrase, we are now at "the threshold of the New Testament age."[5]

In addition to this increased study of the law, the Jews deepened their commitment to absolute monotheism. In such a view, individuals are given to the Lord alone and shun anything that might detract from their worship of him. For example, the prophet Isaiah made strong statements against idolatry while affirming that Yahweh alone is God (Isa. 44; 46). The prophet Jeremiah likewise taught the people that the Lord is one and that idolatry is inconsistent with belief in him (Jer. 1:16; 2:13; 8:19). Ezekiel spoke to the community in exile with these words, "You say, 'We want to be like the nations, like the peoples of the world, who serve wood and stone.' But what you have in mind will never happen" (Ezek. 20:32).

Another important religious development that characterized Judaism was the observance of the Sabbath. Although the law had commanded such, it had not been widely practiced (Jer. 17:19–27). Isaiah called upon the people to be faithful in keeping the Sabbath, which is the mark of a godly Jew (Isa. 56:2–7). True observance of the Sabbath is learning to delight in the things of the Lord, so that the Sabbath is a lesson in godliness (58:13). Ezekiel singled out the Sabbath commandment as a particular commitment that ought to be kept: "They are to keep my laws and my decrees for all my appointed feasts, and they are to keep my Sabbaths holy" (Ezek. 44:24).

Finally, the covenant community learned to live in isolation from the pagan culture, lest it adopt elements of false worship.[6] At the same time, Jews learned to interact with the pagans, both in their business endeavors and in the arts. This tension between religious isolation and cultural interaction would become a crucial issue during the centuries between the Exile and the coming of Jesus Christ.

CONCLUSION

The Exile was an expression of the Day of the Lord, that is, of God's eschatological judgment in time. Both Israel and Judah experienced the wrath of God because for hundreds of years they had failed to respond to God's love, mercy, and patience. The Exile was God's fatherly process of selecting a remnant for himself. This remnant responded to the exilic experience of God's wrath and alienation by returning to him, by reflecting on their past, and by hoping in a new era of God's favor. Through the fire of judgment the godly experienced a renewal, and the elements of this rekindled devotion prepared the exilic community for the new challenges the postexilic people of God were to face under Persia, Greece, the Seleucids, and Rome. Judaism with its distinctive emphases was beginning to take shape, including a concern for the unity of God and for the Torah, the temple, the uniqueness of Israel's mission, the Sabbath, and circumcision.

CHAPTER 25

The Postexilic Restoration

After what must have seemed an eternity, a new era dawned. Cyrus, the Persian king, decreed in 538 B.C. that all exiles were permitted to return to their native countries and worship their native gods. The pious Jews rightly interpreted his decree as an act of God (Ezra 1:1–4). Finally they were permitted to return! Few, however, were interested in returning to their native land. The first return under Sheshbazzar, Zerubbabel, and Joshua numbered only fifty thousand. They took with them the temple vessels (vv. 9–11), and one of their first acts consisted in the rebuilding of the altar of the Lord in preparation for the reconstruction of the temple (3:1–9). How great was their joy, but also how short-lived was their sense of wonder and fulfillment because of their experiences of enmity and of the harshness of life. In this chapter we shall explore (1) the prophetic description of the new era; (2) the reality of the new era, with its tension between promise and fulfillment; and (3) hope in a more glorious era.

THE NATURE OF THE NEW ERA

The new era is clearly to be set apart from the events before the Exile. The postexilic people themselves recognized that restoration was a watershed in the history of redemption. They could not possibly return to preexilic conditions because God had again marvelously moved in history with his mighty hand.

The old era was characterized by sin, judgment, and sorrow. Isaiah speaks of a shroud that covered the people, signifying their sorrow caused by deprivation, desolation, disgrace, and death (Isa. 25:7). They had lost much because of the Exile: their relationship with the Lord and the temple, the blessings that the Lord had promised his people, their loved ones, and all their possessions, homes, and cities. The prophets spoke about the great sorrow of God's people. For example, Jeremiah expressed the deep pathos of the situation:

> This is what the LORD says:
> "A voice is heard in Ramah,

mourning and great weeping,
Rachel weeping for her children
and refusing to be comforted,
because her children are no more."
(Jer. 31:15)

Isaiah asked the people to forget the former things because God will do a new thing (Isa. 43:18–19). Micah prayed that the Lord might remove the sins of the people by forgiving them completely (Mic. 7:18–20). Isaiah affirmed that God will forget the offenses of Judah and Israel (65:16). Even as the Israelites forgot the troubles of their stay in Egypt and celebrated God's mighty redemption from Egypt as he led them into the Promised Land, so also God's people will remember the restoration from exile as a great moment in redemptive history. They will no longer think about their exilic troubles nor about their sinful lives before the Exile. In fact, they will consider the redemption from Egypt less significant than the redemption from exile:

> "So then, the days are coming," declares the LORD, "when people will no longer say, 'As surely as the LORD lives, who brought the Israelites up out of Egypt,' but they will say, 'As surely as the LORD lives, who brought the descendants of Israel up out of the land of the north and out of all the countries where he had banished them.' Then they will live in their own land." (Jer. 23:7–8)

The new era of restoration from exile may be described by four characteristics: divine initiative, divine favor, reestablishment of God's kingdom and covenant, and the power of the Spirit.

God's Initiative

Redemption is accomplished by God's free and sovereign grace. In Isaiah's prophecy, the Lord is portrayed as the Creator-Redeemer, who, as King of the universe, has power to control nations and their kings:

> Surely the nations are like a drop in a bucket;
> they are regarded as dust on the scales;
> he weighs the islands as though they were fine dust.
> (Isa. 40:15)

As the everlasting God, he is able to renew and strengthen his people (Isa. 40:28–31). He will control events in order to achieve this purpose. Based on his covenant with his people, God takes the initiative to redeem them by raising up Cyrus of Persia:

> I will raise up Cyrus in my righteousness:
> I will make all his ways straight.
> He will rebuild my city
> and set my exiles free,

301

> but not for a price or reward,
> says the LORD Almighty.
>
> (45:13)

As the one who has formed Israel, the Lord lays claim on his people:

> I am the LORD, your Holy One,
> Israel's Creator, your King.
>
> (Isa. 43:15)

God's Favor

The new era expresses God's favor. One way of distinguishing the new era is by the word "loyalty" *(ḥesed)*. The Lord affirms to his people that he will renew his covenantal love in such a way that the time of present judgment and wrath will seem a trifle in comparison with their future blessedness. Isaiah states how the Lord hid his face from them with a little wrath, but also how he will love them with an everlasting love (Isa. 54:8). The time when God renews his love is also known as the year of God's favor. Isaiah uses this concept to denote the time in which God proclaims to his people a message of comfort and reconciliation (49:8; 61:2).

God's favor consists of reconciliation and forgiveness. The people in exile were under God's anger and needed the assurance that he would forgive them. In response to their need, he answers:

> Comfort, comfort my people,
> says your God.
> Speak tenderly to Jerusalem,
> and proclaim to her
> that her hard service has been completed,
> that her sin has been paid for,
> that she has received from the LORD's hand
> double for all her sins.
>
> (Isa. 40:1–2)

Reestablishment of God's Kingdom and Covenant.

The Exile brought into question the very rule of God. The Solomonic temple had become the symbol of his rule, but the temple was destroyed, and Israel was disgraced in exile. "Where is your God?" the nations asked Israel, insinuating that the God of Israel was powerless in his rule. But Isaiah proclaims to Zion, "Your God reigns!" (Isa. 52:7), and he explains how this reign will be expressed. The Lord will restore his people from exile (v. 8; cf. v. 11; 48:20, 21), demonstrate his comfort for them (52:9), and save them in the sight of all nations (v. 10). Even though God acts through the instrumentality of nations and kings, it is he alone who can deliver his people:

He saw that there was no one,
    he was appalled that there was no one to intervene;
so his own arm worked salvation for him,
    and his own righteousness sustained him.

(59:16)

The prophet goes on to describe how the Lord is a Warrior-King who puts on a breastplate of righteousness, a helmet of salvation, garments of vengeance for clothing, and zeal as a cloak (59:17). The armor of God illustrates his plans for his people. They will receive their reward and will experience his royal care, "He tends his flock like a shepherd: He gathers the lambs in his arms and carries them close to his heart; he gently leads those that have young" (40:11).

The new era also confirms the renewal of the covenant that had been broken by God's people.[1] Because of his loyalty to his people, God had promised a future renewal of the covenant (see Jer. 31:31). This covenant renewal should be understood not merely in terms of Jesus' coming to the earth but also in the historical context of God's ancient covenant people. Because they had broken the covenant and had been judged, they must also experience a renewal of the covenant after the Exile. Otherwise, the Jewish people were without a covenant between the Exile and the coming of Jesus Christ. Isaiah thus encourages God's people to come freely and enjoy God's benefits, which are expressions of his everlasting covenant—"my faithful love promised to David" (Isa. 55:3).

The Era of the Spirit

At the same time, we must realize that covenant renewal brings a significant change. Not only does the renewal mark the beginning of the era of restoration, it is also characterized as an era of the Spirit. The prophets declare that the Spirit will come upon God's people and upon their descendants (Isa. 44:3; Joel 2:28–29). Before the Exile, Solomon recognized the people's need of a heart to obey God (1 Kings 8:23, 38–39). The prophets taught that God would send his Holy Spirit to seal the people's redemption and sanctify them to himself. Isaiah spoke of this change in terms of purification and holiness (Isa. 4:2–6). He also prophesied that, with the renewal of the covenant, the Spirit would help God's people to be more faithful (59:21; see also Acts 1:8; Eph. 5:18–20; Col. 3:16–17).

The work of the Spirit in spiritual renewal is the very sign of covenant renewal. It is God's guarantee that the heavens and the earth will be restored. Just as previous covenant administrations had signs (the rainbow in the Noahic covenant, circumcision in the Abrahamic, and the Sabbath in the Sinaitic), so the sign of the new covenant is his Spirit:

And afterward,
  I will pour out my Spirit on all people.
Your sons and daughters will prophesy,
  your old men will dream dreams,
  your young men will see visions.
Even on my servants, both men and women,
  I will pour out my Spirit in those days.

(Joel 2:28–29)

THE TENSION BETWEEN REALITY AND HOPE

The period of restoration is characterized by a clear tension between promise and fulfillment, reality and hope. Here I examine how the two-sided nature of restoration is evident in both the history and the theology of the postexilic period.

Reality: The Beginnings of Progressive Fulfillment

The Book of Ezra begins with the affirmation that the Lord "moved the heart of Cyrus" to make a decree permitting the Jews to return to the land, just as Jeremiah had prophesied (Ezra 1:1). God's judgment had come on Babylon, whose seventy years were now over (Jer. 25:11–12; 29:10)! Babylon fell in 539 B.C., when Cyrus marched into Babylon. Cyrus, of whom the prophecy of Isaiah has spoken (chaps. 44–45), permitted the Jews to return and rebuild the temple in Jerusalem. Approximately fifty thousand Jews returned to the land in 538 B.C. under Sheshbazzar, Zerubbabel, and Joshua. Upon their return they found a land that was desolate and full of ruined cities and houses. They began with the restoration of the temple and celebrated the Feast of Tabernacles, but soon their joy was spoiled by the Samaritans (Ezra 1–6). The work on the temple was stopped. Yet, the godly remnant had occasion to rejoice in the Lord. The psalmist asks God's people to remember what it was like when they came from captivity. They were filled with sorrow but soon saw their dream fulfilled and their sadness turned into joy:

When the LORD brought back the captives to Zion,
  we were like men who dreamed.
Our mouths were filled with laughter,
  our tongues with songs of joy.
Then it was said among the nations,
  "The LORD has done great things for them."
The LORD has done great things for us,
  and we are filled with joy.

(Ps. 126:1–2)

304

The continual rejoicing and the certainty of God's blessing are rooted in prophetic statements in which God swears that he will renew his covenant mercy to his people.

Some twenty years after the decree of Cyrus, in 516 B.C., the temple and the priesthood were fully restored. Another fifty years later Jerusalem's walls were completed, and the city was repopulated with representatives from all the towns of Judea (Neh. 4; 7). The people responded readily to the challenges, as the Spirit of God was working in their hearts. The Books of Haggai, Zechariah, Ezra, Nehemiah, and to some extent even Malachi witness to the readiness of God's people to meet the needs at hand:

> So the LORD stirred up the spirit of Zerubbabel son of Shealtiel, governor of Judah, and the spirit of Joshua son of Jehozadak, the high priest, and the spirit of the whole remnant of the people. They came and began to work on the house of the LORD Almighty, their God. (Hag. 1:14)

Though the glory of God's people was not great, their joy was evident to the nations, who could see the mighty things God had done for them (Ps. 126:2). The Lord used the nations when he established his people in the land and renewed the worship of God. Kings such as Cyrus, Darius, and Artaxerxes were instruments of the Lord in this work. From this time onward we find an increase in proselytes, who join the Jews in the worship of Yahweh, and the beginnings of God-fearers, who want to learn more about the God of Israel.

Hope: Living with a Partial Fulfillment

The reality was far from what could be expected in light of the prophetic word. The tension that the people experienced was between the "now" and the "not yet," between this age and the age to come. Three important factors we should consider when discussing the nature of partial fulfillment and the reasons why the people had to keep hoping for a greater fulfillment of God's kingdom are the issue of holiness, the presence of the nations, and the call to faith.

Although we have seen how the prophetic word promises the filling of the Spirit, in reality the returning remnant was far from the holiness that the Lord desires. They did not give freely to the priests but kept for themselves whatever they could; they failed to give the best sacrifices to the Lord (Hag. 1; Mal. 1). Even the priests were not fully devoted to the Lord, for they did not teach the full implications of the law (Mal. 2:1–9). One example of the priests' lack of commitment was the case of Tobiah, the Ammonite, who received sanctuary in the temple (Neh. 13:4–9). The people did not properly observe the Sabbath, as Nehemiah discovered (vv. 15–22). Moreover, they intermarried with the peoples of the land, raising serious doubts regarding the future of God's people as a holy nation (Ezra 9:2).

A second factor that helped cause tension between reality and hope was the presence of the nations. In Isaiah 44:26b–45:6, for example, Yahweh promises to control the nations so that Israel may return to the land. Other passages indicate that the nations would respond positively to the reestablishment of Zion (45:14; 49:22, 23). As Ezra describes, however, the nations were opposed to the Jews (see Ezra 4).

The third factor is that the people of God have the obligation to proclaim the good news of salvation so that others may hear and share in the grace of God. Just as the Servant of God came to preach good tidings of liberty and joy (Isa. 61:1–3), so also God expects his people to call upon others to join them in preparing for the coming of God:

> Pass through, pass through the gates!
> Prepare the way for the people.
> Build up, build up the highway!
> Remove the stones.
> Raise a banner for the nations.
>
> (62:10)

Faith and Obedience: Godly Living Within the Tension

Generations after the decree of Cyrus, pious Jews were still waiting for a greater fulfillment of the promises. Alas, as time went on, many Jews had become perfunctory in their religious expressions, and some had adopted a secular lifestyle. With the separation of faith from everyday life, cynicism set in.

Malachi responds to the growing cynicism by entering into a dialogue with current issues, such as, Does God love us? or Is God just? It seemed as if the prophetic word had been frustrated by the power of the Persians. God had given the people a foretaste of the blessings, without telling them how the blessings would become reality. From the return from exile onward, the Word of the Lord through the prophets (Haggai, Zechariah, Malachi, and possibly Joel) had attempted to encourage the people so that they would not be lost in their despondency. Ezra provided dynamic leadership by upholding the supremacy of the law. Beginning with Ezra's ministry it became imperative to apply the law to everyday life. The law therefore did not remain static; it became the means by which new decrees or decisions could be made in order to adapt to new situations.

Even though the people were encouraged to be faithful, their questions are not inappropriate for true believers in God. They asked, most basically, "Why has God delayed the fullness of salvation?" Isaiah, particularly, gives us some insight into the mind of God when he reminds us that the Lord himself is intent on establishing his kingdom and that he will hasten the fullness of the kingdom at the appointed time (Isa. 60:22). Jesus Christ also reminded the apostles that the time of the establishment of the kingdom is in the Father's hand (Acts 1:7).

Furthermore, the sins of the people have a delaying effect on the progression of the kingdom. Isaiah affirms that the Lord has the strength to save immediately (Isa. 59:1) but that he does not respond, because of the sins of the people (v. 2). He does not listen to their prayers nor does he fulfill the promises until his people learn to live more holy lives. In chapter 58, Isaiah declares that, when God's people learn to live according to his Word, they will experience the fulfillment of the prophetic promises.

THE EXILIC AND POSTEXILIC HOPE

The postexilic era of restoration had brought about a new community in the land of Canaan. The people had indeed witnessed restoration, as the prophets had promised. But the experience of the godly was bittersweet. Life in the era of transformation, of the progression of God's kingdom, was disappointing in comparison with the glorious visions of the prophets. God's people had to adjust to the progressive nature of the fulfillment. Moreover, they also had to adjust to the real world of political shifts, involving Persia, Greece, the Seleucids and Ptolemies, and finally Rome. In view of all these uncertainties, the godly learned to depend on the Word of God. During the lengthy period from about 400 B.C. to the coming of the Messiah and the establishment of the church (known to us as the intertestamental period), the people of God lived, worked, and prayed for the coming of the kingdom of God. I summarize in this section the prophetic hope that sustained the godly—and that still sustains us today, as we too await the kingdom of God.

The Renewal of God's People

The proclamation of the gospel and the reconciliation of God to his people had a profound effect on the remnant. This proclamation was conveyed by means of several important phrases and images relating to renewal.[2] In order to appreciate the varied aspects of the renewal, we shall consider (1) the renewal of covenantal status, (2) the reaffirmation of the patriarchal promises, (3) the reaffirmation of the Davidic covenant, (4) the renewal of the priesthood, and (5) the purposes of renewal.

The Renewal of Covenantal Status

The people begin to grasp the truth that they are indeed the people of God. They had been reckoned as "not my people" (Hos. 1:9), and now they are declared again to be the people of God's choice (Isa. 61:6).

Jeremiah repeatedly affirmed that God renews his covenant mercy by taking them again to be his people (Jer. 30:22; 31:1). The Lord expresses his love to the covenant people who had grievously sinned against him, and he renews them as if he found them again in the desert, even as he originally found Israel in the wilderness and established her as a holy nation after the redemption from Egypt (v. 2).

The Reaffirmation of the Patriarchal Promises

The language with which the returning exiles are assured that their descendants will increase draws heavily on the promises in Genesis.[3] They will be so numerous that their borders will extend into the territories of the nations (Isa. 54:2). No longer will they be regarded as a small nation (60:22). The people will be gathered from east, west, north, and south (43:5–6). The descendants will be heirs of the covenant and will be instructed in the covenant from generation to generation (54:13). No longer will they be uprooted. The era of restoration signifies that God's people will inherit the earth forevermore (60:21). The people of God will experience the blessings and the presence of God. The glory and light that comes to them by virtue of their covenantal status will be recognized by the nations (60:1–3). The Jews will be a blessing to the nations to the extent that the nations may be incorporated into the covenant (55:5; cf. 2:3).

A new aspect in the era of restoration is that the mission of proclaiming the gospel to the Gentiles is made more explicit. The Lord confirms to the people that they are his servants (Isa. 41:8; 44:21), and as his servants they are to be a light to the Gentiles (42:6). Now that they have been redeemed from exile and have tasted of the mighty works of God, they are witnesses to the strength and love of God (43:10; 44:8). For this reason, judgment rests upon those nations and kingdoms that will not respond to the glorious rule of God (60:12).

The Reaffirmation of the Davidic Covenant

God's promise to remain loyal to David and his house obsessed the prophets! Several passages specifically mention David as the messianic king (Jer. 23:5–6; 30:9; 33:17; Ezek. 34:23–24; 37:24; Hos. 3:5; Amos 9:11) and the ongoing validity of "my faithful love promised to David" (Isa. 55:3). Often, however, the prophets speak only in general terms of the glory of the Messiah as he will establish his government on earth (9:7) and be a light and banner to the nations (vv. 2–3; 11:10).[4] He will come with the Spirit and wisdom of God and proclaim the good news to those who are in need (61:1–3). There will be no end to his rule of peace and righteousness (9:6–7; 11:5–9). The messianic era is characterized by the knowledge of the Lord, victory, and the everlasting rest of his people throughout the earth (11:9; 14:1–3).

The prophets teach that the Messiah's glory must follow his humiliation. The one who will come from Bethlehem (Mic. 5:2) will also take the path of human suffering (Isa. 52:13–53:12). He will bear the distress of his people and the wrath of God in order to redeem his people. Zechariah speaks of the King who comes with humility (Zech. 9:9). He alludes to the piercing of the Messiah, which may have a salvific effect (12:10).

The Renewal of the Priesthood

Through the prophets, the Lord confirms the continuity of both the priesthood and the temple. His covenant with the descendants of Aaron had been described as everlasting (Num. 25:13), and now the Lord reaffirms his covenant with the house of Levi (Mal. 2:4–7). After the Exile, they continued to serve the Lord in the temple, according to the prophecy of Jeremiah (Jer. 33:18, 21). Zechariah shows how the priesthood of Joshua and the leadership of Zerubbabel were to be regarded as a postexilic fulfillment of the prophetic word: "These are the two who are anointed to serve the LORD of all the earth" (Zech. 4:14; see also 6:13).

In addition to the continuity, however, there are also some discontinuous elements. Isaiah speaks of all of the Lord's people as being priests. He states,

> And you will be called priests of the LORD,
> you will be named ministers of our God.
> You will feed on the wealth of nations,
> and in their riches you will boast.
>
> (Isa. 61:6)

He goes further in claiming that the whole of the earth is God's temple, and therefore God is not to be limited to the temple in Jerusalem (66:1; see 1 Kings 8:27).

There is also the new expectation regarding sacrifices. The Lord desires that people offer him a contrite spirit (Isa. 66:2), rather than the sacrifice of bulls, lambs, or other offerings (vv. 3–4). Even the Gentiles will bring offerings to the Lord, and out of them he will choose priests and Levites (vv. 20–21). The temple will continue to be on the holy mountain, but now with greater emphasis as the central place where both Jews and Gentiles will worship him:

> For my house will be called
> a house of prayer for all nations.
>
> (56:7)

The Purposes of Renewal

The purposes of God in renewing his people are threefold. First, he intends to *glorify himself* in the presence of all the nations (Isa. 61:3; 66:19). The very name and honor of the God of Israel is at stake; he will not leave his honor to anyone else.

Second, God intends to *glorify his people*. The possibility of glorification is grounded in the Lord himself (Isa. 45:24–25; 46:13). Glorification consists of the process that begins with God's bringing his people back from exile and extends to the fullness of the restoration of heaven and earth. This process continues from generation to generation (51:8) until Israel finds its consummation in the presence of God (60:19–20).

Third, God intends to *sanctify his people*. God's people are called upon to put on beautiful garments because they are the holy city of God (Isa. 52:1). The new garments show that they have been refined and tested (48:10; 61:10). Zechariah looks forward to the time when everything on earth will be holy (Zech. 14:20–21).

The Renewal of the Earth

The great prophetic expectation was that the Lord would renew the earth when he restored his people from the Exile. The Exile was a period of desolation in which the land of Canaan, especially as it had been formed to make a home for God's covenant people, had been desolated and defiled. The renewal of the land as well as the return of God's people to the land were to be signs of the restoration of the entire earth. The restoration thus asserted God's kingship over both Israel and the whole earth and affirmed his lordship over both redemption and creation.

The Relationship Between Redemption and Renewal

From the prophetic perspective, the sins of Israel, Judah, and the nations require the just judgment of God. But because the earth is also polluted by the sins of the nations, the judgment on the nations also affects the earth. The renewal of the land is a picture of what God will do in the renewal of nature. Hosea speaks of the renewal of God's favor in a metaphor derived from nature (Hos. 14:4–8). This picture receives greater credibility because of the prior affirmation that the Lord will renew his covenant with nature *for the sake of* his people (2:21–23). Creation and redemption are truly interrelated motifs, as Isaiah suggests:

> I have put my words in your mouth . . .
> in order to set the heavens in place,
>> and to lay the foundations of the earth,
>> and to say to Zion, "You are my people."
>> (Isa. 51:16; my translation)

Similarly, Isaiah encouraged God's people to look on the existence and continuity of the earth as the very ground for hope, even in exile:

> Shout for joy, O heavens;
>> rejoice, O earth;
>> burst into song, O mountains!
> For the LORD comforts his people
>> and will have compassion on his afflicted ones.
>
> (Isa. 49:13)

The Progressive Nature of Renewal

The relationship between creation and redemption should be viewed in a progressive way. Isaiah clearly prophesied that the Redeemer would come to Zion, indicating that the Jews, as such, would be a part of the new order (Isa. 59:20). The apostle Paul interpreted this text as having significance for both the past and the future salvation of the Jews (Rom. 11:26–27). And both Isaiah and Paul affirm the inclusion of the Gentiles in the people of God (Isa. 42:1, 4; Rom. 11:25–26). The notion of progression or process is therefore inherent in the prophetic and apostolic word: *God's goal is not only the salvation of the Jews but the full establishment of his kingdom on earth.* The progression began with Cyrus, who was called by the Lord to free his people so that they might rebuild Jerusalem and the temple (Isa. 44:28; see also 44:26–45:13). The work of the Servant must continue "till he establishes justice on earth" (42:4). Progression is inevitable because the scope of redemption is the whole earth and not just the Jewish people in Palestine.

CONCLUSION

The prophets affirm that the restoration from exile marks the present realization of redemption. Even though the redemption was not complete when the Jews returned from exile, they were always to remember that it was the *beginning* of their restoration. The era of God's favor extends from the Exile to the return of Jesus Christ and to the complete restoration of all things. We must not limit the "now" of redemption to the New Testament era of the gospel proclamation but must view it in light of God's gracious offer after the Exile. Isaiah uses the word "now" several times to indicate that the time of God's favor has arrived:

> See, I am doing a new thing!
>> Now it springs up; do you not perceive it?
> I am making a way in the desert
>> and streams in the wasteland.
>
> (Isa. 43:19)

311

The return of the exiles to Judah was thus a real fulfillment of God's promise to restore the people to their land. The prophetic proclamation of this redemption (even before the Exile) called for faith on the part of the people. In this sense we should understand the words of Psalm 95:

> Today, if you hear his voice,
>   do not harden your hearts. . . .
>   (vv. 7–8)

Rather, God's people should recognize him as "the great King above all gods" (v. 3) and come to him with thanksgiving (v. 2).·

Men such as Sheshbazzar, Joshua, Zerubbabel, Ezra, and Nehemiah will always be remembered because of their faith in God's promises. They set out in obedience to do God's will and never saw the fruition of their acts. But they built in the hope that the Lord would be faithful to his Word. The story of the postexilic restoration marks an important new stage in preparation for the coming of Jesus Christ. The very existence of the intertestamental period, however, serves as a reminder that God builds his kingdom slowly. The successes of the postexilic period had to be tested over time, and with the deterioration of human institutions, the Spirit of God eventually moved again to bring in a greater evidence of restoration toward the final and climactic goal.[5]

CHAPTER 26

The Intertestamental Period

The intertestamental period is silent with respect to canonical books of the Bible, but it was not a quiet period otherwise.[1] For about four hundred years God sent no further revelation. The prophetic voice ceased (see Ps. 74:9; 1 Macc. 4:46; 14:41; Syr. Bar. 85:3). During this time the writings forming the Old Testament were collected, studied, copied, and brought together into the present canon under the guidance of the Holy Spirit (2 Tim. 3:16–17). Through the study of noncanonical primary sources and archaeological discoveries, we have gained an increasing amount of light on this period, which is also known as the second temple period.[2] (See table 12.)

TABLE 12. THE INTERTESTAMENTAL PERIOD

Date	Political Power	Cultural and Religious Developments
400 B.C.	**Persian Empire**	Diaspora; syncretism; importance of Torah and temple; opposition of Samaritans
332 B.C.	**Macedonian Empire**; struggle between Seleucids and Ptolemies	Hellenism; Torah viewed as lawbook; importance of synagogue
165 B.C.	**Hasmoneans**	Rise of Sadducees, Pharisees, Essenes, Zealots; apocalyptic literature popular
63 B.C.	**Roman Empire**	Jerusalem destroyed in A.D. 70

Our understanding of the second temple period is complicated by the relative lack of sources and by a web of political intrigues and religious responses that would determine the social, political, cultural, and religious context of our Lord's ministry on earth. Judaism was not an isolated community in Palestine but was related to a much broader world. Judaism in Palestine was in contact with Jews and God-fearers from the Diaspora (Egypt, Babylon, Persia, Asia Minor, and Europe) through pilgrimages and trade relations.[3] It was also greatly affected by decisions made at the political centers to which it was successively subject: Susa, Damascus, Alexandria, and Rome. Judaism was forced to respond to the political changes due to the conquest of Alexander the Great, the division of his empire, the wars between Seleucids and Ptolemies, and the conquest by Rome—especially to Hellenism and to the Roman occupation. Judaism at the end of the Old Testament writings was confined and comfortable, but Judaism some four hundred years later was cosmopolitan and constantly adjusting to change. The Jewish world in the time of Jesus and the apostles was in flux and hence shows little in common with the era of Ezra and Nehemiah.

The intertestamental period links the last books of the Old Testament with the Gospels. This era deserves much more attention than the short treatment given here, which intends only to provide a bridge between old and new, to show more clearly the relationship between, on the one hand, Law, Prophets, and Writings and, on the other hand, Gospels, Acts, Epistles, and Apocalypse.[4] Far too often, negative reflections on Judaism, Jewish interpretations of the Old Testament, and the law are generalized in an anti-Semitic, Marcionite manner. It is regrettable that the reader of the Gospels has typically not read the Apocrypha or reflected on the conditions and aspirations of the second temple era. The Reformers encouraged the reading of the Apocrypha, noting that it provided a sense of historical and religious connection between Old and New Testaments.[5] As it is now, we have often had a negative or suspicious attitude toward the Apocrypha, which has a bearing not only on how the New Testament is understood but also on the growing chasm between the two Testaments. With the decreasing interest in the intertestamental period, understanding of the exilic and postexilic era has diminished as well. The silent four hundred years have become the silent six hundred years!

Together with the fall of the Judean monarchy and the Exile, the postexilic restoration is too often treated as a postlude in Old Testament redemptive history, rather than as the inauguration of the restoration.[6] The significance of this era finds expression in Matthew's genealogy of Jesus, as he records the genealogy in a structural division of three periods: from Abraham to David, from David to the Exile, and from the Exile to Jesus (Matt. 1:1–16). Of these three periods, the last is generally the least known. We shall briefly examine both the political and the religious developments during the historical periods of the Persians, Greeks, and Romans.

JEWS UNDER THE PERSIANS

The decree of return by Cyrus opened up the way for restoration of the temple, the law, and a distinct Jewish culture (led particularly by Zerubbabel, Haggai, Zechariah, Ezra, and Nehemiah). Through the prophets and theocratic leaders, the Jews in the Persian province of Judea (Aramaic *Yehud*) had developed a sense of identity around the temple and Torah. They had maintained a separation from the Samaritan community, which was composed of people groups transplanted by the Assyrians, and had successfully resisted the threats of other neighbors.[7]

Little is known of Judaism in the Diaspora. Many Jews had settled in Assyria, Babylon, Persia, and Egypt. Business records from Babylon and Persia, as well as the correspondence from the Jewish community at Elephantine, a small island in the Nile in Upper Egypt, throw a little light on an otherwise undocumented period. At Elephantine, Jews had built a temple dedicated to Yahu (the Lord). They maintained close ties with the Jews in Yehud and were evidently dependent on the religious leadership in Jerusalem as well as on the Jerusalem temple.

Though Yehud was fully incorporated as a Persian administrative district, the Jews there and in the Diaspora enjoyed relative freedom of religious expression. The policy of noninterference begun by Cyrus remained in effect.

THE GREEK EMPIRE AND HELLENISM

In the last decades before the coming of Alexander the Great, the Persian empire was troubled by continual internal unrest. By 334 B.C., the situation had deteriorated to the point that Alexander was able to push his way into Phoenicia, Philistia, and Egypt. The conquest of the Persian Empire brought Judaism directly into contact with the world of Hellenism, which was to have a lasting impact on Judaism and Christianity.[8]

Political and Cultural Developments

With the birth of the Greek (or Macedonian) Empire, new markets were opened up. The world of commerce brought with it the Greek culture (Hellenism). Greek dress, customs, ways of thought, and language were imported by means of the Greek colonies and cities throughout the empire.[9] The provinces of Judah and Samaria were not exempt. Greek cities were established there, placing the surrounding villages under their jurisdiction and influence. Although the Greeks did not at first impose their culture on the subject population, Hellenism was attractive. In addition to Aramaic and Hebrew, Greek was commonly used.[10]

315

At Alexander's death, the Macedonian Empire was broken up by his generals. Judea became a political and military battleground between the Ptolemies, who ruled Egypt, and the Seleucids, who ruled from Syria to Persia. Judaism in the Diaspora was greatly affected by the breakup of the empire, as some groups were aligned with Macedonia (Europe), others with the Seleucid kingdom, and still others with the Ptolemaic sphere of power.

The Jews were suddenly forced to involve themselves politically, leading to syncretism, subterfuge, political intrigue, and eventually the fall of Jerusalem in A.D. 70. Moreover, the location of Judea made it an ideal battleground between the Ptolemies and the Seleucids, so that the peace and prosperity of the Persian era was swept away. In order to finance the incessant wars, the Jews had to pay exorbitant property taxes in addition to the usual tribute required of subject peoples. This requirement gave rise to the practice of appointing Jews of aristocratic background to be "tax farmers" (tax collectors, or publicans).

Judah enjoyed a relative autonomy, even though it was a satellite state.[11] The aristocracy enjoyed political and financial favors because of their position. All during this period Hellenism crept in, a different form of life that gradually altered the unity of Judaism. Judaism was already broken up politically by the division of Alexander's empire (and even the Romans did not regain full control over parts of the Persian Empire, such as Parthia); it was further segmented both culturally and religiously. The Greek rule and culture were advanced by the establishment of Hellenistic (Greek) cities, even in Palestine: Antiochia, Panias, and Seleucia in the north; Gadara, Berenice, Gerasa, and Philadelphia in Transjordan; Gaza, Ascalon, Azotus, Jamnia, Joppa, Apollonia, Strato's Tower, and Ptolemais by the Mediterranean coast; and Marisa, Antiochia, Samaria, Scythiopolis, Nysa, and Itabyrium in the hill country of Judah, Samaria, and Galilee.[12] Judaism was forced into contact with a sophisticated culture that was considered superior by all who sought after it.

Religious Developments and the Sects

In Samaria the Samaritans distinguished themselves from Hellenism by setting up their own temple on Mount Gerizim. The previous tensions between Jews and Samaritans developed into overt hostility (see Nehemiah); Samaritans no longer recognized Jerusalem and its temple. The Jews were also forced to distinguish themselves from Hellenistic culture. Some separated themselves by a strict application of the Torah and considered their oral and written interpretations as authoritative as the Torah of Moses. Such was the case with the community that produced the Book of Jubilees, the Essene (Dead Sea) community, and the Pharisees.

316

From the initial contact with the Persian legal system, the Jewish concept of Torah had begun to change. The original concept of Torah, denoting "instruction," or divine guidelines whereby people might live righteously before a holy God, gradually gave way to the Persian concept of *dat*, or unalterable, incontrovertible decrees that formed a rigid legal system. The Greek *nomos* and Roman *lex* perpetuated this influence, the final result being that Torah became "law." From this point it was only a short step from "guidelines" to "the way of salvation." To this written Torah the Essenes and Pharisees added their own oral traditions as legally binding upon their adherents.

The *Essenes* were probably descendants of the earlier Hasidim, a group of "mighty men" who were "zealous for the law" and who willingly supported the Maccabean Revolt (1 Macc. 2:42; 7:13).[13] Their community at Qumran dates approximately from an altercation with the Hasmonean John Hyrcanus over his holding the high priesthood concurrent with the kingship.[14] The Essenes were barred from participation in the temple cult and eventually came to view the whole temple service as corrupt. They developed a rigid system of self-denial, ritual immersion, prayer, and the study and reading of Scripture as a substitute to the defiled animal sacrifice taking place in the temple. Their doctrinal emphases included communal living, outward purity, separation from the world (which included celibacy), the imminent coming of the kingdom of God, and an apocalyptic intervention of the Divine Warrior, who would destroy the oppressors and make the Essenes rulers and priests of the new world order.[15]

Another group is the *Pharisees*, who are more familiar to us from the Gospels and who, like the Essenes, had probably descended from the Hasidim.[16] Their name derives from the Hebrew *pāraš*, which could mean either "the interpreters" or "the separate ones." Because of their activity in teaching and interpreting the Torah, they naturally became leaders in the synagogue. Of all the sects, their influence among the common people seems to have been the greatest, and this position gave credence to their particular interpretations and applications of the written Torah. In their attempts to counteract the pressure of acculturation, they were quick to apply principles that they felt were inherent in the Torah itself to every conceivable circumstance of life. A whole body of oral rulings thus developed that was intended to be guidelines by which the righteous should "walk" (thus the technical term "Halakah"). In this way they sought to insulate the divine Torah from being broken unwittingly. The weight of tradition eventually established this body of oral material as coequal with the written Torah. Both were believed to have been given to Moses at Sinai (Pirqe Aboth 1:1).[17] In the New Testament this body of material is called "the tradition of the elders" (Matt. 15:2; Gal. 1:14).

The *Sadducees*, like the Pharisees and Essenes, had their beginnings in the period of the Maccabees.[18] They were most likely priestly-aristocratic families who formed a sort of council to the king. This council eventually evolved into what we know as the Sanhedrin, and only later, after they had obtained a great deal of popular support, did the Pharisees have any voice here. The designation "Sadducee" derives from the high-priestly name "Zadok"; the members of this sect must therefore be seen as the descendants and supporters of the high-priestly families who controlled the temple. Unlike the Pharisees and Essenes, the Sadducees had no belief in predestination, oral law, immortality of the soul, angels, demons, resurrection, heaven, or hell. Their influence in politics was at times great, but they were never as popular with the people as were the Pharisees. When the temple was destroyed their power base went with it, and they ceased to be a moving force in the development of Judaism.[19]

In the power vacuum that resulted from the destruction of the temple in A.D. 70, the Sadducees lost the source of their power, and the Essenes were either destroyed by the Romans or fled to Pella and Damascus. The Pharisees, or rabbis of the synagogues, were reconstituted at Yavneh by Rabbi Yohanan ben Zakkai. The tradition of the elders, or Mishnah, was eventually written down in A.D. 200 and as such now forms the heart of the Talmud.[20] Today it remains the infallible interpretation of the Old Testament for the purposes of faith and practice for all orthodox Jews.

Judaism and Hellenism

In their discussions with Hellenists the Jews developed an apologetic that encouraged discussion of their religion and yet kept them apart from the Greeks. They knew that the religion revealed to Moses was different from and superior to Greek polytheism. They spoke of Yahweh no longer by the personal name revealed to Moses and Israel but by the general designation "Lord" *(kurios)*, "the supreme Being" *(ho theos)*, or usually as "the Most High" *(ho hypsistos)*. The titular reference to deity weakened the closeness between God and man as regulated by the covenantal relationship. God became better known as the Creator-God and the Ruler of the universe than as "my Father" or "our Father." We may thus think that Jesus' teachings seemed revolutionary to the Jews of his day, whereas the Old Testament already contained such truths (Isa. 63:16).

The Septuagint (LXX), or the Old Testament translated into Greek, was a major accomplishment.[21] Not only did it make the Old Testament available to all who read Greek, but it also made the "book of the Jews" the basis for dialogue with Gentiles and fostered a greater sense of unity

318

among the Jews in the Diaspora, as they enjoyed the Bible in the vernacular.

In their contacts with the outside world, the Jews showed a laudable concern for non-Jews. While at times they may have adapted Judaism to the Hellenic environment, they were also motivated by a desire to see proselytes and God-fearers adopt or respect the way of Torah and temple. In this period of transition, the prophetic word was being fulfilled. Thousands of Gentiles joined in the worship of the Lord throughout the Diaspora (Mal. 2:6). The Torah was thus going out from Zion (Isa. 2:1–4), even though the era of peace had not yet arrived.

Nevertheless, syncretism was pervasive. The impact of Hellenization could not be avoided because the language, literature, philosophy, manners, and scientific discoveries associated with Greek culture challenged Judaism on a daily basis. The slow but inevitable process of acculturation had begun. The conflict between Judaism and paganism came to a head during the reign of Antiochus IV (Epiphanes, "the exalted one"), who forced the Jews to worship Zeus and who desecrated the temple in Jerusalem by sacrificing a pig on the altar in 167 B.C. The Jewish response came quickly. Under the leadership of the Maccabees (see 1 Macc. 2:1–4:59), Jerusalem and her temple were again consecrated, in 165–164 B.C.[22] The rededication of the temple was to be celebrated every year on the twenty-fifth day of Kislev as the feast of Hanukkah ("rededication"), the "Feast of Lights." With the Maccabean victory, Judaism was encouraged to define more clearly its relation with the outside world, as it walked the tightrope between conservatism and syncretism. In that challenging environment Jewish groups reacted differently to the reality of Hellenism and to one another. Judaism gradually became more and more fragmented.

The synagogue and the Jewish educational system developed as a positive outgrowth of the interaction between Judaism and Hellenism. Pharisaic Judaism expected all young men to learn the Torah and a craft (Pirqe Aboth 2:2). The encouragement of religious learning also advanced the interaction between Jewish and Greek learning, as was the case with Philo of Alexandria, a Jewish philosopher from Alexandria, Egypt, who developed a philosophical system aimed at integrating Torah and philosophy.

THE ROMAN EMPIRE

The Political Scene

The challenge of syncretism was further intensified when Judah became a Roman province.[23] At the death of Alexander Jannaeus (103–76 B.C.), civil war broke out in Judah. Sadducees and Pharisees together with the masses became embroiled in a succession quarrel between his two sons, Hyrcanus and Aristobulus. At stake were the kingship and the high priesthood. Both parties finally appealed to Rome for help, and Rome responded in 63 B.C. by sending Pompey, who incorporated Judah into the empire as a Roman province. Despite the rather shameful demise of the Hasmonean dynasty, later generations idealized this period to the point of viewing it as a picture of the messianic era. This development eventually affected messianic expectation, as the coming one was cast in terms of the old Maccabean rulers, who brought military victory and political autonomy. By the time of Jesus, this yearning for the golden age of the Maccabees had become an accepted tenet of faith. The tension it caused in the ministry of Jesus can be seen, for example, in John 6:15; 10:22–24; and Acts 1:6.

By 39 B.C., the kingship was successfully wrested away from the Hasmonean dynasty by an Edomite sympathizer with Rome, Herod the Great (Antipater).[24] With the appointment of Herod as king of Judah, Judaism had to face the issue of the relationship between state and religion. Because Herod and his successors placed imperial above national interests, and political above religious concerns, the parties in Judah faced a continual·challenge to adjust to the new situation. Their limited self government, the priesthood, and religious life were dependent on the approval of a king who by profession was Jewish but who in loyalty was first and foremost a Roman.

Religious Developments

Into this world of political favoritism, corruption of Old Testament institutions, religious schisms, and discord, our Lord Jesus Christ was born. The Judaism of his time showed little resemblance with that of the early postexilic era. It was segmented into many factions by politics, religious idealism, and varying degrees of acculturation. The Pharisees formed a minority of 5 percent, while the Sadducees and Essenes made up only 2 percent of the Jewish population in Palestine. Moreover, divisions existed within each of these groups.[25]

Study of the Torah

Two major Pharisaic schools developed in the first century B.C.: the school of Hillel and the school of Shammai. Both men developed rules for applying the Torah to everyday life. Hillel's understanding of the complexities of the new world showed greater perception. In its development, Pharisaic Judaism was gradually molded more by Hillel's approach than by that of Shammai.

Men who occupied themselves with the Torah and its interpretation became known as "scribes" *(sōferîm)*. Often the man who aimed at becoming a scribe enrolled at a school taught by a master ("rabbi") and studied until he had obtained a full grasp of that rabbi's teaching. He then continued his education with other masters until he had enough knowledge of the traditional forms of interpretation, application, and explanation to be recognized as an authority. In time he would be sufficiently recognized so as to draw his own circle of young scholars and establish his own school. The teachers of the Torah obtained a significant place in the synagogue, as the community respected them for their learning and sought them out as arbiters in disputes. The Jewish community was isolated from the temple, but even in isolation it formed a close-knit communion in the synagogue. At the remotest places in the Diaspora, Jews could meet together for fellowship and encouragement of their Jewish identity in the synagogue.[26] In spite of political, linguistic, and geographical barriers, the Jews were united by the institution of the synagogue, the Torah (in the Greek Septuagint), and an educational system whereby tradition was crystallized into a large body of legal discussions and decisions.[27] The written law was interpreted in the light of human traditions.

Temple and Priesthood

Many Jews became disillusioned with the temple cult because of the corruption and high-handedness of the priests.[28] The complicity of high priests Jason and Menelaus in political affairs, the close ties of the Sadducees with the priests, the non-Zadokite priesthood, political machinations, and formalism led to a disenchantment with the temple. The Essenes completely separated themselves from the temple and established communities at Qumran, Damascus, and elsewhere, waiting for the Messiah and the reinstitution of the Zadokite priesthood. Others maintained a formal allegiance with the temple, while being openly critical of it. Still others looked for the messianic age with a concern for the revelations of the apocalyptic mysteries with which the pseudepigrapha are replete.[29]

The fall of the temple in A.D. 70 dealt a final blow to the Essenes, Sadducees, and apocalypticists. Judaism slowly developed what G. F. Moore called "normative Judaism."[30] Such a position was rooted in Pharisaic Judaism, but only as it became crystallized after the fall of the temple. For many of the Pharisees with their emphasis on Torah, the fall of Jerusalem and the burning of the temple were no great loss. Torah survived, and the Jewish traditions were reestablished at Jabneh (Jamnia) with the Pharisees under the dynamic leadership of Rabban Yohanan ben Zakkai. Having witnessed the impact of Jerusalem's fall, Judaism developed into a coherent way of Torah life under Yohanan's leadership. Their decisions formed the basis of normative Judaism, and their influence remains until this day.

Four Focuses

In addition to the various parties and approaches to the new world in which Judaism found itself, major theological perspectives had developed around law, wisdom, the prophetic, and the apocalyptic. The approaches opened up by law, wisdom, and prophecy were natural developments growing out of the biblical perspectives. The apocalyptic, however, had its own distinctive rise, and it occupied a significant place within Judaism between 200 B.C. and A.D. 100.[31] During this time it deeply affected Judaism by being an approach to the tensions created by the complex world of politics and culture. The apocalyptic arose as a literary contribution from the view of the oppressed, as it provided a comforting perspective on God, human history, the angelic world, life after death, the messianic kingdom, and the end time.[32] The apocalyptic employed predominantly symbolic language and imagery to communicate the traditions concerning the creation of the world, the history of Israel, and the end of the nations.

As prominent a teacher as Rabbi Yohanan ben Zakkai was, he was given to speculative tendencies, as was his disciple Rabbi Eliezer the Great.[33] The pseudepigrapha, the writings of the Essenes,[34] as well as several apocryphal allusions—2 Esdras 14:13, 26, 46 refer to seventy apocalyptic writings—witness to the significance, if not to the popularity, of the apocalyptic.[35] John's Revelation is in the form of the apocalyptic, testifying to the general popularity of this mode of writing. Only with the fall of Jerusalem, the enthronement of Torah-Judaism, and the dialogues with Christians on messianic interpretation did normative Judaism, represented by Rabbi Judah the Prince, seek to curtail the apocalyptic.

In addition to the Torah and apocalyptic emphases, wisdom made a major contribution to the shaping of Judaism. Ben Sira accorded a place to wisdom in an attempt to find balance in this complex world. For him wisdom required neither slavish adherence to the law nor devotion to the temple but to a pursuit of wisdom. Other thinkers desired to apply the prophetic word to the future, to a world beyond Hellenism and paganism, and so the apocalyptic movement was born. Another group—the Zealots—found meaning in looking for political alternatives and sabotaging the ruling powers.[36] Judaism became divided and splintered by all kinds of factions and interest groups, each vying for popular support and each considering its way superior to the others. The world into which our Lord came was not characterized by a careful application of the Old Testament. Political, social, economic, regional, and sectarian interests combined to create a complex web of interpersonal relations.

Conclusion to Part 8

The world of the postexilic era is overshadowed by great leaders such as Ezra, a religious mover, and Nehemiah, a political mover. Both men were occupied with ideals and united by a common adherence to the Torah and a common vision for a holy nation that could enjoy the presence of God. Such was also the hope of the postexilic prophets (Haggai, Zechariah, and Malachi). However, all three prophets had already pointed out that the world of postexilic Judaism was only a partial fulfillment. The prophetic word was still largely to be fulfilled. The Lord had to bring in another shaking of heaven and earth (Hag. 2:6; see also Heb. 12:26). Jerusalem had to become the object of contention among the nations, and the Messiah had to come and introduce the kingdom (Zech. 14:4–9). The Servant of the Lord would come and purify a people to the Lord; then the godly would receive a great reward, and the wicked would be judged (Mal. 4:1–3). The postexilic prophets spoke of a greater era of fulfillment to come and called on the people of God to prepare for it by acts of devotion, by expecting the Lord's coming with rewards and great glory, and by practicing justice, righteousness, and love in preparation for his coming.

The idyllic world of isolation was suddenly broken up by Hellenism and the real world of Roman politics. After 323 B.C., Judaism had to confront the many faces of the enemy without and within. The world of the prophets had become complex and tense. Jews reacted differently, and out of the different reactions over hundreds of years, different ideologies, schools, and parties were born.

The world of the New Testament was vastly different from that of the postexilic era. With Hellenism a new form of idolatry came into being. Judaism had learned its lessons from the exilic experience, so that the idolatry against which the prophets repeatedly spoke was no longer a great temptation for those who loved the Torah. Hellenism, however, introduced a more seductive form of idolatry. By acculturation to the Greek way of life and thinking, one could obtain power and wealth. In view of the secularization of the ancient world, Judaism had to respond to the realpolitik of the Greeks and later the Romans. Some groups were drawn into the system, others played with the system and lost, and still others reacted strongly to the new world.

With the increase of documentary and archaeological information on the world of the New Testament, it becomes apparent that the first century A.D. was a most complex era. We cannot ask what the Jews believed as a group, because there were so many groups. Even as today there are many denominations, groups, and sects, each undergoing its own process of schism, maintaining its own system of cherished beliefs, and relating differently to political issues, cultural involvement, and understanding of the biblical writings, so also first-century Judaism must be portrayed as a dynamic and complex religion in flux.

This outline of the intertestamental period suggests the need for reevaluating the relationship of Jesus to the Jews and the Jewish leaders. Too often the harassment of Jesus came from certain groups or even from segments of a group. To judge all Jews or all Pharisees for what some did is an injustice to the New Testament writers and to the Jewish people!

This reevaluation must also include a renewed emphasis on the continuity of Jesus and the Old Testament. It is often assumed that Jesus taught a different doctrine from what is found in the Old Testament. Instead, it has become increasingly apparent that Jesus restored the authentic voice of God in the Law, the Prophets, and the Writings. The voice of God had become muffled by systematization and by polemic and party concerns. Each group had its own system for applying and interpreting the Word, and each sought to show the other *the* way to be a true child of Abraham. The emphases were many—Torah, temple, apocalypticism, pragmatism, and realism—and each had its own schools, leaders, and historical justification. Through hundreds of years of facing political, cultural, and religious changes, the Old Testament message had become muddled. Jesus came to restore the teaching of Scripture as the voice of God through Moses and the prophets, not merely through human contingencies!

Part 9

Jesus and the Kingdom

Introduction to Part 9

The situation of the Jews in the first century left much to be desired. God's people had been without a prophetic voice for several centuries. They had experienced the oppression and unrest of the Seleucid-Ptolemaic period and were now under the power of Rome. The messianic era, of which the prophets had so vividly spoken and for which the Jews had so expectantly waited for centuries, had not yet come. With the coming of John the Baptist and our Lord, however, God again spoke to his people.

The New Testament authors witness to the climactic revelation of God in Jesus Christ. The Father revealed himself in the past through Moses and the prophets, but Jesus Christ is the very Son and image-bearer of the Father (Heb. 1:3; 3:6). This era of redemptive history culminates the expectation of the past era and enlarges new vistas and hopes of a greater era to come. The New Testament corroborates with the Old Testament, witnessing to the great and glorious restoration in Jesus Christ. It is a grave error to limit the Scriptures to the New Testament, because the apostles and gospel writers thought of themselves as heirs of the Old Testament message. The people of God before Christ, together with the New Testament saints, form one household, "built on the foundation of the apostles and prophets, with Christ Jesus himself as the chief cornerstone" (Eph. 2:20).[1]

The Gospel of Luke clearly illustrates the continuity of the Old Testament prophetic hope and the New Testament proclamation that, in Jesus the Messiah, all promises of the Old Testament will be fulfilled. By including Mary's Magnificat, Zechariah's prophecy, Simeon's blessing, and Anna's sharing the good news of his birth, Luke expresses the longing of the last of the Old Testament saints for the redemption to come. The birth narrative in his first two chapters forms a link between the Old Testament and the New, connecting the ministry of John and Jesus with the Old Testament and confirming the continuity between the prophets and the ministries of John and Jesus.[2]

In the Lucan birth narrative Jesus comes to care for the humble in Israel so that they might experience the forgiveness of sins, serve God without fear in holiness and righteousness, and know that their salvation will be a revelation to all the Gentiles, in accordance with God's Word to Abraham, David, and the prophets. The connection between the Old Testament prophets and Jesus is amply made because the prophets proclaim that, in the messianic era, the benefits of God's forgiveness will be experienced by his people (Isa. 40:1–2; 43:25; 44:22; Jer. 31:34). It is an era characterized by light, not only for Israel, but also for the Gentiles (Isa. 60; 62). The messianic era also marks the end of all enmity and evil that has disturbed God's people in the past. They will be able to worship him in peace. The inclusion of these songs and expectations in Luke's prologue is theologically important because he prepares the Jewish reader to see in Jesus the fulfillment of the Old Testament prophetic word. In like manner, Paul declares that, in Jesus, all the promises of God are assured: "For no matter how many promises God has made, they are 'Yes' in Christ. And so through him the 'Amen' is spoken by us to the glory of God" (2 Cor. 1:20).

Excitement with the new era lies in the coming of the Christ, the center of redemptive history. Saints from the old era join together with the saints of the new era in the worship of the Christ, with the hope that he will introduce the kingdom of God in a unique and glorious way. The focus on Jesus is given to us by the four gospel writers, and this fourfold perspective contributes to a broader and deeper understanding of who Christ is and what he began to do while cn earth.

The era of the King forms a watershed in redemptive history; from this point onward, the history of redemption rushes on toward its final goal—the restoration of the world. We shall examine the significance of this period by considering the literary, canonical, and redemptive-historical features of this era. The Gospels witness to:

1. the actuality of Jesus' ministry on earth;
2. the purpose and impact of his mission;
3. the authority of the Messiah of God;
4. the continuity of God's plan;
5. the need for an individual response to Jesus the Messiah;
6. the nature and mission of the new people of God ("the church"); and
7. Jesus as the hope of the messianic people.

CHAPTER 27

The Gospel of Jesus Christ

The four Gospels are essentially the only extant literary materials that have a bearing on the life and teachings of our Lord. The word "gospel" is a literary designation for a particular type of literature.[1] The Gospels form a composite portrait of Jesus Christ, designed and drawn by four different men, each being inspired by the Holy Spirit. The literary design reveals a unified plot in each gospel that employs many of the features used in the development of a story. Leland Ryken observes that the literary approach must begin with the conviction that the Gospels are stories of a mixed form; that is, they include biography, historical chronicle, fiction (the parables), oration, sermon, dialogue (or drama), proverb, poem, tragedy, and comedy.[2] By means of selectivity, interpretation, restructuring, and contrastive highlighting, each gospel writer presents an individual interpretive portrait of Jesus.[3]

The Gospels record Jesus' fond use of the parabolic form in his teaching. The parable may be a short, pithy saying, an expression characterized by the wisdom genre, or a short story. The short story category goes beyond the simple analogy to a more complex teaching point. The conviction that the parables are "masterpieces of popular or folk storytelling" leads Ryken to look beyond the simple, realistic elements of the story. He identifies the parable with allegory and finds that each parable has several themes. He thus rejects the modern canon of interpretation that each parable has only one main point.[4]

MATTHEW

How did Matthew structure his material? To what extent did he depend on other sources, such as Mark, and how did he rework these materials so as to make an independent contribution to the portrait of Jesus, the Messiah? Although these questions have occupied New Testament scholars for a century, there is as yet no consensus regarding the answers—honestly said, it is not clear how Matthew has structured his gospel. Attempts at a literary analysis have been made but thus far have failed to reveal convincingly the internal structure.[5] In comparison with Mark, Matthew pays greater attention to the prologue and epilogue of Jesus' ministry on earth. Moreover, he has arranged the materials of the gospel into literary clusters of proclamation *(kerygma)* and teaching *(didachē)*: the Sermon on the Mount (chaps. 5–7), the mission of the disciples (chap. 10), parables (chap. 13), parables and teachings on the church (chap. 18), woes to the Pharisees (chap. 23), and the Mount Olivet Discourse (chaps. 24–26).

A comparison of the Synoptics reveals that Matthew has greatly expanded the material of Mark. According to Kümmel, about 50 percent of Matthew has no parallel in Mark, 28 percent has a parallel with Luke, and 22 percent is unique to Matthew.[6] The material unique to Matthew reveals five theological concerns of the writer: (1) the fulfillment of the prophetic word, (2) the separation of Christianity from Judaism, (3) the continuity of Christianity with Judaism, (4) the radical nature of obedience and discipleship, and (5) the eschatological judgment.

First, Matthew displays interest in the *fulfillment* of the prophetic word. He employs extensively the so-called fulfillment quotations (1:22–23; 2:5–6, 12–15, 17–18, 23; 4:14–16; 8:17; 12:17–21; 13:35; 21:4–5; 27:9–10).[7] The frequent reference to fulfilled prophecies reflects a typological approach to the Old Testament. For Matthew, Jesus is the fulfillment not only of particular Old Testament prophecies but—in his descent from Abraham, his coming out of Egypt, his wilderness stay, and his ministry and rejection—of the general outlines of Israel's history.[8]

Second, Matthew reveals a familiarity with the beginning of a *separation* of Christianity from Judaism. He makes clear that Jesus' concern was with sinners, whether Jewish or Gentile (1:21; 9:13; 11:19). The guilt for Jesus' death is on the Jews (27:25), and "the kingdom of God will be taken away from" the Jews and "given to a people who will produce its fruit" (21:43). Jesus warned the Jews of his generation that "the subjects of the kingdom will be thrown outside, into the darkness, where there will be weeping and gnashing of teeth" (8:12). Matthew uses the word *ekklēsia* ("church") to denote the new community (16:18; 18:17) and shows great care in presenting Jesus' teaching on the new community (chap. 18).[9] The authority given to Peter and the officers of the new community of believers exists separately from the synagogue but is continuous with Jesus' authority to forgive sin and to exercise discipline (9:1–8; 16:19; 18:18).[10] At the final judgment the separation of the sheep from the goats is based on adherence to Jesus' words and expression of love for Jesus (25:31–46). At the end of Matthew, "'the Jews,' especially their leadership, stand over against the church."[11] (See 21:31–32, 45–46.)

Third, Matthew is also concerned with the *continuity* of Christianity with Judaism. Christ did not reject the Jews (10:5–6) but encouraged them to seek God's kingdom as he exemplified it and to follow him (6:33; 11:28–29). He invited every "teacher of the law" to learn of him, while holding on to the old (13:52; see also 5:17). Matthew leaves open a future for the Jews, as he quotes Jesus on how the Jews will welcome him at his return (23:39).

Fourth, Jesus' coming brings with it an emphasis on the *radical nature* of obedience and discipleship. In spite of the elements of continuity, Jesus' mission was to separate the righteous to himself (10:34–39), to call for absolute loyalty to himself (vv. 37–42; 16:24–26), and to require unconditional submission to the will of the Father (7:21–23; 12:50; 13:41–43; 25:31–46). Jesus did not come to free people from God's eternal law (5:17–20), binding for both Jews and Gentiles. The law is no longer to be limited to Moses as the final authority but is to be understood particularly in the light of Jesus' mission (11:28–30). Jesus is *the* interpreter of Moses. Childs has correctly stated, "The law of Moses is not a temporary measure that has now been superseded in the kingdom of heaven, but rather represents the eternally valid will of God."[12]

Fifth, the *eschatological judgment* focuses on the role of Jesus as the teacher of the will of God. He will judge between the sheep and goats (25:31–46), and his judgment is based on loyalty to him and to his teaching (7:21–23; 13:41–43). Jesus does not call for an easy-believ-ism. He calls for discipleship of the most radical nature—the denial of self and the taking up of one's cross (8:22; 10:38–39; 16:24–25) and the absolute allegiance to his will (7:21; 25:31–40).

The literary structure of Matthew unfolds these five emphases in its five divisions, each ending with a formulary conclusion "when Jesus had finished saying these things" (7:28; 11:1; 13:53; 19:1; 26:1). (See figure 20.) Though such schematization is subject to criticism, it gives a convenient summary of the history of redemption as God's expectations for Israel are fulfilled in the ministry and life of Jesus, the Son of God.[13] The theme throughout the book and connecting its various parts is the theological principle of promise and fulfillment.[14] The fulfillment is here and now, but it is also eschatological. Matthew thus subsumes all aspects of his message under the umbrella of eschatology.

MARK

The Gospel of Mark is structured geographically. The story of Jesus begins with his activities in Galilee (1:14–9:50), expands with brief periods outside Galilee (in Tyre [7:24], Tyre and Sidon [v. 31], and Caesarea Philippi [8:27]), and comes to a climax with his journey toward

Jerusalem, including his ministry of teaching and suffering in and around Jerusalem (10:1−16:8). (See figure 21.)

Introduction (chaps. 1−2)
   Jesus and: the Old Testament law (chaps. 3−7)
              discipleship (8:1−11:1)
              the kingdom (11:2−13:53)
              the new community, the church (13:54−19:2)
              the eschaton, the new hope (19:3−25:46)
Climax (chaps. 26−28)

Figure 20. The Literary Structure of Matthew

Introduction (1:1−13)
   Jesus in Galilee (1:14−5:43)
      Jesus around Galilee (chaps. 6−9)
         Jesus to Jerusalem (chap. 10)
      Jesus around Jerusalem (chaps. 11−13)
   Jesus in Jerusalem (14:1−16:8)
Ending (16:9−20)

According to the best textual witnesses, Mark's ending (16:9−20) is not authentic.

Figure 21. The Literary Structure of Mark

The geographical structuring is based on a theological-literary perspective.[15] Mark portrays Jesus as having come from Galilee, having ministered in Galilee, and returning to Galilee after his suffering and resurrection in Jerusalem (14:28). His ministry around Jerusalem, together with his passion and resurrection, forms the background for his resurrection ministry as the risen Lord.

The brief extension of Christ's ministry outside of Galilee and his teaching on the future mission to the Gentiles affirm the importance Mark places on the Gentile mission. Galilee represents the world of the Gentiles, far away from Jerusalem, whereas Jerusalem represents the rejection of Jesus by institutionalized forms of Judaism. Kümmel observes at this point that "the transfer of salvation from the unbelieving Jews [is] to the believing Gentiles . . . he is addressing himself to Gentile Christianity, which no longer has any relationship with Jerusalem and the Jews there."[16]

Little consensus has arisen on the purpose of the gospel, whether it is liturgical, catechetical, or polemical. Too often it is assumed that the gospel writers purposely set out to explain who Jesus is in a manner consistent with the early church. The assumption that Mark explains the variance between the doctrine of Christ in the early church (the so-called Hellenistic Christ) and the Jesus who actually lived and ministered in Galilee (the so-called Palestinian Jesus) by the postulate of the "hidden Christ" is highly doubtful. Such views adopt a critical position toward Mark. No distinction should be made between the Hellenistic Christ and the Palestinian Jesus, because Mark aims clearly at setting forth the risen Christ for the purpose of winning people over to the Christian faith. In Childs's words, "The forms of the pre-resurrected and the post-resurrected Jesus belong together, and there is no way to divorce the two, either in the past or the future."[17] The Christ who conceals, as well as reveals, his true identity before the resurrection is the same after the resurrection.

In his pre-resurrection teaching and miracles, Jesus reveals the authority of the incarnate Christ, whose kingdom is not of this earth (1:22; 9:14–29; 10:46–52; 11:12–33). The "gospel" (1:1) of the kingdom consists of proclaiming the living Christ, who will come to perfect all things. The very opening words, "The beginning of the gospel about Jesus Christ, the Son of God," introduce Jesus' mission in relation to the Old Testament prophetic word (1:2–3; see Isa. 40:3; Mal. 3:1). The title "Son of God" is, according to Bornkamm, Mark's "clearest and most important expression of his understanding of Christ."[18] But Jesus' mission is also to be understood in terms of the eschatological Parousia, or coming. To this end the eschatological discourse (Mark 13) introduces the passion narrative, as if in his passion "Christ's eschatological kingdom is anticipated and already experienced before his final victory."[19] In the later proclamation of the gospel of Jesus, the good news will spread to all nations. The eschaton and the universal, the temporal and the spatial dimensions, converge in Jesus, the exalted Messiah.

LUKE

Luke's distinct historical awareness comes out in his prologue (1:1–4), in which he explains how he intends to write an orderly gospel based on a careful investigation of everything pertaining to Jesus "from the beginning." This focus corresponds to a similar statement in Acts, "I wrote about all that Jesus began to do and to teach until the day he was taken up to heaven" (1:1–2). More than the other gospel writers, Luke seems to be preoccupied with Jesus' place in redemptive history.[20] This concern also explains why Luke wrote a history of the presence of the Spirit in the early church (Acts) as a sequel to the gospel.

The life of Jesus unfolds in stages and reflects temporal and geographical concerns.[21] Luke presents Jesus' life in the geographical pattern introduced by Mark (Galilee, Judea, and Jerusalem) and then projects the mission of the apostles as beginning in Jerusalem and extending to Judea, Galilee, and the ends of the world (Acts 1:8). Temporally, the good news of Jesus is also a further development in the history of redemption: "The Law and the Prophets were proclaimed until John. Since that time, the good news of the kingdom of God is being preached" (Luke 16:16). In Acts, Luke further develops the next stage as the period of the Spirit (Acts 1:4–5). Each epoch shows continuity with the preceding one. Luke's quotation of Jesus on his mission in relation to that of Moses clarifies the integral relationship: "It is easier for heaven and earth to disappear than for the least stroke of a pen to drop out of the Law" (Luke 16:17). As the eras of the Mosaic administration and the presence of God's kingdom in Jesus are distinct, so is Jesus' ministry on earth distinct from the age of the Spirit (Acts 1:1–5). Within the distinctives, however, there are vital elements of continuity.

Many scholars have drawn the inference that Luke wrote his work out of disappointment with the failure of Christ to return. The evidence from the gospel, however, does not support this assertion. First, the Spirit was powerfully present in the ministry of Jesus (Luke 4:18–22). In the proclamation of the gospel, Jesus fulfilled the prophetic word, and in this way the glorious future is present in Jesus.

Second, although Luke does not portray Jesus as "*the* eschatological event," he has a clear perception of eschatology. He clarifies the future of Christ's kingdom as being in the Father's authority (Acts 1:7) and holds that Jesus will certainly and unexpectedly return: "The certainty of the future derives from the plan of God who visits the people with his presence in judgment and redemption, and thus calls forth a continuing response to the imperatives of discipleship."[22] Luke contributes a historical awareness to the imminence of Christ's return. With a view to the persecution of the churches, Luke calls on the church to persevere until the kingdom is fully introduced. Like "the times of the Gentiles" (Luke 21:24), Jesus' coming in glory and the fullness of the kingdom are in God's hands, but the Christian community must stand ready to give witness before the authorities who will try them (vv. 12–19). In fidelity to Jesus, they must live in the expectancy of the redemption that is drawing nearer as the troubles on this earth increase (v. 28). They may thus await his return busily and fearlessly.

Luke, while interested in historical schematization, develops the life of Jesus as a fulfillment of the promises. He works from the schema of progressive fulfillment, as all of Jesus' life—from the birth narratives to his post-resurrection appearances—has been foreshadowed in the Old Testament. In Jesus' words, "Everything must be fulfilled that is written about me in the Law of Moses, the Prophets and the Psalms" (24:44).

In his quotations from the Old Testament, "the Scriptures of the Jews provide the context from which Jesus' life is read and understood. Above all, Luke does not attempt to Christianize the Old Testament, but to let it speak its own voice of the coming salvation."[23] The shift is from eschatology and imminence to continuity. The proclamation of the church includes both old and new: Moses, the Prophets, the Writings, and the Good News of the kingdom (see 16:16; 24:44–45). (See figure 22.)

Prologue (1:1–4)
   Birth and childhood narratives (1:5–2:52)
     Beginning of Jesus' ministry (3:1–4:13)
      Jesus in Galilee (4:14–9:50)
       Travel toward Jerusalem (9:51–19:27)
        Death, resurrection, and postresurrection (19:28–24:53)

Figure 22. The Literary Structure of Luke

JOHN

John contributes a different perspective on Jesus. He is more interested in the words of Jesus and in the sign value of his miracles than in the events of Jesus' life. The words of Jesus mold John's gospel. Even though John may have paraphrased Jesus' words more than the other three gospel writers, he consciously adapted Jesus' words to his argument that Jesus is the Word of God, by whose light men and women are taken out of darkness, which symbolizes judgment. Those who believe on him have life, receive the Spirit of God (the Comforter), are regenerated, and will understand that Jesus is the manifestation of the Father's love and glory. There is no other way to come to the Father except through the Son. The theme running throughout the gospel is thus the necessity to believe on Jesus (see 20:30–31). After all, Jesus is the great I Am: the bread of life (6:35, 48), the light of the world (8:12), the gate (10:7, 9), the good shepherd (10:11, 14), the resurrection and the life (11:25), the way and the truth and the life (14:6), and the true vine (15:1, 5). The gospel may be divided into four parts.[24] (See figure 23.)

Prologue (1:1–18)
   Jesus in the world (1:19–12:50)
   Jesus' return to the Father (chaps. 13–20)
Epilogue (chap. 21)

Figure 23. The Literary Structure of John

The fourth gospel presents the challenge to express faith in Jesus. He is the messianic prophet (4:19, 44; 6:14; 7:40; 9:17). Jesus bears a typological relationship to the Old Testament prophets Elijah and Elisha, by whom God's blessing and curse came on Israel. In structuring the miracles, John evokes the power of the prophets in presenting one greater than Elijah (see 1:19–27). Elisha, for example, purified water at Jericho (2 Kings 2:19–22), and Jesus changed the water into wine (John 2:1–11). Elijah and Elisha brought a child back to life (1 Kings 17:17–24; 2 Kings 4:18–37), and Jesus healed the official's son (John 4:46–54). In these and many other parallels, John invites the reader to faith in one greater than Elijah and Elisha![25]

John's gospel calls on individuals to receive Jesus as the Messiah. It is difficult to determine who the original audience was, whether Diaspora Jews, sectarian groups, people under the spell of docetic teaching, or Gentile believers. The gospel is general enough to call forth a response of faith in each generation. The prologue and the epilogue, for example, present Jesus as the Christ, to whom one must respond in either faith or unbelief. The purpose throughout the gospel is to present the Jesus of faith.[26] The historical dimension, so characteristic of the narrative sections in the other gospels, is therefore suppressed. John is not antihistorical, but he assumes the historical integrity and truth of the other gospels in presenting Jesus as the Christ.

Those who follow him and those he meets are confronted with the living Messiah, who demands a faith response.[27] The reaction of people to Jesus thus becomes highly significant—people such as Nicodemus, the Samaritan woman, Thomas, Peter, the official at Capernaum, and the man born blind.

The gospel also speaks to those who did not have the advantage of being confronted with the living Christ. Jesus speaks frequently of his glorification and of the coming of the Holy Spirit.[28] With the glorification of Jesus after the resurrection and the coming of the Spirit at Pentecost, the Spirit will instruct all who believe on him so that they too may gain special insight into Jesus' earthly ministry and his present state of glorification. Each section of the gospel calls forth a faith response to the Christ, who is now present through the Spirit in the church and who will come in glory. The incarnate Word expects from his disciples no less than love. This love takes the cross as its starting point and model and necessarily reaches out to the world.[29]

A HARMONY OF THE GOSPELS

The four Gospels present a multiple witness to Jesus, the Christ.[30] The apostle John's comment about the deeds of Jesus—"If every one of them were written down, I suppose that even the whole world would not have room for the books that would be written" (21:25)—expresses the unusual ministry of our Lord. Any attempt to put his life into a simplistic reconstruction or harmonization is resisted by the intricate relations of the four Gospels. The church received four Gospels and has never shown an interest in unifying them into a single account. Each gospel is a literary unit, whose value is independent of the others. Yet, the very existence of four Gospels deepens our comprehension of Jesus. The combined effect of their multifaceted witness is greater than an analysis of the constituent parts. The integrity of each gospel must therefore be left unaltered.

The multiformity of the four Gospels moves each generation to ask the question, Who is Jesus of Nazareth? The purpose of the canonical and redemptive-historical approach will be to enhance our understanding of Jesus' ministry in its canonical context as well as in its relationship to the Old Testament. This approach preserves the integrity of each gospel. Each account contributes to the kaleidoscopic witness to Jesus, the Son of God. The uniqueness of the Gospels lies in their canonical place as *confessional* statements; in them is "faith proclaimed *as* a story about Jesus. . .thus the story of his past never lost its contemporary relevance but acquired ever fresh significance."[31]

CHAPTER 28

John and Jesus

JOHN THE BAPTIST

John the Baptist was born to an elderly priest, Zechariah, and his wife, Elizabeth. John was the appointed forerunner of our Lord Jesus Christ and was set apart before birth to be God's prophet (Luke 1:15). By going out in the spirit and power of Elijah, he was to turn the hearts of the fathers to the children and to call upon the remnant to have the faith and loyalty of Abraham, in order that they might be prepared for the coming of the Messiah (v. 17; see Mal. 4:5–6). Upon his son's birth, Zechariah, filled with the Holy Spirit, named the child John (meaning "the Lord is gracious") and identified him with the prophet of the Most High, of whom Malachi had spoken (Luke 1:76; Mal. 3:1).[1]

John's unequivocal call for repentance was matched by his austere living (Matt. 3:4). His ministry consisted of preaching repentance and baptizing all who repented of their sins and awaited the messianic age. John's baptism of repentance (Luke 3:3) was to assure the godly that their sins were forgiven. This repentance was not a mere emotional demonstration but required outward expression, which only then assured forgiveness. Those who submitted themselves to baptism were expected to do good works consistent with repentance (v. 8).

John's preaching announced the coming of the Messiah.[2] He pointed his followers to a new era about to be inaugurated: the era of the Spirit. With the coming of the Messiah the eschaton was inaugurated, whose sign is the baptism "with the Holy Spirit and with fire" (Luke 3:16). The coming of Jesus ushers in an era of the greater manifestation of the Holy Spirit, who was revealed at Pentecost in the form of tongues of fire (Acts 2:1–3). To those who believe on the Messiah, the Spirit-fire signifies that they already have passed through the judgment of God, whereas to those who do not believe, the Spirit-fire symbolizes their condemnation.

John expected the coming one to introduce both an era of salvation and an era of judgment. These two aspects of the prophetic message find their focus in the incarnate Christ. John described the Messiah as the one who is mightier than he (Luke 3:16). Whereas John baptized with water, the Messiah would baptize with the Holy Spirit and fire. John likens the coming of Jesus to an ax placed by the roots of a tree (v. 9). The tree that bears good fruit will not be cut down, whereas one that has not borne fruit will be removed. The winnowing process provides a further analogy. The Messiah will cleanse the threshing floor of the chaff but will gather the righteous unto himself (v. 17). John's mission, therefore, was clearly in fulfillment of God's Word to Malachi, namely, that "the messenger" (John) would precede the coming of "the messenger of the covenant" (the Messiah) and that the Messiah would purify God's people to himself (Mal. 3:1–3).

Citizenship in the new messianic kingdom required the works of righteousness necessary to complement faith. John called on the rich to share their wealth with those who had nothing, the tax collectors to collect only what was their due, and the soldiers not to oppress or intimidate anyone and to be content with their wages (Luke 3:11–14). John's expectations of holiness, justice, righteousness, love, and peace were fully consistent with those of the prophets.

John's redemptive-historical place is that of a prophet. Unlike the prophets of old, who spoke of the eschaton as the day of salvation and judgment, John referred to the coming one as being already here. The eschaton rushes forward in the incarnation of Jesus, who is the fulfillment of the Old Testament hope. The very submission of Jesus to John's baptism shows the continuity between old and new: John, the last prophet of the Old Covenant, baptized Jesus. In his ministry Jesus developed the message of the prophets, namely, the call to repentance. He charged his apostles to continue the prophetic and messianic ministry, when he called them and his followers to go out preaching, teaching, and baptizing in his name (see Matt. 28:18–20). The commission of his disciples after his resurrection only strengthens the bond between the pre- and post-resurrection ministry and between Jesus, John, and the Old Testament prophets. The difference between old and new, between John and Jesus, lies in the greater evidence of the Spirit of God in those who are baptized in the name of Jesus (see Acts 4:12; 10:44–48). Hence, there can be no return to the baptism of John (18:25).

Jesus' testimony concerning John the Baptist is important in that it affirms the significance of John's ministry (see John 10:41). According to our Lord Jesus Christ, John was "the Elijah who was to come," of whom the prophet Malachi had prophesied (Matt. 11:14).[3] John was also the greatest prophet of the old era because he had witnessed the new era. His greatness lies not in the number of his prophecies but in his unique position as one on the threshold between the old and new eras. Nevertheless, Jesus looks forward to the future as he promises that the least in the kingdom of God is greater than John (Luke 7:28). John was a shining lamp to which people must respond (John 5:35), but Jesus' works testify that he is greater than John and that the Father himself has sent Jesus as the Son (vv. 36–37). John's popularity extended far into the first century, as he still had a disciple, Apollos, and twelve followers in Ephesus (Acts 18:24; 19:1–7). The testimony of the Gospels concerning John reveals a humble, devout saint, a prophet of God who spoke of the Messiah. Jesus is the Messiah sent by the Father, and John is thus a link between the pre-Christian and the Christian eras.[4]

THE SELF-DISCLOSURE OF JESUS

The Gospels present the birth and ministry of Jesus.[5] As we have already seen, the synoptic presentation of our Lord is complex. Indeed, there are several reasons for what Ladd calls "the Messianic Problem." First, Jesus was clearly reticent to proclaim his messianic mission.[6] Second, each of the Gospels presents different aspects of his ministry in different vocabulary. Third, the focus of the Gospels is different from Jesus' original mission. While Jesus directed his words to a strictly Jewish audience bound to the Mosaic law, the Gospels represent the concern of the early church for the proclamation of Jesus as the Messiah and the Savior of the world.

A "messianic secret" surrounds the Gospels.[7] Who is this Jesus of Nazareth? Jesus speaks at length on the fatherhood of God, the kingdom, and the way to God, but he is cautious in speaking about himself and his mission on earth. At times, especially in the Gospel of Mark, Jesus instructs those whom he has healed not to speak about what has happened. It appears that Jesus was concerned not to be misunderstood. In light of the variety of Jewish expectations, some groups would conceivably have identified him with their particular views. The complexity of the concept of the Messiah in Judaism was due to the various parties, but in general, it had developed an earthly, political character.[8] They would not have comprehended the greater import of the messianic mission of our Lord. When Jesus' mission is properly perceived against the background of the first century, the Gospels present a clear, unambiguous witness to the nature of the Christ. They do so by the narratives, by allusions to the Old Testament, and by the use of various names for Jesus, which collectively convey the significance of his self-disclosure and of his mission on earth.

Messiah

By the title "Christ" (Heb. *māšîaḥ*, "anointed one," or "messiah") the Christian community has expressed the office of Jesus as well as his relationship to the Old Testament. The title is what Ladd calls "the most important of all the christological concepts . . . , because it became the central way of designating the Christian understanding of Jesus."[9] The title "messiah" derives from the Old Testament promises to David (2 Sam. 7:12–13; Ps. 132) and from the Old Testament prophets. The Davidic covenant was the basis for hope in the continuous rule of God's anointed servant, the Son of David. The Old Testament prophets, through their Spirit-filled message, gave hope in the restoration and in the ministry of the Davidic king, whose rule would be aligned to the rule of God over his people. Over the centuries the Jews began to speak of the Davidic king, the messiah of David, through whom the Lord would introduce an era of Jewish supremacy and peace.

Matthew quotes extensively from the Old Testament (some fifty direct quotations as well as many allusions) to demonstrate that Jesus is the fulfillment of the Old Testament expectations. He patterns Jesus after the history of Israel, but unlike Israel, Jesus is obedient to the Father; unlike Israel, Jesus is the Son of God, the Son of David, the Son of Abraham. He is born to be the King of the Jews (Matt. 2:2). Matthew powerfully demonstrates that this Jesus is the Messiah by quoting extensively from Jesus' teachings on the kingdom (4:12–7:29; 11:27–13:52). The thrust of his argument is against the common messianic expectation among the Jews, who thought of the messiah as some kind of a political figure, by whom God would send his redemption. Though the Jews disagreed on points of detail, they agreed in giving the term "messiah" political associations. But Jesus had no political ambitions and remained reticent in disclosing himself as the Messiah.

The significance of the title "messiah," or Christ, lies in the meaning that Jesus himself gave to it. He gradually changed the popular misconceptions until the word came to denote a person totally different from that of the popularly awaited messiah. In the revised meaning, Jesus is the long-awaited Deliverer, who himself had to suffer for human sin. The evidence that he is the Messiah, the Son of God, the key by whom the restoration of all things will take place, is found in his teaching, in his miracles (Matt. 11:3–5; see also 8:1–11:1), and in his passion and resurrection. The Messiah who came to suffer is the Son of David, the Son of God (9:27; 12:23; 15:22; Mark 12:35–37, a quotation from Ps. 110:1). In all of his interactions Jesus did not reject the popular recognition of his being the Messiah, the Son of David—as when the people exclaimed, "Hosanna to the Son of David!" (Zech. 9:9; Matt. 21:1–11). This emphasis accords with the theology of the early church, according to which the ground of fulfillment of the prophetic word lies in Jesus' being the Son of David (see Acts 2:25–36; 13:22–37).

Jesus the Messiah came to reveal God's concern for his people in the inauguration of the messianic era. The eschatological kingdom receives a concreteness in Jesus' ministry (Matt. 6:10, 14–15; 11:2–6). The intrusion of the kingdom, however, is not separate from Jesus' suffering.

340

The Gospels help us understand how Jesus planned his ministry around his crucifixion, burial, and resurrection. He actively fulfilled the Father's plan. The Messiah had to die and be raised again (Matt. 16:21; 17:22). Only after Jesus had experienced complete humiliation would he appear in glory as the victorious King (24:30; 25:31).

The many allusions, references, and implicit connections to the Old Testament link the Jesus of the Gospels with the Old Testament messianic expectation. The conception of Jesus in the early church agrees with this interrelationship of the Messiah, the kingdom, and the church.[10] According to Acts 2:36, Jesus is the "Messiah-Lord, i.e., an enthroned Messiah as contrasted with a suffering Messiah."[11] The theme of Christian preaching is the proclamation that Jesus is the Christ (5:42). There is no separation between Jesus' lordship and his messiahship. In fact, the Book of Acts concludes on the motif of the proclamation of the kingdom and the present messiahship of Jesus. Though Paul does not develop the kingdom or the messianic office of Jesus in his epistles, it is clear that he also views Jesus as the risen, glorious, and victorious Messiah. Paul represents all Jews who were forced to change their Jewish perception of the Messiah (2 Cor. 5:16). With Paul we witness the beginning of the use of the two names, Jesus Christ or Christ Jesus, in a formulary way. The confession that Jesus is the Christ has bound Christians together throughout the history of the church.

Son of God

While Jesus is the Davidic Messiah, it is because he is also the *only begotten of the Father* that his messiahship is efficacious.[12] During his ministry Jesus demonstrated his sonship by doing the works of the Father in his flesh—healing the blind, the lame, and the sick and teaching the Word of the Father regarding the kingdom of God and the way of salvation. But the ultimate sign of Jesus' being the only begotten of the Father is his death on the cross and resurrection. Jesus is clearly the God of the Old Testament incarnate, as he claims that he is the great "I Am." Whenever Jesus says of himself "I Am" (without a predicate following) or describes himself as "the door," "the bread of life," or some other similar phrase, he is identifying himself with Yahweh in the Old Testament (cf. Exod. 6:6–7; 20:1, 5; Isa. 41:4; 43:10; Hos. 13:4; Joel 2:27).[13]

In his birth our Lord fully identified himself with the human race. Even in his birth and life on earth, however, he is still the Son of God. The Lord of glory emptied himself of his glory for the purpose of living among humankind (Phil. 2:6–11). Although sharing our humanity with us, he differed in that he was conceived by the Holy Spirit (Matt. 1:20). The mystery of the incarnation is that God fully became man, having been born of a woman, and was still fully God (11:27). This truth is best expressed in the title "Immanuel" ("God is with us"; see Isa. 7:14; Matt. 1:23). Mary knew the secret of his conception, having received the announcement by the angel, and also knew by revelation that "the holy one to be born will be called the Son of God" (Luke 1:35). He is the Son of God precisely because God, by the power of the Spirit, was the Father of Jesus.

In his incarnational sonship, the Son of God has the authority to invite others to share in a deeper way the covenantal relationship with the Father (Matt. 11:27). Israel had already received the privilege of adoption, as Moses had proclaimed, "You are the children of the LORD your God" (Deut. 14:1; see also Exod. 4:22; Rom. 9:4). Jesus extends the privilege of adoption to all who receive him, whose birth, like his, is by the Spirit of God (John 1:11–12). Those who are the children of God are in a unique sense his brothers and sisters. As children of God all members of the covenant in Christ are expected to be actively obedient to the Father, even as Jesus the unique Son of God was fully obedient to his Father's will (Matt. 12:50). Privilege without obligation is impossible. Sonship signifies obedience to the Father's will.

Related to the messianic office is the designation "Son of God," in fulfillment of God's promise to David (2 Sam. 7:16; see also Ps. 2:7). In Luke's prologue Mary calls the child that she is to bear "the Son of the Most High," who will inherit the throne of David and rule the kingdom of God forever (Luke 1:32–33). The angels likewise proclaim to the shepherds in Bethlehem that Jesus is Christ the Lord, who will be the Savior of Israel (2:11). His baptism is the beginning of his messianic mission (Mark 1:2–13). From the outset of Jesus' ministry, Mark looks at him as the Son of God. Jesus is the Son of God because he is "the Lord," whose coming is announced by John the Baptist and confirmed by the Father: "You are my Son, whom I love; with you I am well pleased" (v. 11). Even the demons recognize his authority, as did the man with the evil spirit, who cried out, "What do you want with us? . . .I know who you are—the Holy One of God" (v. 24; see also 3:11; 5:7).

Jesus' sonship reveals a messianic mission. He was appointed by the Father and empowered by the Spirit of God. In his messianic sonship he was completely obedient to the Father, as evident in the temptation narratives. Toward the end of his mission the Father glorified his Son in preparation for his suffering. On the Mount of Transfiguration he again confirmed his messianic sonship (Mark 9:2–13).[14] His obedience and suffering without cause even evoked a response from a pagan centurion at the cross: "Surely this man was the Son of God!" (15:39). The Father, evil spirits, and Gentiles witness to Jesus' being the Son of God.

The designation "Son of God" gets to the heart of Jesus' mission. Vos has given a perceptive analysis of Jesus' self-disclosure and concludes that Jesus was fully conscious of his unique oneness with God and of his messianic mission as the glorious Messiah.[15] Because of possible misconstruction he does not use the designation "messiah" of himself and reserves the fuller revelation of his nature for the disciples and through them to the church. As we have already seen, Luke portrays the earthly ministry of Jesus from the perspective of the glorified Messiah. The conception of Jesus as *the* Son of God introduces the mystery of the incarnation. God became a man! Jesus, the Son of God, has already received greater glory and authority as the Messiah who will establish God's kingdom! He is the hope of his church because he is the very focus of the Old Testament message. The Old Testament spoke of the era of the restoration of all things, of forgiveness, of the subjugation of the enemies, and of the messianic kingdom. Jesus explained to his disciples that he is the fulfillment of the Old Testament hope (Luke 24:44–47).

Son of Man

The expression "Son of Man" is our Lord's favorite way of speaking about himself and his mission.[16] Its use is limited to the Gospels, except for Acts 7:56. Jesus' use of the title as a self-designation was an attempt to force his audience to shed their wrong messianic concepts and to consider other passages of Scripture, such as Daniel 7:13–14. In Daniel's vision the Son of Man is of heavenly origin and receives the universal kingdom from God. Jesus also includes the idea of suffering as a fulfillment of the Servant passages in Isaiah (52:13–53:12). "The Son of Man" is our Lord's phrase for everything the Messiah must do, avoiding the stereotypes of Jewish messianic ideology. The phrase brings before us every aspect of Jesus' ministry: his earthly ministry, his suffering, and his coming in glory.

First, the Son of Man comes from heaven, has authority from the Father, and executes his mission on earth.[17] His heavenly origin is expressed in his authority to forgive sin (Mark 2:10), his interpretation of Sabbath regulations (vv. 27–28), and his call for worldwide loyalty to himself (Matt. 13:37). Though he has authority, he humbled himself so as to live on earth and to complete his earthly ministry. His life was fully human, eating and drinking as others (11:19), but he also experienced deprivation, having no place to call his own (8:20; see also Phil. 2:5–11).

Second, the Son of Man came to suffer on earth. Our Lord has come to provide an eternal ransom for sin. His very mission consists of seeking and saving what is already lost (Luke 19:10). In order to accomplish his mission, he reveals to his disciples that he must suffer in Jerusalem (Mark 8:31–32). The whole road of humiliation was in fulfillment of the Old Testament prophets.

Third, the Son of Man will come and reveal the glory and authority that is his by virtue of his messianic office. The ministry and suffering of our Lord reflect the glory of the Son of Man in his servant role and anticipate an even greater revelation of his glory and majesty. The apostles witnessed this glory in his life (John 1:14), on the Mount of Transfiguration (Matt. 17:1–13; 2 Peter 1:16–18), and in his ascension to glory. Upon the completion of his mission the Son of Man returned to glory, where he assumed the divine authority, seating himself at the right hand of the Father in preparation for assuming full authority over the earth when he comes in glory, as evidenced by the presence of angels (Matt. 16:27; 26:64; Mark 8:38; 13:26–27). His coming will be unexpected (Matt. 24:27, 36; Luke 12:40), and it will visibly introduce the final stages in redemptive history (Matt. 19:28; 25:31–32, 46).

Lord

From a post-resurrection perspective, Luke presents Jesus as the incarnate Lord of glory. For him, "Lord" signifies no other one than the exalted Jesus, who is seated at the right hand of the Father (Acts 2:36). The use of "Lord" in the Gospel of Luke thus presupposes this exalted connotation (Luke 7:13, 19; 10:1; and many other references). Luke alone reports the story of the two men from Emmaus and their affirmation to the disciples: "It is true! The Lord has risen and has appeared to Simon" (24:34). The Lord who arose is no one other than God himself, incarnate, of whom the angels said, "Today in the town of David a Savior has been born to you; he is Christ the Lord" (2:11). Jesus, in his messianic office is Lord (Ps. 110; Matt. 22:41–45).

John also shows a deep awareness of the risen Christ, as he speaks of him as "the Lord" (John 4:3; 6:23; 11:2). The confession of Thomas expresses John's conviction regarding the true nature of Jesus: "My Lord and my God!" (20:28).

The usage of Luke and John is in accordance with the view held by the early church that Jesus is Lord (Acts 1:6, 24; 4:29; 9:5; 10:4, 14; 22:8, 19). For example, Peter presents Jesus as the Messiah of God: "God has made this Jesus, whom you crucified, both Lord and Christ" (2:36).

Savior

Jesus Christ is the gospel incarnate. The position of Jesus as the Son of God explains the Good News. He did not come to force his rule over people or to tell them how they might live a better life; he came, primarily, that he might serve humankind, particularly through his sacrificial death on the cross. Jesus declared, "For even the Son of Man did not come to be served, but to serve, and to give his life as a ransom for many" (Mark 10:45). Here, then, is the essence of the ministry of

Jesus, from Mark's perspective. God himself came in the flesh and took upon himself the form of a man. The incarnational ministry of Jesus sought to reconcile individuals to God and to atone for the sins of mankind (John 4:42).

Two passages in the Gospels call Jesus "Savior" (Luke 2:11; John 4:42).[18] The designation "Savior" denotes much more than his ability to redeem from sin. He is the Deliverer-Ruler who establishes his rule with power, glory, and vindication. The Babe of Bethlehem is the Divine Warrior, the Savior, the Messiah, the Lord (Luke 2:11)!

With the coming of Jesus Christ, the era of the restoration is so much nearer. It must be observed that Mark intended to give us "the beginning" of the gospel, up to the resurrection and ascension of Jesus. The pouring out of the Holy Spirit and the apostolic mission mark the next stage in the gospel of Jesus, which continues until it has been preached to all nations (Mark 13:10).

Son of David

Related to the messianic office is the designation "Son of David," in fulfillment of God's promise to David (2 Sam. 7:16). To this end both Matthew and Luke give the genealogy of Jesus (Matt. 1:1–16; Luke 3:23–38), but Matthew's "genealogy of Jesus Christ the Son of David" (Matt. 1:1) more clearly relates Jesus to David's lineage. Matthew reflects on the popular use, according to which Jesus is the messianic Son of David, whose messiahship was apparent even to Gentiles who expressed faith in the Jewish messiah.[19] But Jewish leaders were responsible for the Jewish rejection of the Son of David (chap. 23).

Jesus

The name "Jesus" (which means "salvation") signifies all that the names of our Lord mean singly and in totality. At his birth Mary called him "Jesus" (Matt. 1:23), which Matthew associates with the Immanuel sign of Isaiah 7:14. The presence of God in Jesus is evident in so many ways that the name "Jesus" evokes the association of each of the titles: Jesus the Son of Man, Jesus the Son of God, Jesus the Messiah, Jesus the Lord, and Jesus the Savior. God revealed his name in the Old Testament as Yahweh, and the New Testament affirms that Yahweh is present among people in the God-man whose name is Jesus. "In his name" the new people of God are baptized (Matt. 28:19), assemble together for worship (18:20), do good works (Mark 9:41; see Col. 3:17), and experience the joy of answered prayers (John 14:13; 16:24). The Christian lives in anticipation of the great revelation of Jesus' glory, when every knee will bow to him and every tongue confess that he is Lord of all (Phil. 2:9–11).

CONCLUSION

The titles of our Lord convey a message. The sum total of the titles do not give the totality of who Jesus is. Each title gives a distinct impression, and each title is related to the others. Thus, the apostles reflect on Jesus as the revelation of God. Jesus' self-revelation contributes to our understanding of the God-man, but there is no understanding apart from commitment. Jesus' teaching and self-revelation bring us into the very presence of God. He cannot be shoved aside or rejected, as Israel had resisted the prophets in their times. Jesus makes the bold claim that he is God incarnate. He is the Son of God, the Son of Man, the Messiah of God! He promises deliverance and glory to those who listen, but judgment and shame to all who reject him. May we respond to his claims as Thomas did, as he cried out, "My Lord and my God!"

CHAPTER 29

The Kingdom of God

Jesus' teaching on the kingdom forms his most distinctive message.[1] Through explicit and parabolic teaching Jesus presents the present aspect of the kingdom of God as well as its future glory. The kingdom concept in Jesus' teaching interrelates with the messianic concept as two focuses by which the mystery of Jesus' mission and work may be apprehended. Jesus presents a multifaceted understanding of the kingdom: it is both present and future, spiritual and political, earthly and heavenly. We consider here four aspects of the kingdom of God in light of the person and work of Jesus Christ.

THE OLD AND THE NEW

Historical Development

The kingdom of God was already a reality in the Old Testament.[2] There the Lord revealed himself as the great King over all of his creation. He continues to sustain and bless richly the whole realm of his rule with food, drink, beauty, and the blessing of procreation. He is indeed the Creator-King. But he is also the Redeemer-King, who reveals himself to be the Divine Warrior, whose rule extends over the nations in salvation and in judgment. He had shown Israel his mighty deeds in the Exodus, the crossing of the Red Sea, the Conquest, and many other great acts of deliverance. They had come to know him as their King (Exod. 15), who had constituted the people of Israel to be his "royal priesthood," or a kingdom of priests that were characterized by holiness. They were his kingdom on earth. In order to advance his rule, he covenanted with David that David's dynasty would establish a lasting kingship, serving as the Lord's undershepherd over his people. Through the Davidic kingship the Lord intended to benefit his people with a rule of peace, righteousness, justice, wisdom, prosperity, and exaltation above the nations. These characteristics largely prevailed during the era of David and Solomon, when Israel had become "the royal nation."

Because of the division of the kingdom into North and South, the continual rejection of the Lord and his prophets, and the persistent idolatry, God set Israel aside for a while in the Exile. The Lord's fidelity and love, however, kept the twelve tribes from becoming extinguished. The Lord did as he had promised. He brought a remnant of the people back to the Promised Land; restored their cities, fields, and orchards; and reaffirmed the covenants, including the commitment of God's rule over his people. The theocracy—but not the monarchy—was restored. Though the Lord reconfirmed his commitment in this direction by giving Zerubbabel the promises of David (Hag. 2:23; Zech. 4:14), Zerubbabel died without hereditary succession of his authority.

For some five hundred years the Jewish people were subject to other nations and failed to see a great realization of the prophetic word about a new era of fulfillment, restoration, and universal messianic rule. There were, however, clear evidences of the truth of the prophetic message: the Lord had restored the remnant of the twelve tribes, the temple worship flourished, the presence of the Lord was their protection and guidance, and the Spirit of God had transformed the syncretistic and pagan hearts of their ancestors to hearts desirous of the law and of doing the will of God. Even during the best years, however, the hearts of the pious Jews were beating hard in anticipation of the great era of deliverance and vindication. Though there was little agreement on the form of that era, their hope was fixed on the Lord, at whose command the Messiah would appear and inaugurate the kingdom of God in a more magnificent manner than the era of David and Solomon. The messianic era was also known as "the age to come," in contrast to "the present age."[3]

Theological Dimensions

The Old Testament presents us with a threefold perspective on the kingdom. First, God is the great King over all of his creation. His realm extends from shore to shore, over animals and humans, over subject and hostile nations. He is the sovereign Creator-King. Second, the Lord has established his kingdom in Israel (Ps. 114:2) and his "footstool" in Jerusalem (Ps. 132:7, 13–15). He is the covenant God who is the Redeemer-King, by whose acts Israel receives provision, protection, and guidance (vv. 15–16). To this end, he also covenanted himself with David, confirming the promise of his glorious rule through the dynasty of David (vv. 17–18). The third aspect is the prophetic perspective: God's kingdom is yet to come in fullness. Throughout the Old Testament the people of God long for a greater fulfillment of the promises, knowing that the present reality is a shadow in comparison with things to come.

With Jesus' coming, the angels, John the Baptist, and the heavenly voice from the Father all attest that the kingdom of God is present among human beings. In the Gospels, Jesus presents himself as the one sent by the Father to inaugurate the messianic kingdom. As we have seen, the messianic titles reveal Jesus as the heavenly King, who, after his self-humiliation and suffering, arose and ascended to his sublime glory, which he will make known at his glorious coming, or Parousia. It is noteworthy that Jesus' teaching on the kingdom assumes the *newness* and what we may call the *nowness* of the kingdom. The kingdom is Jesus Christ, and Jesus Christ is the kingdom.

Jesus and the Kingdom

The close identification of Jesus with the kingdom as well as his emphasis on the kingdom have given the impression that the kingdom is new, unlike anything God has done before. Ladd allows for God's kingdom activities in the Old Testament, but hesitantly writes, "In some real sense God's Kingdom *came* into history in the person and mission of Jesus."[4] Vos rightly ascribes this *de novo* emphasis in the Gospels as arising from the historical situation. The preaching of the kingdom presents us with the reality and the presence of the King, continuous with the Old Testament proclamation, but discontinuous with the contemporary expectations.[5] Moreover, the eschatological flavor of Jesus' teaching about the kingdom relates to that of the prophets and differs from the eschatological views of his contemporaries. While one may thus easily gain the impression of newness and difference from the Gospels, a closer look at Jesus' teaching does not warrant that impression. Three passages are representative of the nowness and newness of the kingdom: Matthew 3:1–2; 11:12–13; and Luke 16:16.

According to Luke 16:16, Jesus contrasts the Old Testament era—the period of "the Law and the Prophets"—with his presence, "the good news of the kingdom of God." The context of this passage sets Jesus in dialogue with the Pharisees, who wanted to keep both the law and the material benefits of this world. Jesus had just given them an ultimatum: either God or money (v. 13). Whereas the Law and the Prophets were sufficient for the people, the ministry of John the Baptist and the coming of Jesus required that they also listen to the proclamation of "the good news of the kingdom of God." In this way Jesus means to call them away from their self-sufficiency (they "loved money" [v. 14]) and to call them to a renewed devotion to and understanding of the Law and the Prophets. The contrast here is not between Old Testament and kingdom but between the Old Testament and Jesus Christ, or, even better, between the common misconceptions about the Old Testament and Jesus, the interpreter of the law of God. This function comes out in his ruling, "Anyone who divorces his wife and marries another woman commits adultery, and the man who marries a divorced woman commits adultery" (v. 18).

The second passage is very similar to the first. In Matthew 11:12–13, our Lord speaks with commendation about John, before whom "the Prophets and the Law prophesied" and after whom "the kingdom of heaven has been forcefully advancing." It is no small wonder that the Old Testament and the kingdom could be viewed in a contrastive way. Upon closer reading, our Lord is persuading the crowds that a new era is here, one in fulfillment of the prophetic word. John the Baptist was not just another ascetic but a fulfillment of God's Word to Malachi (3:1; 4:5). He is the Elijah, whom the Jews were expecting to inaugurate the new era (Matt. 11:14). There is no turning back in the history of redemption because, beginning with John, the growth of the kingdom is more evident. Our Lord demonstrates that the kingdom's *progress* was now rapid and unexpected. He does not teach that God's kingdom has no reality in the Old Testament. Instead, he sets off the Old Testament stage of the kingdom from the new manifestation in himself as the dawn of a new age, but suggests that the inauguration of the new age was not without opposition.[6]

The third passage relates to the first two. In Matthew 3:1–2, John the Baptist proclaims that the kingdom of God is near. That proclamation assumes that the kingdom has not been in existence before, that it is new, and that its beginning is to be traced to Jesus. Here again, however, I stress that the Jews knew their Old Testament and spoke about the kingdom of God as a present reality. They idiomatically called their observance of the Torah the act of taking the yoke of the kingdom.[7] John calls for repentance and baptism in the light of the coming of the Messiah, the messianic era, and the Day of the Lord. For him the coming of the kingdom signifies the inauguration of the last days: the Day of the Lord in salvation and judgment. The theme of the nearness of the kingdom is associated with repentance and confession of sin. For the gospel writers the presence of Jesus signifies the beginning of a new era of the last days, one that prepares for the final revelation of the Day of the Lord.

THE UNIVERSAL CONCERN

The Christ of the New Testament is the Creator-Redeemer-King. The incarnate Son of God came to redeem what was lost, and his mission extended to *everything* that is lost. The kingdom of God signifies primarily the actual rule of God over all of his creation. In the Old Testament God expressed his rule over Israel by mighty acts of deliverance (Exod. 15:1–18; Pss. 93–94; 96–99; 103:19; 145:11). The people of God longed for a greater manifestation of the rule of God, especially on the basis of the promises of God and on the message of the prophets (Pss. 2; 47; 67–68; 72; Isa. 2:1–4; 4:2–6; Zeph. 3:14–20; Zech. 14). The Lord established his rule through his servants Moses,

Joshua, the prophets, and the Davidic dynasty. In the coming of the Messiah, however, there is renewed excitement with God's working in redemptive history. The Lord will establish a universal kingdom through the Messiah, according to his Word (Luke 1:68–79).[8]

The gospel writers record this universal concern of Jesus' mission for both Jews and Gentiles. We have already emphasized that the Gospels are not anti-Semitic, because the door for the Jews is always kept ajar. Though individuals and groups fall under condemnation, Jesus came "to give his people the knowledge of salvation" (Luke 1:77), and through him the Lord leads Israel in the fulfillment of his covenant (vv. 54–55). The fidelity of God extends to Israel, in spite of their rejection of Jesus. However, Jesus' mission also concerns the nations. He has come

> to shine on those living in darkness
> and in the shadow of death.
>
> (1:79)

He is

> a light for revelation to the Gentiles
> and for glory to your people Israel.
>
> (2:32)

The kingdom concept entails God's universal rule over his creation through the Messiah. To this end, our Lord taught us to pray,

> your kingdom come,
> your will be done
> on earth as it is in heaven.
>
> (Matt. 6:10)

The goal of the kingdom is nothing less than the extension of God's absolute rule over the earth, the sphere of his creation and redemption. Ridderbos has well said,

> The idea of the kingdom of God is more comprehensive exactly because it is not only oriented to the redemption of God's people, but to the self-assertion of God in *all* his works. Not only does it place Israel, but also the heathen nations, the world, and even the whole creation, in the wide perspective of the realization of all God's rights and promises.[9]

THE SUBJECTS OF THE KINGDOM

Jesus came to call out men and women, boys and girls. The kingdom inaugurated a further development in the selection process by which the true children of the kingdom would be identified. The Lord had set forth the requirements of the kingdom to the children of Abraham through Moses. Listening to Moses was equivalent to listening to the Lord. In the revelation of the Son, the Father reveals again what he expects of all true children of Abraham, if they are to be heirs of the kingdom.

First, the children of the kingdom must *evidence a childlike faith* (Matt. 19:14). There is no other entrance into the kingdom than by the exclusive path of faith in Jesus as "the way" (John 14:6) and by the birth of the Spirit of God (1:12; 3:3–8).

Second, the children of the kingdom must continually and diligently apply themselves to *seek the kingdom* (Matt. 6:33). External forms of piety such as fasting, prayer, and almsgiving do not qualify (vv. 1–18). True godliness is a spiritual quality resulting in conformity to God and in close alignment with his Son, the Lord Jesus Christ (Matt. 19:23–24; Luke 18:29–30; 2 Thess. 1:5). Instead of external requirements, our Lord renews the prophetic call for regeneration, internal renewal, and true spirituality. He expects nothing less than faith, good works, observance of the law of Jesus (discipleship), spirituality, and persevering prayer (Matt. 8:10–12; 10:37–39; 12:50; 16:24–25; 25:31–46), regardless of the cost (13:44–46). Bonhoeffer calls this requirement "the cost of discipleship."

Third, the children of the kingdom must *recognize that their access is given by Christ*; it never comes through their own works (Luke 22:29). As long as the two kingdoms remain, the heirs of the everlasting kingdom must be willing to suffer and experience humiliation (Matt. 5:3–10; Acts 14:22; 2 Thess. 1:5). The kingdom is a kingdom of righteousness, whose source and goal is God himself. Entrance into the kingdom is a gift and stands radically opposed to any attempt to save oneself or to pacify God.

Fourth, the children of the kingdom *are blessed*. They know God as their Father. They have received justification, life, and forgiveness. Living harmoniously with the rules of the kingdom leads to blessed benefits (Matt. 5:3–10). The rewards for kingdom living span both the present life and the life to come, and they touch upon both material and spiritual aspects. Even when being "persecuted because of righteousness," a child of God has reason to "rejoice and be glad" (vv. 10, 12).

Fifth, the children of the kingdom *enjoy a foretaste of the future*. Their lives are lived under the shadow of the eschaton. The kingdom reflects like a mirror the age to come in the present. Jesus is the key to the era of restoration. The newness of life, sealed by the Spirit of God, is a token of the future restoration. The church, the act of preaching, individual sanctification (personal ethics), and societal expressions of the kingdom are all part of the radical transformation bringing in the new heaven and the new earth.

PRESENT AND FUTURE

One of the main issues in any discussion about the kingdom is whether it is present or future.[10] The prophets proclaimed that the kingdom was future, while there was already a real, concrete, institutionalization of the kingdom in the monarchic theocracy. Our Lord spoke of the kingdom as present, as growing, as cataclysmic, and as future. Partly because much of his teaching on this subject is in parables, it is not easy to categorize. The New Testament evidence is subject to interpretation.

According to the parables of the weeds and the yeast, the kingdom grows slowly (Matt. 13:24–43; cf. Mark 4:26–29). Our Lord taught the certainty and inevitability of the progression of the kingdom in the parable of the mustard seed (Mark 4:30–32), along with pointing out the personal responsibility in responding to the Word of our Lord in his parable of the sower (Matt. 13:1–23). He taught the ultimacy of the kingdom as an obtainable goal in the parables of the hidden treasure and the pearl (vv. 44–46). Together with the future separation of the wicked from the righteous (the parable of the dragnet, in vv. 47–50), the parable of the wheat and the weeds recognizes the coexistence of the righteous and the wicked in the world (Mark 4:26–29).

The presence of the kingdom is uniquely concentrated in our Lord (cf. Matt. 19:27 with Luke 18:29; see also Acts 8:12; 28:31). In a certain sense Jesus himself is the kingdom of God because he reveals the dynamic and spiritual power of the kingdom in healing the sick, in casting out of demons (Matt. 12:28), in forgiving sins (Mark 2:10), in binding Satan (Matt. 12:29; see also Luke 10:18), and in proclaiming the gospel (Luke 4:16–21). The issue is not whether the kingdom is present or future, or whether he teaches realized eschatology or future eschatology. As a matter of fact, Jesus teaches both a present and a future coming of the kingdom. Jesus himself is interested neither in time nor in the manner of the progression of the kingdom (Acts 1:7). He points people to himself as the Messiah of God.

In Jesus' presence the reality of the prophetic expectation is unmistakable. There is also a hidden dimension, however, as the full manifestation of his glory has not yet appeared. The fullness, or reality of the fulfillment of the prophetic word, still awaits us. This fact keeps us from saying that Jesus fulfilled the prophetic word—the word is still in a state of being fulfilled. Presently, the believer looks at Jesus with the eyes of faith, believing that he is the Alpha and the Omega, "the Root and the Offspring of David, and the bright Morning Star" (Rev. 22:16). In response to the presence of the messianic kingdom and in anticipation of a greater revelation of his glory, the believer clings to the Law, the Prophets, the Writings, and the Gospels because they harmoniously bear witness to the glorious future awaiting the believers, the church, and the world of creation (see Luke 16:16–17, 31; 21:27–28; 24:44–47). Even while awaiting the fullness of salvation and divine vindication, the Christian knows that the kingdom is here!

Jesus' inauguration of the kingdom is a stage in the progression of the kingly rule of God, set in motion from the time of Adam and Eve's expulsion from the garden. Through the revelation to Israel—the covenants, promises, and mighty acts of the Lord—he extended his kingly rule. Through the prophets he encouraged his people by saying that he would extend his kingdom from heaven to earth. The election of Abraham, the Exodus, the Conquest, the Davidic monarchy, the temple, and the restoration from exile marked highlights in the progression of the kingdom. With the coming of our Lord, God more dramatically and effectively stirs the earth to receive his kingly rule. Heaven and earth are called into action, either to receive or to reject his kingship. Jesus forces acceptance or rejection.

CONCLUSION

Jesus' teaching on the kingdom is a central and unifying theme in the Synoptics. His presence on earth and his glorification model the presence and future glory of God's kingdom on earth. God's kingdom is present and more evident in the incarnation of the Son of God; Dodd concludes, "In the ministry of Jesus the timeless, the eternal, the transcendental has entered history."[11] But God's act in Jesus is one event, though climactic, in a series of events, and the series of God's acts reveals the kingship of God. Jesus' incarnation and proclamation are thus neither the beginning of the kingdom nor its full realization. Instead, the new kingdom stage in Jesus' coming is one element in the *progression* of God's royal acts. This view is close to Ladd's thesis that "the kingdom of God is the invasion of the God of heaven into human history for the purpose of establishing his reign among men." Ladd has two stages: the veiled coming of the kingdom in Jesus' mission and the glorious coming at the consummation. To this schema I add a prior stage: the kingdom of God in Israel. In the coming of the kingdom to Israel as confirmed in the Mosaic and Davidic covenants, God's expectations of his theocratic community differed little from what Jesus requires. However, they have been heightened in the light of Jesus' authoritative interpretation and teaching about God's kingdom as well as in view of the constant reminder that the glorious kingdom is still future. We may agree with Ladd, however, that "the Kingdom of God means that God will bring heaven to earth, and that the earth will share the heavenly life and glory."[12]

Several points bring out the precise nature of the kingdom as it was manifested in Jesus:

1. Jesus came to be victorious over Satan (Matt. 12:28).
2. The mystery of the kingdom is at work and visible to the eyes of faith (Mark 4:11).
3. The nature of the kingdom is most evident in the community of believers (Luke 17:21).
4. The people of God are sent to witness to the world that Jesus is the Christ (Acts 8:12).
5. The growth of the kingdom is inevitable (Matt. 13:24–30).
6. The personal fruit of the kingdom within the heart of the Christian is humility (Matt. 5:3).
7. The hope of the kingdom lies in the coming of Jesus Christ (Matt. 19:28).

CHAPTER 30

Jesus' Messianic Mission

THE "SERVANT" IN OLD TESTAMENT PERSPECTIVE

The unexpected intrusion of the messianic age took place in Jesus' coming as the "servant" of God. The Jews expected the glorious messianic age to introduce a new political entity. In contrast, Jesus taught that the Old Testament also revealed the humiliation and suffering of the Messiah.[1] This teaching that the Messiah must suffer comes to unique expression in Jesus' identification of himself as "the servant of God." It is clear from Acts that the early church confessed Jesus as the servant of God (Acts 3:13, 26; 4:27–30).[2] To a limited extent the early Christians applied the servant passages of Isaiah to Jesus' suffering, as did Philip when giving the gospel to the Ethiopian eunuch (8:26–40; cf. Isa. 53).

The apostles showed an understanding of Jesus' teaching on his servant role (see Matt. 8:17 [Isa. 53:4]; Matt. 12:18–21 [Isa. 42:1–4]; Luke 22:37 [Isa. 53:12]). The word "servant" has a threefold connotation in both Old Testament and New Testament: closeness in relationship, authority, and active obedience in carrying out the instructions given. In this sense the designation "Son of God" explains the incarnational obedience of our Lord to his heavenly Father.[3] The Father had appointed Jesus to be his obedient Son, as he declared at his baptism and at the Transfiguration, when he spoke from heaven, "This is my Son, whom I love; with him I am well pleased" (Matt. 3:17; cf. Isa. 42:1). The very combination of Jesus as the Suffering Servant and as the Lord of Glory is a paradox. But this paradox is the Good News![4]

The parable of the tenants (Luke 20:9–18) explains in parabolic form Jesus' mission. In this story the son must complete the mission of the servants. The servants are the prophets and teachers of the law, who were persecuted for the sake of God. The son as the heir of the kingdom would not escape suffering but would have to undergo death. Jesus as a servant thus fulfilled the Father's will and accomplished his purpose.

Even as God had spoken through his servants Moses and Elijah, representatives of the epochs of the Mosaic covenant and the prophetic ministry, and had made and confirmed his covenant with them at Mount Sinai (Exod. 24; 1 Kings 19:9–18), so the Lord confirmed the covenant by Jesus. His suffering serves to renew the covenant, which Israel has broken. At the Last Supper, Jesus spoke of his imminent suffering and of the blood of the covenant by which the kingdom of God would come: "This is my blood of the covenant, which is poured out for many. . . . I will not drink again of the fruit of the vine until that day when I drink it anew in the kingdom of God" (Mark 14:24–25).

THE "SON" AND THE CHURCH IN THE KINGDOM OF GOD

In addition to the concept of servant, the Gospels speak of the "Son" in his relation to the church. Matthew's concern with the presence of the eschatological kingdom and the glorified Christ is directly related to his interest in the church. He alone uses the word *ekklēsia* to denote Jesus' institution of the community of believers who perpetuate his ministry until his return (Matt. 16:13–20). His kingdom rule in the church is not a limitation of his kingship but rather a manifestation of his rule. Matthew brings together Jesus the Messiah with the concepts of the kingdom, the church, and the gospel mandate to make disciples of all nations (28:16–20). Jesus is the fulfillment of the Old Testament. He began this fulfillment in his earthly ministry. He is still fulfilling it, and he will come again to establish the kingdom fully. Because he has received all authority in heaven and on earth, he rules over his church and will appear with great glory to gather his elect (24:30–31; 28:18). His kingdom is forever!

The Gospel of Matthew furthers a better understanding of the affinity between the kingdom of God and the church of Jesus Christ. Jesus called all Israel to repent and to look upon him as the one sent by God. But as becomes clear in the parable of the tenants (Matt. 21:33–44), he was rejected by them. The kingdom would consequently be taken away and given to others. To this end Matthew also witnesses to the prophetic continuity of Jesus' ministry. He came as the Son, sent by the Father. The rejection of the Son, like that of the servants the prophets, signified a rejection of the Father and the certainty of divine judgment (25:31–46; see also 8:11–12). Those who preach the message of the Son are given authority in the name of Jesus to be ambassadors of the Father in proclaiming judgment or blessing (10:11–15). The mission of Jesus was given to the church in the proclamation of the kingdom in the Christ of God. Those who proclaim, worship together, and have a common faith in Jesus as the Messiah of God constitute the "remnant," or the "new people": the church of Jesus Christ (see 16:19). The church is rooted in

God's redemptive work in the Old Testament; note that the Greek *ekklēsia* corresponds to the Hebrew *qāhāl*, or congregation of Israel.[5]

The church is composed of all who believe on Jesus and suffer for him.[6] It has received authority from Jesus (Matt. 10:40; see also Mark 9:37). It extends forgiveness or divine discipline in the name of Jesus (Matt. 16:19). The authority of Jesus is thus given to the officers of the church, as they administer discipline: "I tell you the truth, whatever you bind on earth will be bound in heaven, and whatever you loose on earth will be loosed in heaven" (18:18).

What is the connection between the kingdom of God and the church of Jesus Christ? Over the last fifty years this question has been debated in evangelical circles. Here I will say only that the kingdom is a broader category than the church. The church is composed of people who follow the Messiah as his disciples, worship together, witness to him, and wait for the full establishment of the kingdom of God (Matt. 24:14; 28:18–20). Those who are members of Jesus' church must continue the mission of Jesus, and to the extent that the gospel will flourish, the kingdom will be more or less evident.

The kingdom of God is the rule of God over heaven and earth. That rule is in continuity with the Old Testament and will last forever and ever. The goal of redemptive history, however, is the full establishment of the kingdom of God on a renewed earth (Matt. 19:28). The kingdom of God was, is, and ever will be. His kingdom rule was represented in the theocracy of Israel. Those who now belong to the church may experience the power of the kingdom. Ultimately, all sin will be removed, the wicked will be cast out, and the kingdom will appear in its full splendor (13:31–50). This differentiation has been well expressed by Ladd, "There can be no kingdom without a church—those who have acknowledged God's rule—and there can be no church without God's kingdom; but they remain two distinguishable concepts: the rule of God and the fellowship of men."[7] The early church's conception of Jesus accords with this interrelationship of the Messiah, the kingdom, and the church. According to Acts 2:36, Jesus is the "Messiah-Lord, i.e., an enthroned Messiah as contrasted with a suffering Messiah."[8]

JESUS' RESURRECTION AS THE CLIMAX OF HIS MISSION

The center and meaning of redemptive history is the resurrection of Jesus Christ. Without the resurrection there is no Christianity, no basis for Christian preaching, and no hope. Each of the gospel writers moves us to the resurrection hope, as the crucified Christ is raised by the power of God. The resurrection is the turning point from creation to the new creation, from the old to the new. The resurrection validates the promises of God. "It is a turning point that ensues from what preceded and that at the same time prepares for the consummation."[9] The resurrection of Jesus validates the incarnation, the mission, and the authority of Jesus the Messiah (see Acts 2:36). Each gospel writer wrote from the perspective of the resurrected and glorified Christ, as he set forth the urgency in believing that Jesus alone is the Messiah of God. Ladd captured the meaning of the Resurrection, as he wrote with great insight:

> In short, earliest Christianity did not consist of a new doctrine about God nor of a new hope of immortality nor even of new theological insights about the nature of salvation. It consisted of the recital of a great event, of a mighty act of God: the raising of Christ from the dead.[10]

The resurrection of Jesus as an eschatological event is the pivot around which the future glorification, consummation, and renewal revolves.[11]

THE CONTINUITY OF JESUS' MISSION

The Son of God came to be the Savior of the world, as the angel proclaimed on the night of Jesus' birth (Luke 2:11). Indeed, the central verse in the entire Gospel of Luke is the proclamation, "For the Son of Man came to seek and to save what was lost" (19:10). Luke demonstrates Jesus' concern for the lost through the parables of the lost sheep and the lost son (chap. 15), which also show the Father's great love for sinners. He also stresses that Jesus has come for *all* who are lost—for Jews, for Samaritans (9:52–56; 17:11–19), and for Gentiles (2:32; 3:6, 8; 4:25–27; 7:9; 24:47). Jesus came to save people, irrespective of their ethnic group or social class. He came for the outcasts of society, such as prostitutes, lepers, and tax collectors. Moreover, the gospel of Jesus Christ is a holistic gospel that deals with both body and soul. Jesus brings words of forgiveness even as he heals those who are sick or lame. He is thus truly the Savior of the world.

The Church's Call to Mission

He called his disciples to *continue* his mission.[12] The Son, sent by the Father, appointed the disciples to establish his kingdom: "I confer on you a kingdom, just as my Father conferred one on me, so that you may eat and drink at my table in my kingdom and sit on thrones, judging the twelve tribes of Israel" (Luke 22:29–30). In addition, they received power to proclaim the gospel, insight into the Old Testament in the light of Jesus' ministry, and power to offer God's forgiveness in the name of Jesus (24:44–47). He expects his followers to give full devotion to him, because "we owe to God such allegiance and devotion and love. Our love for God must be so great that all other loves by comparison are but hatred."[13] Jesus promised to send "power from on high" to his church in the person of the Holy Spirit, who continues the presence of the glorified Christ. At his Parousia Jesus will bring about the restoration of all things: "At that time they will see the Son of Man coming in a cloud with power and great glory. When these things begin to take place, stand up and lift up your heads, because your redemption is drawing near" (21:27–28).

The Spirit's Work in the Church

The era of the Spirit—between the Incarnation and the Consummation—is preparatory and anticipatory to the full revelation of the glorious Messiah. Jesus as the Son of God is one with the Father (John 17:20–21), shares in the glory of God (v. 24), and shares his glory with all his followers by sending the Holy Spirit (14:15–27; 16:14–15; 20:21–23). The Holy Spirit's mission is to share the benefits of the glorified Christ with those who believe on Jesus. The Spirit reveals the Christ, teaches, and consoles (15:18–16:15). The Spirit is the helper who assures the church that Jesus has not forsaken his own (14:26). He is the Spirit of truth who comes from the Father as well as from the Son (15:26) and convicts the world of sin, righteousness, and judgment. In so doing, the Spirit comes to sanctify God's people (17:17–19), to keep them from the world, which is condemned already (16:8–11), and to prepare them for the great glory awaiting them.

THE NEW LIFE IN CHRIST

Another important focus of Christ's sonship is his gift of a new way of life to his people. He is the Good Shepherd, who fulfills the promise of the Davidic covenant in that the Davidic Messiah was to be a shepherd for his people. Jesus is the shepherd who takes care of his sheep (John 10:2–4) and sacrifices his life for them (vv. 11, 17–18). The sheep are all those who hear the voice of the shepherd, Jews as well as Gentiles. They are the two groups of sheep that have to be brought together into one flock (v. 16). The flock of Jesus Christ is characterized by its spiritual transformation. The sheep are the children of God who have been regenerated by the working of the Holy Spirit. They are not born of flesh and blood only, but they are born by the Spirit of God (1:12–13; 3:1–8; 8:39–41). Those who have been born by the Spirit of God will experience a new way of life. They need not be afraid, even in his physical absence, because he assures them of his victory: "I have told you these things, so that in me you may have peace. In this world you will have trouble. But take heart! I have overcome the world" (16:33).

The new way of life is characterized by being filled with the Holy

Spirit and by being satisfied with Jesus. The child of God no longer desires worldly satisfaction for his spiritual thirst, because Jesus now satisfies his needs (John 4:13–15; 6:35; 7:37–38). The newness leads to an abundant life, from which the child of God will show a deeper commitment of love (13:34–35; 17:26; 21:15–19). Love is the expression of obedience to Jesus: "Whoever has my commands and obeys them, he is the one who loves me. He who loves me will be loved by my Father, and I too will love him and show myself to him" (14:21). The child of God, in union with the Father and the Son, must become a fruitful branch of the vine, bearing fruit by doing what Jesus has commanded (15:1–13). This obedience encompasses all of life in that it follows the example of Jesus Christ, who willingly gave his life for others.

Conclusion to Part 9

The Gospels are the Good News proclamation by and for the church to witness to the person and work of Jesus the Christ. His several titles, as well as the teachings and miracles of his earthly ministry, all point to the fact that Jesus of Nazareth is the focus of the whole of the Old Testament and the center of the redemptive plan of God. In Jesus, God has inaugurated a new era in the plan of salvation, and Jesus has commissioned the church to do the work and proclaim the word of his kingdom until he returns in glory. The King has come, declaring the good news of the gospel. He has also accomplished the work necessary to give that gospel power and life. Even as his church serves him, he rules as the King of the universe, awaiting the day when all his enemies will be made a footstool for his feet and every knee shall bow and "every tongue confess that Jesus Christ is Lord, to the glory of God the Father" (Phil. 2:11).

Jesus teaches the sufficiency of the Law and the Prophets as preparation for the coming of the kingdom of God (Luke 16:19–31). He affirms that the Law and the Prophets were proclaimed until John the Baptist and that, since that time, the kingdom of God has been preached (v. 16). Jesus is not saying that, with the proclamation of the kingdom of God, the Law and Prophets are set aside. Instead, they continue to witness to the Messiah and to the messianic era. If one is sensitive to the Old Testament Scriptures, then one will respond to God's revelation in Jesus Christ.

Jesus embodied the kingdom of God within himself, for the kingdom has been given to him (Luke 22:29). Those who desire to be included in the kingdom must seek the kingdom in order to find it (Matt. 6:33). On several occasions Jesus compared the kingdom to a treasure to which one may devote great expense and time. His kingdom is not merely one of flesh and blood, but of the Spirit. Those who follow him may do so only in the power of the Spirit of God, not for the sake of human reward. Righteousness, prayer, fasting, and acts of love are valid only when practiced for the sake of God (vv. 6, 18).

The kingdom of God has not yet come fully to earth. Jesus' disciples thought that the kingdom would come instantly (Luke 19:11), but Jesus revealed that he would first have to leave the earth. In his physical absence, the apostles and the church could continue his mission by using what had been given to them (vv. 12–27). The parable of the mustard seed demonstrates the triumphant growth of the kingdom, as does the parable of the leaven (13:18–21). The parable of the wheat and the weeds (Matt. 13:24–30), however, shows how the righteous will have to live together with the wicked. Within Jesus' teaching a tension exists between the triumph of the kingdom and the progression of the kingdom in this world. At times the kingdom may not be clearly distinguishable because of the presence of evil in the world. Jesus makes clear, however, that a reward is given to those who persevere in seeking his kingdom and in developing the gifts they have received. Jesus promises that whoever has sacrificed anything on behalf of the kingdom will be greatly rewarded both in this life and in the life to come (Luke 18:29–30).

Jesus' inauguration of the kingdom was in continuity with the kingdom of God before his advent. Indeed, he taught that Abraham, Isaac, and Jacob, as well as the prophets, were part of the kingdom of God (Luke 13:28). The Gospels reveal, however, that in Christ a new era of restoration and fulfillment within the kingdom has taken place. The Old Testament idea of kingdom fulfillment focused primarily on the establishment of God's rule in the world through his people Israel. The advent of Jesus demonstrated a broader perspective. Jesus the Messiah brings complete victory, even over Satan (Luke 10:18–20; John 12:31). Satan's power is already weakened in this world (Matt. 12:28–29). Now all men and women, not just Israelites, may receive the blessings of God's kingdom rule in Jesus Christ.

Jesus' call for repentance has an eschatological dimension.[1] The transformation of the present order is *radical*. It can take place only through divine judgment on the earth and the separation of sinners from the righteous, the goats from the sheep. The Jesus of the Gospels demands a radical obedience, just because the eschaton is experienced in the anticipation of his return, the general resurrection, and the judgment to come.

363

Part 10

The Apostolic Era

Introduction to Part 10

The New Testament gives us an account of Jesus' ministry, the preaching of the gospel of the kingdom, and the extension of the people of God. The Books of Luke and Acts have a unique place among the New Testament writings as they mirror redemptive historical developments of the New Testament as a whole. Moreover, the Luke-Acts corpus represents a theological perspective of Jesus as the risen and glorified Christ from three vantage points: the ministry of the glorified Messiah while on earth, the ministry of the glorified Messiah at the right hand of the Father, and the ministry of the glorified Messiah in the Spirit. The focal point of Luke-Acts is Jesus, who through suffering obtained the glorious inheritance and who shares the benefits of his victory with his church, composed of Jews and Gentiles. The Epistles witness to (1) the involvement of the triune God in the application of redemption, (2) the extension of the kingdom, (3) the establishment of churches, (4) the adaptation of the gospel to the Gentile world, and (5) the hope in the glorious kingdom that is to come.

In order to capture a sense of how Acts and the Epistles testify to these things, we shall consider the literary contribution of Acts and the Epistles in relation to the canonical situation, namely, the development of the kingdom from Judah to the Gentile world. The importance of this period lies in the continuing ministry of Jesus Christ, the extension of the gospel, the ministry of the the Spirit, and the progressive fulfillment of the prophetic word. In these chapters we shall consider the following themes:

1. the apostolic confession of Jesus as Christ and Lord;

2. the continuity of the ministry of Jesus in the church by the power of the Holy Spirit in giving gifts to the members, in providing officers to the body, and in uniting the varied membership into one body;

3. the greater reality of the kingdom of God in the Spirit of Jesus and thus the closeness of the eschaton;

4. the progression of the kingdom in the church of Jesus Christ;

5. the apostolic *paradosis*, or tradition, concerning the work and ministry of Jesus Christ (i.e., the gospel);[1]

6. the apostolic preparation for a new age of church leadership; and

7. the apostolic hope that Jesus will return and will fully and gloriously accomplish his mission.

CHAPTER 31

The Apostolic Witness to the Risen Christ

The New Testament writings attest to the importance of Jesus' incarnation, but even more to his being glorified as the Lord of Lords and the Kings of Kings. He is the Messiah of God and the Lord Jesus Christ. The Acts of the Apostles together with the Epistles teach, apply, and give insight into the mystery of the Incarnation, the Atonement, and of the glorious place of the Messiah in the plan of God the Father. The purpose of these writings is basically to present Jesus as the one by whom the promises and covenants of God will come to complete fulfillment. The Acts and the Epistles are the revelation of God the Father, as they witness to the Christ, and this revelation is fully in accord with the Old Testament Scriptures. Both Old Testament and New Testament witness to the glorious things spoken about the Christ.

In this chapter I consider the canonical function of Acts, Hebrews, and the Catholic Epistles. These books present us with the new era of the Spirit of Christ, the church, and the apostles. In reviewing the canonical function, the reader should come to a greater appreciation of:

1. the continuity of Jesus' ministry as the glorious Lord and Messiah;
2. the continuity of Jesus' ministry in the Spirit;
3. the continuity of Jesus' ministry in the church;
4. the expectation of Jesus' coming in glory, bringing both judgment and deliverance;
5. the apostolic authority of Peter, John, and Paul in the establishment of the church universal and leaders such as James and Jude, brothers of our Lord;
6. the gradual shift from the synagogue to the church, from the Jews to the Gentiles; and
7. the permutation from the apostolic authority to the leadership of elders and deacons in the churches.

THE ACTS OF THE APOSTLES

Acts is a continuation of the Gospel of Luke.[1] The gospel ends with Jesus' affirmation of the Father's promise of the Spirit and a charge to

368

remain in Jerusalem (Luke 24:48–49).[2] The prologue to Acts establishes the connection between the two books. The gospel sets forth "all that Jesus began to do and to teach until the day he was taken up to heaven" (Acts 1:1–2), whereas Acts presents us with what Jesus *continued* to do and teach through the ministry of his apostles.

The Book of Acts was not primarily written to record the history of the early church.[3] Though the historical information is reliable, Luke's primary concern was theological.[4] He shows a concern for the continuity of the ministry of Jesus in the apostolic ministry. To this end, he uses sermons, alludes to miracles of the apostles, and provides summary narratives as literary devices to connect the ministry of Jesus in the Gospels with the ministry of the resurrected Christ. The reader of Acts is thus brought to the conclusion that Jesus is present in the Spirit.[5]

Sermons and Speeches

Sermons and speeches are a prominent feature of the Book of Acts.[6] Nearly one-third of the book is given to the spoken word. (See table 13.) Rather than presenting merely a sampling of apostolic preaching, Luke has a theological purpose. First, the sermons and speeches show that the preaching of the apostles is *in continuity* with the teaching of Jesus. Jesus preached in the context of the synagogue, as well as outside, and so did the apostles.[7] Jesus focused on the gospel of the coming kingdom. His followers preach Jesus as the Messiah of God and perform mighty miracles in his name (Acts 4:30; 16:18). They quote extensively from the Old Testament as they set forth the gospel of Jesus the Messiah: his death, resurrection, and present messianic rule.[8]

TABLE 13. SERMONS AND SPEECHES IN ACTS

Text	Speaker	Occasion
2:14–41	Peter	Sermon at Pentecost
3:11–26	Peter	Sermon in Solomon's Portico
4:8–12; 5:29–32	Peter	Speeches before the Sanhedrin
7:1–53	Stephen	Defense before the Sanhedrin
10:34–43	Peter	Sermon at Cornelius's house
13:13–48	Paul	Sermon in Pisidian Antioch
14:15–17	Paul	Appeal to the crowd at Lystra
17:22–34	Paul	Sermon on the Areopagus
20:17–35	Paul	Address to the Ephesian elders
22:1–21	Paul	Defense before the crowd in Jerusalem
26:2–27	Paul	Defense before the authorities
28:25–28	Paul	Defense before the Jewish leaders

Second, the sermons and acts of the apostles also testify to a *progression* in the history of redemption. In his sermon at Pentecost, Peter explains the outpouring of the Spirit as the new act of God in fulfilling his word (Acts 2:16–21). The presence of the Spirit is the evidence of Jesus' resurrection and ascension to glory (vv. 22–35; cf. 7:55). Peter invites the representatives from the Diaspora ("God-fearing Jews from every nation under heaven" [2:5]) to share in the new age by faith in Jesus and the gift of the Holy Spirit. They may enter the new age, for theirs is the promise (v. 39), but only upon repentance and baptism "in the name of Jesus Christ" (v. 38).

Third, the *shift* from Peter to Paul highlights the theological perspective of Acts. Peter is a transition figure between the ministry of our Lord and Paul. Through his ministry the church was established (Acts 2:38–41), it prospered (vv. 42–47), it gave testimony to the power of the glorified Christ (5:12–16), and it opened its doors to the Gentiles (10:1–11:18). At the council in Jerusalem, the apostle Peter gave a persuasive speech concerning the grace of God saving both Jews and Gentiles (15:6–11). With the growth of interest in the Gentile mission and the success granted to Paul, however, the position of the apostle Paul becomes more important in the latter half of the book.

Paul is the apostle to the Gentiles and the apostle of freedom, who understood more clearly the prophetic expectation (especially in Isaiah), who had a special call from Christ, and who focused more sharply on the theological issues raised by the churches during his missionary journeys.[9] From a canonical perspective the place of Paul gains in prominence as the representative of the apostles and continues in this role for each successive generation of Christians. Moreover, the present location of the Pauline Epistles after the Acts of the Apostles witnesses to the place reserved for Paul.[10] Childs correctly notes that the reading of the Epistles must be within the theological perspective of Acts:

> The canon has retained the Pauline letters, but within the framework of Acts which provides hermeneutical guidelines for their interpretation. . . . However, Acts instructs the community of faith in one direction in which to move by translating the significance of Paul's original life and message for a different generation of readers who did not share in Paul's historical ministry.[11]

Miracles

In addition to the literary use of the sermons and speeches, Luke also employs the "proof from miracle" method to demonstrate that the mission of Jesus finds a greater fulfillment in the apostolic era.[12] Peter healed the crippled man "in the name of Jesus Christ of Nazareth" (Acts 3:6). The apostles "performed many miraculous signs and wonders" (5:12). People even carried their sick into the streets in hope that Peter's shadow might heal them (v. 15). The apostolic reputation brought the sick to Jerusalem from surrounding towns. It was evident to all that Jesus' followers had the power to heal and the authority to cast out demons (v. 16).[13] The power of Christ also attended the ministry of Paul to the Gentiles, as the mere touching of handkerchiefs and aprons healed those who were sick and cast out demons (19:11–12). The apostles performed the signs and wonders in the name of Jesus, giving honor to his name, so that they were used as an evangelistic tool: "In this way the word of the Lord spread widely and grew in power" (v. 20; see also v. 17).

The outpouring of the Spirit, the evidences of the Spirit, and the mighty signs of apostolic authority powerfully establish that the apostolic era is the second phase of Jesus' appointed mission to bring in the fullness of the restoration. The fulfillment of the prophetic word is Jesus, whose authority is established in the outpouring of the Holy Spirit on the church. The Spirit is the gift of the ascended and glorified Messiah and inaugurates "times of refreshing" (3:19).

Summary Narratives

The so-called summary narratives form a characteristic literary device. Rather than provide a full-blown account of life and worship in the early church, Luke presents the reader with several brief glimpses of the church (Acts 2:42–47; 4:32–37; 5:12–16, 41–42; 8:1–8; 9:31; 16:5). The newly established community of believers in Jesus Christ prospered by the superintendence of the Holy Spirit. The church was not a separatist or radical community but consisted of people who loved Jesus, lived in harmony with each other, and were rejected by institutionalized Judaism (see, e.g., 8:1–3).

The outline of Acts flows with movement. The book has a geographical movement from Jerusalem to Rome (see 1:8), with an orientation around the Jerusalem church, the Pauline missionary journeys, and his incarceration by the Roman authorities from Jerusalem to Rome. (See figure 24.)

Prologue (1:1–5)
Ministry in Jerusalem (1:6–5:42)
   Extension and persecution (6:1–9:31)
      Extension and the Gentile mission (9:32–20:6)
      Conclusion of Paul's Gentile mission (20:7–21:17)
   Paul's incarceration (21:18–28:10)
Ministry in Rome (28:11–31)

Figure 24. The Literary Structure of Acts

THE EPISTLES

The Epistles make up about one-third of the New Testament. Of the twenty-one epistles, thirteen claim to come from Paul: Galatians, 1–2 Thessalonians, 1–2 Corinthians, Romans, the Prison Epistles (Philemon, Colossians, Ephesians, and Philippians), and the Pastoral Epistles (1–2 Timothy and Titus). The other epistles are Hebrews and the General, or Catholic, Epistles: James, 1–2 Peter, 1–3 John, and Jude.

The epistolary genre was common in Greek and Latin literature. The secular epistle was a relatively short and artificial tractate on a literary, philosophical, or scientific topic.[14] The New Testament epistles, compared with secular epistles, are generally much longer, were addressed to congregations, and contained theological and practical advice. The Pauline Epistles, for example, reveal the warmth and compassion of a teacher-preacher who dictated each letter (see, e.g., Rom. 16:22) and added a personal greeting in his own handwriting to authenticate the epistle (1 Cor. 16:21; Gal. 6:11; Col. 4:18; 2 Thess. 3:17; Philem. 19). The Epistles generally follow a stylized form: salutation and prayer, the epistle proper, and a conclusion with a signature. Several epistles, including Hebrews, James, 1–2 Peter, 1 John, and Jude, have very few personal references and thus are close to the Roman literary form of tractates.

The Epistles reveal a highly complex picture of the first-century church. In this chapter and the next, I consider the canonical function of the Epistles, as each one contributes its own color to the fabric of New Testament writings and impresses on the churches the authentic claims of Jesus. The apostles present the glorious Christ as Lord, explain the nature and application of Christ's redemption, present the place of the Spirit in preparing God's people for the restoration, and exhort God's people to prepare themselves for that glorious day. Moreover, they warn the churches by example and by direct teaching to ward off any false teaching that does not perpetuate the sacred connection between the Old Testament, Jesus Christ, and the apostolic *paradosis*, or transmission of the gospel.[15]

The apostles are the sacred transmitters of the gospel from Jesus to the early church. They received their authority from Christ, exerted their apostolic rights, and readily gave up the mantle of their authority, both to the rising leadership and to the churches at large. Ever since the end of the apostolic era, the full responsibility for the preservation of the *paradosis* has rested with each new generation of believers in Jesus the Messiah.

In the present canonical ordering, the epistles of Paul follow Acts, linking closely Jesus' ministry and Paul's mission to the Gentiles. According to another tradition, the Catholic Epistles followed Acts in the early church. The major difference between the Pauline and the Catholic Epistles is that Paul's letters were generally first addressed to particular congregations, after which they were circulated. The Catholic Epistles were by their nature circular letters, addressed to a larger body of believers. Regardless of their destination, the churches heard the voice of Christ and preserved these writings, as inspired by the Spirit of God, for the benefit of succeeding generations of Christians. I first consider Hebrews and the Catholic Epistles, and then in the following chapter, the Pauline Epistles.

Hebrews

This epistle, written perhaps around A.D. 68, is one of the most problematic books of the New Testament. The authorship, audience, historical context, theological framework, and literary genre all represent issues of scholarly discussion.[16] The designation "Hebrews" or "to the Hebrews" is probably not authentic but serves as a summary of the book's major emphasis. If so, the book addresses believers who were well acquainted with Judaism, probably from birth, and who needed to be instructed on the relationship and differences between the administration under Moses, God's servant, and Jesus, God's Son. The difference is not the Old Testament versus the New Testament, because the same God who has spoken through the Son spoke to Moses and the prophets (Heb. 1:1–5). The divergence lies in the *excellence* of the Son in his present ministry before the Father.

On the matter of authorship, many names have been suggested, including Paul, Barnabas, Luke, Apollos, Silas, Philip, Priscilla, and Clement. Though theological criteria are often advanced in favor of Paul's authorship, no general consensus has been reached. The author is very familiar with the Old Testament and cites the Septuagint to prove a point, sometimes in midrashic fashion. The assumption of the superiority of Melchizedek's priesthood has suggested the author's familiarity with Essene thought.[17]

Hebrews does not follow the formal elements of an epistle, as it omits an introductory salutation and prayer. In form it is closer to a sermon and could be designated as a tractate or as an epistle written in sermonic style. In broad outline the epistle presents the exaltation of Jesus over angels (by virtue of his victory over Satan; chaps. 1–2), over Moses (3:1–4:13), and over the Aaronic priesthood (4:14–10:18). The author also appeals to the faithful to submit themselves to Christ (10:19–13:25). The superiority of the covenantal administration of Christ over the previous administration lies at the heart of the epistle. The author argues that the superiority is *christological* and *eschatological*, because the eschaton is so much closer now that Jesus has entered into the heavenly tabernacle.[18]

The theological sections are broken up by hortatory (or parenetic) segments. The interchange of theological and practical sections encourages the readers to persevere in their faith in the Son, by whom the Father has spoken in an ultimate way and in whom salvation from the great judgment is found (12:18–27).

The General (or Catholic) Epistles

The designation "catholic" (i.e., general) may be traced back to Eusebius, who referred to the seven epistles as universal in intent, since they were not addressed to a particular congregation. Most of these books have raised questions of authenticity and canonicity at one time or another during the history of the church.

James

The canonical function of James bears on the continuity of the Old Testament and Jesus' teaching. The present canonical place given to Paul's Epistles may give the impression that Paul was *the* theologian and that the Catholic Epistles are mere addenda. But James's powerfully written epistle presents wisdom as the essence of godliness. He does not get drawn into the controversy of law and grace, the righteousness of human beings over against the righteousness of God, or works and faith. For Paul, grace, the righteousness of God, and faith are primary motifs in defending the essence of the gospel. The apostle Paul wrote as Christ's apologist, but James writes pastorally. For him faith is both trust in God and works, because he operates from the Hebraic conception that faith is nothing but loyalty to God in Christ Jesus. James thus resists pat answers or simplistic harmonizations with Paul's teaching.[19] Essentially, he is in agreement with Paul, but the canonical witness of the Epistle is complementary to Paul. James is clearest when read in the light of Jesus' teaching.

James presents a Christian understanding of how the Old Testament is to be understood in the light of Jesus' coming and mission. James extends Matthew's understanding of the Old Testament.[20] His message may be set in a period before the Gentile mission introduced the issues of what God requires of Christians. It is also possible to argue in favor of a date in the early 60s, as Childs does:

> His letter is not just a check against a misunderstanding of Paul, but a positive witness for hearing the synoptic sayings in post-Pauline Christianity. The letter bears witness that, correctly interpreted, the Old Testament continues to function as a norm for Christian living even after the resurrection.[21]

James wrote primarily to "the twelve tribes scattered among the nations" (1:1)—that is, Jewish Christians. Their concern was not with the gospel or who Jesus was but with how the Old Testament functioned within the Christian life. To this issue James effectively responds by holding forth the continuity between the Law and Prophets and the coming of Jesus. In Jesus freedom is found, but the freedom is for the purpose of practicing "the royal law" (2:8), which is "the word planted" within the hearts of the believers (1:21). The one who is wise responds to "the perfect law that gives freedom, . . . not forgetting what he has heard, but doing it—he will be blessed in what he does" (1:25). That one is a person of faith, that is, of fidelity; there can be no fidelity if one's speech and actions do not conform to one's inner being.

1–2 Peter

The authenticity of both books, attributed to Peter, is questioned by modern critical scholarship.[22] In spite of issues of authorship, theories of pseudepigraphical writing, and questions of literary structure and audience, the united witness of the early church attributed these two books to the apostle Peter. The first epistle, written probably in the early 60s, is addressed generally to "God's elect in the world, scattered throughout Pontus, Galatia, Cappadocia, Asia and Bithynia" (1:1). The contents, too, while addressed to a specific historical situation, are of a general nature. The thrust of the epistle is to encourage the faithful to persevere, regardless of the persecutions and prevailing heresies. Peter summons and heartens the Christian community to remain loyal. By their calling and their new birth, Christians share in the hope of the fullness of salvation at the revelation of Jesus Christ (1:3–12), for which reason they have been called to be a holy people (1:13–3:11), ready to suffer for the sake of the gospel (3:12–4:19). The final appeal to the elders and young men (5:1–9) carries a canonical role similar to Paul's Pastoral Epistles.[23] Peter, too, prepares the Christian community for his departure by giving his blessing on the leaders of the church.

The second epistle, written between A.D. 65 and 68, has raised even more issues but must also be received as canonical. Here, more than in 1 Peter, we hear the apostolic voice, as Peter, aware of his impending departure from this life (1:14), calls on the early Christian community to live holy lives (vv. 3–11), to authenticate the gospel of Jesus in the light of the Scriptures (vv. 12–21), and to keep the gospel untainted from heretical teaching and teachers (chap. 2). In so doing, they may prepare themselves for the Day of the Lord (chap. 3). Childs correctly assesses the canonical role of these epistles in the light of Paul's farewell speech to the elders at Miletus (Acts 20:17–38) and of the Pastoral Epistles.[24] The difference lies in Peter's catholic concern with the churches at large, rather than with the leadership. In view of their impending death, the apostles gave the mantle of leadership to the church and its leaders.

Their writings function canonically as witnesses to the continuity of the ministry of Jesus and the ministry of the postapostolic churches.

Both Peter and Paul demonstrate a great concern for the continuing authority of the Old Testament Scriptures, the effectiveness of the gospel of our Lord, and the growth and stability of the Christian community. Although they turn over their authority to the faithful community, they require strict adherence to the apostolic *paradosis* and call for a constant vigilance in preparation for the return of Christ.

1–3 John

John's concern is similar to Peter's, as he too is about to lay aside the apostolic mantle. In his three letters, written A.D. 85–95, he reminds the Christian community of what he has taught them concerning Jesus.[25] Through the incarnate Christ, the children of God may have fellowship with the Father (1 John 1:1–4), being assured of forgiveness of sin and being required to walk as children of light (1:5–2:14). Fellowship with Christ requires separation from the world (2:15–17) and from heretical teachings concerning the Christ (vv. 18–27).

The Epistles of John are also truly catholic epistles, as the apostle addresses the broad concerns of the Christian community, even while writing in a particular historical context. In the second and third epistles, the apostle is equally insistent on the importance of loyalty and love.

Jude

The final witness comes to us from Jude, the brother of James (v. 1), quite likely a brother of our Lord (see Acts 1:14; 1 Cor. 9:5; Gal. 1:19).[26] He too addresses his epistle generally, "to those who have been called, who are loved by God the Father and kept by Jesus Christ" (Jude 1). In its canonical role, the epistle reverberates with a warning against apostasy, foretold by "the apostles of our Lord Jesus Christ" (v. 17). Jude stands one step removed from the apostolic authority, but he accepts the apostolic traditions and teachings, and with his authority as brother of our Lord, he summons the Christian community of any age not to forsake the teaching of the apostles but to persevere in the gospel of Jesus. The apostolic tradition is elevated to the status of "the faith that was once for all entrusted to the saints" (v. 3).[27] He also adds the eschatological perspective, encouraging the godly: "Keep yourselves in God's love as you wait for the mercy of our Lord Jesus Christ to bring you to eternal life" (v. 21).

CONCLUSION

The apostolic witness—in proclamation, by means of signs (of Jesus' power), in the presence of the Spirit, in teaching the apostolic *paradosis*, and through the Epistles—communicates the dynamic continuity between our Lord and his church. But there are also clear signs of discontinuity: the coming of the Spirit, the Gentile mission, and the freedom not to observe Jewish precepts. In spite of the marks of discontinuity, however, the apostles spoke of Jesus from the prophetic word in the light of his teaching, of his resurrection, and of his exaltation to glory.

CHAPTER 32

The Pauline Witness to the Risen Christ

Paul's epistles set forth clearly the nature of the benefits of Jesus, the fellowship of mature sons with the Father, and our life in the Spirit.[1] More than any other New Testament writings, the Pauline Epistles clarify the inclusion of the Gentile believers into the Old Testament heritage found in Jesus Christ. As a pastor-teacher Paul writes to the churches with the hope that the apostolic *paradosis* be continued, even after his departure (1 Cor. 15:3–8; Col. 2:8). The apostle is zealous that the churches go forward in their walk with the Spirit and not revert to Judaism or pervert the gospel to what is no longer the gospel. To accomplish these ends, he wrote letters to the churches in the Gentile world.

He wrote Romans to the Christians in the world capital, presenting an exposition of the *righteousness* of God in Jesus Christ and all the benefits that the Father bestows on his children in Christ through the Spirit. The Father expects his children to respond with lives devoted to him (Rom. 12:1–2). The apostle's teaching is continuous with that of our Lord, as he too upholds Christian ethics, consisting of living to the glory of God and of being filled with anticipation of the redemption to come.

In the Epistles to the Corinthians the apostle vindicates his *apostolic authority*, all in the interest of the apostolic *paradosis*. He calls on the Corinthian Christians to manifest the fruits of the Spirit of Christ: unity, faith, hope, love, and a readiness to serve one another with the gifts of the Spirit. He develops more clearly the nature of the church, whose head is Christ but whose members are diverse, having different gifts but only one Spirit. Christian living is Spirit-filled living in anticipation of the resurrection of the body and the full establishment of the kingdom of God.

To the Galatian Christians the apostle upholds the *freedom* of the children of God. Their status before God is different from that of the children of God in the Old Testament because of two related truths: the coming of Christ, the Son of God, and the outpouring of the Spirit of God. The new creation is a reality in Jesus. A reversal to an observance of Jewish Halakah (interpretations and norms derived from the law) is wholly contrary to the very purpose of Christ's coming.

In the Epistles to the Thessalonians Paul develops the nature of Christian *hope*, focusing on the Day of the Lord, the Rapture, and the glory awaiting the Christian community.

The Prison Epistles (Ephesians, Philippians, Colossians, and Philemon) were written during adverse conditions. In them, the reader witnesses a spirit of *joy and triumph* in Jesus Christ, as the apostle speaks of the glory awaiting those who persevere. He is thankful for any prayers and physical support, but even under duress, Paul shows an even greater concern for the churches and for people. He prays for the marks of the Spirit in the church: love, unity, and purity. He warned the Philippians of the Judaizers, and the Colossians of a heresy that minimized the work of Christ as Creator-Redeemer.

In the Pastoral Epistles (1–2 Timothy and Titus) the apostle affirms the importance of *sound doctrine* and the continuity of the apostolic *paradosis*. The future of the church depends no longer on the work of the Spirit in him but on the Spirit in Timothy and in the succession of faithful elders and deacons of the churches. They must be reliable men, who care for the church of Christ. Like the other apostles, Paul in his last letters thus hands over his apostolic mantle. With the death of Paul, Peter, James, Jude, John, and the other apostles and leaders of the early church, the future of the church lies in the hands of a new generation. The canonical function of the Pauline letters, together with the other epistles, is to assure that the *paradosis* will be preserved and that the leadership raised up by the Spirit of God may advance the peace, purity, and love of the church of Jesus Christ.

THE MAJOR EPISTLES

The apostle Paul was an apostle to the Gentiles. He came to know Jesus as the Messiah several years after his resurrection, about A.D. 34.[2] From 47 to 56, he made three missionary journeys, bringing the gospel of the Christ to Asia Minor and Greece. During his journeys he kept in constant contact with the work and life of the churches. Out of his interest in the new messianic congregations and the issues raised by them, the Epistles developed. The Epistles are more than literary forms of communication. They reflect on the apostolic tradition of Jesus, the apostolic understanding of the new age in the light of the Old Testament Scriptures, and the hope of the future awaiting the children of God.[3] The voice of God is heard in them, and because of their inspiration, the church has read, shared, and collected the writings of the apostle as the Word of God to all ages.

Romans

At the end of his third missionary journey the apostle Paul wrote an epistle to the church at Rome, between A.D. 57 and 59. This epistle is more theological in nature and has shaped the theology of Christianity, especially the doctrine of justification by faith. Paul's motive for writing is more than just doctrinal, however, for the eschatological and soteriological concerns as well as the practical exhortations convey Paul's interest in giving the apostolic tradition to the church at Rome.[4] The apostle does not give a full-blown theological treatise but presents an adequate account of the gospel of Jesus Christ as it confronts a pagan, as well as a Jewish, belief system.[5]

The canonical shape differs from that of the other epistles, in that Romans begins with a lengthy personal greeting and introduction (1:1–17) and concludes with a benediction, greeting, and doxology (16:20–27). In the introduction the apostle affirms that he is an apostle of the gospel of Jesus Christ, the resurrected Lord, by whose authority Jews and Gentiles are invited "to belong to Jesus Christ" (1:6). Those who belong to Jesus Christ are saved by faith. The gospel reveals both the power and righteousness of God (vv. 16–17). It is a new event in salvation history, but not a sudden denouement, because God "promised beforehand through his prophets in the Holy Scriptures" (v. 2).

The same emphases are restated in the doxological conclusion.[6] The gospel has been revealed to Paul, not as a completely new revelation, but as a message already "made known through the prophetic writings by the command of the eternal God." The gospel proclamation pertains to "all nations"—both Jews and Gentiles—and expects a response of faith and obedience to Jesus Christ (16:26).

The framing of the epistle brings out the christological and universal concern of the apostle. The gospel includes the message of human sin and of Jesus' atonement, but also contains much more. Paul affirms that this gospel of Jesus is in continuity with the Old Testament prophets. The gospel proclaims the risen Lord, the Messiah of whom the prophets had predicted. In this light we must understand the many citations from, allusions to, and analogies with the Old Testament Scriptures and people (e.g., Adam and Abraham).[7] The Old Testament finds its focus in Jesus Christ, the risen Lord, who will usher in the fullness of the promises given in the Law and the Prophets.[8] The prophets bore witness and still testify to God's righteousness, salvation, and the cosmic transformation. From this point of view, Paul expands the understanding of the gospel to include a call for a new obedience, a new relationship with God, the ministry of the Spirit, the cosmic implications on creation, and the application to both Jews and Gentiles. Jesus is the Messiah-Lord

380

to whom all authority is given—the risen Christ whose dominion extends over all nations.

1–2 Corinthians

In A.D. 57, toward the end of his sojourn at Ephesus during his third missionary journey, Paul wrote to the Christians at Corinth. He had written on a previous occasion (1 Cor. 5:9) but had been misunderstood. The second letter, our First Epistle to the Corinthians, was largely in response to issues raised by the congregation and reported to him by "Chloe's household" and by a delegation of Stephanas, Fortunatus, and Achaicus (1:11; 16:17). The various concerns help explain the somewhat choppy style as the apostle moves from subject to subject. Throughout Paul reveals a pastoral concern "without a trace of legalism or casuistry."[9]

The epistle reveals the apostle's involvement with the life of the churches. In this epistle Paul stands out as a theologian of the church, by whose apostolic authority matters were settled. His authority was derived from Christ (5:3–5; 7:10; 11:23). Yet, Paul remains human as he writes (see 7:6, 12, 25, 40; 10:15) and thus deals with the issues as a pastor-theologian.

Another major contribution of the letter lies in its connection between everyday Christian living and the hope of Christ's return. Paul prays for the Corinthian Christians and, thereby, for every generation of believers to live holy lives in anticipation of the revelation of Jesus Christ (1:7–9). Unity, holy and wise living, and peace with all men exemplify the new way of life in anticipation of the future glory (2:9; 4:5; 10:11). The eschatological concern leavens the theology and Paul's response to the issues raised by the Corinthians.[10]

The new life is therefore best summarized under the triad of faith, hope, and love. Faith pertains to the expression of commitment to the triune God revealed in the gospel of the risen Christ (15:1–11). Hope produces a commitment to God's sovereignty in Jesus Christ and also creates a yearning for the fullness of redemption. Love finds expression in sanctified relationships (chap. 13) and is the greatest of Christian attributes. There can be no love *(agapē)* without faith, nor can love exist without hope in the full establishment of the kingdom of God in Christ Jesus.

The Second Epistle to the Corinthians has occasioned more serious problems. The references to an additional visit from the apostle and to a sorrowful letter help explain what may have transpired between the two epistles. It seems that the apostle had returned to Corinth for a visit (see 2 Cor. 12:14; 13:1–2) and had met with great resistance. Upon his departure, he had written a strongly worded letter (no longer extant) that had caused him great grief (2:4; 7:8).

By the time of the writing of the second epistle, the apostle was in Macedonia completing his third missionary journey. The long-sought repentance of the Corinthians had come about, and the apostle rejoiced in hearing about God's work of grace in their hearts (2:3; 7:5–8).

Galatians

The issue of law and gospel came to a focus in Galatia.[11] The historical issues that have arisen pertaining to the identity of the Judaizers, the location of the church, and the relation of the epistle to the Jerusalem Council have too often become the central focus, while the canonical significance, which brings out much broader concerns, has been neglected.

The present literary form of Galatians, written perhaps between A.D. 48 and 56, gives enough of the argument to reconstruct the issues: law and gospel, freedom and the Spirit, the carnal interpretation of the law and the spiritual application of the law, and the law of Christ and the law of the Judaizers. The epistle's polemic-apologetic form and style present a defense of the gospel, not only against the Judaizers (the occasion for this letter) but against any attack on the faith. The literary contribution thus lies in its being a classic statement of the gospel. For Paul, Christianity is bound to a confession of the Christ, an adherence to his law of love, to a more mature relationship with the Father as sons, and to the freedom of the Spirit. In addition, the epistle supports Paul's authority as an apostle of Jesus Christ. The polemic form is based on the canonical and redemptive-historical perspective. The church hears the voice of Christ confirming the authority of his servant Paul and the authority of Paul's message of faith, justification, sanctification, and the new life in the Spirit.[12]

1–2 Thessalonians

These two epistles were written on the apostle's second missionary journey, in A.D. 51–52, one shortly after the other.[13] The first epistle is unique in that chapters 1–3 consist of an extended thanksgiving and prayer that the Christians may live a holy life (3:13). The prayer for holiness flows into a hortatory section (chaps. 4–5) in which Paul encourages the believers to prepare themselves for the coming of the Lord. He concludes with a prayer for sanctification and then the benediction: "May God himself, the God of peace, sanctify you through and through. May your whole spirit, soul and body be kept blameless at the coming of our Lord Jesus Christ" (5:23). The canonical role of the first epistle encourages thanksgiving, hope, and sanctification in the Christian life.

The second epistle was occasioned by problems arising out of the first letter. The apostle balances the emphasis on the imminence of Christ's return with signs (2:1–12), an encouragement to persevere (chap. 1; 2:13–17), and practical exhortations (3:6–15).[14] The differences in emphases and lack of apparent continuity between these two epistles have occasioned an extensive debate on the authorship, authenticity, and formation of the epistle.[15] From a canonical perspective, the second epistle creates a tension in the eschatological expectations.

THE PRISON EPISTLES

Ephesians

The Epistle to the Ephesians may have been written about the same time as Colossians (A.D. 59–61), as both letters mention Tychicus (Eph. 6:21–22; Col. 4:7–8).[16] The absence in the salutation of "in Ephesus" in several early manuscripts has occasioned serious problems pertaining to authorship, audience, and purpose. Again, the historical circumstances of the epistle's provenance are secondary to its great statement on Christ, the work of the Spirit, the church, and the new walk of faith. The canonical function lies in the apostolic concern for young believers in Christ. He assures them that they also have received the Holy Spirit, guaranteeing them their salvation in Christ (1:13–14). The canonical function of Ephesians is an encouragement to all believers, but particularly to all who have recently come to know Jesus as the Messiah, including non-Jews. All who are in Christ are heirs of the promises and the covenants (2:1–21; 3:6).

With apostolic warrant Paul calls on all new believers to be "imitators of God" and to "live a life of love, just as Christ loved us" (5:1–2). He instructs them, "Do not grieve the Holy Spirit of God, with whom you were sealed for the day of redemption" (4:30). The basis and the practice of the Christian life is trinitarian (chaps. 4–6). Each new believer, each church, and each generation is thus called upon to make personal identification with the working of God in Jesus Christ and in the Holy Spirit. "Paul is desirous that the new generation of Christians understand the nature of God's present exercise of power in their lives according to the divine purpose which he accomplished in Christ and which encompasses the universe."[17]

Philippians

Issues of authorship, composition, and date have at times become the focus of discussion.[18] The epistle conveys the apostle's gratitude to the Philippians for their remembering him in his physical need. He thanks them for their kindness (4:10, 14) and encourages them to be united (2:2; 4:2) and to resist the Judaizers (chap. 3). His experience of suffering has taken on a new light for him (1:12–30), as he reflects on our Lord's suffering and exhorts the Philippians to imitate our Lord's model of living a life of self-sacrifice (2:1–18).[19] Childs proposes that this epistle is the apostle's "last will and testament," because the apostle's hope is fixed on the imminence of Christ's coming and the reality of God's present peace being upon those who follow our Lord (4:4–7).[20] The canonical import lies in the call for perseverance, self-sacrifice, and suffering for the sake of Christ in a christological and eschatological context.

Colossians

The Epistle to the Colossians was written about the same time as the letter to Philemon, A.D. 60, as both contain the identical names of Paul's friends (Col. 1:1; 4:9–14, 17; Philem. 1–2, 23–24).[21] In between the opening salutation, thanksgiving, and prayer (Col. 1:1–14) and the concluding instructions and greetings (4:2–18), the epistle reveals some major differences from Paul's other epistles. The vocabulary, style, and view of Christ differ, resulting in questions of authorship and the Colossian heresy. In spite of the academic problems concerning the date, the heresy, and literary criticism, the epistle has a canonical function.[22] False teaching threatens the essence of Christianity: Jesus Christ! Paul responds by stating clearly that Jesus is the Ruler, the Creator, and the Sustainer of the world, and especially of his church (1:13–18). Jesus is the *plērōma*, or "fullness," of God, whom Paul glorifies in the celebrated hymn in verses 15–23).[23]

The epistle is a canonical witness to the risen Christ as *Lord of Lords*, whose work involves both the church and the world, redemption from sin and redemption of creation, and liberation both from Jewish rituals and from pagan ascetic practices. The sum and substance of the Christian faith is Jesus Christ, who, in his self-sacrifice, has become the Head. He is the Mediator between God and this world (1:20).[24]

Philemon

The Epistle to Philemon has the same formal features that characterize the larger epistles, although it deals with the mundane matter of a runaway slave, Onesimus, who had absconded with Philemon's money. The epistle became a tractate on social transformation, since in Christ there is neither slave nor free (see 1 Cor. 7:17–24; Gal. 3:28).[25]

THE PASTORAL EPISTLES: 1–2 TIMOTHY AND TITUS

Serious critical issues have been raised pertaining to the authorship of the pastorals.[26] Differences in style, vocabulary, and theology have been subjected to careful exegesis and, all too often, have led to negative conclusions. Over against the critical theory that these epistles are pseudonymous, conservatives have argued in favor of Paul's using a trusted scribe and giving him some freedom in wording.[27]

Critics agree on the formal similarities between these writings and Paul's epistles and on the many allusions to Paul's life and ministry (e.g., 1 Tim. 1:1, 3, 16; 2 Tim. 1:11; 3:11; Titus 1:3, 5). Yet, the atmosphere of the pastorals is different. The apostle is more formal, more theological, and less inclined to make personal application. The major canonical contribution of the Pastoral Epistles consists of Paul's transferring his authority to other men, as he did when he addressed the elders at Ephesus (Acts 20:17–35). The colaborers of Paul are hereby charged with perpetuating the apostolic traditions (the teaching about Christ, the ministry of the Word, resistance to heresies) and with encouraging the development of local leadership in the elders and deacons (1 Tim. 3; Titus 1:5–9).

First, the apostle stresses his concern with *sound doctrine* (1 Tim. 6:3; 2 Tim. 4:3). This doctrine pertains to the apostolic tradition that Paul has been carefully teaching the churches. With the ending of his ministry, he ascertains that the teachings pertaining to Christ and his redemptive work must be perpetuated as the basis of the doctrine and practice of the churches. Sound doctrine, consisting of "trustworthy sayings" (see 1 Tim. 1:15; 3:1; 4:9; 2 Tim. 2:11; Titus 3:8), begins and ends with Jesus Christ.[28] Jesus came to redeem sinners (1 Tim. 1:12, 15; 4:10). He alone is the Mediator between God and man (2:5–7) and will return at the appointed time (6:13–16; see also Titus 2:13).

Second, the officers of the church are charged with the *transmission* of the faith to each new generation, with the cultivation of godliness, and with the purity of the church (2 Tim. 4:1–5). To this end, the apostle charges Timothy and, in him, all leaders of the church: "What you heard from me, keep as the pattern of sound teaching, with faith and love in Christ Jesus. Guard the good deposit that was entrusted to you—guard it with the help of the Holy Spirit who lives in us" (1:13–14).

Third, the apostle encourages all to avail themselves of the grace of God by developing *godliness*. He is discharging his duties with the hope that godly men will take over so that they may live and work in the presence of God and of the Lord Jesus. Paul says confidently, "There is in store for me the crown of righteousness, which the Lord, the righteous Judge, will award to me on that day—and not only to me, but also to all who have longed for his appearing" (2 Tim. 4:8).

CONCLUSION

The Pauline Epistles, considered against the background of the Acts of the Apostles, Hebrews, and the Catholic Epistles, unfold a significant development in the history of redemption. On the one hand, the church had to adjust to the absence of the Christ and the presence of the Spirit. The Spirit brings freedom, maturity, and greater assurance, but also expects greater evidence in holiness, love, peace, unity, and spiritual desire. On the other hand, the church had to adjust to the inclusion of Gentiles. Gentiles, too, could be sons of God, receive the Holy Spirit, enjoy all the rights and privileges of covenant life, read the Old Testament Scriptures as the words of the Spirit of God, and hold leadership positions. Along with the Book of Acts, Paul's epistles witness to the tensions of the people of God, living between Pentecost and the time of the revelation of the glorious Christ. They not only are witnesses but have a canonical function, as each epistle establishes the authoritative import of Jesus' incarnation and glorification and calls forth a new life in the Spirit of the individual members of the church and of the Christian community as a whole.

CHAPTER 33

The Apostolic Message About Jesus

APOSTOLIC PREACHING

The Book of Acts is a vital link between the ministry of Jesus and the establishment of the Gentile church. The movement of the book throws light on the formation of the church of Jesus Christ at Pentecost, the outpouring of the Spirit on the church, and the growth of the church from Jerusalem (chap. 2) to Rome (chap. 28). The expansion of the church was due to Spirit-filled preaching of the gospel, or the kerygma.[1] God's faithful word of promise given in the past has found fulfillment in God's Messiah and the coming of the kingdom.

Through the foolishness of what was preached, Jesus established his church (1 Cor. 1:21). Central to that proclamation was the gospel of Jesus Christ (15:1–2), and central to the gospel is the cross and the resurrection of our Lord (Acts 1:22; 4:33; 17:3; 24:21; 1 Cor. 1:18; 15:1–8). Luke's reporting of apostolic preaching in Acts brings out more clearly what Jesus had taught: Jesus, the Servant of God, the Messiah, the Son of Man, is the glorious Ruler over the messianic kingdom and brings in the kingdom of God through his present rule (1 Cor. 15:25–28). His power is fully established by the Spirit of God among Jews and Gentiles in fulfillment of the prophetic word. The apostolic preaching is a theological statement of Jesus' authority over heaven and earth.

The Suffering Servant of God

The apostle Peter, having witnessed the life of Jesus, preached that Jesus is the Messiah of whom the prophets had spoken. The crucifixion of Jesus was not an accident. The path of suffering that led to his death was in accordance with God's will and had been predicted by the prophets (Acts 2:23; 3:18; 4:28). Those who crucified him were therefore guilty of putting to death the Servant of God. Stephen's speech complements Peter's sermons, as he charges the people with a history of resistance to God. Their forefathers had persecuted and killed the prophets, the servants of God. The prophets had predicted the coming of "the Righteous One," but the present generation had not stopped at murdering the Son of Man, to whom the prophets had witnessed (7:51–53). In preaching Jesus as the Servant, the church is thus the true and continuing people of God.

Jesus is the Suffering Servant, who through his humiliation proved himself worthy of his messiahship (Acts 3:13–14, 26; 4:26–27). The kerygma of the early church clearly includes the vital elements of the gospel: the vicarious suffering of the Lord's Messiah—in accordance with the plan of God and the prophetic word—is for forgiveness, reconciliation, restoration, and for anointing with the Holy Spirit. The resurrection and present glory of Jesus the Messiah and Servant of God assure all who repent of their sins and are baptized in the name of Jesus the Messiah that they already belong to the eschatological age (2:38; see also 3:6; 4:10; 8:12). The eschaton, already operative in Jesus' life, is powerfully evident in his glorification to kingly rule, of which the Holy Spirit is the token. The Suffering Servant, after all, is "the Holy One" of God (3:14; 4:27, 30).

The Risen Lord and Messiah

The Resurrection is central to the preaching of the apostles. The truth of the gospel rests on the historicity and the meaningfulness of the Resurrection as a redemptive-historical event of the greatest significance.[2] The apostles were fully persuaded that Jesus arose, and they presented Jew and Gentile with the risen Jesus as the only hope. Faith in a Jesus who did not rise from the dead gives no perspective on the future, and the presentation of "the historical Jesus"—a result of critical scholarly work with the gospel literature—may give an anchor in history but provides no hope for tomorrow.

The resurrection of Jesus signifies the beginning of his *glorious rule as the Messiah* of God. While the Ascension marks the actual enthronement, the Resurrection proves that Jesus is the Messiah whom the Father had appointed for rule. Death could not lay hold on him, because he is the Messiah of God of whom the prophets had spoken (Acts 2:22–36). The Resurrection is the Father's testimony that Jesus, rejected by his people, is "Lord and Christ" (v. 36). The New Testament language of the Resurrection overwhelmingly demonstrates that Jesus arose by the will and the power of the Father. His involvement in the Resurrection proves that the work of Christ was a perfect atonement and that Jesus is the Messiah. The messianic activity of Jesus did not cease with his death but continues on account of his having been raised from the dead. He is both Lord and Messiah-King.

The Resurrection also marks the intrusion of the eschaton into time. Ladd rightly calls it "an eschatological event."[3] Through the preaching of the Word and miracles, the Lord continued his ministry. The continuity of the apostolic ministry with the ministry of our Lord and the apostles witnessed to the continuing presence of the Christ. Jesus' resurrection confirmed the inauguration of the kingdom during his earthly ministry and established the presence and nearness of the eschaton. The apostle Peter urged his audience to believe in Jesus, because he opens up the future promised by the prophets (Acts 3:24–26).

The resurrection of our Lord also guarantees that the new people of God are heirs of the New Covenant. It signifies the imperishable, eternal nature of the covenant, the covenant benefits, and the victorious future for the members of the church of Jesus Christ.

The Ascended King

The ascension of Christ demonstrates that all the benefits of his resurrection hold true.[4] The Father accepted his work on earth when he returned home as the victorious one, having accomplished his mission. Just as Elijah ascended to glory as confirmation of his ministry (2 Kings 2:11), so also Jesus has ascended to glory. In addition, he has received the glory from the Father by being seated at his right hand (Acts 2:33; 7:55).

In his ascension, Christ continues the work he began on earth. All the benefits of his ministry hold true because the Father has acknowledged him and his work. Jesus' ascension is, therefore, the ground of forgiveness and of the prophetic promises of restoration. The Ascension marks the victorious completion of the ministry of our Lord as the suffering servant, while affirming the continuity of his ministry in his glorious resurrection body (see John 3:13). The designation "Son of Man," though used only once in Acts, fittingly characterizes Jesus' closeness to the Father and his glory and authority. He is "the Son of Man standing at the right hand of God" (Acts 7:56).

The Messiah of God

Jesus is Lord and Messiah (Acts 2:36). If he is Messiah, where is his kingdom? Is the kingdom a future event, or is there a present reality to his being the Messiah? The question is quite complex. In the Gospels the nearness and presence of the kingdom lies in Jesus' coming. He is the kingdom in himself. Yet, how can one explain the virtual omission of references to the kingdom of God in the Book of Acts and the Epistles?

First, the proclamation of the gospel is the proclamation of the kingdom. The usage of "kingdom" in Acts gives us a clue. According to Acts 8:12; 19:8; 28:23, the preaching of the good news of Jesus is equivalent to preaching the kingdom. The meaning of these words is brought out more clearly by Luke, the author of the gospel and of Acts, as Ladd concludes, "It is of great interest that Luke summarizes the content of Paul's preaching to the Gentiles by the utterly non-Hellenistic phrase 'the kingdom of God.' "[5]

Second, the messianic enthronement of Jesus at the right hand of the Father signifies the Father's appointment of Messiah and his present messianic rule over his kingdom. There is no ambiguity in the apostolic preaching regarding Jesus' present messianic office. The apostolic argument, as we have seen above, stresses the appointment of Jesus as the Davidic Messiah as well as his glory and victory. The victorious rule of the Christ, however, is present in the Spirit and in the church. He is not a political ruler, yet we know that he will come to judge the world and all kingdoms shall submit to him.

Third, the extension of the church into Gentile territory required an adaptation of language about the kingdom. The word "kingdom" had negative connotations within the Roman Empire. To Jewish ears it represented a prophetic expectation, but to Gentile ears it suggested insurrection and a political ideology foreign to the Romans. Even as Jesus had been careful not to call himself "Messiah" because of the political associations, so the apostles adapted their message in the Diaspora so as not to arouse suspicions of political subterfuge. The confession that Jesus is the Messiah maintained its relevance in the Jewish-Christian dialogue.

Fourth, with the beginning of the apostolic era, the issue is no longer the inauguration of the messianic kingdom but the new aspects of his kingdom. The radically changed vantage point of the post-resurrection and ascension preaching focuses on the immediate benefits of the death of the Messiah: the reality of forgiveness, the church, and the presence of the Holy Spirit. The apostles assume the existence of the messianic age as well as the presence of the kingdom, on the basis of the resurrection and glorification of the Messiah. The designation "Christ" thus becomes a part of the fixed phrase "Jesus Christ," or "Christ Jesus." The apostles assume all that is true about Jesus the Messiah and see no further need for establishing his messianic claims. The existence of his kingdom is presupposed in their gospel.

Jesus Is Lord

Already in the last two chapters of the Gospel of John it becomes apparent that the resurrected Christ is the Lord of glory. Whereas John employs the designation "Lord" as a reference to Jesus only three times in the first nineteen chapters of his gospel (4:3; 6:23; 11:2), he uses the title "Lord" as many as nine times in chapters 20 and 21. For him, Jesus is none other than the very glorious presence of God himself. The apostolic practice in Acts also recognizes Jesus' lordship. The word "Lord" (*kurios*) is more than a general reference or title such as "sir." The preaching that Jesus is *kurios* calls on people to accept the truth that

390

Jesus is God. He is the source of salvation (Acts 2:20–21), the giver of the Holy Spirit (v. 33), the forgiver of sins (5:31; 10:43), the Holy One (3:14), the Righteous One (3:14; 7:52), and the Judge of all people (10:42). His authority is symbolized by his being seated at God's right hand (2:33–36).

In the apostolic preaching Jesus is both Lord and Messiah. Peter warned, "Therefore, let all Israel be assured of this: God has made this Jesus, whom you crucified, both Lord and Messiah" (2:36). He is the Messiah of God, and he is God the Messiah. From the speeches in Acts, Morris concludes, "There is every reason, then, for holding the first Christians freely spoke of Jesus as 'Lord.'"[6] No distinction exists between his being the Savior, the Davidic Messiah-King, and the Lord of glory. His lordship requires submission, faith, devotion, and worship.

The Present Savior

Jesus is Messiah, Lord, and the Prince of Life. He is also the "Savior," a title that is not separate from his authority as Messiah-King. He is Lord, but not apart from his being the Savior (Acts 4:12) who has the power to forgive sins (2:38; 13:38). The resurrection and ascension of Jesus guarantee the present effectiveness of his rule. Salvation is that experience of the blessing of God in the present life in anticipation of the fullness of the restoration to come. Salvation is also that experience in which a believer knows that he or she has received justification in Jesus Christ. Jesus as the Savior has authority to pardon an individual from sin and from the judgment of God. He is just and has the authority to justify in a much grander way than the law of Moses foreshadowed (13:39).

The presence of Jesus and the presence of the eschaton is most clearly revealed in the coming of the Holy Spirit. The victorious rule of our Lord was initiated by the giving of gifts to his church, even as he had promised while on earth. When he was with Cornelius, Peter "remembered what the Lord had said: . . . you will be baptized with the Holy Spirit" (Acts 11:16). As Paul commented, "He who descended is the very one who ascended higher than all the heavens, in order to fill the whole universe. It was he who gave some to be apostles, some to be prophets, some to be evangelists, some to be pastors and teachers" (Eph. 4:10–11). All such offices are expressions of gifts of the one Spirit (1 Cor. 12:4–11).

The coming of the Holy Spirit is a sign of the very establishment of Jesus' messianic kingdom (Acts 2:32–36; 10:44–48; 11:15–17). Throughout the book, Luke brings out the working of the Holy Spirit in the Jews, the God-fearers, and the Gentiles. The Holy Spirit works in apostles as well as members of the church. He does not discriminate between Jew or Gentile, apostle or layperson. The Holy Spirit is present in all who are saved and gives evidence of their new relationship with the Father and Jesus (11:17).

The Coming King

The lordship of Jesus Christ has received greater glory in that Jesus, having been raised from the dead, was glorified by the Father. Jesus is seated on the throne of God at his right hand (Acts 2:30–33). He is known as the Author of Life, Prince, and Savior (3:15; 5:31), who has authority both to bring in the era of restoration in its final and climactic form and to extend the future blessings right here and now. Peter calls upon the Jews to embrace Jesus as the Messiah and the Prince of Life so that they may receive the blessings of God in Jesus and share in the times of refreshing before the coming of the era of restoration (3:19, 21). When that era of restoration comes, it may be too late to embrace this Jesus, who will return to execute judgment upon those who have not received him in faith. The apostle Paul brings out clearly that Jesus will come one day to judge the world in righteousness: "For he has set a day when he will judge the world with justice by the man he has appointed. He has given proof of this to all men by raising him from the dead" (17:31).

APOSTOLIC TEACHING

The apostolic epistles contribute to a better understanding of the significance of Jesus' coming and of the inauguration of the final age. Though no single record is left of the apostolic tradition, or *paradosis*, the Gospels, Acts, and the Epistles harmoniously contribute to a multifaceted presentation of Jesus the Messiah.[7] In a previous chapter we have considered the use of and meaning of the titles of Jesus our Lord. Now we will examine how the Pauline and Catholic Epistles contribute to our perception of the person and work of Jesus.

Jesus in the Pauline Epistles

The apostle Paul had met Jesus on the road to Damascus. He knew himself to be the last of the apostles to have witnessed the risen and glorified Christ (1 Cor. 15:8), but he too could claim the apostolic office by the grace of God (vv. 9–11; see Acts 1:22); he had received a direct revelation of the Christ (Gal. 1:12); and he had received from his teachers, including Gamaliel, "the traditions of my fathers" (v. 14). With the transforming experience of the Christ, however, he had learned to read the Old Testament in the light of a new "tradition," which included the essentials of the gospel—"For what I received I passed on to you as of first importance: that Christ died for our sins according to the Scriptures" (1 Cor. 15:3). His revelation from Christ changed his life and theology, but Paul's theological evaluation of Jesus, while different in emphasis, is fully in agreement with the Jesus presented in the Gospels and Acts.[8]

The Suffering Servant

Paul proclaimed Jesus as the Messiah who had to die and be raised again before he was glorified. It was impossible for Paul to separate Jesus' messiahship from his death and resurrection (1 Cor. 15:3–4).[9] Paul knew that the message of the Cross was a stumbling block to Jews and foolishness to Gentiles (1 Cor. 1:18–25), yet he maintained that the message of the Cross is the power of God to salvation (Rom. 1:16; 1 Cor. 1:18). The Cross is the very expression of Jesus' love, for upon it he gave himself for his church (Gal. 2:20). Jesus demonstrated his love for us by being the Righteous One who died for the ungodly (Rom. 5:6). Jesus came to serve human beings by giving himself for sinners (1 Cor. 15:3; Phil. 2:6–11). The Cross thus reveals the righteousness of God (Rom. 3:21–26) in that God himself is justified, even as he justifies believers who share in the glory that belongs to the Messiah through grace alone. The teaching on Jesus' suffering as a servant is more clearly brought out in Romans (4:25; 8:32–34), but the glory of the Resurrection shines through in Paul's treatment of Jesus' servanthood.[10]

The message of the resurrection and ascension of Jesus also confirms the renewal of life in which all believers may share. Jesus came in the likeness of sinful flesh (Rom. 8:3), did not sin (2 Cor. 5:21), died for sinners, but rose again. For Paul, the resurrection of Jesus is of central importance because it gives hope for this life and for the life to come. Christ's resurrection gives believers the assurance that their faith is not futile. Their sins are forgiven (1 Cor. 15:17), and those who have died will be raised to life (vv. 20–21). Believers can therefore face their own death, knowing that, when Christ returns, they will receive a glorious, incorruptible, spiritual body (vv. 35–49). Paul affirms that the general resurrection means the death of death and the victory of God's people through Jesus Christ (vv. 50–58).

The Glorified, Victorious Lord

The Paul of the Epistles rarely refers back to the *paradosis* of Jesus' life and ministry on earth. He knows the exalted and risen Lord, and thus his theology develops around the future revelation of Jesus Christ, the so-called eschatological Jesus. He knows the elements of the tradition, but he works out the implications of Jesus' work on the basis of his exaltation and glory to be revealed at his coming. Ladd observes,

> Paul knows something of the tradition about the life of Jesus (1 Cor. 11:23ff.); but because his own experience with Jesus is not with the

393

Jesus of history but with the exalted Lord, he is able under the leading of the Spirit to draw out the implications of the divine person of Jesus.[11]

In the first place, the apostle has found in Jesus the beginning of the new age, the *messianic era*. Though he rarely speaks of the kingdom of God, his theology flows out of the conviction that the kingdom is here. The use of "Christ" as a proper name has given way to a title—Jesus Christ or Christ Jesus—which does not mean that Jesus is not the Messiah. To the contrary, in his treatment of Jesus' relationship to the world, the church, and to individual believers, it is apparent that Jesus is the exalted Messiah.[12] Writing to the believers at Ephesus, Paul speaks of Jesus as "our Lord Jesus Christ, who has blessed us in the heavenly realms with every spiritual blessing in Christ" (Eph. 1:3). He defines the blessings as election, adoption, grace, forgiveness of sins, wisdom, salvation, and the seal of the Holy Spirit (vv. 4–14).

That these gifts represent the eschaton is clear from Paul's reference to a point "when the times will have reached their fulfillment" and to "the promised Holy Spirit, who is a deposit guaranteeing our inheritance until the redemption of those who are God's possession" (Eph. 1:10, 13–14). Moreover, the gifts are also evidences of the present rule of the Christ, as Jesus has authority "in the heavenly realms"; Paul describes him there as seated "far above all rule and authority, power and dominion, and every title that can be given, not only in the present age but also in the one to come" (vv. 20–21).

Second, for Paul, Jesus himself is *king over the whole world* (1 Cor. 15:25). He originally created everything (Col. 1:16–17), he has triumphed over Satan and the principalities and powers (2:15), and he will come "to bring everything under his control" (Phil. 3:21), especially death (1 Cor. 15:26). He has been raised and is now seated at the right hand of God in heaven, above all rule and authority, power and dominion (Eph. 1:20–21). The Father himself has exalted the Son and has given him authority over all the nations, awaiting the day when every nation and language will confess that Jesus Christ is Lord (Phil. 2:9–11).

For Paul, finally, Jesus is the *glorious incarnation of God*. The title "Lord" also refers back to the appellation *Adonai* in the Hebrew Old Testament.[13] The Septuagint did not distinguish between the name Yahweh and the title *Adonai* ("Master"; "Lord"). The Jews had become hesitant to use the name of their covenant God, for fear of breaking the commandment against using God's name in vain. By the time the Old Testament was translated into Greek, the custom had been adopted of substituting the title "Lord" (spelled "LORD" in the NIV) for Yahweh. *Adonai* often denotes God as the Master-Ruler of the universe, who judges all humankind (Ps. 2:4; Isa. 6:1). Yahweh is both the King of the world and the covenant God who has established his dominion among his own people (Ps. 114:2). For the apostles, including Paul, the eschatological hope of the Old Testament found an anchor in their belief that Jesus is Lord, as a comparison of several passages reveals:

> He is the one whom God appointed as judge of the living and the dead. (Acts 10:42)

> For he has set a day when he will judge the world with justice by the man he has appointed. (Acts 17:31)

> Christ died and returned to life so that he might be the Lord of both the dead and the living. (Rom. 14:9)

> For he must reign until he has put all his enemies under his feet. (1 Cor. 15:25)

The hope of the Christian community lies in the Aramaic prayer for the full establishment of Jesus' lordship: *Maranatha*, "Come, O Lord!" (1 Cor. 16:22; see also Rev. 22:20).[14]

Jesus in the Catholic Epistles

The Catholic Epistles do not contribute significantly to the christology of the New Testament. They affirm and confirm the traditions of the Gospels, Acts, and the Pauline Epistles. The titles of Jesus, except for rare exceptions, have a formulary use. The concern of the authors is generally more with the application of the truth of Jesus' coming than with the defense of who Jesus is. For example, Peter develops the motif of Jesus as the Suffering Servant (1 Peter 1:11, 19; 2:21–25; 3:18; 5:1) as a ground for self-denial and for perseverance in suffering (2:13–3:22; 4:12–19).

One of the more fruitful contributions is made by the author of the Epistle to the Hebrews. He presents a distinctive understanding of Jesus' incarnation and humanity as well as his exalted status. He holds in careful tension Jesus' ministry and that of his Old Testament forerunners. While he presents past, present, and future aspects of our Lord's work, the eschatological flavor dominates his treatment of Jesus. Jesus came to save sinners (Heb. 2:14, 17) and lived a life without sin, though tempted as a man (4:15). He suffered greatly, while submitting himself to the Father and being faithful to the end (5:7–10). His death provided for the present and the future benefits of the people of God (3:1; 6:4–5; 9:26; 10:10, 12). The exalted Christ is himself the eschaton already here (i.e., the realized eschaton) by his sacrifice on the cross "at the end of the ages" (9:26).

CONCLUSION

The apostolic preaching and teaching reflect variety as well as unity. The apostles adjust to the Gentile world in the proclamation of who Jesus is. Moreover, they accommodate themselves to the changing scene, as the leadership of the church changes hands from the apostles to a new generation. From the variety of confessional expressions and traditions, Dunn concludes that the apostolic witness was not intended to be transmitted apart from personal involvement. Each generation was to address itself to the issues of its day and confess who Jesus is: "Each community of the Spirit and each generation of the Spirit felt the responsibility laid upon it by the Spirit to interpret the received tradition afresh and in relation to its own situation and needs."[15]

CHAPTER 34

The Church: The Ministry of Jesus in His Spirit

The ministry of the apostles is the second stage of Jesus' ministry.[1] The Gospel of Luke records the life of Jesus from his birth to his ascension into heaven. In his sequel, the Acts of the Apostles, Luke quickly summarizes Jesus' incarnational ministry and the presence of the kingdom of God in his life (Acts 1:3). The kingdom of God has come in the person of the great King, Jesus Christ himself. This same Jesus, according to Luke, taught his disciples to expect the expansion of his kingdom beyond Jerusalem, Judea, and Samaria, to include the whole world (v. 8). This goal serves as a framework of Acts, which records the growth of the kingdom of Jesus Christ from Jerusalem (chaps. 1–7) to Samaria (8:5–25), to the Gentiles (vv. 26–40; chaps. 10–11), and ultimately to the nations, when Paul became the apostle to the Gentiles (9:15). Even before the gospel went out to the Gentiles, the Lord had already established churches in Judea, Galilee, and Samaria (v. 31). The conclusion of the Book of Acts gives us a picture of the apostle Paul still fervently witnessing to the kingdom of God in Jesus Christ (28:23, 31). Jesus is the kingdom of God!

The early church is characterized by the ministry of the apostles, who were chosen by Jesus (Acts 1:2) and who were intimately acquainted with the ministry of Jesus from his baptism to his resurrection and ascension (v. 22). The apostolic witness is empowered by the Holy Spirit, who came in fulfillment of Jesus' promise (v. 5). Through the Holy Spirit the apostles evidenced the new era of restoration; like their Lord, they were known for doing wonders and signs (2:43; 3:6; 4:33; 5:12). This activity demonstrates the continued presence of our Lord, who had promised, "I tell you the truth, anyone who has faith in me will do what I have been doing. He will do even greater things than these, because I am going to the Father" (John 14:12). Jesus was at the right hand of the Father and present with his church in the Spirit. The apostolic teaching and ministry of healing was in continuity with Jesus' ministry but gradually changed from a mainly Jewish church to a Gentile church. The Book of Acts records the geographic and racial development of the apostolic church in order to demonstrate the presence of the Holy Spirit, as he continued the work of Jesus through the apostles' leadership and forced the church away from her provincial roots.[2]

The Epistles reflect theologically upon the work of the Holy Spirit. For Paul, the ministry of the Holy Spirit in the church relates to other central motifs such as the person and work of Christ, eschatology, and the nature of the kingdom of God. We explore here the Pauline understanding of the church in three areas: the people of God, the kingdom of God, and the gifts of the Spirit.

THE CHURCH AS THE PEOPLE OF GOD

The characteristic word for "church" is *ekklēsia*, which designates the local congregation (1 Cor. 1:2; 2 Cor. 1:1) as well as the universal church, of which Christ is the head (Eph. 1:22; Col. 1:18). "Church" refers to an eschatological concept, namely, the people of God whom Jesus will present to the Father. Because of the interrelationship of the doctrine of the church and the doctrine of the future, Ridderbos concludes that the universal church is primary in any discussion about *ekklēsia*:

> For if the concept of *ekklēsia tou Theou* [the church of God] has above all a redemptive-historical content and speaks of the church as the true people of God, the manifestation of the (Messianic) congregation of the great future, then it is clear that for Paul . . . the thought of the universal church is primary and the local church, the house-church, and the church gathering can be denoted as *ekklēsia* because the universal *ekklēsia* is revealed and represented in them.[3]

The Pauline doctrine of the church reveals a continuity with the Old Testament concept of the people of God. In the Old Testament the phrase "the people of God" is synonymous with "congregation" (*qāhāl*), translated in the Septuagint by *ekklēsia*. For Paul the church is the *ekklēsia* of God, or what Ridderbos calls "the Messianic congregation of the end time."[4] The difference between the old and new is that the church is more clearly an eschatological concept. It consists of Jews and Gentiles, who together form the body and constitute God's goal of redemptive history: one people from all the nations! The *ekklēsia* is an organic whole, in which "the local congregation is no isolated group but stands in a state of solidarity with the church as a whole."[5] The organic element comes to expression in several metaphors for the church as the people of God: the body of Christ, the temple of God, Zion, and the Israel of God.

The Body of Christ

By the metaphor of the body the apostle expresses both the unity and the diversity existing within the church. Unity and diversity are, however, not abstract concepts that can be understood apart from Christ. The church is one body in Christ and shows a diversity in Christ. The *unity* of the church represents the plan of God to unite all things in Jesus (Eph. 1:10). It is an eschatological goal, as the church already enjoys what God has purposed for all creation: one God and one spiritual people of God (4:4–6), composed of Jews and Gentiles (1 Cor. 12:12–13). All members of the church must relate to one another in allegiance to Jesus Christ, the one head (Eph. 4:15; Col. 1:18).

Paul also develops the *diversity* within the body (Rom. 12:3–8; 1 Cor. 12:14–31). The diversity expresses itself in the gifts and offices of the church. The Spirit sovereignly bestows on individuals the gifts (vv. 7, 11) for the common good of the body. Through the diverse gifts, the Spirit works out renewal in individuals and in the church as a token of the restoration to come. The greatest manifestation of body life occurs when the members of the body seek to serve, rather than be served; to love, rather than be loved; and to humble themselves, rather than humble others (Rom. 12:3; 1 Cor. 12:31; 13:13; Phil. 2:1–4).

The Temple of God

A closely related metaphor is the temple of God.[6] The church is God's spiritual temple (Eph. 2:21–22) because it is a habitation of the Holy Spirit and is characterized by the Spirit's work. The Spirit of God cleanses and sanctifies the people to himself (1 Cor. 3:17). In Christ all of God's children are members of the same household and are fellow citizens (v. 9). In Christ God has brought together into his temple those who were far and those who were near (Eph. 2:14–22).

Zion

The apostle refers to "the Jerusalem that is above," in contrast to Mount Sinai (Gal. 4:25–26). Jerusalem is called "our mother," a concept derived from the prophetic expectation that Jerusalem will be so greatly inhabited that her population cannot be numbered (Zech. 2:10–13; see also Isa. 54:1–15). The Lord dwells in her and blesses both Jews and Gentiles with his presence. So also the exquisite poetic expression of Psalm 87 includes Gentiles as having been born in Zion, whose names are recorded in "the register of the peoples" (vv. 4–6).[7] Zion is the city of the faithful (see Isa. 60:1–22; 66:7–13). The Old Testament association with Zion is reflected in Paul's understanding of Zion.[8] She is the fountain of life, salvation, and joy—"a river whose streams make glad the city of God" (Ps. 46:4; 87:7; Isa. 12:3; Ezek. 47:1–12; Rev. 22:1–5); for him, "the Jerusalem that is above is free, and she is our mother" (Gal. 4:26).

The Israel of God

On the one hand, the apostle Paul clearly saw continuity in the church's relation to the covenants, redemptive history, and the Old Testament people of God. In this sense, the church is the Israel of God (Gal. 6:16). On the other hand, Paul had not yet witnessed the separation of church and synagogue, of Christians from Jews. The lines were hardening, but the door between the synagogue and church had largely remained open. In the sense of historic and national continuity, Israel is still the people of God, even in their rejection of the Messiah (Rom. 11:15–16). The hope of Israel's repentance and faith in Jesus the Messiah comes from Paul's understanding of Isaiah, according to whom the eschatological moment brings Jews and Gentiles together into one body. Because of the present rejection of Israel, the prophetic word that salvation will go out from the Jewish people must still come to fulfillment (v. 26; see Isa. 27:9; 59:20). He believes that the acceptance of the Redeemer will bring salvation to the Gentiles and that this will usher in a new era likened to "life from the dead" (Rom. 11:15).

THE CHURCH AND THE KINGDOM OF GOD

The headship of Jesus Christ over his church finds further expression in the concept of the kingdom of God.[9] Paul writes to the Colossian church that God has "rescued us from the dominion of darkness and brought us into the kingdom of the Son he loves" (1:13). In Paul's usage, the church is a particular expression of the kingdom of God.[10] Jesus is King over the whole world because God has given him the kingdom, but in a real sense the church, like the people of God in the Old Testament, is a visible manifestation of the kingdom of God on earth.

We may use several words to characterize the kingdom of Jesus Christ. In Romans 14:17, Paul describes the kingdom as consisting not of food and drink but of "righteousness, peace and joy in the Holy Spirit." To these descriptions may also be added love, hope, and glory. First, in Jesus Christ, the believer has received the *righteousness* of God (4:22–25). By his obedience, Jesus, the Second Adam, transformed the triad of disobedience, condemnation, and death into obedience, justification, and life. Because of the obedience of Jesus Christ, those who believe on him share in his righteousness and therefore in life (Gal. 3:26–27; Rom. 5:21).

Second, the believer in Jesus Christ has *peace* with God (Rom. 5:1).

The believer has been saved from the wrath of God and has been reconciled to God through Jesus Christ (vv. 9–11; 1 Thess. 1:10; Eph. 2:16–18; Col. 1:21–22). The members of the kingdom love peace and follow the admonition, "Let us therefore make every effort to do what leads to peace and to mutual edification" in the church (Rom. 14:19).

Third, the kingdom of God is also defined by *joy*. Especially in the Epistle to the Philippians, Paul argues that the joy we have in Jesus Christ must be reflected in our way of life. Our joy is closely linked with our progress in the faith and has a place in the worship of God (1:25; 3:3). We therefore must rejoice always, even in the face of difficulties, knowing that we receive God's peace through prayer (3:1, 3; 4:4–6).

Fourth, the kingdom of Jesus Christ is also the kingdom of *love*. God has loved us in Christ and has promised that nothing can separate us from his love (Rom. 8:31–39). Not only has he loved the Gentiles in Jesus Christ, but he has committed himself also to be loyal to the Jews so that one day they too may be the very objects of his love in Christ (chaps. 9–11). Love is the evidence of our union with Christ and manifests itself in the exercise of our spiritual gifts (1 Cor. 13). Moreover, love, like peace and joy, is a fruit of the Spirit in the Christian life (Gal. 5:22). Love fulfills the law of Christ (v. 14).

Fifth, the kingdom of God is the kingdom of *hope*. The Scriptures have been written so that, through endurance, we may have hope (Rom. 15:4). The promises have been given to Jesus Christ, and thus the promises of God have been confirmed to all those who are in Jesus Christ. Paul prays, "May the God of hope fill you with all joy and peace as you trust in him, so that you may overflow with hope by the power of the Holy Spirit" (v. 13).

Sixth, the *glory* of God has been revealed in Jesus Christ. The church of Christ is already glorious because it is heir to the gifts and the benefits of Jesus Christ and to all the glory God has prepared for his people. There is both a present glory and also a future glory for which creation is groaning, waiting for that day of redemption, or restoration (Rom. 8:18). The believer is complete in Jesus Christ (Col. 2:9–10) and as such shares in the glory of Jesus Christ, who is God in the flesh and Ruler over all powers (see Eph. 1:4–6, 12, 14).

THE CHURCH AND THE GIFTS OF THE SPIRIT

There is a significant difference between the fruit of the Spirit and the gifts of the Spirit. All who are in Christ must walk in the Spirit (Gal. 5:16, 25), and by living in the newness of life, they will develop the fruit of the Spirit. The fruit of the Spirit are those *qualities of life* that conform to the image of God, reflected in Jesus Christ (Rom. 8:29; 2 Cor. 3:18): love, joy, peace, patience, kindness, goodness, faithfulness, gentleness, and self-control (Gal. 5:22–23; Eph. 5:9). All Christians without exception have the high and holy calling of cultivating such spiritual fruit.

The gifts of the Spirit, however, pertain to the *variety of functions* within the body of Christ.[11] The apostle stresses the diversity within the body, as we have already seen, and amplifies this practically in his teachings on the diverse gifts (Rom. 12:6–8; 1 Cor. 12:8–10, 28–30; Eph. 4:11). The variety of gifts reveals that all the members of the church of Christ are baptized with the same Spirit (1 Cor. 12:13; Eph. 4:4). These gifts are the charismata, or spiritual gifts. They are sovereignly endowed by the Spirit of God for the building up of the body (vv. 12–13).

The individual receives a unique calling to serve within the church. Paul's listing of the gifts is not theoretical but functional: apostle, prophet, teacher, evangelist, preacher, and so forth.[12] The gifts are not for individual enjoyment but for the development of the whole body. The gifts of the Spirit bring unity, and where unity is, Jesus is present among his people. Where Jesus is, spiritual maturity comes to expression, "until we all reach unity in the faith and in the knowledge of the Son of God and become mature, attaining to the whole measure of the fullness of Christ" (Eph. 4:13).

CONCLUSION

The church of Jesus Christ was built through the preaching and teaching of the Word, the powerful presence of the Spirit, the evidence of the miracles, and the transformation of lives. The church was a continuation of the people of God in the Old Testament, but with the coming of Jesus only those who confessed that Jesus is the Messiah of God could belong to his messianic assembly. There is no salvation other than what the Father grants in the name of Jesus. Paul uses many metaphors expressing the continuity and the unity of the people of God. The new element is the joining together of Jews and Gentiles within the one body of Jesus Christ. Jesus is the head over all creation and, in a special sense, over his church. He has richly endowed its members, and the sign of his victorious rule lies in the gift of the Holy Spirit. The Spirit of God is in all members of the body of Christ but cooperates with and encourages the diversity within the body by granting a variety of gifts.

The people of God as his temple, or those who enjoy the privileges of being free citizens of Zion, are members of the kingdom of Jesus Christ. The kingdom is coextensive with the church of Christ but extends far beyond it. The followers of Jesus have the kingdom within: righteousness, peace with God, joy, love, hope, and glory. But they are united in the hope that one day their Lord will return in greater glory, bestowing his glory upon the children of the kingdom and extending to them the privilege of rule over the earth.

For now, the church is the agency for promoting the kingdom of Jesus Christ by the operation of the Holy Spirit. The church is distinct from Israel but maintains dialogue with Israel as with an elder brother. The church is not Israel but has received the privileges that were natural to the Jews (Rom. 9:4–5). They were cut off from their privileged position but must be treated as holy (11:16) and "loved on account of the patriarchs" (v. 28).

The members of the church of Christ regularly meet together in local churches, which are characterized by the marks of the church of Jesus Christ: prayer, preaching, fellowship, and the administration of the sacraments. In this way the church in each century is in continuity with the early church and hence in continuity with Jesus' earthly ministry through the operation of the Holy Spirit.

CHAPTER 35

The Work of God in Salvation

Salvation is the complex act of the triune God whereby the benefits of Christ's work are applied here and now in anticipation of an even greater fulfillment. The words "regeneration," "salvation," "sanctification," and "new creation" denote a transformation of the individual, on the basis of which God looks on the person as imperishable (1 Peter 1:23), eternal (John 3:16–18), holy (Rom. 6:22), and glorified (8:21). In Christ, the Father looks at his children as those who are forgiven from sin, freed from the powers of this world, and liberated to serve him in anticipation of eternity. For this reason, personal salvation is eschatological in nature (v. 23; Eph. 4:30).

The biblical teaching concerning "union with Christ" relates the Trinity to the work of salvation. Believers are guaranteed redemption and all its benefits as they are in union with Christ. The nature of this union was a mystery in the Old Testament but is now revealed with the suffering and glorification of our Lord (Rom. 16:25–27; Eph. 5:32; Col. 1:26–27). To all who believe on his Son, the Father grants forgiveness, fellowship with God, and the privilege of adoption to sonship (Eph. 1:3–14). They are the elect "in Christ," and because of his unique relationship with the Father, they are heirs together with Christ (1 Cor. 3:22–23). Through him, not only do they have fellowship with the Father, but in some mystical sense, the Father together with the Christ dwells in the believer, on the condition of love for Christ and obedience to his Word (John 14:23; 1 John 1:3). The Spirit of God brings together the many believers into one body and one Spirit (Rom. 8:9–11; 1 Cor. 6:17; 12:13; 1 John 3:24; 4:13), even as Jesus desired, "I pray also for those who will believe in me . . . , that all of them may be one, Father, just as you are in me and I am in you. . . . May they be brought to complete unity" (John 17:20–21, 23).

The word "covenant" also amplifies the nature of this relationship. Jesus opened the way for a fuller appropriation of the benefits of the New Covenant, or *the sovereign administration of grace and promise by which Jesus consecrates his people by his blood and guarantees the benefits by the gift of his Spirit.* The covenants made with creation, Abraham,

Moses, and David are all confirmed in Jesus Christ (Heb. 9:16–17). The Old Covenant refers to the administration of the covenant prior to Jesus, not to its being antiquated or irrelevant. Under the Old Covenant the Lord expected his people to display love and loyalty, provided for the atonement of their sins, and gave them the gifts of sonship, forgiveness, and life. Under the New Covenant the grace of God is more evident in Jesus Christ, by whom the Father reconciles sinners to himself and gives them redemption in the Son. The superiority of the New Covenant is not that it provides forgiveness but that it offers a greater realization of the restoration and fulfillment of the promises.[1] The covenant with humankind is new insofar as it is renewed in Jesus Christ. The benefits of this covenant flow from the triune God as the Father, Son, and Holy Spirit apply the benefits of Christ's incarnation to man.

THE WORK OF THE SON: ATONEMENT

The meaning of "atonement" has little to do with the popular etymology "at-one-ment." The becoming "at one" with God is only one aspect of atonement, better known as reconciliation. Atonement consists of expiation, reconciliation, and redemption.

Expiation

The death of Christ is a part of the gospel message (1 Cor. 15:3).[2] Jesus "died for our sins" in fulfillment of the Old Testament sacrifices and priestly system (Rom. 3:24–26; 8:3). His death satisfied the wrath of God, evoked by our sinful condition (Rom. 5:9). The death of the Christ was thus vicarious; he died for us rather than for himself (v. 8; Gal. 3:13; Eph. 5:2; 1 Thess. 5:10; Heb. 9:11–10:18). The death of Christ was foreshadowed by the expiatory offerings in the Old Testament (the sin and guilt offering) and is efficacious for salvation and sanctification (13:10–13).

Jesus fully identified with the human condition in his incarnation in that he took God's judgment of sinners on himself (Gal. 3:13). In his death for others he, as the last Adam, represented the human family so that he in his life might bring the benefits of his substitutionary death to all who are in him (Rom. 5:12–6:14).[3]

The effect of Christ's sacrifice is nothing less than what God had promised to his Old Testament people: covering of the sin, forgiveness, and cleansing. In the Old Testament the priestly system, the regulations of holiness and purity, and the sacrificial system foreshadowed the death of the Christ. The Old Testament people of God truly experienced forgiveness, cleansing, and the joy of their salvation because the wrath of God was propitiated in anticipation of the final work of our Lord.

How much greater privileges belong to the Christian, who can rest in the final and climactic sacrifice by the Son of God! Jesus fully satisfied the Father's demands for obedience, righteousness, justice, holiness, and absolute love. In him sinners may find the full expiation for all their sins (1 John 2:1–2). Moreover, through his sacrifice the Father's wrath is appeased, making reconciliation possible.

Reconciliation

Through Jesus' sacrifice at the cross and the appeasing of the Father's wrath, the sinner may be reconciled with God (Rom. 5:10–11).[4] Reconciliation signifies the divine acts of removing barriers and of permitting an individual to approach the Father so that one may have peace with God (Rom. 5:1; Eph. 2:13; Col. 1:20). Our condition apart from Christ calls forth God's wrath and condemnation (Rom. 5:6). We are under God's wrath because we are condemned to experience the Day of the Lord as the great and terrible day of judgment and vengeance (2 Peter 3:10; Rev. 6:16–17). We are alienated from God because of our sin, guilt, and ungodliness (Rom. 1:18). But all who are in Christ are not only redeemed from God's wrath, they are also reconciled to God (Rom. 5:8–11; 2 Cor. 5:18–20). As Ladd concludes, "It is God who has both initiated and in Christ accomplished reconciliation." Marshall adds, "God has thus dealt with the sin of the world, and in so doing has rendered his wrath inoperative against those who accept his act of reconciliation."[5]

Redemption

Jesus the Redeemer is none other than the great Divine Warrior-King, by whose authority all powers in heaven and earth will be subjected to the Father's will (1 Cor. 2:6; 15:24–25; Col. 2:15; Heb. 2:8). Those who belong to him receive gifts in anticipation of his final victory, of which the Holy Spirit is the seal of redemption. The term "redemption," however, is all-embracing and denotes a process that takes place in time and extends to Jesus' glorious coming.[6] Redemption has three aspects: ransom, liberation, and glorification.

Ransom is the work of Christ whereby he redeems a sinner from the bondage of sin (Heb. 9:14; Rev. 5:9) and from the condemning power of the law (Gal. 3:13; 4:4–5). Jesus came for this purpose (Mark 10:45) and accomplished his mission of giving himself as a ransom (1 Tim. 2:6). God required nothing less than the blood of his own Son to accomplish this aspect of redemption (Eph. 1:7). Through his ransom he made atonement for sin. He appeased the wrath of God, expiated human sin, and opened up reconciliation with the Father.

Redemption also involves *liberation* as a benefit deriving from the ransom of Christ. Liberation effectively frees the Christian from the guilt and power of sin and sets one free to serve the living God (Rom. 6:11, 14; 8:21). Our Lord has already triumphed over Satan, and the triumph at the end is secure (John 12:31; Col. 2:15; Heb. 2:14–15). The Christian is no longer a slave to sin and to the structures of this world but now is totally free to serve the living God (1 Cor. 6:19–20; 7:22–23; Gal. 5:1–18).[7]

From God's perspective, the redeemed already have received *glorification* in Christ, but in our experience on earth we long for the full redemption of our body and the fullness of the inheritance (Rom. 8:23; Eph. 1:14; 4:30). The hope of the Christian lies in the final victory of Christ over evil and Satanic powers, when the full glory of the children of God will be revealed (Rom. 8:17–18), including the resurrection of the body (1 Cor. 15:43).

THE WORK OF THE FATHER

Election

The apostolic teaching on election connects the grace, omnipotence, and purpose of God. It affirms that the Father has a purpose from beginning to end and that the history of redemption reveals some aspects of that purpose. Throughout this history the Lord has acted freely and sovereignly in blessing and in cursing.

Israel's privileges are due not to any inherent righteousness (Deut. 7:6–9; 9:4–5) but solely to the free grace promised to Abraham (Rom. 4:1; Gal. 3:15–29). Moreover, physical descent from Abraham does not guarantee election, inasmuch as God has looked from the beginning for those who were his children by faith (Rom. 9:8). Those who looked to the God of the promise for their ultimate reality were God's children of promise (Gal. 4:28).

In accordance with his purpose the church, composed of Jews and Gentiles, had to come into being. His purpose is nothing less than the bringing in of the fullness of the Jews and Gentiles. Their fullness, however, is in direct proportion to the revelation of God in Christ in the fullness of time. His purpose, therefore, is most evident in the incarnation and exaltation of our Lord Jesus Christ, in whom alone redemption is to be found and who alone is the foundation of the church (1 Cor. 3:11). The revelation of God's eternal purpose to choose the church took gradual shape through the ministry of the prophets and the apostles (Eph. 1:4; 2:20), and especially in Jesus Christ, "a lamb without blemish or defect. He was chosen before the creation of the world, but was revealed in these last times for your sake" (1 Peter 1:19–20).

Calling

The Father also initiates the calling of those who belong to Christ according to his purpose (Rom. 8:30). He invites us to the fellowship with his Son and is faithful in maintaining the relationship (1 Cor. 1:9; Rom. 11:29). The purpose of his calling is to prepare us for our eternal heritage (Phil. 3:14; 2 Tim. 1:9; Heb. 3:1). It has pleased the Father to call people to himself through the foolishness of preaching (1 Cor. 1:21), to which they must respond. The Father's calling is a mystery: it is unconditional and effective, but at the same time it requires human assent and the expression of faith. The mystery of God's call is beyond man's comprehension, but what is important is that all who are in Christ have been invited by the Father. This is good news!

Justification

The apostolic teaching on justification is grounded in the Old Testament.[8] Abraham was justified by faith (Gen. 15:6; Rom. 4:1–3). Justification is a legal (or forensic) term, designating one's right to stand in the presence of a holy God because of pardon and restoration. By justification the sinner may please God, whereas without being justified it is impossible to please the Father (Rom. 8:8). God expects nothing less than true faith and genuine repentance from the person whom he has called, and when this response is given, he freely justifies the sinner who has been dead in his or her trespasses and sins. This act presupposes the involvement of the Holy Spirit, by whose operation people are regenerated, having become sensitized to their sinfulness and need of salvation (John 1:13; 3:5; 1 John 2:29; 3:9; 5:1, 4, 18).

Justification is the Father's pardon and the legal framework in which the fullness of reconciliation (see above) and all its benefits are granted to the forgiven sinner. The Father's favor rests on those who have been justified. The righteousness of Christ and the Father's rewards to the Son (life, glory, and victory) thus belong to all whom the Father justifies in his Son (2 Cor. 5:21). Since the fullness awaits us, it is also proper to say that justification is eschatological.

Adoption

By God's act of creation he has established a special relationship with the world of creation. It is permissible to say that he is the Father of all humankind both in the sense of origination and in the sense of rule (Acts 17:27–28). He has established a closer relationship with his own people, however, typified by that of Father and son. Israel had already enjoyed this privilege (Isa. 1:2; Jer. 3:19; Hos. 11:1; Rom. 9:4), evidenced in God's love and care for Israel (Deut. 32:5–6, 10–12), beginning in Egypt and extending to the coming of our Lord. In Christ,

408

the Father has extended his family to include Gentiles together with those of Israel and has also made the privileges more explicit.

Glorification

Adoption is the prerequisite for glory. In order to share his glory with us, Jesus had to bring us into the family of God, sanctify us, and share the glory the Father had bestowed on him (Heb. 2:5–11). All of these benefits were possible because of his suffering. On the one hand, "glorification is the final phase of the application of redemption," an inference from Romans 8:30.[9] On the other hand, while glorification is an eschatological concept, it has a real bearing on the present experience of Christians, as they already share in the glory of our Lord, who is the radiance of God's glory (Heb. 1:3; James 2:1). The many benefits of glorification in this life include the freedom of the Christian (Rom. 8:21), the ministry of the New Covenant (2 Cor. 3:9–10), the grace of God (Eph. 1:6), spiritual strengthening (Eph. 3:16), joy (1 Peter 1:8), the glorious transformation of the Christian "into his likeness with ever-increasing glory" (2 Cor. 3:18; see also 2 Thess. 2:14), the Spirit of glory (1 Peter 4:14), and adoption (Heb. 2:10).

THE WORK OF THE HOLY SPIRIT

Regeneration

Isaiah spoke of the work of renewal or restoration of the world as that of the Spirit (Isa. 32:15–20). He was present at creation (Gen. 1:2) and will be involved in the whole process of the renewal of the earth. The Spirit was present in the Old Testament when Israel received the law and constructed the tabernacle of the Lord's presence (Exod. 35:31). He was there when Israel came out of Egypt and when they returned from exile (Hag. 2:5). The renewal begun in the Old Testament, however, was dramatically magnified through the ministry of our Lord, the outpouring of the Spirit, and the inclusion of the Gentiles—all indicative of the eschatological era of renewal.

The Spirit is the Spirit of renewal. Through the operation of the Holy Spirit the spiritual birth takes place. He takes what is sinful, polluted, and dead in trespasses and renews it in the image of God's Son (John 1:13; 3:8; 1 John 2:29). Regeneration is the first stage in the process of spiritual renewal. The Spirit introduces us to the new life and to our participation in the New Creation (2 Cor. 5:17; Gal. 6:15). He is the God-given sign of adoption and of the hope of glory (Rom. 8:1–17).

Sanctification

The Holy Spirit also furthers the work of Christ in the process of sanctification. Through him the ministry of the New Covenant is much more glorious than the ministry revealed under the older covenant, because his ministry embraces the gradual transformation of every believer into the likeness of Jesus, "with ever-increasing glory" (2 Cor. 3:18). Through him Jesus continues his ministry of giving his disciples freedom, spiritual guidance, insight, application of spiritual truth, and spiritual maturity (v. 17; John 16:12–15; 1 Cor. 2:6–16; Phil. 2:12–13). The transformation into the image of the Son is effected as believers walk in the Spirit (Gal. 5:16, 25). They increasingly demonstrate the newness in life as the fruit of the Spirit. The Holy Spirit also helps believers in being more significantly aware of their adoption to sonship (Rom. 8:15–16; Gal. 4:6; see above). The children of God are united together by the Spirit into one body, and to this purpose he has given them a variety of gifts.

THE CHRISTIAN LIFE

For the apostle Paul, the world is characterized by unrighteousness. In its present form the world will certainly pass away to make way for a new world (1 Cor. 7:31). Those who live wickedly in this world will not inherit the kingdom of God (6:9–11). The Christian life, however, is characterized by renewal.[10] When the Spirit of God comes into one's life, he brings renewal (Rom. 8:11). This new life affects one's whole being—one's thoughts, language, attitudes, and actions (Eph. 4:23–24). The Christian is justified, having been under God's condemnation to die (2:1–3), and now has become a new creature in Jesus Christ (2 Cor. 5:17). Having been renewed by the regenerating work of the Holy Spirit and having been justified by the Father, the believer receives his adoption into the family of God, thus becoming heirs with Jesus Christ (Rom. 8:15–17). The newness of life evidences the work of Christ in the Spirit in wisdom, love, freedom, and likemindedness.

Wisdom

Paul defines true wisdom (or godliness) as the pursuit of the triune God. He speaks of wisdom as a walking with God the Father, the Son, and the Holy Spirit. He calls upon Christians to walk worthy of God (1 Thess. 2:12; 4:1–8), to be filled with the fullness of God (Eph. 3:19), to put on the Lord Jesus Christ (Rom. 13:11–14), to live in Jesus Christ (Col. 2:6–7), and to walk in the Spirit (Rom. 8:4–11). Paul contrasts the life in the Spirit with the carnality of the world (1 Cor. 3:1–4; 10:1–10; Gal. 5:16–21). The newness of life is theocentric and produces nothing less than a godly way of life, as evidenced by the fruit of the Spirit (Rom. 6:22; Eph. 5:1–2; Gal. 5:22–23; Col. 1:9–10).

Love

The second characteristic of the Christian life is the life of love. Paul contends that love is the fulfillment of the commandments (Rom. 13:8–10; 1 Cor. 13), affirming the words of Jesus Christ, who identified the most important commandments as those requiring love of God and love of one's neighbor (Mark 12:29–31). Paul does not deny the validity of the moral law of God but rejects the traditions of the rabbis. Law by itself works death instead of righteousness. Since the coming of Jesus, Christians are called to a life of love in which they sacrifice themselves to serve their Master.

The law of love is concretely expressed in two principles: abundance and equity. When God grants individuals more than they need, they have the responsibility for sharing (2 Cor. 8:7; 9:5–13; Gal. 6:6–10). The principle of equity teaches that, if one is in need, then that one's brother has a responsibility to take care of that need. The result of this mutual dependency in the body is that no one is lacking and that all have enough (2 Cor. 8:14).

Freedom

The freedom of the Christian life is a precious truth. Because Jesus has redeemed his own with his blood, no human system can control the Christian. Christians are free in what they eat, drink, or whatever they do to the glory of God (Gal. 4:26; 5:1; Col. 2:16–17; 1 Tim. 4:3–5). The apostle Paul insists that no human system be allowed to interfere with the freedom principle. He argues strongly against those who bind the conscience with human rules and expectations. At the same time, however, he gives guidance in terms of how freedom is to be enjoyed. One may enjoy life in the freedom of the Spirit as long as one acts in faith and in gratitude (Rom. 14:6) and is sensitive to the feelings of the community (1 Cor. 10:29, 33).

Likemindedness

The Christian life is also defined by likemindedness (Rom. 15:5–6; Phil. 1:27; 2:2).[11] The body of Christ is composed of Jesus' followers, whose minds have been renewed to "the mind of Christ" (1 Cor. 2:16; see also Phil. 2:5). The renewal of the mind puts an end to all unrighteousness, expressed through selfish ambition and divisiveness (Eph. 4:23–24; Col. 3:10; Phil. 2:3–4). Paul's antidote to selfishness within the community of the saints is submissiveness and humility, on the model of Jesus Christ himself (Eph. 5:21; Phil. 2:5–8).

411

Conclusion to Part 10

Salvation is the work of the triune God in calling, renewing, justifying, reconciling, sanctifying, and glorifying the people of God. Redemption is both present and future, both forensic and relational, both individual and collective, and affects both people and the world of creation. In a general way, redemption pertains to the whole work of God.

Redemption is a series of acts of divine grace. The history of redemption unfolds the story of God's grace, and God's grace is manifest in Jesus Christ, by whom the Father constitutes a new community *(ekklēsia)* of all who are united to the Christ. Kümmel observes: "The saving event and the lordship of Christ are present realities within the world in the life of the church. Founded by God's saving act, it lives solely by grace."[12]

The present application of redemption takes place within the individual and in the community by the operation of the Spirit of restoration. He renews and keeps on renewing till the inauguration of the new creation. Sanctification, therefore, is not complete until the fullness of the redemption promised by the prophets, the Christ, and the apostles. The Christian community lives in tension between the present enjoyment of the benefits of Christ and the hope for future glory.

Part 11

The Kingdom and the Church

Introduction to Part 11

With the end of the apostolic ministry, the Lord sovereignly brought to an end the apostolic witness to the risen Christ. The end of the apostolic era, however, did not signify the termination of the Spirit's work, the presence of the Christ, or the working out of the Father's purposes in the church. The study of church history helps one to see how great the Father's patience is, how deep the love of Christ is for his church, and how effectively the Spirit continues to transform individuals, churches, and societies. The work of the triune God has brought the light of the gospel of Jesus to the ends of the earth!

In this part we shall look at the people, events, and movements that have shaped the present evangelical world. I do not intend to be exhaustive or to replace the many works available on the history of the church. These few pages serve to provide a connection between the previous stages of redemptive history and the final, climactic revelation of Jesus Christ.

The complexity of issues and the cultural conditioning of people, ideas, and movements require a sympathetic ear. It is far too easy to judge any part of this story from a twentieth-century vantage point. The history of the church witnesses to the vitality of the institution of the church and to the continuing work of the triune God in and through the church and beyond. In this survey I attempt to avoid judgmentalism, myopia, and exclusiveness. Judgmentalism of the past often disregards what God has done over the past nineteen centuries. Myopia closes our eyes to our own culturally conditioned responses. Exclusiveness fosters a spirit of pride for the tenets and practices of our own group.

The triune God is at work in the persecution of the saints; the hammering out of doctrines in the wake of heresies; the awakenings, revivals, and reform movements; and in saving and sanctifying his people for eternity. For the outworking of his purposes it has pleased God to use humans, frail institutions, cultural expressions, denominations and schismatic movements, and even secularization. Imperfect and unreliable as his people are, he remains faithful!

CHAPTER 36

The Church in the World

Christianity inherited from the Jewish Diaspora the concern over how to adapt to the world.[1] Jews had to learn how to apply the Scriptures to a changing world, both to Hellenism and to the Roman Empire. Christianity faced first the matter of Gentile membership. Next, the church had to adjust to the growing separation from the synagogue and Judaism. Third, Christians had to cope with the pressures of Rome and paganism. As the church began to stand on her own, she was continually faced with the problem of living as Christians in a hostile world. (See figure 25.)

CHRISTIANITY FACES THE ROMAN EMPIRE

Witness and Perseverance

Early Christians followed the apostolic example of witnessing to their faith in Jesus their Messiah. Their eagerness to speak about their faith was matched by their readiness to die for Christ. Roman officials and citizens were at a loss to understand the commitment of Christians. Faith in Christ spread rapidly, in spite of the outbursts of hatred for Christians and in spite of Christianity's having been outlawed.

During the rule of Nero (54–68), Domitian (81–96), Marcus Aurelius (161–80), Decius (249–51), and Diocletian (284–305), Christians were persecuted for the cause of Christ. The martyrdom of Polycarp is a moving example of perseverance in the face of persecution. The aged Polycarp confessed Christ before his tormentors: "For eighty-six years I have served him [Jesus], and he never did me any wrong: How can I blaspheme my King who saved me?" (9.3). He died while praying, "I bless thee, because thou has deemed me worthy of this day and hour, to take my part in the number of martyrs, in the cup of thy Christ, for resurrection to eternal life" (14.2).

The growth of the church throughout the Roman Empire was remarkable, even with the occasional violent persecutions. During this time some rose to a position of prominence: the apologists Justin Martyr (c. 150), Tatian (c. 150), and Tertullian (c. 200) defended the gospel, while the polemicists Irenaeus (c. 175), Clement of Alexandria (c. 175), Origen (c. 225), and Cyprian (c. 250) set forth more clearly the contents of the faith.

Date	Period/Event
A.D. 29–500	Early church
29	Death and resurrection of Jesus
70	Fall of Jerusalem
100	End of apostolic era
312	Emperor Constantine's conversion
325	Council of Nicea
400	Augustine
500–1350	The church and power
800	Charlemagne
1054	Church schism into east and west
1096–1272	Crusades
1350–1600	Renaissance and Reformation
1517	Luther's Ninety-five Theses
1536	Calvin's *Institutes*
1600–present	Modern era
1611	King James Bible
1648	Westminster Confession
1750	Wesleys; the Great Awakenings
1750–	Rise in Protestant missions; social reform; biblical and theological studies; humanism, rationalism, and the Enlightenment

Figure 25. Highlights of Church History

General Acts of Devotion

Early Christianity gave itself to prayer, the Word, and the public confession of sins.[2] According to the Didache, a second-century document, believers confessed their sins as often as every Sunday. Beginning in the fourth century, Christians set apart the Lord's Day for public worship services and developed festivals (especially Easter and Pentecost) in a liturgical calendar. With the legal recognition of Christianity in the fourth century, the celebrations became more numerous and more public. Through the establishment of holy sites in Palestine, relics were brought back and functioned as visible reminders of Jesus and the apostles. Too often they became objects of veneration, and special powers were attributed to them.

Gradually, expressions of piety differentiated Eastern and Western

Christianity. In the East the believers were more mystically inclined, developed their own liturgical calendar, and made highly artistic expressions (icons) of Jesus and of the apostles for public and private worship. This practice provoked heated controversy, as a result of which the icon was retained as an established tradition of Christian piety in the Eastern churches.

Asceticism

Asceticism had a strong appeal to Christians long before the Reformation. Partly because of the persecutions, the belief in the immanent return of Christ, the corruption of state and church, and the influence of heresies such as Manicheism, believers were drawn to the rigors of a disciplined lifestyle. Ascetic regimens included abstinence from marital relations, eating only coarse or dried food, and sometimes even a denial of water. A more extreme form was taken by hermits, who left family and work altogether to live on the fringes of civilization.

Manuals and Creeds

Christians needed instruction in the faith. To this end, manuals on the Christian faith, worship, and life were written. One such manual was the Rule of Faith, consisting of questions and answers. Other forms developed in which young believers recited their faith with the formula "I believe . . . ," as in the Apostles' Creed. As these manuals were copied and widely used, churches developed a unity of belief and practice. Although the manuals and catechisms were helpful for young believers, they did not deal with every issue. Gradually, Christians were forced to clarify themselves on many issues, including their doctrine of God, Jesus, the Spirit, the Trinity, salvation, the nature of man, and the authority of Scripture. These formulations developed in light of heresies from within and worldly philosophies from without.

Creeds arose in response to these challenges. With each heresy, issue, and council, the body of theology increased—but also furthered the separation of each generation from the apostolic church. Positively speaking, theological definition and creedal statements provide coherence and precision, without which later generations would have been forced to cover the same ground that earlier believers had adequately dealt with. Moreover, the Spirit of God was at work in raising up able leaders, by whose writings and deliberations significant advances were made in understanding the Bible. Negatively, a chasm developed between the leaders and the laity, between those instructed in theology and philosophy and those who were not. This separation left the laity dependent on the clergy.

Toleration and Vitality of the Church

Latourette has observed that the decree making Christianity the official religion of the Roman Empire was "a greater menace than the earlier policy of persecution."[3] Not only was the church in danger of becoming subordinate to the state, but also it identified too readily with the Hellenistic-Roman cultural legacy. This identification of Christianity with a certain cultural expression bound its witness to the geographical area of the Roman Empire and kept it from readily expanding eastward.

With the Christianization of the Roman Empire in A.D. 313, Christianity came perilously close to being reduced to an arm of the state. The process was dangerous, as it produced a secularization of the Christian faith. Fourth-century separatist groups such as the Novatianists and Donatists demanded purity and strict adherence to their traditions of godliness. In the Eastern church Christians withdrew themselves from the church and the world in order to enjoy fellowship with God through ascetic rigors. Gradually these lonely monastics were brought together into communities by Basil of Caesarea (d. 379), by whose regulations communities of Christian brotherhood were established and received some stamp of ecclesiastical legitimation. The movement gradually spread westward as far as Ireland by the fifth century. Some were reclusive and given to spiritual matters only; others were like Jerome (c. 347–420), an erudite monastic who exemplified a high level of scholarship. He translated the Bible into Latin (the Vulgate) and wrote commentaries on books of the Bible.

Latourette has commented about the spiritual dangers of this time: "Christianity was put in jeopardy by its very success. Through its first great triumph it had come to be so closely associated with the Graeco-Roman world that the disintegration of the one might well be the precursor of the demise of the other."[4] But at the collapse of the Roman Empire, the church showed its resilience. Its spiritual strength came from the presence of the Spirit of God and not from its political and structural unity. The Christian faith triumphed over the political and cultural structures, even though its identity was largely wrapped up with them. The great moving force that overcame persecutions, politicization of the church, acculturation, and all of the weaknesses associated with people remained Jesus Christ. The five hundred years from his birth to the medieval church witness to the vitality of Jesus' teaching and the transforming hope of his glorious return. He overcame the Roman Empire, paganism, the barbarian invasions, the heresies, and the spiritual struggles of the growing church.

CHRISTIANITY FACES THE WORLD

Monasticism, asceticism, deeper life, and missions were legitimate expressions of the Christian faith in response to the challenge posed by secularization. Spiritual renewal came through and outside of the church. The Lord of the church guided his people, even during the centuries when Christianity was not making much progress. But secularization took its toll as certain regions fell to Islam and as the Eastern (Orthodox) church and the Western church gradually drifted apart, forming two branches of Christianity. Corruption and politicization of the priesthood and papacy further adulterated the spirituality of the church. Moreover, the persecuted minority in turn became the persecutors of pagans when Christianity became a majority. By A.D. 1000, Christianity seemed to be at a low.

Monasticism

The monastic movement was a positive vehicle for bringing a certain group of devotees together around a common goal. Though the Reformation rejected the perpetuation of this form of Christianity, it left a positive mark in the history of the church. Maintaining a spiritual fervor during times of severe decline, monasticism produced reformers who began with the church. Among these was Martin Luther, an Augustinian monk who sought and found peace with God.

Monasticism functioned as a beacon of light during a dark era. In the midst of secularization and corruption, monastic orders responded positively to the evil of their days. They provided a source of spiritual, academic, and cultural renewal, based on the teachings of Jesus rather than on increasing accommodation to the changes. For example the monastery at Cluny encouraged the monks to be involved with society by providing ideals for society, education, and politics. Bernard of Clairvaux and the Cistercians observed St. Benedict's rule of poverty and withdrawal from the world but expected all monks to occupy themselves with manual labor to avoid idleness. The order of St. Francis, with its rules of poverty and asceticism, was a wholesome reminder of the original ideals of the monastic orders. The monastery of St. Dominic expected the monks to devote themselves to a life of poverty, preaching, and teaching. Each monastery attempted to make some such contribution to society.

Missions in Northern and Eastern Europe

A more aggressive expression of Christianity is represented by the missionary movement. The Roman Empire was decimated by waves of barbarians, who even destroyed Rome in 410. In this context, Augustine, bishop of Hippo, wrote *The City of God*, in which he explained that "the City of God" was a higher ideal than "the City of Man." This concern for the establishment of the kingdom of God motivated missionaries to respond to the challenge of presenting the barbarian tribes with the gospel: Ulfilas (311–383), Martin of Tours (316–396), Patrick (389–461), Augustine (c. 575 [not the bishop of Hippo]), Columba (521–597), Boniface (c. 725), Willibrord (658–739), Anskar, and others carried the gospel to the Goths, Celts, Britons, Scots, Franks, Frisians, and as far as Norway. By the year 1000, most of Western Europe had become Christianized.[5]

CHRISTIANITY FACES LEARNING

Out of concern for Christian culture, educational institutions arose for the express purpose of teaching the basic skills. The French rulers were especially instrumental in having a vision of educating Europe. To this end Charlemagne (c. 800) established "palace schools." Through this institution basic education was provided in the West, which led in time to the development of a university system.

About the same time, Islam had transformed the dead heritage of the Greeks into a living culture by the translation and study of Greek literature, science, geometry, and philosophy. Through the writings of Aristotle, Western culture was about to be transformed to a rational, scientifically open society.

The philosophical and linguistic accomplishments of the Arabs were carefully studied and adapted by Jewish scholars, especially Ibn Ezra and Maimonides. Through their widespread influence Judaism became open to a more consistent approach to studying the Bible. The *pᵉšat* ("simple") method encouraged a careful study of the biblical text through the usual canons of grammar and literary convention, rather than by sheer repetition of traditional forms of interpretation. The more philosophical interpretation was in vogue in certain circles but did not make a lasting contribution to Judaism. Both forms of interpretation, however, had an impact on Christian scholars who came into contact with these methods of understanding the Old Testament text.

In addition, the Crusades and trade with the East brought ancient literature and learning into the West. Travel necessitated by a search for ever-widening markets introduced the West to the limits of their own civilization. The frontiers were opening and were challenging Western society to rethink its familiar structures.

Scholasticism and the Renaissance

Education, scientific exploration, exposure to a wider world, and an opening of the treasures from a distant past transformed Western medieval culture. The familiar patterns of thought, interpretation, and understanding of the world were being challenged. Medieval society reflects a highly complex world, with a mixture of paganism, superstition, fear of the unknown, confidence in human capacities, excitement with the unknown, love and distrust of the church, spiritual corruption and new spiritual life, extension of the worldly power of king and pope, and a growth of the church. As people became more intoxicated with learning, they showed a greater perception of God, man, and the world. Though the common person may have despaired from the many changes, the world of the Renaissance gave birth to the Reformation!

Scholasticism denotes a medieval movement that occupied itself with the interrelation between Aristotelian philosophy and theology. The so-called schoolmen were divided on the place of reason, the place of the church and learning, and the relation of faith and learning. Out of their concerns the university system arose, with cathedral schools (Notre Dame in Paris) and universities (Paris, Bologna, Padua, Oxford, Cambridge, Vienna, Prague, Leipzig, Heidelberg, Basel, and Louvain).

From the eleventh through the fourteenth century, scholasticism developed as a unifying system, created out of Christian theology and Aristotelian philosophy. Anselm of Canterbury, Peter Abélard, Peter Lombard, and Thomas Aquinas each contributed to the holistic perspective. Aquinas, particularly, is known for his pyramidal, hierarchical structuring of the world of God and man. God was equated with "the supreme good," and man was set in the context of animate and inanimate objects. In between the being (God) and the world of reality was a "chain of being" from the greater to the lesser. Man is good to the extent that he resembles God. Aquinas assumed that the world is orderly and rational, that all of nature reflects the divine mind, and that the Christian must use proper logic to draw near to God. A more empirical scholasticism developed among the Franciscans, whose Robert Grosseteste and Roger Bacon began experimenting with light in prisms, mirrors, and the rainbow in the development of modern scientific theory.

The *Renaissance* ("rebirth") was a most significant movement during the fourteenth to the sixteenth century.[6] It developed in Italy and spread quickly to northern Europe. It affected the human spirit in rekindling a joy in life, as reflected in painting and literature (Giovanni Boccaccio, Leonardo da Vinci, Raphael, Michelangelo) and in a resurgence of classical studies (Johann Reuchlin, Thomas More, Erasmus). The Renaissance gave birth to a form of Christian humanism, in which human nature was realistically assessed as having been affected by sin and in need of divine grace. At the same time there was a wholesome appreciation of humankind's past and present cultural accomplishments, connected with an optimism about human potential. The Renaissance and humanism gave rise to a new synthesis of

Christianity and Aristotelianism, in which the final authority was not the church, but man. In this context the Reformation arose.

Mysticism

Another positive development was found in the stress on a mystical relationship with Christ through the teachings of Eckhart, Tauler, the Friends of God, the *Theologia Germanica*, John of Ruysbroeck, the Brethren of the Common Life, and the monastery of Windesheim. One of the greatest literary contributions from the Brethren of the Common Life is *The Imitation of Christ*, by Thomas à Kempis (c. 1450), a Dutch mystic, whose manual of devotion is a guide to a life of fellowship with God.

The effects of translating the Bible into the vernacular were felt by the fifteenth century. Not only did Wycliffe translate the Bible, he also trained others for preaching the Word. Other pre-Reformation leaders were John Hus in Bohemia and Jiménez de Cisneros in Spain.

THE REFORMATION

The Reformation signifies a most significant development in the history of the church. Out of it the Lutheran, Reformed, Presbyterian, Baptist, and Anglican churches developed. At the heart of the Reformation was the concern for one's immediate relationship with God. The ground for this concern came out of the Epistle to the Romans, in which Paul clarifies the nature of justification by faith. The victory of the Reformation was the freedom of letting Scripture speak without the overshadowing of traditional interpretation or the authority of the Roman Catholic church. For Martin Luther, whose famous theses were nailed on the door of the Wittenberg church in 1517, the Reformation came as a surprise, as he did not know how the Holy Spirit had prepared the world for renewal. He loved Jesus, the Word of God, and held dearly to the conviction of the priesthood of all believers. As he stood his ground against the authorities of the church, Luther affirmed with increasingly greater clarity the *sola*s of the Reformation: *sola fide* ("by faith alone"), *sola Scriptura* ("Scripture alone"), *solus Christus* ("only Christ"), and *sola gratia* ("by grace alone"). The Reformation faith quickly spread over Western Europe. Luther had not set out to revolutionize the world, but the effects of God's work through him are still with us. Thank God for Martin Luther!

The Reformation era stimulated the development of new confessions and catechisms. The great variety in Protestant Christianity goes back to the understanding of the Bible by the primary and secondary Reformers. The development in doctrine, however, was not without polemics. Each group defined its distinctives in relation to its Catholic background and in relation to at least one other separatist group. For example, Lutheranism developed in contradistinction to Rome, Calvinism, and the Anabaptists.

Although Luther, Calvin, and the other Reformers found it difficult to reconstruct a unified Christian world view, the affirmation of the priesthood of believers was an important beginning. Each Christian man and woman was called by God to develop and practice his or her gifts to the glory of God. On a more practical level, Lutheranism and Reformed theologians differed on the nature of the priesthood of all believers, which stemmed from a different conception of nature and grace.

In Lutheranism a distinction is made between nature and grace, between culture and Christ. This distinction flows out of a reaction to Aristotelian philosophy and theology. In Aquinas's view, human cultural accomplishments are a part of the natural world, conforming to natural law. Grace adds whatever is lacking to make it of lasting value—hence, the distinction between nature and grace. Luther, in reacting to the medieval consensus view, played down the human spirit ("nature") and stressed human sinfulness and the consequent need for grace. Culture and human accomplishment have no ultimate value. Christians live in hope of God's pleasure with their work at the return of Christ. The Anabaptists were even more pessimistic about humankind's cultural accomplishments. They, too, emphasized the sinfulness of man and the impossibility of a Christian culture.

Calvin, on the other hand, wrote from the perspective of the kingdom of God and the victorious work of Jesus Christ. He saw that God had been reclaiming this world from the moment of Adam and Eve's fall. Though human beings are sinners, those who are redeemed receive the grace of Christ to make a significant cultural contribution.

A new form of scholasticism ossified the Reformation movement from the sixteenth to the nineteenth century. Time did not stand still, however, as the spirit of humanism continued to free man. The Christian humanism of the Reformers, combining convictions about human gifts and sinfulness, developed into a humanism that allowed no limitations on human abilities and reason. The Enlightenment spirit eliminated God from the world under investigation and led to deism; Immanuel Kant chained religion to reason. Secularism and humanism characterize the present era, which is an outgrowth of a long process extending from the fourteenth century to the present. Christianity and humanism have been together, but they are strange bedfellows. An intoxication with man leads to humanism; a despair of man, to existentialism. Only a faith in Christ, the God-man, affirms the kingdom of God on earth.

THE MODERN ERA

The Development of the Modern Mind

Scholastic Protestantism in the seventeenth and eighteenth centuries did not produce significant scientific or philosophical developments, while the humanistic movement begun in the Renaissance made giant strides. In the beginning, scholars—in awe of the human cultural legacy, human abilities, and scientific exploration—were still associated with the church.[7] Humanism was a movement still very much related to the church and to education. The Christian humanist learned how to live in and adjust to the world, which was now getting both smaller and larger. By the eighteenth century, however, humanism increasingly divorced itself from Christianity. Rationalism flourished, as thinkers deified reason and became more intoxicated with human abilities. Out of this context the Enlightenment developed. Kant's work *Religion Within the Bounds of Reason Alone* (1793) represents the spirit of the time. In his *Critique of Pure Reason* (1781), Kant argued that a person gains knowledge through reason and the categories of human understanding. He virtually excludes revelation, holding that knowledge of God is impossible.

Kant's categories of human understanding, especially his space-time continuum as well as his criticism of the arguments for the existence of God, have had a tremendous impact on the subsequent development of theology. In spite of the corrective attempts of Karl Barth (1886–1968), who developed a theology around the thesis that the hidden God is revealed in Christ through the Spirit and through the Word, Western religious thought could lead only to a gospel of secularization and the "God-Is-Dead" movement. Critical study of the Old and New Testaments further broke up any sense of unity between message and purpose. The focus had shifted from exegesis to source analysis and to a comparative-religions approach. The Bible had become one of many writings and was studied from a humanistic perspective.

The Evangelical Response

Out of concern for the truth of the gospel and purity of the church, a Protestant scholasticism developed. The refinement of theological thinking and doctrinal precision marked the seventeenth and eighteenth centuries. Protestants were little involved with missions and were not aware of the gradual advance of the spirit of secularism. Formalism and dead orthodoxy set in. In response to such coldness in the establishment churches, the Spirit of God raised up movements that greatly affected the course of the Protestant churches.

Pietism and Revival

The Moravians, under the dynamic leadership of Count von Zinzendorf, formed an evangelical movement within the Lutheran, and later the Anglican, church during the eighteenth century. Facing the challenges of formalism and rationalism, the Moravians set out on a path of spiritual renewal by mutual encouragement, the study of the Scriptures, and evangelism. They held a high view of Scripture and were strongly committed to missions. Through them missionaries were sent to the newly colonized areas. Through their widespread influence, too, John Wesley was converted, and the evangelical fire was spread by the Wesleys to America.

Concurrent with the Moravians was the Great Awakening in the American Colonies (1725–60). The Spirit of God used a Congregationalist pastor, Jonathan Edwards, and especially George Whitefield in bringing revival to the New England area. Though they met great resistance within the Presbyterian churches, the new movement took hold of many Presbyterians and others. Through the Great Awakening educational institutions were started (Princeton, Brown, Rutgers, Dartmouth, and the University of Pennsylvania) and a mood of toleration across denominational lines enhanced sensitivity concerning social issues such as slavery and the treatment of Indians.

The Lord used the Wesley brothers, Charles and John, in publicly calling men and women from all classes to the gospel of Christ. Influenced by the Moravians, the Wesleys showed a remarkable evangelical zeal. Charles preached in churches and prisons, and wrote 7,270 hymns besides! John was an open-air preacher who itinerated between London, Bristol, and Newcastle-upon-Tyne. Though originally intent on bringing the fires of spiritual awakening to the Church of England, John formed "societies" of Methodists, which in turn developed into the Methodist church.

Missions

Protestants developed a concern for missions after receiving external stimulus from parachurch organizations. The Moravians and the Great Awakening were largely responsible for sensitizing them to the need for evangelism at home and abroad. The concern for missions continued in the mainline denominations, even though interfaith missions remained strong.

> The prominence of private enterprise in the propagation of Christianity in the nineteenth century was only a phase of the multiplicity of organizations privately formed to attack the evils of society and to promote the improvement of individuals and society.[8]

Education and Culture

The Reformation gave a new impetus to the integration of faith and learning. The Reformers emphasized the authority of Scripture and the responsibility of the individual (which derived from the doctrine of the priesthood of believers). Education was open to all, even though advanced education was still limited to highly talented or monied students. Lutheranism operated from a grace-nature distinction, according to which culture and the realm of nature were unrelated to concerns of the Spirit. Calvinism, on the contrary, did not recognize the nature-grace dichotomy, nor did it accept the hierarchical system of Aquinas. All things were under the dominion of God in Christ and hence were profitable for study, as everything revealed the handiwork of God. By the 1800s, however, education was passing out of the hands of the church into the state, leaving many untaught in the basic principles of the faith. Life became more and more secularized, even though there had not been startling philosophical or scientific discoveries forcing a new change on Western society.

With the increasing secularization and involvement of the state in education, society, and culture, parachurch organizations, schools, and universities developed. Next to the church and often cooperating with the churches were individuals and institutions that were God-sent reminders of the spirituality of the church and of its exalted mission. Unfortunately, many of these organizations were quickly secularized, because they had no connection with or supervision from any church or denomination. "It was usually only when a fairly close relation was retained with some one of the churches that a Christian purpose was clearly conserved."[9]

The American Experience

The Protestant influence from England (Anglican/Episcopalian), Germany and the Scandinavian countries (Lutheran), and the Netherlands and Scotland (Reformed and Presbyterian) together with the Catholic influence have brought about an interesting admixture of ideas, liturgies, theological perspectives, and church polity in the Americas. In the United States, episcopalianism, congregationalism, and presbyterianism exist side by side as the major forms of church organization. In addition to the greater diversity of theological perspectives and forms of church government, the American experience was greatly affected by the spirit of revivalism and by the Great Awakening: "From the Awakening a distinctly American revivalist tradition emerged; it was marked by emotional evangelism with emphasis on sin, salvation, and dramatic conversion experience."[10]

The impact of personal piety also affected society. Especially after the

Second Great Awakening (1795–1830), the churches became more involved in reform movements, missions, and education (including colleges, universities, seminaries, and Sunday school). Around the turn of the twentieth century, however, Christians generally retreated from education and from the new intellectual climate, narrowing their concerns to redemption at the expense of the integration of creation and redemption. This suspicion of intellectualism became known as "Fundamentalism." Askew and Spellman observe,

> Fundamentalism as a movement would eventually reflect as much a state of mind and cultural configuration as a set of theological propositions. . . . Its adherents . . . tended to regard themselves as a "saving remnant," loyal to traditional American Christian values and scornful of "modernism" in thought and behavior.[11]

George Marsden distinguishes between the Fundamentalist and the Evangelical on historical grounds. He sees a progressive separation in the 1950s, when the strict separatists applied the term "Fundamentalism" to themselves and separated their groups from the mainstream of what came to be called "Evangelicalism."[12] Evangelicalism accordingly has become a transdenominational movement characterized by a variety of theological perspectives and ecclesiastical forms, by certain transdenominational convictions and by a variety of so-called parachurch organizations. What characterizes the evangelical mind? In addition to the above transdenominational concerns, the Evangelical adheres to basic Bible teaching, namely, the authority and inerrancy of Scripture, the historical reality of divine revelation, and the importance of salvation, missions, evangelism, and personal piety.[13]

CHAPTER 37

Key Questions in the Church

The church is composed of people with various ideas and is surrounded by a world filled with different philosophies. Over the centuries Christians had to define the faith delivered to them by the apostles. Christians had to explain their faith in relation to the Bible. The Bible is not a collection of creeds, nor does it address specifically each new issue. In the course of twenty centuries, Christians faced Gnosticism, Neoplatonism, Aristotelianism, humanism, and rationalism. Each new wave of ideas affected the ways Christians expressed their faith, but each also had adverse effects. After all, the human factor was very important in the process of transmitting "the faith." Since humans are fallible, have strong personalities, and interpret the Bible differently, disagreements arose, resulting in a wide scope of issues and widely diverging developments. The church eventually faced East versus West, Protestant versus Catholic, denominationalism, and numerous contrasting theological positions. In spite of human institutions and opinions, however, the story of the Christian church reveals the operation of the Spirit.

Some methods of interpretation and adaptation were readily adopted, whereas others were gradually forgotten. Early in the history of Christianity the Christians faced heresies relating to the place of the law (Ebionites), the nature of the knowledge of God and the world (Gnostics and Neoplatonists), the extent of biblical authority and inspiration, and the nature of Christ and the Godhead. From the days of the apostles till the present, the Christian community has faced issues raised from within and without. Each challenge posed grave dangers, but from a historical perspective the heresies forced Christianity to adapt to the changing world. According to Cairns,

> False teachings that arise through the attempts of ambitious men to assert their authority, or through overemphasis and consequent misinterpretation of certain Scriptures, or through loveless treatment shown to an erring minority by the Church—these did not finally weaken the Church but forced it to think out its belief and to develop organization.[1]

The Spirit of Jesus Christ guided the church throughout the centuries in the variety of doctrinal expressions and in the differences that arose between East and West, Catholic and Protestant, Reformed and Lutheran, and the various forms of church government. As strongly as we may hold our particular convictions, we can never go back to the first-century church, but we may disagree in love with those who differ, and we may treasure the fellowship with those who are likeminded.

In this chapter we shall ask these questions:

1. What is the canonical authority of the Scripture?
2. How do we interpret the Bible?
3. How do we adjust biblical interpretation to a changing world?
4. Who is God, and how do the persons of the Trinity relate to each other?
5. How is the Atonement applied?
6. How is a person justified before God?
7. What are the sacraments?

BY WHAT STANDARD?

Christianity has inherited from Judaism a concern for the oracles of God. It calls on individuals to be transformed by the power of the Word, which it has received by revelation from the Spirit of God. The Bible did not drop out of heaven but was given to us in space and time and through human languages and cultures. The Word of God is therefore also the word of man. This fact raises the question not only of the mode of revelation but also of the extent and interpretation of that revelation. How does one interpret the Word, since it was received in the context of a very different cultural situation? Not only was the Bible read and preached in a Gentile context, it also became subject to the canons of tradition in the church context. The authority of the Bible was gradually reduced, in sensitivity to the cultural context as well as by a high regard for the tradition and acceptable norms of interpretation. The "book of God and man" was increasingly bound by human limitations.

The Bible in the Early Church

While the early church was being persecuted for the sake of Christ, it was forced to hammer out significant theological issues. In the process of its growth and theological reflection, it returned to the Scriptures as its authority. To some extent tradition already played a role, as the church fathers, both before and after the Council of Nicea, had received

429

a significant heritage. Underlying their theological discussions was a devotion to the revealed Word of God in Scripture and to Jesus Christ.

Three historical circumstances forced early Christians to determine the books of the Bible they would use to develop their faith, practice, and worship. First, in dialogue with the Jews, the Christians defended their position from Scripture, that is, the Old Testament. The Jews, however, considered that the Old Testament Scriptures belonged to them and insisted that theirs was the proper interpretation. In the first century the Hebrew Bible was not yet in its present form, as the text consisted only of consonants. Though the Septuagint, the Old Testament in Greek, was complete, Jews readily returned to the Hebrew text as the preferred authority. Gradually they introduced a system of marking the vowels so as to ensure the "proper" reading of the text. This process ended up in a normative text, known as the Masoretic (from *massôrâ*, or "tradition") Bible.

Not only did the Jews force the matter of the text, they also argued for their view of the canon. In dialogue with Jews, Christians discovered that the Septuagint contained more books in the Old Testament than the Hebrew Scriptures, having added the so-called Apocrypha. It is small wonder that the debate between Christians and Jews ceased in the second century, as Christians insisted on the Septuagint as the "oracles of God" and as they interpreted even the most literal passages with a spiritual and often christological sense. Moreover, Gentile Christians inherited many biases against the Old Testament narratives and events from the Hellenistic background. They attempted to explain away at all costs whatever was offensive as Jewish.[2] As long as dialogue with Jews took place, Christians learned from the Jews canon, text, and interpretation. But when Christianity went its own way, dialogue ceased, and a grand gulf developed between Judaism and Christianity. Not until the later Middle Ages were Christians attracted to Jewish learning; out of this dialogue the Reformation developed.

Second, Marcion in the second century forced the issue of Jewish versus Christian, Old versus New Testament, law versus gospel. His heresy is associated with Gnosticism, the "gospel" of the spiritual. Through liberating oneself from the material world and especially the flesh, one could find salvation. God is spirit and did not create the world. The physical creation came from the Demiurge, a demigod. Marcion identified the Lord (Yahweh) of the Old Testament with the demiurge, and Christ became the Redeemer of humankind from the Old Testament, from Yahweh, from the flesh, and from the world. The Christ did not come in human flesh but *appeared* in the flesh. From this theological basis Marcion argued that the Old Testament canon is Jewish, evil, and unprofitable. Even certain sections of the New Testament were grouped as Jewish and hence as less than Christian. He adopted only the Gospel of Luke and ten Pauline Epistles (excluding Timothy and Titus) as embodying the spirit of Christ.

The ante-Nicene fathers responded quickly to Gnosticism and to Marcion's teaching. On the one hand, they affirmed that the Lord, the Father of Jesus Christ, created heaven and earth and that Jesus was actually born of a woman (i.e., he had flesh and blood). On the other hand, they affirmed the Scriptures of the Old Testament and began a process of reflection on the canon of the New Testament. The former finds expression in the Apostles' Creed: "I believe in God the Father Almighty; Maker of heaven and earth. And in Jesus Christ his only Son our Lord; who was conceived by the Holy Ghost, born of the Virgin Mary, suffered under Pontius Pilate, was crucified, dead, and buried. . . ."

The latter finds expression in lists of canonical books and a defense of the Old Testament canon. The Jewish canon of the Old Testament was accepted as confirmed by our Lord and the apostles.[3] Moreover, lists were drawn up defending the traditions pertaining to the New Testament writings. The most significant list of the New Testament books is that given in A.D. 367 in the Easter letter of Athanasius, bishop of Alexandria. It is the earliest list that includes all the books of the present New Testament. Other writings (apocryphal, spurious, and apocalyptic) were rejected. Issues were raised with respect to Hebrews, James, 2 Peter, 2–3 John, Jude, and the Revelation of John, but these books were generally accepted. Distinction was made, however, between a practical canonicity and theological reservation. Even as late as the Reformation, Luther expressed candid reservations concerning Hebrews, James, Jude, and the Apocalypse!

Third, the Roman persecutions also drove the Christians to reflect on the books of the canon. During the persecutions the Romans at times demanded that Christians destroy or desecrate the books of Scripture. In A.D. 300, Emperor Diocletian issued four edicts, two of which required the Christian Scriptures to be burned or destroyed. If a book was not canonical it caused no problem, but if it was part of the canon, then a decision had to be made. One group of Christians, known as the traditores, evaded this issue by freely handing over the Scriptures to be burned. At the recognition of Christianity in A.D. 313 by Emperor Constantine, the issue rose to a head as the Donatists separated themselves from the traditores, charging the latter with apostasy. The Donatists avoided any fellowship with leaders and churches that had not maintained the purity of the faith during the recent persecutions. Though this movement was largely confined to North Africa, it ruptured the unity of the church. Over time the Donatists became a minority. With the Moorish invasion of North Africa, the separatist movement was soon forgotten.

431

Church and Tradition

As the church developed, it was only natural that it formulated creedal expressions. The canon was the regulative principle, but as new issues arose (e.g., the nature of Christ, the Godhead, the Holy Spirit), a consensus gradually developed in the form of traditions and confessional statements. This consensus bound Christianity together and became the standard for future generations. It was inevitable that, with the development of canon and creed, a growing tradition also arose.

Tradition became tied in with a hierarchical system of church order. This system had the advantage of offering unity and theological solidarity, as the smaller churches received guidance from the larger churches. The New Testament churches had enjoyed the leadership of the apostles, elders, and deacons, as well as the apostolic representatives Timothy and Titus. As the church developed, a distinction was made between the larger and the smaller congregations. The larger ones enjoyed the service of a "bishop," supported by presbyters (priests), deacons, and subdeacons (acolytes). The responsibility of the bishop included all the churches of his city. The position of the bishop increased, depending on the importance of the city or the recognition among his peers. The bishops of the larger and more affluent cities enjoyed a good salary, permitting them to extend their influence, whereas the country clergy barely survived on their income. Among the bishops, the bishop of Rome gradually ranked higher because he could boast that Rome was the burial ground of Peter and Paul. The church councils recognized Alexandria, Antioch, Carthage, Constantinople, and Rome as the capitals of the church.

For some time, Rome and Constantinople rivaled each other for prominence, but with the division of the empire into East and West (with the capitals in Constantinople and Rome), the competition between the bishops of the two cities came to an end. The secular division of the empire forced the spiritual division. By 1054, the schism between the Eastern and Western churches was formal; after the Crusaders captured Constantinople in 1204, the split was irreparable. Even when the East sought reconciliation with the West in hope of military support against the Moslem Turks, the papacy in Avignon was at first not interested. In the end a decree of union was signed but was not accepted by the East until shortly before the fall of Constantinople in 1453.

The position of the bishop of Rome had become increasingly more secure through the Tome of Leo I (400–461) and the extension of papal jurisdiction under Gregory the Great (540–604). The Roman bishop took advantage of the weakness of the Roman emperors in extending his authority in civil matters and in modeling the ecclesiastical world on the

432

imperial organization. By developing canon law, using Latin as the language of the church, making papal edicts, and fashioning the ecclesiastical organization with archbishops, cardinals, and a papal council (the curia), the ecclesiastical structure of Rome would survive the imperial structure. Innocent III (1160–1216) transformed the church and the position of the pope into an institution whose power would extend to every facet of life and to every church. He also called the Fourth Lateran Council (1215), during which the role of the church in ecclesiastical and secular matters was defined and a policy was formulated against heretics, including the Jews.

The power of the Roman See was now enhanced by the institution of the Inquisition. Jews, heretics, and others who threatened Rome were persecuted and killed in the name of Jesus. The papacy itself witnessed a decline because of political and material interests. Authority was by now intimately tied in with the church and the pope. In this context the Reformation arose. Each group arising out of the Reformation responded to the issue of authority.

The Bible from the Reformation till Today

The Renaissance brought with it a renewed concern with the Scriptures and exegesis over against the traditions of the church (see, e.g., the work of Nicholas of Lyra).[4] Moreover, its renewed emphasis on man and on human reason encouraged the separation of the individual from the authority of Rome. In the Reformation era, the issue of justification by faith was the occasion for the rift between Martin Luther and Rome. But the biblical doctrine of justification was related to the doctrines of God, man, grace, the sacraments, the Scriptures, faith, and the priesthood of believers. The Reformation challenged many cherished traditional views that had developed over the centuries. The "tradition tree" of the church was effectively cut by the ax of Scripture.

This ax had been sharpened for several centuries. The Renaissance had awakened an excitement with the original languages of the Bible and a new sensitivity for the method of interpretation. The change from a system of interpretation that found several meanings for a given passage to a consistent interpretation of a biblical text was most problematic because its conclusions were at variance with current practices of interpretation. Even more disturbing was the wedge the "new hermeneutic" drove between tradition and Scripture, between church authority and the witness of the Spirit of God, and consequently between the right of private interpretation and the authority of ecclesiastical dogma. These issues finally led to the Reformation with its triumphant cry: *Sola Scriptura!* Implied in this position was the assumption that the Holy Spirit is the final authority and not the church, that the Scriptures are perspicuous (clear) in matters of faith and practice, that the Bible must be available in the vernacular language of the people, and that the interpretation of Scripture must be guided by rules that make sense out of the whole Bible.

The motto *sola Scriptura* marked a return to biblical studies for the sake of hearing afresh the Word of God to Israel and to the church. The Reformers shared the Renaissance spirit with its literary, cultural, and historical investigations for its own merit. Out of the wide exegetical spectrum of the Jewish hermeneutical modes (literary-grammatical, allegorical, homiletical, and esoteric) and the Christian approaches to Scripture (literal, allegorical, tropological, and anagogic), the Reformers pleaded for a more thoughtful approach to the Scriptures so that the Word of God could be opened rather than obscured by ingenious methods and by individualistic insights.[5] The Reformers held the position that the Scriptures have *claritas*, or "clarity." This affirmation was an important step in reducing the power of the priest in the Catholic church of the Middle Ages and undergirded the renewed emphasis of the Protestants on the priesthood of all believers.

The Reformers shook the sixteenth century with a renewed emphasis on biblical exegesis, by which they supported the doctrines of the unique importance of Christ, of grace, and of faith. In the interpretation of Scripture they were guided by the assumption that Scripture is generally clear in what God expects of men and women. The Reformers also shared the Renaissance spirit in being open to new facts. All of creation was the handiwork of God and was a means of divine revelation. The study of God's revelation in nature by means of the arts and sciences also led to revolutionary conclusions that challenged longstanding traditions. Luther and Calvin equally insisted on the acquisition of a broad background as a requisite for more fully understanding God's Word. Out of this emphasis on the historical and philological approach to Scripture was born *historical-grammatical exegesis*.

The Reformers, then, did not aim at the doctrine of *sola Scriptura* as an end in itself. It relates to their theological reflection and dialogue with the tradition. They cannot be charged with naïveté, since they did not aim at returning to the primitive church, as if 1,500 years had not elapsed between them and the apostolic church. Moreover, they were fully aware that all revelation is not equally clear. The doctrine of the perspicuity of Scripture together with the renewed emphasis on the presence of the Holy Spirit in interpretation required a new kind of listening to the Bible for salvation and sanctification—to "those things which are necessary to be known, believed, and observed for salvation."[6] The Reformers did, however, emphasize that the new way of understanding required the due use of ordinary means, which involves submission to the Holy Spirit, prayer, hearing the Word proclaimed, and a diligent personal study of God's Word.

The issue of authority has repeatedly arisen with the development of the Enlightenment in the eighteenth century and Higher Criticism in the nineteenth century. In response, evangelical Christians have continued to affirm the authority, inerrancy, and infallibility of the Word of God. The problem remains regarding how inerrancy and infallibility may provide a proper framework for interpreting the Bible. The definition of these terms must provide enough room for continuing study of the Scriptures in the light of the literary and cultural milieu in which they arose. The church in the early centuries may have erred in emphasizing the Scriptures as the oracles of God to the detriment of considering the human authors and the literary and historical-grammatical methods of studying the Bible. The danger today is also with relegating the Bible to a theological system or to a set of propositions. The Bible as the book of God and man requires the modern reader to be sensitive to the witness of the Spirit of God and also to the ways in which these ancient men of God wrote and intended to be understood (the literary perspective), as well as to how God's people heard the voice of God in the sacred Scriptures (the canonical perspective).

WHO IS GOD?

For centuries the Christian church wrestled with the complex definition of Jesus' human and divine natures, as well as with the relationship of the three persons of the Godhead. The doctrine of the Trinity that came out of these discussions has bound all branches of Christianity together as a truly catholic doctrine. The trinitarian doctrine is a mature reflection of what the Bible teaches on the persons of the Godhead. Evangelical Christians today confess with the historic Christian church through the centuries their faith in the triune God: Father, Son, and Holy Spirit.

Whereas the Apostles' Creed affirms a trinitarian formula, it was left to other creedal formulations to hammer out more precisely the relationship between the persons of the Trinity as well as the nature of the divine and the human in Jesus Christ. Some heresies originated as an attempt to preserve uniquely the humanity or the deity of Jesus Christ. Others started from the assumption of the unity of God.

Many views on the nature of Jesus were rejected over hundreds of years of theological reflection. *Arianism* (A.D. 250) held that the nature of Christ was substantially different from that of the Father. It was strongly condemned at the First Council of Nicea in 325. Apollinarius, bishop of Laodicea (c. 375), was influenced by pagan literature and the Alexandrian philosophical orientation. He taught that the Christ is a

435

union of the Logos and of the flesh of Mary. The Logos is fully God and has no human soul. *Apollinarianism* was rejected at the Council of Constantinople (381), where the church affirmed that Christ is wholly human, including his soul, and also wholly divine. Nestorius drew a distinction between the two natures of Christ, affirming that Jesus was two persons, one human and one divine, and that Mary was the mother of his human side. *Nestorianism* was rejected at the Council of Ephesus in 431.

Eutychianism is associated with Eutyches, who stressed the single, divine nature of the Christ. In reaction to Nestorianism, his views represent an early *Monophysitism*, or the position that Christ essentially had one divine nature. This view was condemned as unsatisfactory to the mystery of the Incarnation at the Council of Chalcedon in 451. A related movement, *Monotheletism*, tried to solve the mystery of the two natures by positing two natures but only one will. This position also was rejected as an unbiblical way of understanding the Incarnation, at the Third Council of Constantinople (680).

Closely related to the crux of Jesus' humanity and deity was the nature of the Godhead. *Monarchianism* was an attempt at comprehending the unity of God and the deity of Jesus Christ. Adoptionist (Dynamic) Monarchianism viewed Jesus as a divinely inspired man. At his baptism, God adopted him as his son. Modalistic Monarchianism (or Sabellianism), was more subtle and has had its representatives to this day. The incarnation of God was a mode adopted by God the Father. In Sabellian theology God is one, but he has the freedom to represent himself variously as the Father, the Son, or the Holy Spirit.

In the early discussions little concern was shown for defining the relationship of the Holy Spirit to the other persons of the Trinity. It was generally assumed that the Spirit is a person of the Godhead. For example, Tertullian taught that the Holy Spirit is God, being one with the Father and the Son. The confession of the Spirit in the Apostles' Creed and at Nicea left open the nature of the Holy Spirit. In this doctrine also, erroneous teachings forced the church to reflect. For example, Macedonius denied the deity but not the personality of the Holy Spirit. At Constantinople (381) the Nicene definition was further enlarged to refer to "the Holy Ghost, the Lord and Giver of Life; who proceedeth from the Father; who with the Father and the Son together is worshiped and glorified; who spake by the prophets."

The phrase "who proceedeth from the Father" occasioned further discussion, ultimately leading to another conciliar decree and the division of the Eastern (Orthodox) and the Western (Catholic, or Roman) branches of the church. At the Synod of Toledo (589), the Western churches supported the addition of "and the Son" *(filioque)* to the clause "who proceedeth from the Father," whereas the Eastern churches rejected it.

WHAT HAS THE CHRIST DONE?

As the creeds on the nature of the Trinity, the Christ, and the Holy Spirit were developing in response to serious challenges from within the church, a new set of issues arose that would further divide the church. These issues relate to the nature of human sin, grace, the atonement of our Lord, and the sacraments.

The Nature of Man

Discussion about the nature of man was occasioned by Pelagius, a contemporary of St. Augustine (c. 400). Pelagius taught that the human will is neutral, that people have the freedom to do good or evil, and that they must avail themselves of divine grace. For him grace is not a supernaturally bestowed gift but is readily available to everyone. Individuals must cultivate grace, as they must any gift. Pelagius placed the emphasis on human responsibility, rather than on the culpability of the human race.

Augustine responded critically to Pelagius's teaching on divine grace and human nature. For him, individuals can experience their humanness only while in fellowship with God. On account of man's fall and sin, a person cannot naturally enjoy fellowship with God. People by their very nature are lovers of self rather than of God! Augustine further taught that, since the fall of man, human nature is such that an individual cannot but sin *(non posse non peccare)*. Not only Adam and Eve were affected by sin and God's judgment, but their act of rebellion against God and the divine condemnation affect the whole human race. Their sin may be compared to a seed that germinates, develops, and produces nothing but its own kind: sinners.

Augustine thus placed a great emphasis on divine grace. Because man needs renewal, God alone can convert the soul. Having been wonderfully transformed (or regenerated) by the Spirit, the person who has received God's grace can and must say with Augustine, "Give what thou commandest, and command what thou wilt."[7]

Augustine's position on divine grace was on a collision course with the church's understanding of itself as the dispenser of grace. Though his view triumphed over Pelagianism, church theologians developed a middle-of-the-road position over the course of centuries. After lengthy debates and several councils, Pelagianism as a system was condemned at the Council of Ephesus in 431, but the issues that flowed out of the debate have remained with us to the present: How depraved is man? Can a person cooperate with God's grace? What is the nature of predestination? How can predestination and human responsibility both be true? Is a person free to do good? How can God be the Father of all his creation and elect only some?

The Nature of the Atonement

The issues of human sin, the grace of God, and the work of Christ came together in *Cur Deus homo?* (Why did God become man?), an epochal theological study by Anselm of Canterbury in the eleventh century. Before him the church had tolerated a wide variety of views. In the ransom view Jesus paid a ransom to Satan. The forensic view held that Christ satisfied divine justice. The propitiation view taught that Christ's death was for atonement of human sin. Orr observes,

> There can be no reasonable question, therefore, as to the general faith of the church in the truly atoning virtue of the death of Jesus Christ; but as yet there had been no systematic attempt to bring the various aspects of Christ's saving work into unity, or to give them the necessary theological grounding.[8]

Anselm attempted to represent the biblical data more systematically by arguing that man has wronged God in sinning and consequently deserves God's just punishment. The Father cannot be satisfied with human efforts, because his wrath is too great to be placated by man's individual or collective accomplishments. The Father is satisfied with the obedience of Christ, however, who fulfilled God's requirements, especially in the voluntary act of suffering and death to the honor of the Father. This sacrifice was accepted by the Father, and through Jesus' death sinful individuals may now gain entrance into the Father's presence.

Anselm maintained a place for merit and for balancing merits and demerits, debts and rewards. Anselm's view was not as widely accepted as the moral influence view of Abélard (c. 1100). According to Abélard, individuals who reflect on Christ's death should be moved to repent from their sins, love Jesus, and learn from his example.

From the turbid waters of merit and morality, the Reformation arose. The Reformers argued that Christ fully identified with the human condition so as to bear our sin and guilt, that Christ's sacrifice was expiatory, that man had transgressed the law of God, that individuals could not merit salvation, and that a person may be justified only on the basis of the finished work of the Christ.

The Reformers rejected Abélard's theory of the Atonement as unsatisfactory to the biblical teaching. They refined Anselm's understanding by emphasizing properly the law of God, man's condemnation, and the heinousness of sin. Sin was nothing less than rebellion against God. They explained the death of Christ as his satisfying the wrath of

God and also as his bearing the guilt of human sin. Only by faith and by grace could one lay hold of justification. Justification was not the result of human effort but was *sola fide, sola gratia, solus Christus!*

Another aspect of the discussion is the extent of the Atonement. Here the Reformers were not in agreement. Two groups arose: the generalists (Luther, Melanchthon, Bullinger, and, according to some, John Calvin) and the particularists (Calvinists). According to the generalist view the Atonement was for all humankind, but only those who come to faith benefit from its application. The particularists hold that Christ's death was beneficial only for those who come to faith. This latter position was developed from Calvin's teaching and was set forth in the Canons of Dordt (1618–19).[9]

The question about the extent of the Atonement relates also to the biblical doctrines of election and predestination, sin and the nature of depravity, and man's ability and divine grace. The heritage of the Reformers was quickly divided by many parties, each claiming to have an authentic line back to a particular Reformer, while wrestling with the teachings of Scripture (see, e.g., Amyraldianism, Socinianism, and Arminianism).

The Sacraments

Other present-day ecclesiastical and practical divisions originated with the various views on the sacraments. The Reformers commonly opposed the Roman understanding of the sacraments. Rome had generally accepted the Augustinian definition of "sacrament" as an outward sign of an inward grace, dispensed by the church of Christ. For the Reformers the sacraments were only those signs that Christ had instituted. Instead of the seven sacraments developed within the Catholic "sacramental theology" (baptism, the Eucharist, confirmation, penance, extreme unction, holy orders, and matrimony), the Reformers agreed that there were essentially only two sacraments instituted by our Lord: baptism and the Lord's Supper.

Moreover, the Reformers were agreed on the necessity of the sacraments as means of grace, on the complementary nature of the written Word (Scripture), and on the sign value of the sacraments. They also agreed that the sacraments were to be dispensed through the church by means of duly ordained officers. They differed greatly, however, on the meaning and application of the sacraments.

CONCLUSION

In addition to the issues of Scripture, God, the Atonement, justification, and the sacraments, Christians have discussed—and disagreed over—many other subjects. We as Evangelicals have a common heritage that binds us together, but within the evangelical heritage diversity exists. The diversity extends to every aspect of theology, church government, Christian piety, and the understanding of the relationship between nature and grace, creation and redemption, past and present, and present and future. Yet, we have a common heritage: the *historic Christian faith*.[10] This heritage we have received freely, and we have been charged with the responsibility of transmitting that heritage in a dynamic and fresh way to the new generation. As in the past, the Lord expects his people to respond wholeheartedly with heart and mind, knowing that the Spirit of the risen Christ keeps on transforming individuals and congregations to be renewed in the image of Jesus Christ and to respond to the challenges to the gospel in each generation.

CHAPTER 38

Present and Future Issues

As the church moves into the twenty-first century, it faces at least seven major issues. First, *the place of the Bible* is debated within liberal and conservative Christianity. The future of an immanent Christianity is not great, as it degenerates into secularism. Liberal forms of Christianity will have to seek ways of adjusting to the biblical legacy, whether in the forms of biblical theology, social or personal transformation (Wink), demythologization (Bultmann), existentialism (Kierkegaard), or forms of biblical criticism. For evangelical Christians it is equally important to hold to an evangelical commitment and to a critical-exegetical methodology that will not undermine the faith. Instead of standing on the sidelines, Evangelicals are entering the arena of biblical scholarship, interacting positively with critical scholars.

Second, *political and social involvement* has become a legitimate expression of the Christian faith in this century. Even with the conviction that church and state must be separate, many have become involved politically. The outcome of such activism is unpredictable and hence not only puts the Christian community at odds with society but also frequently pits one Christian group against another. By focusing on the main mission of the church and by the use of parachurch organizations, polarization and isolation may be avoided. The greatest danger, however, lies not so much in the involvement of the church as in its identification with a particular cultural, political, or societal structure for the purpose of obtaining certain goals. Niebuhr encouraged political involvement as a way of protecting the interests of each community.[1] The dangers of political involvement, however, must be carefully weighed against the advantages. The editors of the *Eerdmans' Handbook to the History of Christianity* conclude,

> The greatest challenge that confronts the church in the last decades of the century is to apply Christianity to practical life in a world plagued by poverty, social injustice, racial discrimination and oppression, and ridden by secularism and materialism.[2]

Third, we must face *the relation of American Christianity to the rest of the world*. In an age of secularism, nationalism, and internationalism (note, e.g., the status of the United Nations), it is not popular to argue in favor of the distinctiveness of the Christian faith. The recent examples of Karl Barth and Emil Brunner and of Evangelicalism continue to witness to the distinct light coming from faith in Jesus as the Christ.

The church may serve as God's agent in cross-cultural communication.[3] Dunn has reminded us of how the early Christians adapted their confession to a changing world, from Judaism to a Gentile milieu.[4] John M. L. Young, who served as missionary to Japan, and other missiologists challenge us continually not to equate the gospel with any one culture and to express the gospel by using meaningful contextualization.[5]

The growth of the church outside Europe and America will require an adjustment, as the Western church must recognize the churches in Third World countries. The West will have to accommodate to mission strategies as well as contribute to theological formulation and methodology, inspired by Third World leaders. Moreover, Christian missionaries from whatever country will have to distinguish between Christianity and their own culture. Much of our Christian expression, liturgy, theology, and ethics is so culturally conditioned that it is difficult to separate between the essentials and the nonessentials. Os Guinness soberly reminds us that

> the Western church is not the whole church. It is only the older church, a church that handed on its torch just as it was taken captive by the world it had helped to create. But what if that torch were handed back to the old church by the new, burning more brightly than when it was given?[6]

Fourth, the Christian community will also have to face up to *the challenge of responding to Jews, Arabs, and the state of Israel.* The exegetical and theological issues surrounding the modern nation of Israel may lead the church to renewal as it faces the question of how best to respond to a living situation. While some communities may want to right every wrong of Israel, others avoid the issue altogether out of theological bias. The time for covenant, promise-fulfillment, and dispensational theologians is now! With the rise of interest in Messianic Judaism, Christians and Jews have a unique opportunity to build bridges, develop dialogue, and renew the discussions between church and synagogue that have been suspended since the second century A.D. At the same time the church must respond positively to the challenge of a changing Moslem world.

Fifth, *changes in the religious world* since Vatican II (1962–65) are most important. There are visible changes not only within the structures of the Roman church but also within the world of Eastern Orthodoxy. The ecumenical spirit is here to stay and calls for an evaluation of the criteria under which fellowship between denominations may be reestablished. On the one hand, established denominations merge into new bodies and dialogue continues within official and nonofficial channels. On the other hand, the challenge to Third World countries also comes from the direction of Pentecostalism. In Africa and Latin America, Pentecostalists represent the largest group of non-Catholic Christians. Pentecostalism brings with it an emphasis on the Spirit, spiritual renewal, and Spirit-filled living. Its strength lies in its cross-cultural, pansocial, and transdenominational concern with the new life.

Sixth, Christianity continually faces the *danger of identifying with the culture* of which it is a part. The witness of Moses, the prophets, our Lord, and the apostles presents us with the dawn of a new age: the kingdom of God. We must face the same challenge as first-century Christians: God or Caesar, Jesus or Wall Street, the kingdom of God or the Democratic (or Republican) party, the vision of the New Jerusalem or the humanistic platform of the twenty-first century. Boice speaks of the culturally limited vision of the church, as he asks that we "lead in 'demythologizing the state' and calling on individuals to be different."[7]

The opening of the world and space, together with exposure to new approaches and methods of study and evangelization, poses a challenge to the modern Christian of living in this world, filled with opportunity while maintaining and developing a hope for the future.[8] Pragmatism and secularism easily rob the church of the hope of its existence: Christ Jesus. On the one hand, Christianity may join so-called liberation theology (see Gutierrez, Jose Miranda) by extending a helping hand to the poor and oppressed in other countries, but in doing so it may advance a Marxist philosophy. For liberation theology, neither the Bible nor the Christian hope in justice at Christ's return is the proper starting point. Impatiently, they point to the present and aim at righting the present wrongs autonomously.

The options of the Reformation era are still open to us. On the one hand, some are pessimistic, taking a prophetic view that all awaits transformation and glorification at the return of Christ. C. S. Lewis is representative of those who continue to separate the two realms of nature and grace.[9] Others have a mildly optimistic, redemptive outlook, trusting that God's kingdom is being worked out in Christ and that the Christian can make a significant contribution in subduing all things to Christ.[10]

Finally, the challenge as we move into the twenty-first century lies in how evangelical Christianity adjusts to *confessing its faith in Christ in a meaningful way*. Biblical faith was never formulated in terms of an eternally valid creed. It is dynamic, as God communicates to human beings in particular cultural contexts. His Word is true, but our perceptions continue to change as we view the mosaic-like qualities of

443

the infallible Word of God given and transmitted in the fallible world of man.

Dunn relates the renewal of the church to the continual adjustment of confessions to each new context. "New situations call forth new confessions. A Christianity that ceases to develop new confessional language ceases to confess its faith to the contemporary world."[11] To this end Hendrikus Berkhof has contributed to a new type of theologizing in *The Christian Faith*. Donald Bloesch also makes a significant contribution in relating the categories of theology to past and modern issues.[12] We may admire the ambitious effort that calls for a total integration: "The American today must be involved in his faith. He must approach it through his business, his politics, his neighborhood, schools, and city."[13] To this end, too, Harvie Conn calls for a new way of doing theology in a cosmic context. This theology gives a greater place to the dynamic interaction of a God-centered perspective with a concern for people:

> Theologizing becomes symphonic. . . . each of the parts contributing to the whole, the whole becoming in the process of harmonization more than simply the sum of the parts. Multiperspectivalism as a theological methodology becomes a style of life, a hermeneutic, a way of thinking in which one takes a limited number of starting perspectives and uses them to see the whole.[14]

In confessing Christian faith, the church must heed Francis Schaeffer's appeal for a renewed concern for unity and ecumenicity as true expressions of "visible love." He comments, "Love—and the unity it attests to—is the mark Christ gave Christians to wear before the world. Only with the mark may the world know that Christians are indeed Christians and that Jesus was sent by the Father."[15]

Part 12

The New Jerusalem

Introduction to Part 12

The history of redemption is the story of God's involvement with man's redemption and of man's response to the promises of the Lord. God promises, performs mighty acts, and works out his purpose in salvation and in vindication. The history of redemption displays the interaction between God's revelation and his acts. The two aspects complement each other and reveal God's purpose in creation and redemption. He faithfully executes his purpose for the good of his people (Rom. 8:28). The nature of that "good" becomes increasingly clear in the progress of redemptive history.

Each period in redemptive history reveals God's fidelity in promise, covenant, and fulfillment. As the Lord discloses a new era, he reveals aspects of his royal being, responses he expects from his people, and his overall plan of redemption. Revelation as an act of God reveals our God, with all of his goodness and perfections. The history of redemption thus looks to the revelation of God and particularly to Jesus Christ as the focus. Each book of the Bible contributes to the disclosure of our God in creation and redemption. Each act of God points to the God who saves and to a greater and more lasting fulfillment of his promises. Each act relates to God's purpose in Jesus Christ. That purpose may not be clearly discernible, but the eye of faith looks forward to the great future God has prepared for his people in Jesus Christ. Faith is directed to the Lord, the author and finisher of our salvation, and hence faith is eschatological in nature.

Throughout redemptive history, the Lord encouraged his people to develop a sense of the future. He gave his promise at all stages: to Adam, Abraham, Israel, and the church. He spoke through Moses, the prophets, our Lord, and the apostles, calling for a faith commitment to himself and to his kingdom. Through their ministry the Lord has given us glimpses of his purpose; their words are inscripturated as an abiding witness to his fidelity. This revelation is trustworthy, even when our understanding is limited and fallible.

Though the Bible is one book, it is composed of many books. We have seen that the many books reflect on and witness to an unfolding of the plan of God in the history of redemption. With the changes in the story of salvation from the Garden of Eden to the New Jerusalem, the Lord reveals a grand design. As usual, the retrospective vision sheds light on the connecting points between the diverse constituent parts. In this book I have so far described eleven periods in redemptive history. The major moments in these periods are creation in harmony and then in alienation, the covenant with Abraham, the consecration of Israel and Moses' mediatorial role in the Sinaitic covenant, the ministry of Samuel in relation to the establishment of kingship, the granting of the Davidic covenant, the secession of Israel from Judah and the development of the prophetic office since Elijah, the Exile and the postexilic restoration, John the Baptist and the incarnate ministry of our Lord, and the apostolic mission.

Throughout the program of redemptive history, the Lord chose people to further the unfolding of his plan. God's servants in the Old Testament (Moses and the prophets), side by side with his messengers in the New (his Son and the apostles), bear witness to the coming transformation of all things (Heb. 1:1–3). Transformation is the effect of God's involvement as King with his world in judgment and in deliverance, culminating in the new heavens and earth.[1] Throughout redemptive history the Lord has been working out his purpose, and each act of God has anticipated the final transformation of all things. God's people in both Old and New Testaments collectively experience life between the two horizons of creation in harmony and creation in restoration. They receive adoption to sonship, God's blessings, the good news of his love and compassion, the tokens of his goodness, and the experience of forgiveness, peace with God, and newness of life. All these benefits of covenant membership are theirs on account of Jesus the Messiah. They are God's irrevocable gifts (Rom. 11:29). It would be a mistake, however, to view them as exhaustive. They serve to comfort his children in their pilgrim existence, as they await the glorious revelation of their inheritance. The present blessings are evidence of his largess, sustaining and nurturing in his people an increase in faith and hope for the final transformation of all things.

The message of radical transformation came progressively into focus through the ministry of Moses, Samuel, Elijah, and the prophets. Toward the end of the Old Testament canon it was clear that only God's Messiah could bring deliverance, vindication, and a permanent era of peace. Jesus thus taught his disciples that Moses and the prophets witness to him (Luke 24:44–47) and that the mission of the church continues his work. How did the purpose of God advance in the progression of redemptive history to the coming of Jesus Christ? What was the message of transformation? What did God reveal concerning the future of his people, the enemies of his kingdom, and the restoration of creation? I address these issues in this final part.

447

CHAPTER 39

The Day of the Lord

The motif of the Day of the Lord revolutionizes the biblical conception of history. Biblical events are moments in the outworking of God's plan of redemption. Each event has a theological and an eschatological significance, but the totality of events as a revelation of God does not provide all the data needed for a historical reconstruction. Biblical history reveals the pattern of God's redemption and, together with the history of the church, unfolds the plan of God. History from the biblical perspective focuses on the acts of God in Christ, but even more, it points to the future transformation of all things. Redemptive history thus gains meaning when events are viewed in the light of the future.

Redemptive history considers the acts of God on two levels. The first is the level of human history, where the history of God's people is related to that of God's world. Redemptive history, too, has an interest in the events as they form a part of the human story. The second is the level of the plan and mind of God. History has an eschatological dimension, for all events have meaning in the light of the plan of God. But we do not know that plan and therefore need revelation. God revealed himself through the instrumentality of people: Moses, the prophets, the servants of God, the apostles, and above all his Son (Heb. 1:1–3). Through divine revelation the Lord reminds human beings that they are responsible for their acts and that his judgment will bring to light all things done in the body. Through divine revelation the Lord calls on everyone to repent and to seek refuge in him and in his Messiah. He exhorts his people to purify themselves in preparation for the glory prepared for them. Through divine revelation the Lord encourages and comforts his people, pointing out both the great benefits they already have and those that await them. For the believer, therefore, history unfolds *his story*, operating in two continually intersecting levels: the horizontal and the vertical. From our perspective, the vertical is an intrusion of the eschaton.

Only gradually did the Lord reveal how radical the break would be between the world of creation and the world of restoration. He

448

sustained his children throughout redemptive history with his blessings, promises, acts of protection, and provision. All acts of his special grace were tokens of the eschatological blessing and protection. On the other hand, all acts of judgment also express the sovereignty and kingship that he will establish at the end of the age.

Also gradually, the Lord made explicit the nature of the salvation to come. The Old Testament witnesses to the seeming shift from a concern for the future at the horizontal level to the revolutionary teaching that this present world must be re-created. Everything moves to the moment of God's final judgment of the wicked; the vindication, deliverance, and rewards of the righteous; and the establishment of a new heaven and new earth. We explore here (1) the variation in emphasis from Moses to John the Baptist, (2) the prophetic message of the Day of the Lord, and (3) the concepts of the kingdom of God, the church, and Israel.

FROM MOSES TO JOHN THE BAPTIST

In the process of accommodating himself to humankind's needs, the Lord gradually revealed more of his glorious plan. In the history of redemption, several great servants of God solemnly and faithfully spoke the Word of God. Moses was God's foremost servant in the Old Testament—the "fountainhead" of the prophets. He is the *covenant mediator*, who interceded on two separate occasions for Israel (Exod. 32–34; Num. 14), who challenged Israel to covenant loyalty, and who put before Israel the blessings and curses of the covenant.

Several centuries later the Lord raised up Samuel as the role model of the prophets. Samuel addressed God's Word both to all Israel and to the newly installed king. The prophet served as counselor and accuser, depending on the context.

Again several centuries later Elijah and Elisha ministered God's Word to a people who had a history of rebellion. Elijah was ready to abandon the theocratic ideal, as he accused Israel in God's presence at Mount Horeb. But the Lord revealed how the prophet must serve his message to Israel as *covenant prosecutor*, charging the covenant community with violation of the covenant, warning Israel to prepare for the coming era of judgment, and calling forth a remnant of godly people (1 Kings 19:10–18). The Lord knows his own, and he shall build his kingdom out of the remnant! The remnant will return from exile and enjoy restoration, namely, the renewal of God's covenant with his people.

The major and minor prophets before and after the Exile had a new message: the coming of God's kingdom, the establishment of the messianic rule, the introduction of a new era in which Jews and Gentiles together will worship the Lord, the transformation of hearts, the renewal of the covenant, and the presence of God. They were God's trumpeters, heralding the new age that would be re-created out of the old. The last of such prophets was John the Baptist. Malachi had predicted his ministry of preparation before the day of our Lord (Mal. 3:1; 4:5). John was the transitional figure between the Old Testament prophets and the New Testament apostles. He pointed to and saw the Messiah (John 1:29), while preaching the judgment of God and his deliverance (see Matt. 3:12; Luke 1:76).

THE DAY OF THE LORD: TRUMPET

The *yôm Yahweh*, or "Day of the Lord," inaugurates the revelation of God's glory, holiness, and authority over his creation. Originally Israel looked forward to the establishment of God's kingdom on earth because they assumed that, with the fuller establishment of his rule, their position would be greatly advanced among the nations. As long as Israel had a horizontal view of eschatology, they expected the blessings, promises, and covenantal benefits to increase. They ignored the fact that the Lord also expected a response from them of commitment and devotion.

Through the prophets the Lord introduced teaching on transformation, purification, and redemption of a remnant to himself. Through the remnant and the purging of all things, the Lord planned to reestablish his kingdom on earth. The prophets introduced the radical teaching of God's vertical intrusion into human history. God will bring down his judgment not only on the nations but also on his own covenant people. Moses, Joshua, and Samuel had warned Israel of the curses of the covenant, but the Lord revealed to Elijah the nearness of his judgment in response to Elijah's formal complaint against Israel (1 Kings 19:10–18).

The Lord made it clear to Elijah that he planned to purify a remnant to himself. His displeasure with his people would evidence itself in wars, pestilence, earthquake, famine, and exile. Through the processes of judgment, a remnant would be sifted out like kernels separated from the chaff (Amos 9:9–10). This era of judgment, purification, vengeance, vindication, and redemption is also known as the Day of the Lord. The horizontal plane continuously intersects with the vertical until the final judgment in the form of vengeance and vindication.

Amos was the first classical prophet to redefine the popular concept of the Day of the Lord. The people had believed that the prosperity of the age of Jeroboam II could only get better. Their new-found power and prosperity seemed to prove to them that their economic, political, and social systems were all acceptable. Over against their popular expectations of a more glorious future, Amos describes the terror of God's involvement in human affairs. The Day of the Lord is characterized by psychological anguish and despair, loneliness, and inescapable troubles (Amos 5:18–20). The proper preparation before that day can only be repentance. Repentance includes returning to the Lord as well as living with justice and righteousness, in accordance with the rules of the kingdom (vv. 14–15).

In the Day of the Lord, Yahweh confronts the systems of the world. The leaders may secure political alliances, economic systems of checks and balances, international trade, technology, and religious values, but on the day of accountability, all human values will be brought down, and only the Lord will be exalted as the great King (see, e.g., Isa. 2:6–22). Not only Israel and Judah but all of humankind must prepare to meet the great King (Hab. 2:20; Zeph. 1:7). The day is compared to a great slaughter (Isa. 63:1–6), to the ravages of war (Zeph. 1:10–13), and to an earthquake (Isa. 13:13).

On the other hand, the Day of the Lord introduces the era of restoration. The great King comes to rescue his own and to vindicate them by taking revenge on all who have denied him. The Warrior-Judge avenges himself and his people against his enemies, opponents, and all who have not fully submitted to his reign. The acts of restoration and endearment to his children portray him as the Warrior-Deliverer of his people. He is both!

The prophets, John the Baptist, our Lord, and his apostles all witness to the age of restoration, which I summarize here with the acronym TRUMPET:

Total restoration
Rule of God
Unbroken covenants
Messianic blessing
People of God renewed
Enemies avenged
Transformation by the Spirit

The TRUMPET acronym serves as a pathway through the biblical teaching on the Day of the Lord, an era of judgment and liberation, condemnation and justification, vindication and salvation, destruction and renewal. All these aspects pertain to what God has done and will accomplish in Jesus Christ.[1]

Total Restoration

Creation is the sphere of human operation. Within the world of creation, redemption takes place. Redemption is not a deliverance from the material world but the reestablishment and sanctification of it.

On the one hand, a catastrophic view of creation is destructive to the Christian faith. According to this view, creation is evil, and the Lord must completely destroy this earth. The New Testament, however, does not support this dualistic perspective. The form of this world must indeed pass away (1 Cor. 7:31), but it will be transformed into a holy and righteous habitation of the saints of God (2 Peter 3:13), where the Father and the Son will dwell among the people of God (Rev. 22:3). Jesus promised that the meek will inherit "the earth" (Matt. 5:5) and prayed for the coming of God's kingdom on earth (6:10). Berkouwer put it aptly,

> It is precisely ordinary earthly existence that is redeemed. . . . Then life on this earth is not devaluated, but called. The new earth is never a strange and futuristic fantasy, but a mystery that penetrates into this existence and will make itself manifest there, where steadfast love and faithfulness meet . . . , and where the lines which seem blurred to us now will come more clearly into focus.[2]

On the other hand, an overly optimistic view of the gradual sanctification and betterment of the earth is equally destructive to the Christian faith. The Bible holds the present world and the new creation in tension. In one sense, the new creation is already here! Christians are responsible for fulfilling the creation mandates to subdue the earth, develop culture, and establish Christian families. Through obedience to Christ's expectations of righteousness, justice, love, and peace, the Christian community can be the salt of the earth, or an agency of transformation. However, the call of Christ and the mission of the church must be held in balance with the biblical teaching on the intrusion of God's judgment. The world and its structures must fall! Otherwise, the gospel is reduced to ethics or to a politics of revolution (such as liberation theology) or to a theonomic, reconstructionist view.[3]

The nature of the new is like and unlike the old. The new will be characterized by perfections: peace, justice, righteousness, fidelity, holiness, the presence of the Lord, and his blessings and universal rule. It can also be negatively expressed as the absence of war, injustice, unrighteousness, infidelity, evil, uncleanness, Satan, curse, or physical or temporal limitation (Rev. 21:8, 27).

The confession of the ancient church "I believe in the resurrection of the body" summarily expresses the Christian conviction that the transformation extends even to the human body. The resurrection is an aspect of renewal of heaven and earth. The God who created humankind as male and female, body and spirit, renews his image in the resurrection of man. A human being is not an immortal soul, limited by the physical body. A person is body and spirit. The resurrection of our Lord grounds the good news that man also will be raised from the dead. The resurrection affirms the inherent goodness of the material order, when renewed by the power and salvation of God.

In Christ the wrath of God has passed by the believer (1 Thess. 1:10), and in Christ he or she has hope of the resurrection *to life*. That hope is grounded in Jesus, the "firstfruits" of those raised to eternal life (1 Cor. 15:20; Col. 1:18). Moreover, the Holy Spirit sustains their hope in the resurrection and the glory of the world to come (Rom. 8:11). The nature of the resurrection body is far from clear in Scripture (see 1 Cor. 15), but the glory associated with it and the enjoyment of the presence of Christ encourage believers to remain loyal to their Savior and God. Unbelievers, however, have no ground for hope, and in the judgment their false confidence will give way to a confession of Jesus' lordship. But it will be too late, because God's judgment holds him accountable for all deeds done in the body.

Rule of God

The kingdom of God is both present and still to come. It is present in the benefits of the covenant, the fulfillment of the promises, the presence of the Lord in the temple, the Davidic dynasty, the mighty acts of God, the biblical representations of the Lord as the Divine Warrior (Exod. 15:1–18; Ps. 98), and in the very existence of the people of God. Israel experienced his kingship. The prophets foretold the greater realization of his kingship in his mighty acts of delivering the remnant of Judah and Israel out of exile and extending his kingdom of blessing, peace, and righteousness to the Gentiles.

The rule of God is from everlasting to everlasting. He rules by virtue of being the Creator. He is the Lord *(Adonai)*, the Lord of Hosts, the great King, whose glory extends to the ends of the earth (Isa. 6:1; Mal. 1:11, 14). From a redemptive-historical perspective, creation and redemption are intertwined. The Creator is the Redeemer, and the Redeemer is the Creator. The point of intersection is in the designation of God as the Ruler. The great King rules in judging and avenging his enemies and in delivering and vindicating his people.[4] As the Divine Warrior, the Lord's kingly role comes to expression in his acts of deliverance of his saints and in his acts of vengeance on those who do not submit themselves to his rule.

> I trampled the nations in my anger;
> in my wrath I made them drunk
> and poured their blood on the ground.
> (Isa. 63:6; see also 66:14–16; Zeph. 3:15–17)

Berkouwer integrates the *visio Dei* ("vision of God") with the *visio mundi* ("vision of the world") as expressions of the kingdom of God.[5] The *visio Dei* is hope in the reality of God's promises pertaining to the fullness of redemption—cosmic, corporate, and individual. The hope lies in the God who brings about his New Jerusalem in time and space and who prepares a day for the full revelation of the New Jerusalem on a new earth, where he will be present among his own people. Regrettably, the distinction between spiritual and material, heaven and earth, and the vision of God and the vision of the world has obscured a most fundamental teaching of Scripture. This matter has been well expressed by Martin Buber:

> So it is not only with his thought and his feelings, but with the sole of his foot and the tip of his finger as well, that he may receive the sign-language of the reality taking place. The redemption must take place in the whole corporeal life. God the Creator wills to consummate nothing less than the whole of his creation.[6]

Unbroken Covenants: Creation and Redemption

The covenants are temporal expressions of God's commitment to his people and to the earth as a whole.[7] The Noahic covenant, made with all of life, reveals the broader concerns of the Creator-Ruler, whose glory rests even on animals and people outside the covenant of grace (see Ps. 104). God's love for his creation is never isolated from his love for his children (Hos. 2:18–23). Isaiah also intertwines the motifs of creation and redemption, portraying God's election and love of his people as rooted in creation and also in God's design for the world. The prophet integrates the restoration of Israel with the renewal of the land and nature (Isa. 35:1–2).

Throughout the history of redemption the Lord pledges his commitment by means of four covenants. In the Noahic covenant he affirms his continued fidelity to the world of creation. In the Abrahamic covenant he promises his blessing to Abraham's descendants and to all the clans of the earth who would submit themselves to the God of Abraham. In the Mosaic covenant he confirms and extends the promises to the nation of Israel. In the Davidic covenant the Lord guarantees the blessings of prosperity and peace to his anointed king and through him to Israel and to the world.

The promises of these covenants were renewed and enlarged throughout the history of redemption, even when the external conditions of the covenant relationship changed. McComiskey concludes, "The elements guaranteed by the promise covenant undergo amplification and enrichment in their expression in the major administrative covenants."[8]

The prophets had great expectations for covenant renewal. Through the Exile, the Lord purified a part of his people, renewing his commitment to those who sought him. In this context the prophets proclaim the benefits of the new age in many ways, all expressing God's commitment to covenant renewal. The prophets employ, adapt, and transform motifs from the covenant-promise language. They hold up the promises in the light of renewal, in which the renewed covenants become even more glorious than the old ones. Without binding the fulfillment to a specific time, they encourage, comfort, and exhort the people of God to be faithful, to wait, and to find refuge in the Lord, because he is faithful. (See table 14.)

TABLE 14. THE DIVINE COVENANTS IN PROPHECY

Covenant	Promises	Metaphor	Prophetic Message
Noahic	Governance; sustenance; involving relief from anxiety, sickness, and death	Father	*Transformation*, involving blessing, harmony, and integration of creation and redemption
Abrahamic	Land of blessing, relief from curse, multiplied seed, personal blessing, blessing to all nations	Shield	*Vindication and blessing*, realizing the presence of God and of people from all nations
Mosaic	Holy priesthood and royal nation; glory of the nations; forgiven and blessed	Divine Warrior	*Rule of God* in glory, (Sinaitic) justice, righteousness, and love; *people of God* who are cleansed, holy, faithful
Davidic	Royal nation endowed with glory and blessing through the Davidic Messiah; reign of love	Shepherd	*Victory, glory, peace* under universal rule of Messiah and the rule of the people of God with Messiah

Messianic Blessing

For practical purposes we may distinguish between the kingdom of God and the kingdom of Christ. The prophets speak of God's establishing his rule on earth as well as of the messianic kingdom. On the one hand, the Lord sets up the kingdom of peace, justice, righteousness, blessing, and the prosperity of his people, while establishing his law, or divine will, on earth (e.g., Isa. 2:1–4; Jer. 32:37–33:13; Dan. 2:44–45).

On the other hand, the Lord establishes his kingdom in the Davidic Messiah, "the Branch" and the "Root of Jesse" (e.g., Isa. 9:2–7; Jer. 33:14–26; Hos. 3:5). The messianic concept in the Old Testament is complex, but from the perspective of Jesus' incarnation the complexity has begun to unfold. The Messiah was to bring in the era of peace, prosperity, universal rule over the nations, righteousness, and justice, with the evidences of the Spirit of God on his ministry. In Zechariah 9:9, the identity of the king riding lowly on a donkey is far from clear, but from the perspective of Palm Sunday, it becomes apparent that this verse refers to the lowly, human nature of the Messiah (Matt. 21:1–11).

Isaiah more fully develops the suffering of the Messiah, to whom God gives glory and spoils, but it is not quite perceptible that this Servant of the Lord is the Messiah until the actual suffering of Jesus. The messianic concept shifts between the Divine Warrior (with the associations of victory, blessing, and cosmic transformation that characterize the kingdom of God), the human Messiah (the Davidic Messiah), and the Davidic priestly Messiah (cf. Ps. 110; Jer. 33:22; Zech. 4; 6:9–15). The prophets operate from the theological perspective represented in Psalms 2, 45, 72, 110, and 132. In Psalm 2 the Messiah is the Son of God appointed to subdue all nations, bring *shalom* to the people of God as well as to the cosmos, and rule from shore to shore (see also Ps. 72; Zech. 9:10). Psalms 45 and 72 celebrate the glory, justice, and righteousness of the Davidic dynasty, as God's means of establishing justice for the needy and blessing the nations (Ps. 72:12–14, 17). In Psalms 110 and 132 the close relationship between the Davidic king and the temple or priesthood intimates the close relationship between the Messiah's royal and priestly roles. In Jesus is the presence of the messianic kingdom! His kingdom inaugurates the eschaton more fully than does any previous era. In Jesus lies the hope for the saints to enjoy the benefits of the messianic rule.

People of God Renewed

Ever since Adam and Eve's expulsion from the Garden of Eden, the Lord has involved himself in redeeming humankind to himself. Redemption includes all the acts of God, including his promises, covenants, and the setting apart of Israel as his own people. A thread connecting all epochs of redemptive history is God's promise to be the covenant God of a people whom he has elected and through whom he works out his eternal purpose: "Now if you obey me fully and keep my covenant, then out of all nations you will be my treasured possession. Although the whole earth is mine, you will be for me a kingdom of priests and a holy nation" (Exod. 19:5–6; see also Deut. 26:18–19; 1 Peter 2:9–10).

Through the ministry of Moses, the prophets, the apostles, and especially our Lord Jesus, the Father called out a people to himself. The people of God before and after Christ share certain qualities, privileges, and hopes. The clarity and depth of their relationship varies, depending on the epoch of redemptive history in which they live. Paul well knew how great a privilege God had given them (Rom. 9:4–5).

In preparation for the coming of the Christ, the Lord gave his Old

Testament people a real experience of his presence in the temple institution, a revelation of his glory, an assurance of their special status as children of God by adoption, and a future guaranteed by the promises. They enjoyed forgiveness, special joys in this life, and a hope in the life to come, while awaiting the greater salvation and permanent liberation from the enemies and especially from evil, injustice, and unrighteousness. The Lord himself had marked them to be his holy people out of all the nations of the world.

Even in the darkest hours of Israel's apostasy, the Lord maintained his purpose, preserving a remnant for himself (see 1 Kings 19:18). To this end, the Lord sent prophets to call out and encourage a remnant. The prophets reveal that the Lord prefers a love for himself to a slavish adherence to the commandments. The commandments were instruments to teach God's standards of holiness, justice, righteousness, and love. God—not the commandments—is the end. Salvation was never based on an adherence to the law but on the love of God (Deut. 6:5).

Through the Old Testament writings we come to know God in intimate relationship with his people. They experienced forgiveness, salvation, and the joy of godly living and were richly rewarded. The Old Testament encourages such living and reveals that God looks for righteous and mature children. For this reason the apostle Paul still holds out the Old Testament to Timothy, the pastor-teacher of the Christian church, as the inspired Word of God whose use has not ceased with the incarnation of the Son of God: "All Scripture is God-breathed and is useful for teaching, rebuking, correcting and training in righteousness, so that the man of God may be thoroughly equipped for every good work" (2 Tim. 3:16–17).

With the first coming of Jesus the people of God enter the eschatological era with greater certainty than in any previous generation. With his coming, they realize that all the benefits of God's people before and after Christ are rooted in the atoning death of the Messiah. In his death the wrath of God is revealed, but as great as his wrath is, so much greater is his love, grace, forgiveness, and purpose to renew a people to himself.

Jesus came with no other message than that of the prophets; he did not come to alter the divine expectations of men and women. Instead, he revealed again the original intent of the Father: loyalty, love, submission, and commitment to God's kingdom rather than to any human kingdom. What is new and revolutionary is Jesus' explicit teaching that the love of God and the submission to his kingdom require us to be *disciples* of Jesus. His disciples must learn to follow the king and his "royal law" (James 2:8). This royal law is the law of love, requiring humility and a diligent practice of godliness, righteousness, and the present realization of the kingdom of God on earth. The new people of

457

God also live in expectation of Jesus' coming. His people pray in the Spirit, "Maranatha," or "Come, O Lord" (1 Cor. 16:22; Rev. 22:17, 20), while purifying themselves for his Parousia, or glorious return.

The New Jerusalem denotes the fellowship of the saints who live in harmony with the rules of God's city. God has set forth the requisites of holiness, justice, righteousness, peace, love, and gentleness. These qualities are spiritual, produced by the working of the Spirit of God in his people; they are not natural human qualities (see Rom. 1).

In both Old and New Testaments the Lord has had the same expectation of those who love him, which may be summarized in God's words to Abraham, "Walk before me and be blameless" (Gen. 17:1). The walk before God is that attitude of heart whereby the believer is continually aware of living in the presence of God. The standard of the new creation is the law of love of God and man (Lev. 19:18; Deut. 6:5), humility (Isa. 2:11–15), righteousness, justice, fidelity, holiness, and a love of peace (1:17; Mic. 6:8). This new way is also known as the knowledge of the Lord (Isa. 11:9), designating not only knowledge about the Lord but also the experience of his salvation and submission to his kingship (Hos. 3:5).

Enemies Avenged

Eschatology—the totality of the teaching of Scripture on the redemption of God—goes far beyond a personal hope. It is also related to this world, over which God still rules and over which Jesus will fully establish his lordship. Eschatological expectation engulfs the whole world.

The new world belongs to the righteous who have been persecuted, oppressed, maligned, and unjustly dealt with in life. The righteous cry out for justice and thirst for righteousness, awaiting the full establishment of God's righteousness and justice (Ps. 37:9–11, 34). The hope of the righteous is in God's justice, whereby he will judge evil and vindicate his own (vv. 39–40).

The final judgment reveals the righteousness of God. The biblical passages pertaining to the judgment affirm that it is general, for the purpose of vindicating the children of God and revealing the nature of the reward or punishment, depending on the deeds done in the flesh (Matt. 13:40–43; 25:31–32; Acts 17:31; Rom. 2:5–6; 1 Cor. 6:2–3; 2 Cor. 5:10; 2 Thess. 1:7–10; 1 Peter 1:17; 2 Peter 3:7; Rev. 20:12; 22:12).

Transformation by the Spirit

The Spirit of God is also involved in the processes of renewal. The Old Testament prophets speak of the Spirit as operative in the renewal, guidance, comfort, and indwelling of God's people (e.g., Isa. 44:3; Ezek.

36:26–27; Hag. 2:5). Moreover, he is the agent of restoration, by whom the Lord renews all things to a state of blessing and *shalom* (Isa. 32:15–20; Ps. 104:30).

The Spirit of God is particularly associated with the messianic age. David was endowed by the Spirit of God (2 Sam. 23:2; cf. 1 Kings 3:5–15). Kingship in Israel was a sacral office because the Davidic king was an extension of Yahweh's rule on earth. The Messiah, too, was invested with special authority by the presence of the Spirit (Isa. 11:2). The Lord Jesus was empowered by the Spirit at baptism (Matt. 3:16), when the Father confirmed his messianic mission (see Isa. 11:1; 61:1). The Spirit of God is evident in miraculous healing and in the casting out of demons, the sign of the intrusion of the eschaton: "If I drive out demons by the Spirit of God, then the kingdom of God has come upon you" (Matt. 12:28). The Holy Spirit is the eschatological sign of the presence of the messianic age, characterized by "the Holy Spirit and . . . fire" (Luke 3:16), of which Gaffin writes,

> This baptism as a whole involves nothing less than the eschatological judgment with its dual outcome of salvation and destruction. Messianic Spirit-and-fire baptism is of a piece with God's great discriminating activity of cleansing the world threshing floor or, to vary the metaphor slightly, harvesting the world-field, at the end of history.[9]

Jesus gives the sign of the Holy Spirit to his church for comfort (John 14:16), for instruction and guidance (v. 26; 15:26; 16:13), and for a renewing power (Acts 1:8). The presence of the Holy Spirit in the apostolic church wonderfully transforms Peter, brings in the Gentiles, does wonders and signs, and witnesses to the presence of the messianic age (Acts 2:38; 4:31; 6:5; 7:55; 10:9–48; 11:27–28; 13:1–2; 16:6–7). Through the Spirit each believer shares in the eschaton, as he or she already has the Spirit of adoption and sonship (Rom. 8:9, 14–15; Gal. 4:6; Eph. 2:18). The individual Christian is bound together in the fellowship of the saints, which is the body of Christ on earth (Rom. 5:5; 2 Cor. 5:17). The present age is the age of the Spirit (2 Cor. 3:6–18), the revelation of God's glory in the New Covenant:

> Now the Lord is the Spirit, and where the Spirit of the Lord is, there is freedom. And we, who with unveiled faces all reflect the Lord's glory, are being transformed into his likeness with ever-increasing glory, which comes from the Lord, who is the Spirit. (vv. 17–18)

The Spirit prepares the church for the final glory. He is the "firstfruits" or "deposit" of the new age (2 Cor. 1:22; 5:5; Eph. 1:13–14; 4:30), in whom we groan for the day of redemption (Rom. 8:23). The Spirit of Christ given to the church is closely associated with Jesus' glorification (John 7:39). Unlike at any previous time, the Spirit quickens, reassures, and keeps alive the hope of the great and glorious kingdom that is to come, the mission of the church, and also the goal of personal sanctification. The Spirit keeps the individual believer and the church moving toward the restoration of all things, as Gaffin concludes: "In the 'firstfruits' power of Pentecost the church lives eloquently in the hope of the glory to be revealed (Rom. 8:18–25), confident in its expectation of a new heaven and a new earth in which righteousness dwells (2 Peter 3:13)."[10]

THE KINGDOM OF GOD, THE MESSIANIC KINGDOM, ISRAEL, AND THE CHURCH

"Kingdom" as an Eschatological Concept

The kingdom of God is an eschatological concept, linking creation with the new creation. It refers to the dynamic and beneficent presence of God in heaven and on earth, whereby he rules in righteousness, justice, and peace from everlasting to everlasting (Ps. 74:12; 93:2; 145:13). The Hebrew words *malkût* and *mamlākâ* and the Greek term *basileia* ascribe to God the authority to rule, the perfections and power of his rule, the realm of his rule (creation), the extent of his rule (heaven and earth), and the irresistible, victorious, and glorious establishment of his authority. God visibly establishes his authority over earth throughout the history of redemption by promises, covenants, tokens of his presence, experiences of fulfillment, and reality. The acts of God witness to his ever-present rule and to his concern in redeeming a new humanity for the new heaven and new earth.

The Reality of the Kingdom

The kingdom is a future event (we pray, "Thy kingdom come") and also a present reality. The experience of God's kingship goes back to man's fall, when God reveals his royal concern with rebellious humankind in blessing and in his sovereign limitation of human autonomy (Gen. 3–11). It is regrettable that New Testament scholarship often isolates Jesus' proclamation of the kingdom from the previous acts of God in the history of redemption. New Testament discussion about the nature of Jesus' kingdom was stimulated by J. Weiss and A. Schweitzer, who argued that Jesus expected the imminent end of the world. C. H. Dodd, on the other hand, reasoned that the kingdom is real in the presence of Jesus, a view known as "realized eschatology." Kümmel's position has attracted a wide following, because he tried to do justice to the evidence for both the nearness and the futurity of the kingdom. Ladd's view is a further development of Kümmel in his presentation of Jesus' kingdom as a fulfillment of the Old Testament

460

expectation and as a guarantee of the consummation. This view creates a tension between the present manifestation of the kingdom on the one hand and the consummation and cataclysmic transformation on the other.[11]

The emphasis on the inauguration of the kingdom needs modification, on the basis of the very evident kingship of God directly (in the theocracy) and indirectly (through the Davidic dynasty) over Israel. In the theocratic phase the Lord was the Divine Warrior who ruled over the nations, avenged his enemies, and delivered Israel repeatedly. In the messianic phase, our Lord Jesus more fully displayed the presence of God's kingdom by exorcisms, beneficent miraculous acts, his victorious resurrection, and now in his present glorious rule. Jesus' coming intensifies the tension, as Satan himself opposes the inauguration of a new stage in the development of the kingdom. The church has inherited this struggle, as Ladd observes,

> The church is the focal point of the conflict between good and evil, God and Satan, until the end of the age. The church can never be at rest or take her ease but must always be the church in struggle and conflict, often persecuted, but sure of the ultimate victory.[12]

The intrusion of God's kingdom in its fullness will inaugurate the final stage in the history of redemption, characterized by glory, victory, and reward for the saints of Christ and shame, defeat, and humiliation for his enemies.[13]

The Kingdom of Christ

The present stage in the history of redemption unfolds the kingdom of Christ with its universal proclamation of the gospel and the universal application of the benefits of Christ to all who believe. The Spirit of God, the Spirit of renewal, has been poured out on all persons who have called on the name of the Lord Jesus. He prepares the church of Jesus Christ for the new heavens and new earth by changing each believer into a new creature, born of the imperishable seed by the Spirit and the Word (John 3:3–8; 1 Peter 1:23). The kingdom of Christ is a temporal expression of the eternal kingdom of God. It is temporal because Jesus came in time, inaugurated his kingdom, and rules gloriously as the King of Kings, seated at the right hand of the Father. He will rule till all principalities, powers, and nations are subject to him (1 Cor. 15:23–28; Heb. 2:5–9). He is the Rider on the white horse, by whose warrior-like power the kingdoms of the world, together with the Satanic host, will fall (Rev. 19:11–21). The rule of Christ is an administrative aspect of the rule of God for the purpose of restoring the kingdom of the Father over all creation. There is no tension or conflict between the kingdom of God and the kingdom of the Christ. Berkouwer correctly insists,

Far from being a devaluation of Christ and His Kingdom, this in fact accents their glory and majesty at the point when Christ delivers the Kingdom to God the Father. No dilemma of Christocentrism versus theocentrism or regnum Christi versus regnum Dei arises. Everything centers on the fulfillment of what becomes salvation-laden reality.[14]

Kingdom, Old and New

There is a connection between the kingdom of God in the Old Testament (the theocratic phase) and the present expression of the kingdom (the messianic phase). From what has preceded it should be clear that:

1. God's kingdom is from eternity to eternity.

2. God's kingdom was a reality in the Old Testament in his cosmic rule, in his rule over his people, and in his rule through the descendants of David.

3. In Moses, the covenants, and the prophetic word, the Lord promised to establish an everlasting kingdom of blessing, righteousness, and peace over all his creation.

4. The messianic kingdom would fulfill his promise to David and establish his kingdom on earth.

5. Every act of blessing and curse, justification and condemnation, and life and death anticipated the kingdom to come.

The theocratic phase of the kingdom in the Old Testament thus established God's kingdom on earth. The hope of the kingdom was Jerusalem (Zion) with her temple and the Davidic dynasty, but the focus of the hope was the presence of the great King, God himself (Ps. 46:4–11; 132:13–18).

The Kingdom and Israel

Does God have a special kingdom program for the Jews apart from the church? Yes and no. The gospel went first to the Jews. They were privileged to see and hear the mighty acts of God in the Messiah, born of the Jews. The apostolic mission began with the Jewish people. Paul, the apostle to the Gentiles, always went first to the Jews (Rom. 1:16). The mission to the Jews was by and large unsuccessful because of their rejection of the Messiah and of the Resurrection as the sign of Jesus' messiahship. The apostle Paul theologizes on the problem of the Jews and the growing distance between the church and the synagogue in Romans 9–11. In these chapters he stresses the clarity and the mystery of God's purpose in the Christ. God's purpose is clear with regard to the extension of the gospel to the Gentiles and the gathering of Jews and Gentiles into one body, the church of Jesus Christ (10:1–13). The purpose of God is as yet unclear, however, with regard to the inclusion of the Jews in large numbers (11:25). The apostle returns to the hope given in the prophetic word that the Redeemer will come to and come out of Zion to bless the Jews and the nations (vv. 26–27; see also Ps. 14:7; Isa. 2:3; 59:20–21). Ultimately, he grounds his argument on the fidelity of God: "God's gifts and his call are irrevocable" (Rom. 11:29).

According to Romans 11, the restoration of the Jewish people will take place toward the end of the age. Even in the present state of rebellion, the Jews are still considered holy and beloved. In God's wisdom and according to his purpose, the fullness of the Jews will be added to the fullness of the Gentiles, resulting in a renewal of the body of Christ. He likens this renewal to the grafting back of the natural branches on the olive tree. The apostle, however, does not limit God's acts of grace to the Jews to the future, as Hoekema observes,

> There is nothing in the passage that would rule out such a future conversion or such future conversions, as long as one does not insist that the passage points only to the future, or that it describes a conversion of Israel that occurs after the full number of Gentiles has been gathered in.[15]

Elsewhere I have argued that the apostolic period gives no ground for identifying the church with Israel.[16] The apostles recognized Israel as the naturally endowed means by which the acts of God in Christ were to be proclaimed to the Gentiles. However, they faced the enigma of Israel's hardening. In view of the dialogue and living witness to the Jews, the apostolic church, or *ekklēsia*, saw itself in continuity with the old people of God, which was also known as the *ekklēsia*("assembly") in the Septuagint. They also saw discontinuity, however, because of their faith in Jesus the Messiah. The way remains open for Israel, however, to turn to their Messiah.

The Kingdom and the Church

The church is the present manifestation of the kingdom of Christ. Vos rightly insists that "our Lord looked upon the visible church as a veritable embodiment of his kingdom."[17] It is local and universal, consisting of all who submit themselves to Jesus' lordship and prepare themselves individually and corporately for the glorious revelation of their Messiah. The headship of Christ over the church represents his cosmic headship. Jesus has authority over all creation as the administrative head over the whole world (Col. 1:17–20). Christians are members of the church of Jesus Christ. In their identity with Christ and his church, they worship the triune God, grow spiritually, and further the kingdom of Jesus through the church. Recognizing Jesus' cosmic headship, Christians also look at the whole world as under Christ. They anticipate the glorious transformation of all things, but now they look at all of life as under Jesus. In continuity with its Lord, the church proclaims the gospel of the kingdom to the world, puts down the dominion of Satan (Rom. 16:20), and reflects the spiritual qualities of the kingdom, which are "righteousness, peace and joy" (14:17) and "faith, hope and love" (1 Cor. 13:13).

The kingdom, on the other hand, reflects the rule of Christ over all areas of life: the arts, sciences, humanities, industry, commerce, and politics. As Ladd concludes,

> The kingdom creates the church, works through the church, and is proclaimed in the world by the church. There can be no kingdom without church. . .and there can be no church without God's kingdom; but they remain indistinguishable concepts: the rule of God and the fellowship of men.[18]

The Goal of the Kingdom

The goal of the kingdom is partly revealed and partly hidden. The kingdom is theocentric, dynamic, and universal. The great King moves toward establishing his kingdom over all created things in heaven and on earth through the Messiah. Through the institution of the church and the operation of the Holy Spirit, the Father calls men and women, boys and girls, Jews and Gentiles to fellowship with himself in Jesus Christ. They become his children, united to his Son and regenerated by the Spirit of God. As new creatures they already partake of the new heavens and the new earth. They enjoy the newness of life, forgiveness and reconciliation, adoption to sonship, and the blessings of being fellow heirs with Jesus Christ. In turn, the newness of life must show itself in a submissive, theocentric, incarnational, joyful, and hopeful way of life, to the praise of the triune God and to the proclamation of the kingdom.[19] The prophets, our Lord, the apostles, and especially Revelation 21–22 communicate (in metaphors and in the language of accommodation) the glory and bliss of the kingdom of God on earth. Any skepticism concerning the purpose and goal of God is out of the question for the heirs of the kingdom. They have received the word of promise that the kingdom will most certainly be established. The manner of the establishment, however, remains in the Father's hands. He knows when and how (Acts 1:7), but for now he counts on his children to live obediently, expectantly, and triumphantly while awaiting the day of the glorious revelation of his Son, the Day of the Lord, and the transformation of heaven and earth. To this end Paul commented and prayed, "The God of peace will soon crush Satan under your feet. The grace of our Lord Jesus be with you" (Rom. 16:20).

CHAPTER 40

Eschatology and the Christian Life

Eschatology is the complex of all that the Bible says about the future. The Bible treats the subject of the future as interrelated with the biblical teachings about God, the Lord Jesus, the Holy Spirit, the people of God, the church of Jesus Christ, salvation and sanctification, and the nature of divine revelation. The study of the future (or the eschaton) intersects with all the topics in the Bible and also with the purposes of divine revelation involving salvation, Christian living, and hope. In this regard, the study of the future, like all of the Bible, calls for a commitment, a transformation of one's life. It is not neutral, as Berkouwer observes:

> The eschatological promise and expectation as portrayed in the Bible is not something essentially independent, neutral, or supernatural impart-ing a special knowledge to the believer and endowing him with insight into future events. . . . Eschatology is not a projection into the distant future: it bursts forth into our present existence, and structures life today in the light of the last things.[1]

Our major concern with biblical eschatology comes from within the purposes of Scripture. The revelation of God through Moses, the prophets, Jesus, and the apostles has three essential goals: instruction, encouragement, and exhortation. The teaching about the future in the Bible aims at giving hope and comfort and calls forth the response of living in conformity to our Lord.

ETHICS

Ethics and eschatology embrace.[2] First, the prophetic message contains a rebuke and the consequent judgment of God, expressing the Day of the Lord. But even though God's judgment is inevitable, the invitation still goes forth:

> Come now, let us reason together. . . .
> Though your sins are like scarlet,
> they shall be as white as snow.
>
> (Isa. 1:18)

465

The people to whom he will extend the covenants, promises, and the future hope are those who form a new city:

> Afterward you will be called
> the City of Righteousness,
> the Faithful City.

(v. 26)

The redeemed of the Lord are called holy (4:3); they form "Zion of the Holy One of Israel" (60:14), the New Jerusalem (65:18).

Theocentric Living

Theocentric living requires submission to the great King. A submissive spirit manifests itself in a readiness to let God be God and to be humble in his presence. Theocentric living also reveals itself in one's personal life style, one's home life, and one's language and actions. The motivating factor in *doing* lies in one's *being*. Acts of piety cannot arise out of a need for a sense of self-worth, a desire for rewards, or selfish ambition, but only from a delight in the Lord. This delight is the motivation behind a godly home life, sacrificial service in the kingdom, and faithful preaching, teaching, and evangelism.

The children of the kingdom are committed to seek the glory, honor, and righteous establishment of God's will in their lives. Jesus required nothing less than this commitment when he called on all to seek the kingdom of God. Vos observes,

> The supreme importance that Jesus in virtue of this God-centered conception attached to righteousness may be inferred from the fact that its pursuit is spoken of in equally absolute terms as the seeking of the kingdom. It is the highest concern of the disciple.[3]

The Spirit of Christ advances the theocratic interests of the Trinity in establishing God's kingdom. The Spirit sanctifies, purifies, motivates, produces the fruits of the Spirit, and equips the church with gifted people. God rules his people through the Spirit to be a theocentric people. The Spirit breaks through human institutions that no longer advance Jesus' kingdom interests. Wright has stated,

> It can be argued that God through the work of the Spirit has always been at war with human institutionalism, because the institution becomes idolatrous, self-perpetuating, and self-worshiping, because church membership becomes synonymous with the new birth, because man tries to make the Spirit follow law and assume that it is only mediated through rite, etc.[4]

466

Incarnational Living

In *The City of God*, Augustine explored the coexistence of God's kingdom with that of man in terms of the city of God and the city of man. Christians are citizens of the city of God, but they live in the city of man. The city of God is obedient to the great King, whereas the citizens of the city of man are self-willed, egocentric, and selfish. The uniqueness of the city of God lies in its ruler. The great King serves! He enjoys doing good to his subjects. In this spirit Christ came as the Man for others. Christ came into the city of man ready to do the will of God. In full obedience to the Father, he sacrificed himself for human beings. He called on his followers to take the same road and to take upon themselves the cross (Matt. 16:24–25).

The requisite for inclusion in the kingdom program is nothing less than a complete submission to God's rule and a manifestation of Godlikeness. Only those who call on him, fear him, and love him are the objects of his salvation, righteousness, and love. The requisites of the messianic kingdom consist of nothing less than abandonment, self-denial, and commitment to God's kingdom purpose. The incarnational model of our Lord serves to call all who would enter the kingdom to follow in his footsteps (Phil. 2:1–11).

The children of the kingdom must evidence a childlike faith (Mark 10:15). The only entrance into the kingdom is by the path of faith in Jesus as the way (John 14:6) and by the rebirth of the Spirit of God (John 1:12; 3:5). Regeneration is the work of the Spirit, quickening the human being to be a child of God and re-creating that one for the new creation (John 3:1–8, 36). The New Birth evidences itself in devotion to the Christ, repentance, and good works. The way to the kingdom is not hard, but it is narrow (Matt. 7:13–14).

Instead of external requirements, our Lord renews the prophetic call for regeneration, internal renewal, and true spirituality. He expects nothing less than faith, love, good works, resistance of evil, observance of the law of Jesus (discipleship), readiness to forgive, spirituality, and persevering prayer (Matt. 12:50; 16:24–25; 18:35; 25:31–46). Jesus calls for a total commitment of the life (Luke 17:33). The one who loses oneself in Christ will witness the power of the glorious name, of the one who is King of Kings and Lord of Lords (Rev. 19:16).

Paul continually interrelates Christian living with the glorious hope. Suffering for the sake of the kingdom is worth it, when compared with the greater "glory that will be revealed in us" (Rom. 8:18). The glorious teaching on justification is related to sanctification, or the doctrine of practical righteousness, according to which the Christian lives as a slave to righteousness (5:21; 6:13–23), hoping for the revelation of God's righteousness (Gal. 5:5). Paul's teaching on the Day of the Lord integrates ethics and hope. He called upon the Thessalonian believers to prepare themselves for Jesus, who would return "like a thief in the night" (1 Thess. 5:2), by cultivating self-control, faith, love, hope, peace, encouragement, support, patience, kindness, joy, and gratitude (vv. 6–18). The two-thousand-year history of the church, the ambiguity of the signs of the age, and the delay in the Parousia have brought the church dangerously close to forgetting to wait for the Lord.

Visions of the Apocalypse also encourage godly living. The glorious Jesus calls upon the seven churches of Asia Minor to be loyal, to persevere, to prepare for his coming, and to overcome (Rev. 2–3). The preparation for his coming keeps the church alive and composed so as to be ready whenever he comes. Great are the rewards to those who overcome this world in anticipation of the New Jerusalem, the new heaven and the new earth (Rev. 2:7, 11, 17, 26; 3:4–5, 12, 21)!

ATTITUDES

Waiting, hope, patience, and perseverance are aspects of eschatology. The history of redemption provides insights into God's establishment of his kingdom, as the day of God's vengeance on the nations and of the glorious redemption of his children. That day is past, present, and future. The Lord showed his power in Egypt, in Israel's crossing the Red Sea, in the Conquest, and during the reigns of the various kings. He put down Aram, Assyria, Babylon, Persia, Greece, the Ptolemies, the Seleucids, Rome, as well as the Moors, the Crusaders, Napoleon, and Hitler. Facing injustice, unrighteousness, and evil in this world, the godly learn not to depend on arms, political solutions, or economic hedging, but to put their trust on the Lord:

> In repentance and rest is your salvation,
> in quietness and trust is your strength,
> but you would have none of it. . . .
> Yet the LORD longs to be gracious to you;
> he rises to show you compassion.
> For the LORD is a God of justice.
> Blessed are all who wait for him!
> (Isa. 30:15, 18)

Isaiah, the prophets, and the Psalms ascribe kingship to the Lord and encourage the saints to wait for God to establish his kingdom on earth:

> For the LORD is our judge,
> the LORD is our lawgiver,
> the LORD is our king;
> it is he who will save us.
> (Isa. 33:22)

468

On the eve of Jerusalem's fall to Babylon, the Lord encouraged the godly to persevere, waiting faithfully for his salvation (Hab. 2:3–4). Our Lord Jesus renewed the call to wait at the occasion of the Mount Olivet discourse (Matt. 24:42) and in the parable of the ten virgins (25:1–13).

The expectation of the glorious establishment of God's kingdom creates a tension between joy-filled living in the presence of God and anticipation of what God has prepared for his children. In anticipating the glorious future, the child of God before and after Christ conforms to God's expectations by cultivating joy, hope, and praise as well as by maintaining confidence in prayer and Bible study.[5]

Joy

Trust in God brings quietness, purpose, and joy. As long as we toss about for meaning, self-identification, and self-assertion, the soul cannot rest. Joyous exuberance over God's kingship exposes one's inner peace with God. God's child does not manufacture some enthusiasm for programs or doctrinal truths. The Christian is not "high" because of personal popularity or success, but is intoxicated with the knowledge of God. Such knowledge refers to relationship with God, confidence in God, and trust in God's purposes. Joy floods the heart when one senses something of the vastness of divine activity and the magnificence of God's nature. This attitude filled the psalmist when he exclaimed,

> Great is the LORD and most worthy of praise;
>   his greatness no one can fathom.
>
> (Ps. 145:3)

The Christian life reflects a harmonious balance between election and God's universal fatherhood, which extends to the whole realm of his rule. God's fidelity, covenant love, goodness, and compassion go far beyond the covenant community to all of his creatures. Those who experience the joy of the Lord have discovered an experiential truth. They need not be the judge, guide, or manipulator of others. They live in the presence of God and for the service of God. They restrict their vision to what God has asked them to do and do not clutter their mind with possibilities, hypothetical situations, and doubts. They look at God's vastness rather than at human limitations. They are at peace with other people because they are at peace with God! Within the world of God's creation they have a sense of mission. The mission is so great that they sense their own unworthiness, exclaiming with joy,

> What is man that you are mindful of him,
>   the son of man that you care for him?
>
> (Ps. 8:4)

A theocentric and messianic perspective on the world brings about a change of attitude toward it. The world is not dirty or evil. It belongs to God, regardless of who is king or what economic, philosophical, political, or scientific systems vie for dominance. Hoekema stresses the place of the Christian vision in all areas of life:

> Being a citizen of the kingdom, therefore, means that we should see all of life and all of reality in the light of the goal of the redemption of the cosmos. This implies, as Abraham Kuyper once said, that there is not a thumb-breadth of the universe about which Christ does not say, "It is mine." This implies a Christian philosophy of history . . . of culture . . . of vocation: all callings are from God, and all we do in everyday life is to be done to God's praise, whether this be study, teaching, preaching, business, industry, or housework.[6]

Hope

The goal of God's kingdom is the establishment of God's absolute sovereignty over heaven and earth. From the expulsion from the garden till the glorious coming of the Messiah, God prepares a people to himself. This people desires to do his will on earth and awaits with hope the transformation of this world. The present world is scarred by the effects of sin and judgment, but the restoration of the world inaugurates the consummation of God's purposes.

Our God established Israel to be his priestly kingdom (Exod. 19:6). Israel was the only nation actually belonging to his rule, having been instructed to do his will on earth. Through them he would rule the nations (Deut. 28:12–13). The humble in Israel looked forward to enjoying the fullness of God's presence and his blessings on the new earth, as they had been promised:

> The meek will inherit the land
> and enjoy great peace.
> (Ps. 37:11)

Jesus extends the privileges of royalty and rule to all who belong to him, including Gentile believers. Though the Christians may be persecuted and suffer in life, Jesus has assured them that they will rule with him on this earth (Luke 12:32; Rom. 5:17; Rev. 1:6; 5:10; 20:6).

Hope is a most vital element in the kingdom. It calls the subjects of the kingdom to theocentric living and keeps the present enjoyment of the kingdom of God and the future unfolding of its glory in dynamic tension. The children of the kingdom enjoy a foretaste of the future, but their lives are still in the shadow of the eschaton. Jesus has inaugurated the final stage in the history of redemption. Moreover, newness of life, sealed by the Spirit of God, is a token of the future restoration. The Spirit works in individuals and corporately in the church. The church is the messianic assembly instituted by Jesus Christ for the purpose of calling others to faith in himself and for adorning its members with the hope of his glorious coming. The church is presently the manifestation of the kingdom. The preaching of the Word and the administration of the sacraments keep the blessed hope alive. The involvement of individual Christians in society can be a responsible expression of Christian citizenship, as long as it does not deny the radical transformation bringing in the new heaven and the new earth. Christ promises transformation. He expects reformation, not reconstruction.

Hope in the kingdom to come lies at the center of Christ's teaching, ministry, and kingdom (Matt. 6:10; 25:1–13). The proclamation of the Good News—that the kingdom is here in the Christ who gave himself a ransom—is incomplete unless it has the corollary preaching of the glorious coming of the Messiah.

The kingdom is imminent (Matt. 16:28; Luke 17:20–21; 21:31). Differences of interpretation will continue to exist among well-meaning Christians regarding the manner of his coming, the signs of the times, and the interpretation of the prophetic word in relation to the teaching of Jesus and the apostles. Hope creates a tension between our understanding of the Word and the freedom of God in working out his purpose even more gloriously than we might expect.

In conclusion, the meaning of the prophetic word is not exhausted by the coming of the Lord. It is all the more imperative to study the prophetic Scriptures, because they speak of the glories of the messianic age (1 Peter 1:11). Peter admonishes the churches to wait and to encourage one another with the hope of the inheritance prepared for the saints at Jesus' coming (vv. 3–4, 8). The elements of that hope include the glorious appearing of our Lord, the resurrection of the body, the glorification of the people of God, the vengeance on the enemies of God's Messiah, the fullness of Jews and Gentiles in the church of Christ in accordance with God's promises and purpose in Christ, the presence of the triune God, and the renewal of heaven and earth. Hope fills the Lord's Prayer, especially the petition, "Thy kingdom come."[7]

Praise

The revelation of God's design for the future is also for the purpose of praise. We may join together with Moses, Isaiah, the Psalms, Paul, and John in the Apocalypse in singing praise to the infinite wisdom and love of the Lord, by whose counsel all things were made and will be subjugated to Christ's lordship. Through the prophets the Lord is giving his people a beatific vision of the glory prepared for them, of the kingdom of God in Christ, of the new world characterized by righteousness, justice, and holiness.

Isaiah's song is representative as he leads the godly to join with him in the praise of God, the King and Divine Warrior, by whose triumph the godly are fully delivered and who condescends in his holiness to dwell among his redeemed:

> Sing to the LORD, for he has done glorious things;
>   let this be known to all the world.
> Shout aloud and sing for joy, people of Zion,
>   for great is the Holy One of Israel among you.
>   (Isa. 12:5–6; see also Zeph. 3:14–17)

Paul rejoices that in Christ the victory is being secured and that through Christ the church participates in the spoils of victory (Eph. 4:7). In Christian praise the new work of God in the Messiah becomes prominent, as Jesus is the agent divinely appointed to bring in the new era (Phil. 2:6–11). According to Paul, the Christian must learn to respond to the work of God in Christ not only in acts, prayers, and a development of the glorious hope but also in singing. Singing represents one expression of godliness by which the whole community can encourage one another with the acts of God in the past, present, and future, employing the inspired psalms and hymns of Scripture as well as "spiritual songs" composed by later believers, reflective of the greatness of God in Christ (Eph. 5:19–20).

The apostle John adds further insight into the wonderful designs of God in Christ by including the praise of the saints, elders, and angelic host around the throne of Christ in heaven. These expressions of praise, hope, and triumph inspire the saints on earth with hope as well as heartfelt joy as they anticipate the victory of Christ over the kingdoms of this world, the establishment of his rule, and the full, uninhibited joy of the saints (Rev. 5:9–10; 7:15–17; 15:3–4; 19:1–2, 6–8).

Confidence in Prayer and Bible Study

Our Lord illustrates the necessity of persistent prayer in the parable of the widow who kept on appealing to a judge for justice (Luke 18:1–5). The woman represents the children of God awaiting the world of righteousness as they are persecuted and dealt with unjustly in this world. The judge represents the world's imperfect system of justice. After our Lord taught the parable he explained the thrust from minor to major by encouraging the godly with the truth that the Father cares much more than any human judge. He always hears the prayers of his children. Prayer is the believer's communication with God on high while being mistreated, misunderstood, ridiculed, harassed, and discriminated against. Prayer is also the expression of faith and persistence, as the godly do not give up, but persevere in waiting for their redemption.

The prayers of the Old Testament saints, prophets, and psalmists and of New Testament saints witness to the fidelity and promises of God.

Through prayer they capture a glimpse of the acts of God. Habakkuk, for example, first questions God in his complaint (Hab. 1:2–2:1) but then ends with prayer, rejoicing in the Lord in the face of historical uncertainties (3:16–19).

The longing of the believer expresses itself not only in prayer but also in the study of God's promises. The Lord instructed the prophets at times to seal their oracles for the sake of further study and contemplation in successive generations. For the sake of the Lord's disciples, Isaiah sealed the prophecy so as to bring judgment on those who had not responded to the Word of God (Isa. 6:10; 8:16). The godly will take courage in the assurance that all of his designs will come about:

> The grass withers and the flowers fall,
> but the Word of our God stands forever.
> (40:8; see also 34:16–17; 55:11)

The study of the prophetic word in the Old and New Testaments develops hope and gives a unique perspective. The study of the Bible should not be oriented primarily toward a construction of detailed speculations concerning how and when all the pieces of the prophetic puzzle fit together. Our Lord's answer to the apostles' question about the inauguration of the kingdom should also give us a proper regard for what belongs to God (Acts 1:7). The power of the Holy Spirit enables, guides, comforts, and gives hope to accomplish the mission Christ has given to the church (v. 8). The study, teaching, and preaching of the Word has an eschatological dimension whenever the practical effects of the Word prepare us for the glorious return of the Christ (Titus 2:11–15). The study of Scripture involves more than a contemplation of the future for its own sake but is highly practical. It encourages holiness, faith, hope, and love: "Blessed is the one who reads the words of this prophecy, and blessed are those who hear it and take to heart what is written in it, because the time is near" (Rev. 1:3).

Conclusion

The story of redemption reveals the grand design of the acts and revelation of God in Jesus Christ. The Son is the Mediator of the relationship between the Father and the people of God. The Spirit of God is given to all the children of God as a token of the restoration to come. He bears witness to the glory in which the children of God will share together with the Lamb. Though we have purposely avoided formulating detailed schematic systems of how the salvation of God will be worked out in the future, Moses, the prophets, our Lord, and the apostles witness harmoniously to the reality of the eschaton. The Christian faith is by nature eschatological, but it is also christological. There is no eschatology without christology, even as there is no christology without eschatology.

Regrettably, evangelical Christians have locked horns on the precise details of interpretation and, even more regrettably, have defined Evangelicalism in terms of a particular millennial perspective.[8] Each of the millennial positions suffers from not hearing the whole prophetic and apostolic witness. Out of concern for the total witness, we must strive for unity even while recognizing diversity. Christ calls us to persevere in living our lives as Christians in preparation for the blessed hope. Our calling is not to work out the details of the blessed hope. Hope may express itself differently, because we are still looking through a glass darkly. Depending on our position, we have various vantage points from which we look at eternity as the one horizon and at the interpretation of the Bible as the other horizon. But we cannot be indifferent to the future or to the interpretation of the prophetic word. We have been called upon to develop the blessed hope and to encourage one another. To this end, the Holy Spirit has been given to deepen within us the longing for the redemption that is to come.[9] With him we cry, "Come, Lord Jesus! Maranatha!"

Abbreviations

AB	*Anchor Bible Commentary.*
BJRL	*Bulletin of the John Rylands Library.*
BSC	*Bible Student's Commentary.*
BT	Vos. *Biblical Theology. Old and New Testaments.* Grand Rapids: Eerdmans, 1948.
CaC	W. J. Dumbrell. *Covenant and Creation: An Old Testament Covenantal Theology.* Exeter: Paternoster, 1984.
CBQ	*Catholic Biblical Quarterly.*
CC	O. Palmer Robertson. *The Christ of the Covenants.* Grand Rapids: Baker, 1980.
CF	H. Berkhof. *The Christian Faith.* Grand Rapids: Eerdmans, 1979.
CP	Thomas E. McComiskey. *The Covenants of Promise: A Theology of the Old Testament Covenants.* Grand Rapids: Baker, 1985.
EBC	*Expositor's Bible Commentary.*
EDT	*Evangelical Dictionary of Theology.*
EJ	*Encyclopaedia Judaica.*
EQ	*Evangelical Quarterly.*
FRLANT	*Forschungen zur Religion und Literatur des Alten und Neuen Testaments.*
HB	Norman K. Gottwald. *The Hebrew Bible: A Socio-Literary Introduction.* Philadelphia: Fortress, 1985.
ICC	*The International Critical Commentary.*
IDB	*The Interpreter's Dictionary of the Bible.*
IDBSup	*IDB Supplementary Volume.*
IHCIP	Willem A. VanGemeren. "Israel as the Hermeneutical Crux in the Interpretation of Prophecy," pt. 1, *WTJ* 45 (1983): 132–45; pt. 2, ibid., 46 (1984): 254–97.
IJH	J. H. Hayes and J. M. Miller, eds. *Israelite and Judean History.* Philadelphia: Fortress, 1979.
IOTS	Brevard S. Childs. *Introduction to the Old Testament as Scripture.* Philadelphia: Fortress, 1979.
ISBE rev.	*International Standard Bible Encyclopedia*, rev. ed.

JBL	*Journal of Biblical Literature.*
JETS	*Journal of the Evangelical Theological Society.*
JNES	*Journal of Near Eastern Studies.*
JSOT	*Journal for the Study of the Old Testament.*
JSOTSup	*JSOT* Supplement Series.
LXX	*Septuagint.*
MT	Masoretic Text.
NCB	*New Century Bible.*
NEB	New English Bible.
NICNT	*New International Commentary on the New Testament.*
NICOT	*New International Commentary on the Old Testament.*
NIGTC	*New International Greek Testament Commentary.*
NIV	New International Version.
NKJV	New King James Version.
NTCI	Brevard S. Childs. *The New Testament as Canon. An Introduction.* Philadelphia: Fortress, 1984.
NTI	Donald Guthrie. *New Testament Introduction.* Downers Grove: InterVarsity, 1970.
NTS	*New Testament Studies.*
NTT	Donald Guthrie. *New Testament Theology.* Downers Grove: InterVarsity, 1981.
OTL	*Old Testament Library*
OTS	William S. LaSor, David A. Hubbard, and Frederic W. Bush. *Old Testament Survey.* Grand Rapids: Eerdmans, 1982
OTTCC	Brevard S. Childs, *Old Testament Theology in a Canonical Context.* Philadelphia: Fortress, 1986
SBT	*Studies in Biblical Theology*
SEA	*Svensk Exegetisk Årsbok*
SNT	Robert H. Gundry. *A Survey of the New Testament.* Grand Rapids: Zondervan, 1970
StBib	*Studia Biblica et Theologica*
TB	*Tyndale Bulletin*
TDNT	*Theological Dictionary of the New Testament*
TNT	George E. Ladd. *A Theology of the New Testament.* Grand Rapids: Eerdmans, 1974
TOTC	*Tyndale Old Testament Commentaries*
TOTT	Walter C. Kaiser, Jr. *Toward an Old Testament Theology.* Grand Rapids: Zondervan, 1978
UD	James D. G. Dunn. *Unity and Diversity in the New Testament: An Inquiry into the Character of Earliest Christianity.* Philadelphia: Westminster, 1977
VT	*Vetus Testamentum*
VTSup	*VT Supplements*

Abbreviations

WBC	Word Biblical Commentary
WTJ	Westminster Theological Journal
ZAW	Zeitschrift für die altestamentliche Wissenschaft
ZNW	Zeitschrift für die neutestamentliche Wissenschaft

Notes

Preface

¹G. E. Ladd, *The Pattern of New Testament Truth* (Grand Rapids: Eerdmans, 1968), 110–11.

Introduction

¹For a survey, see Alan R. Millard, "Approaching the Old Testament," *Themelios* 2 (1977): 34–39.

²Eugene F. Klug, Foreword to *The End of the Historical Critical Method*, by Gerhard Maier (St. Louis: Concordia, 1977), 9.

³G. Ebeling, *Word and Faith*, trans. James W. Leitch (Philadelphia: Fortress, 1963), 308.

⁴For further discussion see Anthony C. Thiselton, "Hermeneutics and Theology: The Legitimacy and Necessity of Hermeneutics," in *The Two Horizons: New Testament Hermeneutics and Philosophical Description* (Grand Rapids: Eerdmans, 1980), 85–114; Roger Lundin, Anthony C. Thiselton, and Clarence Walhout, *The Responsibility of Hermeneutics* (Grand Rapids: Eerdmans, 1985).

⁵James Barr, *Old and New in Interpretation* (New York: Harper & Row, 1966), 190.

⁶Emil Brunner, *The Christian Doctrine of Creation and Redemption*, vol. 2 of *Dogmatics* (Philadelphia: Westminster, 1952), 213.

⁷B. S. Childs, "On Reading the Elijah Narratives," *Interpretation* 34 (1980): 128.

⁸B. S. Childs, *The Book of Exodus*, OTL, x.

⁹B. S. Childs, "Interpretation in Faith," *Interpretation* 18 (1964): 437, 438. Hermeneutic theory increasingly recognizes the place of the individual in interpretation.

¹⁰Ibid., 444.

¹¹See W. VanGemeren, "IHCIP," pt. 1; idem, "Perspectives on Continuity," in *Continuity and Discontinuity: Perspectives on the Relationship between the Old and New Testaments in Honor of S. Lewis Johnson, Jr.,* ed. John S. Feinberg (Westchester: Crossway, 1988); W. C. Kaiser, Jr., *Toward Rediscovering the Old Testament* (Grand Rapids: Zondervan, 1987), 35–46. Kaiser approaches the subject of the unity of Old and New Testaments after a careful analysis of the Old Testament promises and concludes, "There was just one people of God and one program of God even though there are several aspects to that single people and single program" (*TOTT*, 269).

[12] Friedrich Delitzsch, *Die grosse Täuschung* (Stuttgart: Deutsche Verlags-Anstalt, 1920–21), 2:52, quoted in E. G. Kraeling, *The Old Testament Since the Reformation* (New York: Harper & Row, 1955), 158. For a discussion, see A. C. Cochrane, *The Church's Confession Under Hitler* (Philadelphia: Westminster, 1962).

[13] David W. Lotz, "Sola Scriptura: Luther on Biblical Authority," *Interpretation* 35 (1981): 258–73.

[14] Quoted in Emil G. Kraeling, *The Old Testament Since the Reformation*, 16.

[15] Calvin, *Institutes* 2.9–11; Anthony A. Hoekema, "The Covenant of Grace in Calvin's Teaching," *Calvin Theological Journal* 2 (1967): 133–61.

[16] See VanGemeren, "Perspectives on Continuity."

[17] Calvin, *Institutes* 2.9.3.

[18] Ibid.

[19] Ibid. 2.11.2.

[20] For a discussion concerning the center in biblical theology, see Kaiser, *TOTT*, 20–32; Gerhard Hasel, *Old Testament Theology* (Grand Rapids: Eerdmans, 1972), 123–30. On the problem of biblical theology, see Brevard S. Childs, *Biblical Theology in Crisis* (Philadelphia: Westminster, 1970). For a current reassessment and contribution, see idem, *Old Testament Theology in a Canonical Context* (Philadelphia: Fortress, 1986), 1–17.

[21] Bruce C. Birch, "Biblical Hermeneutics in Recent Discussion: Old Testament," *Religious Studies Review* 10 (1984): 1–7.

[22] Kaiser, *TOTT*, 39; see also pp. 32–40.

[23] See P. D. Hanson, *The Diversity of Scripture* (Philadelphia: Fortress, 1982).

[24] Brevard S. Childs, *IOTS*, 671; cf. Fritz Stolz, *Interpreting the Old Testament* (London: SCM, 1975), 140–43.

[25] See Kaiser, *Toward Rediscovering*, 101–20.

[26] See E. D. Hirsch, Jr., *The Aims of Interpretation* (Chicago: University of Chicago Press, 1976); L. Berkhof, *Principles of Biblical Interpretation* (Grand Rapids: Baker, 1950); G. B. Caird, *The Language and Imagery of the Bible* (Philadelphia: Westminster, 1980). For an evaluation of the use and limitations of this method, see the contributions from various vantage points in Donald K. McKim, ed., *A Guide to Contemporary Hermeneutics: Major Trends in Biblical Interpretation* (Grand Rapids: Eerdmans, 1986).

[27] Bernard Ramm, "Who Can Best Interpret the Bible?" *Eternity*, November 1979. vol. 30., pp. 25, 28, 43.

[28] Thomas F. Torrance, *The Mediation of Christ* (Grand Rapids: Eerdmans, 1984), 27.

[29] See John Barton, *Reading the Old Testament: Method in Biblical Study* (Philadelphia: Westminster, 1984); Peter W. Macky, "The Coming Revolution: The New Literary Approach to New Testament Interpretation," *Theological Educator* 9 (1979): 32–46; Robert Alter, *The Art of Biblical Narrative* (New York: Basic, 1981); idem, *The Art of Biblical Poetry* (New York: Basic, 1985). Tremper Longman III, *Literary Approaches to Biblical Interpretation* (Grand Rapids: Zondervan, 1987).

[30] Childs, *IOTS*, 533.

[31] Sidney Greidanus, *Sola Scriptura: Problems and Principles in Preaching*

Historical Texts (Kampen: Kok, 1970); Theodore Plantinga, *Reading the Bible as History* (Burlington, Ont.: Welch, 1980).

³²W. Kaiser, *The Old Testament in Contemporary Preaching* (Grand Rapids: Baker, 1973); idem, *Toward an Exegetical Theology* (Grand Rapids: Baker, 1981); G. Maier, *The End of the Historical-Critical Method* (St. Louis: Concordia, 1977).

³³Peter Stuhlmacher, *Historical Criticism and Theological Interpretation: Towards a Hermeneutics of Consent*, trans. Roy A. Harrisville (Philadelphia: Fortress, 1977), 85–87. See also James D. Smart, *The Strange Silence of the Bible in the Church* (Philadelphia: Westminster, 1970).

³⁴Stuhlmacher, *Historical Criticism*, 65.

³⁵Richard L. Rohrbaugh, *The Biblical Interpreter: An Agrarian Bible in an Industrial Age* (Philadelphia: Fortress, 1978), 7, 8–9.

³⁶Ebeling, *Word and Faith*, 311.

³⁷Thiselton, *The Two Horizons*.

³⁸*Chicago Statement of Biblical Hermeneutics.*

³⁹Brunner, *Doctrine of Creation and Redemption*, 212.

⁴⁰David J. Hesselgrave, "The Three Horizons: Culture, Integration, and Communication," *JETS* 28 (1985): 443–66. See Walter C. Kaiser, Jr., "Legitimate Hermeneutics," in *Inerrancy*, ed. Norman Geisler (Grand Rapids: Zondervan, 1980), 117–47.

⁴¹Bernard L. Ramm, "Biblical Interpretation," *Baker's Dictionary of Practical Theology*, ed. Ralph G. Turnbull (Grand Rapids: Baker, 1967), 101.

⁴²H. Berkhof, *Christ, the Meaning of History*, trans. L. Buurman (Grand Rapids: Baker, 1979).

NOTES TO PART 1: CREATION IN HARMONY

Introduction to Part 1

¹"The only essential thing is that the Bible includes among God's works the beginning and the end as the framework for the history of salvation, and that for the Bible it is essential to God's deity that he is the first and the last, that his activity includes everything" (Claus Westermann, *Beginning and End in the Bible*, trans. Keith Crim [Philadelphia: Fortress, 1972], 39).

²"Yahweh" is the name of God given by self-revelation to Israel (Exod. 3:13–19; 6:2–8). It signifies that God is faithful to his promises by redeeming his people and showing the mighty wonders in Egypt; it is the Old Testament equivalent of "Father." In chap. 11, I discuss further the significance of the name.

Chapter 1: A Theocentric Focus on Creation

¹I agree with Childs (*IOTS*, 145) that the critical division should not be made after Gen. 2:4a. Verse 4 is a *superscription* of the second narrative.

²1William S. LaSor, David A. Hubbard, and Frederic W. Bush, *OTS*, 71.

³For helpful works on literary conventions, see Robert Alter, *The Art of Biblical Narrative* (New York: Basic, 1981); idem, *The Art of Biblical Poetry* (New York: Basic, 1985).

⁴Note Martin Buber's comment regarding purposeful repetitions: "The

measured repetition that matches the inner rhythm of the text, or rather, that wells up from it, is one of the most powerful means for conveying meaning *without expressing it*" (quoted in Alter, *Biblical Narrative*, 93, emphasis mine).

[5] For a discussion of dissonance, see ibid., 100–101.

[6] Meredith G. Kline, "Because It Had Not Rained," *WTJ* 20 (1957): 146–57.

[7] Parallelism is a convention in Hebrew that relates words or ideas to each other by stating the same idea in different words (synonymous parallelism), in complementary terms (synthetic parallelism), or in a contrastive way (antithetic parallelism). See Alter, *Biblical Poetry*, 3–26; James L. Kugel, *The Idea of Biblical Poetry* (New Haven: Yale University Press, 1981).

[8] See Alter's treatment of Gen. 2 (*Biblical Narrative*, 141–47).

[9] The cultural mandate includes the command to raise a family, populate the earth, and be involved creatively with God's creation. See John Murray, *Principles of Conduct* (Grand Rapids: Eerdmans, 1964), 27–44.

Chapter 2: The Canonical Perspective—God's Word to Israel

[1] See A. Heidel, *The Babylonian Genesis* (Chicago: University of Chicago Press, 1963); James B. Pritchard, ed., *Ancient Near Eastern Texts Relating to the Old Testament*, 3d ed. (Princeton: Princeton University Press, 1969), 4–5.

[2] W. Foerster, *"Ktizō," TDNT* 3:1006, 1010.

[3] Gen. 1:26 ("let us make") does not disprove this position, because the phrase brings out a declaration of divine intent. Certainly the angelic host did not give him counsel. See Gerhard F. Hasel, "The Meaning of 'Let Us' in Gen. 1:26," *Andrews University Seminary Studies* 13 (1975): 58–66.

[4] Augustine was one of the first to warn against the dogmatic approach to creation. He properly viewed the language of Genesis as a form of accommodation to the human mind (*The City of God* 11. 30). Still today we must humbly admit that the finite cannot comprehend the infinite. The concern with theories of origins, the antiquity of the world and of humankind, and the synthesis of science and the Bible is important. But if no distinction is made between the theological significance and the scientific significance of creation, the contribution of Christians in scientific pursuit will be limited. Biblical interpretation of the creation account involves both a total interpretation of the Old Testament teaching on creation and a readiness to admit the mystery of creation. This requires a willingness to limit theological inquiry if necessary as Warfield did in his classic essay ("On the Antiquity and the Unity of the Human Race," *Biblical and Theological Studies* [Philadelphia: Presbyterian and Reformed Publishing Co., 1952], 238–61), in which he persuasively argued that the theological concern of Genesis 1–11 is the unity of the race and not the antiquity. This also requires a willingness to be in dialogue with science, as Davis Young concludes: "Our alternative involves thorough exegesis of all of Scripture, and does not build a scientific theory on a few selected texts as does neo-catastrophism. We recognize science for what it is and allow it to develop in a natural way without forcing discovery into a preconceived mold. To be sure problems still remain, but our approach is faithful to both Scripture, God's special revelation, and nature, His general revelation. Only an approach that is faithful to all of God's works has any real hope of resolving any problems in the fascinating area of the

relationship between geology and the Bible" (*Creation and the Flood: An Alternative to Flood Geology and Theistic Evolution* [Grand Rapids: Baker, 1977], 213. But dialogue does not mean a slavish following of scientific trends, as James M. Houston writes, "creation can thus never be a rival hypothesis to the latest scientific theories, since God has given man the faculty of intelligence to develop science as well as regulate the structure of reality he can perceive" (*I Believe in the Creator* [Grand Rapids: Eerdmans, 1980], 47). See Davis Young, *Christianity and the Origins of the Earth* (Grand Rapids: Zondervan, 1982).

⁵ James M. Houston, *I Believe*, p. 57; so also H. Berkhof, "But this stumbling block for the mind becomes much greater yet when we are faced not only with something irreducible, but with an irreducible break, a discontinuity in existence, a jump of the infinite into the finite. The created world is an imperfect world, a reality happening in time. It comes from the perfect and eternal God. . . . We can think only in the categories of space and time, which implies that we cannot comprehend what it means that God is the ground of our existence. We cannot penetrate this mystery, we can only make it our starting point" (*CF*, pp. 152–53).

Chapter 3: Creation as a Preamble to the History of Redemption

¹ See Thomas F. Torrance, *Divine and Contingent Order* (Oxford: Oxford University Press, 1981), 4. Shamai Galender argues that creation is the materialization of God's justice, in "Justice and the Order of Creation" (in Hebrew), *Beth Miqra* 97 (1984): 158–79.

² According to Torrance, however, the order is not "a static or predetermined programming but as a dynamic function of its contingent processes in a mutual involution of form and being, giving rise to ever richer patterns of order which may be understood only in terms of the natural onto-relational structures" (*Divine and Contingent Order*, 110).

³ Ibid., 64–65, 68.

⁴ See Henry F. Lazenby, "The Image of God: Masculine, Femine, or Neuter?" *JETS* 30 (1987), 63–70.

⁵ For a full discussion of the covenant of creation, see O. Palmer Robertson, *CC*, 67–87; cf. W. J. Dumbrell, *CaC*.

⁶ Isa. 27:11; 43:7, 15, 21; see also Exod. 34:10; Ps. 95; W. Foerster, *"Ktizō,"* *TDNT* 3:1006–7.

⁷ H. Berkhof, *CF*, 170.

⁸ Ibid., 169.

⁹ Ibid., 170.

¹⁰ Houston has developed a stimulating, reformational perspective on the biblical teaching of living in the presence of God: "Man's identity does not lie in his work as *homo faber* assumes but in the creator-redeemer who calls him to a vocation of service . . . meditation as well as work, contemplation as well as action, being as well as doing, companionship with God as well as service for God . . . these are the creative mandates of man" (*I Believe*, 162).

¹¹ Claus Westermann, *Beginning and End in the Bible*, trans. Keith Crim (Philadelphia: Fortress, 1972), 37.

NOTES TO PART 2: CREATION IN ALIENATION

Introduction to Part 2

[1] H. Berkhof, *CF*, 170.

Chapter 4: The Generations from Adam to Terah

[1] Gen. 2:4; 5:1; 6:9; 10:1; 11:10; 11:27; 25:12, 19; 36:1; 37:2.

[2] The phrase "these are the generations of" is not to be interpreted as a colophon, or closing phrase. P. J. Wiseman, *Creation Revealed in Six Days* (London: Marshall, Morgan & Scott, 1949), 46–53; D. J. Wiseman, ed., *Ancient Records and the Structure of Genesis: A Case for Literary Unity* (Nashville: Nelson, 1985); followed by R. K. Harrison (*Introduction to the Old Testament* [Grand Rapids: Eerdmans, 1969], 548–51) and others have sought to establish the antiquity of Genesis by proposing that the accounts were separate stories, each of which ended with a colophon, or brief designation of the contents. In this view Moses used clay tablets, at the end of which an ancient scribe had marked an idea of the contents. This proposal, however, does not agree with the actual usage in Genesis. See M. G. Kline, "Genesis," in *New Bible Commentary* (Grand Rapids: Eerdmans, 1970), 80; W. H. Gispen, *Genesis* (Kampen: Kok, 1974), 1:95; D. S. DeWitt, "The Generations of Genesis," *EQ* 48 (1976): 196–211.

[3] For another schematization with the flood narrative as the center, see Walter Brueggemann, *Genesis* (Atlanta: John Knox, 1981), 23.

[4] See G. J. Wenham's fascinating argument for the unity of the Flood narrative in "The Coherence of the Flood Narrative," *VT* 28 (1978): 336–48.

[5] Gary V. Smith has proposed an alternative approach, concluding with similar theological motifs, in "Structure and Purpose in Genesis 1–11," *JETS* 20 (1977): 307–19.

[6] William S. LaSor, David A. Hubbard, and Frederic W. Bush, *OTS*, 83.

[7] Claus Westermann, *Creation*, trans. John. J. Scullion, S. J. (London: SPCK, 1971), 49. Such blessing, as it relates to humankind, is called "common grace" in theology (see C. Van Til, *Common Grace and the Gospel* [N.p.: Presbyterian & Reformed, 1973]).

[8] The narratives and genealogies do not give a complete history of humankind, nor do they provide sufficient data for establishing the antiquity of man. Moreover, one should not use the narratives in any other way than they have been originally intended—that is, to demonstrate the unity and the solidarity of mankind (see B. B. Warfield, "On the Antiquity and Unity of the Human Race," in *Biblical and Theological Studies* [Philadelphia: Presbyterian & Reformed, 1952], 238–61). See also James Barr, "Why the World Was Created in 4004 B.C.: Archbishop Ussher and Biblical Chronology," *BJRL* 67 (1985): 575–608.

[9] Nahum M. Sarna, *Understanding Genesis* (New York: Schocken, 1970), 24–28.

[10] A. Heidel, *The Gilgamesh Epic and Old Testament Parallels* (Chicago: University of Chicago Press, 1963).

[11] Sarna, *Understanding Genesis*, 55.

Chapter 5: Israel and the Nations

[1] Gen. 6:18; 7:7, 13, 23; 8:16, 18.

[2] Umberto Cassuto, *A Commentary on the Book of Genesis* (Jerusalem: Magnes, 1964), 2:175–80. Note that the story of Nimrod (10:8–12) is a parenthetic account and if included would increase the number to seventy-two. See Daniel Grossberg, "Number Harmony and Life Spans in the Bible," *Semitics* 9 (1984): 49–57.

[3] Whereas the NIV reads "May Japheth live in the tents of Shem," the preferable understanding of "he" is "the LORD," as others have argued (e.g., Walter Kaiser, *TOTT*, 82). The goal of redemptive history remains the presence of God on earth, which Israel experienced in the form of the tabernacle.

Chapter 6: Man's Revolution and God's Rule over the Earth

[1] In Gen. 6:6, the word for God's "pain" (Heb. ʿeṣeb) is similar to the word used for Adam and Eve's "painful toil" (3:16–17; Heb. ʿiṣṣābôn). Brueggemann observes, "The text affirms that God is decisively impacted by the suffering, hurt, and circumstance of his creation. God enters into the world's 'common lot'" (*Genesis*, 78).

[2] Davis Young expresses a proper note of caution against a scientific reading of the narratives that describe the Fall and the Flood. With respect to the effects of sin on creation, he notes, "It cannot be proved from the Scripture that the curse resulted in anything other than pain, sorrow, agonizing labor, and death for man and degradation for the serpent. Ideas about structural changes in the animals, death among animals, and drastic transformations in the laws of nature such as laws of the thermodynamics must from a Scriptural perspective forever remain pure speculations" (*Creation and the Flood: An Alternative to Flood Geology and Theistic Evolution* [Grand Rapids: Baker, 1977], 168). In response to the widespread influence of Flood theology (see, e.g., John C. Whitcomb and Henry M. Morris, *The Genesis Flood: The Biblical Record and Its Scientific Implications* [Philadelphia: Presbyterian & Reformed, 1961]), Young persuasively argues against the catastrophic-flood theology in favor of a careful exegetical approach in conjunction with scientific exploration.

[3] G. Vos calls it "minimum grace" and argues in favor of its continuity: "Without at least some degree of divine interposition, collapse of the world-fabric would have resulted" (*BT*, 56); see also Arthur H. Lewis, "Jehovah's International Love," *JETS* 15 (1972): 87–92.

[4] Brueggemann, *Genesis*, 61.

[5] For a full discussion of the views, problems, and possible interpretations of 6:1–4, see Willem A. VanGemeren, "The Sons of God in Genesis 6:1–4 (an Example of Evangelical Demythologization?)," *WTJ* 43 (1980): 320–48.

[6] Vos observes, "The continuity of the race is preserved. God saves enough out of the wreck to enable him to carry out His original purpose with the self-same humanity He had created" (*BT*, 62).

[7] Dumbrell's connection of the Noahic covenant with Genesis 1 and 2 is exegetically correct (*CaC*, 20–33). See also Michael V. Fox, "The Sign of the Covenant," *Revue Biblique* 81 (1974): 557–96.

[8] At Pentecost representatives of the nations heard about the Messiah in their

own language (Acts 2:5–12). John portrays the diversity in the praise of God as an assembly of the redeemed "from every nation, tribe, people and language, standing before the throne and in front of the Lamb" (Rev. 7:9).

[9]The phrase "I will wipe from" (Gen. 6:7) is equivalent to "I curse." God's curse on the earth (3:17), however, will be lifted for the sake of his people.

[10]Kaiser, *TOTT*, 78.

[11]Berkhof, *CF*, 200.

[12]For a similar perspective, cf. Carol L. Meyers, "Gender Roles and Genesis 3:16 Revisited," *The Word of the Lord Shall Go Forth*, ed. Carol L. Meyers and M. O'Connor (Winona Lake: Eisenbrauns, 1983), 337–54. See also Susan T. Foh, "What Is the Woman's Desire?" *WTJ*, (1974–75): 376–83.

[13]Moreover, the translation should carry the ambiguity of the tense in Hebrew. The imperfect mood of the verbs "crush" and "strike" could also be translated modally as "may," "could," or "should." Finally, the difficulty in translation lies in the etymology and meaning of the verb *šûp*. The NIV translates the one root with two separate verbs, whereas it seems that this rare verb is chosen for poetic effect and that the emphasis lies on the contrast between "head" and "heel." See Vos, *BT*, 55.

[14]Ibid., 67.

[15]Genesis 2–11 appears to support an ancient Jewish tradition expecting the nations to observe at least the Noahic laws, the basic moral guidelines given to Noah in Genesis 9 and listed above. The apostle Paul gives credibility to this teaching in his expectation that the Gentiles should respond to the revelation of God in nature rather than "suppress the truth by their wickedness" (Rom. 1:18). The Council of Jerusalem also appeared to uphold these basic rules (Acts 15).

[16]See John Murray, *The Imputation of Adam's Sin* (Grand Rapids: Eerdmans, 1959).

NOTES TO PART 3: ELECTION AND PROMISE

Chapter 7: Promise in an Alienated World

[1]W. Zimmerli, quoted in D. J. A. Clines, *The Theme of the Pentateuch, JSOTSup* 10 (1978), 77–78.

[2]See the extensive bibliographies in Claus Westermann, "Promises to the Patriarchs," trans. Keith Crim, *IDBSup*, 693; and in William G. Dever and Malcolm Clark, "The Patriarchal Traditions," in *IJH*, 70–148. Walter Kaiser has organized his entire Old Testament theology around the concept of promise *(TOTT)*; Thomas E. McComiskey *(CP)* has given a penetrating analysis of the "promise" element in the structural development of the covenants.

[3]On two occasions Ishmael is the object of a "seed" promise (Gen. 16:10; 17:20). He never receives this word himself, however (as do the patriarchs), and he does not receive any form of promise of a land or blessing. The very frequency of the promises highlights the importance of Abraham and Jacob.

[4]C. Westermann has observed that, in several cases of God's assurance of his presence, God promises to be with the person on a journey. It is given as a part of the command to move (Gen. 46:1–3) or to remain (26:1–3) or to return

(31:3) (*The Promises to the Fathers: Studies on the Patriarchal Narratives*, trans. David E. Green [Philadelphia: Fortress, 1980], 141).

[5] Both Vos (*BT*, 89–93) and Kaiser (*TOTT*, 87) bring out this movement.

[6] An excellent work dealing with historical, archaeological, and critical issues related to the historicity of the individual patriarchs is A. R. Millard and D. J. Wiseman, eds., *Essays on the Patriarchal Narratives* (Leicester: InterVarsity, 1980). Note that the *toledot* structure focuses on families instead of individuals. The account of Terah (11:27–25:11), for example, is named after Terah because Abraham, the main character, must deal with Lot, a grandson of Terah, and Abraham's son Isaac marries a great-granddaughter of Terah.

[7] For a literary-critical discussion of the Joseph narrative, see Hans-Christoph Schmitt, "Die Hintergründe der 'neuesten Pentateuchkritik' und der literarische Befund der Josefsgeschichte, Gen. 37–50," *Zeitschrift für die alttestamentliche Wissenschaft* 97 (1985): 161–89.

Chapter 8: The God of the Fathers Is the God of Promise

[1] F. G. Smith, "Observations on the use of the Names and Titles of God in Genesis," *EQ* 40 (1968): 103; W. F. Albright, "The Name Shaddai and Abram," *JBL* 54 (1935): 173–204; G. J. Wenham, "The Religion of the Patriarchs," *Essays on the Patriarchal Narratives*, ed. D. J. Wiseman (Leicester: InterVarsity, 1980), 157–88.

[2] Commentators have long debated the intent of Exodus 6:3. If it means that the patriarchs did not know the name at all, what are we to do with passages where the name is on the patriarch's lips (e.g., Gen. 14:22; 26:22; 32:9) or where God himself says "I am Yahweh" (15:7; 28:13)?

[3] Brevard S. Childs, *The Book of Exodus*, OTL, 112–14.

[4] John Murray, *The Covenant of Grace* (London: Tyndale, 1954), 31. This definition of covenant is amplified by O. Palmer Robertson, who defines it as "a bond in blood sovereignly administered" (*CC*, 4).

[5] Childs, *IOTS*, 151.

[6] D. J. A. Clines, *The Theme of the Pentateuch*, JSOTSup 10 (1978), 46.

Chapter 9: Promise, Grace, and Fidelity

[1] A. Van Seters, "God and Family: From Sociology to Covenant Theology," *Themelios* 5 (1980): 4–7.

[2] Vos is fond of pointing out that Isaac's passivity reflects his role as the middle patriarch. "The middle stage is a stage of suffering and self-surrender, and is therefore passive in its aspect" (*BT*, 106). D. Kidner agrees: "Isaac too comes briefly into his own—not by what he does but by what he suffers. Here, it seems, is his role, undistinguished though he may be in himself." He demonstrates "God's pattern for the chosen 'seed': to be a servant sacrificed" (*Genesis: An Introduction and Commentary, TOTC*, 143).

[3] An excellent treatment of this difficult hermeneutic issue is by O. Palmer Robertson, "Genesis 15:6: New Covenant Expositions of an Old Covenant Text," *WTJ* 42 (1980): 259–89. The contrast in James 2:14–26 is "between faith minus works, and works minus faith—not between faith and works" (James B. Adamson, *The Epistle of James*, NICNT, 132).

4Dumbrell, *CaC*, 78.

NOTES TO PART 4: A HOLY NATION

Chapter 10: The Literary Record of Promise and Fulfillment

1Childs, *IOTS*, 176.

2"For Israel to learn the will of God necessitated an act of self-revelation. Israel could not discover it for herself" (ibid., 174). See also Dale Ralph Davis, "Rebellion, Presence, and Covenant: A Study in Exodus 32–34," *WTJ* 44 (1982): 71–87.

3"The status of a holy people, separated unto God, does not only control Israel's relation with the deity, but extends into the realm of human relations" (Childs, *IOTS*, 185). J. Milgrom recognizes the fusion of ethics and cult: "However, Leviticus is not just a collection of rituals. On the contrary, the ethical element fuses with and informs the ritual so that one may seek a moral basis behind each ritual act" ("Leviticus," *IDBSup*, 541).

4G. Mendenhall, "The Census Lists of Numbers 1 and 26," *JBL* 77 (1958): 52–66.

5I agree wholeheartedly with Childs's conclusion that "in spite of its diversity of subject matter and complex literary development the Book of Numbers maintains a unified sacerdotal interpretation of God's will for his people which is set forth in a sharp contrast between the holy and the profane" (*IOTS*, 199).

6N. Lohfink isolates other small narrative units and concludes that "a cloak of narration was thrown around the book" as a means of bringing together a collection of speeches ("Deuteronomy," *IDBSup*, 229). Childs made a major breakthrough in his literary analysis by asking how the various parts of Deuteronomy function in their present form (*IOTS*, 213–21). On the theology of Deuteronomy as a whole and on its distinctive contribution, see J. G. McConville, *Law and Theology in Deuteronomy, JSOTSup* 33 (1984). I agree with Ernest W. Nicholson that Deuteronomy should not be structured according to the treaty form (*God and his People. Covenant Theology in the Old Testament* [Oxford: Clarendon, 1986], 71–82). For an example of this approach, see Meredith G. Kline, *Treaty of the Great King; The Covenant Structure of Deuteronomy: Studies and Commentary* (Grand Rapids: Eerdmans, 1963).

7See Gordon Wenham's significant contribution on the date of Deuteronomy, "The Date of Deuteronomy: Linch-pin of Old Testament Criticism," *Themelios* 10 (1985): 15–20; 11 (1985): 15–18.

8See Gordon J. Wenham, "The Deuteronomic Theology of the Book of Joshua," *JBL* 90 (1971): 141–42. See also Robert G. Boling, "Levitical History and the Role of Joshua," in *The Word of the Lord Shall Go Forth: Essays in Honor of David Noel Freedman,* ed. Carol L. Meyers and M. O'Connor (Winona Lake: Eisenbrauns, 1983), 241–61.

Chapter 11: The Revelation of Yahweh and the Consecration of Israel

1The Lord responds to the cry of Israel in Egypt (Exod. 2:24; 3:7) and shows his fatherly love and compassion for them (19:4; Deut 4:20). Yet, he was also full of anger so as to destroy murmurers, rebels, and those who were complacent. Israel lived because of God's patience but could be judged in his wrath (Exod. 33:3; Num. 11:10). In spite of all of Israel's shortcomings as a rebellious, stiff-necked people, however, they are still the people of God (Exod. 33:13).

2 W. L. Moran, "A Kingdom of Priests," in *The Bible in Current Catholic Thought*, ed. J. L. McKenzie (New York: Herder & Herder, 1962), 7–20. For a different approach, see E. Fiorenza, *Priester für Gott* (Münster: Aschendorff, 1972). In J. H. Elliott's study linking the Old and New Testaments, he remarks about this text, "Not priestly function but priestly character is weighted here" (*The Elect and the Holy* [Leiden: Brill, 1966], 56). Dumbrell comments, "The theology of the kingship of God is here prominently displayed. But kingship and covenant are . . . coordinates since the presupposition of covenant is divine rule, while covenant in and through Israel is the implementation of divine kingship in national polity" (*CaC*, 90).

3 J. Gerald Janzen, "What's in a Name? 'Yahweh' in Exodus 3 and the Wider Biblical Context," *Interpretation* 33 (1979): 227–39. Debate has arisen over the precise pronunciation of the name. The name was freely used in the biblical literature and in nonbiblical materials before the Exile. After the Exile, however, the Jews were so concerned that they might unwittingly break the third commandment that they introduced substitutions such as "Lord" (*Adonai*), "heaven," and "the place." The Jews of Jesus' time continued this practice, and he adjusted to their habits. When Christianity separated from Judaism, there was no need not to continue the old practices. The Reformation era reintroduced a familiarity with the tetragrammaton (YHWH) of the Hebrew text but unfortunately read the vowels of *Adonai* with YHWH, resulting in *Jehovah*. Modern scholars are not agreed on the precise vocalization, but since the use of Yahweh is now well established, it is preferable to translate YHWH as Yahweh (see W. VanGemeren, "Tetragrammaton," *EDT*, 1079–80).

4 Charles D. Isbell, "The Divine Name as a Symbol of Presence in Israelite Tradition." *Hebrew Annual Review* 2 (1978): 101–18; Charles R. Gianotti, "The Meaning of the Divine Name YHWH," *BibSac* 142 (1985): 38–51.

5 F. M. Cross, "Yahweh and the God of the Patriarchs," *Harvard Theological Review* 55 (1962): 225–59, developed further in his *Canaanite Myth and Hebrew Epic* (Cambridge: Harvard University Press, 1973), 3–75.

6 For a similar construction see Exod. 33:19: "I will have mercy on whom I will have mercy, and I will have compassion on whom I will have compassion." See Th. C. Vriezen, " 'ehje 'ašer," *Festschrift für Alfred Bertholet*, ed. Baumgartner, Eissfeldt, Elliger, Rost (Tübingen: Mohr, 1950), 498–512.

7 W. Zimmerli, *Ezekiel 1*, trans. R. E. Clements (Philadelphia: Fortress, 1979), 37–38.

8 J. Goldingay, " 'That you may know that Yahweh is God': A Study in the Relationship Between Theology and Historical Truth in the Old Testament," *TB* 23 (1972): 58–93.

9 George E. Mendenhall, *The Tenth Generation. The Origins of the Biblical Tradition* (Baltimore: Johns Hopkins, 1973), 29.

10 The motif of "holy War" has been carefully studied since von Rad's seminal work (*Der heilige Krieg im alten Israel* [Göttingen: Vandenhoeck und Ruprecht,

1969). See P. D. Miller, Jr., "El the Warrior," *Harvard Theological Review* 60 (1967), 411–31; idem, *The Divine Warrior in Early Israel* (Cambridge: Harvard University, 1973). See also Tremper Longman, III, "Psalm 98: A Divine Warrior Victory Song," *JETS*, 27 (1984), 167–74.

[11] Tremper Longman, III, "The Divine Warrior: the New Testament Use of an Old Testament Motif," *WTJ*, 44 (1982), 290–307.

[12] "The coexistence of these two elements, that of trustful approach to God and that of reverence for the divine majesty, is characteristic of the Biblical religion throughout" (Vos, *BT*, 167).

[13] J. G. McConville, "God's 'Name' and God's 'Glory'," *TB*, 30 (1979), 149–63.

[14] Meredith G. Kline treats the Mosaic covenant as a parenthesis in God's gracious and promissory dealings (*The Structure of Biblical Authority* [Grand Rapids: Eerdmans, 1972], 94–110), as does Mark Karlberg ("Reformed Interpretation of the Mosaic Covenant," *WTJ* 43 [1980–81]: 1–57). For a perspective on the truly gracious elements, see Murray, *Covenant of Grace*.

[15] For a study of the formal parts of the treaty or covenant, see George E. Mendenhall, "Covenant Forms in Israelite Tradition," *Biblical Archeologist* 17 (1954): 50–70, summarized in LaSor, Hubbard, and Bush, *OTS*, 145; K. A. Kitchen, *The Bible in Its World: The Bible and Archaeology Today* (Downers Grove: InterVarsity, 1977), 79–85. For studies on law, see A. Alt, "The Origins of Israelite Law," in *Essays in Old Testament History and Religion* (Oxford, Blackwell, 1966); D. Daube, *Studies in Biblical Law* (Cambridge, Cambridge University Press, 1947).

[16] T. McComiskey, *CP*, 73. See pp. 94–137 for an excellent treatment of the relation between law and grace, old and new.

[17] John Murray, *Principles of Conduct* (Grand Rapids: Eerdmans, 1957), 181–201.

[18] Childs, *IOTS*, 132–35.

[19] Gordan Wenham, "Grace and Law in the Old Testament," *Law, Morality and the Bible*, Bruce Kaye and Gordon Wenham, eds. (Downers Grove: InterVarsity, 1978), 3–23; Norbert Lohfink, "Law and Grace," *The Christian Meaning of the Old Testament*, trans. R. A. Wilson (London: Burns and Oates, 1968).

[20] For recent studies on this subject, see Gordon Wenham, "Law and Legal System in the Old Testament," in *Law, Morality, and the Bible*, 24–52; Walter C. Kaiser, Jr., *Toward Old Testament Ethics* (Grand Rapids: Zondervan, 1983); Christopher J. H. Wright, *An Eye for an Eye: The Place of Old Testament Ethics Today* (Downers Grove: InterVarsity, 1983); Dale Patrick, *Old Testament Law* (Atlanta: John Knox, 1985).

[21] Kaiser, *Ethics*, 81–95; idem, "Decalogue," *Baker's Dictionary of Christian Ethics*, ed. C. F. H. Henry (Grand Rapids: Baker, 1973), 165–67; J. J. Stamm, M. E. Andrew, *The Ten Commandments in Recent Research* (Naperville: Allenson, 1967).

[22] Kaiser, *Ethics*, 96–137. I appreciate Kaiser's holistic approach. Beginning with the chapter "Holiness as a way of life" (139–51), he goes into the various areas of life: family and society, regard for life, marriage and sex, wealth and possessions, truth, and especially "motive and heart" (*Ethics*, 152–244).

[23] Bernard S. Jackson, "The Ceremonial and the Judicial: Biblical Law as Sign and Symbol," *JSOT* 30 (1984): 25–50.

[24] W. VanGemeren, "Feasts and Festivals, OT," *EDT*, 409–12; Childs, *OTTCC*, 162–63.

[25] Vos's treatment of the place and typological value of the offerings is still highly relevant (*BT*, 172–90). See also H. Gese, *Essays on Biblical Theology*, trans. Keith Crim (Minneapolis: Augsburg, 1981), 81–95; B. A. Levine, *In the Presence of the Lord: A Study of Cult and Some Cultic Terms in Ancient Israel* (Leiden: Brill, 1974).

[26] For a more extensive treatment of the categories and occasions of offerings, see N. H. Snaith, "Sacrifices in the Old Testament," *VT* 7 (1957): 308–17; A. F. Rainey, "The Order of Sacrifices in Old Testament Ritual Texts," *Biblica* 51 (1970): 485–98; Willem A. VanGemeren, "Offerings and Sacrifices in Biblical Times," *EDT*, 788–92.

[27] W. Kaiser, *Ethics*, 235–44.

[28] Brevard S. Childs, *The Book of Exodus*, OTL, 541–42; idem, *OTCC*, 70-2; J. Siker-Gieseler, "The Theology of the Sabbath in the Old Testament: A Canonical Approach," *StBib* 11 (1981): 5–20.

[29] Matitiahu Tsevat, "The Basic Meaning of the Biblical Sabbath" *ZAW 84 (1972), 447–59.*

[30] "The Sabbath brings this principle of the eschatological structure of history to bear upon the mind of man after a symbolical and a typical fashion" (Vos, *BT*, 156).

[31] One of the finest illustrated books on the tabernacle is Moshe Levine's *The Tabernacle. Its Structure and Utensils* (New York: Socino, 1969). See also F. M. Cross, "The Tabernacle," *The Biblical Archaeologist* 10 (1947): 45–68; A. Rothkoff, "The Tabernacle," *Encyclopaedia Judaica* 15:679–88.

[32] Arthur H. Lewis, "The New Birth Under the Old Covenant," *EQ* 56 (1984): 35–44.

Chapter 12: God's Kingdom and His Promise

[1] George E. Mendenhall, "Early Israel as the Kingdom of Yahweh: Thesis and Methods," in *The Tenth Generation: The Origins of the Biblical Tradition* (Baltimore: Johns Hopkins University Press, 1973), 1–31.

[2] For "love" (*ḥesed*) as "loyalty," see Dumbrell, *CaC*, 124.

[3] J. L. McKenzie, "The Elders in the Old Testament," *Analecta Biblica* 10 (1959): 388–406.

[4] D. J. McCarthy, "The Theology of Leadership in Joshua 1–9," *Biblica* 52 (1971): 165–75.

[5] Childs, *OTTCC*, 145–53; M. Greenberg, "A New Approach to the History of the Israelite Priesthood," *Journal of the American Oriental Society* 70 (1950): 41–47.

[6] K. W. Whitelam, *The Just King: Monarchical Judicial Authority in Ancient Israel*, JSOTSup 12 (Sheffield: *JSOT* Press, 1979).

[7] W. Brueggemann, *The Land: The Place as Gift, Promise, and Challenge in Biblical Faith* (Philadelphia: Fortress, 1977).

[8] Dumbrell concludes that the vision of Canaan's fertility in Deut. 26 reflects

a restoration to Eden motif, "One can hardly escape the impression that what is being depicted through such references is Eden recaptured, paradise recovered" (*CaC*, 120).

⁹For the issues arising out of the Conquest stories and the differences between the world of the Conquest and of the judges, see Y. Kaufmann, *The Biblical Account of the Conquest of Palestine,* trans. M. Dagut (Jerusalem: Magnes, 1953); A. Alt, "The Settlement of the Israelites in Palestine," in *Essays on Old Testament History and Religion,* trans. R. A. Wilson (Oxford, 1966), 135–69; M. Weippert, *The Settlement of the Israelite Tribes in Palestine* (Naperville: Allenson, 1971), 21.

¹⁰See W. Kaiser, *TOTT,* 129–30; M. H. Woudstra, *The Ark of the Covenant from Conquest to Kingship* (Philadelphia: Presbyterian & Reformed, 1965).

¹¹See Kaiser, *TOTT,* 133–34. The era of David and Solomon signifies an important fulfillment of these promises. Nevertheless, the prophets develop the hope of a greater manifestation. In Jesus Christ the glory, presence, and fullness of God was revealed in a greater manner. Our hope still is for the New Jerusalem, without a tabernacle or temple, because the triune God will then *dwell* in the midst of the new people (Rev. 21:3).

NOTES TO PART 5:
A NATION LIKE THE OTHER NATIONS

Chapter 13: A Story with Little Movement

¹Most critics agree that the literary materials are the result of generally reliable traditions that were edited from a deuteronomistic perspective. See, e.g., C. A. Simpson, *Composition of the Book of Judges* (Oxford: Blackwell, 1957). For a brief description of the theology behind these books, also known as deuteronomic history, see W. Kaiser, *TOTT,* 122–24.

²E. O'Doherty, "The Literary Problem of Judges 1.1–3.6." *CBQ* 18 (1956): 1–7.

³M. Weinfeld, "The Period of the Conquest and of the Judges as Seen by the Earlier and the Later Sources," *VT* 17 (1967): 93–113; G. E. Wright, "The Literary and Historical Problem of Joshua 10 and Judges 1," *JNES* 5 (1946): 105–14.

⁴For additional background material, see A. Malamat, "The Period of the Judges," *A History of the Jewish People,* ed. B. Mazar (New Brunswick, N.J.: Rutgers University Press, 1971), 3:129–63; A. D. H. Mayes, *Israel in the Period of the Judges* (Naperville: Allenson, 1974); E. Robertson, "The Period of the Judges," *BJRL* 30 (1946): 91–114.

⁵See Norman K. Gottwald, *HB,* 255–60. The major judges were Othniel, Ehud, Deborah (Barak), Gideon, Jephthah, and Samson; the minor judges, Shamgar, Tola, Jair, Ibzan, Elon, and Abdan.

⁶A. Malamat, "The War of Gideon and Midian: A Military Approach," *Palestine Exploration Quarterly* 85 (1953): 61–65. Childs observes that Samson "personifies the tension between promise and fulfillment, ideal and actuality, freedom and servitude which also constitutes the tragedy of the nation under the judges" (*OTTCC,* 115).

[7] A rich literature has considered the hymn of Deborah. See, e.g., J. Blenkinsopp, "Ballad Style and Psalm Style in the Song of Deborah: A Discussion," *Biblica* 42 (1961): 61–76; G. Gerleman, "The Song of Deborah in the Light of Stylistics," *VT* 1 (1951): 168–80; A. Globe, "The Literary Structure and Unity of the Song of Deborah," *JBL* 93 (1974): 493–512. See also J. Blenkinsopp, "Structure and Style in Judges 13–16," *JBL* 82 (1963): 65–76; and J. L. Crenshaw, *Samson: A Secret Betrayed, A Vow Ignored* (Atlanta: Knox, 1978).

[8] On the three stories pertaining to Bethlehem ("the Bethlehem trilogy (Judg. 17–18; Ruth), see Eugene H. Merrill, "The Book of Ruth: Narrative and Shared Themes," *Bibliotheca Sacra* 142 (1985): 130–41. See also Leif Hongisto, "Literary Structure and Theology in the Book of Ruth," *Andrews Univ. Sem. Stud.* 23 (1985): 19–28.

[9] Childs observes that history and redemptive history "flow easily together when viewed from the theological perspective of a God from whom all causality ultimately derives" (*IOTS*, 567–68).

[10] John A. Martin, "The Structure of 1 and 2 Samuel," *Bibliotheca Sacra* 141 (1984): 28–42.

[11] See Childs, *IOTS*, 271–78. LaSor, Hubbard, and Bush comment, "In contrast with Judges and especially Kings, the editorial framework is hardly discernible. . . . The final author rarely intruded his own observations" (*OTS*, 228–29).

[12] S. Abramsky, "Saul and David—the Pursued: The Significance of the Stories of David and Saul's Meeting for Understanding the Beginning of Israelite Monarchy" (in Hebrew), *Beth Mikra* 100 (1984): 48–68.

[13] For a study of Saul's rise to power, see J. M. Miller, "Saul's Rise to Power: Some Observations Concerning I Sam. 9:1–10:16; 10:26–11:15 and 13:2–14:46," *CBQ* 36 (1974): 157–74; J. Blenkinsopp, "The Quest of the Historical Saul," in *No Famine in the Land: Festschrift for John L. McKenzie*, ed. J. W. Flanagan and A. W. Robinson (Missoula: Scholars, 1975), 75–99.

Chapter 14: Lessons from Israel's History

[1] For a background to Canaanite theology and cultic practices, see Elmer B. Smick, "Israel's Struggle with the Religions of Canaan," in *Through Christ's Word*, ed. W. Robert Godfrey and Jesse L. Boyd, III (Phillipsburg: Presbyterian & Reformed, 1985), 108–18.

[2] J. L. Crenshaw, *Samson: A Secret Betrayed, A Vow Ignored* (Atlanta: Knox, 1978).

[3] *OTCC*, 115.

[4] W. F. Albright, "Reconstructing Samuel's Role in History," *Archaeology, Historical Analogy, and Early Biblical Tradition* (Baton Rouge: Louisiana State University, 1966), 42–65.

[5] A. F. Campbell, *The Ark Narrative (1 Sam. 4–6; 2 Sam. 6): A Form-Critical and Traditio-Historical Study*. SBL Dissertation 16 (Missoula: Scholars Press, 1975); P. D. Miller and J. J. M. Roberts, *The Hand of the Lord: A Reassessment of the "Ark Narrative" of Samuel* (Baltimore: Johns Hopkins, 1977).

[6] W. J. Dumbrell, "In those days there was no King in Israel; every man did

what was right in his own eyes. The Purpose of the Book of Judges Reconsidered," *JSOT* 25 (1983): 23–33; R. G. Boling, "In those days there was no King in Israel," *A Light unto my Path: Old Testament Studies in Honor of Jacob M. Myers* (Philadelphia: Temple University, 1974), 33–48.

⁷For a study on this era, cf. H. Haag, "Gideon-Jerubbaal-Abimelek," *ZAW* 79 (1967), 305–14.

⁸B. Lindars, "Gideon and Kingship," *Journal of Theological Studies* 16 (1965): 315–26.

⁹J. H. Grønbaek, *Die Geschichte vom Aufstieg Davids (1 Sam. 15–2 Sam. 5): Tradition und Komposition* (Copenhagen: Muksgaard, 1971); A. Weiser, "Die Legitimation des Königs David," *VT* 16 (1966): 325–54.

Chapter 15: God's Faithfulness and Israel's Unresponsiveness

¹Terence E. Fretheim, "Divine Foreknowledge, Divine Constancy, and the Rejection of Saul's Kingship," *CBQ* 47 (1985): 595–602.

NOTES TO PART 6: A ROYAL NATION

Chapter 16: Yahweh Is the Rock of Israel

¹N. Gottwald, *HB*, 319.

²Walter Brueggemann, "David and His Theologian," *CBQ* 30 (1968): 156–81.

³David M. Gunn, *The Story of King David: Genre and Interpretation*, *JSOTSup* 6 (1978).

⁴2 Sam. 9–20; 1 Kings 1, 2 are also known as the "succession narrative." Instead, we chose to discuss these chapters as David under judgment. For material on the succession narratives, see J. W. Flanagan, "Court History or Succession Document? A study of 2 Sam. 9–20 and 1 Kings 1–2," *JBL* 91 (1972): 172–81; D. M. Gunn, "David and the Gift of the Kingdom (2 Sam. 2–4, 9–20, 1 Kgs. 1–2)," *Semeia*. 3 (1975): 14–45; idem, "Traditional Composition in the 'Succession Narrative'," *VT* 26 (1976): 214–29; R. N. Whybray, *The Succession Narrative: A Study of II Sam. 9–20; I Kings 1 and 2.* (London: SCM, 1968). For a criticism, cf. Childs, *IOTS*, 275–78.

⁵William J. Dumbrell favors a separate edition of Chronicles ("The Purpose of the Books of Chronicles," *JETS* 27 [1984]: 266).

⁶Raymond B. Dillard, "The Literary Structure of the Chronicler's Solomon Narrative," *JSOT* 30 (1984): 85–93.

⁷Dumbrell, "Purpose of Chronicles," 266; R. L. Braun, "Solomonic Apologetic in Chronicles," *JBL* 92 (1973): 503–16; G. Goldingay, "The Chronicler as a Theologian," *Biblical Theology Bulletin* 5 (1975): 99–126.

⁸B. Porten, "The Structure and Theme of the Solomon Narrative (1 Kings 3–11)," *Hebrew Union College Annual* 38 (1967): 93–128; J. Liver, "The Book of the Acts of Solomon," *Biblica* 48 (1967): 75–101.

Chapter 17: God's Presence in the Kingship of David and Solomon

[1] Moshe Weinfeld, "The King as the Servant of the People," *Journal of Jewish Studies* 33 (1982): 189–94.

[2] H. Tadmor, "United Monarchy," *A History of the Jewish People,* ed. H. H. Ben-Sasson (Cambridge: Harvard University Press, 1976), 101–4.

[3] For a detailed study of the temple, the priesthood, and the tabernacle, see Menahem Haran, *Temples and Temple-Service in Ancient Israel* (Oxford: Clarendon, 1978). See also idem, "The Ark and the Cherubim," *Israel Exploration Journal* 9 (1959): 8.

[4] Carol L. Meyers concludes that the pillars had both a religious and a political function. As political symbols they communicated visually to the bureaucrats and visiting emissaries that the Davidic dynasty carried out God's will in the administration of Israel and the adjacent territories ("Jachin and Boaz in Religious and Political Perspective," *CBQ* 45 [1983]: 167–78).

[5] See R. B. Y. Scott, "Solomon and the Beginnings of Wisdom in Israel," *VTSup* 3 (1955): 262–79. W. Kaiser concludes that, in light of internal and external linguistic evidence, it is reasonable to argue for Solomonic authorship (*Ecclesiastes: Total Life* [Chicago: Moody, 1979], 25–29). But cf. M. Eaton, who holds to an editor-author who admired Solomon (*Ecclesiastes: An Introduction and Commentary* [Downers Grove: InterVarsity, 1983], 23).

Chapter 18: The Covenant with David

[1] For further discussion, see W. Kaiser, *TOTT,* 149–64; T. McComiskey, *CP,* 21–25; O. Palmer Robertson, *CC,* 229–69. For a comparison of the Abrahamic and Davidic covenants, see R. E. Clements, *Abraham and David: Genesis XV and Its Meaning for Israelite Tradition* (Naperville: Allensen, 1967), 47–60.

[2] D. J. McCarthy, "II Samuel 7 and the Structure of the Deuteronomic History," *JBL* 84 (1965): 131–38; J. L. McKenzie, "The Dynastic Oracle: II Sam. 7," *Theological Studies* 8 (1947): 187–218; H. Gese, "Der Davidsbund und die Zionserwählung," *Zeitschrift für Theologie und Kirche* 61 (1964): 10–26.

[3] T. N. D. Mettinger, "The Last Words of David: A Study in Structure and Meaning in II Samuel 23:1–7," *SEA* 4–42 (1976–77): 147–56; S. Mowinckel, "Die letzten Wörter Davids, II Sam. 23, 1–7," *Zeitschrift für die alttestamentliche Wissenschaft* 45 (1927): 30–58; H. N. Richardson, "The Last Words of David: Some Notes on II Sam. 23:1–7," *JBL* 90 (1971): 257–66. See Moshe Weinfeld, "Covenant, Davidic," *IDBSup,* 190.

[4] See M. Noth, "Jerusalem and the Israelite Tradition," in *The Laws in the Pentateuch, and Other Studies* (Philadelphia: Fortress, 1967), 132–44; Jon D. Levenson, *Sinai and Zion. An Entry into the Jewish Bible* (Minneapolis: Winston, 1985); J. J. M. Roberts, "Zion in the Theology of the Davidic-Solomonic Empire," in *Studies in the Period of David and Solomon,* ed. T. Ishida (Winona Lake: Eisenbrauns, 1982), 93–108.

[5] For an illuminating though critical study, see Heinz Kruse, "David's Covenant," *VT* 35 (1985): 139–64. For its bearing on the progression of redemption, see W. C. Kaiser, Jr., "The Davidic Promise and the Inclusion of

the Gentiles (Amos 9:9–15 and Acts 15:13–18): A Test Passage for Theological Systems," *JETS* 20 (1977): 97–111.

⁶See Haran, *Temples and Temple-Service*; C. J. Davey, "Temples of the Levant and the Buildings of Solomon," *TB* 31 (1980): 107–46.

⁷A. Malamat, "Aspects of the Foreign Policies of David and Solomon," *JNES* 22 (1963): 1–17.

NOTES TO PART 7: A DIVIDED NATION

Chapter 19: Literary Perspectives

¹Norman K. Gottwald asserts critically that the annals were "patchily and arbitrarily excerpted" (*HB*, 338).

²G. Van Groningen, "Joshua–II Kings: Deuteronomistic? Priestly? Or Prophetic Writing?" *JETS* 12 (1969): 3–26.

³See Childs, *IOTS*, 293; G. von Rad, *Old Testament Theology*, 2 vols. (New York: Harper & Row, 1962, 1965), 1:344–47.

⁴"Because the writer of Kings does not restrict the presence of God to either the temple or the land, the possibility of renewed blessing is left open to the hope of future generations" (Childs, *IOTS*, 294).

⁵The exact date is contested, and proposals vary from 520 B.C. to 250 B.C. The author shows a clear familiarity with the postexilic community and writes for their benefit (see J. M. Myers, *I Chronicles*, AB, lxxxvii–lxxxix).

⁶D. N. Freedman, "The Chronicler's Purpose," *CBQ* 23 (1961): 436–42; Sara Japhet, "The Historical Reliability of Chronicles," *JSOT* 33 (1985): 83–107.

⁷See R. R. Wilson, *Genealogy and History in the Biblical World* (New Haven: Yale University Press, 1977); R. Braun, "Solomonic Apologetic in Chronicles," *JBL* 92 (1973): 503–16; H. G. M. Williamson, "The Accession of Solomon in the Books of Chronicles," *VT* 26 (1976): 351–61.

⁸P. R. Ackroyd, "History and Theology in the Writings of the Chronicler," *Concordia Theological Monthly* 38 (1967): 501–15; id. "The Theology of the Chronicler," *Lexington Theological Quarterly* 8 (1973): 101–16; id. "The Chronicler as Exegete," *JSOT* 2 (1977): 2–32; E. W. Barnes, "The Midrashic Element in Chronicles," *Expositor* 5 (1896): 426–39.

⁹Note the treatment of Azariah (2 Chron. 15:2–7), Hanani (16:7–9), Jahaziel (20:15–17), Elijah (21:12–15), some anonymous prophets (25:7–9, 15–16), and Oded (28:9–11).

¹⁰Richard Pratt, "Royal Prayers and the Chronicler's Message" (Ph.D. diss., Harvard University, 1987).

¹¹J. M. Myers, "The Kerygma of the Chronicler," *Interpretation* 20 (1966): 259–73.

¹²R. Braun, "The Message of Chronicles: Rally Round the Temple," *Concordia Theological Monthly* 42 (1971): 502–13; H. G. M. Williamson, "Eschatology in Chronicles," *TB* 28 (1977): 115–54.

Chapter 20: Israel and the Prophetic Ministry

[1] Wayne A. Brindle, "The Causes of the Division of Israel's Kingdom," *Bibliotheca Sacra* 141 (1984): 223–33; J. H. Hayes and J. M. Miller, *IJH*, 385.

[2] On the theological function of Jerusalem, see R. de Vaux, "Jerusalem and the Prophets," in *Interpreting the Prophetic Tradition*, ed. H. M. Orlinsky (Cincinnati: Hebrew Union College, 1969), 296; G. Fohrer, "Zion-Jerusalem in the Old Testament," *TDNT* 7 (1971): 293–319; Donald E. Gowan, *Eschatology in the Old Testament* (Philadelphia: Fortress, 1986).

[3] J. Debus, *Die Sünde Jeroboams: Studien zur Darstellung Jeroboams und der Geschichte des Nordreichs in der deuteronomistischen Geschichtsschreibung, FRLANT* 93 (1967).

[4] C. F. Whitley, "The Deuteronomic Presentation of the House of Omri," *VT* 2 (1952): 137–52.

[5] J. M. Miller, "The Fall of the House of Ahab," *VT* 17 (1967): 307–24.

[6] Y. Kaufmann, *The Religion of Israel*, trans. Moshe Greenberg (New York: Schocken, 1972), 60–149.

[7] The literature on this period is extensive; see R. P. Carroll, "The Elijah-Elisha Sagas," *VT* 19 (1969): 400–415; J. M. Miller, "The Elisha-Cycle and the Accounts of the Omride Wars," *JBL* 85 (1966): 441–54; H. H. Rowley, "Elijah on Mount Carmel," *BJRL* 43 (1960–61): 190–219.

Chapter 21: Judah and the House of David

[1] Hayes and Miller, *IJH*, 444; cf. E. Nicholson, "The Centralization of the Cult in Deuteronomy," *VT* 13 (1963): 380–89.

[2] Hayes and Miller, *IJH*, 467; F. M. Cross and D. N. Freedman, "Josiah's Revolt Against Assyria," *JNES* 12 (1953): 56–68.

Chapter 22: Prophetism

[1] See C. Westermann, *Basic Forms of Prophetic Speech*, trans. H. C. White (Philadelphia: Westminster, 1967).

[2] For a further study in Old Testament prophetism and interpretation, see W. VanGemeren, *Interpreting the Prophetic Word* (Grand Rapids: Zondervan, forthcoming).

[3] For a more extensive treatment of Isaiah from the perspective of the progressive-fulfillment hermeneutic, see my commentary on Isaiah in *Evangelical Commentary of the Bible,* ed. Walter Elwell, (Grand Rapids: Baker, 1988).

[4] For a summary of Jeremiah and his time, see Willem A. VanGemeren, "Jeremiah," *Bible History,* June 1987.

[5] For a summary of his message, see W. A. VanGemeren, "Ezekiel," *Evangelical Dictionary of the Bible* (Grand Rapids: Baker, forthcoming).

[6] For a brief commentary, see W. A. VanGemeren, "Zephaniah," *Evangelical Commentary on the Bible* (Grand Rapids: Baker, 1988).

[7] Willem A. VanGemeren, "Daniel," in *Illustrated Guide to the Bible,* ed. David I. Payne (Basingstoke: Pickering, forthcoming).

NOTES TO PART 8: A RESTORED NATION

Introduction to Part 8

[1] See H. L. Ellison, *From Babylon to Bethlehem* (Atlanta: John Knox, 1979).

[2] P. R. Ackroyd, *Exile and Restoration* (Philadelphia: Westminster, 1968); Charles F. Whitley, *The Exilic Age* (Philadelphia: Westminster, 1958); D. F. Morgan, "Captivity," *ISBErev.*, 612–15.

Chapter 23: The Literature of the Exilic/Postexilic Era

[1] Gottwald, *HB*, 411.

[2] Ibid., 410–13; Hayes and Miller, *IJH*, 480–503.

[3] For a discussion about authorship, see R. K. Harrison, *Introduction to the Old Testament* (Grand Rapids: Eerdmans, 1969), 1069–70; *OTS*, 617–18.

[4] S. Japhet, "The Supposed Common Authorship of Chronicles and Ezra-Nehemiah Investigated Anew," *VT* 18 (1968): 330–71; and D. N. Freedman, "The Chronicler's Purpose," *CBQ* 23 (1961): 436–42.

[5] F. M. Cross, Jr., "A Reconstruction of the Judean Restoration," *JBL* 94 (1975): 4–18.

[6] Childs, *IOTS*, 631–37; Edwin M. Yamauchi, "The Reverse Order of Ezra/Nehemiah Reconsidered," *Themelios* 5 (1980): 7–13.

[7] Childs, *IOTS*, 637.

[8] Neh. 8–12; *IOTS*, 635; *OTS*, 655–58.

[9] P. R. Ackroyd, "God and People in the Chronicler's Presentation of Ezra," in *La notion biblique de Dieu*, ed. J. Coppens, Bibliotheca Ephemeridum Theologicarum Lovaniensium 41 (Paris, 1976), 145–62. Gottwald notes that Chronicles "validates a vigorous recovery of national traditions and communal practices that was both a form of accommodation to the colonial status under Persia and also an act of national resistance by marking off a religiocultural identity for Jews that was drawn so tightly that in the end it excluded fellow Jews, such as the Samaritans, who did not fully succumb to the reform leadership in Judah" (*HB*, 521–22).

[10] Ran Zadok, "On the Historical Background of the Book of Esther," *Biblische Notizen* 24 (1984): 18–23; idem, "The Historical Background of Esther," *Beth Mikra* (1984–85): 186–89 (Hebrew).

[11] H. Ringgren, "Esther und Purim," *SEA* 20 (1956): 5–24; B. W. Anderson, "The Place of the Book of Esther in the Christian Bible," *Journal of Religion* 30 (1950): 32–43; J. L. Crenshaw, "Method in Determining Wisdom Influence upon 'Historical' Literature," *JBL* 88 (1969): 129–42.

[12] For the date see W. J. Dumbrell, "Malachi and the Ezra-Nehemiah Reforms," *Reformed Theological Review* 35 (1976): 42–52; W. Kaiser, *Malachi* (Grand Rapids: Baker, 1984), 15–17; Andrew E. Hill, "Dating the Book of Malachi: A Linguistic Reexamination," in *The Word of the Lord Shall Go Forth* (Winona Lake: Eisenbrauns, 1983), 77–89. See also James A. Fischer, "Notes on the Literary Form and Message of Malachi," *CBQ* 34 (1972): 315–20.

[13] See James A Fischer, "Notes on the Literary Form and Message of Malachi," *CBQ* 34 (1972), 315–20; and W. VanGemeren, "Malachi," *Evangelical Commentary on the Bible* (Grand Rapids: Baker, 1988).

[14] For a discussion of the views, see R. K. Harrison, *Introduction to the Old Testament* (Grand Rapids: Eerdmans, 1969), 876–79; Leslie C. Allen, *Joel*, *NICOT*, 19–25.

[15] Willem A. VanGemeren, "The Spirit of Restoration," *WTJ*, forthcoming.

[16] Childs, *IOTS*, 393.

Chapter 24: Exilic Perspectives

[1] See Ackroyd, *Exile and Restoration*; for a technical study of Jeremiah, see E. W. Nicholson, *Preaching to the Exiles: A Study of the Prose Tradition in the Book of Jeremiah* (New York: Schocken, 1970).

[2] Childs defines sin as "a willful affront to God which opens up the floodgates of universal rebellion and initiates a cosmological chain of disasters which far exceeds any human intent" (*OTTCT*, 230).

[3] James B. Pritchard, ed., *A New Anthology of Texts and Pictures* (Princeton: Princeton University Press, 1976), 1:54, 222.

[4] Dumbrell concludes, "In 587 B.C. all the tangible marks of the empirical Israel had thus vanished and the question which the Exile raised was really, what was the nature of the true Israel and was such a body tied to any necessary political forms?" (*CaC*, 165).

[5] Ibid., 166.

[6] H. Tadmor, "The Period," *A History of the Jewish People*, ed. H. H. Ben-Sasson (Cambridge: Harvard University Press, 1976), 163.

Chapter 25: The Postexilic Restoration

[1] For a discussion of this matter, see Dumbrell, *CaC*, 172–88; W. C. Kaiser, "The Old Promise and the New Covenant," *JETS* 15 (1972): 11–23; idem, *TOTT*, 228–35.

[2] Dumbrell, *CaC*, 164–200; Donald E. Gowan, *Eschatology of the Old Testament* (Philadelphia: Fortress, 1986), 59–96.

[3] Kaiser, "Kingdom of the Promise," in *TOTT*, 236–49.

[4] According to Childs, "Because David's rule had become a type of God's reign, an adumbration of the eschatological rule of God, mythopoetic language could be applied to the reigning monarch as the emisssary of God's righteous rule" (*OTTCC*, 120).

[5] Tadmor concludes, "This first Jewish diaspora attempted to impose its own self-image on the community of Judah—as evidenced by the activities of Ezra and Nehemiah—and this self-assertion, to one degree or another, became a central facet of the relationship between the homeland and the diaspora that has characterized Jewish-existence up to the present day" ("Period," 182).

Chapter 26: The Intertestamental Period

[1] See M. Avi-Yonah, *The Holy Land from the Persian to the Arab Conquests: A Historical Geography* (Grand Rapids: Baker, 1966); S. W. Baron, *A Social and Religious History of the Jews*, 2 vols. (New York: Schocken, 1952); E. J. Bickerman, *From Ezra to the Last of the Maccabees* (New York: Schocken, 1962); D. S. Russell, *Between the Testaments* (Philadelphia: Fortress, 1960); idem., *The Jews from Alexander to Herod* (Oxford: Oxford University Press, 1967); S. Safrai

and M. Stern, eds., *The Jewish People in the First Century,* vols. 1, 2. *Compendia Rerum Iudaicarum ad Novum Testamentum* (Philadelphia: Fortress, 1974).

[2] See the listing of Hebrew, Aramaic, Greek, Latin, New Testament, papyri, and archaeological sources in "Sources," *Compendia* 1:1–62.

[3] M. Stern, "The Jewish Diaspora," *Compendia* 1:117–83; S. Safrai, "Relations Between the Diaspora and the Land of Israel," ibid., 184–215.

[4] J. J. Scott, Jr., "On the Value of Intertestamental Jewish Literature for New Testament Theology," *JETS* 23 (1980): 315–23.

[5] See Bruce M. Metzger, "An Introduction to the Apocrypha," in *The Oxford Annotated Apocrypha,* ed. Metzger (New York: Oxford, 1965); R. H. Pfeiffer, *History of New Testament Times with an Introduction to the Apocrypha* (New York: Harper, 1957).

[6] For excellent treatments of this era, see Hayes and Miller, *IJH,* 489–677; M. Stern, "The Period of the Second Temple," in *A History of the Jewish People,* ed. H. H. Ben-Sasson (Cambridge: Harvard University Press, 1976), 185–295. For a more popular treatment see H. L. Ellison, *From Babylon to Bethlehem* (Exeter: Paternoster, 1976).

[7] M. Stern, "The Province of Judaea," *Compendia* 1:308–76; F. M. Cross, "Aspects of Samaritan and Jewish History in Late Persian and Hellenistic Times," *Harvard Theological Review* 59 (1966): 201–11.

[8] M. Hengel, *Jews, Greeks, and Barbarians: Aspects of the Hellenization of Judaism in the Pre-Christian Period,* trans. John Bowden (Philadelphia: Fortress, 1980); V. Tcherikover, *Hellenistic Civilization and the Jews,* trans. S. Applebaum (New York: Atheneum, 1975).

[9] D. Flusser, "Paganism in Palestine," *Compendia* 2:1065–1100.

[10] C. Rabin, "Hebrew and Aramaic in the First Century," *Compendia* 2:1007–39; G. Mussies, "Greek in Palestine and the Diaspora," ibid., 1040–64.

[11] S. Safrai, "Jewish Self-Government," *Compendia* 1:377–419.

[12] M. Rappaport, "The Hellenistic Cities and the Judaization of Palestine in the Hasmonean Age" (in Hebrew), in *Commentationes Benzioni Katz Dedicatae,* ed. S. Perlman and B. Shimron (Tel Aviv: University of Tel Aviv, 1967), 219–30.

[13] Menahem Mansoor, "Essenes," *EJ* 6:899–902.

[14] See F. F. Bruce, *Second Thoughts on the Dead Sea Scrolls* (Grand Rapids: Eerdmans, 1961); M. Mansoor, *The Dead Sea Scrolls* (Grand Rapids: Eerdmans, 1964); J. T. Milik. *Ten Years of Discovery in the Wilderness of Judaea,* trans. J. Strugnell (London: SCM, 1959).

[15] Josephus, *Antiquities* 18. 1. 5; idem, *Wars* 2. 8. 2–13. See also Philip R. Davies, "Eschatology at Qumran," *JBL* 104 (1985): 39–55.

[16] R. Travers Herford, *The Pharisees* (Boston: Beacon, 1962); L. Finkelstein, *Pharisaism in the Making* (New York: Ktav, 1972); idem, *The Pharisees: The Sociological Background of Their Faith,* 2 vols. (Philadelphia: Jewish Publication Society, 1962).

[17] Ephraim Urbach, "Halakhah and History," in *Jews, Greeks, and Christians,* ed. Robert Hamerton-Kelly and Robin Scroggs (Leiden: Brill, 1976), 112–28.

[18] M. Mansoor, "Sadducees," *EJ* 14:620–22.

[19] Josephus, *Antiquities* 13. 10. 6; 18. 1. 4; idem, *Wars* 2. 8. 14; see also Acts 23:8.

[20] An excellent translation of the Mishnah is still H. Danby, *Mishnah* (London: Oxford, 1938). See S. Safrai, "The Era of the Mishnah and Talmud (70–640)," in *A History of the Jewish People*, ed. H. H. Ben-Sasson (Cambridge: Harvard University Press, 1976), 307–82. For an introduction, see Hermann L. Strack, *Introduction to the Talmud and Midrash* (New York: Atheneum, 1974).

[21] R. A. Kraft, "Septuagint," *IDBSup* 807–15; Sidney Jellicoe, *The Septuagint and Modern Study* (Oxford: Clarendon, 1968); E. Tov, *The Text-Critical Use of the Septuagint in Biblical Research* (Jerusalem: Simor, 1981).

[22] M. Stern, *Documents on the History of the Hasmonean Revolt* (in Hebrew), 2d ed. (Tel Aviv, 1972).

[23] E. Mary Smallwood, *The Jews Under Roman Rule: From Pompey to Diocletian* (Leiden: Brill, 1976).

[24] M. Stern, "The Reign of Herod and the Herodian Dynasty," *Compendia* 1:216–307.

[25] David S. Russell, *The Method and Message of Jewish Apocalyptic* (Philadelphia: Westminster, 1964), 22; Jacob Neusner, *Early Rabbinic Judaism: Historical Studies in Religion, Literature, and Art* (Leiden: Brill, 1975).

[26] S. Applebaum, "The Social and Economic Status of the Jews in the Diaspora," *Compendia* 2:701–27.

[27] S. Safrai, "The Synagogue," *Compendia* 2:908–44; idem, "Education and the Study of the Torah," ibid., 945–70.

[28] S. Safrai, "The Temple," *Compendia* 2:865–907; M. Stern, "Aspects of Jewish Society: The Priesthood and Other Classes," ibid., 561–630.

[29] The term "pseudepigrapha" refers to apocryphal writings that were never included in a canonical listing of the Greek or Latin Bibles (such writings include, e.g., 1 Enoch, the Book of Jubilees, the Testament of the Twelve Patriarchs, the Psalms of Solomon, the Assumption of Moses, the Martyrdom of Isaiah). For an introduction, see J. H. Charlesworth, *The Old Testament Pseudepigrapha and the New Testament* (Cambridge: Cambridge University Press, 1985); Russell, *Method and Message*; R. H. Charles et al., *Apocrypha and Pseudepigrapha of the Old Testament*, 2 vols. (New York: Oxford University Press, 1913).

[30] G. F. Moore, *Judaism in the First Centuries of the Christian Era*, 2 vols. (1927–30; reprint, New York: Schocken, 1971); E. E. Urbach, "The Sages," *EJ* 14:636–55.

[31] G. E. Ladd, "The Revelation and Jewish Apocalyptic," *EQ* 29 (1957): 94–100; idem, "The Place of Apocalyptic in Biblical Religion," ibid. 30 (1958): 75–85; idem, "The Origin of Apocalyptic in Biblical Religion," ibid., 140–46.

[32] Russell, *Method and Message*, 205–390.

[33] Israel Levi, "Apocalypse dans le Talmud," *Revue des Etudes Juives* 1 (1880): 108–14; Jacob Neusner, *First-Century Judaism in Crisis: Yohanan ben Zakkai and the Renaissance of Torah* (Nashville: Abingdon, 1975), 126–32.

[34] G. Vermes, *The Dead Sea Scrolls in English* (Hammondsworth: Penguin Books, 1970).

[35] Russell, *Method and Message*, 28–33.

[36] Josephus, *Antiquities* 18. 2. 6.

NOTES TO PART 9: JESUS AND THE KINGDOM

Introduction to Part 9

[1] For the use of the Old Testament in the New, see R. N. Longenecker, *Biblical Exegesis in the Apostolic Period* (Grand Rapids: Eerdmans, 1974); James D. G. Dunn, *UD*, 81–102.

[2] Willem A. VanGemeren, "IHCIP," pt. 2, pp. 285–86; Raymond Brown, *The Birth of the Messiah* (Garden City: Doubleday, 1977), 499.

Chapter 27: The Gospel of Jesus Christ

[1] Meredith G. Kline, "The Old Testament Origins of the Gospel Genre," *WTJ* 38 (1975–76): 1–27.

[2] Leland Ryken, *How to Read the Bible as Literature* (Grand Rapids: Zondervan, 1984), 131–32; idem, ed., *The New Testament in Literary Criticism* (New York: Ungar, 1984), 84–129.

[3] See Robert A. Guelich, "The Gospels: Portraits of Jesus and His Ministry," *JETS* 24 (1981): 117–25; David Rhoads and Donald Michie, *Mark as Story: An Introduction to the Narrative of a Gospel* (Philadelphia: Fortress, 1982); George Wesley Buchanan, *Jesus: The King and His Kingdom* (Macon: Mercer University Press, 1984).

[4] Ryken, *Bible as Literature*, 144. For further treatment of this matter, see Raymond E. Brown, "Parable and Allegory Reconsidered," in *New Testament Essays* (Garden City: Doubleday, 1968), 321–33; G. B. Caird, *The Language and Imagery of the Bible* (Philadelphia: Westminster, 1980), 160–71; M. D. Goulder, "Characteristics of the Parables in the Several Gospels," *Journal of Theological Studies*, n.s., 19 (1968): 51–69; L. Ryken, *The New Testament*, 78–83, 255–72, 285–94).

[5] Donald Guthrie, *NTI*, 29–33, 48–50; K. Stendahl, *The School of St. Matthew and Its Use of the Old Testament* (Philadelphia: Fortress, 1968), 20–29; H. J. Bernard Combrink, "The Structure of the Gospel of Matthew as Narrative," *TB* 34 (1983): 61–90.

[6] W. G. Kümmel, *Introduction to the New Testament,* trans. A. J. Mattill, Jr. (Nashville: Abingdon, 1966), 108.

[7] See A. T. France, "The Formula Quotations of Matthew 2 and the Problem of Communication," *NTS* 27 (1980): 233–51; Stendahl, *School of St. Matthew*, 39–217.

[8] See R. H. Gundry, *The Use of the Old Testament in St. Matthew's Gospel, Novum Testamentum Supp.* 18 (Leiden: Brill, 1967); Buchanan, *Jesus*, 291–311.

[9] Terry Spearman, "An Exegetical Study of Matthew 16:18," (M.A. thesis, Reformed Theological Seminary, 1983); James P. Martin, "The Church in Matthew," *Interpretation* 29 (1975): 41–56.

[10] Hans Conzelmann, *An Outline of Theology of the New Testament* (London: SCM, 1969), 145–49; cf. Childs, *NTCI*, 77–78.

[11] Kümmel, *Introduction*, 115.

[12] Childs, *NTCI*, 72.

[13] B. W. Bacon, " 'Five Books' of Matthew Against the Jews," *Expositor*, 8th

ser., 15 (1918): 56–66; Childs, *NTCI*, 63; Marianne Meye Thompson, "The Structure of Matthew: A Survey of Recent Trends," *StBib* 12 (1982): 195–238.

[14] W. G. Kümmel, *Promise and Fulfillment: The Eschatological Message of Jesus* (London: SCM, 1961).

[15] B. van Iersel argues in favor of a fivefold structure—desert, Galilee, way, Jerusalem, and tomb—in "Locality, Structure, and Meaning in Mark," *Linguistica Biblica* 53 (1983): 45–54; see also Ryken, *New Testament*, 214–20; Guthrie, *NTI*, 63–69.

[16] Kümmel, *Introduction*, 89.

[17] Childs, *NTCI*, 86.

[18] Günther Bornkamm, *The New Testament: A Guide to Its Writings*, trans. Reginald H. Fuller and Ilse Fuller (Philadelphia: Fortress, 1973), 55.

[19] Childs, *NTCI*, 91. For Conzelmann, the gospel "points to the parousia, but not beyond" (*Outline of Theology*, 141).

[20] According to Conzelmann, "The continuity of the salvation history is clear from the law: the first age is the time of the law and the prophets. Then Jesus develops the law by his preaching of repentance and his commandments. These remain in force for the church, but now it is given *in addition* the preaching of the kingdom of God (Luke 16.16) and the spirit" (*Outline of Theology*, 151; italics mine).

[21] S. J. Kistemaker, "The Structure of Luke's Gospel," *JETS* 25 (1982): 33–40; for other structures see Ryken, *New Testament*, 190–92.

[22] Childs, *NTCI*, 110. Conzelmann writes, "For Luke's salvation-historical conception, too, the foundations are: Israel, the church as a church between resurrection and parousia" (*Outline of Theology*, 150); see I. Howard Marshall, *Luke: Historian and Theologian* (Exeter: Paternoster, 1970).

[23] Childs, *NTCI*, 115.

[24] For other forms of structuring, see Ryken, *New Testament*, 164–69.

[25] Buchanan, *Jesus*, 304–5.

[26] Daniel Roy Mitchell, "The Person of Christ in John's Gospel and Epistles" (Ph.D. diss., Dallas Theological Seminary, 1982).

[27] See the study on discipleship in John by Jeffrey S. Siker-Gieseler, "Disciples and Discipleship in the Fourth Gospel: A Canonical Approach," *StBib* 10 (1980): 199–227.

[28] David Earl Holwerda, *The Holy Spirit and Eschatology in the Gospel of John* (Kampen: Kok, 1959); cf. Hans Windisch, *The Spirit-Paraclete in the Fourth Gospel*, trans. James W. Cox (Philadelphia: Fortress, 1968).

[29] Leon Morris, "Love in the Johannine Epistles," in *Through Christ's Word*, ed. W. Robert Godfrey and Jesse L. Boyd, III (Phillipsburg: Presbyterian & Reformed, 1985), 23–37.

[30] Jack Dean Kingsbury, "The Gospel in Four Editions," *Interpretation* 33 (1979): 363–75.

[31] Günther Bornkamm, *The New Testament*, 41.

Chapter 28: John and Jesus

[1] Werner Georg Kümmel, *The Theology of the New Testament, According to Its*

Major Witnesses: Jesus—Paul—John, trans. John E. Steely (Nashville: Abingdon, 1973), 22–36.

[2] For a careful study of John's conception of the kingdom, see Herman Ridderbos, *The Coming of the Kingdom* (Philadelphia: Presbyterian & Reformed, 1976), 18–60. Ridderbos treats the kingdom teaching under five rubrics: theocentric, dynamical, messianic, future, and present. Vos's contribution on John the Baptist is still highly significant ("The Ministry of John the Baptist," in *Redemptive History and Biblical Interpretation. The Shorter Writings of Geerhardus Vos,* ed. Richard B. Gaffin, Jr. [Phillipsburg: Presbyterian & Reformed, 1980], 299–303).

[3] Walter C. Kaiser, Jr., "The Promise of the Arrival of Elijah in Malachi and the Gospels," *Grace Theological Journal* 3 (1982): 221–33.

[4] See K. Brower, "Elijah in the Markan Passion Narrative," *Journal for the Study of the New Testament* 18 (1983): 85–101.

[5] For relevant books about Jesus' revelation of himself, see G. Vos, *The Self-Disclosure of Jesus* (Philadelphia: Presbyterian & Reformed, 1975); Leon Morris, *The Lord from Heaven* (London: InterVarsity, 1964); and especially the volumes in *The Jesus Library,* ed. Michael Green (Downers Grove: InterVarsity).

[6] T. W. Manson, "The Life of Jesus: Some Tendencies in Present-Day Research," in *The Background of the New Testament and Its Eschatology,* ed. W. D. Davies and D. Daube (Cambridge: Cambridge, 1964), 211–21; R. H. Fuller, *The New Testament in Current Study* (New York: Scribner, 1962); S. Kistemaker, *The Gospels in Current Study* (Grand Rapids: Baker, 1980).

[7] J. D. G. Dunn, "The Messianic Secret in Mark," *TB* 21 (1970): 92–117.

[8] G. R. Beasley-Murray, *Jesus and the Kingdom of God* (Grand Rapids: Eerdmans, 1986), 46–68.

[9] G. E. Ladd, *TNT,* 135. For a fuller treatment of the title "messiah," see Donald Guthrie, *NTT,* 236–52; Morris, *Lord from Heaven,* 29–32; Dunn, *UD,* 41–45.

[10] Donald L. Jones, "The Title Christos in Luke-Acts," *CBQ* 32 (1970): 69–76.

[11] Guthrie, *NTT,* 246.

[12] For a fuller treatment, see G. E. Ladd, *TNT,* 159–72; I. H. Marshall, "The Divine Sonship of Jesus," *Interpretation* 21 (1967): 87–103; Vos, *Self-Disclosure of Jesus,* 141–70.

[13] Eduard Schweizer, *Ego Eimi* (Göttingen: Vandenhoeck & Ruprecht, 1939); Raymond Brown, *The Gospel According to John,* AB, 2 vols., 1:533–38; Philip B. Harner, *The "I Am" of the Fourth Gospel: A Study in Johannine Usage and Thought* (Philadelphia: Fortress, 1970), 37–65.

[14] J. A. Kirk, "Messianic Role of Jesus and the Temptation Narrative," *EQ* 44 (1972): 11–29, 91–102; Morris, *Lord from Heaven,* 34.

[15] Vos, *Self-Disclosure of Jesus,* 141–42.

[16] For fuller treatment, see Ladd, *NTT,* 146–58; Guthrie, *NTT,* 270–91; B. Lindars, *Jesus Son of Man* (Grand Rapids: Eerdmans, 1983).

[17] M. D. Hooker, *The Son of Man in Mark* (London: SPCK, 1967), 181; R. Maddox, "The Function of the Son of Man According to the Synoptic Gospels," *NTS* 15 (1968): 45–74; idem, "The Function of the Son of Man in the Gospel

of John," in *Reconciliation and Hope: New Testament Essays on Atonement and Eschatology*, ed. Robert Banks (Grand Rapids: Eerdmans, 1974), 186–204.

[18]G. Turner, "Soteriology in the Gospel of John," *JETS* 19 (1976): 271–77.

[19]J. M. Gibbs, "Purpose and Pattern in Matthew's Use of the Title 'Son of David,'" *NTS* 10 (1963): 446–64.

Chapter 29: The Kingdom of God

[1]G. R. Beasley-Murray, *Jesus and the Kingdom* (Grand Rapids: Eerdmans, 1986). George Eldon Ladd, *The Presence of the Future* (Grand Rapids: Eerdmans, 1974); idem, *The Pattern of New Testament Truth* (Grand Rapids: Eerdmans, 1968), 41–63.

[2]John Bright, *The Kingdom of God* (Nashville: Abingdon, 1953).

[3]Ridderbos, *Coming of the Kingdom*, 8–13; Ladd, *TNT*, 45–48.

[4]Ladd, *TNT*, 69.

[5]Vos, *BT*, 399.

[6]"The Prophets and the Law prophesied until then, and, implicitly, prophesied of this new era. And from that time on, the fulfillment of prophecy, the kingdom itself, has been forcefully advancing" (D. A. Carson, "Matthew," in *EBC* 8:268).

[7]Berakhot. 2.2, 5; Aboth 3. 5.

[8]"One of the most distinctive facts that set Jesus' teaching apart from Judaism was the universalizing of the concept [of the kingdom]" (Ladd, *TNT*, 64).

[9]Ridderbos, *Coming of the Kingdom*, 23.

[10]Ibid., 61–103; Ladd, *Presence of the Future*.

[11]C. H. Dodd, *The Parables of the Kingdom* (London: Nisbet, 1935), 107–8.

[12]Ladd, *Pattern of Truth*, 63.

Chapter 30: Jesus' Messianic Mission

[1]L. Sabourin, "About Jesus' Self-Understanding," *Religious Studies Bulletin* 3 (1983): 129–34.

[2]R. T. France, "The Servant of the Lord in the Teaching of Jesus," *TB* 19 (1968): 26–52. For the problems associated with the title in Acts, see Guthrie, *NTI*, 264–65.

[3]On the Son of Man, his suffering, and his kingdom, see Beasley-Murray, *Jesus and the Kingdom*, 219–312.

[4]Herman Ridderbos ephasizes John's "contrasting duality of divine glory in the true flesh and blood of the man Jesus" ("The Word Became Flesh," in *Through Christ's Word. A Festschrift for Dr. Philip E. Hughes,* ed. W. Robert Godfrey and Jesse L. Boyd III (Phillipsburg: Presbyterian and Reformed, 1985), 14.

[5]K. L. Schmidt, "Ekklēsia," *TDNT* 3:530–31. Hunter concludes that "Jesus during his Ministry gave himself to the high purpose of creating a new people of God" (*The Message of the New Testament* [Philadelphia: Westminster, 1944], 65).

[6]Birger Gerhardsson correlates Jesus' sacrifice, the church, and discipleship in "Sacrificial Service and Atonement in the Gospel of Matthew," in *Reconciliation and Hope*, ed. Banks, 1–35.

[7]Ladd distinguishes between the kingdom and the church in three ways: the

kingdom creates the church, the church witnesses to the kingdom, and the church is the custodian of the kingdom (*TNT*, 113–19).

[8] Guthrie, *NTT*, 246.

[9] H. Berkhof, *CF*, 319.

[10] Ladd, *TNT*, 317. On the empty tomb, see James C. DeYoung, "Event and Interpretation of the Resurrection," in *Interpreting God's Word Today*, ed. Simon Kistemaker (Grand Rapids: Baker, 1970), 127–75; M. C. Tenney, "The Historicity of the Resurrection," in *Jesus of Nazareth: Saviour and Lord*, ed. C. F. H. Henry (Grand Rapids: Eerdmans, 1966), 135–44.

[11] Grant R. Osborne contributes to the richly varied theological understanding of the Resurrection by correlating the life of Jesus, salvation, eschatology, and the mission of the church (*The Resurrection Narratives: A Redactional Study* [Grand Rapids: Baker, 1984]).

[12] Contrary to Dunn (*UD*, 104–6), I hold that "the community of Jesus" was inherent in Jesus' earthly ministry.

[13] Morris, *Lord from Heaven*, 42.

Conclusion to Part 9

[1] See John Painter, "Eschatological Faith in the Gospel of John," in *Reconciliation and Hope*, ed. Banks, 36–54.

NOTES TO PART 10: THE APOSTOLIC ERA

Introduction to Part 10

[1] The *paradosis* is the total of the essential apostolic teaching concerning the Christ (see Mark 7:5, 8–9, 13; Col. 2:8). This tradition is represented in the canonical New Testament writings.

Chapter 31: The Apostolic Witness to the Risen Christ

[1] S. Brown, "The Role of the Prologues in Determining the Purposes of Luke-Acts," in *Perspectives on Luke-Acts*, ed. C. H. Talbert (Danville, Va.: Association of Baptist Professors of Religion, 1978), 99–111.

[2] F. F. Bruce, "The Holy Spirit in the Acts of the Apostles," *Interpretation* 27 (1973): 166–83; Richard B. Gaffin, Jr., *The Centrality of the Resurrection: A Study in Paul's Soteriology* (Grand Rapids: Baker, 1978); G. W. H. Lampe, "The Holy Spirit in the Writings of St. Luke," in *Studies in the Gospels: Essays in Memory of R. H. Lightfoot* (Oxford: Blackwell, 1955), 159–200.

[3] Guthrie considers five views of the purpose of Acts: narrative of history, gospel of the Spirit, apology, defense brief for Paul's trial, and a theological document (*NTI*, 349–54). I favor the second view, whereas Guthrie argues for the first.

[4] I. H. Marshall, *Luke: Historian and Theologian* (Exeter: Paternoster, 1970); P. S. Minear, "Dear Theo: The Kerygmatic Intention and Claim of the Book of Acts," *Interpretation* 27 (1973): 131–50; J. C. O'Neill, *The Theology of Acts in Its Historical Setting* (London: SPCK, 1970).

[5] R. F. O'Toole, "Activity of the Risen Jesus in Luke-Acts," *Bibl* 62 (1981): 471–98.

⁶F. F. Bruce, *The Speeches in the Acts of the Apostles* (London: Tyndale, 1942); idem., "The Speeches in Acts, Thirty Years After," in *Reconciliation and Hope: New Testament Essays in Atonement and Eschatology*, ed. Robert Banks (Grand Rapids: Eerdmans, 1974), 53–68; W. W. Gasque, "The Speeches in Acts: Dibelius Reconsidered," in *New Dimensions in New Testament Study*, ed. R. N. Longenecker and M. C. Tenney (Grand Rapids, Zondervan, 1974), 232–50.

⁷J. W. Bowker, "Speeches in Acts: A Study in Proem and Yalammedenu Form," *NTS* 14 (1967–68): 96–111.

⁸Cf. R. N. Longenecker, *Biblical Exegesis in the Apostolic Period* (Grand Rapids: Eerdmans, 1975); M. Rese, "Die Funktion der alttestamentlichen Zitate und Anspielungen in den Reden der Apostelgeschichte," in Kremer, *Les Actes*, 61–79.

⁹On the name Paul as cognomen, see Colin J. Hemer, "The Name of Paul," *TB* 36 (1985): 179–93. On his distinctive call, see J. W. Bowker, "Merkabah Visions and the Visions of Paul," *Journal of Semitic Studies* 16 (1971): 157–73; C. W. Hedrick, "Paul's Conversion/Call: A Comparative Analysis of the Three Reports," *JBL* 100 (1981): 415–32.

¹⁰See J. Knox, "Acts and the Pauline Letter Corpus," in *Studies in Luke-Acts*, ed. L. E. Keck and J. L. Martyn (Nashville: Abingdon, 1966), 279–87; Peter R. Jones, "1 Corinthians 15:8: Paul the Last Apostle," *TB* 36 (1985): 3–35.

¹¹Childs, *NTCI*, 240.

¹²G. W. H. Lampe, "Miracles in the Acts of the Apostles," in *Miracles*, ed. C. F. D. Moule (London: Mowbray, 1966), 163–78; F. Neirynck, "The Miracle Stories in the Acts of the Apostles: An Introduction," in *Les Actes des Apôtres*, ed. J. Kremer (Leuven: University Press, 1979), 169–213.

¹³Simon the Sorcerer, who had gained a reputation in Samaria for his "miracles," was overwhelmed by the evidences of the signs (Acts 8:9–24). Desiring to gain special apostolic powers, he tried to bribe the apostles. They placed a curse on him, however, and departed. This story dramatically reveals how evident was the continuation of Jesus' ministry in the apostles, both in Judea and in Samaria!

¹⁴Kümmel, *Introduction to the New Testament*, trans. A. J. Mattill, Jr. (Nashville: Abingdon, 1966), 247–52. Stanley K. Stowers has shown that letters of friendship, family, praise and blame, and exhortation and advice were much more common than previously supposed (*Letter Writing in Greco-Roman Antiquity* [Philadelphia: Westminster, 1986]).

¹⁵E. Earle Ellis, "Paul and His Opponents: Trends in Research," in *Christianity, Judaism, and Other Graeco-Roman Cults: Studies for Morton Smith at Sixty*, ed. J. Neusner (Leiden: Brill, 1975), 264–98.

¹⁶There is no general agreement on the date, but the association of Hebrews with Essene thought, the assumption of the existence of the temple, and the concern to leave organized Judaism favor a date shortly before the fall of Jerusalem; see P. E. Hughes, *Hebrews* (Grand Rapids: Eerdmans, 1977); George Wesley Buchanan, "The Present State of Scholarship on the Hebrews," in *Christianity, Judaism*, 299–330.

¹⁷M. Barth, "The Old Testament in Hebrews," in *Current Issues in New Testament Interpretation: Festschrift for O. Piper*, ed. W. Klassen and G. F. Snyder (New York: Harper, 1962), 53–78; S. Kistemaker, *The Psalm Citations in the*

Epistle to the Hebrews (Amsterdam: van Soest, 1961); P. E. Hughes, *Hebrews* 10–32; I. W. Batdorf, "Hebrews and Qumran: Old Methods and New Directions," *Festschrift in Honour of F. W. Gingrich*, E. H. Barth and R. E. Cocroft, eds. (Leiden: Brill, 1972), 16–35; F. F. Bruce, "To the Hebrews" or "To the Essenes," *NTS* 9 (1962/3): 127–32; J. Carmignac, "Le Document de Qumran sur Melkisedeq," *Revue Qumran* 7 (1970): 348–78; A. S. van der Woude, "11Q Mechizedek and the New Testament," *NTS* 12 (1962/3): 301–26; "Melchisedek als himmlische Erlosergestalt des neugefundenen eschatologischen Midrashim aus Qumran Hohle XI," *OTS* 14 (1965): 354–73; Y. Yadin, "The Dead Sea Scrolls and the Epistle to the Hebrews," *Scripta Hierosolymitana* 4 (1958), 36–55; for a critical reevaluation, see Richard Longenecker, "The Melchizedek Argument of Hebrews," Ladd *FS*, 161–85.

[18] C. K. Barrett, "The Eschatology of the Epistle of the Hebrews," in *The Background of the New Testament and its Eschatology: Festschrift for C. H. Dodd*, ed. D. Daube and W. D. Davies (Cambridge: Cambridge University Press, 1964), 363–93; G. W. MacRae, "Heavenly Temple and Eschatology in the Letter to the Hebrews," *Semeia* 12 (1978): 179–99; James C. De Young, *Jerusalem in the New Testament: The Significance of the City in the History of Redemption and in Eschatology* (Kampen: Kok, 1960).

[19] For a treatment of James and Paul, see J. Jeremias, "Paul and James," *Expository Times* 66 (1954–55): 368–71; P. Stuhlmacher, *Gerechtigkeit Gottes bei Paulus*, FRLANT 87 (1965), 191–94; W. Schmithals, *Paul and James*, trans. Dorothea M. Barton (Naperville: Allenson, 1965). James Dunn perpetuates this antithesis in *UD*, 251–57.

[20] For a listing of similarities between Jesus' teaching in Matthew and the Epistle of James, see Guthrie, *NTI*, 743, who refers to M. H. Shepherd, "The Epistle of James and the Gospel of Matthew," *JBL* 75 (1956): 40–51.

[21] Childs, *NTCI*, 438. James was written before A.D. 50 or perhaps in the early 60s. For a critical discussion concerning authorship and date, see Guthrie, *NTI*, 736–64; Robert H. Gundry, *SNT*, 343–45. P. Davids gives a convincing case for an early date between A.D. 40 and the Jerusalem Council (*The Epistle of James*, NIGTC, 2–22).

[22] Kümmel, *Introduction*, 421–34; Guthrie, *NTI*, 771–862.

[23] Guthrie, *NTI*, 771–863.

[24] Childs, *NTCI*, 469–74.

[25] On the relation between the Gospel of John and the Epistles of John, see C. H. Dodd, "The First Epistle of John and the Fourth Gospel," *BJRL* 21 (1937): 129–56; W. F. Howard, "The Common Authorship of the Johannine Gospel and Epistles," *Journal of Theological Studies* 48 (1947): 12–25; W. G. Wilson, "An Examination of the Linguistic Evidence Adduced Against the Unity of the First Epistle of John and the Fourth Gospel," ibid., 49 (1948): 147–56.

[26] Jude is dated to A.D. 65 or 80, depending on its relationship with 2 Peter (see Guthrie, *NTI*, 906–27).

[27] See E. E. Ellis, "Prophecy and Hermeneutic in Jude," in *Prophecy and Hermeneutic in Early Christianity* (Grand Rapids: Eerdmans, 1978), 221–36.

Chapter 32: The Pauline Witness to the Risen Christ

[1] For Paul's theology, see Günther Bornkamm, *Paul*, trans. D. M. G. Stalker (New York: Harper, 1971), 109–239; Werner Georg Kümmel, *The Theology of the New Testament, According to Its Major Witnesses: Jesus—Paul—John* (Nashville: Abingdon, 1973), 137–254; Herman Ridderbos, *Paul: An Outline of His Theology*, trans. John Richard de Witt (Grand Rapids: Eerdmans, 1975).

[2] Guthrie, *NTI*, 386–91; Richard N. Longenecker, *Paul, Apostle of Liberty* (New York: Harper, 1964). For an intriguing explanation of Paul's Pharisaic background in Merkabah mysticism and his conversion, see J. W. Bowker, "Merkabah Visions and the Visions of Paul," *Journal of Semitic Studies* 16 (1971): 157–73. For further background in Merkabah mysticism, see W. A. VanGemeren, "The Exegesis of Ezekiel's 'Chariot' Chapters in Twelfth-Century Hebrew Commentaries" (Ph.D. diss., University of Wisconsin, 1974).

[3] For an excellent summary of Paul's theological development, see Ridderbos, *Paul*; Richard B. Gaffin, Jr., "Paul as Theologian: A Review Article," *WTJ* 30 (1967–68): 204–32.

[4] See Gundry, *SNT*, 290. For a variety of views concerning the focus of Romans—polemic, conciliatory, doctrinal, summarizing present experience, and addressing the needs of the church—see Guthrie, *NTI*, 398–99.

[5] According to Childs, "The praescript and concluding doxology serve to establish a christological context from which to interpret Paul's missionary activity to the Romans. . . . Any interpretation which abstracts the content from the kerygmatic centre into timeless truths misses the eschatological thrust of the message" (*NTCI*, 255).

[6] L. W. Hurtado, "The Doxology at the End of Romans," in *New Testament Textual Criticism: Essays in Honour of Bruce M. Metzger*, ed. E. J. Epp and G. D. Fee (New York: Oxford University Press, 1980), 185–99.

[7] See Robert Paul Martin, "Paul's Use of Old Testament Quotations in Romans" (Ph.D. diss., Southwestern Baptist Theological Seminary, 1983).

[8] Childs gives an excellent summary of the role of the OT in Romans (*NTCI*, 258–60); cf. E. E. Ellis, *Paul's Use of the Old Testament* (Grand Rapids: Eerdmans, 1957).

[9] Günther Bornkamm, *A Guide to Its Writings*, trans. Reginald H. Fuller and Ilse Fuller (Philadelphia: Fortress, 1973), 95.

[10] Childs, *NTCI*, 276–79; see also D. J. Doughty, "The Presence and Future of Salvation in Corinth," *ZNW* 66 (1975): 61–90; A. C. Thiselton, "Realized Eschatology at Corinth," *NTS* 24 (1977–78): 510–26.

[11] For the issues pertaining to the date, see Guthrie, *NTI*, 457–65. I am not concerned here with the precise identification of the Galatian churches, whether in the north or in the south. For a discussion of the views, cf. Kümmel, who takes a northern Galatian view (*Introduction*, 295–98), and Gundry, who espouses the southern Galatian theory (*SNT*, 260–62).

[12] For further discussion, see D. Betz, "Spirit, Freedom, and the Law: Paul's Message to the Galatian Churches," *SEA* 39 (1974): 145–60; F. Hahn, "Das Gesetzesverständnis im Römer-und Galaterbrief," *ZNW* 67 (1976): 29–63; Richard N. Longenecker, "The Pedagogical Nature of the Law in Galatians 3:19–4:7," *JETS* 25 (1982): 53–61.

[13]The date of the second epistle is more debated but may be placed about half a year after the first, or ca. A.D. 52; see Guthrie, *NTI*, 566–67, 575–78; Gundry, *SNT*, 270–71.

[14]For the relation of 2 Thess. 2 and Mark 13, see G. R. Beasley-Murray, *Jesus and the Future* (New York: St. Martin's, 1954), 232–34. For the eschatology of Paul, see Ridderbos, *Paul*, 487–563; O. Cullmann, "Der eschatologische Charakter des Missionsauftragen und des apostolischen Selbstbewusstseins bei Paulus," in his *Vorträge und Aufsätze, 1925–1962* (Tübingen: Mohr, 1966), 305–26.

[15]See Guthrie, *NTI*, 569–75; Childs, *NTCI*, 360–66; J. A. Bailey, "Who Wrote II Thessalonians?" *NTS* 25 (1978–79): 131–45.

[16]For a discussion of the problems associated with the dating and authorship, see Guthrie, *NTI*, 472–516.

[17]Childs, *NTCI*, 325.

[18]The date depends on whether Paul's imprisonment was in Ephesus, Caesarea, or Rome; see Guthrie, *NTI*, 522–40; Childs, *NTCI*, 331; Gundry, *SNT*, 314–18.

[19]Our Lord's making himself nothing (i.e., his *kenosis*; see Phil. 2:7) refers to the self-emptying of his royal and glorious prerogatives for the sake of presenting himself an atonement for humankind. For literature, see Ridderbos, *Paul*, 68–78; G. Howard, "Phil. 2:6–11 and the Human Christ," *CBQ* 40 (1978): 368–87.

[20]Childs, *NTCI*, 337.

[21]For a discussion of the issues, see Guthrie, *NTI*, 545–59; Childs, *NTCI*, 341–44; Kümmel, *Introduction*, 340–46.

[22]Guthrie gives as many as six views: christological, philosophic, Jewish, and respective emphases on angelology, the spirit-world, and exclusive claims (*NTI*, 546–50). Gundry concludes in favor of a blending of several of the above elements, combining Greek, oriental, and Jewish ideas (*SNT*, 307-8). See also E. P. Sanders, "Literary Dependence in Colossians," *JBL* 85 (1966): 28–45.

[23]G. Delling, "Plērōma," *TDNT* 6:288–311; R. P. Martin, "An Early Christian Hymn (Col. 1:15–20)," *EQ* 36 (1964): 195–205; B. Vawter, "The Colossian Hymn and the Principle of Redaction," *CBQ* 33 (1971): 62–81.

[24]A. J. Bandstra, "Did the Colossian Errorists Need a Mediator?" in *New Dimensions in New Testament Study*, ed. R. N. Longenecker and M. C. Tenney (Grand Rapids: Zondervan, 1974), 329–43; Childs, *NTCI*, 344–50.

[25]For critical issues, see Guthrie, *NTI*, 635–40. See also U. Wickert, "Der Philemonbrief–Privatbrief oder apostolisches Schreiben?" *ZNW* 52 (1961): 230–38; Childs, *NTCI*, 399.

[26]Guthrie, *NTI*, 584–624; Childs, *NTCI*, 378–86; E. E. Ellis, "The Authorship of the Pastorals: A Resume and Assessment of Current Trends," *EQ* 32 (1960): 151–61. Titus and 1 Timothy are generally dated A.D. 63–65, and 2 Timothy shortly before the apostle's death (67 or 68).

[27]See Gundry *SNT*, 322–23; cf. Childs, *NTCI*, 378–86.

[28]George W. Knight, *The Faithful Sayings in the Pastoral Letters* (Kampen: Kok, 1968).

Chapter 33: The Apostolic Message About Jesus

[1] R. N. Longenecker, *Biblical Exegesis in the Apostolic Period* (Grand Rapids: Eerdmans, 1975), 79–103; Leon Morris, *The Apostolic Preaching of the Cross* (Grand Rapids: Eerdmans, 1965); C. H. Dodd, *The Apostolic Preaching* (New York: Harper, 1964). Hunter defines the apostolic kerygma as consisting of (1) fulfillment of the Old Testament prophetic word; (2) an exposition of the life, death, and exaltation of Jesus; and (3) a summons to repent (*Message*, 29–38). For a more extensive study of the apostolic kerygma, see Dunn, *UD*, 11–32.

[2] Richard B. Gaffin, Jr., *The Centrality of the Resurrection: A Study in Paul's Soteriology* (Grand Rapids: Baker, 1978).

[3] Ladd, *TNT*, 327.

[4] John F. Maile, "The Ascension in Luke-Acts," *TB* 37 (1986): 29–59.

[5] Ladd, *TNT*, 333.

[6] Morris, *Lord from Heaven*, 58. For Hunter, the title "Lord" summarizes the "essential christology in the New Testament" (*Message*, 48).

[7] See A. M. Hunter's selection of unifying themes in *The Message: One Lord, One Church, and One Salvation*. Cf. Dunn, "The Role of Tradition," in *UD*, 60–80; Kümmel, *Theology of the New Testament*, 96–136.

[8] L. Cerfaux, *The Christian in the Theology of St. Paul*, trans. Lilian Soiron (London: Chapman, 1967); Ridderbos, *Paul*, 44–90. Guthrie concludes, "Paul has more to say about the divine nature of Christ than about his humanity. . . . He rather assumes the humanity, because without it neither the work of Christ on the cross, nor his glorious exaltation, would make sense" (*NTT*, 225–26). So also Morris, *Lord from Heaven*, 66.

[9] H. Ridderbos considers 1 Cor. 15:3 the kerygma of the Atonement ("The Earliest Confession of the Atonement in Paul," in *Reconciliation and Hope*, ed. Banks, 76–89).

[10] Richard N. Longenecker, "The Obedience of Christ in the Theology of the Early Church," in *Reconciliation and Hope*, ed. Banks, 142–52.

[11] Ladd, *TNT*, 411–12.

[12] Martin Hengel, *Between Jesus and Paul*, trans. John Bowden (Philadelphia: Fortress, 1983), 65–77.

[13] F. F. Bruce, "Jesus Is Lord," in *Soli Deo Gloria: New Testament Studies in Honor of William Childs Robinson*, ed. J. M. Richards (Richmond: John Knox, 1968), 23–36.

[14] For a discussion of the exegetical issues, see Guthrie, *TNT*, 295–96; Ladd, *TNT*, 341; R. N. Longenecker, *The Christology of Early Jewish Christianity* (Naperville: Allenson, 1970), 121–24.

[15] Dunn, *UD*, 92.

Chapter 34: The Church: The Ministry of Jesus in His Spirit

[1] For a helpful summary of the apostolic period, see Donald Guthrie, *The Apostles* (Grand Rapids: Zondervan, 1975); Everett F. Harrison, *The Apostolic Church* (Grand Rapids: Eerdmans, 1985).

[2] The apostolic community, however, continued the community of Jesus, even if it was a development. According to Dunn, "The Pauline concept of

church and ministry *differs from the discipleship of Jesus' earthly ministry* in that it was a concept of charismatic community" (*UD*, 114).

³Ridderbos, *Paul*, 330; cf. Ladd, *TNT*, 743.

⁴Ridderbos, *Paul*, 328.

⁵Ladd, *TNT*, 537.

⁶Ridderbos, *Paul*, 429–32; Ladd, *TNT*, 539–41.

⁷The LXX of Ps. 87:5 (cf. "Zion shall be called a mother / in whom men of every race are born" [NEB]) may lie behind Paul's designation of Jerusalem as "mother."

⁸Anthony A. Hoekema writes, "Once again we find that the New Testament widens the understanding of these terms ["Jerusalem" and "Zion"]. . . . The term Jerusalem, therefore, used in the Old Testament of the people of Israel, is used in the New Testament of the entire church of Jesus Christ" (*The Bible and the Future* [Grand Rapids: Eerdmans, 1979], 199).

⁹Hunter equates the ideas of being "in the kingdom," being "in Christ," and having "eternal life" (*Message*, 20).

¹⁰According to Hengel, "The *Sitz im Leben* of Pauline theology is the mission of the apostle among the 'nations.' He understands it as a worldwide eschatological proclamation of the rule of the Kyrios" (*Between Jesus and Paul*, 63).

¹¹Dunn explains the variety in ministry as an expression of "Christ-mysticism," according to which the "distinctive characteristic of the disciple of Christ is the experience of sharing in Christ's sufferings as well as the sharing of his life" (*UD*, 195).

¹²For an excellent study of the offices, see Ridderbos, *Paul*, 446–63; see also Ladd, *TNT*, 534–37.

Chapter 35: The Work of God in Salvation

¹L. Morris, *The Atonement: Its Meaning and Significance* (Downers Grove: InterVarsity, 1983), 39.

²I do not distinguish between propitiation (i.e., the turning away of God's wrath) and expiation, as atonement always includes propitiation; see L. Morris, "Propitiation," *EDT*, 888.

³James D. G. Dunn argues in favor of the substitutionary significance of Jesus' death in "Paul's Understanding of the Death of Jesus," in *Reconciliation and Hope: New Testament Essays on Atonement and Eschatology Presented to L. L. Morrison on His Sixtieth Birthday*, ed. R. Banks (Grand Rapids: Eerdmans, 1974), 125–41.

⁴Morris, *Atonement*, 132–50; Ridderbos, *Paul*, 182–204; I. Howard Marshall, "The Meaning of Reconciliation," in *Unity and Diversity in New Testament Theology: Essays in Honor of George E. Ladd*, ed. Robert E. Guelich (Grand Rapids: Eerdmans, 1978), 117–32.

⁵Ladd, *TNT*, 451; Marshall, "Meaning of Reconciliation," 130.

⁶Morris, *Atonement*, 132–50; Ridderbos, *Paul*, 182–204; Marshall, "Meaning of Reconciliation."

⁷See Jacques Ellul, *The Ethics of Freedom*, trans. and ed. Geoffrey W. Bromiley (Grand Rapids: Eerdmans, 1976).

[8]Morris, *Atonement*, 177–202; Ridderbos, *Paul*, 17–174. On the relation between law and righteousness, serious challenges have recently been made to the traditional position by E. P. Sanders, *Paul and Palestinian Judaism* (Philadelphia: Fortress, 1977), and by D. P. Fuller, *Gospel and Law: Contrast or Continuum?* (Grand Rapids: Eerdmans, 1980).

[9]John Murray, *Redemption: Accomplished and Applied* (Grand Rapids: Eerdmans, 1955), 174.

[10]William Barclay, "The One, New Man," in *Unity and Diversity in New Testament Theology: Essays in Honor of George E. Ladd*, ed. Robert E. Guelich (Grand Rapids: Eerdmans, 1978), 73–81.

[11]See John B. Webster, "The Imitation of Christ," *TB* 37 (1986): 95–120.

[12]Kümmel, *Theology of the New Testament*, 176.

NOTES TO PART 11:
THE KINGDOM AND THE CHURCH

Chapter 36: The Church in the World

[1]James D. G. Dunn, "Earliest Christianity: One Church or Warring Sects?" in *The Evidence for Jesus* (Philadelphia: Westminster, 1985), 79–102.

[2]Roger T. Beckwith, "The Daily and Weekly Worship of the Primitive Church," *EQ* 56 (1984): 65–80, 139–58.

[3]Kenneth Scott Latourette, *The Unquenchable Light* (London: Eyre & Spottiswoode, 1945), 3.

[4]Ibid., 15–16.

[5]"Never was that West fully Christian. Always a tension existed between the high calling of Jesus and the actual practice of Western culture" (ibid., 44).

[6]See William R. Estep, *Renaissance and Reformation* (Grand Rapids: Eerdmans, 1986).

[7]Roland H. Bainton, "Enlightenment and Revival," in *From the Reformation to the Present*, vol. 2 of *Christendom* (New York: Harper & Row, 1966), 98–128.

[8]Latourette, *Unquenchable Light*, 87.

[9]Ibid., 89.

[10]Thomas Askew and Peter W. Spellman, *The Churches and the American Experience: Ideals and Institutions* (Grand Rapids: Baker, 1984), 51.

[11]Ibid., 152–53.

[12]George Marsden, "Introduction," in *Evangelicalism and Modern America*, ed. Marsden (Grand Rapids: Eerdmans, 1984), xiv. See J. I. Packer's definition of "Fundamentalism" in *"Fundamentalism" and the Word of God: Some Evangelical Principles* (Grand Rapids: Eerdmans, 1958), which reflects the understanding of the term in the 1950s.

[13]Marsden, "Introduction," ix–x. For the variety of groups within Evangelicalism and their relationship to society and contemporary issues, see the challenging essays in *Evangelicalism and Modern America*. For a critical perspective on Evangelicalism, see James Barr, *Fundamentalism* (Philadelphia: Westminster, 1978).

Chapter 37: Key Questions in the Church

[1] Earle E. Cairns, *Christianity Through the Centuries: A History of the Christian Church* (Grand Rapids: Zondervan, 1954), 113.

[2] See Tim Dowley, ed., *Eerdmans' Handbook to the History of Christianity* (Grand Rapids: Eerdmans, 1977), 101.

[3] The issue of a Palestinian versus an Alexandrian canon has recently been dismissed in the epochal study by Roger Beckwith, *The Old Testament Canon of the New Testament Church* (Grand Rapids: Eerdmans, 1985).

[4] Eugene H. Merrill, "Rashi, Nicholas de Lyra, and Christian Exegesis," *WTJ* 38 (1975–76): 66–79; A. S. Wood, "Nicholas of Lyra," *EQ* 33 (1961): 196–206.

[5] See Menachem Elon, "Interpretation," *EJ* 8:1413–29; K. Grobel, "Interpretation," *IDB* 2:718–24; D. P. Fuller, "Interpretation, History of," *ISBErev.*, 2:863–74.

[6] Westminster Confession 1.7.

[7] Augustine, *Confessions* 10.19, 31, 37.

[8] James Orr, *The Progress of Dogma* (Grand Rapids: Eerdmans, n.d.), p. 220.

[9] For a thorough treatment of the particularist perspective, see J. Owen, *The Death of Death in the Death of Christ* (London: Banner of Truth, 1963), especially the introductory essay by J. I. Packer, pp. 1–25.

[10] Such concern for the historic Christian faith lies at the heart of J. Gresham Machen's writings, e.g., *Christianity and Liberalism* (New York: Macmillan, 1923); *What Is Faith?* (Grand Rapids: Eerdmans, 1946); *The Christian Faith in the Modern World* (Grand Rapids: Eerdmans, 1936).

Chapter 38: Present and Future Issues

[1] Reinhold Niebuhr, *Moral Man and Immoral Society* (New York: Scribner, 1960); see also Gabriel Fackre, "Reinhold Niebuhr," in *Reformed Theology in America*, ed. David F. Wells (Grand Rapids: Eerdmans, 1985), 263–79.

[2] Dowley, *Handbook*, 640.

[3] D. J. Hesselgrave, *Communicating Christ Cross-Culturally* (Grand Rapids: Zondervan, 1978); B. J. Nichols, *Contextualization: A Theology of Gospel and Culture* (Downers Grove: InterVarsity, 1979).

[4] Dunn, *UD*, 226–31.

[5] John M. L. Young, "Cross-Cultural Witness: Conflict and Accommodation," in *Interpretation & History: Essays in Honor of Allan A. MacRae,* ed. R. L. Harris, Swee-Hwa Quick, J. Robert Vannoy (Singapore: Christian Life, 1986), 281–90.

[6] Os Guinness, *The Gravedigger File* (Downers Grove: InterVarsity, 1983), 236.

[7] Boice, "The Future," 309. Boice here alludes to Jacques Ellul, *The Political Illusion*, trans. Konrad Kellen (New York: Vintage, 1972).

[8] For the challenge of religion and science, see Landon Gilkey, *Religion and the Scientific Future* (New York: Harper, 1970), 160.

[9] See Jacques Ellul, *The Meaning of the City* (Grand Rapids: Eerdmans, 1970); J. H. Yoder, *The Politics of Jesus* (Grand Rapids: Eerdmans, 1972); C. S. Lewis, "Christianity in Culture," in *Christian Reflections*, ed. Walter Hooper (Grand Rapids: Eerdmans, 1967).

[10] See A. Kuyper, *Lectures on Calvinism* (Grand Rapids: Eerdmans, 1961); Cornelius Van Til, *Common Grace and the Gospel* (Nutley: Presbyterian & Reformed, 1973); Francis A. Schaeffer, *How Should We Then Live?* (Old Tappan: Revell, 1976).

[11] Dunn, *UD*, 58.

[12] Donald G. Bloesch, *Essentials of Evangelical Theology*, 2 vols. (San Francisco: Harper & Row, 1978–79).

[13] Thomas F. O'Meara and Donald M. Weisser, eds., *Projections: Shaping an American Theology for the Future* (Garden City: Doubleday, 1970), 224.

[14] Harvie M. Conn, *Eternal Word and Changing Worlds. Theology, Anthropology, and Mission in Trialogue* (Grand Rapids: Zondervan, 1984), 337. See Vern S. Poythress, *Symphonic Theology. The Validity of Multiple Perspectives in Theology* (Grand Rapids: Zondervan, 1987).

[15] Francis A. Schaeffer, *The Great Evangelical Disaster* (Westchester: Crossway, 1984), 182; idem, *The Mark of the Christian* (Downers Grove: InterVarsity, 1970), 35.

NOTES TO PART 12: THE NEW JERUSALEM

Introduction to Part 12

[1] Meredith G. Kline, "The Intrusion and the Decalogue," *WTJ* 16 (1953): 1–22.

Chapter 39: The Day of the Lord

[1] For a theological treatment of the topics of eschatology, see works on systematic theology and also specialized works such as G. C. Berkouwer, *The Return of Christ*, trans. James VanOosterom (Grand Rapids: Eerdmans, 1972); Robert G. Clouse, ed., *The Meaning of the Millennium* (Downers Grove: InterVarsity, 1977); Anthony A. Hoekema, *The Bible and the Future* (Grand Rapids: Eerdmans, 1979).

[2] Berkouwer, *Return of Christ*, 234.

[3] See C. H. Cox, *The Secular City* (New York: MacMillan, 1966); Greg L. Bahnsen, *Theonomy in Christian Ethics* (Nutley: Craig, 1977).

[4] The Divine Warrior motif is found throughout Scripture (e.g., Exod. 15:1–18; Num. 10:35; Josh. 23:9–10; Isa. 51:9–10; Rev. 19:11–21). See William H. Brownlee, "From Holy War to Holy Martyrdom," in *The Quest for the Kingdom of God: Studies in Honor of George E. Mendenhall*, ed. H. B. Huffmon, F. A. Spina, and A. R. W. Green (Winona Lake: Eisenbrauns, 1983), 281–92.

[5] Berkouwer, *Return of Christ*, 385.

[6] Martin Buber, "The Faith of Judaism," in *The Writings of Martin Buber*, ed. W. Herberg (1956), (Cleveland: World, 1956), 265.

[7] Cf. H. Berkhof: "For centuries the Bible has been read as if it teaches that the renewal of the world is entirely discontinuous, as a break with this world and history. Closer investigation shows, however, that even in the most discontinuous statements, the background and framework is always the continuity" (*Christian Faith*, 519, 520).

[8] T. McComiskey, *CP*, 172.

⁹Richard B. Gaffin, *Perspectives on Pentecost* (Phillipsburg: Presbyterian & Reformed, 1979), 15.

¹⁰Ibid., 38.

¹¹J. Weiss, *Jesus' Proclamation of the Kingdom of God*, trans. and ed. Richard Hyde Hiers and David Harrimore Holland (Philadelphia: Fortress, 1971); A. Schweitzer, *The Kingdom of God and Primitive Christianity*, trans. L. A. Garrard (New York: Seabury, 1968); C. H. Dodd, *The Parables of the Kingdom*, 2d ed. (London: Nisbet, 1935); W. G. Kümmel, *Promise and Fulfillment*, trans. Dorothea M. Barton (London: SCM, 1961); George Eldon Ladd, *The Presence of the Future* (Grand Rapids: Eerdmans, 1974), 218.

¹²Ladd, *Presence of the Future*, 338.

¹³For a good survey of alternate views concerning the realization and future of the kingdom, see Hoekema, *Bible and the Future*, 288–316.

¹⁴Berkouwer, *Return of Christ*, 437.

¹⁵Hoekema, *Bible and the Future*, 147.

¹⁶W. VanGemeren, "IHCIP," pt. 2, p. 287.

¹⁷G. Vos, *The Kingdom: The Teaching of Jesus Concerning the Kingdom of God and the Church* (Nutley: Presbyterian & Reformed, 1972), 87.

¹⁸Ladd, *TNT*, 119.

¹⁹A. I. deGraaf, *The Kingdom of God in the Preaching and Work of Jesus* (Potchefstroom: Potchefstroom University, 1982).

Chapter 40: Eschatology and the Christian Life

¹Berkhouwer, *Return of Christ*, 18–19.

²See the significant essay by Günther Bornkamm, "Future and Present, Eschatology and Ethics," in *Paul*, trans. D. M. G. Stalker (New York: Harper, 1969).

³Vos, *The Teachings of Jesus*, 63.

⁴G. Ernest Wright, *The Rule of God* (Garden City: Doubleday, 1960), 108.

⁵It is regrettable that so much attention has been given to the millennial question. Regardless of one's perspective, eschatology has a bearing on life, as Berkhouwer observed: "The unity of this expectation has often been threatened in the Christian church by the constant arguments about pre-, post-, and a-millennialism. . . . The issue is not just one of how to interpret Rev. 20, but one that bears on the entire philosophy of history" (*Return of Christ*, 234).

⁶Hoekema, *Bible and the Future*, 54.

⁷See my articles on the future of Israel in Reformed theology and prophetic interpretation, "IHCIP," pts. 1 and 2. See also Raymond E. Brown, "The Pater Noster as an Eschatological Prayer," in *New Testament Essays* (Garden City: Doubleday, 1968), 275–320.

⁸The millennial issue was pointedly raised in a recent report of a Christianity Today Institute, "Our Future Hope: Eschatology and Its Role in the Church" (*Christianity Today*, Feb. 6, 1987). The moderator, Kenneth Kantzer, wisely concluded that we must recognize legitimate differences, continue our work as students of the Word, and remain in dialogue together. See this article for works representing the various positions on the millennium.

⁹Willem A. VanGemeren, "The Spirit of Restoration," *WTJ*, forthcoming.

Select Bibliography for Further Study

OLD TESTAMENT STUDIES

General Commentaries

Series

Bible Student's Commentary (BSC). Grand Rapids: Zondervan, 1982–.
Calvin's Commentaries on the Old Testament. Grand Rapids: Baker, 1979.
Gaebelein, F. E., gen. ed. *The Expositor's Bible Commentary (EBC)*, vols. 1–7. Grand Rapids: Zondervan.
Harrison, R. K., gen. ed. *New International Commentary on the Old Testament (NICOT)*. Grand Rapids: Eerdmans.
Hubbard, D. A., and G. W. Barker, gen. eds. *Word Biblical Commentary (WBC)*. Waco: Word.
Keil, C. F., and F. Delitzsch. *Commentary on the Old Testament*. Grand Rapids: Eerdmans, 1971.
Wiseman, D. J., gen. ed. *Tyndale Old Testament Commentary (TOTC)*. Downers Grove: InterVarsity.

One-Volume Commentaries

Elwell, W. A., gen. ed. *The Evangelical Commentary on the Bible*. Grand Rapids: Baker, forthcoming.
Guthrie, D., and J. A. Motyer, gen. eds., *The New Bible Commentary*. Rev. ed. Grand Rapids: Eerdmans, 1970.

Bible Dictionaries

Bromiley, Geoffrey W., gen. ed. *International Standard Bible Encyclopedia*. Rev. ed. Grand Rapids: Eerdmans, 1979–88.
Douglas, J. D., ed. *The New Bible Dictionary*. Grand Rapids: Eerdmans, 1979.
Douglas, J. D., gen. ed. *The Illustrated Bible Dictionary*. Sydney and Auckland: InterVarsity, 1980.
Elwell, Walter, ed. *Evangelical Dictionary of Theology*. Grand Rapids: Baker, 1984.
_____. *Evangelical Dictionary of the Bible*. Grand Rapids: Baker, forthcoming.
Tenney, Merrill C., ed. *The Zondervan Pictorial Dictionary*. Grand Rapids: Zondervan, 1967.
_____. *The Zondervan Pictorial Encyclopedia of the Bible*. 5 vols. Grand Rapids: Zondervan, 1975.

Bible Atlases

Aharoni, Yohanan, and Michael Avi-Yonah. *The Macmillan Bible Atlas*. Rev. ed. New York: Macmillan, 1977.

Frank, Harry Thomas, ed. *Hammond's Atlas of the Bible Lands*. Maplewood: Hammond, 1977.

May, Herbert G., ed. *Oxford Bible Atlas*. New York: Oxford University Press, 1984.

Commentaries on Old Testament Books

Genesis

Aalders, G. C. *Genesis*. BSC. 1981.

Cassuto, Umberto. *A Commentary on the Book of Genesis*. Translated by Israel Abrahams. 2 vols. Jerusalem: Magnes, 1961–64.

Kidner, Derek. *Genesis: An Introduction and Commentary*. TOTC. 1967.

Westermann, Claus. *Genesis: A Commentary*. Translated by John J. Scullion. 3 vols. Minneapolis: Augsburg, 1984.

Exodus

Cassuto, Umberto. *A Commentary on the Book of Exodus*. Jerusalem: Magnes, 1967.

Childs, Brevard S. *The Book of Exodus*. OTL. 1974.

Cole, Robert A. *Exodus*. TOTC. 1973.

Gispen, W. H. *Exodus*. BSC. 1981.

Leviticus

Mays, James L. *The Book of Leviticus and the Book of Numbers*. Richmond: John Knox, 1963.

Noordtzij, A. *Leviticus*. BSC. 1982.

Snaith, Norman H. *Leviticus, Numbers*. NCB. 1967.

Wenham, G. J. *The Book of Leviticus*. NICOT. 1979.

Numbers

Budd, Philip J. *Numbers*. WBC. 1984.

Noordtzij, A. *Numbers*. BSC. 1983.

Noth, Martin. *Numbers*. OTL. 1968.

Wenham, G. J. *Numbers: An Introduction and Commentary*. TOTC. 1981.

Deuteronomy

Craigie, Peter C. *The Book of Deuteronomy*. NICOT. 1976.

Kline, Meredith G. *Treaty of the Great King*. Grand Rapids: Eerdmans, 1963.

Rad, Gerhard von. *Deuteronomy*. OTL. 1966.

Thompson, John A. *Deuteronomy: An Introduction and Commentary*. TOTC. 1974.

Joshua

Butler, Trent C. *Joshua*. WBC. 1983.

Soggin, Juan Alberto. *Joshua. OTL.* 1972.
Woudstra, Marten. *The Book of Joshua. NICOT.* 1981.

Judges

Boling, Robert G. *Judges. AB.* 1975.
Cundall, Arthur E. *Judges. TOTC.* 1968.
Soggin, Juan Alberto. *Judges: A Commentary. OTL.* 1981.

Ruth

Campbell, Edward F., Jr. *Ruth. AB.* 1975.

1–2 Samuel

Hertzberg, H. W. *I and II Samuel. OTL.* 1964.
Klein, Ralph W. *I Samuel. WBC.* 1983.
Lange, Johann Peter. *Commentary on the Holy Scriptures: Samuel–Kings.* Grand Rapids: Zondervan, 1960.

1–2 Kings

Gray, John. *I and II Kings. OTL.* 2d ed., 1970; 3d ed., 1977.

1–2 Chronicles

Myers, Jacob M. *I and II Chronicles. AB.* 1965.
Williamson, H. G. M. *I and II Chronicles. NCB.* 1982.

Ezra-Nehemiah

Clines, David J. A. *Ezra, Nehemiah, Esther. NCB.* 1984.
Fensham, F. C. *The Books of Ezra and Nehemiah. NICOT.* 1982.
Kidner, Derek. *Ezra and Nehemiah: An Introduction and Commentary. TOTC.* 1979.

Esther

Clines, David J. A. *The Esther Scroll: The Story of the Story. JSOTSup* 30. 1984.
Moore, Carey A. *Esther. AB.* 1971.

Job

Andersen, F. I. *Job. TOTC.* 1976.
Eaton, J. H. *Job.* Old Testament Guides. Sheffield: *JSOT* Press, 1985.
Ellison, H. L. *A Study of Job: From Tragedy to Triumph.* Grand Rapids: Zondervan, 1972.
Gordis, Robert. *The Book of Job.* New York: Ktav, 1978.
Habel, Norman C. *The Book of Job: A Commentary.* Philadelphia: Westminster, 1985.
Pope, Marvin H. *Job. AB.* 1st ed., 1965; rev. ed., 1973.

Psalms

Allen, Leslie C. *Psalms 101–150. WBC.* 1983.

Select Bibliography for Further Study

Craigie, Peter C. *Psalms 1–50. WBC.* 1983.
Kidner, Derek. *Psalms. TOTC.* 1975.
VanGemeren, Willem. *Psalms. EBC,* vol. 5. Forthcoming.
Weiser, Artur. *The Psalms. OTL.* 1962.

Proverbs

Kidner, Derek. *The Proverbs: An Introduction and Commentary. TOTC.* 1964.
McKane, William. *Proverbs: A New Approach. OTL.* 1970.
Scott, R. B. Y. *Proverbs and Ecclesiastes. AB.* 1965.

Ecclesiastes

Eaton, Michael A. *Ecclesiastes. TOTC.* 1983.
Gordis, Robert. *Koheleth–the Man and His World: A Study of Ecclesiastes.* New York: Schocken, 1973.
Kaiser, Walter. *Ecclesiastes: Total Life.* Chicago: Moody, 1979.
Kidner, Derek. *A Time to Mourn and a Time to Dance.* Downers Grove: InterVarsity, 1976.

Song of Songs

Pope, Marvin H. *Song of Songs. AB.* 1977.

Isaiah

Kaiser, Otto. *Isaiah 1–39. OTL.* 2 vols. 1972, 1974.
Westerman, Claus. *Isaiah 40–66. OTL.* 1969.
Oswalt, John N. *The Book of Isaiah. Chapters 1–39.* Grand Rapids: Eerdmans, 1986.
Young, E. J. *The Book of Isaiah.* 3 vols. Grand Rapids: Eerdmans, 1965–72.

Jeremiah

Bright, John. *Jeremiah. AB.* 1965.
Carroll, Robert P. *Jeremiah: A Commentary.* Philadelphia: Westminster, 1986.
Harrison, R. K. *Jeremiah and Lamentations: An Introduction and Commentary. TOTC.* 1973.
Thompson, J. A. *The Book of Jeremiah. NICOT.* 1980.

Lamentations

Hillers, Delbert R. *Lamentations. AB.* 1972.
Kaiser, Walter. *A Biblical Approach to Personal Suffering.* Chicago: Moody, 1982.

Ezekiel

Craigie, Peter C. *Ezekiel.* Philadelphia: Westminster, 1983.
Eichrodt, Walther. *Ezekiel. OTL.* 1970.
Ellison, H. L. *Ezekiel: The Man and His Message.* Grand Rapids: Eerdmans, 1956.
Taylor, John B. *Ezekiel: An Introduction and Commentary. TOTC.* 1969.
Zimmerli, Walther. *Ezekiel.* Hermeneia. 2 vols. Philadelphia: Fortress, 1979.

Daniel

Baldwin, J. G. *Daniel. TOTC.* 1978.
Young, E. J. *The Prophecy of Daniel.* Grand Rapids: Eerdmans, 1949.

Minor Prophets

Allen, Leslie C. *The Books of Joel, Obadiah, Jonah, and Micah. NICOT.* 1976.
Andersen, Francis I., and David Noel Freedman. *Hosea. AB.* 1980.
Baldwin, Joyce. *Haggai, Zechariah, Malachi. TOTC.* 1972.
Hillers, Delbert R. *Micah: A Commentary on the Book of Micah.* Philadelphia: Fortress, 1984.
Kaiser, Walter. *Malachi: God's Unchanging Love.* Grand Rapids: Baker, 1984.
Maier, Walter. *The Book of Nahum.* St. Louis: Concordia, 1959.
Mays, James L. *Amos. OTL.* 1969.
———. *Hosea. OTL.* 1969.
———. *Micah. OTL.* 1976.
Mitchell, Hinckley; Thomas Gilbert; J. M. Powis Smith; and Julius A. Brewer. *A Critical and Exegetical Commentary on Haggai, Zechariah, Malachi, and Jonah. ICC.* 1912.
Petersen, David L. *Haggai and Zechariah 1–8: A Commentary.* Philadelphia: Westminster, 1984.
Smith, Ralph L. *Micah–Malachi. WBC.* 1984.
Verhoef, Pieter A. *The Books of Haggai and Malachi. NICOT.* 1987.
Wolff, Hans Walter. *Hosea.* Hermeneia. Philadelphia: Fortress, 1974.
———. *Joel and Amos.* Hermeneia. Philadelphia: Fortress, 1977.

General

Childs, B. S. *Old Testament Books for Pastor and Teacher.* Philadelphia: Westminster, 1977.
Goldingay, John. *Old Testament Commentary Survey.* Leicester: Theological Students Fellowship, 1982.

NEW TESTAMENT STUDIES

Introduction and Theology

Brown, C., ed. and trans. *The New International Dictionary of New Testament Theology.* 3 vols. Grand Rapids: Zondervan, 1975–78.
Gundry, Robert H. *A Survey of the New Testament.* Grand Rapids: Zondervan, 1970.
Guthrie, Donald. *New Testament Introduction.* Downers Grove: InterVarsity, 1970.
———. *New Testament Theology.* Downers Grove: InterVarsity, 1981.
Ladd, G. E. *A Theology of the New Testament.* Grand Rapids: Eerdmans, 1974.
Ridderbos, Herman. *Paul: An Outline of His Theology.* Translated by John Richard DeWitt. Grand Rapids: Eerdmans, 1975.
Stott, John R. W. *Basic Introduction to the New Testament.* Chicago: InterVarsity, 1964.

Tenney, Merrill C. *New Testament Survey.* Rev. ed. Edited by Walter M. Dunnett. Grand Rapids: Eerdmans, 1985.
Theological Dictionary of the New Testament. Abridged in one volume by G. W. Bromiley. Grand Rapids: Eerdmans, 1985.

General Commentaries

Bruce, F. F., gen. ed. *The New International Commentary on the New Testament (NICNT).* Grand Rapids: Eerdmans. 1962–1984.
Calvin's New Testament Commentaries. Grand Rapids: Eerdmans. 1960.
Gaebelein, F. E., gen. ed. *The Expositor's Bible Commentary (EBC)*, vols. 8–12. Grand Rapids: Zondervan, 1976–84.
Hendriksen, W., and S. J. Kistemaker, eds. *New Testament Commentary.* Grand Rapids: Baker.
Hubbard, D. A., and G. W. Barker, gen. eds. *Word Biblical Commentary (WBC).* Waco: Word, 1984.
Tasker, R. V. G., gen. ed. *Tyndale New Testament Commentaries.* Grand Rapids: Eerdmans.

Commentaries on New Testament Books

Matthew

Carson, D. A. "Matthew." In *Expositor's Bible Commentary*, vol. 8. Grand Rapids: Zondervan, 1984.
Gundry, R. H. *Matthew: A Commentary on His Literary and Theological Art.* Grand Rapids: Eerdmans, 1982.
McNeile, A. H., ed. *The Gospel According to St. Matthew.* London: Macmillan, 1961.
Mounce, R. H. *Matthew.* San Francisco: Harper & Row, 1985.
Plummer, A. *An Exegetical Commentary on the Gospel According to St. Matthew.* Grand Rapids: Eerdmans, 1956.

Mark

Plummer, A. *The Gospel According to St. Mark.* Grand Rapids: Baker, 1982.
Schweizer, E. *The Good News According to Mark.* Atlanta: John Knox, 1970.
Wessell, W. W. "Mark." In *Expositor's Bible Commentary*, vol. 8. Grand Rapids: Zondervan, 1984.

Luke

Ellis, E. Earle. *The Gospel of Luke.* Grand Rapids: Eerdmans, 1981.
Geldenhuys, Johannes Norval. *Commentary on the Gospel of Luke. NICNT.* 1952.
Liefeld, W. L. "Luke." In *Expositor's Bible Commentary*, vol. 8. Grand Rapids: Zondervan, 1984.
Marshall, I. H. *The Gospel of Luke. NIGTC.* 1978.
Plummer, A. *A Critical and Exegetical Commentary on the Gospel According to St. Luke. ICC.* 1902.

John

Brown, Raymond E. *The Gospel According to John. AB.* 2 vols. 1966–70.
Bruce, F. F. *The Gospel of John.* Grand Rapids: Eerdmans, 1983.
Tenney, M. "John." In *Expositor's Bible Commentary,* vol. 9. Grand Rapids: Zondervan, 1981.
Westcott, B. F. *The Gospel According to St. John.* Grand Rapids: Eerdmans, 1964.

Acts

Bruce, F. F. *Commentary on the Book of the Acts. NICNT.* 1954.
Neil, W. *The Acts of the Apostles.* New Century Bible. London: Marshall, Morgan & Scott, 1973.
Williams, David John. *Acts.* San Francisco: Harper & Row, 1985.

Romans

Cranfield, C. E. B. *The Epistle to the Romans. ICC.* 2 vols. 1975.
_____. *Romans: A Shorter Commentary.* Grand Rapids: Eerdmans, 1985.
Hodge, C. *Commentary on the Epistle to the Romans.* New York: Hodder & Stoughton, 1882.
Kasemann, E. *Commentary on Romans.* Translated by G. W. Bromiley. Grand Rapids: Eerdmans, 1980.
Luther, Martin. *Lectures on Romans.* Translated by Wilhelm Pauck. Library of Christian Classics, vol. 15. Philadelphia: Westminster, 1961.
Murray, John. *Romans.* 2 vols. *NICNT.* 1959–64.

1–2 Corinthians

Barrett, C. K. *A Commentary on the First Epistle to the Corinthians.* London: A. & C. Black, 1968.
_____. *A Commentary on the Second Epistle to the Corinthians.* New York: Harper & Row, 1973.
Bruce, F. F. *I and II Corinthians. NCB.* 1980.
Hughes, Philip E. *Paul's Second Epistle to the Corinthians.* Grand Rapids: Eerdmans, 1962.
Martin, Ralph P. *2 Corinthians. WBC.* 1986.

Galatians

Bruce, F. F. *The Epistle to the Galatians. NIGTC.* 1982.
Burton, E. D. *The Epistle to the Galatians. ICC.* 1920.
Guthrie, D. *Galatians.* London: Nelson, 1969.

Ephesians

Lloyd-Jones, D. M. *An Exposition of Ephesians.* 4 vols. Grand Rapids: Baker, 1972–79.
Westcott, B. F. *St. Paul's Epistle to the Ephesians.* Minneapolis: Klock & Klock, 1978, reprint.

522

Philippians

Lightfoot, J. B. *St. Paul's Epistle to the Philippians*. Grand Rapids: Zondervan, n.d., reprint.
Martin, R. P. *Philippians*. London: Oliphants, 1976.

Colossians and Philemon

Eadie, J. *Commentary on the Epistle of Paul to the Colossians*. Grand Rapids: Zondervan, 1957, reprint.
Lightfoot, J. B. *St. Paul's Epistles to the Colossians and to Philemon*. Grand Rapids: Zondervan, 1961, reprint.
Martin, R. P. *Colossians*. Exeter: Paternoster, 1972.
O'Brien, P. T. *Colossians, Philemon*. WBC. 1982.

1–2 Thessalonians

Bruce, F. F. *1 and 2 Thessalonians*. WBC. 1982.
Marshall, I. H. *I and II Thessalonians*. Grand Rapids: Eerdmans, 1983.
Ward, R. A. *A Commentary on 1 and 2 Thessalonians*. Waco: Word, 1974.

1–2 Timothy and Titus

Kent, H. *The Pastoral Epistles*. Chicago: Moody, 1958.
Ward, R. A. *A Commentary on 1 and 2 Timothy and Titus*. Waco: Word, 1974.

Hebrews

Hughes, P. E. *A Commentary on the Epistle to the Hebrews*. Grand Rapids: Eerdmans, 1977.
Kistemaker, Simon J. *Exposition of the Epistle to the Hebrews*. New Testament Commentary. Grand Rapids: Baker, 1984.
Lane, W. L. *Call to Commitment*. Nashville: Nelson, 1985.
Westcott, B. F. *The Epistle to the Hebrews*. Grand Rapids: Eerdmans, 1952, reprint.

James

Davids, P. *The Epistle of James*. Grand Rapids: Eerdmans, 1982.
Hiebert, D. E. *The Epistle of James: Tests of a Living Faith*. Chicago: Moody, 1979.
Mayer, J. B. *The Epistle of St. James*. Grand Rapids: Baker, 1978.

1–2 Peter

Hiebert, D. E. *First Peter*. Chicago: Moody, 1984.
Kelly, J. N. D. *Commentary on the Epistles of Peter and of Jude*. London: A. & C. Black, 1969.
Kistemaker, Simon J. *Exposition of the Epistles of Peter and of the Epistle of Jude*. NCC. Grand Rapids: Baker, 1987.
Mounce, R. H. *A Living Hope: A Commentary on 1 and 2 Peter*. Grand Rapids: Eerdmans, 1982.

1—3 John

Boice, J. M. *The Epistles of John.* Grand Rapids: Zondervan, 1979.
Brown, R. E. *The Epistles of John.* Garden City: Doubleday, 1982.
Bruce, F. F. *The Epistles of John.* New York: Revell, 1970.
Westcott, B. F. *The Epistles of St. John.* Introduction by F. F. Bruce. Grand Rapids: Eerdmans, 1966.

Jude

Kistemaker, Simon J. *Exposition of the Epistle of Peter and of the Epistle of Jude.* NCC. Grand Rapids: Baker, 1987.
Manton, T. *An Exposition of the Epistle of Jude.* London: Banner of Truth Trust, 1958.

Revelation

Barclay, William. *The Revelation of John.* 2 vols. Philadelphia: Westminster, 1961, 2d. ed.
Hendriksen, William. *More Than Conquerors.* Grand Rapids: Baker, 1965.
Sweet, J. P. M. *Revelation.* Philadelphia: Westminster, 1979.
Swete, H. B. *The Apocalypse of St. John.* New York: Macmillan, 1907.

HISTORY OF THE CHURCH

General

Aland, Kurt. *A History of Christianity.* Philadelphia: Fortress, 1985.
Austin, Bill R. *Austin's Topical History of Christianity.* Wheaton: Tyndale, 1983.
Cairns, Earle E. *Christianity Through the Centuries.* Grand Rapids: Zondervan, 1981. 2d. ed.
Gonzalez, Justo L. *The Story of Christianity.* 2 vols. San Francisco: Harper & Row, 1984.
Latourette, Kenneth Scott. *Christianity Through the Ages.* New York: Harper & Row, 1965.
_____. *The Unquenchable Light.* London: Eyre & Spottiswoode, 1945.
Meyer, Carl S. *The Church: From Pentecost to the Present.* Chicago: Moody, 1969.
Renwick, A. M., and A. M. Harman. *The Story of the Church.* Grand Rapids: Eerdmans, 1985.
Thompson, Ernest Trice. *Through the Ages: A History of the Christian Church.* Richmond: CLC, 1965.
Treadgold, Donald W. *A History of Christianity.* Belmont: Nordland, 1979.

Dictionaries and Handbooks

Cross, F. L., and E. L. Livingstone, eds. *The Oxford Dictionary of the Christian Church.* 2d ed. New York: Oxford University Press, 1974.
Douglas, J. D., ed. *The New Interational Dictionary of the Christian Church.* Grand Rapids: Zondervan, 1978.
Dowley, T., ed. *Eerdmans' Handbook to the History of Christianity.* Grand Rapids: Eerdmans, 1977.

Keely, Robin, org. ed. *Eerdman's Handbook to Christianity in Today's World.* Grand Rapids: Eerdmans, 1985.

————. *Eerdmans' Handbook to Christian Belief.* Grand Rapids: Eerdmans, 1982.

Doctrine

Bromiley, Geoffrey W. *Historical Theology: An Introduction.* Grand Rapids: Eerdmans, 1978.

Fisher, George Park, *History of Christian Doctrine.* New York: Edinburgh: T. & T. Clark, 1902.

Kelly, J. N. D. *Early Christian Doctrines.* New York: Harper, 1959.

Noll, Mark A.; Nathan O. Hatch; George M. Marsden; David F. Wells; John D. Woodbridge, eds. *Eerdman's Handbook to Christianity in America.* Grand Rapids: Eerdmans, 1983.

Orr, James. *The Progress of Dogma.* London: Hodder & Stoughton, 1901.

Seeberg, Reinhold. *Textbook of the History of Doctrines.* Translated by C. E. Hay. Grand Rapids: Baker, 1964.

Toon, Peter. *The Development of Doctrine in the Church.* Grand Rapids: Eerdmans, 1979.

Periods

Early

Bainton, Roland H. *Early Christianity.* Princeton: Van Nostrand, 1960.

Brown, Peter Robert Lamont. *Augustine of Hippo: A Biography.* London: Faber, 1967.

Chadwick, Henry. *The Early Church.* Grand Rapids: Eerdmans, 1968.

Frend, W. H. C. *The Early Church.* Philadelphia: Lippencott, 1966.

Petry, R. C., ed. *A History of Christianity: Readings in the History of the Early and Medieval Church.* 2 vols. Englewood Cliffs: Prentiss-Hall, 1962–64.

Middle

Cragg, Gerald R. *The Church and the Age of Reason, 1648–1789.* New York: Atheneum, 1962.

Estep, William R. *Renaissance and Reformation.* Grand Rapids: Eerdmans, 1986.

Green, V. H. H. *Renaissance and Reformation: A Survey of European History Between 1450 and 1660.* 2d. ed. New York: St. Martin's, 1964.

Strayer, Joseph R., and Dana C. Munro. *The Middle Ages, 395–1500.* New York: Appleton-Century-Crofts, 1970.

Reformation

Bainton, Roland H. *The Age of the Reformation.* Princeton: Anvil, 1956.

————. *Christendom.* New York: Harper & Row, 1966.

————. *Erasmus of Christendom.* New York: Scribner, 1969.

————. *Here I Stand: A Life of Martin Luther.* New York: Abingdon, 1950.

————. *The Reformation of the Sixteenth Century.* Boston: Beacon, 1952.

Chadwick, Owen. *The Reformation.* Grand Rapids: Eerdmans, 1965.

Estep, William R. *Renaissance and Reformation.* Grand Rapids: Eerdmans, 1986.

McNeill, J. T. *The History and Character of Calvinism*. New York: Oxford University Press, 1954.

Parker, T. H. L. *John Calvin: A Biography*. Philadelphia: Westminster, 1975.

Stevenson, William. *The Story of the Reformation*. Richmond: John Knox, 1959.

Modern

Cragg, Kenneth. *Christianity in World Perspective*. New York: Oxford University Press, 1968.

Latourette, Kenneth Scott. *Challenge and Conformity: Studies in the Interaction of Christianity and the World of Today*. New York: Harper & Brothers, 1955.

————. *Christianity in a Revolutionary Age*. 5 vols. New York: Harper & Row, 1958–62.

Manschreck, C. L., ed. *A History of Christianity: Readings in the History of the Church from the Reformation to the Present*. Englewood Cliffs: Prentiss-Hall, 1964.

Miller, Perry. *Jonathan Edwards*. New York: Meridian, 1959.

Nichols, James H. *History of Christianity, 1650–1950*. New York: Roland, 1956.

Vidler, Alec. *The Church in an Age of Revolution*. Vol. 5 of *History of the Church*. Baltimore: Penguin, 1961.

Christianity in America

Ahlstrom, Sydney E. *A Religious History of the American People*. New Haven: Yale University Press, 1972.

Brauer, Jerald C. *Protestantism in America: A Narrative History*. Philadelphia: Westminster, 1965.

Herberg, Will. *Protestant, Catholic, Jew*. Garden City: Anchor, 1960.

Hudson, Winthrop. *American Protestantism*. Chicago: University of Chicago Press, 1961.

Inch, Morris A. *The Evangelical Challenge*. Philadelphia: Westminster, 1978.

Noll, M. A.; N. O. Hatch; G. M. Marsden; D. F. Wells; and J. D. Woodbridge, eds. *Eerdman's Handbook to Christianity in America*. Grand Rapids: Eerdmans, 1983.

Thompson, Ernest Trice. *Presbyterians in the South*. Vol. 1, *1607–1861*. Richmond: John Knox, 1963.

Wells, David F., ed. *Reformed Theology in America: A History of Its Modern Development*. Grand Rapids: Eerdmans, 1985.

Other

The Cambridge History of the Bible. 3 vols. Cambridge: Cambridge University Press, 1963–70.

Neill, S. C. *A History of Christian Missions*. Baltimore: Penguin, 1964.

Packer, J. I. *"Fundamentalism" and the Word of God*. Grand Rapids: Eerdmans, 1958.

Scripture Index

Subject and Person Index